I ALSO HAD MY HOUR

DALE AHLQUIST

I ALSO HAD MY HOUR

An Alternative Autobiography of G. K. Chesterton

IGNATIUS PRESS   SAN FRANCISCO

Cover:
Portrait of G. K. Chesterton taken at
Harris & Ewing Photographic Studio
in Washington, D.C., in January, 1931.
Private collection of Dale Ahlquist.
Published here for the first time.

Cover design by Pawel Cetlinski

© 2025 by Ignatius Press, San Francisco
All rights reserved
ISBN 978-1-62164-773-7 (PB)
ISBN 978-1-64229-349-4 (eBook)
Library of Congress Control Number 2025934383
Printed in the United States of America ∞

To Geir Hasnes

CONTENTS

Acknowledgments	9
Introduction: When Fishes Flew: The Paradox	11
Prologue: Some Moment When the Moon Was Blood: The Chesterton Timeline	27
1 Then Surely I Was Born: An Alternative Autobiography	141
2 With Monstrous Head: All I Survey	302
3 The Devil's Walking Parody: An Alternative Biography	329
4 All Four-Footed Things: The ChesterBelloc	341
5 Ancient Crooked Will: The Devil	361
6 Starve, Scourge, Deride Me: The Accusation	368
7 I Keep My Secret Still: The Echoes of Words	387
8 Fools: A Brief Word on Critics	394
9 I Also Had My Hour: Manalive	400
10 One Far Fierce Hour and Sweet: The Man Who Was Sunday	438
11 There Was a Shout About My Ears: The Convert	446
12 And Palms Before My Feet: The Path to Holiness	462

ACKNOWLEDGMENTS

John Peterson was the early inspiration for this project. He started two features in his *Midwest Chesterton News* (a monthly newsletter published from 1990 to 1997): "Glimpses" and "Fragments of an Autobiography." The former gave us, indeed, glimpses of Chesterton from people who knew him or met him; the latter gave us glimpses of Chesterton where he talks about himself when talking about something else. I continued both of these features in *Gilbert* magazine (published since 1997 by the American Chesterton Society—now the Society of Gilbert Keith Chesterton) under the headings "Our Mr. Chesterton" and "GKC on GKC."

I have been part of a small group of people who have been gathering the ungathered Chesterton for a long time. First in finding it and collecting it and then slowly getting it all into a computer database. It is and will be an incredible tool, allowing readers and researchers to search for all the writings and other relevant material of one of the most prolific authors who ever lived. But building the tool involved the effort and sacrifice of some specific people. The late Father Ian Boyd first started publishing uncollected Chesterton pieces in the *Chesterton Review*, which he began editing in 1974, the centennial of Chesterton's birth. The late Aidan Mackey and the late Denis Conlon began the search for the "other" Chesterton writings and soon discovered there was seemingly infinitely more than anyone had imagined. Two other great Chestertonians who are no longer with us, Frank Petta and Ann Stull, were great treasure hunters and collectors and enthusiastic helpers. Peter Floriani created the first computer database in about 1996, when computers were still gas-powered and screens were mostly black and green. Geir Hasnes spent over three decades putting together the complete Chesterton bibliography, which was finally published in 2022 (three volumes, twelve hundred pages). While I worked closely with him, he was especially assisted by John Holland and an army of volunteers, hunting down obscure items and typing everything up. Special mention must be made of Nancy Brown for her many hours of research and many wonderful discoveries. Michael Lavrisha has been creating a search engine for this expanded database, which will be available to everyone through Chesterton.org, the website of the Society of Gilbert Keith Chesterton.

But I should point out that these latest developments have occurred after I had done almost all the research and assembling of the material for this book. I suppose it would have been a lot less work to wait. While it is very convenient now to have so much at my fingertips in the comfort of my comfortable study, I miss those days of spending hours in libraries across the U.S., Canada, and England, looking through yellowed newspapers, dusty file folders, crumbling bound periodicals, and scratchy microfilm. Finding Chesterton has been a great adventure.

INTRODUCTION

When Fishes Flew:
The Paradox

It is not in a man's biography that we can read his life.

—G.K. Chesterton, *Life*, April 20, 1916

The Gothic arch defies gravity. It uses gravity against itself in order to soar into the heavens. The fountain, too, contradicts gravity and even standard metaphors. It is water running uphill.

G.K. Chesterton also defies gravity. "Angels can fly because they can take themselves lightly."[1] Since it is mostly impossible not to quote *Orthodoxy*, and nearly as impossible not to quote one of the greatest lines in *Orthodoxy*, I thought it best to get that out of the way at the beginning. The goal of the rest of this book is to avoid quoting Chesterton books, but to quote from everything else he wrote.[2] The goal is to assemble Chesterton's testimony about himself by sneaking up on him.

But there is no avoiding paradox in this project—or in any other project. "Paradox lies at the very roots of existence; we are all born the children of paradox, just as we are all born the children of two

---

[1] "The Eternal Revolution," *Orthodoxy*. As for the Chesterton sources, we will use the ACS format as opposed to the Chicago style. "ACS" formerly referred to the American Chesterton Society, which is now the Society of Gilbert Keith Chesterton, but also known as the Apostolate of Common Sense—thus retaining the same TLA (Three Letter Acronym). The ACS format for books gives the chapter name and book title; for journalism, the title of the publication and the date. And speaking of TLA's, we will often use GKC to refer to Chesterton.

[2] This is the rule we are going to attempt to follow. We are going to avoid using Chesterton's books as source material, unless a particular essay or passage originally comes from Chesterton's journalism, speeches, and other uncollected writings or direct quotations. There will be a few exceptions and most of them will be in this introduction.

isolated and irreconcilable sexes."[3] Though we all live the paradox, G.K. Chesterton lives it more than others. And one of the most notable paradoxes connected to him is his *Autobiography*. Completed just before his death in 1936, he fills it with many good things, but he seems to swerve around the main topic, which happens to be himself, and divert attention toward the other people in his life. He manages to insert a few details about Gilbert Keith Chesterton, but not enough to paint a self-portrait. However, in his boundless writings about everything else, especially in his vast and largely uncollected journalism, he leaves fragments of an autobiography. I have tried to cobble together from this mountain of words a new version of Chesterton's life. And I have committed another paradox, the paradox of writing someone else's autobiography, after he has already written one—and after he has been in his grave for ninety years, an alternative autobiography. But it is not alternative in the sense that it is going to be a completely different picture of the man from the one we have. But possibly it will give us a more complete account of our Mr. C. It will fill in some blanks and shed new light on our subject, the light that he has perhaps unwittingly shone on himself.

Dumas Malone wrote six volumes on the life of Thomas Jefferson with far less material available to him than we have for G.K. Chesterton. He studied Jefferson his whole life, and his last volume was published when he was in his nineties. An exhaustive biography of Chesterton would fill many more volumes than that and would require more lifetimes than mine to complete. In the meantime, here is a condensed version of that material. On the one hand, I have been laboring on this book for over thirty-five years. On the other hand, I do not consider it labor at all. I have reveled in the hours and days and weeks and months of listening to G.K. Chesterton talk about everything—and occasionally I have caught him talking about himself.

The more that I consumed his thousands of essays, the more I realized that this was the body of writing where he reveals more of himself than anywhere else. Other biographers of Chesterton have admitted that they have really not dealt with his journalism. This is ironic. Chesterton considered himself a journalist before anything else. They were missing a gold mine of material. But one of Chesterton's contemporaries may

---

[3] *Daily News*, Dec. 25, 1901.

have figured out the same thing I have. Literary critic Holbrooke Jackson says early on: "Chesterton is his own Boswell."[4]

Equally neglected to Chesterton the journalist is Chesterton the speaker. This is understandable because so few actual transcripts of his speeches survive. However, there are innumerable newspaper accounts of his speeches, and these have been overlooked until now. Most of these reports capture quite well the main points and main quotations from his talks, where he might share a memory of his youth or, more often, will contradict his introducer with a different introduction of himself.

Of course, one could argue (and some *have* argued) that Chesterton is sometimes untrustworthy when writing or talking about one particular subject: himself. It is quite evident that certain descriptions of himself are more for effect, comic effect, and maybe exaggerations. But as he himself says, "Only the truth can be exaggerated. Nothing else can stand the strain."[5] One thing Chesterton is not: a liar. His honesty is one of the most obvious qualities of his writing. It is what wins so many readers over, because along with honesty is humility.

He is a secular writer who happens to write about God. He is a religious writer who writes for a secular audience. He is always putting things in the wrong envelopes. It is jarring for the reader, whether it be the self-confident but self-questioning literary humanist who suddenly has to grapple with God as a reality, or the settled and certain religious representative who unexpectedly has to wrestle with the ambiguity of art—and the clarity of justice.

While there have been great artists who have excelled at self-portraits, turning the mirror of nature on themselves, Chesterton is not among these Rembrandts and Van Goghs, who repeatedly and intently studied themselves as subjects. Chesterton says, "The precept 'Know Thyself' did not fall from heaven; it fell upstairs from the other place. I decline to know myself; he is not in my set. He is an unknown benefactor of mine, who prefers to remain anonymous."[6] Yet we hope to discover who this unknown benefactor is and kindly ignore his preference to stay anonymous.

---

[4] *Bystander*, Feb. 18, 1914.
[5] "The Time of Transition," *Charles Dickens*.
[6] *World*, Sept. 13, 1904.

In writing his biography (if it can be called a biography) of Saint Francis of Assisi, Chesterton says his approach is "to use what is understood to explain what is not understood."[7] To do the same thing with Chesterton himself presents a problem: Even what is understood about him is not understood. He has been mostly misunderstood, but also misrepresented, mischaracterized, and then ... misplaced. This is also a paradox. He is one of the clearest writers ever to grace the page. But he is a giant, and giants do not fit into small things such as books. G. K. Chesterton had a fascinating life that is never satisfactory in the telling of it. He lived a life of the mind, of the word, but he clearly lived it in the flesh and blood, with a robust appreciation of the created world and of the creatures who were his fellow men.

Nonetheless, I will pay Chesterton the same honor he pays other writers, and the same respect he pays his readers. He assumes they know something about the subject already, and he assumes they have some sympathy for the subject. So the readers of this book should at least know this much at the outset: G. K. Chesterton loves God, and so he loves creation. He loves people, and so he loves justice.

Known in his own lifetime as a journalist and praised as a poet, Chesterton is largely forgotten as both. He is chiefly remembered as a writer of detective stories. This, of course, would have pleased him. "I will not destroy the pleasures of those who read detective stories; for the simple and selfish reason that I am one of them myself."[8]

In exploring the mystery of G. K. Chesterton, we are tempted to explore his mysteries. We could follow him as he manifests himself in the form of his detectives, not only the humble Father Brown, but the poet Gabriel Gale, the joking Rupert Grant, the overburdened Horne Fisher, and the paradoxical Mr. Pond—all pursuing the truth. Combine their general motive and their peculiarities, and we have the complexity of Chesterton: He hunts you down in order to forgive you; he will expose your insanity; he will laugh at your error; he is weary of your corruption; he will unsettle what you have settled.

But there is another well-known mystery story, one that extends into a novel. Setting aside Innocent Smith from *Manalive* as his most obvious fictional self-portrait, his cosmic detective tale, *The Man Who*

---

[7] "The Problem of St. Francis," *St. Francis of Assisi*.
[8] *Illustrated London News*, Nov. 7, 1908.

Was Thursday, might be the most revealing when it seems to be concealing. It is a book of masks, where each character appears to be something he is not. In the end, there are no masks, but there still seem to be many different faces. They all join to reveal not only the fullness of creation but also the Man Who Was G. K. Chesterton. It is perhaps the most artful retelling of the Book of Job that has ever been written, the final riddle about the book of riddles, because "the riddles of God are more satisfying than the solutions of man." Is Chesterton Gabriel Syme, a man with confidence and wit and courage, being put to the test, confronting a world that looks like a nightmare? Everything that could go wrong goes wrong, yet his enemies turn out not to be his enemies. But there is still an actual adversary, who follows him from beginning to end. In the meantime, our hero is too amusing, too jolly, too joyful to let us see his suffering. But he has been suffering all along, thus his kinship with Job. When he finally has his face-to-face meeting with his creator, who invites him to sit down at the table with him, the drink the host serves is ... more suffering. But he learns that while he has been suffering, his mysterious creator has been suffering with him.

Chesterton says that in a novel, every character is only the author in disguise. So even GKC's portrayal of Sunday can be considered somewhat autobiographical. The large man in the dark. The man who set us on the chase is himself the man we are chasing. And when we get hold of him, he turns out to be even bigger than we imagined. He is too big to get a hold of. He looms so large that he fills up our vision so that we are wondering if he blots out the common light of the sun,[9] replacing it with a radiance of his own. And then we wake up. We realize that as large as he is, he is still pointing to something larger than himself.

As appealing and intriguing as his formula-breaking mysteries are, winning him the devotion of fans of detective fiction, Chesterton also delves into the greater mystery, which is why he is known to a different crowd as a Defender of the Faith. He enjoys a good argument, and the bigger the stakes, the more enjoyable the argument. "A good cause deserves to be defended by a good argument."[10] He

---

[9] "Walking down Fleet Street some day you may meet a form who vastness blots out the heavens." A. G. Gardiner, "Gilbert K. Chesterton," in *Prophets, Priests, and Kings* (J. M. Dent, 1908), p. 331.

[10] *Illustrated London News*, Dec. 17, 1921.

would be pleased to know that his written legacy has kept the argument going, and that his thrusts and parries are as swift and surprising as ever: "That dangerous and sometimes soul-destroying phrase that there are two sides to a question is true, but is emphasised untruly. It is emphasised, that is to say, without the truth that balances it. There are two sides to a question, but there is only one answer to a question; that is, only one right answer."[11]

Just as Chesterton is many characters who turn out to be the same character, he is many different writers who turn out to be the same writer. To call him a polymath makes him sound like a sideshow attraction. For some odd reason it is more impressive to be good at one thing than to excel at many. But the fact is, Chesterton is a master at every genre he touches. He is accomplished as a mystery writer and a novelist, but also as a critic and a commentator. He is a poet and a playwright. He is a historian wrapped in the past, but also a social reformer absorbed in the present. He is a philosopher in the halls of reason and a theologian in the halls of faith. But he excels most of all as an essayist. No subject escapes his notice, and he illuminates every topic he considers. His masterly essays are the product of his humble profession as a journalist. It is as a daily writer that he earns his daily bread.

Though newspapers get thrown away, many (but far from all) of his essays extend their life by being bound together in books. He compares his essays to gargoyles. In fact, he had wished that his volume of collected essays *Alarms and Discursions* had instead been published under the title *Gargoyles*. "I really have a notion of why I have collected all the nonsensical things there are.... This row of shapeless and ungainly monsters which I now set before the reader does not consist of separate idols cut out capriciously in lonely valleys or various islands. These monsters are meant for the gargoyles of a definite cathedral. I have to carve the gargoyles, because I can carve nothing else; I leave to others the angels and the arches and the spires. But I am very sure of the style of the architecture and of the consecration of the church."[12] Thus he reveals that though his essays stand out individually, they are an integral part of a single work. It is only his

---

[11] *Illustrated London News*, June 3, 1911.

[12] "On Gargoyles," *Alarms and Discursions* (based on an essay that originally appeared in the *Daily News*, Jan. 16, 1909).

humility that prevents him from admitting that he has also contributed angels and arches to the grand edifice of his sacred project.

The journalist must maintain the discipline of writing daily and of writing for the day. But the more he sharpens his focus on the times, the less timeless he is. Or so it would seem. It sometimes takes patience for the reader to see that Chesterton truly understands history as it is happening. His insider's perspective is often more useful than the academic analysis that is detached by decades from the same events. Chesterton stands apart from the reporters who merely react. He has an acute sense of anticipation. He sees not just yesterday's events but tomorrow's. And he never loses his eternal perspective. The challenge of the journalist is to make things interesting. For Chesterton, everything *is* interesting. He is not chasing a truth that flees, but warning a people that flee the truth. The new truths might be news, but they are not truths. The old truths that do not change can often be found to be shockingly relevant. Chesterton's gift is to make the familiar things startle us. During his lifetime, his impact resulted in him being a journalist who was himself news. Paradoxically, that is precisely the part of him that has been forgotten. His novelty wore off. But now he is starting to catch on as a classic.

His overlooked journalism is an essential part of him, where he reveals perhaps the most of himself. Not only his stated opinions, which are, of course, the windows to his mind, but the philosophy he takes for granted, which is the window to his soul. His newspaper columns are arguably more honest and unrehearsed than the autobiography he deliberately set down in the closing months of his life. Chesterton maintains that journalism, the article written under a deadline, is always "honester."[13] (However, one could argue that even his autobiography was written under a deadline.)

His journalistic essays are pages from the diary he never wrote, a record of what "can be achieved with a commonplace existence and the sacred spectacles of exaggeration."[14] But such writing is also a task, a job; it has something of the onerous quality of *work* to it. He once even refers to it as "sending articles to hell."[15] Poems, on the

---

[13] *Illustrated London News*, July 20, 1912.
[14] Introduction to *Tremendous Trifles*.
[15] Quoted in John O'Connor, *Father Brown on Chesterton* (Frederick Muller, 1937), p. 91.

other hand, are a holiday, written as a reward to himself. Thus we are going to devote a too small chapter to the neglected genre that represents a gigantic portion of Chesterton's writing: his poetry. Many of his poems are also pages from his diary. It is in a poem where he confesses, "Alas, my trade is words,"[16] a profound reflection on his vocation as a writer. He has no other gift to give.

I would argue that his most famous poem is latently autobiographical. I suppose this whole book is that argument. The poem is "The Donkey."

> When fishes flew and forests walked
> And figs grew upon thorn,
> Some moment when the moon was blood
> Then surely I was born.
>
> With monstrous head and sickening cry
> And ears like errant wings,
> The devil's walking parody
> On all four-footed things.
>
> The tattered outlaw of the earth,
> Of ancient crooked will;
> Starve, scourge, deride me: I am dumb,
> I keep my secret still.
>
> Fools! For I also had my hour;
> One far fierce hour and sweet:
> There was a shout about my ears,
> And palms before my feet.

---

[16] "To M.E.W.," a dedicatory poem to Mildred Wain, a friend of his who married another friend of his, Waldo D'Avigdor of the Junior Debating Club. Later the poem contains these lines: "I give a hand to my lady, another to my friend, / To whom you too have given a hand; and so before the end / We four may pray, for all the years, whatever suns be set, / The same two prayers worth praying—to live and not forget."

"My lady" refers to Frances, to whom GKC has given his hand in marriage. "My friend" is Waldo, who is now married to Mildred. And he hopes they will remain lifelong friends. GKC would dedicate the first *Father Brown* book to this couple. For anyone who thinks it important, Waldo was Jewish. But much more important is that this poem offers one of the very rare glimpses in GKC's prayer life. He says that the only two prayers worth praying are "to live and not forget"—that is, to embrace the gift of life at this moment, along with the memory of every other moment already lived.

G.K. Chesterton, the walking paradox, who also seems to be a walking joke, with his monstrous head and his two extra legs in the person of Hilaire Belloc, is a spectacle. He stubbornly does not conform. He even becomes an object of scorn to some. Nobody really knows what is behind that absurdly comical appearance. In spite of his unlikely beginnings, he suddenly finds himself in the midst of a jubilant celebration. And those who once dismissed him as a buffoon or an irrelevancy are shocked to discover that he has brought Christ into their presence.

Of course, my own critics, who stay closer to me than anyone else, will no doubt point out the absurdity of this argument due to the fact that when Chesterton penned this sweet little poem, most of his life was still unwritten because he had not lived it yet. As usual, I dismiss them with a wave of my hand.

Chesterton the poet makes even his prose poetic—and for good reason. "I have never understood why it should be a progress for poetry to become prosaic. It seems to me that it would be more of a progress for prose to become poetical."[17] And that is what Chesterton does with his words. Consider this description of the dawn that seems to come from a poem but does not: "White morning lay about the grey stoney streets like spilt milk."[18] Or this of the other end of the day: "A sickly sunset clung weakly to the horizon, as if pale with reluctance to leave the world in the dark. And as it faded more and more the skies seemed to come closer and to threaten."[19] Or this passage from a travelogue that seems to be an extraction from the climax of an epic poem: "And the Lord of the laurels, clad in his somber crimson, looked down into that darkness and then looked up, and saw that all the stars in his own sky were dead. They were deities no longer but only a brilliant dust, scattered down the vain void of Lucretius."[20]

As for travel, both of Chesterton's American tours are triumphs. His visits to each city are anticipated for weeks, and he plays to packed houses with enthusiastic responses nearly everywhere. Yet both visits are marred by negative reviews of books just published about a previously visited country. In 1921, *The New Jerusalem* is published, and

---

[17] *Illustrated London News*, Jan. 30, 1926.
[18] "The Songs of the Car Club," *The Flying Inn*.
[19] *Daily News*, Oct. 7, 1905 (which became "The Secret of a Train," in *Tremendous Trifles*).
[20] *Daily Telegraph*, Sept. 7, 1920 (which became "The Endless Empire," in *The New Jerusalem*).

in 1931, *The Resurrection of Rome*. The former is used to misrepresent his position about the Jews, and he is called anti-Semitic. The latter is used to misrepresent his position on Mussolini, and he is called a "half shamed-faced Fascist." Perhaps the problem is that neither book is up to Chesterton's standards when the subject matter certainly demanded that it be. Jerusalem and Rome? What could be more richly fruitful and inspirational for GKC's eloquent observations and insights? But he is overwhelmed by both places, and the books are underwhelming. He writes better about the things he finds in his pockets. Chesterton is large, but in general he manages to enlarge everything else, rather than make it small. He only makes himself small. However, when it comes to the Holy Land and the Eternal City, the two major crossroads of history, the two centers of everything, he cannot manage to make them larger in a way that transcends time. Instead, he puts them too much into the time in which he writes, when the pressing political questions and current grievances beg to be addressed more urgently and therefore unsatisfactorily. His mistake is that he does not step back far enough to see them, as he does when he writes *The Everlasting Man*, when he steps back far enough to see "The Strangest Story in the World" in its entirety.

In *The Everlasting Man*, GKC proposes alternative categories for understanding the history of the world and the development of religious thought. It is different from a purely chronological approach. "The worst argument in the world is a date."[21] He says his suggested categories apply not only to the history of the world but also to the history of each nation, and even to the history of each person, and that the categories are usually present at the same time in some degree:

1. God
2. The gods
3. The demons
4. The philosophers

The first category is easiest to explain and the most difficult to grasp. It is God—the Creator; the monotheism behind even polytheism.

---

[21] *Illustrated London News*, July 13, 1935. GKC wrote a book on the history of England with no dates in it. And he did not date his letters. And because of the consistency of his style and his philosophy, his writings are often difficult if not impossible to date.

The second category refers to the pagan efforts to understand the ultimate without the benefit of revelation but only the use of imagination: mythology; the poetry of the shepherds looking up at the night sky. The third category is the very real and alluring evil that manifests itself in a time of degradation and decline. And the fourth category contains the attempts to use reason rather than imagination to find the truth: logic; science; the wisemen who also search the stars.

As all four categories are present in different proportions in different people, they are also present in the subject of this autobiography. First, as his friend and first biographer, W. R. Titterton, testifies, Chesterton "was always thinking about God." He is thankful to God in all things. Prayer is present in all his acts.

> You say grace before meals. All right.
> But I say grace before the play and the opera,
> and grace before the concert and pantomime,
> and grace before I open a book,
> and grace before sketching, painting, swimming,
> fencing, boxing, walking, playing, dancing;
> and grace before I dip the pen in the ink.

But we see the second category in Chesterton as he also sympathizes with the pagan whose poetic attempts to pull the secret out of every tree, every branch, and every leaf are still foundational in the universal language of the arts. His imagination is always at work. And his wonder. The whole business of literature, he says, "is to describe the indescribable."[22] But he also sees that neo-pagan literature grows weary by the fact that Pan does not die.

Amid the praise of God and his creation is the darkness of the third category, the troubling encounters with the madness of evil. We will see that Chesterton also knows the Devil—based on personal experience.

And finally, Chesterton takes his place among the philosophers. He will not allow them their agnosticism and doubt but urges them to follow their own arguments. "Thinking means connecting things."[23] He laments the loss of reason in the world and argues that the Church is the only thing left defending it.

---

[22] *Illustrated London News*, June 6, 1931.
[23] "The Maniac," *Orthodoxy*.

But the journey of the wisemen is one of humility. At the beginning of his career, GKC is writing for *The Speaker*. At the end, he is writing for *The Listener*. There is easy confidence and boldness in his early pronouncements as he faces the road ahead, and there is more quiet reflection as he looks back. In the early publication he profoundly lays down proverbs: "Love is drawn to truth by the unerring magnetism of agony."[24] At the other end, he ponders, "It seems to me that Life is the one thing that most modern men never think about all their lives."[25]

As with every other aspect of Chesterton's life—his mystery stories, his economic ideas, his political controversies—his religious ideas are either the only thing people want to talk about or the only thing they do not want to talk about.

His early defense of Christianity in daily newspaper debates gives him fame among the faithful and an attractive notoriety among the London literary crowd. But his conversion to Catholicism in 1922 is, by his own account, the "chief event" of his life. It changes his life without changing his style. He has been defending the Catholic faith long before he becomes a Catholic, an event which many had either anticipated or already assumed to have occurred. As early as 1909, the *Catholic Monitor* calls him a recent convert. I assume they somehow retract that statement. In 1914, in the same publication, Father Robert O'Loughran writes that the more you study the mind of Cardinal Manning, the less surprised you are that he converted. "His best understudy today is G.K. Chesterton. He stands where Manning stood long ago. He refuses to believe in old grandmotherly stories about [the] Church.... He thinks for himself. He investigates the claims of the Church, and today he is at the parting of the ways. He is the Church's most brilliant defender, though he is not yet her son. With him, too, submission is the next logical step. When it comes, to the Catholic onlooker it will give great joy but will cause little astonishment."[26]

In the book *From Chaos to Catholicism*, Reverend W.G. Peck, an Anglican cleric, writes that Chesterton "is the champion of the Catholic Church, arriving when it seemed to outsiders that all the clever

---

[24] *Speaker*, May 18, 1901.
[25] *Listener*, Jan. 31, 1934.
[26] *Catholic Monitor*, June 20, 1914.

people had deserted her ... and his influence has probably been wider and deeper than has yet been anywhere acknowledged.... It is impossible to appreciate Chesterton unless one sees that he is always fighting for the spiritual and sacramental interpretation of human life."[27] This book is from 1920. It is two years before Chesterton's conversion.

After Chesterton finally does become Catholic, it actually sets in for major Anglicans who realize that they have suffered a major loss, and for the Catholics that they have landed a big fish. While the matter of looking into a man's soul is not a public event nor a thing to treat like scorekeeping, G. K. Chesterton's conversion is a chief event in many more lives than his, and he never fails to offer an open view of his soul. Most writers take that risk, even when engaged in the art of concealment.

During their courtship, Frances writes to him, "I think you are the most good-natured soul alive." A review of one of his earliest books says that he "speaks directly, from soul to soul, of the things that preoccupy all men."[28] Another early commentator proclaims: "He is one of the few interesting writers in contemporary literature with something to say ... and the power of compelling a jaded and tired age to listen to his voice."[29] One of his earliest editors observes, "Most of us are creatures of our time, thinking its thoughts, wearing its clothes, rejoicing in its chains." But Chesterton, he says, is not of our time, "but for all times."[30] (GKC might even agree, arguing that it is true not only of himself, but for anyone who has embraced the Catholic faith: "The Catholic Church is the only thing that saves a man from the degrading slavery of being a child of his age."[31])

And one of his very close friends, who looks back after having watched not only the rise to fame but the conversion and the soul-feeding wisdom that flows from his pen, reflects: "It was as if Chesterton had been taught by the Holy Ghost."[32]

---

[27] W. G. Peck, "G. K. Chesterton: The Return to Sanity," in *From Chaos to Catholicism* (Macmillan, 1920), p. 55.

[28] F. Y. Eccles, reviewing *The Wild Knight* in *The Speaker*, December 29, 1900.

[29] C. F. G. Masterman, *Bookman*, February 1903.

[30] Gardiner, "Gilbert K. Chesterton," pp. 331–32.

[31] *Forum*, January 1926.

[32] Rann Kennedy, who lived in Overstrand Mansions at the same time as the newlyweds Gilbert and Frances, quoted in Maisie Ward, *Return to Chesterton* (Sheed & Ward, 1952), p. 73.

Chesterton stands apart as a writer, as a journalist. He reports on the soul—not the typical topic of the daily papers. But his words are not buried in the religion section, where one might expect to find them; they show up everywhere. And from beginning to end. In one of his earliest published pieces for the *Daily News*, Chesterton writes a book review of Graham Balfour's biography of Robert Louis Stevenson.

> When Robert Louis Stevenson was a little boy, Mr. Graham Balfour tells us, he once made the following remark to his mother: "Mother, I've drawn a man. Shall I draw his soul now?" The remark bears some traces perhaps of that over-formalised Scottish religion in which a man's soul was not so much himself as a very delicate younger brother whom he had to save at all costs. But the remark has, nevertheless, a great deal of cogency in the question of all biographies, and especially in the biography of a man like Stevenson. It may be admitted that Mr. Graham Balfour has "drawn a man," or the thing that we ordinarily call a man, the featherless biped who eats and sleeps and pays an income tax. But even if Mr. Graham Balfour's life be the best ever written of one man by another, we cannot escape from the refection of how strange a thing it is to call such a thing a man's life. A man's life is held to mean what he did, the whole external pantomime of his existence. But this is in fact the most lifeless part of him, being the furthest removed from the centre of life. No one can know what Stevenson's life was, except perhaps, Stevenson, who no doubt had glimmerings from time to time. The only biography that is really possible is autobiography. To recount the actions of another man is not biography, it is zoology, the noting down of the habits of a new and outlandish animal. It is most valuable and interesting, but it does not deal with the spring and spirit of a man's existence. It may fill ten volumes with anecdotes, without once touching upon his life. It has drawed a man, but it has not drawed his soul.[33]

Chesterton, a master critic, makes his splash as a book reviewer and captures London's attention by his insightful reading of literature both old and new. But now, long afterward, he is seldom granted the same courtesy he shows other authors. His critics try to make Chesterton smaller. He is too big for them. The real challenge, however, is to make Chesterton even bigger, the same way that Chesterton makes

---

[33] *Daily News*, Oct. 18, 1901.

other authors bigger. I have read enough of Chesterton to figure out that he is smarter than I am. And I have also read enough of his critics to know that he is smarter than all of them. Their criticisms usually focus on one thing: on whatever that critic's pet peeve is. They never see Chesterton as a whole. They only see a hole. They have not even "drawed" the man. They certainly have not "drawed" his soul.

From getting the basic facts wrong to getting the foundational ideas wrong, in most cases the problem is the same. They have not read enough Chesterton. They are myopic and jumpy and oversensitive, relying on reflexes rather than reason. They are guilty of what GKC calls "the worst fallacy of realism," which is "the idea that we come nearer to the soul of a human being by climbing over walls and listening at keyholes, whereas the soul is only to be opened with the key of reverence."[34]

In spite of that, there *has* been an unconscious reverence toward Chesterton. It comes in the many, many times he is quoted. And even misquoted. Already during his lifetime, but certainly ever since, articles, speeches, and scholarly papers have appeared across the spectrum that will, usually at the outset, have a sentence along the lines of "G. K. Chesterton remarks somewhere that ..." or else conclude with "As G. K. Chesterton once said ..." Sometimes the quotation will actually be a version of something that Chesterton actually said. In any case, it is quoted or misquoted without a source. If it is paradoxical or pithy or proverbial, it is a tribute to Chesterton that his wit and wisdom have made a mark on the modern mind that has otherwise dismissed him. It is, shall we say, a paradox, that they call upon him almost as an oracle while rejecting his faith and philosophy.

When they actually have to face the fact that he writes more than epigrams and that he might be a significant Catholic thinker in the modern era, the means by which they reject him has been to hang him not as a heretic but as a hypocrite. They call upon his sins to discredit his creed. The only problem with this approach is that he is guilty of none of the things for which he has been accused. For those who are convinced that he is keeping secrets, who are convinced that this writer of detective stories is trying to mislead them on the trail to his own crimes, they find that the trail leads to a dead end. Those

---

[34] *Daily News*, Mar. 3, 1901.

intent on uncovering scandal are disappointed when they dig into Chesterton's life. The suggestions about his dark desires cannot be followed by any hard evidence. Hard lies have been told, and there are those who wish to believe them: latent homosexual, sadomasochist, adulterer, drunk, glutton, racist, Jew-hater, right-wing Fascist, *and* left-wing Socialist—he has been accused of all these things. It is easy to believe a lie because lies are designed to be believed. "Truth," says Chesterton, "is of necessity stranger than fiction, for we have made fiction to suit ourselves."[35] The accusations made of Chesterton always reveal more about the accuser than the accused.

Those who are friends of Chesterton have had their patience tested by the critics of Chesterton. I suppose I am more Bellocian than Chestertonian in my own response to the critics. I lack the humility and forbearance to deal with such remote and ineffectual, pinched, starved, stuttering, dull, brutish, pedantic, puffed and empty, hypocritical, and, well, *bad* in most senses of the word, critics who have simply conducted an attack of which they are unworthy. Such critics are like bees, who "give their one sting and die."[36] But criticism, says Chesterton, is "only words about words."[37] I find it more useful and delightful to read what Chesterton says than what his detractors say. I prefer to read what he says about everything than to hear someone else miss the point. And after more than four decades of reading GKC, I can say it has been more enlightening to read what he writes about himself rather than what others write about him. That is what I have tried to allow him to do in this book, a thing he tried to avoid doing but did not quite succeed—a happy failure for our benefit. His humility prevented him from realizing that he was the most interesting character he ever encountered. Here for all of us there is a new encounter with G. K. Chesterton. I trust we will discover that the secrets he keeps are not about his sins, but rather about his glories. He is the Donkey. He does not mind being laughed at, does not mind being starved, scourged, and derided, does not mind being considered an ass. He knows he is carrying Christ.

---

[35] "Mr. Bernard Shaw," *Heretics*.
[36] *Daily News*, Aug. 27, 1910.
[37] "The Strangest Story in the World," *The Everlasting Man*.

PROLOGUE: SOME MOMENT WHEN THE MOON WAS BLOOD

The Chesterton Timeline

Only yesterday all these things were to-morrow.
—*Illustrated London News*, August 20, 1932

1874
May 29—Gilbert Keith Chesterton is born in the London suburb of Kensington at 14 (now 32) Sheffield Terrace, the second child to Edward and Marie Chesterton.

July 1—Baptized a few blocks from his home at St. George's Church, Campden Hill, across from the water tower that would figure so prominently in *The Napoleon of Notting Hill*. (The water tower is demolished in 1970.)

1878
July 25—His eight-year-old sister Beatrice dies from typhoid fever.

1879
November 12—Cecil Chesterton is born. "Now I shall have an audience," says the young GKC. Instead, he gets a loyal adversary to hone his debating skills.

During this year, his family moves to 11 Warwick Garden, where he will live for the next twenty years, until his marriage.

1883
Is enrolled at Colet House (later Colet Court), preparatory school for St. Paul's.

*Estimated date.

1887

January—Is enrolled at St. Paul's School.

December—School report: "Has an inconceivable knack of forgetting at the shortest notice, is consequently always in trouble."

1888

July—School report: "Wildly inaccurate about everything: never thinks for two consecutive moments to judge by his work: plenty of ability, perhaps in other directions than classics."

December—School report: "Fair. Improving in neatness. Has a very fair stock of general knowledge."

1889

July—School report: "A great blunderer with much intelligence."

December—School report: "Means well. Would do better to give his time to 'modern' subjects."

1890

July—School report: "Can get up any work, but originates nothing."

July 1—First meeting of the Junior Debating Club (JDC), organized by Lucian Oldershaw at his house, 7 Talgarth Road, West Kensington. Original members include GKC, Edmund Clerihew Bentley, Lucian Oldershaw (GKC's future brother-in-law), B. N. Langdon-Davies, Edward Fordham, Lawrence Solomon, Waldo D'Avigdor, and Francis Bertram. Meetings are held regularly, but there is no record of the meetings till the following January. GKC is elected chairman and Oldershaw secretary. GKC presents the first paper, "On Shakespeare's Methods of Opening His Plays."

December—School report: "Takes an interest in his English work, but otherwise has not done well."

1891

January 23—JDC meeting at Oldershaw's house.

January 30—JDC meeting at D'Avigdor's house. GKC and Oldershaw reelected unanimously.

January 30—JDC meeting at Chesterton's house. GKC reads a paper on "Old Ballads."

February 4—JDC meeting at Fordham's house.

February 6—JDC meeting at D'Avigdor's house. The sixteen-year-old GKC proposes two possible mottos for the club: "Words are the only things that last forever" (from William Hazlitt's *Table Talk* essay, "On Thought and

Action"), or "Reading maketh a full man, conference a ready man, and writing an exact man" (from Francis Bacon's essay "Of Studies").

February 11—JDC meeting at Langdon-Davies' house.

March—First issue of *The Debater* is printed, with GKC's first published essay, "The Dragon." GKC contributes most of the material to the Junior Debating Club's magazine over the next two years.

March 13—JDC meeting at Solomon's house.

March 20—JDC meeting at Fordham's house. Debate about ghosts. GKC doubts secondhand accounts.

April 17—JDC meeting at Chesterton's house.

April 24—JDC meeting at Langdon-Davies' house.

May 1—JDC meeting at H. A. Sam's house.

May 7—JDC meeting at D'Avigdor's house.

May 14—JDC meeting at Fordham's house. Debate on capital punishment. GKC argues that all punishment should be regarded not as a moral equivalent to the fault but as a measure for the safety of society.

May 21—JDC meeting at Chesterton's house. GKC recommends to the club Alfred Church's "Stories from Herodotus" as amusing if not profound reading.

May 28—JDC meeting at Solomon's house.

June 4—JDC meeting at D'Avigdor's house.

June 11—JDC meeting at Langdon-Davies' house.

June 18—JDC meeting at Fordham's house. Debate on forms of government. GKC argues that the French Republic had not failed.

July 1—JDC meeting at Oldershaw's house. First anniversary of the club. Oldershaw makes a speech saying that GKC is the reason for the club's success.

July 8—JDC meeting at Bentley's house.

July 23—JDC meeting at Robert Vernede's house.

July—School report: "He has a decided literary aptitude. But does not trouble himself enough about school work."

September 18—JDC meeting at Chesterton's house.

September 25—JDC meeting at Oldershaw's house. Debate on "The Effect of a Nation's Prosperity on Its Literature and Art." GKC points out that there is probably more literary production at present than in the time of Shakespeare, but it is not necessarily better.

October—GKC's poem "Harmony" is published in *Pauline*, the school's magazine.

October 2—JDC meeting at Fordham's house. GKC reads a paper, written at short notice, on "Three English Dramatists" (Marlowe, Congreve, and Goldsmith).

October 9—JDC meeting at Langdon-Davies' house.
October 16—JDC meeting at D'Avigdor's house. GKC "drew the meeting's attention to Trevelyan's *Life and Letters of Macaulay*, which he describes as giving many interesting glimpses of the history of the formation of essays."
October 23—JDC meeting at Solomon's house.
October 30—JDC meeting at H. A. Sam's house.
November 4—JDC meeting at Avigdor's house. GKC reads a paper on "Literary Cynicism."
November 13—JDC meeting at Bentley's house.
November 20—JDC meeting. Reads a paper on "Nonsense."
November 27—JDC meeting at Chesterton's house. Debate. GKC argues against the proposition that Kipling is the best writer of short stories that England has produced.
December 4—JDC meeting at Solomon's house.
December—Wins the first prize essay at St. Paul's for his essay "Boys' Literature." Chosen by three boys in the Upper 8th.
December 11—JDC meeting at Fordham's house.
December 17—JDC meeting at Oldershaw's house.

1892

January 22—JDC meeting at Chesterton's house. Reelected chairman.
January 26—First meeting of the JDC Paper-cutting Committee. The purpose was to cut out interesting newspaper articles and read them at JDC meetings. GKC regards this as a waste of time.
January 29—JDC meeting at Langdon-Davies' house.
February 1—JDC meeting at Oldershaw's house. The JDC Naturalists' Society is formed, but GKC declines to be a member. They also form a chess club, which GKC does join.
February 5—JDC meeting at Solomon's house. GKC argues against "Evangeline" as being the best of Longfellow's poems.
February 12—JDC meeting at D'Avigdor's house. GKC says that a fairy-tale is formed on the principles of beauty, with vivid pictures illustrating a central moral idea.
February 19—JDC meeting at D'Avigdor's house.
February 26—JDC meeting at Bertram's house. GKC says the Puritans struck a death blow to the minstrels.
March 4—JDC meeting at Vernede's house. Debate. GKC argues that in the matter of education, women should not be treated any differently than men.
March 11—JDC meeting at Solomon's house. Debate. GKC argues that good writers prostitute themselves by writing rubbish articles for magazines.

March 12—Meeting of the JDC Chess Club. GKC beats Langdon-Davies and is beaten by Fordham. At this point in the term, he has won twenty-one out of fifty games.

March—The members meet at Chesterton's house to form the JDC Sketching Club and elect GKC chairman. A subsequent meeting is held at Solomon's house, and GKC reads a paper on Japanese art.

March 18—JDC meeting at Chesterton's house. Debate about *Hamlet*, GKC arguing that Hamlet was not even a little mad, and Polonius was not an utter imbecile.

March 26—JDC meeting at Oldershaw's house. GKC reads a paper on "The New School of Poetry."

April 2—JDC meeting at Fordham's house. Debate. GKC argues that science should be taught along with the classics.

April 8—JDC meeting at Langdon-Davies' house. Debate. GKC argues that *David Copperfield* is the best of Dickens' novels (even though *Pickwick* is splendid).

May 6—JDC meeting at D'Avigdor's house.

May 13—JDC meeting at Solomon's house. Debate. GKC argues that Athens had a better government than Sparta.

May 20—JDC meeting at D'Avigdor's house. Debate. GKC argues that excessive reading of fiction is injurious and that the present age demands serious speculation rather than the preponderance of inferior romance.

May 27—JDC meeting at Bertram's house.

May 28—JDC Chess Club meets. GKC loses to Langdon-Davies and Fordham and beats Maurice Solomon.

May 29—JDC Sketching Club meeting at Phillips' house.

June 10—JDC meeting at Vernede's house. Debate. GKC argues against a national literary academy awarding literary prizes.

June 12—JDC Sketching Club meeting at Hedgeland's house.

June 18—JDC meeting at Solomon's house. Debate in which GKC argues that collaborative writing does not produce good literature.

June 24—JDC meeting at Chesterton's house. Debate about compulsory athletics. GKC argues for individual liberty during play hours.

June 25—JDC Chess Club meeting. GKC defeats Bentley and loses to Maurice Solomon.

June 27—Wins the Milton Prize at St. Paul's for his poem "St. Francis Xavier." Also wins the French Prize. And, at the headmaster's discretion, advances to Eighth (or Senior) Form at St. Paul's and therefore completes school at the end of the term.

July 1—JDC meeting at Oldershaw's house. GKC is called upon to make a speech about the success and growing popularity of the club.

July 8—JDC meeting at Fordham's house. GKC reads a paper on "The Three Stages of Ethical Poetry in Europe."
July 22—JDC meeting at Solomon's. Debate. Virgil vs. Horace. GKC argues that Horace has better command of imagery.
August—His father takes him on a holiday in France. Visits Rouen, Normandy, and Paris.
September 16—JDC meeting at Fordham's house. GKC is reelected chairman, though he is no longer a student at St. Paul's.
September 20—Meeting of the JDC Antiquarian Society at Chesterton's house.
September 23—JDC meeting at Langdon-Davies' house. Debate about illustrations in books. GKC gives the instances in which they are defensible.
September 30—JDC meeting at Vernede's house.
October—Enrolls at Calderon's School for Art in St. John's Wood, which is simply an informal collection of not entirely serious painters.
October 7—JDC meeting at D'Avigdor's house. Debate. GKC argues in favor of the proposition that true humor need not necessarily cause laughter.
October 14—JDC meeting at Solomon's house. Debate. GKC argues in favor of the proposition that articles in magazines should be signed by the authors.
October 21—JDC meeting at Bertram's house. Debate. GKC proposes that advertisement should be restrained by law.
October 28—JDC meeting at D'Avigdor's house. Debate: "That the civilization of the present day is inferior to that which has been." GKC says the way to consider the progress is by how it treats women.
November 4—JDC meeting at Solomon's house. Debate. GKC proposes "that hunting as present practised on foxes, hares, stags and deer is unjustifiable and inhuman."
November 11—JDC meeting at Chesterton's. Debate about the Lord Mayor's Show. GKC argues that pageantry is respectable when it represents an existing authority.
November 19—JDC meeting at Oldershaw's house. Debate. GKC supports the proposition that restraints on political debate be removed.
November 25—JDC meeting at D'Avigdor's house. GKC proposes "that full publicity should be given for the lives of famous men."
December 2—JDC meeting at Fordham's house. Debate. GKC argues in favor of women's suffrage.
December 9—JDC meeting at Solomon's house. GKC reads a paper on "Literary Composition Among Boys."
December 14—JDC Antiquarian Society meeting at Chesterton's house. GKC speaks after a presentation about the Tower of London.

December 16—JDC meeting at D'Avigdor's house. Members discuss the future of the JDC, as many are leaving St. Paul's and *The Debater* is about to cease publication.

December 17—JDC Antiquarian Society tours the Tower of London together, gaining access to parts not open to the public.

December 17—*The Speaker* publishes the poem "A Song of Labour," GKC's first piece published in a major paper.

1893

August—Family holiday in North Berwick, Scotland.

September—Completes the drawings for *The Dictionary of Biography*, a book of clerihews written mostly by Bentley, but also by GKC, other members of the JDC, and even Edward Chesterton. The manuscript is given to Maurice Solomon. It will not be published until 1982 as *The First Clerihews*.

October 6—Begins classes at the Slade School of Art, University of London. Also takes courses in English, French, and Latin. His Latin professor is poet A. E. Housman (just before he achieved fame). GKC's experience at art school throws him into a deep, dark, near suicidal depression, from which he emerges some months later.

1894

March 19–30*—Travels to Italy with some fellow University of London students. Stays at the Hotel New York in Florence and the Grand Hotel de Milan in Milan. Also visits Venice and Verona.

July—Drops out of Slade Art School. Frederick Brown, one of his professors, will say that GKC was writing when he was supposed to be drawing and drawing when he was supposed to be writing.

August—Holiday with his family in North Berwick. Writes a letter to Bentley making reference to coming out of a "meaningless fit of depression," and alludes to what may have been a mystical experience and a divine encounter. "It is embarrassing talking to God face to face, as a man speaketh to a friend." The writing in his personal notebook reveals a new appreciation for existence. And he starts writing about Christ.

October—Continues at the University of London, taking courses in French, English, history, and political economy. His English professor is W. P. Ker.

1895

May—Visits Bentley and Oldershaw at Oxford.

June 22—His first book review ("A Ruskin Reader") is published (unsigned) in *The Academy*.

July—Leaves University of London at the end of summer term.

August—Holiday with the Solomon brothers and their family in Broadstairs, near Margate, and then with his own family in Southwold in Suffolk.

September—Takes a job reading manuscripts for Redway, a publisher of spiritualist literature.

1896

April—At the invitation of Lucian Oldershaw, attends a meeting of the I.D.K. Debating Society at the home of the Blogg family, 8 Bath Road, Bedford Park. Frances is not present. But sometime before he attends his second meeting of the society, he meets his future wife. Lucian will eventually marry Frances' sister, Ethel. What does "I.D.K." stand for? I Don't Know.

Summer—Holiday at Margate, followed by a trip to France. Stays at the Hotel St. Pierre in Ault.

October—Leaves Redway.

November 1—Begins new employment as a reader for the publisher T. Fisher Unwin on Paternoster Row.

December 1—Attends a meeting of the I.D.K. Society at the Blogg home. Frances is present. Speaks in opposition to the motion "that the punishment of crime is unjustifiable." Is elected as a member.

December 17—Attends a meeting of I.D.K. Society (with Frances) at 25 Stile Hall Gardens.

1897

Works at Fisher Unwin, reading thousands of manuscripts; courts Frances; writes.

January 9—Meeting of the I.D.K. Society (with Frances), possibly at 11 Warwick Gardens, GKC's home.

February 2—I.D.K. Society (with Frances) at 5 Stanwick Road, West Kensington. Speaks in opposition to the motion "that a man's character is his fate." Argues that we must take a lenient view of our parents. "Why did they not knock me on the head or throw me out of a third-story window?" (followed by cries of "Why! Why! Hear, Hear!").

February 18—I.D.K. Society (with Frances) at 25 Larkfield Road, Richmond.

March 16—I.D.K. Society at the Blogg home. Frances proposes the motion "that the conduct of Brutus as portrayed by Shakespeare in *Julius Caesar* is indefensible."

November 23—I.D.K. Society at the Blogg home. Digby D'Avigdor is elected a member.

December 15—I.D.K. Society (with Frances) at 28 The Avenue, Bedford Park. Ada Jones (the future Mrs. Cecil Chesterton) attends. E. C. Bentley is elected a member.

1898

Is given editing duties at Fisher Unwin, and ghostwrites *Through New Guinea and Cannibal Countries* by Herbert Cayley-Webster.

January 12—I.D.K Society (without Frances) at 41 Priory Road, Bedford Park. Proposes "that all private life is of public interest." Says that in the great ages of faith, men had always thought their emotion worth declaring openly: the martyrs testified before thousands, while the modern man of sentiment would prefer to be eaten by a lion in his own parlor, with a few friends.

February 3—I.D.K. Society (with Frances) at 28 The Avenue, Bedford Park.

March 2—I.D.K. Society at the Blogg home. Cecil attends.

March 16—I.D.K. Society (with Frances) at 18 Dorville Crescent, Ravenscourt Park.

March 31—I.D.K. Society (with Frances) at Adyar Studio, Flanders Road, Bedford Park.

April 28—I.D.K. Society (with Frances) at 28 The Avenue, Bedford Park. Frances opposes the proposition "that no respect is due to age or sex."

June or July—GKC proposes to Frances on the bridge over a duck pond in St. James Park. Their engagement will last three years.

November 22—I.D.K. Society at the Blogg home.

December 14—I.D.K. Society (with Frances) at 6 Denmark Street, Charing Cross. Standing in for Bentley, opposes the proposition "that family ties are destructive to social progress." Says that the man who carries his aspirations and ideals so that he is discontented with his own world is a traitor to morality and religion.

1899

February 16—I.D.K. Society (with Frances) at Stanford Brook House, Hammersmith. Another former JDCer, Robert Vernede, is elected a member. So is Cecil.

March 21—I.D.K. Society (with Frances) at 28 The Avenue, Bedford Park. (No further record of meetings.)

June 30—Frances' sister Gertrude is knocked from her bicycle and run over by a carriage. The accident occurs at the end of June.

July 2—Gertrude tragically dies of her injuries from the accident.

August—Family holiday in the coastal town of Felixstowe, in Suffolk.

October—Submits book reviews to *The Speaker*, but they are rejected by the book editor, F. Y. Eccles, who concludes, on the basis of GKC's distinctive italic handwriting, that he must be Jewish. At the behest of his University of London classmate, Ernest Hodder-Williams, he begins writing reviews of art books for *The Bookman* (published by the Hodder family). By his own account, he has discovered the easiest of professions and decides he wants to be a journalist.

October 26—Dinner at The Old Cock (Dr. Johnson's pub) with Bentley and Oldershaw.

December—GKC's first *Bookman* review appears.

1900

April—Attends a debate on the Boer War at the studio of painter Archie MacGregor. Is fascinated by a speaker who holds the floor for an hour and a half. GKC says, "I thought it was five minutes." It is Hilaire Belloc. He meets Belloc in person for the first time a few days later at the Mont Blanc tavern, 16 Gerrard Street in Soho (but it is not there anymore). Ironically, F. Y. Eccles is among the several people who will take credit for introducing them.

April—SPEECH, London, Stamford Brook House. Debate on the Boer War. Belloc also gives a speech.

April 28—First *Speaker* review appears, and from now on, his work will be accepted.

October 2—GKC's first book, *Greybeards at Play*, a collection of nonsense verse with his own illustrations, is published. Underwritten by his father.

November 20—*The Wild Knight*, a second volume of poetry, is published. "I ride forever, seeking after God."

December 24—Attends Midnight Mass with Belloc. First time GKC witnesses a Roman Catholic Mass.

1901

January 16—First book review published in the *Daily News* (unsigned).

January 22—Death of Queen Victoria. One of the very few times on record that GKC weeps openly.

March 21—First book review signed "GKC" in *Daily News*.

June 28—Marries Frances (on her thirty-second birthday) at St. Mary Abbotts Church, Kensington; Rev. Conrad Noel presiding. Arrives late because he has to stop to buy a gun. Also misses the train for the honeymoon. The newlyweds finally arrive at Ipswich and stay at the White Horse Inn, and then spend six days in Norfolk.

July—They rent a house at No. 1 Edwardes Square in Kensington, one street over from Warwick Gardens.

October—They move to 60 Overstrand Mansions, Battersea. At some point within the next eight years, they move to number 48.

October 24—SPEECH, Paddington Town Hall. "On Patriotism."

November 28—*The Defendant*, GKC's first book of essays, is published.

December—John Morley, general editor of Macmillan's *English Men of Letters* series, commissions GKC to write a monograph on Robert Browning.

1902

January 22—SPEECH, London, Clifford's Inn Hall. "Why Socialists and Radicals Should Cooperate." (Identifies himself as a Socialist.)

February 1*—SPEECH, Darlington. "On Mere Journalism." Says, "I believe in getting into hot water. I think it keeps you clean."

February 10—SPEECH, London, Passmore Edwards Settlement. "The Future of Liberalism."

March 21—Chairs a meeting of the Christian Social Union at Paddington, where a Miss Mona Wilson delivers a lecture on "Lead Poisoning in the Pottery Trade."

Summer—Spends a weekend in Bourne End, Buckinghamshire, at the home of R. C. Lehmann, editor of the *Daily News*. Another guest the same weekend is poet Alfred Noyes, who later recalls meeting Chesterton, who's standing in the library quoting William Morris. Later, at lunch, Chesterton "suddenly produced from his pocket and arranged on the table before him a number of little brass figures, Mr. Pickwick, Mr. Micawber, Sam Weller, and other characters from Dickens, giving one an almost uncanny sense that Gulliver held them alive in his hands."

September 23—Presides at a meeting of the Pharos Club, where Belloc speaks on The Land Question. (The title of his talk is "The Way Out," which paves the way for what will later be known as Distributism.) GKC apologizes for being late but says he had to pass by the office of a publisher to whom he owed a manuscript.

October 13—*Twelve Types* is published. "I once wrote a rather silly book about twelve historic figures whom I chose to consider symbolic—St. Francis of Assisi, Charles II, Tolstoy, and so on. As a book must have a name, I called the thing *Twelve Types*. I afterwards discovered that it had some sales as a book about technical printing; I found it myself in a library for working printers. I hope the poor brutes didn't read it."

November 20—SPEECH, London, Essex Hall, Humanitarian League. "Humanitarianism True and False." Frank Swinnerton, in his memoirs, says it was at this meeting that he first saw Shaw, who had jumped up and appeased the unruly crowd that had totally misunderstood GKC's speech.

November 21—Attends a meeting with Belloc at the Kensington Town Hall to listen to a lecture by Paul Sabatier on St. Francis of Assisi.

1903

January 25—SPEECH, London, Hotel Cecil, Playgoers Club. "The Harlequinade and the Human Soul." Max Beerbohm presides. GKC talks about the degeneration in both religion and joviality, which he refers to as "conscience and confetti."

February 22—SPEECH, Battersea, Upper Town Hall. "Dogma and Being Dogmatic."

March—Begins a public debate (in print) about Christianity, with Robert Blatchford, editor of the *Clarion*.

March 2—SPEECH, Uxbridge, Town Hall. "The Englishman and His Neighbors."

March 19—SPEECH, Peckham, Hanover Chapel. "On the Advantages of Ceremonial."

March 26—DEBATE, Bexleyheath, Parish Room, Bexley District Literary and Debating Society. "Patriotism and Small Nationalities."

March 28—Is a guest, along with Belloc and Wells, at the March Dinner of the Omar Khayyam Club.

April 19—SPEECH, Watford Labour Church. On behalf of the Bethesda quarrymen.

May 1—SPEECH, London, Caxton Hall. The Westminster Lecture Series (other lectures in the series are by Shaw, Belloc, Yeats, and two others). "Parochial Poetry."

May 19—*Robert Browning* is published.

July—Spends a few days visiting Belloc and family at their rented summer home (called "Bleak House") in Slindon, West Sussex.

August—Spends the only money he has on a good dinner and a bottle of wine, and then goes to his publisher and pitches an idea for a novel. Gets an advance and goes to Scotland to write *The Napoleon of Notting Hill*.

October 19—SPEECH, Hampstead, Parents National Education Union. "Tin Soldiers: The Place of Militarism in Education."

November—Joins the People's League Against Protection, opposing tariffs and protectionist tax on food.

November 8—SPEECH, Croydon, Ethical Society of South Croydon. "The Limits of Progress." "He at once proceeded to turn every conventional idea of progress completely up-side-down, and to make fun of the term as applied to any political party."

November 18—SPEECH, Portsmouth, Lecture Hall, Christ's Church Literary Society. "The Old English Ballads."
December 1—Frances is invited to join the Lyceum Club for Women.
December 3—SPEECH, Keighly Scientific and Literary Society. "The Shyness of the Journalist." Advocates against anonymous journalism. "The world is being led by phantoms and shadows." Meets Fr. John O'Connor for the first time, though they both seem to think their second meeting was their first.
December 8—SPEECH, Avondale Hall, Bellenden Road. Liberal Federation Meeting in anticipation of the election.
SPEECH, Northampton, the Liberal Club. "The Ethics of Patriotism."
December 9—SPEECH, East Dulwich, Imperial Hale, Grove Vale. Liberal Federation Meeting.
December 12—SPEECH, Ludgate-circus, Cafe de Paris, the Modern Club. Toast in honor of Sheridan Jones.
December 22—SPEECH, London, Hotel de Bale, Hatton Garden, City Socialist Circle. "Life and Motive."

1904

Date unknown—Is invited by Sir Oliver Lodge to be the first chair of the Department of English Literature at the University of Birmingham. He politely declines.
January 6—*Daily News* reports that GKC has been engaged to write a monograph on Charles Kingsley for the *English Men of Letters* series (for which he wrote his book on Browning), but no such book ever appears.
January 18—Lunch with Max Beerbohm.
January 28—SPEECH, London, Clifford's Inn, Guild of St. Matthew. Symposium on the representation of Labour and the possibility of a Labour Party.
January 29—SPEECH, Reigate, Public Hall. In support of public libraries.
February 1—Dinner at the home of Fisher Unwin.
February 9—SPEECH, Aberystwyth, Wales, Aberystwyth University, College Literary and Debating Society. "Shall We Abolish the Inevitable?" (*Cambrian News*.)
February 13—Attends the London Fellowship Annual at the Three Nuns.
February 17—Attends a large social event at Sidney Colvin's. "Too many clever people," according to Frances (e.g., Joseph Conrad, Henry James).
February 18—Lunch with Mary Cholomondely and other guests, including Lady Jekyll, whose Oxford son is a great admirer of GKC.
February 23—SPEECH, London, Imperial Restaurant. Guest of publisher John Lane.

March 5—Hosts a dinner party. Guests include Laurence Houseman.
March 8—DEBATE, London, Sion College, Christian Social Union. GKC is scheduled to speak on education, but the subject of Chinese labor in South Africa is introduced instead and big debate ensues.
March 12—Attends a grand dinner party at the home of a Mrs. Franklin. Other guests include Charles Masterman, Herbert Samuel, and Beatrice Webb.
March 17—*G.F. Watts* is published.
March 22—GKC's first novel, *The Napoleon of Notting Hill*, is published. SPEECH, Christo-Theosophical Society. "How Theology Appears to a Christian." Followed by a vigorous debate with Herbert Burrows.
March 29—Attends a large conference at Caxton Hall and supports the condemnation of Turkish atrocities in Macedonia.
March 31—Visits the Steinthals in Ilkley for a few days holiday. He is arrested by two policemen for defacing public property. "I was throwing a big Swedish knife at a tree, practising (alas, without success) that useful trick of knife-throwing by which men murder each other in Stevenson's romances." He is brought before the local constable, who turns out to be a big fan and immediately releases him.
April 5—In Ilkley, Frances meets Fr. O'Connor for the first time. ("He is delightful.") GKC and Fr. O'Connor take their famous walk on the moors.
April 13—SPEECH, Birmingham, Old Central Hall, Ruskin Society. "English Character and English Ballades."
April 26—Dinner party at John Lane's. Other guests include Max Beerbohm, and much of the discussion is about GKC's portrayal of Max as Auberon Quin in *The Napoleon of Notting Hill*.
April 27—Hosts a dinner for the Bellocs and the Noels.
May 7—Dinner with a Mr. and Mrs. Thurston.
May 9—Guest at the Royal Literary Fund Dinner. J.M. Barrie presiding. Frances describes the event as "about the greatest treat I have had in my life." She is so pleased at how well received GKC is among the literary crowd.
May 12—Visits the Carfax Gallery to view Max Beerbohm's caricature of "GKC kissing the world."
May 17—SPEECH, London, Christian Social Union. "The Religious Education Difficulty." GKC raises eyebrows when he says the Education Acts of 1870 and 1902 are the result of the influence of Professor Huxley and Sidney Webb, and "the best of His Majesty's Ministers are Agnostics and the worst are devil-worshippers."
May 22—SPEECH, London, Forest Gate, Earlham Hall, Ethical Church Meeting. "Local Patriotism." He says that everyone has to "begin with absolute realities if they are going to build up humanity again."

June 9—Attends an "at home" at Sidney Webb's. Winston Churchill and Lloyd George also attend. "Nothing but politics," says Frances.

June 11—SPEECH, Oxford, Randolph Hotel. Annual dinner of the University Palmerston Club. Toast.

June 21—Frances attends the first meeting of the Lyceum Club, hosted by Lady Balfour in Picadilly, a ladies club for women "actively engaged in literature, journalism, and the fine arts" (but she makes no mention of it in her diary). One of the other members is Mrs. John Lane, the wife of GKC's publisher.

June 22—Attends a social at the home of Wilfred and Alice Meynell. "Rather dull," says Frances. "I don't really like the 'precious people.' They worry me." (The Meynells will turn out to be great friends and admirers of GKC.)

June 23—Attends a social at the Duchess of Sutherland's. Frances meets Austen Chamberlain and notes his "eagerness" and "vulgarity."

June 30—An "exceedingly select 'at home'" at Graham Robertson's. Frances writes, "I felt rather too uncultivated to talk much.... It was all too grand. No men ought to have so much wealth."

July 4—Attends a meeting of the New Reform Club at Adelphi Terrace, with Frances. The only political club in London that admits women members.

July 5—Visits poet Algernon Swinburne. Frances thinks that GKC "found it rather hard to reconcile the idea with the man."

August—Guest for several days at the Steinthal home, St. John's Wharfemead, near Ilkley. Creates and performs a masque with several children for a birthday party for Francis Steinthal. One of the other guests in attendance is Fr. O'Connor.

August 12—While out walking in the country near Westerham, he runs into the photographer Alvin Langdon Coburn, who makes a famous portrait of him on the spot.

September 10—SPEECH, London, Anderton's Hotel. Dinner in honor of T. Werner Laurie, former manager at Fisher Unwin. Toast.

September 27—Scheduled to give a speech at the Guild of St. Matthew at Sion College on the "The Wrong Kind of Socialism," but cannot attend due to ill health.

October 1—SPEECH, Leeds, Philosophical Hall, Leeds Art Club. "Man, the Great Man, and the Super-Man." Says that the old idea of a hero was "an enormously intensified and extra passionate version of a human being, but the modern conception is a cold, detached non-human being."

October 4—SPEECH, Liverpool, (Anglican) Church Congress: "Aggressive Infidelity." Sixteen hundred people in the audience; the first time GKC has ever faced such a large crowd. He "won everyone over." The same day, Frances addresses the Bradford Mothers' Union at St. Luke's School in Manningham on "The Development of the Town Child."

October 15–November 5—SPEECHES. Delivers a series of six lectures before the Frankfort Academy of Social Science on "English Contemporary Poetry": Tennyson, Browning, Swinburne, and the Neo-pagans; William Morris, Kipling, and W. B. Yeats.

November 13—Supper party hosted by Laurence Housman. His brother, poet A. E. Housman, who according to Frances is "much nicer than he," also attends.

December 8—SPEECH, London, Caledonian Hotel, Adelphi. "The Moderns."

December—Methuen commissions Chesterton to write about the life of Dickens.

1905

Date unknown—Dinner at the Pall Mall Restaurant with H. G. Wells, artist William Rothenstein, and conductor Thomas Beecham.

January 8—SPEECH, Kilburn, Unitarian Church, Quex Road. "Why I Am a Christian."

January 12—Sells a series of sketches called "Men I Have Murdered" for the benefit of the *Daily News* Distress Fund for the benefit of the unemployed.

January 17—SPEECH, London, Essex Hall, Garden City Association. "The Blessings of Abuse" (on the modern city as "monstrous and grotesque").

January 22—SPEECH, Manchester, New Islington Hall. "Liberty vs. Equality." Nearly faints during the lecture, but recovers with great effort and finishes, apologizing for "the thunderbolt from heaven."

January 24—Lolly Yeats (W.B.'s sister) visits.

February 1—SPEECH, London, the Eighty Club.

February 12—SPEECH, London, Hengler's Circus, Argyll Street, Wesleyan West London Mission. "Religion and Equality."

February 13—Joins an appeal on behalf of Polish peasants who have been massacred by Russian soldiers.

February 16—SPEECH, Bradford, Bradford Church Institute. "The Practical Importance of Visions."

February 18—SPEECH, Bradford, District Teachers' Association, Charlton Street School. "The Teaching of Patriotism." Talk arranged by Mrs. Steinthal.

February 24—Visits Ilkley. Third meeting with Fr. O'Connor. This is when Fr. O'Connor claims they met the two Cambridge undergraduates whose reaction to the priest inspired GKC to create the character of Fr. Brown.

March 9—*The Club of Queer Trades* is published.
March 12—SPEECH, London, Whitefield's Central Mission, Men's Club. "What Is a Nation?"
March 14—Lunches at Buxton's. Meets Herbert Asquith.
March 16—SPEECH, London, St. Paul's Church, Covent Garden, London Branch of the Christian Social Union. "Vox Populi, Vox Dei." Frances says it is one of the proudest days of her life.
March 30—SPEECH, London, St. Paul's Church, Covent Garden, London Branch of the Christian Social Union. "The Citizen, the Gentleman, and the Savage." Frances says this sermon was even better than the last one.
April 2—SPEECH, Clapham, Morris Hall. "Why I Am a Liberal."
April 8—Guest at a dinner honoring Frederick Greenwood, founder and editor of the *Pall Mall Gazette*, Trocadero Restaurant. Others attending include J. M. Barrie, Thomas Hardy, George Meredith, Edmund Gosse, Max Beerbohm, Rufus Isaacs. Chesterton sits at a table drawing "a constellation" of his own.
April 9—SPEECH, Ealing, Ealing Congregational Church. "Why I Am a Christian." He says that "all philosophy ended in paradox. The ultimate contradiction waited for them on every obvious road."
May 5—SPEECH, London, Miss Nickell's School Hall, Willesden Green, Liberal Association. The *Daily News* calls GKC "a good political speaker" who has placed his services at the disposal of the Liberal Committee during the election campaign. Ironically, he works hard to get the Liberal candidates elected, and they are the very ones who turn their backs on him and his brother a few years later.
May 10—SPEECH, London, Burlington House, Shakespeare League. "Puck."
May 20—A reunion dinner for the members of the Junior Debating Club.
May 21—SPEECH, London, Westbourne-Park Chapel. P.S.A. "Some Misunderstandings of the English Character."
May 24—Visits the writer George Meredith, at Flint Cottage, Boxhill, Surrey. He is very old and amusing.
June 1—SPEECH, Walworth, St. John's Institute, the Eighty Club, on behalf of C. J. O'Donnell (brother of Hugh O'Donnell), Liberal candidate for Parliament.
June 5—Dinner at Hugh Riviere's, the painter who will do at least two portraits of GKC.
June 6—*Heretics* is published.
June 27—Garden party at the bishop's house, Kensington.
June 29—SPEECH, Guild of St. Matthew. "A rowdy speech," according to Frances.

July—Guest at a party hosted by socialite Ottoline Morrell (chiefly known for her love affair with Bertrand Russell).

July 5—Dinner at the Asquiths'. Meets former Prime Minister Lord Rosebery. Frances thinks that GKC "hated it."

July 16—Guest of Mrs. W.N. Grenfell at Taplow Court. Meets Prime Minister Arthur Balfour, Austen Chamberlain, and George Wyndham.

July 22—SPEECH, London, Hotel Cecil, Old Pauline's Club. Welcoming new High Master of St. Paul's, A.L. Hillard, who is succeeding Mr. Walker. GKC toasts "to the Masters, for whom he had always had a respect, all the more authoritative because, during his boyhood, it was a respect that was by no means reciprocated."

September—Is called to serve on a jury in Battersea. The experience will be the basis of his essay "The Twelve Men."

September 15—Alfred Langdon's portrait of Chesterton is included in an exhibition of photographs at the Royal Academy of Art.

September 24—SPEECH, Battersea Town Hall, National Union of Teachers. "Can We Teach Without Bias?"

September 26—Attends a Guild of St. Matthew meeting at Sion College and participates in a discussion about "popular criticism of the Christian faith."

September 30—Takes over the "Our Note-Book" column in the *Illustrated London News*, for which he will contribute a weekly essay for the next thirty-one years.

October 3—SPEECH, Bury St. Edmunds, the Eighty Club.

October 17—SPEECH, Hampstead, Drill Hall. In support of Liberal candidate G.F. Rowe.

October 24—SPEECH, London, Guildhall School of Music, London Shakespeare League. One of several speakers on the subject "The Best Methods of Presenting Shakespeare's Plays." One of the other speakers is Shaw.

SPEECH, Limehouse, Dalgleish Schools. In support of W. Pearce, Liberal candidate.

October 29—SPEECH, West Hampstead Congregational Church. Pleasant Sunday Afternoon (P.S.A.) Meeting.

November 8—SPEECH, St. Mary Abbott's, Kensington Branch of the Christian Social Union. On society. "What is the first primary fact about Christianity? That it did not lead up from barbarism out of darkness into civilisation. It stepped up to civilisation and told it what it thought of it."

November 27—SPEECH, Nottingham, Christian Social Union. "A racy speech bristling with smart epigrams."

November 29—SPEECH, London, National Liberal Club, League of Young Liberals. With Belloc, who is running for Parliament.
December 1—SPEECH, Greenock, Scotland, Greenock Philosophical Society. "Shall We Abolish the Inevitable?" "His lecture was a novel and interesting way of saying that it is the unexpected that happens."
December 2—SPEECH, Glasgow, Fabian Society. Argues for home rule for Scotland on the grounds that England had been tyrannized over long enough "by the greatest people on earth."
December 3—SPEECH, Glasgow, St. Andrew's Halls, Independent Labour Party. "The New Dangers of Oligarchy."
December 4—SPEECH, Helensburgh.
December 5—SPEECH, Edinburgh, Edinburgh Philosophical Association, Queen's Hall. "The Poetry of the Parish Pump."
December 8—SPEECH, Armistead, Dundee, Kinnaird Hall. "Shall We Abolish the Inevitable?" He says, "Man makes society far more than society makes man."
December 12—SPEECH, London, Cliffords Inn. Opening of an Exhibition of the Clarion Handicrafts Guild.

1906

January 3—SPEECH, London, New Reform Club. Shaw in the chair. "Liberal Watchwords."
January 10—SPEECH, Norwich, St. Andrew's Hall. In support of the Liberal candidate Louis Tillett.
January 12—SPEECH, Hoxton, the Eighty Club.
January 14—SPEECH, London, Anerly Congregational Church. "Shall We Abolish the Inevitable?"
January 27—Attends a banquet at the National Liberal Club to celebrate the victories of the Liberal candidates (including Belloc) for whom he campaigned.
February 3—SPEECH, London, Inns of Court Hotel. Annual dinner of the *Daily News* Companionship and Cricket Club. Toast.
February 4—SPEECH, Saltley, Adderly Road Mission Hall. "The Necessity of Dogma."
February 5—SPEECH, Birmingham, Birmingham and Midland Institute. "Modern Journalism." "Men are ruled by journalistic priesthood, who let out such knowledge as they like, and shut out such knowledge as they like."
February 16—Chairs a meeting of the New Reform Club, London. Speech by Belloc.
February 18—SPEECH, South London Mission. "Religion and Brass Bands."

February 20—SPEECH, Croydon, Aberdeen Road Congregational Church, South Croydon Literary Society. ("Mr. Chesterton began by explaining that he could not find a title for what he was going to say.")

March 3—SPEECH, London, Trocadero Restaurant. Annual dinner of the Association of Correctors of the Press. Toast.

March 4—SPEECH, Woolwich, St. Mary's, Men's Meeting. "Religion and Brass Bands."

March 7—SPEECH, London, Memorial Hall, Dickens Fellowship. "Dickens as Mystery Maker."

March 11—SPEECH, Colchester, Moot Hall, Men's Service.

March 13—Attends a performance of Euripides' *Electra* at the Court Theatre in London.

March 21—SPEECH, Church, Church School, Acerington Christian Social Union. "The Sanity of Christianity."

March 25—SPEECH, Hackney, St. John-at-Hackney Institute. "The Sanity of Christianity."

March 31—SPEECH, London, Bedford Park Natural History and Gardening Society. "Humour."

April 1—SPEECH, Southwark, St. Anne's Church, South Lambeth Road. Service for men.

April 5—SPEECH, Woolwich, Plumstead Library. "Sir Walter Scott and the Romance Element in Novels" ("bright and delightful").

April–Early May—Frances undergoes an operation that will enable her to have children. While she convalesces, GKC stays with the Rivières for five days and is painted by Hugh Rivière. Then he visits Germany and France with Oldershaw. While at a cafe in a small German town, he walks away without paying for his cigar and is unable afterward to make it right with the proprietor who wants to keep giving him another cigar.

May 1—Visits the Place de la Bastille in Paris.

May 2*—Meets George Bernard Shaw at Rodin's studio.

May 9—SPEECH, Tunbridge Wells, Lecture Hall, Christian Social Union. "Why Is Dogma Wanted?"

May 19—Attends the annual banquet of the Savage Club, Hotel Cecil.

May 20—SPEECH, Peckham Rye, Hanover Chapel, a Free Church. "They seemed to me to be charming people; able to listen intelligently to things with which they did not agree."

May 21—The founding of The Anti-Puritan League for the Defence of the People's Pleasures is announced, with GKC as one of its members (along with Fabians Hubert Bland and Edith Nesbit). Cecil is the secretary. The address for the league is 11 Warwick Gardens, where Cecil still lives with his parents.

June 24—SPEECH, Ilkley, P.S.A. Brotherhood. Hosted by the Steinthals. "Christianity and Materialism."

July 9—SPEECH, London, Clifford's Inn Hall, Anti-Puritan League. "The Joy of Life."

August—Sprains his foot ("The Advantages of Having One Leg").

August 30—*Charles Dickens* is published.

September—Holiday in the Isle of Thanet, where he discovers he is in Elfland. Then to Margate, where he receives a letter from Belloc telling him that Margate is a fraud. The same letter contains the poem saying that Chesterton is "the only man I regularly read." Belloc visits him at Overstrand Mansions as soon as GKC returns from his holiday.

September 20—Attends a luncheon in honor of Alice Hegan Rice, American author of *Mrs. Wiggs of the Cabbage Patch*.

September 22—SPEECH, Battersea Town Hall, West Lambeth Association of the National Union of Teachers. "The Education Question from the Socialist Point of View." The problem, he says, is that the rich have been trying to figure out how to educate the poor, but the upper classes have just as bad an education as the working classes.

October 16—SPEECH, Northwood, Northwood Literary Society. "Romance in English Literature." English literature, he says, is a "beautiful chaos.... No nation has produced more poets, but we want a little more clear thinking."

October 21—SPEECH, Acton, Acton Social Union. "The Wrong Kind of Progress."

November 1*—Suffers minor injuries when the hansome cab he is riding in overturns on the Strand.

November 10—An exhibition by the Society of Portrait Painters opens at the New Gallery, featuring a portrait of GKC by Hugh Riviere. A critic describes the gigantic figure as "a kind of inflated Napoleon of Notting Hill looking skyward for more of his inexhaustible and stimulating paradoxes."

November 26—SPEECH, Bradford, St. George's Hall, Christian Social Union.

November 29—Attends a lecture by George Bernard Shaw at Essex Hall and asks questions from the audience.

December 1—SPEECH, London, Inns of Court Hotel. Annual dinner of the *Daily News* Companionship and Cricket Club. Toast.

December 2—SPEECH, Kensington Town Hall, West London Ethical Society. "The Wrong Sort of Progress."

December 3—SPEECH, London. Opening of an exhibit of Christmas books. "On Books." He says that most children's books are written for adults.

December 16—SPEECH, Enfield, Council Schools. "A Critic in Utopia."
December 21—SPEECH, London, Guild of St. Matthew. A response to Bernard Shaw's lecture on "some necessary repairs to religion," which was made on November 29.

1907

January 4—SPEECH, London, Hall of the Institute of Journalists, United Irish League. "The Irish Literary Revival." "It is characteristic of the English people that in all their injustice to Ireland they have always found excuses."

January 15—SPEECH, London, Hotel Cecil. New Vagabonds Dinner. ("He spoke of the difficulty of being a learned man without being a pedant, and of how he had overcome that difficulty triumphantly by steadfastly refusing to become a learned man.") Arthur Conan Doyle is present.

January 18—SPEECH, London, Whitefriars Club. Expresses satisfaction that his fatness has become a legend. First reference to offering his seat to three ladies on a tramcar.

January 19—SPEECH, Manchester University Settlement, Toynbee Debating Society. "Shall We Abolish the Inevitable?"

January 20—SPEECH, Manchester, New Islington Hall. "Why in Politics I Am on the Right Side." Says, "Everybody with any kind of healthy conviction ought to think himself in possession of the truth," and should also be able to see the other side of the question clearly.

January 26—SPEECH, Ilkley, Wesleyan Assembly Room, the Bronte Society. "Charlotte Bronte and the Realists." Mrs. Steinthal presides.

January 31—SPEECH, London, Clifford's Inn Hall, Guild of St. Edmund. "The Sanity of Christianity."

February 8—Attends the Dickens Fellowship Annual Meeting, Memorial Hall, on the ninety-fifth anniversary of the author's birth.

February 9—SPEECH, London, National Liberal Club. Toast in honor of A. G. Gardiner (*Daily News*).

March—C. F. G. Masterman, editor of the *Albany Review*, comes to GKC's flat to collect the poem that GKC has promised him for the next issue. GKC says he has not written it down, so he proceeds to recite the whole thing while Masterman and Frances furiously copy it. It is "The Ballad of Alfred," which will eventually be the first canto of *The Ballad of the White Horse*.

March 9—Attends a dinner at the National Liberal Club in honor of H. W. Massingham, who is departing as editor of the *Daily News* to become editor of the *Nation*. Also present are Winston Churchill and Shaw.

March 18—SPEECH, London, Queen-square Club. "The Critic in Utopia."
April—Visits Ilkley with Cecil. Dinner with Fr. O'Connor. GKC and Cecil get into a long debate about Socialism that lasts for hours. Fr. O'Connor says of Cecil: "He is the reason why Gilbert was never afraid to debate with anyone."
April 20*—Attends a social gathering with the Colonial Premiers (Prime Ministers of Australia, Canada, and the British Virgin Islands).
May 12—SPEECH, Sydenham, Park Hall, Lewisham League of Young Liberals. In support of the Licensing Bill. With Belloc.
June—Spends a holiday in France, Germany, and Belgium, visiting Paris, Bescon, Belfort, Heidelberg, Frankfort. In Paris, attends several plays with an English friend who lives in Paris.
July 7—SPEECH, Saltley, Saltley Christian Fellowship. "The New Theology and the Social Movement." ("He doubted whether any of the philosophical scepticism and unrest of modern thought was good for Social Reform—it was probably the reverse.")
July—Attends a lecture at Oxford with H. G. Wells.
August 1—SPEECH, London, Piccadilly, New Dudley Gallery. "The Superiority of the Pickwick England."
September 25—SPEECH, London, Bishopsgate Institute. "The Tyranny of Wheels." Robert Blatchford presides.
September 30—SPEECH, London, Bishopsgate. Handicraft and Sweated Industries Exhibition. On art. Introducing artist Edith Wynne Mathison, wife of Rann Kennedy.
SPEECH, London, the Actors' Association.
October 3—SPEECH, London. Handicraft Exhibition. Introduced by Robert Blatchford. ("To have these two fast-friends and firm opponents at close quarters was an intellectual treat of the highest order which nobody had expected.")
October 22—Attends a dinner for the Newsvendors' Benevolent and Provident Institution at De Keyser's Royal Hotel. Bram Stoker is also in attendance.
October 23—Presides at a meeting of the New Reform Club. Belloc gives a speech about corruption in politics.
October 30—SPEECH, Bristol, Clifton College, P.N.E.U. "Mother-Wit."
November 2—SPEECH, Maidenhead, Town Hall, the District and Maidenhead Liberal Association. Introduced by Lucian Oldershaw. Billed as "A Liberal Smoking Concert," GKC claims he was invited to speak on "Beer and the House of Lords," which he could not connect as they seemed to be "opposite phases of human existence ... beer being good and the House of Lords being bad."

November 6—SPEECH, London, Hotel Adelphi, New Reform Club. "What I Want the Government to Do."
November 13—SPEECH, Luton, King Street Congregational Church. "Pickwick England." GKC is "as per usual, rampant in paradox and epigram."
November 19—DEBATE, Cambridge Union Society. With three professors from Cambridge. On Censorship.
December 8—SPEECH, Croydon, Gymnasium Hall, Croydon Ethical and Religious Fellowship. "The Sacredness of Revolution."
December 19—SPEECH, London, the Boltons. In aid of the Workrooms' Society. "Browning."

1908

January 18—Dinner at C. F. G Masterman's with Belloc, Baring, and Rann Kennedy. The party moves to Baring's and ends at 2 A.M.
January 19—SPEECH, London, Hampshire House Club. "The Sanity of Christianity."
January 24—SPEECH, Maidenhead, Wesleyan Schoolroom. On behalf of the mayor's poor-box fund. Belloc gives a speech on "The Distribution of Wealth" followed by a short speech from GKC.
February 4—SPEECH, Leeds. About politics as a sport.
February 12—Signs his name on a commemorative vellum to George Meredith on the occasion of his eightieth birthday. Other signatories include Thomas Hardy, Rudyard Kipling, J. M. Barrie, and Jerome K. Jerome.
February 14—SPEECH, University of Leeds, Great Hall, Leeds Arts Club. "What's Wrong with Drama?"
February 28—*The Man Who Was Thursday* is published. Hosts Masterman to dinner. "Gilbert in tremendous form," reciting his own and Belloc's poetry.
March 2—Chairs a debate on Socialism between Rev. A.J. Waldron (against) and Rev. Conrad Noel (for), and says he has special qualifications for the position as he believes neither side.
March 12—DEBATE, Cambridge Union Society. On Imperialism.
March 15—SPEECH, Bedford Park, St. Michael and All Angel's Parish Hall. "The Ethics of Journalism."
March 28—SPEECH, London, National Liberal Club. *Daily News* Dinner. Toast to A. G. Gardiner, editor of the *Daily News*. Also attending are owners and chocolate manufacturers H. T. Cadbury and George Cadbury.
March 29*—D. H. Lawrence, hitherto unpublished, sends GKC an essay, asking for an appraisal. After many weeks, and much to Lawrence's displeasure,

Frances returns the manuscript, with apologies, saying that her husband's workload has prevented him from evaluating the work.

March 30—SPEECH, Kippington, Parish Room, Christian Social Union. "The Sanity of Christianity."

March 31—London. Leads a discussion on censorship, following a lecture by Gertrude Kingston on "Drama and the Public." GKC says, "I made a bet that a recent play would be passed by the censor. All my friends betted that it would not. It was passed. It was passed because the censor glanced through it, and did not see any words which are to be found in Shakespeare and the Bible. The play is of a violently revolutionary character, and the censor passed it because he did not understand it."

April 1—SPEECH, Reading, Parents' National Educational Union. "Motherwit."

April—Visits Belgium, including the towns of Bruges, Mechlin, and Lierre.

May 8—SPEECH, London, the Eighty Club. On Macedonian reform.

May 11—SPEECH, London, Church House, Society for Providing Homes for Waifs and Strays. In support of the society's work. Says, "Nobody reads statistics except Bishops, and nobody reads theology except laymen."

May 12—Chairs a meeting of the League of Young Liberals at Sydenham. Belloc is the speaker. GKC gives a short speech on Christianity and democracy at the conclusion.

May 14—Chairs a meeting at Sion College, where Conrad Noel gives a speech on Socialism.

May 19—SPEECH, London, Portman Rooms, Women's Industrial Council. "A Critic in Utopia."

May 21—Attends a Royal Literary Fund Dinner in honor of Rudyard Kipling.

June 2—Attends the wedding of Charles and Lucy Masterman at Westminster Abbey. Afterward, they greet him in the nave and he wishes to present each of them with one of his books. But he first asks for a pen. On the spot, with a borrowed pen, he writes an original poem in each book, "An Imitation" in *The Napoleon of Notting Hill* (for him), and "A Ballade of Wedding Presents" in *The Man Who Was Thursday* (for her). (Lucy's great uncle was Gladstone.)

June 12—Attends a garden party. Hosted by Prime Minister Asquith at No. 10 Downing Street.

June 13–14—Dresses up as Dr. Johnson for a pageant at the British Exhibition at Agriculture Hall.

June 21—SPEECH, London, Pan-Anglican Congress. "On Anonymous Journalism." Part of a symposium on religion and the press.

June 30—SPEECH, London, Hampshire House Club. "The Prologue." Shows up because he had seen a printed announcement that he was giving a speech with that title, but he had no recollection of actually being invited nor any idea what "The Prologue" referred to.

July—Belloc and Maurice Baring start a paper called the *North Street Gazette* (Baring's address is No. 6 North Street), whose motto is "Out, out, brief scandal!" It folds after one issue but is the forerunner of *The Eye Witness*.

July—Rents a house for one month at 4 Mermaid Street in Rye, next door to the "ambassadorial" Henry James. William James, H. G. Wells, and Belloc all pay amusing visits.

August—Holiday at the seaside town of Lowestoft in Suffolk with his wife and parents. Also visits Great Yarmouth.

August 21—Knollys Blogg is found dead in the River Cuckmere near Seaford, a probable suicide. (He likely had died August 16.) Frances subsequently suffers a nervous breakdown and seeks out a medium to make contact with her dead brother. GKC begins making arrangements to move out of London.

September 2—Cecil's anonymously authored *G. K. Chesterton: A Criticism* is published.

September 10—*All Things Considered* is published, a collection of some of his best *Illustrated London News* essays. "An inconvenience is only an adventure wrongly considered. An adventure is an inconvenience rightly considered."

September 12—Possibly attends the Eucharistic Congress because he is seen near Westminster Cathedral "carrying all the marks of violent inspiration."

September 25—*Orthodoxy* is published. "My elephantine adventures in pursuit of the obvious."

October 3—SPEECH, Sheffield, Dickens Fellowship. Toast. "To the Immortal Memory of Dickens."

October 9—Attends the Book Trade Dinner at the Trocadero Restaurant.

October 23—SPEECH, London, Irish Club. "How Ireland Might Help England."

October 24—Wins a literary competition sponsored by the *Westminster Gazette* for his translation of verses by French poet Charles Guerin. The prize is one guinea.

November 8—SPEECH, Stevenage, men's group. On the Christian Sunday.

November 12—SPEECH, London, Criterion Restaurant. Charles Lamb Memorial Banquet. Toast.

November 13—DEBATE, London, Caxton Hall, Christian Social Union. With Ramsay MacDonald. On Socialism. Says that Socialism is a desperate remedy and works "as smoothly and plainly as negro slavery, because it is very much of the same character.... Socialism has nothing in the world to do with democracy."

November 18—SPEECH, London, Surrey Masonic Hall, South London I.L.P. Council. With Belloc in the chair. "Why I Am Not a Socialist."

December 1—Attends the Follies at the Apollo Theatre.

December 5—Joins an appeal initiated by the Baptist World Congress to erect a memorial to John Bunyan in Westminster Abbey. Other signatories include Thomas Hardy and Stopford Brooke.

December 9—Attends the Lord Mayor's Banquet in commemoration of the tercentenary of Milton's birth. Every notable figure in London is also present.

December 14—Attends the birthday party in Rye of four-year-old Elizabeth Marshall, daughter of Archibald Marshall, literary editor for the *Daily News*. Henry James also attends, and the two of them compose an impromptu song for the little girl. Elizabeth has a pet rabbit named Gilbert Chesterton.

December 31—Lunches at a London club with Belloc and Spencer Leigh Hughes.

1909

January 15—SPEECH, London, National Liberal Club, League of Young Liberals. On the decline of English liberty.

February (date unknown)—Goes to dinner with H. G. Wells, Hilaire Belloc, Maurice Baring, and Ford Madox Ford. When Belloc begins to insult a novelist at the next table, an embarrassed Wells changes the subject by loudly asking Ford to tell everyone about a new writer he has just discovered. Thus does Belloc help launch the career of D. H. Lawrence.

February 8—Attends a meeting of the Synthetic Society at the invitation of Wilfrid Ward. Arrives late and causes a disruption during a speech by Arthur Balfour.

February 9—DEBATE, London, Morley Hall, London and Southwark Girls' Diocesan Association. With Dr. W. Temple. On the redistribution of land.

February 11—SPEECH, London, Piccadilly, Grosevnor Club. Author's Dinner. "If they asked me to choose between being a perfect artist upon no side in particular, and a vulgar journalist on the right side, I should choose the latter. I might say in all modesty that I have chosen it."

February 21—SPEECH, Croydon, Public Hall, Croydon Ethical and Religious Fellowship. "Will Science Be a Tyranny?"

February 23—SPEECH, London, United Arts Club, Poets' Club. "English and Scottish Poets." In 1933, drama critic Hannen Swaffer, an original member of the club, says: "Perhaps the most interesting meeting was when G. K. Chesterton spoke on 'The Ballad' and Shaw and Belloc took part in the debate which followed."

February 28—Dines at the home of Charles and Lucy Masterman.
March 8—SPEECH, Maidenhead, Town Hall, Maidenhead Liberal Association. "On the House of Lords." Says that the House of Lords is a house of knaves.
March 22—SPEECH, London. The Synthetic Society Dinner. (The speech is possibly "England's Peril," which is transcribed in *Great Thoughts* three weeks later.)
March 26—SPEECH, Croydon, Aberdeen Road School, South Croydon Literary Society. "Charlotte Bronte and the Realists."
March 31—Attends a dinner of the Omar Khayyam Club celebrating the centenary of Edward Fitzgerald at the Trocadero Restaurant. Other guests include E. M. Forster and Arnold Bennett.
April 8—SPEECH. First annual dinner of the National Union of Journalists at Anderton's Hotel on Fleet Street. Toast. Says he will join the union.
April 18—SPEECH, Hertfordshire, "a village of great beauty." Arrives very late because he has missed his train and takes a cab from London, but the cab breaks down along the way, making him even further delayed. His talk largely consists of his adventure getting there. The surviving members of the audience are not pleased.
May (date unknown)—SPEECH, London, Criterion Restaurant, Union Debating Club. Fr. O'Connor attends.
May 17—Chairs a debate between Conrad Noel and F. G. Jannaway, "Ought Christians to Be Socialists?," at Memorial Hall, London.
June 13—SPEECH, Parliament Hill Fields, Catholic Crusaders Platform. "Some Errors of Evolution." (This speech had been cancelled the previous summer due to "family bereavement," i.e., Knollys Blogg's death.)
June 14–16—Appears as Dr. Johnson at the Fulham Palace Church Pageant. Visits Charles and Lucy Masterman's home, in full costume, and is invited to stay for dinner.
June 26—SPEECH, Ilkley, Warlbeck. Opening of the Midsummer Fair, for the aid of the Ilkley University Extension Society. Attends a puppet play of *Faust*. Gives a recitation from the *Bab Ballads* and tells a nursery story from J. M. Bullock.
July—Frances is very ill. GKC cancels his travel plans and remains at her side.
August 24—*George Bernard Shaw* is published.
August 30—Holiday includes a stay at Harrow Lane, Maidenhead.
September 23—*Tremendous Trifles* is published.
September 24—Presents testimony at the Joint Committee on Censorship. Herbert Samuel presides.
October 1—Moves out of London to Beaconsfield, renting the house known as Overroads on Grove Road.
October 9—Attends the Dickens Fellowship Dinner in Birmingham.

November 16—Attends the local meeting of the Church of England Men's Society at the Old Rectory in Beaconsfield and participates in a discussion about patriotism.
November 18—DEBATE, Oxford, Oxford Union Society. With members of Oxford faculty. "That the House of Lords Is a Menace to the State." GKC argues for the motion. It is defeated by a vote of 316–308.
November 21—Attends a Liberal meeting in his new neighborhood in Beaconsfield. A local paper notes that he "is not settling down to the life of a literary recluse."
November 24—SPEECH, High Wycombe. Liberal Meeting. "On the House of Lords" (again).
November 30—Chairs a debate between Belloc and Conrad Noel at Caxton Hall, Westminster: "That Socialism Is Not the Best Alternative to the Present System."
December 17—SPEECH, London, *The Times* Library Club. "Romances of the Future."

1910

January 1—SPEECH, Beaconsfield, New Hall. Liberal Meeting. When the meeting is disrupted, he invites the hecklers to come forward so that he may debate them. They decline and disburse.
January 5—Is elected to the National Liberal Club by its members.
January 11—SPEECH, Chalfont St. Peter. In support of Arnold Herbert, Liberal candidate for Parliament.
January 17—SPEECH, Maidenhead, East Berks, Town Hall. In support of Holford Knight, Liberal candidate. Lucian Oldershaw presides.
January 18—SPEECH, Caversham. Outdoor meeting for Philip Morrell, Liberal candidate. One of the other speakers is Rufus Isaacs, who condemns corruption in politics.
January 20—SPEECH, Uxbridge, Old Meeting Schoolroom. In support of Lloyd George to be Chancellor of the Exchequer because he represents the middle class.
January 24—SPEECH, High Wycombe, Workers Education Association. "Does Education Educate?" Defines education as "that part of a human being which has to be added to him by his elders and his natural surroundings, in order to make him a complete human being."
February 3—Opening of the exhibit of the Modern Society of Portrait Painters at the Royal Institute Galleries. Includes a portrait of GKC by Alfred Priest.
February 4—SPEECH, Manchester, Chetam Hospital. Dickens birthday celebration, benefit for Chetam Hospital. "The Limelight on Aristocracy."
February 24—*The Ball and the Cross* is published.

March—Joins the True Temperance Association, an organization opposed to the so-called "Temperance League," which promotes not temperance but prohibition.

March 4—Nominated, without his knowledge or consent, to be parish constable of Beaconsfield. When he learns of it, he protests his unsuitability for the job, arguing that if a riot broke out in his home town, his sympathies would be entirely on the side of the rioters.

March 9—SPEECH, London, Clifford's Inn. Dickens' success as a novelist.

March 18—SPEECH, Liverpool, Adelphi Hotel, Liverpool Ladies' Sanitary Association. "History, Natural and Unnatural."

March 21—SPEECH, Huddersfield, Temperance Hall, Young Men's Christian Association. "Romances of the Future."

March 22—SPEECH, Hull, Royal Institution, Hull Literary and Philosophical Society. "The Meaning of the Grotesque." Says he will try to pour on them as many incongruous and unconnected thoughts as he can manage to do in a short space of time.

March 28*—SPEECH, Oxford. (He "entertained and instructed us with his humorously expressed and thoughtful philosophy.")

April 4—SPEECH, London, Lyceum Club. Dickens Dinner.

April 15—Dresses up as Dr. Johnson and presides over a dinner of the I.D.K. Club at the Cheshire Cheese.

May 5—Attends Royal Literary Fund Dinner.

June 17—SPEECH, Old English Fair at Hampshire House Club, Hammersmith, where several of his drawings are auctioned off to support the club (a working man's social club not connected to any political party).

June 25—Attends the Court Theatre in London to see three Irish plays by Lady Gregory. Sits with Lady Gregory and William Butler Yeats.

June 27—*What's Wrong with the World* is published.

June 30—SPEECH, London, Caxton Hall. Conference on the Defence of Nationalities and Subject Races. An international slate of speakers during the three-day conference defend national autonomy in Ireland, Poland, India, Mexico, Africa, and South America. In discussing "Proposed Remedies," GKC moves a resolution against Imperialism, saying "Mr. Roosevelt is wrong."

July 6—Attends a dinner of British journalists where the guest of honor is Theodore Roosevelt. Sits next to Roosevelt at the former president's request.

July 23—The first *Father Brown* story is published in the *Saturday Evening Post*. The priest-detective makes his debut in America a month before he appears in England. The story is called "Valentin Follows a Curious Trail" but will later be renamed "The Blue Cross."

July 28—SPEECH, Maidenhead. Garden Fete and Coster Fair. Awards prizes to the winners of the costume contest, although he has Frances do it because "distributing prizes is a practical thing, and anything practical I leave to my wife."

September 10—"The Blue Cross" is published in *The Story-Teller* and is immediately hailed as "the literary sensation of the year." It is predicted that Father Brown "undoubtedly will take rank with the most famous detectives of fiction."

October 20—SPEECH. Colchester Oyster Feast. Along with the Archbishop of Canterbury, Sir Lawrence Alma-Tadema, and others. Toast to the Houses of Parliament.

November 3—*Alarms and Discursions* is published.

November 4—SPEECH, Ware, Roman Catholic College of St. Edmund's. "On Chivalry."

November 21—*William Blake* is published.

November 12—SPEECH, London, Cafe Monico, "L'entente Cordiale." "On the French Character." "I think it right that French should be the language of diplomacy, because it is the natural language of quarreling."

November 18—SPEECH, London, United Irish League. "The Neglect of Tom Moore."

November 25—SPEECH, Bedford Park Literary and Philosophical Society. "Progressing Backwards." ("A large and enthusiastic audience.")

December 1*—SPEECH, Beaconsfield. Meeting of the Liberal Party, regarding the upcoming election.

1911

January 11—Signs a petition, along with several others, including Israel Zangwill, given to the Home Secretary, protesting the imprisonment of two men in Leeds for blasphemy, calling it "religious persecution."

January 13—*A Chesterton Calendar* is published.

January 19—SPEECH, Hampstead Town Hall. "The Ideals of Bernard Shaw." He arrives a half hour late. "The elite of Anglicanism were present; together with dear, deaf, old ladies from the front pew of the Baptist Chapel looking a little uncomfortable."

February 7—SPEECH, Hull, Hull Literary and Philosophical Society. "Progressing Backwards." Arrives late. Explains that he has lost his notes and leaves it to the audience to decide if he has lost his head.

February 9—SPEECH, Liverpool, Adelphi Hotel. Benefit for the Ladies Sanitary Association. "Romances of the Future." Says that most prophecy consists in saying that humanity will get more and more like those who prophesy.

The Modern Society of Portrait Painters opens an exhibit in the Institute Galleries in Piccadilly featuring Alfred Priest's portrait of GKC.

February 10—SPEECH, Warrington, Wire-pullers Philomathical Society. "The Coming Slavery."

February 14—SPEECH, Leeds University, Leeds Playgoers' Society. "What's Wrong with the Drama?"

February 17—SPEECH, Sheffield, Temperance Hall, Sheffield Playgoers' Society. "The Nightmare of the Specialist."

February 23—SPEECH, Cambridge, Magdalen College.

February 27—*Appreciations and Criticisms of the Works of Charles Dickens* is published.

March 9—Attends a trial where the *Daily Express* sues the *Penny Illustrated Paper* for libel. The judge is Justice Phillimore, who will later preside at Cecil Chesterton's trial for libel. The jury rules in favor of the plaintiff. The article in question was written by W. R. Titterton, who will go on to be a great friend and admirer of GKC, as well as managing editor of *G.K.'s Weekly*.

March—DEBATE, Leeds. "That All Wars Are Religious Wars." Supported in the motion by Fr. O'Connor.

April 7—DEBATE, London, Small Queen's Hall. With Miss Cicely Hamilton. On women's suffrage. "That the Demand for the Enfranchisement of Women Is a Sign of Progress."

April 8—Contributes £2 2s. to the "Wycombe Footpath Dispute." (Officials had tried to close a popular footpath, resulting in furious protests and mass trespassing until the path was eventually reopened.)

April 10—Helps lead a petition (eventually signed by seventy thousand) to stop the death sentence of Stinie Morrison, a Jew convicted of murder. Winston Churchill, Home Secretary, commutes the sentence to life in prison. *London Monitor* credits Chesterton for saving Morrison's life. Morrison, protesting his innocence, also protests the life sentence and dies in prison in 1921, having starved himself to death.

April—Visits Wilfrid and Alice Meynell in Sussex.

Visits the village of Stilton and learns to his distress that the famous cheese that was invented in that place is no longer made there.

Visits Lincoln and the famous Cathedral there.

June 22—First issue of *The Eye-Witness*, edited by Hilaire Belloc. Its purpose is to expose government corruption. The title of the paper is GKC's idea.

July 27—*The Innocence of Father Brown* is published, which will be his best-selling book ever.

August—Holiday in France. Visits "a small town" and its cathedral. Also visits Wales, "a curious place full of rocks; and the people there *said* it was Wales."

August 14—Adds his signature to a public letter urging the formation of an independent political party.
August 31—*The Ballad of the White Horse* is published.
September 2—SPEECH, Beaconsfield. Open-air meeting of Young Liberals.
September 14—Attends a dog show in Maidenhead for the benefit of the Working Boys' Club. His dog Winkle wins first place.
October 4—SPEECH, London, Queens Hall, Women's Freedom League. "Women's Suffrage: The Last Blow to Democracy." ("In the debate that followed, Mr. Chesterton was warmly heckled.")
October 9—SPEECH, London, Queens Hall. On public houses. Is quoted in a letter to the *Times* as saying that an immense step would have been taken in social reform if all those women who had entered a public house refused point-blank to leave their children outside.
October 12—*Lepanto* is published in the *Eye-Witness*.
October 1—SPEECH, Bristol. "On Dickens."
October 20—Attends a public meeting in Beaconsfield regarding the district council's decision not to allow the erection of telephone poles because they are unsightly in the rural setting. GKC says there are uglier things than telephone poles.
October 27—DEBATE, London, Queens Hall, National Organisations of Girls Clubs. With Mrs. F. T. Swanwick. On women's suffrage.
November—Purchases the field across the road from Overroads, where one day he will build Top Meadow.
November 3—Writes an original paper on Dickens that is read (by someone else) to the Sheffield branch of the Dickens Fellowship. "On the Party System."
November 3—SPEECH, Bedford Park, Southfield-Road School, Bedford Park Literary and Philosophical Society. "On Guy Fawkes." Says another Gunpowder Plot would be "a jolly good thing ... a revolt from below."
November 17—SPEECH, Cambridge, Guildhall. "The Future of Religion." Response to a lecture by Shaw on May 29.
November 30—DEBATE, London, Memorial Hall, Farringdon Street. With Shaw. Belloc in the chair. On Socialism. Shaw defends the resolution: "That a Democrat Who Is Not Also a Socialist Is No Gentleman." Chesterton counters by stating that Socialism and democracy are distinct ideas, that Shaw is no Democrat, and that it is impossible to state what Shaw means by "a Socialist."
December 9—SPEECH, London, Connaught Rooms. The Savage Club Dinner (members were "distinguished in literature, science, and art").
December 11*—SPEECH, London, West-end Jewish Literary Society. ("It is doubtful whether those present at the meeting, or the members of the community in general, took Mr. Chesterton seriously.")

December 14—SPEECH, Beaconsfield, New Hall. Benefit for the Children's Convalescent Home. GKC attends a performance of three one-act plays and is asked to speak during the intermission.

1912

January 8*—SPEECH, Cambridge. With Bishop Gore. On social reform.

January 10—SPEECH, Amersham, Town Hall, Amersham and Coleshill Liberal Association. "He had heard people say that because from time to time he had disagreed with the Liberal Front Bench, he was no longer a Liberal. That was a mistake. ('Hear, Hear.') It was the other people who were not Liberals (*laughter*)."

January 23—DEBATE, London, Queen's Hall, the Institute of Lecturers. With Sir Henry Seton-Carr. "Are the Evils of the Present English Party System Intolerable and Remediable?"

February 1—SPEECH, London, Caxton Hall, Christian Social Union. "The Social Obligations of a Christian."

February 8—Harcourt Williams gives a dramatic recitation of some unpublished ballades by GKC in a matinee at the Little Theatre in London.

February 9—SPEECH, Chichester, Assembly Room, West Sussex Branch for the National League Opposing Women's Suffrage. Says that the vote is not democracy, not self-government, nor the popular will. It is "a broken down machine, perfectly useless for procuring any sort of object whatsoever," and the suffragettes are trying to get a hold of something that has already become quite useless to men.

February 10—SPEECH, Brighton, the Dome. Brighton Municipal Technical College and School of Art awards ceremony. "Romances of the Future." Says, "An artist is a man who tells a lie and brags about it, and a scientist is a man who tells a lie and conceals it. That is what people mean when they talk about the humility of the men of science."

February 15—SPEECH, London, the Pioneer Club. "Dickens and the New Slavery."

February 22—*Manalive* is published. Its hero, Innocent Smith, is perhaps the most autobiographical of all of GKC's fictional characters. He "dealt life."

February 23—SPEECH, Woodford, Woodford Green Lecture Hall, Woodford Liberal Association. "Home Rule."

February 28—SPEECH, London, Caxton Hall, Peasant Arts Fellowship. "The Country vs. The Town." Says, "The peasant is the man nearest the realities of life. If the peasant is strong, the State is strong, even in defeat; if he is not, the State is weak even in victory."

March 14—SPEECH, Glasgow, St. Andrew's Hall, Catholic Social Reform Association. "Fads, or the Revival of Superstition."

March 18—SPEECH, Edinburgh University French Society. "A Plea for Peasant Proprietorship." Introduced by Charles Sarolea as "probably the most popular, and certainly the most original, English man of letters."

March 1—SPEECH, Bradford Mechanics Institute. "Mystery Plays and Problem Plays." GKC says, "You cannot have a great tragedy that is not founded on a great admitted system of morals."

March 20*—While traveling by train with Fr. O'Connor, tells the priest he has made up his mind to be received into the Church and is only waiting for Frances to come with him. It will be ten more years.

April 12—SPEECH, Westminster, Church House, Church Socialist League. Conrad Noel in the chair. George Lansbury also speaks. GKC, speaking as a non-Socialist, urges the need for civil war. Afterward a group marches from Parliament Square to Lambeth Place to present a petition to the archbishop, demanding that the Church of England support the workers' right to strike and a minimum wage. GKC's hymn "O God of Earth and Altar" is sung.

April 12*—Visits exhibition by John Hargrave at the Dudley Galleries in Piccadilly. He expresses his admiration for the work of the eighteen-year-old artist.

May—Contributes a poem for the program of the Titanic Disaster Relief Fund.

May 9—SPEECH, Beaconsfield. A presentation on behalf of the residents to the departing police superintendent.

May 10—SPEECH, University of London Catholic Students Society, Kings College Theatre, the Strand. "The Barbarian, Ancient and Modern." Belloc presiding. Cecil present,

May 23—SPEECH, Boyne Hill, Church of England's Men's Society. "Nonsense and the Newspapers."

May 30—SPEECH, Chenies, Buckinghamshire, Amersham Ruri-Decanal Conference. On peasant proprietorship.

June 7—Cecil is received into the Catholic Church at Brompton Oratory by Fr. Sebastian Bowden.

June 12—Visits Stonehenge.

June—Construction is completed on a studio across the street from Overroads, which one day will become the main room in Top Meadow.

July—Along with Belloc, helps establish the Resistance Defence Fund to oppose the Insurance Act.

July 3—Performs one of his many charades in the studio at Top Meadow, featuring Fr. O'Connor as Canon Cross-keys and Lily Yeats (the poet's sister). While walking back to Overroads, trips over a flower tub in his garden and fractures his arm.

September—The International Exhibition of the London Salon features a photographic portrait of GKC by Hector Murchison.

October—Robert Frost, who was born the same year as GKC, moves into a rented five-room house in Beaconsfield, noting its location "within a mile or two of where Milton finished *Paradise Lost* and a mile or two of where Grey lies buried, and within as many rods as furlongs of the house where Chesterton tries truth to see if it won't prove as true upside down, as it does right side up." He lives there for three years, during which time he writes "The Road Not Taken." Amazingly, the two of them never meet.

October 5—SPEECH, London, Frascati Restaurant, the Dickens Fellowship. "The Immortal Memory of Charles Dickens." (Dickens' daughters are present.) (*Times, Dickensian*.)

October 10—*A Miscellany of Men* is published.

October 14—SPEECH, London, Sion College. University of London Extension Series on English Literature and Culture.

October 31—Final issue of *The Eye-Witness*.

November 2*—SPEECH. Farewell dinner for Canon Liley. "There are people who know everything and experience nothing. They are dons. There are people who experience everything and know nothing. They are journalists."

November 7—First issue of *The New Witness*, edited by Cecil Chesterton. Successor to *The Eye-Witness*.

November 9—SPEECH, Beaconsfield. Inaugural meeting of the Guild of Arts and Crafts.

November 14—SPEECH, Dublin, Trinity College, University Philosophical Society. On social unrest. GKC sends his regrets that he could not be present for the meeting but has sent an "impromptu speech" that he asks be read.

November 19—Appears before the Amersham Assessment Committee appealing the assessment on his house.

November 22—SPEECH, Gerrards Cross, Cranley Court School. Opening of the new school building.

November 27—Committee meeting of the Guild of Arts and Crafts, at the Railway Hotel. GKC is elected chairman.

November 28—Participates in a variety show fundraiser for the Beaconsfield Orchestra, where he is described in the handbill as "armchairman, general mis-manager, and incensor of playwrights."

December 6—SPEECH, Bedford Park Literature and Philosophical Society. "The Narrowness of Breadth." Says that Islam is "an alien poison in Europe."

December 7—Signs a Humanitarian League petition addressed to the Prime Minister opposed to flogging.
December 9—Signs a congratulatory letter, along with other distinguished signers, to Prince Kropotkin on his seventieth birthday.
December 12—Attends the Browning Dinner of the Poetry Society at the Hotel Cecil.
December 19—SPEECH, Chelmsford, Rainsford House School (GKC's friend Mrs. Burke is the headmistress).

1913

January 29—Cecil Chesterton is sued for criminal libel by Godfrey Isaacs, manager of the Marconi Wireless Telegraph Company.
February 4—The papers announce that GKC's next book will be *The Evils of Eugenics*. The volume, under a slightly different name, will not be published till 1922.
February 13—Final column in the *Daily News*. A few days earlier, he had resigned from the paper. The *Daily Herald* announces that GKC will be joining its staff. The event itself is news in several other papers.
February 19—*The Victorian Age in Literature* is published.
February 21—SPEECH, Farnham, Christian Social Union. "The Church and Social Reform."
February 26—Attends the arraignment of Cecil at Bow Street Police Court. Offers to stand as surety for bail, but Cecil is released on his own recognizance. Cecil declines legal representation and acts in his own defense.
April 8—SPEECH, London, Caxton Hall, Insurance Tax Resisters Association. Meeting to demand the abolition of compulsion from the Insurance Act. With Hilaire Belloc.
April 9—SPEECH, Leeds, Insurance Tax Resisters Association. Another meeting to demand the abolition of compulsion from the Insurance Act. With Hilaire Belloc.
April 11—SPEECH, London, Monico Restaurant, Young Liberals Association.
April 17—Attends the wedding of Diana Lister and Percy Wyndham.
May 2—SPEECH, London, Emerson Club. On the complete break-up of the government.
May 5—SPEECH, London, Hotel Metropole, Royal Literary Fund Dinner. Toast following a speech by American Ambassador Walter Page. Says that the literary man is not necessarily a solitary or a lonely being but is as sociable as his cash allowed him to be.
May 6—SPEECH, London, St. Mary's Church. "The Danger of the Great Shops."

May 12—Is made vice president of the *Daily Herald* Cricket Club. "The position is not honorary but symbolical."

May 27—Cecil's court trial begins on the libel suit. Edward Carson and F. E. Smith represent the prosecution. Trial was delayed to this date due to Cecil's laryngitis. GKC attends all the sessions. The Marconi Committee hearings are being held in Parliament during this same time period. The same day the trial begins a claim is brought against Godfrey Isaacs on behalf of the shareholders of the English Marconi company about the sale of five hundred thousand shares by Isaacs in American Marconi.

May 30—SPEECH, Battersea Town Hall. "The Reintroduction of Slavery."

June 6—Testifies at the trial as a character witness on behalf of Cecil.

June 7—Cecil is found guilty of libel and ordered to pay a fine of a hundred pounds plus the expenses of the trial. He is greeted by a cheering crowd as he leaves the court, accompanied by GKC. George Lansbury leads a large protest at Memorial Hall against government encroachment on the right of free speech.

June 13—Marconi Committee publishes its report, finding no fault in any of the minister's actions, reflecting the opinion of the Liberal majority in the House of Commons. However, the minority report concludes they acted with "grave impropriety." Most papers reflect the public sentiment that the report is a "whitewash."

June 18—David Lloyd George and Sir Rufus Isaacs publicly apologize to the House of Commons for their actions. House of Commons votes along party lines not to censure them.

June 27—London, Essex Hall. Chairs a panel discussion sponsored by the New Witness League on "The Meaning of the Marconi Scandal."

July 4—SPEECH, London, Essex Hall. "Why I Am Not an Official Liberal."

July 25—Marches with a large group of "non-militant suffragettes" on the Watling Street Pilgrimage (the route between London and Canterbury). He explains his presence by saying he "wanted to see that the Suffragettes got a good hearing."

August 3—Attends the annual summer meeting of the Liberal Association of Mid Bucks, hosted by the Earl of Buckinghamshire at the historic Hampden House.

September 1*—While strolling on the Salisbury plains, he stumbles into the midst of military maneuvers. Several of the soldiers stop and recognize him.

September 3—SPEECH. Opening of the Olde Englyshe Fayre at Beaconsfield.

October 20*—SPEECH, Reading.

October 29—Chairs a public meeting sponsored by the National League for Clean Government at Essex Hall, London. Sir George Kekewich, former secretary of the Board of Education, speaks on "Corruption in Government."

November 1—Dublin Relief Rally at Albert Hall, London, chaired by George Lansbury. Appears on the platform with James Larkin, George Russell ("A.E."), and others.

November 3—Preview performance of *Magic*, Eastbourne, Devonshire Park Theatre.

November 6—SPEECH, Reading, Corn Exchange Building, National League for Clean Government. With Cecil. They are roundly heckled by a crowd of Liberals.

November 7—*Magic* opens at the Little Theatre, London, to great acclaim. GKC gives a speech of thanks following the performance.

November 15—Is named president of the Beaconsfield Rifle Guild (!).

November 18—SPEECH, London, Catholic Association Rooms, Catholic Social Guild. "The Modern Revolution."

November 29—SPEECH, London, Essex Hall, the New Witness League. On England being badly governed.

November 30—SPEECH, London, Hotel Metropole. Dinner for the Actors' Benevolent Fund. Toast. "The Drama."

December 6—Reelected president of the Guild of Arts and Crafts at Beaconsfield.

December 6—SPEECH, London, Entente Cordiale Society. "Some Differences Between English and French Journalism."

December 12—SPEECH, Bedford Park Literary and Philosophical Society. "That Discipline Will Be Necessary to the Revolution." Says that history shows that nearly all autocracies are not nearly so strong as they appear to be.

December 18—SPEECH, Coventry, Royal Opera House. In aid of the Church Schools Emergency Fund. "The Soul of an Umbrella." The advertisement in the *Coventry Herald* reads: "The title is pure fiction. It was invented when the lecture was arranged. The subject is unknown to anyone except Mr. Chesterton himself, but the audience may rest assured that it does not concern the soul of an umbrella."

In the end, "his remarks were less cast in the form of a lecture than in an easy-going discursive monologue on the conditions of modern society and things in general, the umbrella forming a species of text."

1914

Date unknown—SPEECH, London, City Temple. "The Snob as Socialist." During the question-and-answer session, GKC makes a reference to the Lever Brothers soap manufacturing factory as "corresponding to a slave compound."

January 5—GKC is threatened with a libel lawsuit by Lever Brothers because of his comments at the City Temple lecture. He is fully prepared to go to trial, but the lawsuit is dropped.

January 7—Presides as judge, complete with horsehair wig, at the Edwin Drood Trial, or rather, the Trial of John Jaspers. King's Hall, Covent Garden. Cecil argues for the defense. Shaw is foreman of the jury. The event gets worldwide coverage. GKC rules that everyone present is in contempt of court.

January 12—The run for *Magic* is extended due to popular demand. "The best-reviewed play of the year."

January 16—SPEECH, Beaconsfield Chamber of Commerce. GKC says he knows as much about commerce as he does about astrology.

January 19—DEBATE, London, Little Theatre. "Do Miracles Happen?" with Joseph McCabe et al.

January 20—Travels to Sussex to visit Elodie Belloc, who is very ill. It will be the last time he sees her.

January 22—*The Flying Inn* is published. GKC will later say that along with *Heretics* and *Orthodoxy*, it is the book he most enjoyed writing.

February 2—Elodie Belloc dies.

February 3—SPEECH, Chalfont St. Giles, Primitive Methodist Schoolroom. On peasant proprietorship.

February 5—Attends the funeral of Elodie Belloc in West Grinstead.

March 2—SPEECH, Cambridge, St. Peter's House. "Human Nature and the Supernatural." (Does not address the expected topic but gives "an illuminating talk on the differences between Catholicism and Protestantism.")

March 5—Stays in Lichfield one night at the George Hotel.

March 13—150th performance of *Magic*. Souvenirs are given to the audience.

March 25—Keeps getting elected president of the Beaconsfield Arts and Crafts Guild.

April 23—Attends a fancy dress ball for the London Press Club at the London Opera House.

May 5—SPEECH, London, Whitehall Rooms, Royal Literary Fund. A short speech responding to a toast after a talk about the need to assist poor writers. Chesterton will later bequeath his literary estate to the Royal Literary Fund.

May 8—Guest at a dinner of the Bridge House Estate Committee regarding the bridges of London.

May 9—Attends an all-night "revel" at the London Opera House, a formal social with dancing, drinking, and dining. Though many come in costume, GKC comes as himself.

May 16—SPEECH, Oxford, Board of Medieval and Modern Languages. "Romance." Defines romance as "that mood in literature which combine[s] to the keenest extent the idea of danger and the idea of hope." Attended by Dorothy L. Sayers, who writes to her parents that GKC is "much sounder than I had expected and not so fire-worky.... Altogether, a most pleasant lecture."

May 25—Adds his name to a plea on behalf of the English Dramatists' Club, urging some practical reforms in the regulation of child actors.

June 13—SPEECH, Beaconsfield, Three County Competitive Music Festival (organized in part by Frances). GKC awards the prizes and says he is entirely ignorant about music and therefore was entirely impartial.

June 22—SPEECH, London, Caxton Hall. Introduces Msgr. Robert Hugh Benson, who lectures on modern miracles. The press wonders if GKC has "joined the Church of Rome," since the talk is sponsored by the Catholic Guild.

June 28—Lunches with American critic Alexander Woolcott at Villa Villa, a London Soho restaurant.

July (date unknown)—Speaks at an unpublicized International Peace Conference in a Quaker Hostel, outside of London. Organized by Norman Angell. One of seventy-five delegates from around the world. The Great War breaks out just afterward.

July 9—Contributes sketches for a fundraiser at Witheridge on behalf of the St. Mark's Home for Boys in High Wycombe.

August 10—Attends a public meeting in Beaconsfield at Burnham Hall, called by the rector to discuss how best to prepare for the war.

September 2—Attends a secret and enthusiastic gathering of twenty-five English authors at Wellington House in Buckingham Gate, to discuss how literature can help the war effort. The meeting is convened by the head of War Propaganda, C. F. G. Masterman, and among the attendees are Arthur Conan Doyle, Thomas Hardy, H. G. Wells, J. M. Barrie, John Galsworthy, Robert Hugh Benson, Israel Zangwill, John Masefield, and William Archer. The government proposes to subsidize patriotic books, pamphlets, articles, and lectures by these writers. Arnold Bennett records in his diary that Zangwill talks too much, and Chesterton and Wells are the only ones who talk sense.

September 19—Signs a letter along with the other writers from the Wellington House meeting that is circulated to papers throughout England and America, "Why British Authors Support a War with Germany."

October 13—SPEECH, London Rotary Club, Holborn Restaurant. "Nonsense and the Newspapers." Says that the legends of mankind are much more true than their newspapers.

October 14–27*—Visits friends in Brighton. Frances remains in Beaconsfield.

October 19—*The Wisdom of Father Brown* is published.

November 3—SPEECH, London, Women's Emergency Corps. "Joan of Arc and Emergencies." Says that Joan of Arc is a great example of an emergency person. She took up the position of saying, "If nobody else will do this work, I will do it." She was very representative of her sex, women who rise up and save civilization when something has gone wrong.

November 25—SPEECH, Oxford. "In Defence of the English Declaration of War." Becomes dizzy during the talk and has to leave the platform. Manages to return home to Beaconsfield, where he collapses on his bed with such force that the bed breaks. Thus begins the illness that would last for several months. The press starts to report his illness within a few days.

November 26—The first of his war propaganda books, *The Barbarism of Berlin*, is published.

December 23—A letter, obviously signed earlier, is issued from a group of eminent English authors addressed "to our colleagues in Russia," expressing sympathy in their present position at the outbreak of the war. Other signers include Conan Doyle, Thomas Hardy, H. G. Wells, J. M. Barrie, Henry James, and Alice Meynell.

1915

January 1—The *Times* reports that Chesterton is still seriously ill, "though his strength up to the present is well-maintained." Over the next several weeks, there are daily reports in the press all over England about his condition.

January 7—*Letters to an Old Garibaldian* is published.

February 15—Frances, wondering if Gilbert recognizes her, asks him, "Who is taking care of you?" He answers: "God." A nurse later offers to wash his hands for him, and he responds, "What damned impertinence!" Frances is thrilled by these "characteristic" comments.

February 16—Frances writes to Edith Kennedy that Gilbert is "just emerging from the semi-conscious state.... He is as helpless as a baby and can only say two or three sentences at a time."

March 12—GKC continues to emerge from his semi-comatose state. He is able to get out of bed but cannot walk without the assistance of two people.

April 12 (Easter)—GKC shows marked improvement. Recites the Creed. Frances writes to Josephine Ward: "I feel the enormous significance of the resurrection of the body when I think of my dear husband, just consciously laying hold of life again."

April 20—*Poems* is published (edited by Frances during GKC's illness).
April 27—The *Times* reports that Chesterton is "now able to leave his room and hopes to resume his literary work."
May 22—First *Illustrated London News* column since his illness.
June 10—First *New Witness* column since his illness.
June 21—John Buchan writes to GKC from France: "The other day in the trenches we shouted your Lepanto."
July—Spends "one or two weeks" at Sussex by the sea recovering.
August 5—Sends a letter to dozens of newspapers in England, appealing for donations to the National Committee for Relief in Belgium.
Wine, Water and Song is published.
September 15—At Cecil's request begins a regular column in the *New Witness* under the title "At the Sign of the World's End."
October 21—Participates in a Beaconsfield fundraiser for the Red Cross. Composes an original poem for the occasion, which sells for over £30, while copies sell for £5.
November 16—*The Crimes of England* is published.

1916

January 1—When polled along with other prominent men by the *New York American*, if he thinks the war will last another year, he responds, "Distrust predictions about moral things. It depends on whether Germany finds a better spirit in defeat than in success—probably not."
January 8—Impaneled to serve on the grand jury in Bucks County. When his name is called to take the oath, "there is a general craning of necks to see the great man in the gallery."
January 12—Attends the funeral of Lord Burnham, proprietor of the *Daily Telegraph*, in Beaconsfield.
February 17—Contributes to a benefit for Clunn Lewis, one of the last of the old puppet masters in England.
April 11—Is scheduled to give a public reading of one of his poems at a high society "Poet's Reading" hosted by Elizabeth Asquith, in Piccadilly, in aid of the Star and Garter Fund; but someone else has to do it as GKC is unable to attend.
May 25—SPEECH, London, at Lord Byron's townhouse, the Poetry Society.
June 9—Matinee at the London Coliseum for the benefit of the British Women's Hospital. Included is the cowboy film made by J.M. Barrie starring Shaw and Chesterton. (The footage was shot in 1914 and has, alas, been lost.)
August 2—Signs an appeal for mercy for Irish Revolutionary Roger Casement. Other signers include Arthur Conan Doyle, Israel Zangwill, John

Galsworthy, Rev. E.J. Campbell, and Rev. John Clifford. But Casement is executed the following day.

August 4*—Contributes to a memorial for Rev. John Grant, who was the (Anglican) priest of St. Michael's parish in Bedford Park.

August 5*—Visits the Royal Flying Corps Hospital in Bryanston, London, and meets injured pilot Hugh Paynter, beginning a friendship that lasts for the rest of GKC's life.

September 9*—SPEECH, London, home of Lady Grenfell. She is hosting an old-time puppet show performed by the widow of a famous puppeteer (possibly Clunn Lewis), when the show stops suddenly and GKC is pressed into making an impromptu speech about the art of puppeteering. It turns out the elderly performer had blacked out after having "fortified" herself a bit in excess.

October 12—Is obliged to take over as editor of the *New Witness* as Cecil enlists in the army, joining the Highland Light Infantry, eventually going to France.

October 16—SPEECH, London, Lyceum Club. In aid of Russian refugees, in conjunction with the publication of *The Soul of Russia*. With Edmund Gosse.

November 7—*The G. K. Chesterton Calendar*, a second collection of quotations for every day of the year, is published.

December 29—A version of the English "Mummers" play written by GKC is performed by the children of the Foundling Hospital in London. (The text of the play is considered lost.)

1917

February 12—*Magic* opens on Broadway to good reviews and a successful run of over fifty performances.

February 23—SPEECH, Knightsbridge, Kent House. Benefit of the Children's Aid Society. "The English People." Says it is necessary "to find something that shall stand for the English as the Declaration of Independence stands for America."

April 9—Poet Robert Vernede, an old friend from the Junior Debating Club, is killed in action.

June 9—Cecil is married to Ada (or Alice) Elizabeth (or M.) Jones ("John K. Prothero," pen name) ("Keith," nickname) at Corpus Christi Catholic Church in Maiden Lane. GKC and Belloc attend the wedding and the reception at the Ol' Cheshire Cheese on Fleet Street.

July 2—Signs a letter with other members of the Dickens Fellowship, appealing for funds to build a home for blinded soldiers and sailors. Co-signers include Conan Doyle.

Date unknown—Visits Warsash, along with his secretary, Freda Spencer, and secretary of the Navy, Winston Churchill, who is Freda's cousin. While they are accompanying Churchill on an inspection of seaplanes on the Solent, Freda falls into the water and has to be rescued by her famous cousin.

October 18—*A Short History of England* is published.

November 5—*Utopia of Usurers* is published in America without GKC's permission. There is no English edition.

November 10—SPEECH, Wycombe Abbey School, Loan Fund Committee of the Central Bureau for the Employment of Women.

December 3—Fined ten shillings by the Beaconsfield court under the Defense of the Realm Act for not shading a bedroom light at night on November 18.

December 4*—SPEECH, Beaconsfield, Baptist Chapel, Literary and Social Union. "Tyranny."

December 8—SPEECH, London Poetry Society. On Alexander Pope, for which he is "severely taken to task for daring to bring into vogue again so thoroughly insincere and lifeless a poet," and to which he responds (according to one observer) with "real anger and scorn."

December 14—SPEECH, Kentish Town Day Nursery Benefit, residence of the Marquess of Salisbury. "How the Dickens Tales Come True."

1918

February 1*—Attends a local pantomime in support of the Beaconsfield Convalescent Home.

April 11—SPEECH, London, Essex. About forming the New Witness League.

March 12—Dines with Belloc and Lady Juliet Duff. The Germans conduct a major air raid on London, but Lady Duff reports that the three of them were so absorbed in conversation that they did not hear the bombs.

May 10—SPEECH. Chairs a meeting of the New Witness League.

June 10—Appears before the Aylesbury Medical Board and is classified as unfit for military service.

June 26—Appears as Dr. Samuel Johnson in a pageant at the Old Beaconsfield Fair (for the benefit of the Red Cross) and is ill with the whooping cough at the time. Frances appears as the painter Angelica Kauffman.

July 30—SPEECH, London, Holborn Restaurant, New Witness League. "The Curse of Professional Politics." Says, "People are growing tired of the war. They wish they could be fighting Laplanders or anyone but Germans, because they are so tired of German names. This is our danger. The Prussian has not escaped because he was an assassin or a pirate. Do not let us allow him to escape because he is a bore." Also says that people who point out scapegoats have sordid motives themselves. The scandals they expose have a journalistic motive. "They have a fresh scandal every day, and by their changeableness ye shall know them." Belloc also gives a speech.

August 1—Signs a letter circulated to the press appealing for funds for a home for blinded soldiers and sailors. Other signatories include Conan Doyle and Bernard Vaughan.

September 13—Cecil announces that he will run for Parliament in the next election as an independent candidate endorsed by the National Federation of Discharged Soldiers.

September 17—SPEECH, London, Cannon Street Hotel. With Hilaire Belloc. "The German Financial Octopus."

September 21—Arrives in Dublin to help recruit for the war and to lecture on behalf of Sir Horace Plunkett's War Aims Committee.

September 25—SPEECH, Dublin, Luncheon at the Shelbourne Hotel, Alma War Committee. "On the War Effort."

September 27—SPEECH, Dublin, Theatre Royal. "Poetry and Property."

September 30—SPEECH, Dublin, Central Hotel, Rotary Club. "War Aims."

October 1—SPEECH, Cork, Chamber of Commerce. "War Aims."

October 13—DEBATE, Dublin, Abbey Theatre. "That Private Property is necessary for the welfare of mankind." Against a Mr. Johnston. Shaw shows up unannounced and also participates.

October—Agrees to be president of the Mothers' Defence League (co-founded by Mrs. Cecil Chesterton). The purpose of the League is to defend the rights of motherhood, to secure just treatment for working mothers, and to oppose measures that introduce State control of the family.

November 11—Armistice.

November 26—Cecil announces he is unable to run for Parliament because he is ill in a hospital in Boulogne, France.

December 6—Cecil dies of nephritis in a military hospital (the 55th General) in Boulogne, France, and is buried in Terlincthun British Cemetery in Wimille. He is thirty-nine years old.

December 14—Attends a Requiem Mass for Cecil at the Church of Corpus Christi, Maiden Lane. Fr. Kearney, the rector, presides. Fr. Vincent McNabb preaches. "Open Letter to Lord Reading (Rufus Isaacs)" appears in *New Witness*.

December 14—Opening of an exhibit at No. 8 Duke Street, Adelphi, of "Authors Who Are Artists," featuring work by GKC, Belloc, Arnold Bennett, George Moore, and others. GKC's drawings are "curiously kin to his writing."

December 22—"Without any high moral effort on my part, however, I have managed to catch the influenza; and it is at least a broad, brotherly and human experience uniting me with the masses." (The Spanish influenza epidemic would claim more lives than the Great War, but GKC makes a full recovery.)

1919

January 7—SPEECH, London, Old Vic Theatre. Introduces a Nativity play. (He "filled his hearers with delight.")
January 21—Lends his public support to the English Folk-Dance Society.
February 2—Joins the League of the Arts for National Civic Ceremony and signs a letter appealing for support. Co-signers include Edward Elgar.
February 22—Attends the dedication of the Grenfell Memorial Windows in All Saints Parish, Beaconsfield.
March 14—As part of the St. Sophia Redemption Committee, signs a letter to the Prime Minister, urging the Christian reclamation of the Great Church of St. Sophia from Muslim control in Constantinople.
April 16—SPEECH, London, Old Vic Theatre. Introduces the fifteenth-century morality play *Everyman*. The play is performed once a week during Lent, with a different speaker introducing each performance. GKC partakes in the series again in 1923, 1924, and 1925. Other introducers included J. C. Squire and Sheila Kaye-Smith, and some Anglican bishops.
May 27—SPEECH, London, St. Paul's in Covent Garden. Christian Unity Conferences series. "Liberty and Leisure."
July 10—Leads an elaborate procession (with Frances) urging the public to buy victory bonds.
September—Signs a letter urging the abolishment of the Defense of the Realm Act (war emergency laws) and the complete restoration of civil liberties. He is joined by H. G. Wells, Rev. Dr. Clifford, Bishop Gore, Lord Parmoor, and others.
September 21—Eminent poet and critic Edmund Gosse is presented with a letter of congratulations on the occasion of his seventieth birthday, signed by two hundred famous friends, including GKC, Shaw, Beerbohm, Galsworthy, Kipling, Barrie, and others. Gosse, who was a personal friend and devotee of Robert Louis Stevenson, will later write a letter to GKC filled with effusive praise for his book on Stevenson.
October 17—SPEECH, Edinburgh University, English Association. "On the Differences Between English and Scottish Humor."
October 18—SPEECH, Glasgow University. "Home Rule for England" (on Celtic influences).

October 19—SPEECH, Bridgeton, Scotland, Olympus Theatre, Catholic Guild of Social Study, Sacred Heart. "The Disease of Hygiene."

October 30—DEBATE, London, Writers Club. With Dr. Eric Bayley. "On Hygiene and Liberty."

November 4—*Irish Impressions* is published.

November 19—The Mothers' Defence League, of which GKC is president, distributes a pamphlet to mothers informing them that visits from health officials are not compulsory and can be carried out only with the consent of the mother of the patient concerned.

December 9—SPEECH, Reading, Town Hall. "Poetry and Property."

December 11—SPEECH, Maidenhead, Town Hall. Opening a bazaar.

December 12—Chairs a meeting of the London Society, Hall of the Royal Society of Arts. Speech by Belloc on "The River of London."

December 29—Leaves for the Holy Land. Arrives in Paris. Stays at the Gare de Lyons Palace Hotel. Mrs. Cecil Chesterton serves as interim editor of the *New Witness*.

December 30—Departs from Paris to Rome. Travels overnight on train.

December 31—Arrives in Rome. Stays at the Hotel Royal.

1920

January 1—Tours Roman Forum, Coliseum. Leaves on a night train to Brindisi.

January 2—Arrives in Brindisi. Stays in a private home because all the hotels are full.

January 3—Ship departs from Brindisi.

January 3–7—Steams past Greek coast and Crete.

January 7—Arrives in Alexandria. Stays at the Grand Hotel. Visits the Cathedral of St. Catherine.

January 8—Takes train to Cairo. ("Marvellous," writes Frances in her diary. "Every scene like some picture ... from some illustrated Bible.") Stays at the Hotel National.

January 8–20—Egypt. Tours Cairo, including a visit to the Pyramids on January 14. SPEECH at the Bishop's Chapel. In a letter, GKC says that while the Jews took forty years to cross the desert, the modern Christian can do it in forty hours. He says the trip has been wonderfully easy, with the only mishap being the disappearance of his cigars from his baggage while in Italy. He is very struck by the grace and dignity of Egyptian women carrying earthenware jars on their heads and wonders why English women do not carry their typewriters in a similar fashion.

January 16—SPEECH, Ismailia (headquarters of the Suez Canal), English Club. "Sight-seeing for the Blind."

January 18—SPEECH at the Anglican Bishop's Chapel.

January 19—SPEECH, military barracks.

January 21—SPEECH, Kantara, military camp on the Suez Canal. To soldiers at the camp theatre.
January 22—SPEECH, Port Said. Stays at Hotel Casino.
January 23—SPEECH, Port Tewfik, another military camp on the Suez Canal. Stays at the Hotel Bel Air.
January 24—Returns to Ismalia.
January 25—Arrives in Ludd by train, then to Jaffa by car. Stays at the Hotel Jerusalem.
SPEECH, in the great camp outside the city.
January 26—Arrives in Jerusalem by train, and then enters the city through the Jaffa Gate. Stays at the Grand New Hotel.
January 27—Meets with Dr. David Eder, president of the Zionist Commission. Dines at the governor's house with Col. Storrs.
January 28—Visits Zion Gate, House of Caiaphas, and scene of the Last Supper.
January 29—Visits the Holy Sepulcher.
January 29—*The Superstition of Divorce* is published.
January 30—Visits the Great Mosque, site of the Temple.
January 31—Frances visits the Via Dolorosa alone.
February 3—"We have secured a typist and a typewriter!" (Frances' diary.)
February 6—Visits the Dead Sea.
February 7—Visits the tombs of Godfrey de Bouillon and his brother Raymond.
February 10—Snow in Jerusalem, two feet. All transportation and commerce is shut down.
February 11—Snow continues, over three feet deep. City is paralyzed.
February 15—SPEECH, Jerusalem, English College.
February 16—After a thaw, the city streets turn to rivers. Trees and roofs collapse under the weight of the snow.
February 23—Party at Governor's House. "All of Jerusalem must have been present."
February 26—SPEECH, Jerusalem, after dinner at the OETA office (Occupied Enemy Territory Administration). "On the Arthurian Legend." Sits across the table from Herbert Samuel! What did they talk about?
March 2—SPEECH, Jerusalem, St. George's Church. "On Dickens' England."
March 6—Visits Bethlehem and the Church of the Nativity. (Frances had taken a quick look earlier, but she wanted to save the real visit to be shared with GKC.)
March 7—Visits the countryside and hills with an American couple. Drinks from Jacob's well.
March 9—Visits the Garden Tomb.

March 10—Treacherous drive to visit the Jewish colonies (kibbutzes) about fifty miles from Jerusalem with Dr. Pool of the Zionist Committee. Tea with "a nice Jewish Colonel."

March 11—Attends "Miss Landau's Fancy Dress Ball, though not in fancy dress.... Everyone there, Jews, Turks, heretics and infidels!"

March 14—Attends a baptism at the Armenian Church of St. Gabriel. Frances is asked to be the godmother.

March 19—"A day of adventure ... Jericho, Jordan, and the Dead Sea.... It is impossible to describe the beauty of the scenery and the badness of the roads." (Frances.)

March 21—Visits "beloved" Bethlehem again. (Frances.)

March 24—Frances hosts a big tea party.

March 25—Visits the Church of Ecce Homo, and an American colony.

March 27—Lunches with Dr. Eder and Dr. Chaim Weizmann (who will become the first president of Israel).

SPEECH, military headquarters.

March 28—Palm Sunday. Attends morning service at Christ Church (the Soldier's Church), and Benediction at the Ecce Homo Church.

March 29—Visits the Convent of the Holy Sepulcher.

March 30—Leaves Jerusalem. All-night train to Alexandria.

March 31—Arrives in Alexandria. Stays at the Grand Palais Hotel.

April 1—Boards the *Helouan* for a three-day voyage to Italy. (Herbert Samuel is on board, and Dr. Eder.)

April 4—Easter Sunday. Arrives in Brindisi. Attends Mass. Upon entering a church in Brindisi and seeing a statue of the Virgin and Child, he makes the decision that upon returning to England, he will become Catholic. But it will be three more years before he is received into the Church. Takes an all-night train to Rome.

April 5—Arrives in Rome. Meets Maisie Ward and her mother.

April 6—Visits Ancient Rome: Forum, ruins, etc.

April 7—Visits St. Peter and Sistine Chapel.

April 8—Visits the Catacombs of St. Callixtus.

April 9—Lunches with Italian journalist Emilio Cecchi. Visits St. John Lateran.

April 10—Frances visits Vatican Art Museum.

After a long delay, they finally obtain visas and depart for Europe, going through Paris and then back to Beaconsfield.

April—The Mothers' Defence League (founded by Mrs. Cecil Chesterton to defend mothers whose custody over their children is threatened by government or social service agencies) is sued for libel by the Society for Prevention of Cruelty to Children. GKC pays for the legal expenses of the Mothers' Defence League.

May 1—A revival of *Magic* opens at the Little Theatre in London.
May 13—SPEECH, Oxford Union. On divorce reform.
June 7—SPEECH, South Kensington, British Women's Patriotic League. Fears about the growth of officialism on the English character.
June 20—Attends an outdoor concert in London, sitting on the lawn with Evelyn Waugh.
June 23—Impersonates Sam Weller at a Dickens Fair in Beaconsfield for the benefit of a clergy home for St. Michael's.
July 1—SPEECH, London, First Anglo-Catholic Congress. "The Church and Social and Industrial Problems."
July 7—SPEECH, Oxford, Conference for Rural Teachers. "What Children Read."
July 14—SPEECH, London, Caxton Hall, Mothers' Defence League. Protest against the Bastardy Bill.
July 15—SPEECH, London, Society for the Protection of Ancient Buildings. The only thing that gets mentioned about his talk is his comment that movies are a waste of time.
At about this time, he also joins the Committee for the Rheims Cathedral Restoration Fund, which includes both Cardinal Bourne and the Archbishop of Canterbury, the Duchess of Norfolk, and Fr. Bernard Vaughan.
August 15—SPEECH, London, Soho, St. Anne's. "Ideas from the Past."
September 26*—SPEECH, Sheffield. On marriage.
October 13—SPEECH, London, Halborn Restaurant, Rotary Club. "Nonsense and the Newspapers." His remark that the police news is the most honest part of a newspaper is widely reported.
October 21—*The Uses of Diversity* is published.
October 26—SPEECH, London County School of Arts and Crafts, Southampton Row. "The Pub and the Institute." ("He kept his audience amused for well over an hour without coming to specially close grips with the subject suggested by the title.")
October 27—SPEECH, London, Lyceum Club. "Chaucer and the English."
October 28—*The New Jerusalem* is published.
November 9—SPEECH, London, Church House. In support of the Bede Library.
November 12—Joins the Executive Committee of the Anti-Reprisals Association, and adds his name to a petition, submitted to Prime Minister David Lloyd George, protesting England's policies against Ireland. Other signatories include Arnold Bennett, Walter de la Mare, Havelock Ellis, J. Lowes Dickinson, and E. M. Forster, as well as professors from Oxford, Cambridge, and Birmingham; newspaper editors; and bishops.
November 20*—SPEECH, Beaconsfield. "Problems of Palestine."

November 25—DEBATE, London, 19 Grosvenor Square. With Hugh Walpole. "The Modern Novel Is a Sign of Social Decay." Edmund Gosse presiding.

November 30, December 1—Appears as Old King Cole at a Beaconsfield bazaar (running a tobacco stall) held in benefit of the Children's Convalescent Home. "Chesterton in real life is worth seeing, but it was a great draw to see him attired as Old King Cole."

December 13—SPEECH, Ashley Gardens, the Catholic Women's League. "The Destruction of Freedom."

1921

January 1—Departs from Liverpool aboard the *Kaiserin Augusta Victoria* for New York.

January 8—SPEECH, on board the ship to the passengers on behalf of the Merchants Service Orphanage, which brings in a "record-breaking collection."

January 10—Arrives in New York City to a huge press reception. Says he has come "to lose his impressions of the United States ... to see this country and to talk, to give inadequate after-dinner speeches known as lectures." Stays at the Biltmore Hotel.

January 11—Boston. Stays at the Copley Plaza Hotel.

January 12—SPEECH, Boston, Jordan Hall. "The Ignorance of the Educated."

January 13—Boston.

January 14—SPEECH, Boston, Jordan Hall. "Shall We Abolish the Inevitable?"

January 15—SPEECH, Boston, Jordan Hall. "The Perils of Health."

January 16—SPEECH, New York City, Times Square Theater. "The Ignorance of the Educated." Is introduced by poet Edwin Markham.

January 17—New York City.

January 18—SPEECH, Northampton, Massachusetts, Northampton Academy of Music. "The Ignorance of the Educated." Students from Smith, Amherst, and Mt. Holyoke cram into the theater.

January 19—New York City. Stays at the Biltmore.

January 20—New York City.

January 21—SPEECH, New York City, Times Square Theater. "Shall We Abolish the Inevitable?"

January 22—SPEECH, New York City, Brooklyn Academy of Music. "The Ignorance of the Educated."

January 23—SPEECH, New York City, Times Square Theater. "The Perils of Health."

January 24—New York City.

January 25—New York City.

January 26—SPEECH, New Haven, Yale, Sprague Memorial Hall. "The Ignorance of the Educated." Visits the headquarters of the Knights of Columbus and is presented with a snakewood walking stick. Stays at the home of Prof. William Lyons Phelps.
January 27—SPEECH, Bridgeport, Connecticut, high school auditorium, High School Alumni Organization. "The Ignorance of the Educated."
January 28—SPEECH, Philadelphia, ballroom of the Bellevue-Stratford. "The Ignorance of the Educated." Lunches at the Franklin Inn Club with George Gibbs, author, painter, and illustrator for the *Saturday Evening Post*.
January 29—New York. Dinner at the home of Dr. Nicholas Murray Butler, president of Columbia University.
January 30—SPEECH, New York City, Times Square Theater. "Fads."
February 1—SPEECH, Philadelphia, Bellevue-Stratford. "Shall We Abolish the Inevitable?"
February 2—Philadelphia. Stays at the home of Mr. And Mrs. Henry Anker in Bristol, Pennsylvania.
February 3—SPEECH, Philadelphia, Bellevue-Stratford. "The Perils of Health."
February 4—SPEECH, Baltimore, Lyric Theater. "The Ignorance of the Educated."
February 5—Baltimore.
February 6—SPEECH, New York, Times Square Theater. "Literature as Luggage."
February 7—New York City.
February 8—Pittsburgh. Stays at the William Penn Hotel.
February 9—SPEECH, Pittsburgh, Nixon Building. Luncheon Meeting at the Pittsburgh Press Club.
SPEECH, Carnegie Music Hall. "The Ignorance of the Educated."
February 10—SPEECH, Washington, D.C., National Theater. "The Ignorance of the Educated."
February 11—Washington, D.C.
February 12—New York City.
February 13—Montreal. Stays at the Windsor Hotel.
February 14—Ottawa. Stays with his uncle and aunt, Walter and Martha Chesterton, and cousin, Lilian Chesterton, at 300 Waverly Street. Walter Chesterton, an architect, designed and built the Ottawa Post Office. GKC does not give a speech in Ottawa apparently because his agent could not arrange a venue willing to pay the going rate of a thousand dollars, much to the consternation of several local residents.
February 15—Ottawa.
February 16—SPEECH, Montreal, Windsor Hall. "The Ignorance of the Educated."

February 17—SPEECH, Toronto, Masonic Temple. "The Ignorance of the Educated." Stays at the King Edward Hotel.
February 18—Albany.
February 19—SPEECH, Albany, Vincentian Institute, Catholic Women's Service League. "The Ignorance of the Educated." Introduced by Martin H. Glynn, former governor of New York.
February 20—Buffalo.
February 21—SPEECH, Buffalo, New York, Twentieth Century Club. "The Ignorance of the Educated."
February 22—Chicago.
February 23—SPEECH, Chicago, Orchestra Hall. "The Ignorance of the Educated." Stays at the Blackstone Hotel. Meets John Drinkwater and Sinclair Lewis in a bookstore, and they talk of collaborating on writing a play called *Mary the Queen of Scotch*.
February 24—Columbus, Ohio. Stays at the home of Mr. and Mrs. John Meyers Taylor.
February 25—SPEECH, Columbus, Scioto Country Club, at luncheon in his honor.
SPEECH, Columbus, Crichton Club, Deshler Hotel. "The Ignorance of the Educated."
February 26—Detroit. Stays at the Statler Hotel.
February 27—SPEECH, Detroit, Orchestra Hall. "The Ignorance of the Educated."
February 28—Cleveland.
March 1—Cleveland.
March 2—SPEECH, Cleveland, Hotel Statler. "The Ignorance of the Educated."
March 3—Toronto.
March 4—SPEECH, Toronto, Masonic Temple. "Literature as Luggage."
March 5—Detroit. No speech.
March 6—Dayton, Ohio. Stays at the Miami Hotel.
March 7—SPEECH, Dayton, Victory Theater. "The Ignorance of the Educated."
March 8—SPEECH, Chicago, Orchestra Hall. "Literature as Luggage."
March 9—SPEECH, Madison, Wisconsin, Madison High School. "The Ignorance of the Educated." Visits University of Wisconsin, sponsored by the *Wisconsin Literary Magazine*.
March 10—Madison. Stays at the Park Hotel.
March 11—SPEECH, Duluth, First Methodist Church. "The Ignorance of the Educated." Stops in Eau Claire, Wisconsin, en route. Stays at the Spalding Hotel in Duluth.

March 12—Minneapolis. No speech. Stays at the Radisson. Meets Jack Dempsey in the elevator.

March 13—Minneapolis.

March 14—SPEECH, Omaha, Fontanelle Hotel, Fine Arts Society. "The Ignorance of the Educated."

March 15—Kansas City. No speech.

March 16—Oklahoma City. Stays at the Lee Huckins Hotel.

March 17—Attends the Hamon Murder Trial in Ardmore, Oklahoma. (A millionaire oilman and politician, Jake Hamon, was shot to death by a young woman he had seduced. She was acquitted. GKC makes the national news by saying that she would have been hanged in England, in which case he would have preferred that she had been murdered by the millionaire, which could have been a good murder mystery, leading to the proper hanging of the millionaire.)

SPEECH, Oklahoma City, First Presbyterian Church, Men's Dinner Club. "The Ignorance of the Educated." (There is a speech at a private banquet before the public speech at the church.)

March 19—St. Louis. Stays at the Statler Hotel.

March 20—SPEECH, St. Louis, Sheldon Memorial Auditorium. "The Ignorance of the Educated."

March 21—Nashville. Stays at the Hermitage Hotel.

March 22—SPEECH, Nashville, Orpheum Theater, Centennial Club. "The Ignorance of the Educated." (*Nashville Tennessean.*)

March 23—Indianapolis.

March 24—SPEECH, Indianapolis, Masonic Temple. "The Ignorance of the Educated." Introduced by former U.S. Senator Albert J. Beveridge.

March 25—Indianapolis. Stays at the Hotel Severin.

March 26—Returns to New York City for "a holiday of ten days." He intends to "do nothing sensible.... I shall among joys, have an orgy of theaters and waffles." Stays at the Hotel Chatam, and then moves to a private apartment at 56 86th Street, owned by a Mr. Cushman.

March 27—SPEECH, New York City, Apollo Theater. "The Revolt Against Reason"

March 28–April 2—New York City. Apparently does "nothing sensible," which includes attending a performance of *The Bat*, a detective play featuring a character who is the precursor to Batman.

April 3—SPEECH, New York City, Apollo Theater. "Ireland and the Confederate Parallel." Introduced by Fr. Francis Patrick Duffy, "The Fighting Chaplain of the 69th."

April 4–8—New York City. At some point visits Aline Kilmer, widow of poet Joyce Kilmer.

April 8—Guest at an afternoon tea hosted by novelist Carolyn Wells at the Hotel des Artistes. Over fifty other guests show up, including painter James Montgomery Flagg, and the widow of George Armstrong Custer.

April 9—SPEECH, New York City, National Arts Club. Dickens Fellowship Luncheon. Travels to Poughkeepsie and stays with Rann Kennedy at Millbrook.

April 11—SPEECH, New York City, Central Congregational Church. "Literature as Luggage."

April 12—Departs from New York on the *Aquitania*, one of 1775 passengers, to Southampton, England. Meets explorer Ernest Shackleton on board. Also on board are Florenz Ziegfeld and his wife Billie Burke (who played Glinda the Good Witch in *Wizard of Oz*). Upon his departure, the New York press asks him what most impressed him about America. He answers, "The number of people who came to my lectures."

April 14—In his absence, is elected president of the North Bucks Historical Association. He is already president of the South Bucks Historical Association.

April 15—Attends an onboard lecture by Shackleton, whom he had met the day before.

April 16—SPEECH, on board, Benefit for the Liverpool Seaman's Orphanage. Also participating is movie star Pearl White, of *Perils of Pauline* fame.

April 17—Attends a church service in the ship's lounge hosted by the captain.

April 19—Ship arrives at Southampton.

May 8—Attends the unveiling of the War Memorial in Beaconsfield (to which he had made a generous contribution and prevailed in the controversy that it should include a crucifix).

May 18—SPEECH, Brighton, the Dome, Society for the Propagation of the Gospel. "On American Ideals." Says, "The Declaration of Independence is a creed."

May 25—SPEECH, London, Suffolk Street Galleries, the After Dinner Club (of which he is a founder), on his trip to America. Praises John Drinkwater's play about Abraham Lincoln. Suggests a play should be written about Robert E. Lee.

May 30—SPEECH, London, Architectural Association. "A Layman's View of Architects and Architecture." Says that architecture is the only sane art left.

July 8—The Council of the Dickens Fellowship elects GKC president for 1921–1922.

July 16—SPEECH, Jordans Village, Friends Meeting House, Society of Friends. "On Peace with Ireland."

July 20—SPEECH, Bromley, St. Mary's Hall, for the benefit of the starving children in Europe. "When I Was Young." Says that spontaneous games among children are dying out.

July 21—Portrays Theseus in the local Players' Club production of *A Midsummer's Night Dream* at Hall Barn, produced by Mrs. Margaret Halford, a Jewish woman who had assumed she was not going to like GKC, but did.

September 16—A report from the Manchester Reference Library notes that Chesterton's poetry is checked out more than any other modern poet.

October 6—Fails to show up for a speech at the Ibis Literary Society, where six hundred people are waiting for him. "I am very unbusinesslike."

October 7—SPEECH, London, Colet Court School. Russian Famine Relief Fund.

October 14—SPEECH, London, Connaught Rooms, Dickens Fellowship. Presidential address. The attractions of hell, he believes, are very much overrated.

October 18—SPEECH, London, Church House, Society of the Sacred Mission.

October 22—SPEECH, Wycombe Abbey School, Bucks Historical Association. "Meditations on Monuments." Presidential address.

October 24—SPEECH, London, Authors Club. On noses.

November 4—SPEECH, Hampstead. In support of the Bedford College for Women.

November 14—SPEECH, London. Guest of honor at the Monday Evening Authors Club Dinner. "The Fantastic in Literature." "Few people seem to understand the fantastic when it is used logically upon the principle of reduction ad absurdum."

November 16—SPEECH, London, International Franchise Club. "The Extinction of Liberty."

December 9—SPEECH, London. Benefit for the Maryfield Retreat House.

December 15—SPEECH, London, Irish Literary Society. "Poets and Peasants."

December 16—SPEECH, London. "The Alternatives to Socialism."

1922

January 13—Awards are announced in a competition for amateur photographers sponsored by Kodak. GKC is one of the judges.

January 15*—SPEECH, London, Bethnal Green, Ghetto Social Circle (group of working-class Jews determined to bring the arts to London's East End).

January 26—SPEECH, London, Mayfair Room, League of Arts. On Merrie England. "There has never been any living movement that did not attempt to recover the past."

February 7—SPEECH, London, Connaught Rooms. Dickens Fellowship Dinner. Toast. "The Immortal Memory of Charles Dickens." Dickens' granddaughter is present.

February 7—Adds his name to an appeal from the National Council for Lunacy Reform.

February 8—SPEECH, London, Kingsway, Stoll Picture Theatre Club. "What the public ought to have (in the way of cinema and entertainment)." Belloc presides.

February 23—*Eugenics and Other Evils* is published.

March 3—SPEECH, Oxford, Carlton Club.

March 7—SPEECH, London, P.E.N. Club. ("There is no better after dinner speaker.")

March 11—SPEECH, Manchester Playgoer's Club. "The Miracle Play and the Pantomime."

March 16—SPEECH, Leeds University, Leeds Poetry Society. "The lecture had no title.... It was not strictly speaking, a lecture at all, and he himself never pretended that it was. It was really a conversational monologue—the rich, racy talk of a particularly good talker."

March 26—Embarks on a ten-day speaking tour of Holland (the Netherlands). The lectures are either about Dickens or Browning, but at one that is supposed to be about Dickens, he confuses the audience by talking about Browning.

March 27—SPEECH, Rotterdam, English Association in Holland. "Dickens."

March 28—SPEECH, Haarlem, English Association in Holland. "Dickens."

March 29—SPEECH, Amsterdam, Aula der Universiteit, English Association in Holland. "Browning."

March 30*—SPEECH, Groningen.

March 31—SPEECH, Nijmegen, Concertgebouw "de Vereeniging," English Association in Holland. "Dickens."

April 1—SPEECH, Haag, Pulchri Studio, English Association in Holland. "Browning and Dickens."

April 4—SPEECH, Hilversum, Hotel Jans, English Association in Holland. "Dickens."

April 7—Returns to Beaconsfield.

April 15*—Moves out of Overroads and into Top Meadow, across the road. Says, "Of the moving of many books there is no end." Frances is so ill that she cannot help at all, and she has to be carried in a bed to her new home.

April 26—SPEECH, Royal Society of Literature (RSL). On William Cobbett. "Being on the wrong road is not a matter of degree. There is nothing in it but to turn back." GKC is elected a Fellow of the RSL.

PROLOGUE: SOME MOMENT WHEN THE MOON WAS BLOOD   85

May 4—SPEECH, Plaistow, St. Philip's Church. Patronal Festival.
May 15—Edward Chesterton dies at 11 Warwick Gardens after declining in health for several months. On his deathbed, he whispers to his son: "Even if I were to be a lost soul, life would have been worth living."
June—An exhibition at the Royal Photographic Society features a portrait of GKC by American photographer Pirie MacDonald.
June 6—Introduces a lecture by M. Francis de Croisset at the French Institute in South Kensington.
June 13—SPEECH, London, Burlington House. "The Return of the Guilds." Overflowing crowd.
June 15—SPEECH, London, Belgrave Square, National Council on Lunacy Reform. "Psychology will be the euphemism for tyranny in the future."
June 29—SPEECH, London Commercial Club. "On Prohibition."
July 14—SPEECH, London, Caxton Hall, New Witness League. With Hilaire Belloc. "The Scandal of the Sale of Honours to Benefit the Secret Party Funds."
July 23—SPEECH, London. To Indian students. "On Industrialism, Materialism, and Idealism."
July 30—Makes his first confession and is received into the Catholic Church in a tin and wooden shed adjacent to the Railway Hotel in Beaconsfield. Fr. O'Connor and Fr. Ignatius Rice presiding.
August 1—Attends the wedding of Hilaire Belloc's daughter Eleanor to Reginald Jebb at Westminster Cathedral. Belloc probably does not know that GKC has become Catholic.
August 10—Following a story in the Catholic *Universe*, the *Times* reports that Chesterton has been received into the Catholic Church, and the story is reported in papers all over the world.
September 4—*What I Saw in America* is published.
September 7—Belloc visits Top Meadow. Of GKC's conversion, Belloc says, "I had never thought it possible."
September 21—Lunch with Belloc in London.
September 24—Receives his First Communion from Fr. Thomas Walker at the morning Mass at the Railway Hotel. That afternoon is confirmed along with thirty-eight other candidates by Bishop Cary-Elwes at St. Augustine's, High Wycombe. Takes Francis as his confirmation name.
October 4—Grants interview to Henry Somerville, London correspondent for the *Toronto Star*, in Beaconsfield, about his conversion. Says it was the Protestants who helped convince him to become Catholic.
October 6—SPEECH, London, Kensington Town Hall, New Witness League. With Hilaire Belloc. "The Causes of Our Present Weakness in Foreign Policy and the Attempt During the Great War to Make a Separate Peace."

October 23—*The Ballad of St. Barbara* is published.

October 31—Signs a letter to a judge appealing for clemency in the case of Maude Hibbert, who had been sentenced to prison for attempted suicide. Other signers include Shaw, Wells, Bertrand Russell, and Lady Rhondda (all of whom GKC would debate at one time or another).

November 1—SPEECH, London, Suffolk Galleries, the After Dinner Club. Says that the general election used to be a fight, and then it became a sham fight, and now it is a sham without a fight.

November 2—*The Man Who Knew Too Much* is published.

November 16—SPEECH, London, the Commercial Club. On Parliament. Calls it "a machine out of gear."

November 18—SPEECH, Oxford. Newman Dinner. Guest of honor along with Cardinal Bourne and Hilaire Belloc. Talks about his conversion.

December 3—SPEECH, London, Hotel Cecil. Annual Dinner of the Institute of Journalists. Toast.

December 9—SPEECH, London, Connaught Rooms, the Savage Club. A. A. Milne present. Toast.

December 15—Frances Chesterton's "How Far Is It to Bethlehem?" wins first prize in the *Daily News* Carol-Writing Contest, out of five thousand entries.

1923

January 11—SPEECH, Chorley Wood, Memorial Hall, Chorley Wood Literary and Debating Society. "Chaucer and Dickens." ("His address abounded in those happy asides and witty impromptus which the speaker employs so adroitly.")

January 16—Attends a dinner in honor of C. F. G. Masterman at the Reform Club. Also in attendance are H. G. Wells, T. P. O'Connor, and Frank Swinnerton.

January 21—SPEECH, Cambridge, Guildhall, Mission Committee. "The Place of Religion in the Modern World."

January 25—SPEECH, London, Burns Society Dinner, Prince's Restaurant. "The Immortal Memory of Robert Burns." First after-dinner speech ever broadcast live by BBC Radio.

February 3—SPEECH, Bath, Three Cups Hotel (formerly the Pelican), where Dr. Johnson once stayed. Unveils a commemorative plaque honoring Dr. Johnson's visit. Gives a series of lectures in Bath the following week.

February 28—SPEECH, High Wycombe, Town Hall. St. Augustine's Bazaar.

March 5—DEBATE, London, Cromwell Gardens, Insitut Francais. "That Prohibition Is Anti-Christian and Anti-Social." GKC and Mrs. Baillie Reynolds, for. Lief Jones and G. W. Wilson of the United Kingdom Alliance, against.

March 7—SPEECH, London, Lyceum Club. "The Need for Philosophy."

March 12—SPEECH, London, Grove House. Fundraiser for Lady Chichester Hospital in Brighton.

March 24—SPEECH, London, Old Vic Theatre. Introduces the fifteenth-century morality play *Everyman*.

March 25—SPEECH, Crusader's League. Invited by Arthur Penty. "On the Case for Private Property."

April—An exhibition at the Corcoran Gallery in Washington, D.C., of portraits by Walter Tittle. Includes a drypoint of GKC.

April 27—SPEECH, London, Hyde Park Hotel. Gervase Elwes Fund Dinner, a benefit for musicians. GKC says that in the Middle Ages, England was the most musical country in the world, and he calls for a constructive effort to revive this national tradition.

April 30—SPEECH, Liverpool, St. George's Hall. "The Common Sense of Catholicism." Says, "A society based on the struggle for existence is not really a society at all."

May 4—SPEECH, High Wycombe. Berks, Bucks, and Oxon Music Festival. Distributes prizes.

May 4—Final issue of *The New Witness*.

May 15—DEBATE, London School of Economics. In aid of the hospitals of London. With C. A. McCurdy, K. C., M. P. "Is Modern Journalism Worth the Price We Pay for It?" Says, "I don't ask for a Press that leads us to higher truths. I only ask for a Press that tells the truth—and I don't get it." (The following week Sinclair Lewis debates Ian Hay about "Main Street and High Street.")

May 28—SPEECH, London, Mansion House, Village Clubs Association.

June—The *Illustrated Review*, a new monthly magazine edited by Belloc, is launched. GKC is a regular columnist. The paper lasts for less than a year.

June 2—SPEECH, London, Sodality Hall, Farm Street. "Reasons Why People Do Not Become Catholics."

June 12—SPEECH, Chelsea, home of Mrs. Hugh Spender, Chelsea Poetry Society. On modern poetry, which he says suffers from "affected anarchism."

June 13—SPEECH, Beaconsfield, Orchestral Society. Makes a fund-raising appeal prior to the last piece on the program, a Haydn symphony.

June 14—SPEECH, London, Connaught Rooms, Harveian Society. Toast to the Harveian Society.

June 21—DEBATE, London, St. Martin's Theatre. With George Bernard Shaw and Commander J. M. Kenworthy. On robots and the meaning of the play *R.U.R.*

June 27—SPEECH, London, Queen's Gate-gardens. Toc H Dinner. On reform.

June 28—Chairs a meeting of the National Society for Lunacy Reform. Walter de la Mare is the speaker.

July 6—SPEECH, London, home of Mrs. Arthur Fryer, Eaton Place, the C.W.L. Weaving Society at Bethlehem.

July 11—SPEECH, as the presenter of the Hawthornden Prize in Literature to David Garnett. "On Sham Imagination."

July 25—SPEECH, Uckfield. "Property or Slavery, which is better for national prosperity?" In the morning, attends the prize-giving ceremony at Springfield Park School, Horsham.

July 31—SPEECH, London, French Embassy, Friends of France Society.

August 4—SPEECH, Birmingham. Roman Catholic Congress. "The Catholic Church Does Not Die."

August 6—SPEECH, Birmingham. Roman Catholic Congress. "Anti-Catholic History." Cardinal Bourne present.

SPEECH, Birmingham, Catholic Truth Society. Says that the modern industrial society repudiated slavery in theory but proceeded to apply it in practice.

SPEECH, Birmingham, Guild of Our Lady of Ransom. Criticizes Dean Inge's remark that a Catholic cannot be an Englishman.

August 20—A revival of *Magic*, directed by Harcourt Williams. Opens at the Everyman Theatre in Hampstead to great acclaim.

August 23—Extracts from *Magic* at Everyman Theatre are broadcast by BBC.

Late August–Early September—Holiday in the western harbor towns of Lynton and Lynmouth. Tours Cornwall.

September 6—*Fancies Versus Fads* is published.

September 10—Attends the movie *The Sheik* in the Turret Kinema, Bodmin.

September 11—A regional production of *Magic* opens at the Liverpool Playhouse.

September 17—The London production of *Magic* moves to the Kingsway Theatre in the West End and continues its successful run. Shaw's *The Dark Lady of the Sonnets* is on the same playbill.

September 27—Attends a literary luncheon at the Ritz with Mrs. William Randolph Hearst.

October—SPEECH, Oxford Newman Club. Evelyn Waugh makes it a point to come hear him.

October 16—DEBATE, Cambridge, Cambridge Union Society. Debate on the influence of the press. Other participants: Hamilton Fyfe and Sir John Foster Fraser.

October 18—SPEECH, Nottingham, Mechanics Lecture Hall. Belloc in the chair. "The Need for Modern Journalism."

October 26—*St. Francis of Assisi* is published.

PROLOGUE: SOME MOMENT WHEN THE MOON WAS BLOOD   89

October 26—SPEECH, Birmingham, with Belloc. Together they lay the foundation stone for a new Oratory mission school on Hyde Road, Ladywood. Belloc, who had been a student at the Oratory School in Birmingham, which had been founded by Newman, says that Catholics are exiles in England. GKC says that Catholics are the only people who understand the meaning of human equality, which is a transcendental thing.

October 31—SPEECH, Newcastle. On the newspaper monopoly. "Never before were men ruled by men of whom they knew nothing at all," and, "If there could be a paper that consisted entirely of nonsense, of open and avowed nonsense, I think it would be a glorious institution, and very much more valuable than the papers which exist."

November 2—SPEECH, Glasgow, Trinity Literary Society. "The Press and Public Opinion."

November 5—SPEECH, Edinburgh, Usher Hall, the Scottish Public-House Reform League. "Prohibition and the New Morality."

November 9—SPEECH, Liverpool University, University Catholic Society.

November 10—SPEECH, Liverpool, Picton Hall, Catholic Truth Society. "The Cant of the Age."

November 11—SPEECH, Wigan. Roman Catholic Young Men's Conference. On the nonsense of journalists.

November 14—SPEECH, Blackburn High School, Blackburn Literary Society. "The Return of King Arthur."

November 18—SPEECH, Birmingham, Town Hall, Catholic Young Men's Society. Says, "Modern political views are dominated by fatalism."

December 8—SPEECH, London, Beaufort Gardens. Opening of an "author's auction" benefit organized by Sir Philip Gibbs, for the Orphaned Boys' Home at Maryfield House. Wells, Belloc, Compton Mackenzie, Katherine Tynan, Sinclair Lewis, Cecil Roberts, and Adrian Ross also appear and auction off signed copies of their own books.

December 11—Guest of Lord Burnham at a dinner party at Hall Barn, Beaconsfield, with King George.

1924

January 22—SPEECH, Birmingham, Town Hall. Birmingham Catholic Reunion. On Catholicism as the largest thing in the world.

January 23—DEBATE, London, Law Society's Rooms, Chancery Lane. With Prof. Edward Jenks, principal of the Law Society. GKC moves "that the Idea of Liberty is Declining in English Law."

January 27—SPEECH, London Coliseum, Catholic Women's League. "The Revival of Chivalry." Says that knighthood was originally a Catholic institution. Over eight thousand people attend.

February 29—Signs a petition to the government asking that a Royal Commission be appointed to enquire into the Lunacy Act. Several nobles, bishops, and literary lights also sign, including Shaw, Wells, and Noyes.

March 5—Attends *The Beggars' Opera* in Bath.

March 14—SPEECH, London, Memorial Hall, Metropolitan Catholic Teachers Association. "Expansion of Education." Suggests that it would be an excellent thing if the disreputable classes could be educated—such as politicians, the great financial lords, and the rulers of the modern world.

March 26—SPEECH, Beaconsfield. Opening of the new public library.

April. Date unknown—Appears at the Polish Legation as part of an invitation to join a select committee in support of Poland.

April 2—SPEECH, London, Irish Literary Society. "The Literature of Liberty."

April 10—SPEECH, London, Caxton Hall, Friends of France. "The Need for a Franco-British Alliance."

April 11—SPEECH, London, Caxton Hall, True Temperance Association. On a proposed resolution in Parliament.

April 15—SPEECH, London, Old Vic Theatre. Introduces the fifteenth-century morality play *Everyman*.

April 23—Unveiling of the Queen's Doll House, at the British Empire Exhibition, complete with crown jewels, wine cellar, a working gramophone, pianos, and a two-thousand-book library. GKC, along with other authors, including Barrie, Beerbohm, Maugham, and Housman, contributes a handwritten volume on pages the size of a postage stamp.

May 7—SPEECH, Plymouth, Guildhall, Catholic Evidence Guild. "On the Coming Controversy." Introduced by Bishop Keily of Plymouth.

May 21—SPEECH, London, Institute Francais. Exchanges compliments with Rene Bazin, who says he has read ten of GKC's books in French.

May 22—Attends the opening of an exhibit of art by Frank Brangwyn at Queen's Gate, London. The distinguished guests include the Prime Minister and the French and Japanese ambassadors.

May 23—SPEECH, London, Burlington House, Poetry Society. "A Defence of Rant." Talks about Byron.

June 3—Guest at P.E.N. Luncheon in London, Gatti's Restaurant. Czech playwright Karel Capek (*R.U.R.*) speaks, expressing his thanks to the English writers, including "your genial adventurer, Mr. Chesterton." The two have an "animated discussion" during the luncheon.

June 3—SPEECH, London, New Cross, Goldsmiths College. Commencement address. Receives the "honorary degree" of "Doctor of Distillery" and is crowned with the "Wreath of Bacchus" at the conclusion.

June 4—SPEECH, Beaconsfield, Old Rectory, League of Nations' Union. With George Barnes. "On Labour and the League."

June 8—SPEECH, Chester, Cinema-De-Luxe, Catholic Young Men's Society Conference. "Moral History."
June 12—Appears as Dr. Johnson at the eighteenth-century fair at Old House, Aylesbury. Benefit for the Aylesbury Girl Guides Association.
June 21—Attends a garden fair and school exhibition at Ballinger.
July 24—Attends the Royal Garden Party at Buckingham Palace, hosted by the king and queen. Other guests include American diplomats Frank B. Kellogg and Charles Evans Hughes.
July 30—SPEECH, Beaconsfield. Horticultural Show.
August 1—SPEECH, City of London Vacation Course in Education, Imperial Hotel. On Logic. Says, "Most of my admirers are lunatics," drawing loud laughter.
August 2—SPEECH, Dublin, special guest, along with Compton MacKenzie, at the opening banquet for the revival of the ancient Tailteann Games.
August 4—SPEECH, Dublin. Luncheon meeting of workers in the Sir Patrick Dun's Hospital Forward Movement Campaign, a hospital fundraiser.
August 5—Visits the Irish Industries Fair.
August 6—Is photographed with William Butler Yeats, Compton McKenzie, Augustus John, Sir Edwin Lutyens, James Stephens, and Lennox Robinson in the garden of the Dublin home of Oliver St. John Gogarty.
August 7—Attends the Horse Show at Ballsbridge as a personal guest of President Consgrave.
August 9—SPEECH, Dublin, Royal Irish Academy. With William Butler Yeats. "On Irish Genius." Praises the Irish and calls Imperialism "cannibalism."
SPEECH, Dublin, Central Catholic Library. On Catholic education. GKC says that education which leaves out the Catholic Church and her doctrines is "not only leaving out the truth but the facts."
August 18—SPEECH, Glastonbury Festival. With Laurence Housman. "The Arts of the Middle Ages." Says that the Renaissance and Modernity are responsible for narrowness and specialization.
August 23—An improvised performance of "St. Vanglia, the Witch of Fleet Street," along with a troupe of other well-known journalists who bill themselves as "The Peasant Players of Fleet Street," the Inns at Court Hall, Drury Lane. GKC takes the leading role of King Badula and Famine. Makes a lot of fat jokes. His "quips and gestures ... provoke ... long laughter." Mrs. Cecil plays the role of the witch.
August 31—The London Salon of Photography opens an exhibition, featuring a portrait of GKC in cape, hat, and stick.
September 22—SPEECH, Gerrards Cross, Masonic Hall. Introduces Charles Rouse, a former Anglican clergyman lecturing on the dangers of Spiritism.

September 27—SPEECH, London, Association of the Correctors of the Press. GKC says he speaks "as one whose writings invariably require a vast amount of correction."

October 8—SPEECH, Plymouth, High School for Girls, Plymouth Historical Association. "The Perils of Plutocracy."

October 25—SPEECH, Chiswick, on behalf of J. C. Squire's candidacy for Parliament. Squire loses, doing "much worse than anticipated."

October 27—SPEECH, High Wycombe, Town Hall. Wycombe High School Speech Day.

October 30—SPEECH, Brighton, Brighton Dome. "Spiritualism and the Child." The talk is attended by a mixture of Catholics and hostile Spiritualists. (Conan Doyle lectures there a month later and responds to GKC's criticisms of Spiritualism.)

November 6—SPEECH, London, Aberdeen University Club of London. George MacDonald Centenary.

November 8—A specimen issue of *G.K.'s Weekly* is published, featuring his "Apologia."

November 10—SPEECH, Cambridge, Guildhall. "The Superstitions of the Sceptic."

November 12—SPEECH, Hull, Hull Council of the Knights of St. Columba, Royal Institution. "Christianity and the Counter Revolution."

November 15—SPEECH, London, Westminster Cathedral Hall. Benefit for the building fund of Our Lady of Lourdes Catholic Church, New Southgate. "What Is Wrong."

November 17—Presides as judge at a humorous mock murder trial of "Crechard" (from the story "In the Next Room") at St. Martin's Theatre, London. Jury members include Agatha Christie and Mrs. Cecil Chesterton. W. R. Titterton is the counsel for the defense.

November 19—Attends a performance of an old French play, *Aucassin and Nicollette*, at the Little Theatre, arriving late, and gives a SPEECH at the conclusion of the play.

November 21—SPEECH, Edinburgh. Opens a bazaar, benefit to raise funds for a sports field for an Edinburgh school.

SPEECH, Edinburgh, McEwan Hall, presidential address of the Associated Societies of Edinburgh University. "The Universal University."

November 22—SPEECH, Radio broadcast in Edinburgh. "Unless we make broadcasting broad, it will make us narrow."

November 23—SPEECH, Dumbarton, Scotland, Catholic Guild. "Liberty and Lunacy."

November 24—SPEECH, Greencock, Scotland, Watt Hall, Greenock Philosophical Society. "Truth and Tradition."

November 27—SPEECH, Beaconsfield, Burnham Hall. Bazaar in support of Windsor Hospital.
December 2—SPEECH, Reading, Town Hall. "The Educated and the Sophisticated."
December 10—SPEECH, London, Pall Mall, Suffolk Galleries. Centennial of George MacDonald. GKC is late because of the heavy fog, and Labor leader Ramsay MacDonald fills in with an impromptu speech. GKC finally arrives and "improvised some delicious sentences out of his journey through the fog. He compared the light of Rationalism, which falls on things, with the light of mysticism, which shines through them, and he claimed George MacDonald as one of the truest mystics."
December 16–17—*Piers Plowman's Pilgrimage*, a play by Frances, is performed at Oakdene School in Beaconsfield.
December 17—SPEECH, London, Queen's Hall, Society of Our Lady of Lourdes. "Miracles and the Supernatural" along with a talk by Belloc, "Lourdes and the Modern Mind," and C. C. Martindale, "Bernadette." Cardinal Bourne presides.

1925

January—Spends almost three weeks in the city of Bath as the guest of the mayor, Alderman Cedric Chivers.
January 6—SPEECH, Bath, Royal Literary and Scientific Institution. "The Use and Abuse of Hero Worship."
January 8—SPEECH, Clifton, Pro-Cathedral Hall. Catholic Women's League Charity Fund. "Higher and Lower Criticism."
January 14—SPEECH, Bath. Rotary Luncheon. Says that in starting his new paper, he had thrust himself into a position abnormally remote from his normal mode of life, "which is that of a drifting, not to mention blind and objectless character!"
January 21—DEBATE, Exeter, University College of the South-West (now University of Exeter), the Debating Society. "That an interest in the growth of Spiritualism be deplored." With three members of the university and a priest.
January 23—SPEECH, Bath. Dinner in his honor, as guest of Mayor Cedric Chivers. "There is extraordinarily little self-government in modern civilization."
January 24—Departs Bath.
January 26—SPEECH, Gerrards Cross, Masonic Hall, Literary and Musical Society. "Mystery and Mystery Stories." Says he's thought of writing a book "Fifty Ways of Murdering Your Wife" but so far can only think of fifteen.

January 31—SPEECH, Beaconsfield, Burnham Hall. Presides at a League of Nations meeting and talks about being sympathetic with the patriotism of other nations. Earlier in the day attends the funeral of Field Marshall Lord Grenfell.

February 5—SPEECH, Westminster, Caxton Hall. Inaugural address as the new president of the To-morrow Club. "On Progress." Tells the audience that the only way they can work for the future is to contemplate the past.

March 21—SPEECH, Wolverton, County Secondary School. Teacher's Conference. "Learning and Un-Learning." ("Mr. Chesterton, with a remarkable fund of humour and an extensive vocabulary, kept his audience greatly amused.")

March 21—First issue of *G.K.'s Weekly*.

March 26—SPEECH, London, Trocadero Restaurant, Commercial Club.

March 30—Joins a committee to raise funds to renovate the Sadler's Wells Theatre in North London to an "Old Vic" Shakespearean theatre. Other committee members include Winston Churchill.

April 6—SPEECH, Radio broadcast, "The Saving of Sadler's Wells."

April 11—SPEECH, London, Old Vic Theatre. Introduces the fifteenth-century morality play *Everyman*.

April 20*—Meets with Belloc. Completes in one sitting the illustrations for Belloc's novel, *Mr. Petre*.

April 23—SPEECH, Chelsea, Palace Theatre. Shakespeare Festival. Talks about the "ostentatious apathy of the English public in regard to their greatest poet."

May 14—SPEECH, Hartsbill, St. Dominic's School. "The Arthurian Legends." Is introduced as a legend himself.

May 18—Viscount Burnham, Lord of the Manor, appoints Chesterton as the official Ale-Taster of Beaconsfield. A party is held.

May 28—SPEECH, London. Fishmongers' Company Dinner. "The Art of Journalism." Says that a Code of Honor is needed in journalism.

May 30—SPEECH, London, Inner Temple. Centenary of the birth of Charles Lamb. With Edmund Gosse and J. C. Squire.

June 1—SPEECH, Ilford. Presides, dressed in judge's wig and red robe, in bestowing the Dunmow Flitch (a large piece of bacon), in a six-hundred-year-old ceremony where married couples testify to their "connubial felicity." The jury traditionally consists of bachelors and spinsters. The winner this year is a couple with nine children.

June 4—DEBATE, Oxford Union. "That Contemporary Legislation Tends to Destroy Liberty."

June 11—*Tales of the Long Bow* is published.

June 14—Attends three one-act plays at a private theatre in the garden of the home of Morely Horder, St. John's Wood. John Drinkwater, J. C. Squire, and Sybil Thorndike are also in the audience.

June 26—In a demonstration that *G.K.'s Weekly* is having an impact, Parliament has an open discussion about what can be done to get more people in "our industrialized society" back to the land.

July 14—SPEECH, London, Arlington Gallery, Old Bond Street. Opening of a show featuring caricatures by Raphael Nelson. GKC's only criticism of his own caricature is that it makes him look better than he actually is, and that he could not live up to it. Zangwill also attends.

July 21—SPEECH, Edinburgh, World Federation of Education Associations. Presents himself as "an uneducated man" even though he will receive an honorary doctorate the next day.

July 22—SPEECH, Edinburgh. Receives Honorary Doctorate (L.L.D.) from the University of Edinburgh. Speaks at dinner after the ceremony. Calls himself "an isolated, accidental, and some would say, calamitous journalist."

July 25—SPEECH, Ilkley. Presents prizes at the Ilkley Grammar School and is himself presented with a model catapult.

August—Holiday in Lyme Regis at the Three Cups Hotel. Meets the Nicholl family, a widow and four daughters. He and Frances will return there for the next few summers to rendezvous with the Nicholls until the family comes to live in Beaconsfield.

August 13—Attends the funeral of Mr. Borlase in Beaconsfield, owner of the Railway Hotel, where GKC had been received into the Church.

August 24—SPEECH, London, Faculty of Arts Gallery, Upper John Street, British Model Theatre Guild. Opening of an exhibit of toy theatres, costumes, and theatrical art. GKC says that one of the great tragedies of his life was not being able to get inside his toy theatre as a small boy. If it was impossible then, it is even more impossible now.

September—*The Man Who Was Thursday* is produced, without GKC's authorization, as a play in Vienna—with a Bolshevist interpretation.

September 14—The Dalkeith United Free Presbytery votes unanimously to delete GKC's "O God of Earth and Altar" from the revised Scottish Church Hymnal.

September 30—*The Everlasting Man* is published.

October 5—Is nominated by C. F. G. Masterman to become a member of the National Liberal Club (again) and is duly elected. The purpose is so that GKC can be nominated for the rectorship of Glasgow University.

Attends a lecture by Paul Claudel at the *Institut Francais*.

October 25—Defeated by Austen Chamberlain for the rectorship of Glasgow University.

October 26—SPEECH, London, Royal Institute of British Architects Gallery. Architecture Club exhibit. Introduced by J. C. Squire as "an edifice."

October 29—SPEECH, Reading, Town Hall. "The Cult of the Unreasonable."

November 1—SPEECH, London, Hotel Victoria. Inaugural Dinner of the International Theatre Society.

November 11—Attends the Old English Fayre at St. Augustine's Church in High Wycombe.

November 18—Attends the inauguration of the mayor of Maidenhead, who happens to be GKC's brother-in-law, Lucian Oldershaw.

November 20—*William Cobbett* is published. Fr. O'Connor says that Cecil Chesterton was "Cobbett come again," which may explain GKC's devotion to Cobbett.

December (Date unknown)—SPEECH, Oxford.

1926

January 7—SPEECH, London, Faculty of Arts, Model Theatre Guild.

January 14—DEBATE, London, St. Martin's Theatre. "Madras House."

January 15—Attends a pantomime at Burnham Hall in Beaconsfield.

January 17—SPEECH, Bradford, St. George's Hall, Catholic Women's League. On modern religion.

January 18—SPEECH, Sheffield, Montgomery Hall, Catholic Women's League. "I Don't Think."

January 19—SPEECH, London, Kensington, De Vere Hotel, West London Circle of the Catenian Association Annual Dinner.

January 20—SPEECH, London, Everyman Theatre, following the premiere of the stage version of *The Man Who Was Thursday* (adapted by Mrs. Cecil Chesterton and Ralph Neale).

January 27—SPEECH, Oxford. "Liberty and Lunacy."

January 28—Meeting with Martin Melvin, editor of the Catholic paper *The Universe*, at the Carlton.

January 29—Meeting with Mr. Grove.

February 1—SPEECH, London, Mansion House. Aid for Assyrian and Iraqi Christians.

February 11—Dinner with the Solomon brothers.

February 16—Royal Society of Literature meeting. Dinner with J. C. Squire at the Cheshire Cheese.

February 18—*G.K.'s Weekly* Editorial Board Meeting.

February 23—Lunch at Claridge's with Martin Melvin.

March 7—Performance of a stage version of *The Napoleon of Notting Hill* at Regent Theatre.

March 10—SPEECH, London, Canon Street Hotel. City of London Workers' meeting protesting proposed bus reductions.
March 20—Meets with French journalist Henri Massis in London.
March 25—Dinner with Charles and Dorothy Buxton.
March 31—SPEECH, London, Memorial Hall, Farringdon Street, National Citizens' Union. Regarding the buses agitation. (GKC appears at the request of his friends the Solomon brothers.)
April 20—Arrives in Spain.
April 22—SPEECH, Madrid. "The Romance of History." Attended by the queen of Spain.
April 24—Visits Toledo.
April 27—Arrives in Barcelona. Stays at the Majestic Hotel on the Passeig de Gracia. Tour of Catalan arranged by poet and writer Josep Maria Junoy.
May 3—Opening of the Annual Exhibit of the Royal Academy. Includes bust of GKC by Maria Petrie.
May 5—SPEECH, University of Barcelona. "England Seen from the Outside."
May 6—SPEECH, P.E.N. Club Dinner in GKC's honor at the Barcelona Ritz Hotel.
May 8—Great Coal Lock-Out and General Strike occurs while GKC is in Spain. Titterton, assistant editor of *G.K.'s Weekly*, sides with the strikers and the miners. GKC later backs him up, but several subscribers drop their support for the paper.
May 15—Spends a week in Sitges. Stays at the Hotel Subur on the Passeig Maritim, overlooking the sea. Visits Tarragona.
May 23—Returns to Barcelona for about a week before returning to England.
June 1—DEBATE, London. With film actress Betty Balfour. Benefit for King Edward's Hospital Fund. "Should the Cinema Be Tolerated?"
June 2—SPEECH, London, Lyceum Club, Piccadilly. Inaugural address as president of the Philosophical Society. "All my life I have endeavoured to explain that my sympathies are entirely with the mass of people in their ordinary instincts. I am not a highbrow. I realise that it is this mass of normal people which keeps the world straight and that, without them, the world would soon qualify for a lunatic asylum."
June 8—Meeting with Andrew MacLaren of the Labour Party.
June 11—Meeting with Wilfred Platt, an advocate for Violet Douglas-Pennant, who had served in the Women's Royal Air Force but claimed she was unjustly dismissed for exposing corruption.
June 14—Meets with Mrs. Margaret Halford, founder of the Players' Club at Hale Barn, the local amateur theatrical troupe in Beaconsfield. Agrees to serve as president.

Signs his name to an appeal to raise funds to feed the families of miners during the strike. Other signers include A. A. Milne and H. G. Wells.

June 15—Attends the Anglo-French lunch in London.

June 17—*Incredulity of Father Brown* is published.

Meeting with Martin Melvin and Belloc at office of *The Universe*.

June 18—Attends an "at home" with Lady Beecham.

June 19—SPEECH, Birmingham, Empire Poetry League. Presidential address. Anglican Bishop Barnes is asked to introduce him but refuses because Chesterton is Catholic.

June 20—Frances writes a letter to Fr. O'Connor, informing him she wants to become Catholic.

June 22—A debate is scheduled at the London School of Economics between GKC and J. H. Thomas, M. P., and David Lloyd George (!) presiding: "Is the House of Commons of Any Use?" The debate was to have been broadcast on BBC Radio but is banned by the postmaster general. It is cancelled ("to the relief of many") due to the general strike. GKC apparently had planned to tell both Thomas and Lloyd George what he really thought of them. (In 1928, two proposed debates are banned by the BBC, and GKC says, "On this principle, wireless will soon be left to the witless. Government officials simply propose that nobody shall be controversial except themselves.")

June 24—Meeting with the Sadler's Wells Fund Committee.

June 25—Meeting with Sir Michael Sadler at the London School of Economics.

June 26—SPEECH, London, the After Dinner Club. "Humour."

June 29—Attends an "at home" with the mayor and mayoress of Maidenhead (his in-laws, the Oldershaws).

July 1—Joins the board of the Foundling Estate Protection Society, whose secretary is Mrs. Cecil Chesterton.

July 7—Attends the Royal Society of Literature Dinner.

July 8—SPEECH, London. Soroptimist Club Luncheon, where he also signs a petition for finance reform in the House of Commons. Attends a performance of the play *The Salutation* at St. Pancras Theatre.

July 9—SPEECH, Exeter, Theater Royal. Following a performance of *Magic* by the University College Dramatic Society.

July 13—Attends Evan Morgan's birthday party.

July 17—Attends the Anglo-French lunch at Princes Restaurant in London.

July 18—Mr. and Mrs. Rann Kennedy visit from the U.S.

July 20—Attends a ceremony where Bishop Cary-Elwes lays the cornerstone for a new Catholic church in Beaconsfield.

July 22—By special invitation, attends the King and Queen's Afternoon Party in the garden of Buckingham Palace. Then attends a shareholders' meeting for *G.K.'s Weekly*.

July 28—SPEECH, Beaconsfield, Burnham Hall. "On Elementary Education."

August 1—SPEECH. London, Notting Hill, Convent of the Little Sisters of the Assumption.

August 4—Lunch with Mr. and Mrs. Stephen Johnson at the Whitehall Hotel in London. (Stephen, a son of one of Frances' cousins, spent much time as a young boy with Uncle "Kind Giant.")

August 5—Frances gives a lecture on bird life to school children in Beaconsfield on behalf of the Royal Society for the Protection of Birds.

August 11—Is visited by Bernard Bell, Anglo-Catholic clergyman, president of St. Stephen's College (now Bard College) in New York.

August 18—Lunch with H.V. Lloyd Jones, who had been in the Oxford Union in the 1920s when he befriended GKC.

August 20—Meeting of the Society for the Promotion of the British Charter for the Mines. Meets at the home of Rev. W. E. Orchard in London. GKC agrees to serve as chairman; Orchard as vice-chairman. They create a petition urging a reorganization of the mining industry and better wages and hours for miners. They will eventually get over 140,000 people to sign the petition.

Also attends *G.K.'s Weekly* Editorial Board Meeting.

August 26—Lunch with Mrs. Rann Kennedy.

August 27—Meets with archeologist Denis Grant King at Rev. Orchard's home.

September 3—Meets with writer and publisher F. Garfield Howe, who had been a fellow employee of GKC's at Fisher Unwin. (Howe's wife, Anna, would be the first cello teacher for Jacqueline du Pre.)

September 9—Lance and Rachel Seiveking visit.

September 10—Meeting with Owen Barfield at office of *G.K.'s Weekly*, 20 Essex Street.

September 13—SPEECH, London, Faculty of Arts Gallery. Opening of exhibition by a group of young artists including Nicholas Bentley, Edmund's son.

September 17—SPEECH, London, Essex Hall. With Hilaire Belloc. "The League." First meeting of what will become the Distributist League. Captain Went speaks out against the "horrible" name "Distributism." And also the word "League." Several papers call it a new political party. The *Westminster Gazette* calls it "Distributiveness." GKC will argue for it being called "The League of Little People," but there is too much irony in that title.

September 21—Attends meeting of the Finance Enquiry Petition Committee.

September 24—First committee meeting of "The League" at 20 Essex Street. GKC is elected president. He suggests it be called the League for the Restoration of Liberty by the Distribution of Property. Within months if not weeks, it is referred to as the Distributist League, the name they had been warned about using and one which they will defend and dislike.

Also attends the British Charter Meeting.

September 25—SPEECH, Manchester, Eighth Annual Catholic Conference. "On Intellectual Independence." Receives a standing ovation before he even begins speaking.

September 26—SPEECH, Manchester, Memorial Hall of Our Lady of Ransom. Motion to form a Central Fund for Church Extension.

September 27—SPEECH, Manchester. Eighth Annual Catholic Conference. Toast. "To the Hierarchy."

October 3—SPEECH, BBC broadcast. "A Celebration of St. Francis of Assisi." GKC arranges the whole production, which also involves a chorus and orchestra, which is promoted to "revolutionize" the methods of broadcasting. He gives "a brilliant address" but no recording or transcript exists.

October 4—SPEECH, Kingston-on-Thames.

October 7—SPEECH, London, Guildhouse. "St. Francis of Assisi."

October 8—SPEECH, Downside Abbey.

October 9—SPEECH, Bath, Bath Guildhall, the League. Explains the principles of Distributism, a name that "had been adopted because it was long and pedantic, and for the same reason that people who were wage-earners called themselves proletarians." (*Bath Chronicle.*) Stays a few days as a guest of Cedric Chivers, mayor of Bath. While in Bath, he loses his picturesque cape. "Mourns for it like a lamented friend." Presumably, it was either found or replaced.

October 14—SPEECH, Kensington Poetry Society.

October 15—DEBATE, London, the League. "Have We Lost Our Liberty?" British Charter Meeting.

October 18—SPEECH, London, Radlett Lecture Union.

Meeting with Emile Cammaerts.

October 19*—SPEECH, London, St. Francis Festival, League of the Church Militant (Anglican).

October 20—DEBATE, St. Martin's Theatre, Royal Society of Literature. With Sir Oliver Lodge. Following a performance of *Berkeley Square*, a play about time travel, GKC argues that the instant is immortal.

October 21—SPEECH, London, home of Sir Phillip Sassoon, Park Lane, in his glass ballroom. A meeting organized by Mrs. Cecil Chesterton for developing lodging for homeless women in central London (what will become the Cecil Houses). Fr. McNabb also speaks. Large audience includes H. G. Wells, John Galsworthy, Evan Morgan, Sheila Kaye-Smith, and Lady Lovat.

October 23—Attends a special Mass at Westminster Cathedral in his full academic regalia.

October 27—*G.K.'s Weekly* Editorial Board Meeting.

October 31—Awards prizes at a costume party of the P.E.N. Club. (No report of *his* costume.)

November—Joins the Finance Inquiry Petition Committee demanding an impartial inquiry into the financial affairs of Parliament. Other members include Julian Huxley, H. G. Wells, Sir Oliver Lodge, and the Canon of Westminster Abbey.

November 1—Frances is received into the Catholic Church by Bishop Cary Elwes at High Wycombe.

November 2—Attends a reception at Claridge's for the Irish Free State. Also attending are Shaw and Lord Birkenhead.

November 5—British Charter meeting.

November 11—Attends an Armistice Day ceremony in Bath.

November 12—SPEECH, London, Essex Hall. First formal meeting of the Central Branch of the League. One of many speeches from the over one hundred members present. "Nearly all the others would have spoken if there had been time to hear them. It was a great night."

November 14—Dorothy Collins arrives in Beaconsfield and begins working as GKC's secretary.

November 15—SPEECH, Chatham Town Hall, Melway Branch of the League. "The New Despotism."

November 16—Royal Literary Fund Dinner.

November 19—SPEECH, London, Leighton House, Kensington Art Center. "The Savage in Art." Talks about Gaugin invading the South Seas. "The fine frivolity and splendid levity of the savages has hoaxed the missionaries and professors."

November 24—Attends a meeting of the Royal Society of Literature. The speaker is Emile Cammaerts.

November 29—SPEECH, London, Catholic Citizens Parliament.

November 30—Book Ball is held by the P.E.N. Club in London. GKC comes dressed as Dr. Johnson.

December 2—*The Outline of Sanity* is published.

December 6—Although the miners reach a settlement, the British Charter Society announces that it will continue its work because "no settlement under the present conditions can be lasting."

Attends a Women's Lodging House meeting with Mrs. Cecil Chesterton.

December 8—SPEECH, London, Grosvenor House. For the benefit of the Industrial Law Committee of the YWCA.
December 10—SPEECH, Oxford University, American Club. "English Mistakes About America."
December 13—SPEECH, Fulham, Town Hall. "The Fantastic in Literature."
The Queen of Seven Swords is published.
December 14—Meets with composer Rutland Boughton, who is a sympathizer with the miners.
December 15—Royal Society of Literature meeting.
December 16—SPEECH, London, Eighty Club. "The Real Threat to Liberty."
December 17—SPEECH, London, the Mitre, Cobbett Club.
DEBATE, London, Essex Hall, Distributist League. With Henry Slesser, M.P. "Can We Replace the Trade Union?"
December 20—DEBATE, St. Paul's School.
December 31—Distributist League Meeting.

1927

January—*The Catholic Church and Conversion* is published, though it is dated December 1926.
January 6—SPEECH, "The Romantic Age."
January 7—SPEECH, Westminster, Fabian Nursery Meeting, Tathill Street. "The Problem of Liberty."
January 13—SPEECH, London, French Library. When the French patrons of the library realize GKC is browsing for books there, they surround him and press him to give an impromptu speech, which he does—in French.
January 17—Attends the Wiseman Dining Society at Claridge's Restaurant, London.
January 19—DEBATE, Chatham. With Lt. Cmdr. A. S. Elwell-Sutton, Liberal candidate. Distributism vs. Socialism.
January 21—DEBATE, Croydon, New Gallery. With Sutton again. Distributism again.
January 24—SPEECH, London, Cannon St. Hotel. Men of Sussex Annual Dinner. GKC says that he has adopted himself as a man of Sussex because it is the most beautiful county he has yet to discover, and being a Cockney, he has no recognizable county of his own.
January 27—Frances is confirmed at Westminster Cathedral.
DEBATE, London, Kingsway Hall. With Lady Rhondda. Shaw in the chair. Broadcast on BBC. "The Menace of the Leisured Woman."
January 28—Lunch with Sir Gregory Foster, provost at University College, London.

January 30—SPEECH, Cambridge, Guildhall. Dominican Lecture Series. With Sir Henry Slesser. On the purpose and methods of the League.

January 31—*Hull Daily Mail* reports that GKC may run for Parliament. "The presence of Mr. Chesterton would certainly add to the livening up of the debates, and provide more interesting topics for bored reporters."

February 1—P.E.N. Club Dinner.

February 2—Lunches at the Savoy Grill in London with Rex Stout, creator of Nero Wolfe.

Women's Lodging House Meeting at Mansion House with Mrs. Cecil Chesterton.

February 4—SPEECH, London, the Delphi Coterie. "The Financier as a Figure in History."

February 6—Attends consecration of St. Teresa's Church in Beaconsfield.

February 7—SPEECH, Old Boys' Club, Mile End Road. "Is Journalism Justifiable?"

February 12—SPEECH, London, Messengers of Faith. "The True Reforms."

February 14—DEBATE, London, Essex Hall, the League. With Gordon Selfridge. "The Menace of Monopoly." Other speakers include Belloc and St. John Ervine.

February 17—SPEECH, Venture Society. "An Aspect of St. Francis of Assisi."

February 18—*G.K.'s Weekly* Editorial Board Meeting.

February 22—SPEECH, Westminster, Central Hall. National Society for Lunacy Reform.

February 26—SPEECH, Bethnal Green Men's Institute.

March 1—Attends the Invalids Dinner hosted by J. C. Squire.

March 3—SPEECH, London. Annual Dinner of the National Federation of Retail Newsagents, Booksellers, and Stationers. "I have always found that people who were selling papers and books were people who were worth talking to."

March 7—Attends the wedding of Freda Spencer.

March 8—Meeting with the Polish minister regarding upcoming trip to Poland.

March 11—Meets with Sir James Marchant.

G.K.'s Weekly Board of Directors Meeting.

March 15—Meeting with Mrs. Byass of Chatto and Windus, which is about to publish *The Return of Don Quixote*.

March 18—SPEECH, London, the Friday Club.

March 23—Attends P.E.N. Club Meeting.

March 25—SPEECH, London, the Devereux, the League. The Distributist concept of liberty. Following a speech by Fr. McNabb.

March 27—Attends the opening ceremony of the first Cecil House in London, a shelter for homeless women, founded by his sister-in-law. GKC sits on a stair chuckling at how the many luminaries present pack themselves into the small house. Lady Violet Bonham Carter is one of the speakers. The queen sends a generous donation. The Cecil Houses still operate in London.

March 30—A statue of Pope Pius XI is unveiled at the Ambrosian Library in Milan. GKC, along with Cardinal Bourne and the Duke of Norfolk, is on the English committee that raised funds for the statue.

April 4—Attends the Old Pauline Dinner, London.

April 5—Dinner with the Solomon brothers, Beaconsfield.

April 6—Belloc visits.

April 7—SPEECH, Kings College.

Chairs the P.E.N. Club Meeting.

April 8—SPEECH, Maida Vale Literary Society. "On Certain New Poets." He says, "Though we may think too much of Victorian poets, modern poets think too much of themselves."

April 12—SPEECH, London, Essex Hall. With members of the League. In support of independent bus owners and street stall-holders.

April 23—SPEECH, H.A.C. Dinner. Toast. "England."

April 26—Departs for Poland. A member of the Polish Embassy sees him off from Liverpool Street Station. Arrives in Berlin the next day.

April 28—Arrives in Warsaw. Spectacular reception at train station with military honor guard and large crowd. Stays at the Hotel Europski.

April 29—SPEECH, Polish P.E.N. Club. Attends a play at the National Theatre.

April 30—Attends a dinner in his honor at the British Embassy.

May 1—Visits the towns of Lowicz and Borowo. Visits the estate of former Polish Prime Minister Wladyslaw Grabski.

May 2—SPEECH, Polish P.E.N. Club. Huge dinner in his honor. Frances notes that the speeches by their hosts are delivered in "quite colloquial and very witty" English, showing "a detailed knowledge" of GKC's works far surpassing that of any her acquaintances.

May 3—Attends reception in his honor at the former Royal Palace. "Everybody in Warsaw was there." (Frances' diary.)

May 4—Attends dinner in his honor in "the very famous wine-cellar of the Fukier family which dates from 1610."

May 5—SPEECH, P.E.N. Club. Luncheon meeting. Reduces the audience to tears. Dorothy Collins reports that she has never heard a more inspiring talk. In the evening, meets with Marshall Jozef Pilsudski, leader of Poland.

May 7—Travels to Poznan by overnight train.
May 8—Attends Sunday Mass in Poznan.
May 9—Lunch with the provincial governor.
May 10—Visits a rural area and lunches with a surgeon whose mother was English.
May 11—Meets with Roman Dmowski, leader of the National Democratic Party, Pilsudski's defeated rival, who a few years before had visited Top Meadow.
May 12—Arrives in Cracow.
The Return of Don Quixote is published.
May 13—Attends a play at the national theatre about the destiny of Poland. Before the play a speech is made, praising GKC for all he has done for the Polish people. The audience gives him a standing ovation.
May 14—SPEECH, University of Cracow.
May 15—SPEECH, University of Cracow.
May 16—Visits Zakopane. Buys several walking sticks. On the drive back to Cracow, encounters a car accident, and they drive a man to the hospital.
May 17—Leaves Cracow for Lwow. Stays at the Hotel George.
May 18—SPEECH, University of Lwow.
May 19—Takes a tour of the countryside by a Polish soldier. Visits small villages where everyone comes out to meet him.
May 21—Returns to Warsaw to more huge crowds.
May 22—SPEECH to a Catholic study circle on Catholicism in England. Attends Mass at Chopin's church. Meets Joseph Conrad's niece.
May 23—Takes a night train to Vilna.
May 24—Arrives in Vilna (also known as Wilno and Vilnius), near the Russian border.
May 25—SPEECH, local P.E.N. Club.
May 26—Visits Count Tyszkiewicz, who had been educated in England at Downside and whose huge estate had been burned down by Russian soldiers. Visits a small settlement of four hundred Karaim Jews (who do not accept the Talmud). Attends a service in the synagogue and receives a blessing from the rabbi.
May 27—Visits the Jewish Ghetto in Vilna.
May 28—Leaves on a night train to Warsaw. A crowd sees him off from the station in Vilna.
May 29—SPEECH. Farewell luncheon at the Polish P.E.N. Club. GKC talks about the real dangers of Bolshevism and how the one main thing that has spared Western Europe from "direct and unpleasant contact" with Bolshevism is Poland.
May 31—Leaves Warsaw.

June 1—Arrives in Berlin.

June 2—Gets on the wrong train. Instead of going to Cologne, goes to Aachen.

June 3–9—Arrives in Bruges. Spends a week in Belgium. Visits Ghent and Antwerp.

Arrives back in England about June 10.

June—*Collected Poems* is published.

June 17—*G.K.'s Weekly* Editorial Board Meeting.

June 21—DEBATE, London School of Economics. With Mitchell Banks, M.P., and novelist Rose Macauley. "Is the House of Commons of Any Use?" "The London School of Economics ... should be the very temple of the abstract sciences. But what impressed [me] most in the debate, entertaining and energetic as it was, was that the prevailing process of thought seems to be not so much a pedantic or academic detachment as an almost childish literalism."

June 23—SPEECH, French Club. "The Real Realist."

June 24—SPEECH, Oxford Luncheon Club. "The New Nicholas Nickleby" (i.e., the new tyranny of financial power).

June 28—SPEECH, London, University of London, Great Hall. "Culture and the Coming Peril." He warns about "standardisation by a low standard."

June 29—SPEECH, London, the After Dinner Club.

June 30—SPEECH, Westminster, Cathedral Hall. Annual Meeting of the Converts' Aid Society. (Top Meadow will one day be bequeathed to the Converts' Aid Society and used for housing Anglican clergy who had converted to the Catholic faith.)

July 3—Meets with Polish scholar Roman Dyboski.

July 4—*G.K.'s Weekly* Editorial Board Meeting.

July 6—SPEECH, London. On Shakespeare.

Attends Old Pauline Club at Trocadero Restaurant

July 7—SPEECH, London, Essex Hall, Distributist League. "What Poland Is." Huge crowd. Cardinal Bourne is present.

Also attends the Annual Meeting of the Catholic Prisoners' Aid Society at Caxton Hall.

July 8—Dinner with the Solomons.

July 9—SPEECH, Woking, Hookheath School. Awards prizes.

July 13—Attends Evan Morgan's birthday party. Other distinguished guests include the Sitwells, Alfred Noyes, actress Elsa Lanchester, Lord Balfour, and members of the royal family.

July 14—SPEECH, Horder's Dinner.

July 15—Dinner with the Marquis de Chambrun at Savoy.

July 16—Attends a silver wedding celebration for the Oldershaws.

July 18—*G.K.'s Weekly* Editorial Board Meeting.
July 20—Meeting with James Garvin, editor of *The Observer*.
July 22—SPEECH, Wimbledon, King's College Junior School. Awards prizes. Dinner with Evan Morgan.
July 26—Attends the wedding of Peter Gilbert Belloc, son of Hilaire, at Hove.
August 3—Meeting for Cecil House. Dinner with Evan Morgan at the Ambassadors Club.
August 5—Meets J. P. De Fonseka for the first time at the offices of *G.K.'s Weekly*.
August 6–9—Visits Bath as a guest of Mayor Cedric Chalmers. It is probably on this trip when, en route, he dines at the Spread Eagle Inn in Thame, which is recorded in John Fothergill's *An Innkeeper's Diary*.
August 9—SPEECH, Bath, Concert Hall of the Pump Room. "The Perils of Pantomime."
August 24–28—Visits Brighton with Belloc.
August 26—SPEECH, Brighton, Catholic School. Awards prizes.
September—Contributes to the founding of a School of Drama as part of the University of the South-West (now University of Exeter).
September 2—*G.K.'s Weekly* Editorial Board Meeting. Meets with a Fr. Stephen Brown (a real Fr. Brown).
September 10—Attends the wedding of Joan Mills.
September 15—*The Secret of Father Brown* is published.
September 17—SPEECH, Beaconsfield. Chairs a debate at Burnham Hall between Liberal and Labour Party protagonists.
October 6—SPEECH, London, the Dickens Fellowship (twenty-fifth anniversary). "On the Need of a Modern Satirist."
October 10—Serves as foreman of the grand jury for the Bucks quarter session at Aylesbury.
October 12—SPEECH, Oxford Student Union. On Distributism.
October 14—*G.K.'s Weekly* Editorial Board Meeting.
October 17—SPEECH, Buxton Literary Society. "The Modern Drama."
October 18—SPEECH, Hoylake. "The Modern Novel."
October 19—SPEECH, Liverpool, Congregational Church Literary Society, Great George Street Congregational Church. "Charles Dickens."
October 20—SPEECH, Glasgow Literary Society. "Charles Dickens." Visits Convent of Notre Dame.
October 21—SPEECH, Aberdeen, YMCA Hall. "On the Modern Novel."
October 24—SPEECH, Glasgow. "Some Thoughts on G.B.S."
October 25—SPEECH, Glasgow, Liberal Club of Glasgow University in the Student Union. "The Danger of Modern Organization." He says that Utopia was never a democratic creation.

October 27—The play *The Judgment of Dr. Johnson* is published. It is not performed till 1932.

October 28—SPEECH, London, Wyndham Theatre. Fundraiser for the Cecil House. John Drinkwater presides.

DEBATE, London, Kingsway Hall. With George Bernard Shaw. Belloc in the chair. Broadcast on BBC. "Do We Agree?"

October 29—SPEECH, Temple Bar Restaurant. Dinner for the League. GKC acknowledges a generous donation from Shaw to the League and genially toasts him as "Our Greatest Enemy."

October 31—SPEECH, London, *G.K.'s Weekly* Shareholders Meeting.

November 3—SPEECH, Beaconsfield. Liberal Meeting. "Liberalism as I See It."

November 4—SPEECH, London, Marylebone Hall. Chairs a debate "The Fallacy of Socialism?" between Sir Ernest Benn and John Scurr, M.P. In summing up, GKC says, "I am in hearty disagreement with nearly everything that has been said."

November 8—SPEECH, London, Leighton House, Irish Literary Society. *Robert Louis Stevenson* is published.

November 14—SPEECH, Great Eastern Hotel. General East End Tradesmen's Association Dinner in Aid of the London Hospital. "Sunlight Treatment."

November 17—SPEECH, London, the Tomorrow Club (for literary aspirants). Says the immediate tomorrow is in the hands of vulgar Americans, but the whole intelligent world anticipates the triumphs of the day after tomorrow. Other speakers include Sheila Kaye-Smith.

November 18—Meets with Fr. Vincent McNabb, Adam de Hegotius (editor of a daily paper in Budapest), and Mr. Anthony, a reporter for *Cosmopolitan* magazine.

November 19—Attends the wedding of Ralph Neale at St. Ethelreda's, Ely Place.

November 21—Attends the funeral of C. F. G. Masterman at St. Margaret's Church, Westminster. Also attending are Winston Churchill, Lloyd George, and Herbert Samuel.

SPEECH, Royal Literary Society Meeting. "The Religious Background in Literature."

November 22—Meets with Polish philosopher Wincenty Lutoslawski.

November 23—Attends a lecture by Robert Lynd at the Royal Society of Literature.

November 25—Catholic Writers Day. Mass with Cardinal Bourne. Meets with Fr. McNabb.

SPEECH and conference with Catholic writers.

SPEECH, Hotel Russell. Robert Louis Stevenson Club Annual Dinner. Toast. Quotes Stevenson extensively, all from memory.
November 26—Attends the *Old Girls* play in Beaconsfield.
November 28—SPEECH, Gerrards Cross Literary Society, Masonic Hall. "Progress and Old Books."
November 29—SPEECH, London, Anderson's Hotel. Introduced by Gustaf Hellstrom, Swedish Minister Baron Palmstetna.
November 30—*G.K.'s Weekly* Editorial Board Meeting.
December 3—SPEECH, International Student Movement House Club. "Medieval Monasticism."
December 5—DEBATE, London, Sesame Club. With Selfridge. "What Is the Distributive Future of the Small Shopkeeper?"
December 9—*GK's Weekly* Editorial Board Meeting.
Attends one-act plays at the Players Club in Beaconsfield.
December 14—Attends Royal Literary Society Meeting.
December 15—SPEECH, London. Whitefriars Club Dinner. Toast. "Literature and Poetry."
December 16—SPEECH, London, Cannon Street Hotel, Delphian Coterie. "The Americanization of England." Says if the Kaiser had occupied London, he could not have denationalized it as America has done.
December 17—Is interviewed by a reporter from Budapest. Visits the Victoria and Albert Museum.
December 18—Tea with the Fordhams.
December 19—Cosmo Monkhouse visits.
December 20—Attends Distributist League Christmas Dinner at the Devereux.
December 21—Hugh Paynter visits.
December 22—Elizabeth Belloc visits.
Attends a special screening of Cecil B. de Mille's "The King of Kings" at the Opera House, Covent Garden, with a distinguished audience of mostly clergy and authors.

1928

January 5—SPEECH, London, Wyndham's Theatre. Chairs a debate on the writer William Congreve.
January 6—SPEECH, London. University College, Great Hall, the Nursery School Association. "Some Doubts on Education."
Distributist League Twelfth Night Dinner, Physics Theatre.
January 12—Editorial Board Meeting
January 19—Meeting with the Booksellers Provident Association.
SPEECH, Johnson Society of Pembroke College, Dr. Johnson's House.

January 22—SPEECH, London, Hotel Cecil, the O.P. Club. "Don Quixote and the Puppets."
January 23—Wiseman Society Meeting.
January 27—SPEECH, Aberystwyth, University College of Wales. Presidential address to the Debates Union. "Liberty: The Last Phase." Is greeted by students, carrying javelins, "a guard of honour," and is pulled by other students in a carriage.
February 1—SPEECH, London, Trocadero Restaurant. Catholic Association Dinner. Toast.
February 3—Meeting with Mr. Barnett of the *Jewish Chronicle.*
Sadler's Wells Fund Meeting.
February 4—SPEECH, London School of Economics. Conference on Agriculture and the Small Farmer. "The Fallacy of Mass Production." Other participants include Fr. Vincent McNabb and C. G. Heseltine.
February 8—SPEECH, Writers Club. "Crimes in Literature."
February 9—Attends a "picture show" with David Bomberg, Leicester Galleries.
February 10—Attends one-act plays by the Players Club, Beaconsfield.
February 12—Attends a reception at the archbishop's house following a Vespers service at Westminster Cathedral, commemorating the sixth anniversary of the pontificate of Pope Pius XI.
February 13—Editorial Board Meeting.
February 14—SPEECH, London Day Training College, City Literary Institute. "The Religious Interpretation of History."
Meeting with the Emigration Council.
February 16—SPEECH, London, League of Arts Annual Meeting.
February 20—Meeting with Mrs. Cecil Chesterton.
February 21—Scheduled to be part of a debate at Cambridge about making divorce laws less restrictive, but he sends a telegram of apology: "Suddenly knocked up with a cold. Difficult to expose fallacy of divorce in dumb show."
February 22—Royal Society of Literature Meeting.
February 25—Meeting with Dennis Braybrooke.
February 26—SPEECH, After Dinner Club.
February 29—Attends lecture at Burlington house on Wilkie Collins by his biographer H. W. Garrod.
March 7—Attends the Cobbett Club Annual Dinner at Oxford.
March 9—SPEECH, London, First Avenue Hotel. Catenian Lunch.
March 12—SPEECH, Booksellers Provident Annual Meeting. "Books and the Journalist."
March 13—SPEECH, Winslow, Bucks Clerical Society. "Aspects of the Roman Question."

March 16—Distributist League meeting.
March 21—SPEECH, Eton College Political Society. "The Destruction of Democracy."
March 23—Editorial Board Meeting.
March 29—SPEECH, London, Essex Hall, Distributist League. With W. Mellor (editor of *Daily Herald*) and W. R. Titterton. "Free Speech and the Press."
March 30—SPEECH, Tetbury, Literary and Debating Society. "Mystery in Literature."
April 4—Spends several days in Bath as a guest of Mayor Cedric Chivers.
April 13—SPEECH, Distributist League.
April 15—SPEECH, Dublin, Theatre Royal, Society of St. Vincent de Paul. "Pagan and Modern Rome."
April 19—Attends a performance of *The Mikado*.
April 20—SPEECH, London, Essex Hall, with members of the League and the major political parties. "What Is Wrong with the Mines?"
Meeting with Mr. Barnett of the *Jewish Chronicle*.
April 21—Attends the wedding of Evan Morgan and Lois Sturt at Brompton Oratory, Fr. C. C. Martindale presiding.
April 25—SPEECH, London, Drapers Hall, Throgmorton Street. Drapers Company Dinner.
April 26—Editorial Board Meeting.
April 27—Players Club Annual Meeting.
Distributist League Executive Meeting.
April 29—SPEECH, London, Guildhouse, Eccleston Square. "Beauty in the Commonplace."
May 2—Attends Writers Club Dance, Suffolk Galleries.
May 3—Meeting with J. P. de Fonseka.
May 25—Is visited by Sigrid Undset in Beaconsfield.
May 26—Dinner with Archbishop Bourne, Westminster.
June 1—Meeting with reporter May Bateman.
June 6—DEBATE, London, Lady Beecham's House. With Professor MacBride of the Eugenics Society. "Heredity for Parents and Children." MacBride speaks first, and his supporters walk out when it is Chesterton's turn. He speaks to a half-empty room.
June 12—Attends the Hawthornden Prize Award. Siegfried Sassoon is the recipient.
June 15—Attends the English Association Dinner at the Metropole Hotel. J. P. de Fonseka is the speaker.
June 20—DEBATE, Writers Club. With Rose Macaulay. "That the Value of Faith Has Often Been Overrated."

June 22–23—SPEECH(ES), Beaconsfield, Old Rectory gardens. Open-air performances of "The Pied Piper of Hamelin." Gives a prologue before each performance about the legend of the Pied Piper.

June 26—SPEECH, London, After Dinner Club. Presidential address. "Humour."

June 27—Converts Aid Society Annual Meeting, Cathedral Hall, Westminster.

June 28—SPEECH. Vintners Company Dinner.

July 2—Attends a performance of his play *The Tragic Women* (along with a performance of *The Vice* by Luigi Pirandello) at the Garden Theatre, London. Performed by Barbara Horder.

July 3—Dinner with Mr. and Mrs. Rann Kennedy.

July 4—Belloc visits for a day.

July 5—Dinner with Fr. Walker.

July 8—Meets with Rose Macaulay.

July 9—SPEECH, Railway Hotel. On the occasion of Fr. Walker's Jubilee, and his departure from St. Teresa's Church.

July 11—Sees the movie *The Thief of Bagdad*.

July 12—Visits Brighton for a few days. Sees Belloc.

July 23—SPEECH, London, Victoria and Albert Museum. Inaugural address for a course of lectures to teachers in art schools. "The Relationship Between the Art of the Author and That of the Painter."

July 26—Attends a tea with King George.

July 30—Is visited by William Lyons Phelps.

July 31—Visits the Oldershaws at Maidenhead.

August 7—Dinner with Mr. and Mrs. Reginald Jebb (Belloc's daughter and son-in-law).

August 11–24—Two-week holiday in Bath and Lyme Regis.

August 25—SPEECH, Wormwood Scrubs Prison. "Dickens."

August 29—SPEECH, London, L.C.C. Training School, Southampton Row. "The Meaning of Democracy."

September 6—SPEECH, Toc H. "Distributism."

September 9*—An emergency Editorial Board Meeting for *G.K.'s Weekly* is held in Bath at the home of Cedric Chivers, who is ill; the meeting is actually held in his bedroom. Regarding the paper's drastic financial state. GKC is also taken ill at the same time. Cecil Palmer insists on removing Titterton and the business manager from the paper and forming a new board under his chairmanship.

September 21—Attends the Malvern School Play.

October 4—SPEECH, University Extension.

October 16—Meeting with Methuen.

October 18—*Generally Speaking* is published.

SPEECH, University Extension.

PROLOGUE: SOME MOMENT WHEN THE MOON WAS BLOOD   113

October 20—Dinner with Hugh Paynter.
October 24—SPEECH at a convent (uncertain which convent).
October 26—Meeting for Cecil House.
October 27—Annual Meeting of the Distributist League.
November 1—SPEECH, University Extension.
November 2—Players Club performs three plays.
November 8—Meeting with Fr. Vincent McNabb.
November 9—Distributist League Dinner, Devereaux Restaurant.
November 12—At home with the Bentleys.
November 13—SPEECH, Knights of Columbus Meeting.
November 23—DEBATE, Distributist League.
November 28—SPEECH, London, Hyde Park Hotel, Society of Authors. Toast to James Barrie, who is the new president.
November 29—SPEECH, Royal Society of Arts. "On Cottage Preservation."
November 30—SPEECH, Oxford, Randolph Hotel. Inaugural meeting of the Charles Fox Association.
December 4—Editorial Board Meeting.
December 5—Writers Club Meeting. Discussion on *Magic*.
December 7—Players Club performs *Outward Bound*.
December 10—Meeting with Ivor Nicholson, editor of *Pall Mall*.
December 15—Attends a Woodland Babies nativity program with Frances at Chalfont Hall, Princes Risborough, which includes a performance of "How Far Is It to Bethlehem?"
December 16—SPEECH. Franklin Dyall Dinner. "On Victoria."
December 18—Wiseman's Dining Society, Claridges.
December 19—Meeting with Kenelm Foss, who had produced *Magic*.
December 20—Attends the wedding of Joan Bennett.
December 22—Attends the Merry Masque at Chelsea Palace.
December 24—BBC broadcast of "The Children's Hour" with GKC and Frances.
December 26—Meeting with E. W. Fordham.
December 29—SPEECH, Jordans, Village Hall, Social Guild. "Twelfth Night."

1929

January 3—Lunch with Maisie Ward and Mrs. Wilfrid Ward.
January 4—Sculptor Thomas J. Murphy unveils a bust of GKC and is elected to the Royal Society of Sculptors.
January 7—SPEECH, the Savage Club.
January 14—SPEECH, Chelsea, Chelsea Palace Theatre. Before a performance of *Holy Night*, a play by Gregorio Sierra. Defines Catholic plays as "plays in which Catholic players would not be ashamed to play."

January 15—SPEECH, Rostand's Fantastes.
January 16—SPEECH, London, Swinton House, Kings Cross. London Socialist Forum. "On Distributism."
January 18—SPEECH, London, Simpson's, Thomas More Society.
January 23—Meets with Irish Nationalist politician Tim Healy.
January 29—SPEECH, London, Bank of England Literary Society. "On Dickens' and Hardy's Times."
February 2—Attends the funeral of Cedric Chivers, Bath.
February 12—SPEECH, Hull, Royal Institution, Hull Literary and Philosophical Society, "The Modern Novel." "Not only has the family been broken up in modern fiction, but the individual has been broken up also."
February 13—SPEECH, Bridlington, Lounge Theater. "The Modern Novel."
February 19—SPEECH, Bexhill Literary Society. "The Modern Novel."
February 25—SPEECH, Cromwell Gardens, Alliance Francoise.
February 26—SPEECH, Brighton, Congregational Church, Purley Literary Society. "Dickens."
February 27—SPEECH, London, Royal Society of Arts, Society for the Preservation of Ancient Cottages.
March 11—Lunch with Hilary Pepler. Meeting with Belloc.
March 13—Meeting with Walter de la Mare.
March 15—Attends the official opening of a new Cecil House in London that will accommodate up to sixty women. Home Secretary William Joynson-Hicks presides. Many dignitaries are present.
March 20—Meeting with Belloc.
March 21—DEBATE, London, Wyndham Theatre. "About *Major Barbara*."
April 10—Royal Society of Literature Meeting.
April 13—Signs a public letter urging the establishment of better public houses.
May 3—SPEECH, Distributist Meeting. Opens a debate on "Our Cure for Unemployment."
May 15—Maurice Baring visits.
May 22—Mrs. Digby d'Avigdor visits.
June 4–5—Fr. O'Connor visits.
June 7—Is a guest at the annual meeting of the English Association at Bedford College.
June 20—SPEECH, London, Faculty of Arts Gallery. With Eric Gill, Eugene Goosens, and T. E. Sturge Moore. "On Style." *Daily Herald* reports that GKC "justified using prepositions at the end of sentences."
June 26—Royal Academy Meeting.
June 29—GKC and Frances host a "no adults allowed" children's party.
July 10—Meets with Alfred Noyes.

July 11—SPEECH, London, Allen Hall Seminary. Thomas More Memorial Exhibition. "A Turning-Point in History."
July 25—*The Poet and the Lunatics* is published.
August 1—Lunch with Humbert Wolfe at Villa Villa. Editorial Board Meeting.
August 8—Meets with Prof. Lutoslawski.
August 10—Meets at Oxford with J. P. de Fonseka.
August 17—Writes a public letter appealing for funds on behalf of Bath Orthopedic Hospital that is published in dozens of newspapers.
August 29—SPEECH, London Day Training College, the Co-operative Union. "The Meaning of Democracy."
September 10—Spends a few days in Tenbury Wells, at the home of his cousin Rev. J. A. Chesterton, who is an Anglican vicar. Is visited by Rev. H. E. G. Rope, a Catholic priest. To make things confusing, he also visits Tetbury and stays with Francis' cousins, the Braybrookes.
September 14—SPEECH, London, Hotel Cecil, Catholic Evidence Guild. "Emancipation of an Atheist." Maisie Ward (co-founder of the Guild with her husband, Frank Sheed) is the speaker following GKC, speaking on "The Emancipation of a Protestant." The event is held in conjunction with the Catholic Congress, celebrating the one hundredth anniversary of Catholic Emancipation in England.
September 19—Attends the wedding of Dr. Francis Leslie and Enid Simon at St. Paul's, Knightsbridge.
September 23—Meeting with artist Powys Evans.
October—*The Thing* is published.
October 4—SPEECH, London, Devereaux, the League. "The Philosophy of Distributism."
October 9—Meets with Belloc.
October 15*—SPEECH, Kilmarneck, Scotland, Scottish League of Young Liberals. Hopes for a revival of the Liberal Party.
October 22—Arrives in Rome. Stays at the Hotel Hassler, at the top of the Spanish Steps.
October 31—*GKC as MC* is published.
November 2—Defeated by Winston Churchill in the election for the rectorship of the University of Edinburgh.
November 9—Meets with Emilio Cecchi, who interviews him for *Corriere*.
November 11—SPEECH, Rome, Beda College.
November 15—Private audience with Pope Pius XI. When emerging into the daylight of St. Peter's Square, GKC says, "That frightened me more than anything I have known in my life." Is unable to work or concentrate for several days.

November 18—Attends party in honor of Cardinal Cerretti.
November 20—Meets with Scott Moncrieff.
November 28—SPEECH, Scotch College.
December 2—SPEECH, Anglo-American Convent of the Holy Child, Roma Unitas Society. "Blessed Thomas More and Humanism." ("Attended by one of the most distinguished audiences Rome can muster." Great demand for entry cards, and hundreds are turned away.)
December 3—SPEECH, Scotch College.
December 4—Meets with Princess Doria. SPEECH. Press Club Dinner.
December 5—Lunch with Emilio Cecchi.
December 6—Receives an honorary doctorate, in absentia, from the National University of Ireland in Dublin, along with Hilaire Belloc.
December 6—SPEECH, North American College.
December 8—Visits the Statue of Our Lady in Piazza de Spagna on the Solemnity of the Immaculate Conception. Attends, with a group from England, a semi-private audience with Pope Pius XI, who officially approves the documents for the upcoming beatification.
December 10—SPEECH, Venerable English College.
December 11–13—Visits Assisi, Nemi, Ariccia, and Rocca di Papa.
December 13—Returns to Rome.
December 15—Attends the beatification ceremony of the English Martyrs in St. Peter's Square.
December 17—Venice.
December 18—Rapallo. Visits Max Beerbohm.
December 20—Paris.
December 23—Back in Beaconsfield in time for Christmas.

1930

Sometime before May 1930, on a date no one seems to know, GKC becomes a founding member and is unanimously elected president of the Detection Club, a "secret society" of mystery writers that has been assembled by Anthony Berkeley. Members include Agatha Christie, Ronald Knox, Dorothy L. Sayers, and A. A. Milne. The meetings are held at L'Escargot Restaurant on 48 Greek Street, Soho.
January 10—Distributist League.
January 15—SPEECH, Wokingham. Town Hall, Wokingham Lecture Society. "Crime in Literature."
January 21—First Annual Johnson Society Dinner. Chesterton, as chairman, cannot preside, sending a telegram stating, "I am forbidden by a doctor more despotic than Dr. Johnson." He is confined to bed for the rest of January and February but continues to write his columns.

January 29—Visits the Oldershaws in Maidenhead (apparently against doctor's orders).
February 19—Speech at the Royal Society of Arts is cancelled due to GKC's illness.
March 11—SPEECH, Folkestone, Leas Cliff Hall, the Bouverie Society. "Chaucer."
March 28—Lunch with Douglas Woodruff.
April 4—Meeting with bookseller Gabriel Wells.
April 6—Attends a play written by E. W. Fordham.
April 25—SPEECH, London, Essex Hall. "The Menace of Empire."
April 28—SPEECH, Chelsea Town Hall, Catholic Stage Guild.
April 30—SPEECH, Royal Society of the Arts.
May 3—SPEECH, London, the Distributist League. "The Menace of Bureaucracy."
May 9—Attends the Royal Literary Fund Dinner at the Hotel Victoria and learns that John Masefield has been named poet laureate. GKC responds, "He is an extremely fine poet, and I am very glad to hear it. I hope he will go on writing poems about drunken pirates." Patrick Braybrooke had said a year earlier, "Chesterton deserves to be poet laureate and fortunately never will be."
May 14—Attends the wedding of Henry Northcote, Earl of Iddesleigh, and Elizabeth Lowndes (Belloc's niece) at Westminster Cathedral.
May 23—SPEECH, Reading. "When Is a Poem Not a Poem?"
May 26—SPEECH, London, Russell Square, Anglo-Polish Association. "England, Poland, and the European Crisis."
Lunch with American writer Hoffman Nickerson.
May 29—Belloc visits to celebrate GKC's birthday.
May 30—Attends fundraiser for Cecil Houses at the Shaftesbury Theatre.
June 5—Attends the wedding of Walter de la Mare's son, Rickard.
June 20—DEBATE, London, Essex Hall. With Edwin Scrymgeour, M.P. "The Menace of Prohibition."
June 21–24—Visits Cambridge.
June 24—SPEECH, Cambridge Emigration Society.
June 26—Editorial Board Meeting
June 27—SPEECH, London, Waldorf, Thomas More Society. "Libel and Public Life."
July 2—SPEECH, London, Lyceum Club, Philosophical Society. "Humanism."
July 7—Lunch with Belloc at Villa Villa.
July 18—Attends the wedding of actress Barbara Morley Horder, daughter of architect Percy Morley Horder.
July 23—Meets with Rose Macaulay.

July 24—Attends the Royal Garden Party at Buckingham Palace.

July 27—SPEECH, London, Adelphi Terrace Hotel. Chairs a lively dinner in honor of Belloc's sixtieth birthday.

August 7—Meets with Powys Evans.

August 8–20*—Holiday at the Three Cups Hotel, Lyme Regis.

August 21—*Four Faultless Felons* is published.

August 26—SPEECH. To a group of Americans, probably in anticipation of his trip.

August 27—Meets with American writer Cyril Clemens of the Mark Twain Society.

September 19—Departs from Liverpool for America on the *S.S. Doric*, "one of the smaller P. & O. boats" that crosses the Atlantic and sails all the way up the St. Lawrence River to Montreal.

September 27—Arrives in Montreal, Quebec. Greeted by the mother of a woman who used to live in Overroads, and who drives them around.

September 29—Tea at the Ritz Carleton with the Canadian Authors Association.

SPEECH, Victoria Hall, Montreal. "The New Enslavement of Women."

September 30—Ottawa. Stays two days with his uncle Walter Chesterton and cousin Lilian.

October 1—Visits the National Museum in Ottawa.

October 2—*Come to Think of It* and *The Resurrection of Rome* are published.

October 2—Arrives in Toronto. Reception with the faculty of St. Michael's College. Meets Etienne Gilson. Stays at the King Edward Hotel.

October 3—Lunches with Cardinal Neil McNeil and Etienne Gilson.

SPEECH, University of St. Michael's College. "Culture and the Coming Peril."

October 4—Leaves Toronto. Smuggles a flask of brandy across the border. Arrives in South Bend, Indiana. Stays overnight at the university. The next day moves into the home of Dellhard and Anna Bixler and their family in a small residence at 209 E. Pokagon Street.

October 6–November 14—Guest lecturer at the University of Notre Dame.

Eighteen lectures on Victorian literature, and, on alternate days, eighteen lectures on Victorian history, with a lecture on each subject on Fridays. At the first lecture, he is introduced by university president Rev. Charles L. O'Donnell, C.S.C., who extolls GKC as the greatest of the many famous speakers who have been heard from the stage of Washington Hall.

October 6—Lecture 1 (Lit): Literature of the Victorian Period

October 7—Lecture 2 (His): The History of the Victorian Period—Background

October 8—Lecture 2 (Lit): Classicism vs. Romanticism

October 9—Lecture 3 (Lit): Romanticism
October 9—Lecture 3 (His): Influence of Paganism on the Aristocracy
October 10—Lecture 4 (His): Catholic Emancipation and the Reform Bill
October 13—Lecture 4 (Lit): The Grotesque, the Fantastic, and the Eccentric
October 14—Lecture 5 (His): The Tories
October 15—Lecture 5 (Lit): Macaulay
October 16—Lecture 6 (His): Colonial Difficulties
October 17—Lecture 6 (Lit): Dickens
October 17—Lecture 7 (His): Prince Albert
October 20—Lecture 7 (Lit): Minor Figures in Victorian Literature
October 21—Lecture 8 (His): The Corn Laws and the Irish Famine
October 22—Lecture 8 (Lit): Carlyle
October 23—Lecture 9 (His): Palmerston
October 24—Lecture 9(Lit): Kingsley, Darwin, and the Rationalists
October 24—Lecture 10 (His): The Story of India
October 27—Lecture 10 (Lit): Newman
October 28—Lecture 11(Lit): Thackeray
October 30—Lecture 11 (His): The Whigs
October 31—Lecture 12 (His): Relationship with America
November 3—Lecture 12 (Lit): Trollope and the Victorian Novel
November 4—Lecture 13 (Lit): Bronte and Ruskin
November 4—Lecture 13 (His): Wars and Averted Wars
November 5—Lecture 14 (Lit): Tennyson
November 6—Lecture 14 (His): Gladstone and Disraeli
November 7—Lecture 15 (Lit): Browning
November 7—Lecture 15 (His): The Second-Last Phase of Victorian History
November 10—Lecture 16 (Lit): Pater, Wilde, and the Pre-Raphaelites
November 11—Lecture 16 (His): Politicians vs. Financiers
November 12—Lecture 17 (Lit): Matthew Arnold
November 13—Lecturer 17 (His): Ireland
November 14—Lecture 18 (Lit): Kipling, Shaw, and Wells
November 14—Lecture 18 (His): The Break-up of the Victorian Age (concluding lecture)
October 7—Lunch with Cardinal Hayes of New York, who is at Notre Dame to dedicate the new law building. GKC attends the ceremony.
October 10—Attends the official opening of the Notre Dame Stadium. Knute Rockne gives a speech. GKC is introduced and given a huge ovation.
October 11—SPEECH, Chicago, Orchestra Hall. "The New Enslavement of Women."
October 12—SPEECH, Chicago.
October 15—NBC Radio broadcasts a radio version of the play *Magic*.

October 19—DEBATE, Chicago. With Horace Bridges. "Is the New Woman Enslaved?"
October 25—DEBATE, Chicago, Orchestra Hall. With Horace Bridges of the Chicago Ethical Society. "Is Psychology a Curse?" Introduced by the Anglican Bishop George Craig Stewart.
October 29—SPEECH, Detroit, Orchestra Hall. League of Catholic Women. "The Curse of Psychology." Introduced by Judge William F. Connolly.
November 5—Receives an honorary doctorate at a special convocation in Washington Hall, Notre Dame, by Fr. Charles O'Donnell. The first time an honorary degree is conferred outside of commencement.
November 6—SPEECH, South Bend, St. Mary's College.
November 15—Departs from Notre Dame. Both GKC and Frances have tears in their eyes as they say goodbye to the Bixlers.
November 16—SPEECH, Ann Arbor, University of Michigan, Oratorical Association. "The Age of Unreason."
November 17—SPEECH, Cincinnati, Sinton Hotel Ballroom, Woman's City Club. "The Curse of Psychology." Introduced by Mayor Russell Wilson.
November 18—SPEECH, Pittsburgh, Soldier's Memorial Hall, Duquesne University. "The Inhumanity of Humanism."
November 19—SPEECH, Buffalo, Elmwood Music Hall, Canisius College. "Culture and the Coming Peril." Receives honorary doctorate from Canisius College. Says that Edith Wharton or Thornton Wilder were more deserving of the Nobel Prize than Sinclair Lewis. The remark is widely reported.
November 21—SPEECH, New York City. "The Inhumanity of Humanisim."
November 22—SPEECH, Washington, D.C., Trinity College. "The Age of Unreason."
November 23—DEBATE, New York City. With Cosmo Hamilton. "Is Divorce a Social Asset?"
November 25—DEBATE, New York City, Brooklyn Academy of Music, Brooklyn Institute of Arts and Sciences. Again with Cosmo Hamilton. "Is Immorality in Modern Books Justified?"
November 26—SPEECH, Millbrook, New York, Bennett College, where a Greek drama is performed in his honor. Spends Thanksgiving Day with his old friend, Rann Kennedy.
November 27—SPEECH, New York City, Commodore Hotel. "What I Saw in Rome."
November 27–30—New York City. Stays at the St. Moritz Hotel.
December 1—SPEECH, Cleveland. "What I Saw in Rome."

PROLOGUE: SOME MOMENT WHEN THE MOON WAS BLOOD   121

December 3—SPEECH, Albany. "The Age of Unreason."

December 4—SPEECH, Syracuse, New York. "The Curse of Psychology." Stays at the Mizpah Hotel.

December 5—SPEECH, Philadelphia. Forum, Academy of Music. "The New Enslavement of Women."

December 7—Back in New York City.

December 9—SPEECH, Boston, Symphony Hall. "Culture and the Coming Peril."

December 11—SPEECH, Providence College, Providence, Rhode Island. Stays at the Providence Biltmore.

December 12—SPEECH, Worcester, Holy Cross College, Mechanics Hall. "Some Heresies of Our Mass Production." Is named an Honorary Crusader by the students of Holy Cross.

December 13—SPEECH, Newark.

December 15—SPEECH, Hartford, Connecticut, Horace Bushnell Memorial Hall. "The Curse of Psychology."

December 16—SPEECH, Baltimore, Lyric Theater. Sponsored by St. Mary's Seminary. "Puritanism and Paganism."

December 18—Departs for Canada with Frances. Spends Christmas and New Year's in Ottawa with his relatives. GKC enjoys "a real 'do nothing whatever' time." Dorothy Collins remains in New York on her own.

1931

January 6—SPEECH, New York City, Academy of Music, International Federation of Catholic Alumnae. Benefit for St. Joseph's Day College. "The Curse of Psychology."

January 9—SPEECH, Convent Station, near Morristown, New Jersey, College of St. Elizabeth. "Culture and the Coming Peril." Arrives two hours late because he gets lost. Fulton Sheen is called from the audience to give an impromptu talk during the delay, cleverly performing the difficult task of keeping everyone in good humor.

January 11—SPEECH, New York City, Hotel Astor. Carroll Club Communion Breakfast. "St. Francis of Assisi." Introduced by Mrs. William Brown Meloney, editor of the *New York Herald Tribune Magazine*. During the speech, which is mostly to young women, GKC makes some critical remarks about rotary clubs and other businessmen's "get together" organizations as "vulgar" and "greasy." The national press seizes on it.

January 11—DEBATE, Boston. With Cosmo Hamilton. "Is Divorce a Social Asset?"

January 14—DEBATE, Washington, D.C., Women's Guild of American University. With Cosmo Hamilton. "Is Psychology a Curse?"

January 16—DEBATE, New Haven, New Haven Arena. With Clarence Darrow. "Will the World Return to Religion?"

January 18—DEBATE, New York City, Mecca Temple. With Clarence Darrow. "Will the World Return to Religion?" Audience votes for GKC, 2359 to 1022.

January 21—Frances becomes ill while traveling. They stop in Chattanooga, where she checks into Erlanger Hospital. Dorothy remains with her. GKC goes to Nashville and St. Louis alone.

January 22—SPEECH, Nashville, Fr. Ryan High School. "Culture and the Coming Peril." Stays at the Andrew Jackson Hotel.

January 23—Arrives in St. Louis. Stays at the Hotel Coronado.

January 24—SPEECH, St. Louis, Hotel Jefferson, Gold Room, the Catholic Club. "Rome, the Vatican City."

January 26—SPEECH, St. Louis, Kenrick Seminary. Guest of Archbishop John Joseph Glennon.

SPEECH, St. Louis, the Odeon. "Culture and the Coming Peril."

January 28—Returns to Chattanooga completely a mess, having slept in his clothes, unshaved, nails black. Frances is very ill, near death. GKC has to cancel several lectures, which costs him a lot of money, as he still has to pay a fee to his agent, Lee Keedick, who booked the lectures.

January 31—Frances "off the danger list."

February 5—Frances leaves hospital.

February 7–10—While Frances stays with a nurse in Chattanooga to continue her recovery, GKC and Dorothy Collins take a three-day train trip to the West Coast via New Orleans.

February 11—SPEECH, Los Angeles, Philharmonic Auditorium. Sponsored by Loyola University. "The Ignorance of the Educated." Stays at the Biltmore Hotel.

February 12—Large public reception at the Ambassador Hotel (where Robert F. Kennedy was assassinated). Hosted by Patrick McGill, Irish author and former custodian of the Royal Library at Windsor Castle.

February 12—SPEECH, Santa Barbara. Stays with his cousin, Cyril Chesterton (brother of Lillian, from Ottawa, Canada).

February 12—The House of Commons debates a proposed Prohibition Bill. One M.P. invokes GKC as objecting to the statistics on drunkenness being applied only to the poor, because when the upper classes get drunk, they are sent home in cabs and do not become statistics (*loud laughter*).

February 13—SPEECH, San Diego, Russ Auditorium. "The New Enslavement of Women."

February 14—SPEECH, Long Beach, Municipal Auditorium. "The New Enslavement of Women." Lunch at the Pacific Coast Club.

February 16—SPEECH, Pasadena.

Frances arrives by train after a long journey from Tennessee. Dorothy finds the "perfect" place to stay, La Venta Inn, Palos Verdes, on a hilltop with a view of the ocean. She attempts to negotiate some film deals for *Magic* and *Father Brown* but never pulls off the big one.

February 27—SPEECH, Los Angeles, Knights of Columbus.

February 28—Frances remains in L.A., recuperating while GKC and Dorothy continue on the speaking tour up the coast.

March 1—Arrives in San Francisco after a night journey by train.

March 3—SPEECH, San Francisco, Dreamland Auditorium, Paulist Fathers. "The Ignorance of the Educated."

March 4—Visits a speakeasy in San Francisco.

March 5—SPEECH, Oakland, Oakland Auditorium Theatre. Holy Names Central Girls High School Fund. "Culture and the Coming Peril." Introduced by Robert Gordon Sproul, president of the University of California. Afterword by Archbishop of San Francisco, E.J. Hanna, who tells the audience: "You have listened to one of the world's wisest men."

March 7—Arrives in Portland, Oregon. Stays at the Multnomah Hotel.

March 8—SPEECH, Portland, Oregon, Municipal Auditorium. "Shall We Abolish the Inevitable?"

March 10—SPEECH, Vancouver, British Columbia, High School Teachers' Association. "Culture and the Coming Peril." Stays with childhood friend, Annie Firmin, now Mrs. Robert Kidd.

March 11—SPEECH, Victoria, British Columbia. "The Ignorance of the Educated." Stays at the Empress Hotel.

March 13—SPEECH, Seattle, University of Washington, Meany Hall. "The Ignorance of the Educated." Stays with relatives of Frances.

March 16*—Returns to Los Angeles. Is a guest at the home of Hugh Matier, Manhattan Beach, California. Presents an illustrated poem to Sheila Matier, "The Three Conquistadors." Hugh makes ten full-color copies of the poem.

March 22—Departs from Los Angeles.

March 23—Visits Grand Canyon. Probably stays at the El Tovar Hotel (but Dorothy Collins reports it as the "St. Toras," of which there was not or is not one). Remarkably, he never comments about seeing the Grand Canyon.

March 25—Stops in Kansas City, where they drop off the nurse who had been attending Frances.

March 27—Makes a brief stop at the train station in South Bend, where he is greeted by many friends from Notre Dame, including the Bixlers.

March 28—SPEECH, Toledo, Ohio. "The Age of Unreason."

March 29—Arrives in New York. Stays at the Hotel St. Moritz. Lee Keedick sets up more talks to make up for the ones that were cancelled.

April 15—SPEECH, Morristown, New Jersey, College of St. Elizabeth. "Dickens at the Present Time."

April 17—Departs for England on the White Star liner *SS Majestic*, world's largest ship at that time. Singer Paul Robeson is also on board.

April 24—Arrives in Southampton.

April 29—SPEECH, London, Chartered Surveyors Institution, Council for the Preservation of Rural England. "A Miraculous Relic." Describes America as "a different civilization, or barbarism," and contrasts the ugly small towns to picturesque English villages, provoking bad reactions in the American press. He also says that Prohibition is a disaster for America, causing too much consumption of raw alcohol. The point of the talk, however, is not to complain about America, but to preserve the beauty of the English village.

May 1—SPEECH, London, Carr's Restaurant, The Distributist League. "Cobbett and the Present Crisis." Overflowing crowd.

May 12—SPEECH, London, City Literary Institute. "Mary Queen of Scots." Chesterton says that he makes speeches, he does not give lectures.

May 13—Attends the Detection Club Meeting, D'Escargot Restaurant.

May 15—Cecil Houses Meeting.

May 21—DEBATE, Oxford Union. "That the Law Is an Ass." GKC, for; Lord Darling, against. Amazingly, the audience votes against the motion.

June 6—Lunch with Sir Martin Melvin, Claridge's.

June 12—*G.K.'s Weekly* Meeting.

June 16—SPEECH, London School of Economics. Mock trial for the benefit of King Edward's Hospital Fund. GKC is arraigned on the charge of "perversely preferring the past to the present." He defends himself by saying, "I wrote a history of England in which I described the 15th century as corrupt, diseased and completely decadent. All I have praised is a short time during the very best period of the Middle Ages." But he is found guilty and is sentenced to write another *Father Brown* story.

June 20—SPEECH, Victoria Palace. Westminster Catholic Federation Silver Jubilee. "On the Federation."

June 21—Converts Aid Society Meeting.

June 26—*G.K.'s Weekly* Meeting.

June 3—Meets with Fr. O'Connor.

July 6—Attends the premiere of *The Love Game*, a play by Mrs. Cecil Chesterton and Ralph Neale. The play had originally been banned by the censor.

July 9—BBC airs a radio play of *The Napoleon of Notting Hill*.

Royal Society of Literature Meeting.

July 13—Meets with Langely Taylor, secretary of the Penn County Branch for the Preservation of Rural England.
July 15—Meets with Sir John Simon (who will be appointed foreign secretary in a few months).
July 17—*G.K.'s Weekly* Shareholders Meeting and Editorial Board Meeting.
July 22—Attends Michael Braybrooke's wedding.
July 23—Attends the Royal Garden Party at Buckingham Palace.
July 25—Lunch with Evan Morgan.
July 26—Attends a party hosted by Rose Macaulay.
July 31—Meets with W. R. Titterton.
August 4—Dinner with J. P. de Fonseka.
August 6—SPEECH, London, Prince of Wales Theatre. Between acts of a midnight performance of *The Love Game*. Also speaking is Ellen Wilkinson, M.P.
August 28—Executive Meeting of the Distributist League.
October 13—SPEECH, Glasgow, Glasgow University Student Union. University Branch of the Distributist League. "On Distributism." Fifteen hundred students attend.
SPEECH, Glasgow, Central Halls, the Glasgow Central Branch of the Distributist League. "On Distributism." Four hundred attendees from the general public.
SPEECH, Glasgow University. In support of Compton MacKenzie for rector. GKC tells the students that he cannot claim to be one of the Scottish raiders, but he does have one-quarter Scottish blood (hence the middle name "Keith").
October 14—SPEECH, Aylesbury Education Committee.
October 22—*All Is Grist* is published.
October 29—Philosophical Society Dinner.
October 31—Chairs the Annual General Business Meeting of the League, followed by a dinner at the Temple Bar Restaurant.
November 10—Invalids Dinner (J. C. Squire's cricket team, of which GKC is an honorary member), Cheshire Cheese.
November 12—Inner Temple Dinner.
November 25—Meets with Belloc.
November 27—Chairs an Extraordinary General Meeting of the Distributist League at the Devereux.
December 3—SPEECH, Beaconsfield, Burnham Hall, Penn County Branch for the Preservation of Rural England. On the English countryside.
December 5—A monthly publication, *The Distributist*, begins. Edited by the local branches of the Distributist League and reporting on their activities. It lasts until 1935.

December 10—SPEECH, Wimbledon, Sisters of St. Anne Convent.
December 14—SPEECH. On art.
December 16—*G.K.'s Weekly* Editorial Board Meeting.
December 19—SPEECH, London, Victoria and Albert Museum, League of Arts.
December 25—SPEECH, BBC Radio broadcast to America. "On Christmas and Dickens."

1932

January—Foyle Art Gallery (adjacent to Foyle's Bookshop on Charing Cross Road) holds an exhibit of author-artists, featuring artwork by GKC.
January 20—*The Judgment of Dr. Johnson* premieres at the Arts Theatre Club in London. Gives a SPEECH at the conclusion of the play.
January 26—SPEECH, London, Criterion Restaurant, Johnson Society of London. "It is not your duty to be as untidy as Dr. Johnson, although it is a duty I have carried out myself with complete success. It is not your duty necessarily to dress up as Dr. Johnson, or induce poor actors on the stage to dress up as he did—as I also have done—but it is your duty to keep as close as possible to the truth of things, to treat it sincerely, directly and with courage, so that men will never forget it."
January 30—Belloc visits.
February 2—Anthony Bertram visits. So does Fr. McNabb.
February 5—Meets with Belloc. Editorial Board Meeting at Cheshire Cheese.
February 6—Meets with old JDC friend F.R. Salter, who is also GKC's attorney.
February 9—Invalids Dinner with J.C. Squire, Cheshire Cheese.
February 10*—Luncheon guest of Lord Dunedin, who knew Robert Louis Stevenson.
February 14—DEBATE, London, Duchess Theatre. With Nancy Price. "Are Cinemas Killing Theatre?" "While the drama began with something beyond mankind in the worship of heroes and demigods, the cinema began by assuming that the vast majority of people were really beneath the level of humanity."
February 15—Meeting with Belloc. Sits for James Gunn portrait.
February 17—Meets with Italian diplomat and historian Luigi Villari.
February 18—DEBATE, London, Royal Courts of Justice. "That the One Man Business Is Over."
Meeting with Commander Oliver Locker-Lampson, M.P.
February 19—SPEECH, Holborn Restaurant.
Meeting with Titterton.
March 10—Attends wedding of Basil somebody.

March 11—Attends Catholic Social Guild Meeting.
March 15—SPEECH, Kensington, United Kingdom Benefit Association.
March 16—DEBATE, London, St. Paul's Debating Society. With Ivor Brown. "That Human Nature Makes Pacifism Impossible."
March 17—SPEECH. University of Ireland Club Dinner.
April 2—Dinner at Bentley's.
April 5—Meeting with Gregory MacDonald.
April 6—Meeting with E. V. Lucas.
April 7—Dinner with Fr. O'Connor.
April 8—Dinner with Mr. and Mrs. E. V. Lucas.
April 9—Interview with Mrs. Thais for *Everyman*. Meeting with Gregory MacDonald.
April 11—*Chaucer* is published.
April 12*—SPEECH, People's National Theatre Movement. "On Cinema."
April 14—Meeting with Richard Ellis Roberts.
April 15—Editorial Board Meeting.
April 26—SPEECH, Tetbury, Literary and Debating Society. "On Foreign Influence in England."
April 27—SPEECH, Kingscote, Kingscote Literary Society. "Crime and Mystery Stories."
April 30—The Royal Academy exhibits "The Conversation Piece," the triple portrait of GKC, Belloc, and Baring by James Gunn, which sells on opening day for £1,500 to George Balfour, a Member of Parliament from Hampstead. (His widow will donate it to the National Portrait Gallery.)
May 6—SPEECH, Hampstead, Home of Walter Runciman. Annual Meeting of the Marie Curie Hospital. "Copernicus and Marie Curie."
SPEECH, London, Essex Hall, Distributist League. "The Crash of Capitalism."
May 10—*Sidelights on New England and Newer York* is published.
May 11—Detection Club Dinner.
May 12—Editorial Board Meeting.
Meeting with Titterton at the Victoria Hotel.
May 22—SPEECH, Oxford, Newman Society. "Strategy and Controversy."
May 25—SPEECH, London School of Economics. Mock trial for the benefit of King Edward's Hospital Fund, with GKC as prosecutor against the headmasters of several important schools for "destroying liberty of thought."
June 1—SPEECH, Derby.
June 5—DEBATE, Arts Club. "That Modern Manners Are Deplorable."
June 9—Editorial Board Meeting.
June 15—SPEECH, Lyceum Club. "The Classical Tradition in Poetry."

June 18—Departs from Holyhead and crosses to Dublin for the Eucharistic Congress. Stays at the Viceregal Lodge.

June 21—Attends a garden party at Blackrock with some thirty thousand people. Is widely recognized and cheered by the Irish.

June 22—Attends a house party at the Vicergeal. Hosted by Free-State Governor-General McNeill.

(Does not attend a reception at Dublin Castle hosted by Eamon de Valera, because the governor general was not invited.)

June 23—Attends the Pontifical High Mass in Phoenix Park with three hundred thousand people.

June 27—Returns to England.

July 7—Editorial Board Meeting. Lunch with Mr. Lippman, director of talks for BBC.

July 10—Lunch with Lord Burnham.

July 22—Annie Firmin Kidd visits.

July 25—Meeting with Titterton.

July 28—Dinner with Mr. Lippman of BBC.

July 30—Mrs. Waldo d'Avigdor visits.

August 5—Meeting with Wyndham Lewis.

August 6—Meets with R. Ellis Roberts.

August 20—Meets with Titterton.

August 24—Titterton again.

August 25—SPEECH, Stanway.

August 29—SPEECH, Salisbury.

September 2—SPEECH, Woolhampton, Douai Abbey. Meeting of the Distributist League. GKC has to act as peacemaker between quarreling factions.

October 1—Spends a few days in the coastal town of Bognor Regis, West Sussex, to "recover from a rather serious chill."

October 9—Arrives in Liverpool. A reception is held in his honor at the Town Hall, hosted by the Lord Mayor.

October 10—SPEECH, Liverpool, Picton Hall. Roman Catholic Cathedral Fund. "Present Day Problems."

October 11—Stock Exchange Art Exhibition includes a statuette of a reclining Chesterton by K. Pollock.

October 12—Editorial Board Meeting.

October 22–24—Ellis Roberts spends the weekend at Top Meadow.

October 26—*G.K.'s Weekly* Shareholders Meeting, office of E. S. P. Haynes.

October 29—Distributist League Dinner.

October 31—BBC broadcast, "Some Famous Historical Characters." First of what will be fortnightly book reviews. His "manner at the microphone is pleasant. His voice is deep and slow ... and all the time conversational ... once heard, not easily forgotten."

November 3—Meeting with Titterton.
November 10—*Christendom in Dublin* is published.
November 14—BBC broadcast, "A Batch of Memories." Is photographed by BBC.
November 15—Invalids Dinner, Cheshire Cheese.
November 17—Meeting with Ellis Roberts.
November 24—Attends Authors Dinner, Victoria Hotel.
November 28—BBC broadcast, "Travellers' Tales."
December 6—Dinner with Ellis Roberts at Grecians.
December 7—SPEECH, High Wycombe, Guildhall. "The Church and the Worker."
December 12—BBC broadcast, "The Day Before Yesterday."
Editorial Board Dinner, Carr Restaurant.
December 14—Meeting with Mrs. Cecil Chesterton.
December 15—SPEECH, London, Dorchester Hotel. Dinner in honor of J. C. Squire, editor of *London Mercury*.
December 16—Lunch at the Polish Embassy.
December 26—BBC broadcast. "Books of the Week."

1933

January 9—BBC broadcast, "Architecture in Search of Style."
February 2—SPEECH, London, part of a public protest to prevent the government from demolishing Carlton Terrace, historic buildings overlooking St. James Park. Other speakers include J. C. Squire and Sir William Llewellyn, president of the Royal Academy. The demolition is stopped. The buildings still stand.
February 3—SPEECH, Ealing, Town Hall, Maternity and Child Welfare Committee. Large protest meeting against a town resolution to allow a birth control clinic in Ealing. Over a thousand people attend. "Birth control ... is blind destruction in the dark. You are destroying Shakespeares and Beethovens by every contraception act."
February 14—Meeting with Eric Gill.
February 21—Marie Louise Chesterton dies peacefully at 11 Warwick Gardens. GKC inherits the bulk of her estate, and for the first time in his life is financially secure.
February 22—Meets with Titterton.
March 2—SPEECH. First meeting of High Wycombe Branch of the Distributist League, joining branches in London (Central Branch), Bradford, Birmingham, Leicester, Southampton, Glasgow, Manchester, Bournemouth, and Liverpool.
March 8—Editorial Board Meeting.
March 22—*G.K.'s Weekly* Board of Directors Meeting and Editorial Board.

March 23—*All I Survey* is published.
April 5—*G.K.'s Weekly* Board of Directors Meeting and Editorial Board.
April 28—SPEECH, Oxford.
May 2—Attends the Distributist Meeting at High Wycombe. Eric Gill is the speaker.
May 6—Meets with Lord Burnham.
May 10—Annual Dinner of the Detection Club.
May 16—SPEECH, High Wycombe Distributist Meeting. "Some Criticisms of Distributism."
May 18—SPEECH, London, Westminster Cathedral Hall, South of London Catholic Land Association.
Editorial Board Meeting.
May 20—SPEECH, Dorset, Bryanston School. He discounts the possibility that Fascism would ever come to England. There follows a scathing attack on GKC in *The Blackshirt*, newspaper of the British Fascists.
May 22—SPEECH, Malvern.
May 26—Attends Distributist League Central Branch Meeting. Belloc is the speaker.
May 30—SPEECH, London School of Economics. Mock trial for the benefit of King Edward's Hospital Fund, with GKC as prosecutor against artists for endangering humanity by being fickle and revolutionary: "Artists are more afraid of being connected with a fashion of 10 years ago than women are of being seeing in last year's hat." The artists are represented by Sir Reginald Blomfield, Eric Gill, and Sir William Rothenstein. After hearing GKC's speech, Sir Reginald "turns King's evidence."
June 2—SPEECH, London, Carr's Restaurant, Distributist League. "The Opportunity of the Communist."
June 7—Editorial Board Meeting.
June 15—Meets with Titterton.
June 21—*G.K.'s Weekly* Board of Directors Meeting and Editorial Board Meeting.
July 5—SPEECH, Ditchling. "Communism."
July 12—SPEECH, London, Claridge's Hotel, Royal Society of Literature. Honoring the Canadian Authors Association. Seconds toast by Rudyard Kipling. Broadcast on BBC.
July 15—SPEECH, High Wycombe, Oakley Hall. Distributist League Public Meeting. Other speakers include Fr. McNabb.
July 21—SPEECH, London, Albert and Victoria Museum. Presents diplomas to the Royal Academy of Art students.
July 29—SPEECH, High Wycombe, St. Bernard's Convent School.
August 3—SPEECH, Beaconsfield. Opens a charity bazaar on behalf of the St. Joseph's Convent Hospital.

August 26—Attends wedding of Miss E. Gordon Dunham to Mr. G. H. Phillips at St. Clement Danes, London. GKC lends the bride the veil worn by his mother at her wedding, which was also worn by Frances and by Ada. (Cropped photo of GKC standing next to Ada is always identified as Mr. and Mrs. Chesterton, but the whole photo shows Frances standing nearby.)

September 1—Seventy-eighth annual exhibition of the Royal Photographic Society. Out of over a thousand photographs, first prize goes to Paul Shillibeer for his portrait of G. K. Chesterton.

September 5–18—Holiday at Lyme-Regis, Three Cups Hotel.

September 18–21—Spends a few days in Lincoln on holiday because Frances wants to visit Lincoln Cathedral. Stays at the White Hart Hotel.

September 21—*St. Thomas Aquinas* is published.

September 25—BBC broadcast, "Understanding France."

October—Fr. O'Connor visits GKC and notices how unhealthy he appears and how his breathing is labored.

October 7—Distributist League Dinner and Annual Meeting.

October 9—BBC broadcast, "Prophets and Poets."

October 10—*G.K.'s Weekly* Board of Directors Meeting and Editorial Board Meeting.

October 14—The British Museum is presented with seven portrait medals of English men of letters sculpted by T. Spicer Simson, including one of Chesterton.

October 23—BBC broadcast, "Truth About Ourselves."

October 29—SPEECH, West Wycombe Park, home of Lady Dashwood, Council for the Preservation of Rural England. On the spoliation of the English landscape by ugly advertising posters.

November 1—Editorial Board Meeting.

November 6—BBC broadcast, "Cavaliers and Roundheads."

November 8—SPEECH, King's College. On Polish literature.

November 10—Comes in second in the election for the rectorship of Aberdeen University. The winner is the immortal Walter Elliot, minister of agriculture. Aldous Huxley finishes fourth.

November 12—SPEECH, Harrow. "Romances of Chivalry."

November 14—SPEECH, High Wycombe. Introduces author and historian R. McNair Wilson, who speaks on "The Money Power."

November 16—Arthur Bryant comes for dinner. He will one day succeed GKC as columnist for the *Illustrated London News*.

November 20—BBC broadcast, "Both Sides of the Looking-Glass."

November 27—SPEECH, London, Claridges, Wiseman Dining Society. "The Oxford Movement."

November 30—SPEECH, London. Polish Embassy Luncheon.

December 4—BBC broadcast, "Rebels and Reactionaries."
Meets with Ellis Roberts.
December 6—Dinner at the home of Mr. and Mrs. Walter de la Mare.
December 12—SPEECH, High Wycombe. Introduces Fr. Gerald Flanagan, who speaks on "A Catholic Distributist and the Present Crisis."
December 13—SPEECH, Oxford, Knights of St. Columba.
December 18—BBC broadcast, "Books of the Week."
GKC's datebook at the end of 1933 shows him having refused over forty speaking engagements for 1934.

1934

January 6—Attends a Twelfth Night children's party in Beaconsfield, and a Twelfth Night party with the Distributist League in London at Carr's Restaurant.
January 11—SPEECH, London, Gatti's Restaurant. Luncheon for the Distributist League. Suggests a chessboard pattern for a Distributist shirt.
January 13—SPEECH, BBC Radio broadcast, "Seven Days Hard."
January 26—Editorial Board Meeting.
February 28—Elected to the Aetheneum as a person of distinguished eminence in literature.
March 20—Leaves for Rome. Stays in Rome about two weeks.
March 23—Is interviewed by Emilio Cecchi.
March 27—Letter from Cardinal Bourne conferring "the Knight Commandership with star of the Order of St. Gregory the Great in recognition of the services you have rendered to the Church by your writings."
April 6—Leaves Rome for Naples. There takes a boat overnight to Palermo, Sicily.
April 7—Palermo, Sicily.
April 9—Taormina, Sicily.
April 10–May 13—Syracuse, Sicily. Bedridden with an inflammation from April 22 to May 4.
May 13–23—Visits Malta. Stays at the Osborne Hotel.
May 21—The Archbishop of Malta calls in the evening.
May 24—Vatican officially announces that Chesterton and Belloc have been made Knights of St. Gregory by Pope Pius XI.
May 23—Takes the boat from Malta to Marseilles.
May 24—Spends the evening on the boat with Andre Maurois.
May 25—Arrives at Marseilles in the morning.
May 26—The boat leaves for Gibraltar in the morning.
June 1—Arrives in England at Tilbury.

After GKC returns from the trip, Fr. O'Connor visits him and thinks he looks much more himself than on their previous meeting. It is the last time he will ever see GKC.

June 14—Editorial Board Meeting.
June 16—SPEECH, Oxford, Charles Fox Association.
June 20—Attends a garden party.
June 23—Attends the wedding of Nicholas Durham and Joy Du Pre in Beaconsfield.
June 25—Meets with Maisie Ward.
June 26—Meets with Hugh Walpole.
June 28—Attends a play at Holy Cross School, Gerrard's Cross.
June 30—Meets with E. S. P. Haynes.
July 1—Lunch with Msgr. Smith, rector at St. Teresa's in Beaconsfield.
July 2—Meets with a priest from Sweden, Fr. Dowsett, who was introduced to him by Fr. Martin D'Arcy.
July 14—Visits Abbotsholme School in Derbyshire, where sculptor Maria Petrie is the art teacher.
July 24—Visits Westerham in Kent.
July 26—Tea with Arnold Lunn.
August 14—Meets with Christopher Hollis.
August 20—Tea with New Zealand journalist Ian Donnelly.
September 13—Is photographed by Howard Coster at Coster's studio in London.
Editorial Board Meeting.
September 26—BBC broadcast, "The Return of the Hero."
October 6—SPEECH, Monks Risborough, Whitecross Hall, "Building and Barbarity." On saving the English countryside from ugly building developments, specifically to preserve the view of a famous ancient chalk figure of a cross. The protest is successful, and the land is publicly owned and preserved to this day.
October 10—BBC broadcast, "Popular and Party Heroes."
October 11—SPEECH, London, Essex Hall. With Belloc. "Independence in the Press."
October 24—BBC broadcast, "Eighteenth-century Gains and Losses."
November 7—BBC broadcast, "Revolutionists and Revivalists of the 19th Century."
November 8—*Avowals and Denials* is published.
November 15—Meeting at the American Consulate in London with a Mr. Walker.
Meets with Bentley.
November 16—Cecil Houses Meeting.

November 21—BBC broadcast, "Nothing to Shout About."
December 5—BBC broadcast, "Documents of the Twentieth Century."
December 7—The Hollywood feature film *Father Brown—Detective*, produced by Paramount and starring Walter Connelly, premieres in the U.S.
December 15—Meets with Mr. Robinson, producer of *The Judgment of Dr. Johnson*.
December 19—BBC broadcast, "Victorian Frame and Picture."
GKC's datebook at the end of 1934 shows him having refused over eighty speaking engagements for 1935, but indicates he is considering a trip to South America.

1935

January 2—BBC broadcast, "The Stuarts."
January 16—BBC broadcast, "War and Post-war."
January 30—BBC broadcast, "Remembering Far-off Things."
The Hollywood film *Father Brown—Detective* premieres in England. GKC eventually sees it and diplomatically says that he thinks the acting was good.
February 13—BBC broadcast, "Back to Reason."
February 25—Signs an appeal to the Home Secretary to hold an inquiry about the physical and psychological effects of flogging prisoners. Shaw, Wells, Lansbury, and several bishops also sign.
February 27—BBC broadcast, "Attitudes to Poverty."
March 13—BBC broadcast, "Things We Don't Know About European History."
March 15—Donates money to the Royal Bucks Hospital Building and Extension Fund.
March 20—BBC broadcast, "England and Patriotism."
March 28—*The Scandal of Father Brown* is published.
April—Signs a petition in protest following the hunting of a tame stag through the main street of Beaconsfield.
April 8—SPEECH, Beaconsfield. Opening of Borlase Hall. "Nonsense and the Newspapers."
April 9—Departs for an extended holiday in France, Spain, and Italy. Dorothy takes the car ferry and meets GKC and Frances in Calais. All of his *Illustrated London News* and *G.K.'s Weekly* columns have been written ahead of time.
April 10—Amiens.
April 11—Rouen, then Chartres.
April 12—Chartres, then Blois.
April 13—Brive.
April 14—Palm Sunday, Brive.

April 15—Rocamadour, Montaubon.
April 16—Toulouse, Carcassonne.
April 17—Narbonne, Perpignon.
April 18—Gerona. Car breaks down. Takes two days to repair.
April 20—Barcelona.
April 21—Easter. Pontifical High Mass at Tarragona.
April 22—Barcelona.
April 24–May 3—Stays in Sitges.
April 27—Montserrat.
May 3—Gerona, Narbonne.
May 5—Aix-en-Provence, via Montpellier.
May 6–8—Mentone.
May 9—Santa Margharita.
May 10—Rapallo. Visits Max Beerbohm. Ezra Pound joins them for lunch. Pound discovers that he likes GKC after having prepared himself not to like him.
May 12—Portofino, Pisa.
May 13—Florence.
May 14—SPEECH, Florence, Palazzo Vecchio, Salone dei Duecento. "English Literature and the Latin Tradition." In honor of Luigi Pirandello, who has won the Nobel Prize for Literature.
May 17—Lake Como.
May 20—Lucerne, Switzerland.
May 21—Langes.
May 22—Rheims.
May 23—Arrives back in England.
June 11—SPEECH, London, National Hall. "Freedom" broadcast on BBC Radio.
June 12—Attends garden party for St. Teresa's Church.
June 23—Dinner with Msgr. Smith.
June 26—SPEECH, London, Trade Union Club. "The Right to Strike." Editorial Board Meeting.
July 8—BBC broadcast, "Meet the Detective." On Father Brown.
Meets with Lord Tyrrell, newly appointed president for Board of Film Censors.
July 10—SPEECH, London. With Eric Gill. Meeting of the Catholic Fund for Homeless and Destitute Men.
SPEECH, London, Arundel Hotel, the Keys (Catholic editors). Dinner hosting editors of U.S. Catholic journals. Archbishop of Westminster, Belloc, and C. C. Martindale, guests of honor.
Meets with Lord Howard of Penrith, former British ambassador to the U.S.
Meets with Bentley.

July 11—Tea with Msgr. Smith.
July 13—Mr. and Mrs. Rann Kennedy stay at Top Meadow for the weekend.
July 16—Meets with Ellis Roberts.
July 25—Attends the Royal Garden Party at Buckingham Palace and the wedding of Elizabeth Scott-Ellis, daughter of Lord Howard de Walden, to Count Serge Orloff-Davidoff, at the Russian Orthodox Church on Buckingham Palace Road.
August—Makes a generous donation to a fund intended for building a memorial sanctuary honoring the newly canonized St. John Fisher.
August 8—Visits Hungerford.
August 27—Meets with Ellis Roberts.
August 28—Editorial Board Meeting.
September 3—Tea with Mr. and Mrs. Moses, German/Jewish Catholic converts.
October 3—*The Well and the Shallows* is published.
October 6—SPEECH, London, Queen's Hall. International Congress of the Apostleship of the Sea. "On the Mercantile Marine." Compares the lot of sailors with that of peasants. Other speakers at the congress include Fr. Martindale and Fr. McNabb.
October 12—Lunch with Ellis Roberts.
October 20–29*—Spends several days in Brighton. Is photographed reading on a bench and walking along the pier.
October 30—Editorial Board Meeting.
November 1—SPEECH, Stonor Manor, Christmas Common. He and Frances serve as godparents to Mr. and Mrs. Hugh Paynter, who are received into the Church in the chapel.
November 16—DEBATE, on BBC Radio. With Bertrand Russell. "Who Should Bring Up Our Children?"
November 22—Contributes to the renovation of a sixteenth-century barn in Chesham into a theatre. Other patrons include Cedric Hardwicke, John Gielgud, and Tyrone Guthrie.
November 29—*G.K.'s Weekly* General Meeting.
SPEECH. Thomas More Society Dinner at the Waldorf.
December 2—Attends the *Brentwood Mystery* play performed by the students at Holy Cross Convent at Gerrard's Cross. Awards prizes and certificates to the students.
December 3—SPEECH. Golden Jubilee Luncheon for Fr. McNabb. Calls Fr. McNabb the greatest man in England.
December 4—Attends children's Christmas party hosted by the Invalids and J. C. Squire.
December 12—Meets with John Cargill, Scottish Presbyterian and Distributist.

PROLOGUE: SOME MOMENT WHEN THE MOON WAS BLOOD   137

GKC's datebook at the end of 1935 shows him having refused over ninety speaking engagements for 1936, and he is no longer considering the trip to South America.

1936

January 4—Hosts a children's Christmas party for the Distributist League at the Decca Studio in Chelsea.
January 13—Dinner with Desmond McCarthy.
January 26—Is visited by a Mr. Charop from Polonia.
February 5—Is visited by Msgr. Smith.
February 5—Chesham Bois Farm Theatre opens. The debut show is *Magic*.
February 13—Attends a performance of *Magic* at Chesham Bois Theatre.
February 26—Meets with Maisie Ward.
February 27—SPEECH, BBC Radio, "Hitler's Germany."
March 14—SPEECH, BBC Radio, "The Spice of Life."
March 27—SPEECH, BBC Radio, "The Middle Ages." (GKC's final BBC broadcast.)
April 2—Attends a wedding.
April 8—Belloc visits.
April 18—Belloc visits.
April 20—Dinner at the Nicholls at Christmas Cottage in Beaconsfield.
April 27—Departs from Beaconsfield for a trip to the Continent. Arrives in Dover.
April 28—Passes through Calais and arrives in Rouen.
April 29—Visits the Rouen Cathedral. Arrives in Lisieux for lunch.
April 30—Attends Mass at the Carmel. Visits Alencon, birthplace of St. Thérèse. Arrives at Caen.
May 1—Poitiers and Perigeux.
May 2—Lourdes. Torchlight procession.
May 3—Mass at the Grotto.
May 5—Still in Lourdes. Mass again at the Grotto. Procession of the Blessed Sacrament and another torchlight procession.
May 7—After another visit to the Grotto, departs for Montpellier via Toulouse.
May 8—Arles.
May 9—Menton. Day trip to Nice, which does not impress him. Remains for nine days in Menton.
May 18—Digne.
May 19—Le Puy.
May 21—Clermont Ferrand. Mass at the Cathedral (Solemnity of the Ascension). GKC feels unwell.

May 22—Visits Chartres and Orleans. Arrives at Beauvais, where he stays for two days.

May 24—Mass at the Cathedral in Beauvais and then on to Calais.

May 25—Dover and back in Beaconsfield by evening.

May 30—SPEECH, Beaconsfield, Sisters of Bon Secours. Garden fete to raise money for the extension of a nursing home, the place where Frances would be cared for at the end of her life, two years later. GKC's last public appearance.

June 5—Begins to lose his concentration and starts falling asleep at his desk, even while dictating. A few days later is bedridden.

June 11—*As I Was Saying* is published.

June 12—Receives Extreme Unction and Holy Communion from his parish priest, Msgr. Smith. Is visited by Fr. Vincent McNabb, who sings the *Salve Regina* over him and kisses his pen. Bentley visits Top Meadow but is not allowed to see GKC. At some point, GKC emerges from unconsciousness and says, "The issue is now quite clear. It is between light and darkness and everyone must choose his side."

June 13—Utters his last words, "Hello, my darling," to his wife, and "Hello, my dear," to Dorothy Collins.

June 14—Dies at Top Meadow, Beaconsfield, at 10:15 a.m.

June 17—Burial Mass at St. Teresa's and burial in the Roman Catholic Cemetery, Beaconsfield. The route of the funeral procession is extended, as the streets are lined with mourners.

June 27—Requiem Mass at Westminster Cathedral. Fr. O'Connor presides. Archbishop Hinsley reads a telegram from Vatican Secretary of State, Eugenio Pacelli (who will be Pope Pius XII), expressing the condolences of Pope Pius XI. Msgr. Ronald Knox preaches the panegyric, saying, "It is extraordinary how much love GKC brought to himself."

September 9—The value of Chesterton's estate is announced: £28,389. It is a little less than what he inherited from his mother. He leaves £2000 to Dorothy Collins, £1000 to Mrs. Cecil Chesterton, and £500 to Msgr. Smith. The bulk goes to Frances.

October 1—The first biography of GKC is published: *G.K.C.—A Portrait* by W.R. Titterton. He says Chesterton should be made a saint.

November 5—*Autobiography* is published.

GKC's datebook at the end of 1936 shows him already having refused over a dozen speaking engagements for 1937, but over thirty-five are booked.

1937

February 6—Val Gielgud (brother of John) directs a dramatic presentation of *Lepanto* on BBC, featuring Robert Speaight and Leon Quartermaine and orchestral accompaniment. It is rebroadcast several times.

March 14—"The Blue Cross" is dramatized on BBC. Over the next several months, more *Father Brown* stories will follow.

April 1—*The Paradoxes of Mr. Pond* is published.

October—Eric Gill's sculpted tombstone is placed on Chesterton's grave. Until that time the only marker is a simple 4" × 6" frame with the inscription "Of your charity, pray for the soul of Gilbert Keith Chesterton" followed by Walter de la Mare's poem "Knight of the Holy Ghost..."

1938

September 5—Radio broadcast of *The Man Who Was Thursday* by Orson Welles and his Mercury Radio Theatre. "Welles had great affinity for the works of Chesterton and decided to write the adaptation himself, allowing no assistance." In his introduction to the program, Welles calls Chesterton's prose "shamelessly beautiful."

November 22—*The Coloured Lands* is published.

December 12—Frances dies at the nursing home in Beaconsfield. Fr. O'Connor says, "In all things she was his angel." A local paper describes her as "a sweet presence."

December 16—A Requiem Mass for Frances at St. Teresa's, with Msgr. Smith. She is laid to rest in the same grave as her husband.

Chapter 1

Then Surely I Was Born

An Alternative Autobiography of G. K. Chesterton

Much of my life has been passed in making bad jokes and getting good morals out of them.

—*New Witness*, September 21, 1916

To begin with, I shall disappoint you. I have captured no cities, climbed no ultimate summits. I have not discovered the cure for anything. I think I know what is the cure for the unrest of the world. But I did not discover it. All I did was to discover that somebody else had discovered it long ago.[1]

Objection is often raised against realistic biography because it reveals so much that is important and even sacred about a man's life. The real objection to it will rather be found in the fact that it reveals about a man the precise points which are unimportant. It reveals and asserts and insists on exactly those things in a man's life of which the man himself is wholly unconscious; his exact class in society, the circumstances of his ancestry, the place of his present location. These are things which do not, properly speaking, ever arise before the human vision. They do not occur to a man's mind; it may be said, with almost equal truth, that they do not occur in a man's life. A man no more thinks about himself as the inhabitant of the third house in a row of Brixton villas than he thinks about himself as a strange animal with two legs. What a man's name was,

---
[1] *Daily Sketch*, May 14, 1931.

what his income was, whom he married, where he lived, these are not sanctities; they are irrelevancies.[2]

There is involved here, of course, a new question of what is called unconventional biography; and it is a question about which I am myself conventional. I believe that the very democratic phrase "convention" is here akin to the equally democratic phrase "common sense." But the new method is applied by many other distinguished biographers to many other distinguished subjects; it is applied to living people, and it has lately been much applied to the great dead of the Victorian era. Like most other experiments, it starts from a truth; that the greatness and littleness of man are intermingled; and that sometimes we cannot prove him great without proving him little. But there is a preliminary doubt about whether little things do prove him little; they are often too little to prove anything. A man's life is a mass of details which can easily be represented as a mass of contradictions; but they may still be things that can really be contradicted. I almost fancy that the small things belong to God, and the great things to man. If a man has a hundred wives and murders half of them, he will have a delicate task in disguising from his next-door neighbours the nature of his establishment and the habits of his home life. But if a man has one wife, and his biography records every time he quarrelled with his wife, it will not be unnatural if he quarrels with his biographer. It is not so much that the one thing is slighter; for there may be spiritual abysses in either; but that the public can judge of the one thing and not of the other.[3]

I do not know how I began, nor where I was when the foundations of the world were laid and the sons of God shouted for joy. Possibly I was not there; I wish I had been. I believe, not by experiment but upon authority, that I appeared in a form more or less human on the top of Campden Hill, Kensington, and was christened in the little St. George's Church close to the tall waterworks tower. I trust I do not seem to suggest by the reference that any more water than usual was required to efface the aboriginal iniquity in my case. I merely mention the fact because the tower played a most towering part in the unspoken fairy-tales of my childhood, which I afterwards

---

[2] *Speaker*, Dec. 5, 1901.
[3] *New Witness*, Aug. 22, 1919.

tried to regather in a book called *The Napoleon of Notting Hill*—with conspicuous lack of success.⁴

I was brought up in a fairly typical middle-class English family. My father had been prosperous in business, and he had felt that something more than business was needed to square oneself with the universe.⁵ My father was a sympathetic and very interesting man. He was one of the few lucky people who manage to be good at business and at the same time complete human beings.⁶

---

⁴ *T.P.'s Weekly*, Mar. 21, 1913. GKC was obviously pleased with this account. He reworked it a bit to serve as the opening paragraph of his autobiography in 1936. The waterworks tower, a structure of some architectural significance if not literary significance, was torn down in 1970 and replaced by a block of flats. If it had survived just a few more years, it would likely still be standing today as a protected historical site.

⁵ *Daily Sketch*, May 14, 1931. Ironically, the Chesterton real estate office has survived even if the water tower did not.

⁶ *Churchman*, Oct. 23, 1926. It is generally agreed that G. K. Chesterton got his great wit from his mother and his great kindness and patience from his father. E. C. Bentley said he never knew a man with greater kindliness "in addition to his other sterling qualities." He had a sweetness of character, good humor, and even-temperedness that GKC describes as "Pickwickian."

Edward Chesterton (1849–1922) was a successful real estate agent who probably wanted to be an artist. At the behest of his daughter-in-law Frances, Edward did write one book: *The Wonderful Story of Dunder Van Haedon*, an amusing children's story with lush illustrations. He also designed the bookplate that Gilbert and Frances used in their personal library. Another work of his art that has survived is an intricate colored drawing in pen and ink of the apostles, demonstrating high church artistic sensibilities in spite of his rather undefined low church beliefs. It is interesting that GKC delayed his conversion until after his father's death. It may be a coincidence, but the fact is, he had to first go bury his father before entering the Catholic Church.

GKC says that Edward "knew English literature backwards," which may be why Gilbert had memorized much of Shakespeare long before he understood it. However, his greatest contribution to Gilbert's gigantically receptive mind was to build a toy theatre. He created a fantasy world for Gilbert, painting the landscapes and populating it with tiny people and putting a frame around it. One of those characters carried a golden key. Thus, Chesterton always thought of his father as the man with the golden key, who unlocked the door to a world of wonders.

In spite of the fact that Edward did not outwardly encourage his son to pursue a career as a writer, he did the very encouraging thing of underwriting the costs of publishing Gilbert's first two volumes of poetry. He also kept and dated every drawing that Gilbert had done, wishing perhaps that his own dream of being an artist would be realized through his son. It happened when Gilbert's career as a literary artist took off. Edward saved every article and press clipping by or about Gilbert.

Unfortunately, after Edward died, GKC began cleaning out his father's papers, most of which consisted of Gilbert's writing. He had the rubbish man haul away two truckloads before Dorothy Collins discovered what was happening and was able to stop the total destruction of what would have been the best collection of Chesterton in all of Christendom.

My mother's family as I have always known them, my maternal grandfather in all I can recall about him, were ordinary English people, like my father's family—except that they were partly Scotch. They happened to inherit a name [Grosjean] which must have been French at some time; and one of them happened (for some disconnected and probably fanciful reason) to call a daughter after the Empress Marie Louise. But when I tell you that the names of my mother's elder sisters were Eliza, Harriet and Jessie, the full Parisian flavour of the family will rather abruptly evaporate. In short, that fact alone will show you that I am telling you the reality about the household, as you would have found it if you had walked into the house. You would have thought it an English family, or rather you would never have thought of anything else. Beyond that I am indifferent and very largely ignorant. I have heard that the name came some generations ago from Switzerland, but even then I suppose it must have come originally from France, if anyone can find out anything about it I shall be much interested. If anybody could honestly think that I show the faintest trace of the great Gauls whom I so much admire in the Crusades or the Revolution, I should be most monstrously flattered. But my exceedingly English mother is the reality, and all the reality that I know.[7]

Saved, thankfully, were many of Gilbert's drawings, dating all the way back to his childhood, his early notebooks, and many manuscripts. Lost were all his unsigned journalism, letters to the editor, every review of his work, genealogical information and who knows what else. Re-creating this collection will take several lifetimes and will probably never be completely accomplished. Chesterton scholars—both of them—cry every time they think of that day when their hero decided to make their own lives so difficult.

[7] *New Witness*, Aug. 24, 1916. Marie Chesterton (1845–1933) was born Marie Louise Grosjean, one of twenty-three children. Her mother's maiden name was Keith, which would be the source of the "K" in her son's famous initials. GKC describes his mother as "more swift, restless and generally Radical in her instincts" than his father. His brother Cecil called her "the cleverest woman in London."

Marie was known for her great hospitality. She served "gargantuan" meals and made all her guests eat enormous amounts. Chesterton's many boyhood friends were always welcome at the smallish three-story row house at 11 Warwick Gardens in Kensington, where he lived for twenty years. She would address his friends by their surnames "Oldershaw, Bentley, Solomon" and so on, always adding the word "Darling," from the time they were boys till they were adults. Her unkempt appearance, which included bad teeth, was apparently a little off-putting, but her conversation was always warm and incredibly witty. The house was usually dusty and untidy, but by everyone's account, the home was a place of great happiness and affection.

GKC was closer to his father, and Cecil closer to his mother. But she always spoke of Gilbert as "my beautiful boy," and his high praise of motherhood obviously has a strong

The age into which I was born was a dark period that began vaguely about 1870; that end of the great Liberal epoch, the year when Paris fell and when Dickens died. It spreads equally vaguely up to the retirement of Gladstone and the abandonment of Home Rule, the last Liberal crusade which was unmistakably Liberal and unmistakably dangerous. All that period was filled with emptiness. Oscar Wilde was justly its greatest man; because he alone could really do levity upon a large scale. Its products include many men whom I count as my best friends—myself among others. But I can hardly think of one of them who would not have been both better and happier if he had been born in any other period from the Stone Age to the Reign of Terror. For almost all other ages have set one enthusiasm against another; but of this brief and black age only can it be said that it sneered at enthusiasm simply for being enthusiastic. All men had dreaded the lightning because it was destruction; but these disdained the lightning because it was the light.

It is idle presumably to speculate as to the causes of this queer interregnum and vacuum. The truth, I fancy, is this: that religion and politics (man's chief concerns, almost his only concerns) alternate in history, but are seldom absent simultaneously. A rude society may be rich in saints; or a time of frigid infidelity, such as the eighteenth

---

personal foundation. Edward Chesterton opened up the world of imagination for his son. Marie opened up the world.

The two most important decisions in Chesterton's life were his engagement to Frances and his conversion to Catholicism. In each case, he informed his mother of these life-changing events—by writing her a letter. As to the engagement, he wrote the letter to his mother while she was sitting in the same room with him. He knew that his mother did not entirely approve of his fiancée Frances, for the simple reason that, in Marie's own words, "No mother ever thinks any woman good enough for her son." But Frances and Marie grew closer, especially in Marie's later years. She knew her son needed looking after, and she said more than once how much she appreciated Frances because "she kept Gilbert out of debt."

As for the second letter, Chesterton explained to his mother that one of the reasons for his choosing to become Catholic had to do with protecting the institution of the family, which was coming under increasing attack in the modern world. He thought it would be best defended "by the one fighting form of Christianity."

Marie's religious beliefs are not entirely clear. She seems to have grown slowly and steadily more Orthodox as a result of her son's move in the same direction. One of her nephews said, "Doubtless she had curious opinions of her own—but at heart she was a Christian believer." On her deathbed her main concern was whether her sins were forgiven. We do not know all the details of those last days, but we know that Gilbert and Frances visited her, and said that when she died, she was "at peace with God."

century, may be heroic in politics. But at the particular point I speak of both these waves were spent. Liberty had become legend, and France, its standard-bearer, was struck down. At the same time everyone had drunk in Darwin ceaselessly and silently; men absorbed the idea that we had come from the beasts, which rapidly and popularly transformed itself into the idea that we had not come very far.[8]

The first book that clearly looms in my memory is Charles Kingsley's *Water Babies*. Throughout my childhood, which is not yet over, it has been a great source of comfort. The part I understand now I did not understand then, and I fancy I understood then a part I do not understand now—the light caught first the warp and then the woof.[9] The books of my boyhood, by Manville Fenn and David Ker and Talbot Baines Reid, were really very interesting deposits of many other kinds of labour—of the love of travel, of the teaching of popular science, and of the sincere though not always sufficient contemporary conceptions of history.[10]

I was born towards the end of the Victorian Age; which many modern writers, strangely enough, imagine to have been a time of conservative placidity and of people content with their stations in life. As a fact, it was exactly the opposite. It was the period during which two modern ideas came into the world and fought; a true idea, that we must raise the economic as well as the political status of the poor; and a false idea, that every man must raise his own economic status, even if he kills everybody else and ultimately himself as well. To both of these different things the more earnest Victorians gave the name of "divine discontent." But the mistake of the earnest Victorians was that they tried to make a new morality without having studied any really good philosophy. The thing became rhetoric and sentiment; a thing of words; and they got even the words mixed; as in this case. For the truth is that the one thoroughly bad sort of discontent is divine discontent. We can all sympathise with human discontent. For human discontent means discontent with inhuman conditions. But divine discontent must really mean discontent with divine conditions.[11]

---

[8] *Daily News*, June 26, 1909.

[9] *T.P.'s Weekly*, Nov. 12, 1927.

[10] *Illustrated London News*, Sept. 23, 1922. George Manville Fenn (1831–1909), David Ker (1842–1914), and Talbot Baines Read (1852–1893) were prolific and popular authors of boy's books, adventures, and travel books.

[11] *New York American*, Jan. 28, 1933.

It is said that young people were humbugged in Victorian times; I can only say that young people are being very thoroughly humbugged now on the subject of the Victorian times. Nothing can be more absurd than to say that the Victorians were merely prim people who lived in a happy topsy-turvydom. It may be hundreds of years before we again produce the mood that produced Lewis Carroll and Edward Lear's Nonsense Rhymes; for ages and for ages the Walrus and the Carpenter may never meet again.

Now if I wanted to describe that late Victorian England in which I was a child, I should say that I grew up with the Gilbert and Sullivan operas—they were of much more national importance than the Gladstone and Disraeli debates. W. S. Gilbert once asked an actor to sit down pensively—the actor sat down and broke the chair. (This often happens to me when I sit down in a pensive manner.) Gilbert said: "I said sit down pensively, not expensively."[12]

I do not even know enough of music to describe my own pleasure in musical terms. But the Victorians excelled in throwing off fancies, which were rather dreams relieving the general system than visions breaking it up. They were holidays of the intellect rather than (in the modern sense) emancipations of it.[13] But this very case of Gilbert's wit gives a hint of the danger. This Victorian jollity was too comfortable, and it sometimes stifled the things that were sent by God to make it uncomfortable. We must purge ourselves of this happy habit of saying that all our old domestic satire must have been good-natured satire; that all our foreign allies must have been completely satisfied allies. It will not do. We were all in a very jolly old world

---

[12] *Listener*, Nov. 1, 1933.
[13] "Gilbert and Sullivan," *The Eighteen Eighties*.
Gilbert and Sullivan knew exactly how to play the fool. The effect was not lost on Gilbert Chesterton—not only the foolery but the fantasy. The nonsense had a sacred quality about it, in the sense of being fenced off from the outside world, protected from intrusion. The stage doors were shut. The fantasy literature that grew out of this period and which developed in the twentieth century was, in Chesterton's eyes, a result of the English not being able to mount a real revolution. They could only turn the world upside down in their imaginations. As witty and delightful as the Savoy Operas were, Chesterton thought that W. S. Gilbert's *Bab Ballads* were superior, "a dazzling treasure house," more humorous and—paradoxical. The lyricist repeated the jokes in the Savoy Operas, but they were not as good. And when he tried to be serious, he could only be pathetic. He could not produce a hero. With his detached satire, Gilbert was fighting against all of life's illogicalities, but he was not fighting *for* anything. His namesake, Gilbert Chesterton, coming out of the music hall, was looking for something to fight for.

once, those of us who were Englishmen of the comfortable classes. It seemed like a world in which everyone was satisfied; in which the Walrus and the Carpenter were always walking hand in hand. The fact that we were under-paying the Carpenter and probably exterminating the Walrus didn't trouble us. We never remembered that the Walrus had tusks, or the Carpenter tools. We never allowed anything to have a sharp edge. It was a very jolly world I grew up in, and I love it; there was nothing wrong with it, except that it does not exist.[14]

The man in the top-hat in front of the Ogre's Castle, the man with the red nose in front of the Gates of Fairyland, was incongruous and was justified by his incongruity. He did not have to match his surroundings, but only to sing for his supper. This naturally led to the limelight being concentrated on the actor and not on the scenery; not indeed on the scene; or even on the play. This led to songs and speeches quite separable from the play, and much more connected with the world outside the theatre; songs that could be sung in the streets; topical songs; political songs; songs that one man could pick up from another without even seeing the play at all.[15] In my childhood, it was common for families or chance companies to sing in chorus; and the number of old songs with choruses testifies to the tradition. Only we did not call it communal singing; we called it singing. Nowadays we need official organisation for everything; and there will soon be systematic instruction in communal laughing.[16] The old style in things like pantomime covers so large a number of very different things. It may mean (I hope it does) the old harlequinade, the true substance and body of a pantomime, a real Christmas banquet, by the one noble test—that you can get ill over it. For I have been literally ill with laughing over a clown, a policeman, and a baker's shop.[17]

I happen to have no ear for music, and if ever, by accident or compulsion, I find myself at an opera, I have the wholesome experience of feeling half-witted; it is disgraceful that all that deafening glory should break about my wooden head. But a modern dramatic critic, of the best type, has no more business at a pantomime than I have at a concert. I cannot explain the clown to him any more than he

---

[14] *Listener*, Nov. 1, 1933.
[15] "Gilbert and Sullivan," *The Eighteen Eighties*.
[16] *G.K.'s Weekly*, Aug. 2, 1930.
[17] *Illustrated London News*, Jan. 16, 1909.

can explain the sonata to me. But I at least am wise enough to envy, whereas he is often actually stupid enough to scorn.[18] I happen to be rather above the human average touching books and very much below it touching music.[19] I was reconciled (at the age of seven) to the knowledge that I would never understand a piano.[20] I know only two songs. One is "God Save the King," and the other isn't. I know "God Save the King" because people stand up.[21]

There is a great deal of talk about emancipation from Victorian conventions, and there is some truth along with a great deal of talk. I have never, either here or elsewhere, merely whitewashed Victorian manners in order to blacken modern manners. Some conventions of that particular age and country did confine the human imagination too much to one place. But just as it was confined in one place, so it has only broken out in one place, and generally broken out in the wrong place. The new revolution is quite as narrow as the old convention. And an excellent example of this excrescence or disproportion is the opening of the theatre to serious doubts, while it is still practically closed to serious beliefs. So long as the Victorian drama was really Victorian, in the sense of covering only a certain area of rather artificial life, it did not do much harm either way. The only play of that period in which the spirits of good and evil could be said to put in an appearance was in the quarrel of the Demon King and the Fairy Queen in a pantomime. And there the deepest metaphysical and moral issues were seldom sounded to their depths. But what has happened to-day is this, that the trap-door has been left open for the demon and the skylight has been locked against the fairy. We have had plays opening abysses of insane scepticism and despair, but not, as in the old tragedies and epics, any voice speaking in judgment, or in the name of order and light.[22]

I am just old enough to remember the world before telephones. And I remember that my father and my uncle fitted up the first telephone I ever saw with their own metal and chemicals, a miniature

---

[18] Ibid.
[19] *Bibliophile*, November 1908.
[20] *Daily Herald*, Sept. 13, 1913.
[21] Quoted by Chesterton scholar Rev. Kevin Scannell, *National Catholic Register*, May 10, 1986.
[22] *Illustrated London News*, Apr. 2, 1927.

telephone reaching from the top bed-room under the roof to the remote end of the garden. I was really impressed imaginatively by this; and I do not think I have ever been so much impressed since by an extension of it. The point is rather important in the whole theory of imagination. It did startle me that a voice should sound in the room when it was really as distant as the next street. It would hardly have startled me more if it had been as distant as the next town. It does not startle me any more if it is as distant as the next continent. The miracle is over. Thus I admired even the large scientific things most on a small scale. So I always found that I was much more attracted by the microscope than the telescope. I was not overwhelmed in childhood by being told of remote stars which the sun never reached, any more than in manhood by being told of the empire on which the sun never set. I had no use for an empire that had no sunsets. But I was inspired and thrilled by looking through a little hole at a crystal like a pin's head, and seeing it change pattern and colour like a pigmy sunset.[23]

A Victorian childhood, while a very innocent, was also a very childish childhood.[24] When I was a little boy I enjoyed Norse mythology, as a fairy-tale ought to be enjoyed; and as for the social and religious life of the American Indian, I lived it for weeks at a time in the lilac bushes at the end of the garden, with a toy hammer for a tomahawk.[25] I had a toy-theatre, illuminated in those days by candles (to which perhaps the psychoanalyst will trace my subsequent downfall into ecclesiastical crypts and cloisters) and in the ordinary way I was quite content with this type of illumination, the candles seeming to my barbarous mind to be themselves like a forest of fairy trees, with flames for flowers. There were also yet more rich and rare delights, which were sufficiently rare to those not sufficiently rich. It was sometimes possible to purchase a sort of dark red powder, which when ignited burst into a rich red light. Fire was wonderful enough—but red fire! But then I was only a dull Victorian infant somewhere between five and seven; and I only used red fire rarely; when it was effective. Living under such limitations, my immature brain perceived that it was more suitable to some things than to others; as, for instance, to a goblin coming up through a trap-door out of

[23] *Illustrated London News*, Feb. 8, 1930.
[24] *Columbia*, October 1926.
[25] *G.K.'s Weekly*, Dec. 13, 1930.

the cavern of the King of the Copper Mines, or to the final conflagration that made a crimson halo round the dark mill and castle of the execrable Mad Miller. I should not even then have used red fire in a scene showing the shepherd (doubtless a prince in disguise) piping to his lambs in the pale green meadows of spring; or in a scene in which glassy gauzes of green and blue waved in the manner of waves round the cold weeds and fishes at the entrance to Davy Jones's Locker. Science and progress and practical education and knowledge of the world are necessary before people can make blunders like that. Therefore, that red fire of the nursery still glows in my memory as an inward imaginative revelation, in spite of years, in spite of time, in spite even of passing through the streets of modern London.[26]

When I was a boy I used to start from Kensington, which was my home, and walk up to St. Paul's Cathedral; I walked a great part of the way in the middle of the road, which will serve as a small illustration in the change of traffic within thirty years. As I came to the end of the Strand and the first of the two Strand churches, found myself in an enchanted grove then called Booksellers' Row; where the second-hand bookshops gathered together their rich refuse; seeming to me like a bazaar in the Arabian Nights. Now there we have, so far as I am concerned, a real romance of memory and lost traditions.[27]

In so far as I have in me anything of the sentimentalist, of the antiquary, of the man with hobbies, or generally of the old fool (and I trust I am not without some element of these characters), I can and do lament over the disappearance of Booksellers' Row. It was a part of my boyhood, like horse omnibuses and hansom cabs; and no man has lived who does not connect such things with many purple hours. Booksellers' Row had all the essentials of something in a dear, quaint, picturesque old town. It was dingy, it was untidy, it was at once hugger-mugger and hole-in-a-corner; it was everything I like.[28]

A great part, perhaps the more godlike part, of a boy's life, is passed in doing nothing at all.[29] I know that boys will sometimes

---

[26] *G.K.'s Weekly*, May 16, 1935.
[27] *G.K.'s Weekly*, Oct. 3, 1925.
[28] "The Case for Old London," in *Wonderful London: The World's Greatest City Described by Its Best Writers and Pictured by Its Finest Photographers*, ed. Arthur St. John Adcock (Fleetway House, 1926), pp. 171–72.
[29] *Nation* (UK), Dec. 7, 1907.

quite willingly wade through enormous books much duller than Boswell's Johnson; I can remember myself, about the age of eight, slowly digesting several tons of a History of Scotland. Dr. Johnson himself would scarcely have selected the subject; but at least it was full of fighting, whereas Boswell's book is only full of argument. I did not appreciate two-thirds of Johnson till I was over forty; for three-quarters I had to wait till I was over fifty.[30]

All through my boyhood (which I need hardly say was studious and industrious in an almost feverish degree) I used to wonder why people hit or stoned people with an opposite philosophy. A little experience in the world, however, has taught me that the explanation is simple: the reason is that people with an opposite philosophy are extremely unpleasant. Whether or no heretics are unpleasing to God, there is no doubt at all about their being unpleasing to man.[31]

I was always arguing. I was always arguing with my brother, and he was always arguing with everybody. When I was not arguing with my brother, I was arguing with myself; and most of the things I have done have been the outcome of those well-balanced contests. I do not say I have done nothing else; but, with one or two happy exceptions (which I am so old-fashioned as to prefer to keep to myself), I doubt whether I have ever done anything so well worth doing. For I believe more and more than the modern world has far too little argument of the real sort; and that the aim of any public-spirited person to-day must be to find a stable statement of truth, upon which alone anything socially solid can be built. When I look back on my life, even in the lightest fashion, I can see it only as an attempt to reach such an end.[32] I love questions. I love to ask them and I love to answer them. Anybody can drag me into an argument.[33]

When I was a little boy I had an imagination, though this has long been washed out of me by the wordy abstractions of politics and journalism. For imagination, real imagination, is never a vague thing of vistas. Real imagination is always materialistic; for imagination consists of images, generally graven images. There is a mad literalism about imagination; and when I had it I turned everything that any one mentioned

---

[30] *New York American*, Mar. 24, 1934.
[31] *Illustrated London News*, June 30, 1906.
[32] *T.P.'s and Cassell's Weekly*, Jan. 23, 1926.
[33] *New York Tribune*, Sept. 15, 1912.

into a concrete body and a staring shape. Thus, I would hear grown-up people using ordinary proverbs and figures of speech; pale, worn-out proverbs, battered and colourless figures of speech. But every one of these phrases sprang out for me as fierce and vivid as a motto written in fireworks. Thus, when I heard that my uncle on a sea voyage "had got his sea legs" I pictured the most horrible bodily transformations in my uncle.[34]

When I was a child all plays were fairy plays. By fairy plays I do not mean plays about fairies; but, rather, plays produced by fairies, acted by fairies, written by fairies. It was not that in an elfin drama ladies and gentlemen dressed up as elves. It was rather that in a modern drama elves had dressed up as ladies and gentlemen. The whole play, the whole theatre, the whole fact that there was any play or any theatre, seemed to me to be something produced by a spell or a stroke of the wizard's wand, as Aladdin's palace was produced by Aladdin's lamp. The very shape of the stage, its structure and limitations like those of a closed box, its contained glow like that of a curtained window, all worked up to the crisis of lifting the curtain and looking through a new window into a new world. Every man of my age has had that purely theatrical thrill.[35]

Among the pleasing fancies that occurred to us in those early days was a sense of the poetry of London; and, in the days when I wrote a fortunately forgotten work called *The Napoleon of Notting Hill*, I quite honestly felt that I was adorning a neglected thing, when I felt impelled to write about lamp-posts as one-eyed giants or hansom cabs as yawning dragons with two flaming optics, or painted omnibuses as coloured ships or castles, or all the rest of it. And now, after many years of controversy and complications, and collisions with all sorts of other questions, I come back to the same feeling in a new way, but with something of an undiminished freshness. I still hold, every bit as firmly as when I wrote *The Napoleon of Notting Hill*, that the suburbs ought to be either glorified by romance and religion or else destroyed by fire from heaven, or even by firebrands from the earth. I still hold that it is the main earthly business of a human being to make his home, and the immediate surroundings of his home, as symbolic and significant to his

---

[34] In *Odd Volume*, ed. John G. Wilson (Simpkin, Marshall, Hamilton, Kent, 1910), p. 28.
[35] *Illustrated London News*, Dec. 9, 1922.

own imagination as he can; whether the home be in Notting Hill or Nicaragua, in Palestine or in Pittsburgh.[36]

I had the idea for the *Napoleon of Notting Hill* ever since I was a boy of ten. I and a friend at school used to make up wars and discuss strategic positions. Then I thought—as a joke—of Notting Hill warring against Bayswater, and then I thought, why shouldn't a person love Notting Hill and be ready to fight and die for it? After all, ridicule doesn't kill, and joking is very superficial. It's not a good novel. I am quite unpractised in writing fiction. It didn't read smoothly at all to me. An artistic conception is a horrible nuisance to carry about with you. There is absolutely nothing, when you come to think, that cannot be loved to the point of blood. That is the only reason for wishing to have a sane religion. If you leave the spirit of idolatry running loose, some people might worship anything, even a Bengal tiger or a piece of rotten cheese.[37] Lord, what a bad novel!—in which I made the hero say: "There were never any just wars but the religious wars." It was, perhaps, the only quite sound remark in the whole book.[38]

But I confess that the original idea, in the conscious intellectual sense, was concerned with places of that kind in general; and my book might have been *The Washington of Walham Green*, or *The Kosciuszko of Kennington Oval*, or *The Garibaldi of Gunnersbury*, or *The Charlemagne of Chiswick*, instead of *The Napoleon of Notting Hill*. For I have never been able to conceal entirely from a derisive world the fact that I was driving at something; though I had then got no further than asking in rather a wild way "Is there nothing that will save Notting Hill from being frankly common?" By the way, if it is not too irrelevant, if anybody is interested in those things, a nun had a vision not long ago in Notting Hill.[39]

When I was at school I was constantly in contact with that stoical tradition of the English schoolboy who, if he did like literature, would conceal it as if it were a mortal sin.[40] I went to St. Paul's School, where I did no work but wrote a lot of bad poetry, which has, fortunately, perished with the almost equally bad exercises. I got

---

[36] *G.K.'s Weekly*, Nov. 29, 1930.
[37] *Public Opinion*, Sept. 29, 1905.
[38] *Illustrated London News*, Sept. 12, 1914.
[39] *Week-end Review*, Dec. 20, 1930.
[40] *Book Window*, June 1928.

a prize for one of those prize-poems which stand as the salutary humiliations at the head of many paths of journalism and literature. What a poem! It had a sturdy Protestant tone. It was about St. Francis Xavier, of whom I had never heard.[41]

Like most English boys of my generation, I inherited the speech that Milton spoke and learnt it almost entirely out of Mark Twain.[42]

I was not a great success as a schoolboy. I know I succeeded in doing next to no work, even under the old discipline.[43] I was a poetical and unpleasant little boy.[44]

There is nothing that boyhood or the romantic spirit enjoys so much as preparing for an entirely remote contingency. Scores of young men buy revolvers; they never shoot anybody. Scores of young men carry sword-sticks; they do not run anybody through. When I was a boy, I used to carry chocolate in my pocket; not because I liked it (I didn't), but because I was told that it was a concentrated and sustaining food, and I had always before my mind the extreme probability of being lost in an open boat, lowered down a dry well, snowed up in a hut, or imprisoned in a cellar. I never have been; but I still carry the chocolate, full of an infinite and hungry hope.[45]

The mental digestion of boys is as strong as their physical digestion. They do not heed the cookery of art any more than the art of cookery. They can eat the apples of the tree of knowledge, and they can eat them raw. It is a great mistake to suppose that boys only read boyish books. Not only do they privately revel in their sisters' most sentimental novels, but they absorb cartloads of useless information. One boy in particular, with whose career from an early age we have the best reasons for being familiar,[46] used to read whole volumes of *Chamber's Encyclopaedia*, and of a very musty and unreliable History of English Trade. The thing was a mere brute pleasure of reading, a pleasure in leisurely and mechanical receptiveness. It was the sort of pleasure that a cow must have in grazing all day long.[47]

---

[41] *T.P.'s Weekly*, Mar. 21, 1913.
[42] *G.K.'s Weekly*, Dec. 5, 1931.
[43] *Illustrated London News*, Jan. 21, 1933.
[44] *Illustrated London News*, Sept. 12, 1908.
[45] *Illustrated London News*, Oct. 20, 1906.
[46] He's referring to himself.
[47] *Daily News*, Sept. 26, 1901.

Before I left school I had been a member of a little amateur club[48] with a little amateur magazine, in which the beginnings of intelligence were faintly brighter. Indeed, besides its most unfortunate product, the club has since produced some good work in contemporary letters: two members of it have just brought out two excellent novels. Mr. E. C. Bentley's *Trent's Last Case*, and Mr. R. E. Vernede's *The June Lady*.[49]

The first essay I ever wrote was on the subject of dragons; and I was an object of hearty and healthy derision among my schoolfellows because it began with the somewhat pedantic sentence: "The dragon is the most cosmopolitan of impossibilities," my happy school friends hailing me with such salutation as "Hello! The dragon is the most copper-plated of indigestions," or "What ho! The dragon is the most colly-wobblish of indiarubbers," or what not.[50] I am not sure that I was justified in jumping to the conclusion that the monster was cosmopolitan, though certainly that would be a sufficient justification for killing him. I could still enjoy with enthusiasm an epic in which St. George should kill the dragon of cosmopolitanism. Dragons are found in the decorative and imaginative work of almost all nations and ages; and that is all I meant by the pompous and polysyllabic impertinence of calling him cosmopolitan. But I do profoundly repent and repudiate the childish superstition which led me into calling him impossible.[51]

It must be remembered that I was born a late Victorian, amid all the strange simplifications of that epoch. I was educated in the fairy-tales of science; and very preposterous fairy-tales they often were. One of them was the dear old nursery legend of Natural Selection, or the Darwinian Theory of Evolution. Children in this more enlightened age will find it hard to believe that we all religiously believed it. Our credulity was fed with myths of more mysterious origin; the

---

[48] This was the Junior Debating Club. It was started by Lucian Oldershaw, who will make three more of the most important introductions in GKC's life. He introduces him to *Leaves of Grass*, which helps pull GKC out of a deep pit of depression. He introduces him to another debating society known as the I.D.K. Club, where he will meet Frances Blogg, who will become his wife. (And Oldershaw will marry Frances' sister Ethel.) Finally, he introduces him to Hilaire Belloc.

[49] *T.P.'s Weekly*, Mar. 21, 1913.

[50] *Observer*, Sept. 14, 1919.

[51] *Illustrated London News*, Sept. 18, 1926.

queerest old-wives' tales about the Atom and the Aryan Race and the Anglo-Saxon origin of all the more obvious results of the Roman Empire and the Norman Conquest. But we believed all those simple Victorian myths, because of the simple but very real virtues of the people who taught them to us.[52]

A man may make excellent comedy out of the evasions of a rascal; but a comedy is a totally different conception from an adventure story. There must not obviously be any irony in an adventure story. When I read in my boyhood adventure books, they had to be read with the single eye with which a man sees danger, and not with the stereoscopic squint with which he sees incongruity. I rejoiced wholeheartedly when the brave English sailors captured the slaver; and I was right, because bravery is a good thing and slavery a bad thing. With fuller historical knowledge, I can easily find irony in the incident. But sympathising with St. George against the dragon has to do with cruelty to crocodiles. The child or the boy is quite right in believing that there really is a dragon somewhere, and that the harder he is hit the better.[53]

A lad of seventeen may be an apparently irresponsible moon calf; it may be hereditary, but it may be all sorts of things. Such dullness is sometimes shyness; it is sometimes genius; it is sometimes corruption; it is often a protection; it is very often a pose. Nearly everyone of us can remember a time when schoolmasters or even parents might have thought us not only stupid, but hopelessly stupid; might not only have thought it, but thought it justifiably. Almost every one of us knows that he still is on some point startlingly below the mental average, as if there were a blind spot on his brain.

To take the case I know best, my own, I have a good memory for form and physical proportion, so that I could draw from memory; I have a fairly good eye for distance and direction, so that I could shoot if I had been trained. But in a third sense of proportion, the sense of the passage of time, I am almost an idiot. I could describe in detail scenes and incidents of my recent life; and I have no faintest feeling for whether they happened a week, or three weeks, or three months, or half a year ago.[54]

---

[52] *Illustrated London News*, Sept. 18, 1926.
[53] *Illustrated London News*, Sept. 23, 1922.
[54] *New York Tribune*, Sept. 14, 1912.

Boys, like dogs, have a sort of romantic ritual which is not always their real selves. And this romantic ritual is generally the ritual of not being romantic; the pretence of being much more masculine and materialistic than they are. Boys in themselves are very sentimental. The most sentimental thing in the world is to hide your feelings; it is making too much of them. Stoicism is the direct product of sentimentalism; and schoolboys are sentimental individually, but stoical collectively.

For example, there were plenty of boys at my school besides myself who took a private pleasure in poetry; but red-hot iron would not have induced most of us to admit this to the masters, or to repeat poetry with the faintest inflection of rhythm or intelligence. That would have been anti-social egoism; we called it "showing off." I myself remember running to school (an extraordinary thing to do) with mere internal ecstasy in repeating lines of Walter Scott about the taunts of Marmion or the boasts of Roderick Dhu, and then repeating the same lines in class with the colourless decorum of a hurdy-gurdy. We all wished to be invisible in our uniformity; a mere pattern of Eton collars and coats.[55]

It was the excellent custom at my school to give the boys a half-holiday when it seemed too hot for working. And I can well remember the gigantic joy with which I left off reading Virgil and began to run round and round a field. My tastes in this matter have changed. Nay, they have been reversed.[56]

When I first went to Paris as a mere boy I think the thing that most struck my eye and stuck in my memory was that sculptured circle of the great cities of France, in which the only statue still girt with new garlands and draperies is the lost city of Strasburg. It seemed to be a challenge to the changes of time more momentous and impressive even than the cannon column of Napoleon or the towers of Notre Dame.[57]

I remember in my boyhood, when Swinburne was our (rather too bubbly) champagne, I for one wrote almost as many conscious travesties of Swinburne as unconscious copies of him.[58] Having revelled in Swinburne as a boy, I have known this pessimist notion from boyhood,

---

[55] *Daily News*, Feb. 13, 1909.
[56] *Illustrated London News*, Mar. 1, 1913.
[57] *Daily News*, June 28, 1916.
[58] *Life and Letters*, December 1934.

and never believed in it. As I say, even in youth I always regarded this argument as a Nihilist sophistry of the nineties and did not allow it to disturb in the least my enjoyment of pink faces or moonshine.[59]

If my father had been a Duke, instead of a—NICE MAN—I should have gone to Oxford, and learnt at great expense the insane optimism of the idle rich.[60] Instead, I went to an art school, at about the time when most of my friends went to Oxford, with the somewhat hazy and impressionist idea of learning to draw. At this stage I chanced to review some art books for a literary weekly, and I rapidly discovered how much easier it is to criticise the drawing of anybody than to draw anything. I therefore slid into my present low trade. After that I sank yet lower and became a critic of literature, which is not even describing a picture but only describing a description.[61]

I began by writing little reviews for the *Bookman* about art books at a particularly drifting and futile stage of my life, when I was supposed to be an art student. And not having yet learnt to put a line correctly on paper with a piece of charcoal, of course I sat down and wrote fluently in pen and ink: "Mr. Smith's suggestion about the limitations of Michael Angelo is so far correct that," etc., or "We should be disposed rather to find the defect of Velasquez in," etc.[62]

My first book was a collection of poems which I illustrated myself. Being barely twenty-five at the time, I wrote, of course, about the older generation, because I thought I knew everything that the greybeards were thinking. The title was *Greybeards at Play*. In those days I was out to be an artist. Since then I have, alas, produced other poems.[63] In 1912, I wrote a long poem of which a good many people are still very fond. It was called *The Ballad of the White Horse*, and told the story of King Alfred's war against the barbarians. Toward the end there is a passage which is often quoted because in it I suggest a return to barbarism.[64]

---

[59] *G.K.'s Weekly*, June 16, 1928.
[60] Quoted in John O'Connor, *Father Brown on Chesterton* (Frederick Muller, 1937), p. 29.
[61] *New York American*, May 30, 1935.
[62] *Daily Express*, Dec. 30, 1920.
[63] *Living Age*, June 6, 1925. His wife claimed, in this same interview, that poetry is what GKC most enjoyed writing but had no time to do it.
[64] Ibid. The poem was actually completed and published in 1911. Here in part is the prophetic passage he refers to: "They shall not come with warships, / They shall not waste with brands, / But books be all their eating, / And ink be on their hands. . . . / By terror and the cruel tales / Of curse in bone and kin, / By weird and weakness winning, / Accursed from the beginning, / By detail of the sinning, / And denial of the sin."

There was not a Unitarian tradition in the family. But that was the mode of the age. And I think that from my very junior youth I felt that something more was necessary. I don't think that I myself have ever changed. From the beginning I think I was staggered by the stupendous marvel of existence—by the miracle of sunlight coming through a window, by the miracle of people walking on legs through the streets, by the miracle of people talking to each other. This marvel fascinated me, as it does to-day. I said to myself—or I might have said to myself—well, is that not enough? And Echo might have answered:

"Yes, it is enough. If you see it. And if you will always see it."

Rather a large mouthful for Echo! But, as a matter of fact, that is what Echo said. Which brings me to what was an important event in my life, though thinking led up to it.[65]

Youth is a period when the wildest external carelessness often runs parallel to the most gloomy and concentrated internal cares.[66] To one American man of genius, whom I read in my youth, I owed much of my deliverance from the decadent cynicism that was corrupting most of the young men of my generation. Walt Whitman had his faults, artistic and other, but he did lead the democracy of the *Leaves of Grass* against the oligarchy of *The Green Carnation*. He did set the thousand common things against the two or three perverted and exotic things that had been set up as the idols of that age.[67]

My whole youth was filled, as with a sunrise, with the sanguine glow of Whitman. He seemed to me something like a crowd turned to a giant, or like Adam the First Man. It thrilled me to hear of somebody who had heard of somebody, who saw him in the street; it was as if Christ were still alive. I did not care about whether his unmetrical poetry were a wise form or no, any more than whether a true Gospel of Jesus were scrawled on parchment or stone. I never had a hint of the evil some enemies have attributed to him; if it was there, it was not there for me.[68]

---

[65] *Daily Sketch*, May 14, 1931.

[66] *Illustrated London News*, Aug. 10, 1929.

[67] *Illustrated London News*, Apr. 21, 1928. In one sense, Walt Whitman saved Chesterton's life. This "alternative biography" could have been called "Song of Myself," as a tribute to this writer who was very important to Chesterton but is never associated with him.

[68] *The Criterion*, April 1929. The "hint of evil" was Whitman's homosexuality. Though some micro-minded critics have casually suggested it, there is absolutely no evidence that GKC was homosexual or even inclined in that regard. On the contrary, he states explicitly in the *Autobiography*: "I have never indeed felt the faintest temptation to the particular madness of Wilde."

I got hold [of] *Leaves of Grass*. I call it a revelation. It put in black and white the things that I had always known. The glory and magic of God's universe—the shows of night and day, and, "in the midst, God's beautiful right hand."

Well, very soon I found that those who imitated Whitman's irregular lines missed out the magic of the universe and were definitely antagonistic to God's beautiful right hand. That was disturbing. God was all right, the universe was all right, Whitman was all right. But something had gone wrong.[69]

I did not come in contact with the more painful controversies sometimes raised round the American poet, but even as a boy I doubted the wisdom of his abandonment of metrical form. As many would have said, I liked him for liking everything; I should have preferred him to have liked poetry that would scan. I hated Swinburne's pessimism as I loved Whitman's optimism. The poets who have imitated Whitman have imitated everything except what is great about him. His emotion of hospitality and human sympathy, because it was a mere emotion, has *not* been perpetuated. The writers of free verse have followed him in being writers of fragmentary prose. It is the very reverse of the poetry of acceptance and assimilation. It is the poetry of emetics.[70]

What is called "free verse" has become more common, and is in a sense a progress to which Whitman played the pioneer. If having caused other people to write a vast amount of bad poetry, or of stuff too bad to be called poetry, be a triumph for a great poet, by all means let it be added to his triumphs. But in one respect the remark is indeed relevant. It is very interesting to note that most writers of *vers libre* have

---

In *The Everlasting Man* ("The End of the World"), he writes: "The truth is that one of the weaknesses in nature-worship and mere mythology had already produced a perversion among the Greeks.... Just as they became unnatural by worshipping nature, so they actually became unmanly by worshipping man.... It is true that in one sense there was less inhumanity even in Sodom and Gomorrah than in Tyre and Sidon. When we consider the war of the demons on the children, we cannot compare even Greek decadence to Punic devil worship. But it is not true that the sincere revulsion from either need be merely pharisaical. It is not true to human nature or to common sense. Let any lad who has had the luck to grow up sane and simple in his day-dreams of love hear for the first time of the cult of Ganymede; he will not be merely shocked but sickened. And that first impression, as has been said here so often about first impressions, will be right. Our cynical indifference is an illusion; it is the greatest of all illusions; the illusion of familiarity." (Ganymede was a handsome young Trojan boy who was carried away by Zeus. The term refers to a young man kept for pleasure. The Latin equivalent is catamite.)

[69] *Daily Sketch*, May 14, 1931.
[70] *T.P.'s and Cassell's Weekly*, Jan. 23, 1926.

actually imitated everything in Whitman *except* that great spirit which, in spite of everything, made him great. So far from that enlargement and love of men and things that struggled for expression in him having found any further expression in his followers, the only thing they try to express is exactly the opposite. The whole point of Walt Whitman, right or wrong, is that the great heart of man should be an inn with a hundred doors standing open. It is that there should be a sort of everlasting bonfire of special rejoicing and festivity for all men that come and all things that happen; that nothing should be thought too trivial or too dull to be accepted by that gigantic hospitality of the heart. Something may be said presently about what it was that hampered his genius when it strove to express this giant appetite for acceptance. But his imitators in unmetrical verse do not in the least strive to express this appetite. They strive to express exactly the opposite; they strive to express a complete loss of appetite. Read through any collection of free verse published to-day, and count up the number of utterances that are concerned with some form of distaste or even disgust. On the lines of the old songs of the sea these might be called the songs of the sea-sick.[71]

Certain magazines have symposiums (I will call them "symposia" if I am allowed to call the two separate South Kensington collections "musea") in which persons are asked to name "Books that Have Influenced Me," on the lines of "Hymns that Have Helped Me." It is not a very realistic process as a rule, for our minds are mostly a vast uncatalogued library; and for a man to be photographed with one of the books in his hand generally means at best that he has chosen at random, and at worst that he is posing for effect. But in a certain rather special sense I for one can really testify to a book that has made a difference to my whole existence, which helped me to see things in a certain way from the start; a vision of things which even so real a revolution as a change of religious allegiance has substantially only crowned and confirmed. Of all the stories I have read, including even all the novels of the same novelist, it remains the most real, the most realistic, in the exact sense of the phrase the most like life. It is called *The Princess and the Goblin*, and is by George MacDonald.[72]

---

[71] *Illustrated London News*, June 13, 1925.
[72] Introduction to *George MacDonald and His Wife*, by Greville MacDonald (George Allen & Unwin, 1924), p. 9.

Now about the time when I was a boy, there arose and flourished a race of men who affected to have a feminine sensibility. They called themselves artists; other people called them aesthetes, and many other names much less polite. But the essence of their position was that they professed that the aesthetic motive was with them primary and dominant, as is the moral motive, or the mercantile motive, with most men. They professed that debased Tudor architecture gave them a pain, an eye-ache as definite as a tooth-ache, as sacred as a heart-ache. Big, well-fed men swooned and staggered when they saw the right picture in the wrong frame. Now this exhibition of sensibility never impressed me for a moment because I knew it was an artificial excitement. The women really felt; the men only imagined that it would be fun to feel like the women.[73]

It was at the Slade School that I passed a happy time. It was at the Slade School that I discovered that I should never be an artist; it was at the lectures of Professor A. E. Housman that I discovered that I should never be a scholar; and it was at the lectures of Professor W. P. Ker that I discovered that I should never be a literary man. The warning, alas! fell on heedless ears, and I still attempted the practice of writing, which, let me tell you in the name of the whole Slade School, is very much easier than the practice of drawing and painting.[74]

There was an amount of pessimism in the period when I began to write. In fact, it was largely because of the pessimism that I began to write.[75] When I began to write, I was called an optimist; and may have deserved, or possibly accepted, the epithet. This was not, as will be said by the cynic, the sceptic, the materialist, the modern psychologist, and the whole herd of wild asses, merely because I was young. As a fact, it was precisely because nearly all the other young men were pessimists, that I consented to call myself an optimist. It was precisely because they boasted so arrogantly of being completely in the dark, that I pointed out that there is something to be said for the daylight.[76] I can remember in my ardent youth I carried about in my pocket a large but harmless revolver. Whenever anyone said,

---

[73] *Illustrated London News*, Apr. 25, 1908.
[74] Speech at the University of London, June 28, 1927. Of course, it was not an entirely happy time, as shown in chapter 5. But it was indeed a pivotal time.
[75] *Illustrated London News*, Feb. 18, 1933.
[76] *G.K.'s Weekly*, Feb. 20, 1936.

"Life is not worth living," I produced it, and always with the most satisfactory results.[77]

Literary criticism is largely a string of labels; and at some time, early in my scribbling days, somebody called me an optimist. But he was speaking in the spirit of the time; and when he called me an optimist, he simply meant that I was not a pessimist. He certainly assumed that everybody with any intellectual pretensions was a pessimist. For in my early youth it was Schopenhauer's hour and the power of darkness, and there lay on the whole intellectual and artistic world a load of despair. The liveliest claim that could be made was to call oneself a decadent, and demand the right to rot. The decedents said in substance that everything was bad except beauty. Some of them seemed rather to say that everything was bad except badness. Now the first movement of my mind was simply an impulse to say that being rotten was emphatically all rot. But I began to make for myself a sort of rudimentary philosophy about the thing, which was founded on the first principle that it is, after all, a precious and wonderful privilege to exist at all. It was simply what I should express now by saying that we must praise God for creating us out of nothing. But I expressed it then in a little book of poems, now happily extinct, which described (for example) the babe unborn as promising to be good if he were only allowed to be anything, or which asked what terrible transmigrations of martyrdom I had gone through before birth, to be made worthy to see a dandelion. In short, I thought, as I think still, that merely to exist for a moment, and see a white patch of daylight on a grey wall, ought to be an answer to all the pessimism of that period. But I did do it chiefly as a rebellion against the pessimism of that period. Like every rebel, I was a reactionary; that is, I was mainly reacting against something else.[78]

Does anyone have the right to criticise? No. "Judge not that ye not be judged." You must preserve a power of righteous indignation in public affairs, and a strong sense of the mystery of the soul. I don't think I have any right to judge a man, but I do think I've a right to hang him. Criticism is really the act of a reformer, but the reformer, to be any good, must have enormous enthusiasm and desire to mend things.

---

[77] *Illustrated London News*, Mar. 17, 1906.
[78] *Catholic World*, November 1922.

A reformer must have a love of the thing, not merely disapprove. Is it worth while? I think yes. How is one to know? That is where faith comes in. Primitive enthusiasm. Faith is a prime factor of philosophy. Your first attitude *must* be taken for granted. I don't believe in a man working purely for the sake of art. It does him good to work for bread and cheese. It is putting himself into the stream of life.[79]

Most of my friends went to Oxford, but I went to an art school; having the presumptuous hope of learning to illustrate books, before I fell back in despair upon the lighter task of writing them. For some reason I have never understood, there is nothing that is so definitely dated as art and art schools. Artists are almost the only people who are still so retrograde as to believe in progress. There is art and art criticism of a certain date as there are hats and bonnets of a certain date; they are taken as seriously so long as they are thought dressy; they are dismissed as lightly when they are thought dowdy. I belonged to the period of the Impressionists; their sons had not yet grown up to be Post-Impressionists; just as their grandsons are only now preparing to appear as Post-Post-Impressionists. Impressionism was, I think, an expression of scepticism.

In teaching a man to paint his uncle as an arrangement in grey and purple, it insisted that these patches of tinted shade were all that we actually saw of an uncle; and to prove this the artists would screw up their eyes till they could see nothing at all. But underneath it was the old mad metaphysical question: "What do I know but sense impressions?" And that was why the age which talked of the art of Whistler also talked of the philosophy of Schopenhauer. The chief educational effect of most schools that I went to was to teach me to play truant. But towards this school in its intellectual sense I began to find myself in the uncomfortable position of a mutineer, rather than the more cheerful condition of a deserter. I began to argue with young artists because they were young pessimists. I found myself committed to the alarming task of defending the broad daylight and the breath of life. I had to do my best with desperate paradoxes; and nerved myself to declare firmly that grass is green. Hence I was not content with the philosophy which dissolved the uncle into grey and purple; I felt the need of believing in an uncle of clearer outline and more vivid colour; an uncle really existing

---

[79] *Public Opinion*, Sept. 29, 1905.

elsewhere than on the retina of the eye. I did not know how ancient were the disputes I stirred; or how in the depths of my muddled mind St. Bernard rose against Abelard. But I began to put my arguments into some sort of form; and when a friend and fellow-student, now Sir Ernest Hodder Williams, gave me some art books to review for *The Bookman*, I wrote down the arguments instead of reviewing the books.

That was the beginning of a long career of irrelevance; I became a writer, and however much we may all deplore it, it is too late to alter it now.[80] Very young men often work hard and work well because they have a beautiful terror that the mass of people in this world work hard and work well. Just as the child thinks it splendid to be a lamplighter, the young author imagines that it is hard to be a novelist and responsible to be a Prime Minister. Let the publisher seize the author before that rainbow dream has vanished for ever. A man often does his best work in the time before he discovers that people will put up with his worst. A young author puts very much more of himself into his work than an experienced one. For youth is pre-eminently the time of toil and martyrdom; it is in middle age that men begin really to be frivolous. A young man will take a great deal more trouble in order to fall in love than a man of middle age will take in order to rule the political destinies of an empire. And in literature, as in everything else, youth takes a great deal of trouble: elaborates its theories, piles up its descriptions, multiplies its epigrams. The young man, to use the cant phrase, is always "giving himself away"; he is only saved by the fortunate fact that no one thinks the present of much value. The first effort of a man in any profession is likely to have all the perfection of an ardent ignorance. The first poem, the first speech, the first report, the first novel, is almost certain to be, whatever else it is, full of industry and solemnity and fire. For the terrible secret which we all learn as life goes on, is not the secret of the difficulty of things, but rather the secret of the extraordinary easiness of things. We discover sooner or later that it is by no means difficult to be as clever as the average speaker, or the average reviewer, or the average poet-laureate, or the average Cabinet Minister.[81]

But first I went and read manuscripts in a publisher's office. I became absorbed in the publisher's manuscripts, but not in the right way.

---

[80] *Strand Magazine*, April 1925.
[81] *World*, Mar. 5, 1902.

Everyday my critical reports became of more interest to me and of less use to him, until I suddenly realised the fact that I was some sort of journalist, and bowed myself out. I owe it to my friends and to my luck that, though I had no money in particular and married on very much less than a hundred a year, I never was put to the ultimate Fleet Street test that drives men to intellectual prostitution. By a coincidence, a kind of work came to my hand from a group which, though not prosperous and quite reverse of popular, thought and talked as much as I did so that I felt but little break with the crude convictions of my boyhood. My old friends at Oxford had mingled with a very original and sincere school of politicians who were re-asserting an idealistic Liberalism, a traditional praise of liberty, against both the most powerful fashions of that time.[82]

I began my career as a pamphleteer during the Boer War, when with a few others I set up a violent opposition to that unhappy undertaking. Those were the days when Cecil Rhodes was a hero and when Kipling was at the height of his glory. During that campaign I came to know Hilaire Belloc. Both of us found ourselves in a rather queer position. We were both members of the group of young men who managed and inspired *The Speaker* and who fought against Imperialism; but in that little phalanx Belloc and I constituted a minority which was in rather bad odor. The rest were fighting against Imperialism pure and simple. They were fighting war because it was war. Any war was a bad war in their opinion. They were, in short, what you call defeatists in France and what we call pacifists in England. Belloc and I were fighting against colonial Imperialism. We thought that England did wrong to fight against a little republic, and that the Boers were right in defending themselves. Even in the midst of the country's unpopular minority, we formed a minority more unpopular still.[83]

The negotiations just before the Boer War were really a network of mystery and hypocrisy on both sides; therefore, I waited to make up my mind until I heard the moral arguments. And I decided; because I found that the moral arguments on our side were immoral arguments. Doubtless the Dutch had numberless examples among their individual citizens of rapacity, of double dealing, of secret cruelty

---

[82] *T.P.'s Weekly*, Mar. 21, 1913.
[83] *Living Age*, June 6, 1925.

or sudden injustice. Still their talk was of the truth of treaties, of the sacredness of national boundary, of the simple pride of Republican institutions, of the colossal courage of the weak. That is the talk of a people who are wronged. Doubtless there were among the English fighting in that field (certainly there were, for I knew them) men who lived and died only for a chivalrous fancy, of redressing wrongs, or even more manly principle of professional honour. Still our talk was of the need of expansion, of the hopelessness of the weak resisting the strong, of everything being inevitable, of everything being better in the long run. That is the talk of a people who are doing a wrong. Such a people is condemned not by its crimes; it is condemned by its justification. It was only when I had read the defences of the thing that I saw that it was indefensible.[84]

In those old days of the Boer War (where I learnt to be a democrat by fighting democracy; the only way to learn it) the secrecy of our external policy was insisted on in a sense that logically led to stark nonsense. Everyone must remember that tiresome triple argument. If we criticised a war before it came, we were hampering the high and delicate negotiations of the diplomatists. If we criticised the war during its progress, we were encouraging the enemy and discouraging our country's soldier; who read the Radical papers every day. If we criticised the war after its conclusion, we were opening old wounds and not allowing sleeping (or slaughtered) dogs to lie.[85] It is sometimes easy to give one's country blood and easier to give her money. Sometimes the hardest thing of all is to give her truth.[86]

I took, and take, the Pro-Boer view of the question of the war we waged there; but I always admitted there was a question. The question was, roughly: "Is the *real* motive of the Imperialists, those of them that run the Empire, to rescue Englishmen from being the helots of foreigners? Or is it to get mineral and other monetary advantages for the great Capitalists, most of whom are foreigners themselves? Is it a national or an international action ...?" I always admitted there was a question. The only difference is that now there is an answer. I thought I was right; but now: I know. The practical decision of the

---

[84] *Illustrated London News*, Aug. 29, 1908.
[85] *Daily News*, Nov. 2, 1912.
[86] Letter to his fiancée, Frances, Feb. 2, 1901, day of Queen Victoria's funeral.

whole Imperialist school and movement is now public and beyond parley it is that blood may be thicker than water; but gold is a deal thicker than blood. Believing man to be a moral being (and never more than when he is a rebel) I naturally believed that our immoral experiment would prove itself wrong somehow in the long run.[87]

I was brought up in the old days in the heavy Capitalist system, and of course about the age of eighteen or so I became a Socialist—I imagine every decent man did—and gradually I began to realise that there was something a little wrong with the Socialist, carefully following the career of Bernard Shaw in that discovery; and I found that, as a matter of fact, the fallacy of all these things was quite simple. Property had failed because it had ceased to be property, or to put it even more clearly, private property ceased to be private.[88]

I talked the State Socialism I believed when I was eighteen, and saw through it when I was twenty-three.[89] Divine discontent, of the older sort, was disposed to drive its questions backwards against the movement of existence and discover the causes of things. The old abstract revolutionist would have had the star-defying audacity to ask who it is who really runs the trams or controls the tubes. Most of the young rebels of to-day are content to ask whether they will not soon be made a little bigger or a little quicker or a little more convenient. In other words, the individual has indeed a certain kind of independence but I am not sure that it is the kind of independence which requires most intelligence. I notice, for instance, that these people are always thinking of more or less new notions, and never thinking them out. Their novels and newspapers are full of suggestions and of assumptions, but not of opinions. I mean opinions in the sense that I used to have opinions when I was an exceedingly opinionated young man. We always wanted to state our doctrines in a dogmatic fashion, and state them completely so as to show that they were complete. We wanted to prove to Uncle Humphrey that Socialism was

---

[87] *Daily Herald*, Feb. 14, 1914.
[88] *G.K.'s Weekly*, June 15, 1933.
[89] *Illustrated London News*, Mar. 31, 1923. This seems to be a corollary to the line "If a man is not a socialist by the time he's twenty, he has no heart, and if he's still one when he's forty, he has no mind," which is often attributed to GKC. It's attributed to a lot of people, and no one seems to be able to pin down the original source. Maybe it grew out of any of the sentiments GKC expresses in these passages.

unanswerable, and challenge him to answer it. We wanted to spread the whole fabric of Fabianism before the horrified eyes of Aunt Susan and defy her to pick a hole in it.[90]

My colleague Maurice Reckitt said it is now a bad thing to be a Socialist, but a good thing to have been one. For the purpose of testing this matter, I try to imagine even the ideal Socialist official for whom the Fabians looked so confidently in the days of my youth; and even supposing him to be as thorough as Sidney Webb, as brilliant as Bernard Shaw, and as full of human imagination as H. G. Wells, I still do not think that a machinery worked from the centre by a committee of Webb, Wells, and Shaw, would produce what I call enough variety or enough liberty. But if this be true even of the best that we might get, what shall we say of the worst, which we probably shall get?[91]

I think that I always hated the idea of things being done from a centre. I hated bureaucracy. But they told me that if I wanted to get rid of the manifold iniquities of aggressive Capital, of interest, I must get rid of private property. And so I believed them. Although what I really believed in was the sort of thing that William Morris pictured, with every craftsman running his own show.

Perhaps the catastrophic event—if you want one—was the South African War. There I saw something which seemed to me to be the meanest kind of financial grab supported by the fine sincere fellows like Stopford Brooke (at whose feet I had sat as a child), York Powell, and the Fabians—apparently merely because the British Empire was big and the Transvaal Republic was little. That stirred me up. Why did all these fine men and women go wrong?[92]

At that time at Oxford, everything that was moral was Socialist. Everything that was immoral was Imperialist. Mr. Belloc, Mr. Hammond, Mr. J.S. Phillimore and the rest thus fought with two unpopularities at once; and I do not know whether the tale is exaggerated which describes the Republican Club as consisting of four members at the most, of whom two had generally been expelled, one for Toryism, and the other for Socialism. The outbreak of the South African

---

[90] *Illustrated London News*, Mar. 6, 1926.
[91] *G.K.'s Weekly*, July 30, 1927.
[92] *Daily Sketch*, May 14, 1931.

War seemed to them a sort of signal for a direct defiance of what they thought (as I did, and as I do to this day) the sheer devil-worship of commercial empire and compulsory colonial expansion. They founded the Pro-Boer *Speaker*, a spirited paper from which some of the first books from Belloc and myself were pulled and patched together. My friend, Mr. Oldershaw—now, by all the thundering wheels of time, a J. P.!—pestered these poor people with my articles; and I never shall be so proud of anything again as I was then of my companions and of my cause. Whether I could now be so happy and so universally hated, I do not know; but I would try. The result of this sort of Oxford skirmish was that, when the midnight of Jingoism had passed, and the *Daily News* had been recovered for the older Liberal tradition, the new editor, Mr. R. C. Lehmann, gave me a place upon that paper.

In that paper I have written a vast amount of nonsense and also, I happen to think, a great deal of sense. As the more fanciful parts of the work, the tales and the parables, do not easily lend themselves to any logical exposition, I will confine myself to stating one principle upon which I went in the abstract or controversial passages—a principle, I think, of some genuine value. I was, and am, a Liberal; though the Liberal Party has seceded from Liberalism. But while that danger was only threatening I took a certain view of the nature of that danger, which led me into a large number of extremely agreeable rows. I found that in official and editorial circles there was a strong notion that we must prevent the Liberal Party being split by a controversy. I was quite convinced that it was, in sober truth, being split by the absence of a controversy. I do not mind your calling the phrase paradoxical: the Party was really being split by silence and unanimity. It is really a very simple truth, and is related to the admitted truth about the danger of allowing uncontradicted rumours or unpurged slanders to proceed. The two sections of our Party would not have minded their leaders differing in public. What they minded was the leader they disagreed with making a speech, and the leader they agreed with not being allowed to answer him. A reasonable Imperialist speech directly answered by a reasonable Pro-Boer speech would have united the Liberal Party. It was on this principle that I proceeded in all my own controversies: that nothing could pull us together except public division and debate. At this time I had little more than a desire to be just to the Catholic theory of Christianity. I had not yet discovered the fact that is a key to a hundred conversions and persecutions—I mean the fact that a man cannot be just to the Catholic idea. The moment he begins to be just to it, he begins to like it. But it was the same in all my controversies. It did no harm to Socialism or revolution generally that Blatchford, a secularist, should wrangle with Chesterton, an orthodox person. It did a great harm that Blatchford should wrangle all by himself: it simply meant the secession of all Socialists who were not secularists. This absolute conviction that a controversy not only clears the air, but solidifies the real sympathies I followed persistently on the *Daily News*, until I left it.[93] I, for one, would never write where I was not allowed to write what I believe.[94]

Long ago, before the Balkan Wars or the Russo-Japanese War, I remember writing that there were two forces in the world threatening its peace, because of their history, their philosophy and their externality to the ethics of Christendom: and they were Prussia and Japan. I remember horrifying all my Liberal friends, when I wrote for the *Daily News* in the days of my youth, by saying this about Japan. I did not, however, modify my view then. I am certainly not likely to modify it now.[95]

Incidentally, in Mr. Blatchford's book [*General Von Sneak*, 1918], he preaches a popular crusade against Prussia, with all the hot logic and vituperation of Cobbett. But it is certainly an attack not only on Germany, but on Germans. And I cannot wholly subdue a smile when I recall a controversy,[96] in which I myself took a small part in my youth; a controversy in which Mr. Blatchford, then engaged in popularizing Haeckel, proved as lucidly and logically from the facts of heredity and environment that everybody should be forgiven for

---

[93] *T.P.'s Weekly*, Mar. 21, 1913.

[94] *Daily Herald*, Aug. 23, 1913.

[95] *G.K.'s Weekly*, Mar. 25, 1933. GKC is here repeating a prediction he made much earlier. This is still six years before Hitler invaded Poland and eight years before the Japanese bombed Pearl Harbor.

[96] GKC had been a great admirer of Blatchford. The book *Merrie England* had a profound, shaping effect on him. But as a very young journalist, he locked horns with the august editor of the *Clarion*. Why? Because Blatchford was parading his agnosticism too proudly and sneering at religion in general and Christianity in particular. Their literary back-and-forth helped catapult GKC to fame because of such lines as "I have begun, as you begin, a total Agnostic. I have never seen a miracle; also, I have never seen India. You will say that vast human testimony says that India exists. Oh! be careful, Mr. Blatchford, and take heed to your feet! What does the vast human testimony say about miracles?" (*The Clarion*, Dec. 12, 1903.) Ironically, a decade later Blatchford and GKC would find themselves on the same side in attacking Prussia.

everything, and never blamed at all.⁹⁷ Fashions can fly faster than the shots or arrows. In my youth I made tremendous efforts against a boom in the materialism of Haeckel, as popularized by Mr. Blatchford. Nowadays we never hear the name of Haeckel.⁹⁸

When I was young, I wrote a "Defence of Rash Vows"; a defence I am still ready to defend. But then I meant it in the sense that all vows are rash, even when they are right. In the recent political and moral atmosphere, it seems to mean that vows may be infinitely rash, because nobody intends to keep them. It seems to be the fruit of a modern combination between large views and short memories. It is necessary that every political generalisation should be wide enough to extend to the end of the world, and yet not quite firm enough to extend to the end of the week.⁹⁹

Satire has weakened in our epoch for several reasons, but chiefly, I think, because the world has become too absurd to be satirized.¹⁰⁰ The fact was really stranger than the fancy. I could give a great many other cases even from my own journalistic and literary diary, so to speak. I could tell the remarkable story of the siege of Edwardes Square, where I lived, which was, in many ways, curiously like a story of my own about the siege of Notting Hill, or, more properly, of Campden Hill, with its waterworks tower, under which I was born. There are more examples of absurd ideas that embodied themselves as even more absurd facts. The question is: what are we to do if our civilisation is reduced to an absurdity?¹⁰¹

The waterworks tower still overshadowed me; and I had begun to imagine *The Napoleon of Notting Hill* while I was still going to school at St. Paul's School along the road to Hammersmith. I think I went

---

⁹⁷ *Sun* (NY), Sept. 15, 1918.

⁹⁸ *New Witness*, May 5, 1922. Ernst Haeckel (1834–1919) was a German biologist and eugenicist whose ideas were very much in vogue in the early twentieth century. He provided a scientific basis for racism, which is probably why we do not hear about him much anymore.

⁹⁹ *Illustrated London News*, Jan. 18, 1936.

¹⁰⁰ *Illustrated London News*, Dec. 16, 1911. The world that did exist as Chesterton grew older was one on which it became increasingly difficult to write satire. It was a satire on itself. It was a parody of itself. The things that Chesterton would suggest in jest became distressingly prophetic: divorce ceremonies complete with divorce rings; Shakespeare in modern dress; Islamic influence. But later the jokes could no longer be taken as jokes. They became deadly serious. There was no jollity.

¹⁰¹ *Illustrated London News*, May 2, 1925.

through my schooldays in a sort of trance or sleep of sloth, dimly tracing those first fancies and refusing to put away childish things. Certainly, when I emerged into some sort of sense of citizenship, they still constituted my first comment on current affairs. I wrote that foolish romance about Notting Hill as a protest against the prevalent tendencies towards Imperialism and Internationalism; two tendencies which were then supposed to divide the world, but which seemed to me to unite it in one common lump of cosmopolitan dullness and vulgarity. Thus my politics from the first were strongly nationalist; and were expressed in a sympathy with the Irish over the first Home Rule Bill and afterwards in a sympathy with the Boers over the South African War. Party labels have since come to mean very little. In the controversy in which I was what was called a Pro-Boer, I really began my journalistic career and (what is much more important) made many of my best friends, including Mr. Belloc. I had indeed been unusually fortunate before that, in retaining the friendships of my schooldays more than do most men. Among them were E. C. Bentley, whose very universal brilliancy, familiar in private, is best known in public through the best detective story of our time; and Robert Vernède, who called in very noble verse upon the name of England, before he fell fighting for her in the Great War.[102]

I remember being thought a traitor because I was a Pro-Boer.[103] When the farmers were sacrificed to the financiers, in the South African War, it was the first political event about which I was really old enough to take sides; and it was also the supreme triumphant moment of unchecked and unchallenged financial control. In the intervening years of my life the story has worked itself out from Kruger[104] to Kreuger.[105] It began with the financier killing farmers for a gold mine; and it ended with the financier killing himself to announce the ruin of gold.[106] For me the Franco-Prussian War is history, but the South African War still is politics. I can become quite excited about it, and shout and catcall in my own private drawing room, as I did in the public meetings of my youth. For I was violently opposed to the imperialistic policy of my

---

[102] *Strand*, April 1925.
[103] *G.K.'s Weekly*, Dec. 26, 1931.
[104] Paul Kruger (1825–1904), president of the South African Republic.
[105] Ivar Kreuger (1880–1932), Swedish industrialist known as the "Match King."
[106] *G.K.'s Weekly*, May 14, 1932.

country; and a patriotic person disapproving of his country is one of the most noisy and offensive beings on earth.[107]

The whole of the last Victorian phase was full of Teutonic nonsense; and people were peculiar for not talking it—I confess I am proud to remember that I was one of the peculiar ones.[108]

I have founded many clubs and societies in my time; only I never could get anyone to join them. At an early age, for example, I inaugurated "The Band of the Young Gods of Freedom," the object of which was to encourage the eating of mustard with mutton: but this merely expansive and anarchic stage, as is so often the case, soon passed, and gave way to the more responsible moods of growth.

In this austerity of youth I became the first President and the only member of "The Alphabetic Altruists League," afterwards expanded into "The Cohort of Modesty." The aim of this society was to effect an important change on ethical grounds in the principles of English lettering. It proposed that the capital "I" for the first person singular should be replaced by a small "i," to symbolise humility, and the capital transferred to the beginning letter of the word "you." Arrangements were made for mass meetings in all the great cities, and considerable excitement was anticipated, and even riots were feared.

Then I instituted "The Army of the Avengers of Existence." Each member of this body merely undertook always to carry a revolver in his pocket and to present it suddenly in the face of any person who should, at a tea-table, dinner party, tennis match, or what not, let fall the expression that life was dreary to him, or that he wished he were dead. I tried the thing several times myself upon some quiet conversational pessimist, and it was really most gratifying to see a sudden appreciation of existence leap, as it were, into his eyes. It was a wild optimism, an optimism shrieking like a new-born child; a terrible optimism which the superficial would call mere alarm.

Then I was responsible for the little-known institution which is called "The New Chivalry." I never could be very certain in my own mind whether the practice of the New Chivalry came before or after the theory of it; but the theory of it was this: It rested on

---

[107] *New York American*, July 23, 1932.

[108] *Illustrated London News*, Jan. 24, 1925. He goes on to say that "when the next great war comes as a result of such nonsense" it will have a different name. It was already being called "Nordic" instead of "Teutonic."

the conception that a man is so overwhelmed and confounded by the superiority of woman in her works and graces that he is, so it were, paralyzed and glued to his seat, as wholly unable to offer her his clumsy assistance as he is unworthy to offer it. "Who am I," he seems to say, "that I should presume to open the door for one whose way of opening doors shows her to be a mistress of that subtle art? Shall I, in mere coarse patronage and condescension, pick up her pocket handkerchief, and thus rob the world of that sublime spectacle, that sweeping and seraphic gesture with which she picks it up?" This dream, however, also belongs to the past. Many ladies have told me that they prefer the crude obtrusiveness of the old chivalry.[109]

A man once told me that in twenty years I should find married life very difficult. I told him I had found it in twenty minutes; and was indeed aware of it before I began.[110] The things told to us by our

---

[109] *Daily News*, Aug. 4, 1906.

[110] *New Witness*, July 15, 1915. Just as Chesterton largely left his wife, Frances, out of his *Autobiography* (at her request), he also largely leaves her out of his journalism. Though she is part of his daily life, she is not immediately visible in his daily columns. But she is there. She turns up in his ongoing defense of marriage, his attacks on divorce and contraception and eugenics, in the centrality of the home and family to his philosophy. He makes specific references to her, such as "a lady I know very well," who said that when she tasted tea in America she remarked, "Well, if that's the sort of tea we sent you, I don't wonder you threw it into Boston Harbor." (*Illustrated London News*, Jan. 1, 1935.) And she is his touchpoint, the basis of his generalizations about women. "Women are the only realists; their whole object in life is to pit their realism against the extravagant, excessive, and occasionally drunken idealism of men." (*Nation*, Dec. 7, 1907.)

The most obvious thing that does not show up in his public writing is his most personal, private life. A naturally modest man with a modest wife, even though he was no puritan, he exercises great decorum when he talks about sex.

And so he would never write about what happened on his wedding night, and it is a subject that rightly is no one else's business. But Chesterton's sister-in-law made the imprudent decision to write about it, claiming the marriage was never consummated. And so it must be addressed.

Why would a man who has not consummated his marriage pen a poem like "Creation Day" to his new wife? And why (as his sister-in-law claims) would Gilbert go to Cecil for help? It is not as though his younger, unmarried brother was experienced in these things.

The claim is so outrageous that it has compelled several scholars to rise to defend the honor of Gilbert and Frances. This includes his official biographer Maisie Ward, who knew all the parties involved, and Aidan Mackey, who knew Ada Chesterton and confronted her about it, and Frances' biographer, Nancy Carpentier Brown, who provides strong arguments against Ada's claims. Apparently, Ada held a deep-seated resentment against her happily married sister-in-law. She herself had married the less appealing, less successful brother, and never enjoyed any wedded bliss with him, as he died in France at the end of World War I, less than two years after their wedding. In her indefensible book, *The Chestertons*, even her unkindness to Frances is overshadowed by her lack of glow for her own husband. She had spurned him for over fifteen years and then married him not because he had successfully wooed her but because he had successfully enlisted in the army.

elders were mainly true, but we could not believe them; we shall try to tell them to our posterity, and they will not be believed: "Learning Latin will help you"—what spirited boy ever believed that? Yet Latin is still the language of modern science as much as of eternal literature. "You will feel different when you are married"—what sincere young philosopher ever believed that? Yet it is not only true but the most solid truth on earth. A married man has not only married his wife, he has married the world. Henceforth he looks at the universe from the inside and not from the outside.[111]

It is true that people in marriage go through things for which a soldier would be decorated.[112] But monogamous marriage proves itself right with every step of existence.[113] I am not a suffragist. In the words of a vulgar English song, "My wife won't let me." I was something of a

---

What is worse is that it seems much more likely that the marriage that was never consummated was Cecil and Ada's, and her lurid account of Gilbert's wedding night might well have been merely a projection of Cecil's disappointment rather than his brother's. Ada, who went by the masculine name of "Keith"—who kept the company of male journalists for most of her career, yet never dated, and never remarried, remaining single for ninety-one of her ninety-three years, and who lived apart from her husband for most of their married life—might very well have been asexual. It would explain her rather cold and cynical and nearly nasty outlook about intimate matters.

There is also the problem of envy and not even facing reality. Not only did Ada never go by her own name; she was always hiding behind another identity. In addition to going by "Keith," her pen name was "John K. (or J.K.) Prothero," and last and longest of all, by Mrs. Cecil Chesterton. She knew the Chesterton name was a door-opener, and she made the most of the fact that the papers sometimes even referred to her as "Mrs. G.K. Chesterton." In fact, she was even photographed standing next to GKC, and the caption printed described them as "Mr. and Mrs. Gilbert Chesterton."

After GKC's death, she did a lecture tour of America, giving a talk entitled "G.K. Chesterton—As I Knew Him." Though she portrayed GKC as ever the innocent, to her credit she said he was unaware of his greatness. We must also add that Mrs. Cecil was an admirable and accomplished journalist and eventual Catholic convert. Her strange and regrettable attitude toward Frances should not be used to sum up her character.

The record shows that Gilbert and Frances deeply loved each other, depended on each other, and were proud of each other. And, like every good married couple, argued and laughed together. It was a personal tragedy that they were childless. Frances visited more than one medical specialist to treat her infertility.

Chesterton, a great defender of morality and married love, of babies and large families, does say, however, "Sex is not quite so simple in practice as it is in theory." (*Listener*, Oct. 18, 1933.) No honest person will argue with that. But he also says, "You can never take the tragic element out of sex." (Interview with Margery Rex, Feb. 2, 1921.)

[111] *Daily News*, Mar. 18, 1911.
[112] *Chicago Daily Tribune*, Nov. 29, 1930.
[113] *Daily News*, Oct. 28, 1905.

suffragist before I met her. She has had a great deal to do with forming my ideas on the matter.[114]

God and His Book by the famous Freethinker "Saladin" (a book attacking orthodox Christianity) played no small part in my conversion to Christianity.[115] Nothing so much drives a thinking man to the conviction that Christianity is the moral core of the world than the vast diversity of the fools who attack it.[116] You will find what I believe, expressed with a clearness to which I have no claim, in the Apostle's Creed. What is more important in anybody is his belief. That is not the modern view. It is now held to be right and proper to be proud of one's strength or vain of one's personal beauty; while I hold that the only legitimate ground of vanity in a man is the fact that he believes something. I am not vain about either my personal appearance or my books. Speaking as an old literary critic, I don't think much of my books; and I really cannot undertake to defend my personality—there is so much of it and it is open to attack round so wide an area. These are things I would not trouble to fight about, but I would fight for my opinions because I am quite sure they are right. It is that spirit which has died out of the modern world. What counts most in a man is his view of the universe.[117] The real difference of intellectual method between those who think with me and many who think themselves more rational or more modern is that they cannot even hypothetically detach themselves from their ideas. I can see that Christianity is intellectually disputable: so are mercy and justice. But Mr. Blatchford says (in effect) that it would be kinder if we abolished human justice. That is, he arbitrarily repudiates justice, but unconsciously assumes mercy. He can ask the question, "Why should we punish?" He cannot imagine the question, "Why should we pardon?" The sense of human responsibility, which he denies, is quite as universal and fundamental as the sense of human sympathy, which he takes for granted. That men should be kind is quite as much of a dogma as that they should be punished.[118] When I was young a number of fiery fatalists went about saying that

---

[114] *Daily Oklahoman*, Mar. 20, 1921.

[115] *Daily News*, Mar. 3, 1906.

[116] *Daily News*, Oct. 29, 1910.

[117] *Churchman*, Oct. 23, 1926.

[118] *Daily News*, Mar. 3, 1906. A variation on: "There are two kinds of people: those who are dogmatic and know it and those who are dogmatic and don't know it." (*New Witness*, June 23, 1922.)

all punishment was revenge, and all revenge was cruelty. They said we must not blame anybody for anything; and then proceeded to blame the parsons for blaming. They always talked as if religion had invented revenge. They always talked as if humanity had always regarded the cruelty of revenge as self-evident, as if pardoning everybody for everything were the simplest and most natural thing in the world. But pardon is a paradox; it is one of the paradoxes of Christianity. I do not mean, of course, that nobody ever rose to that particular virtue outside that particular religion. But I do mean that the ordinary jolly heathen left entirely to himself does regard vengeance as a sort of wild justice, and not much the worse for being wild. Anyhow, vengeance, whether it be a wild-flower or a weed, does obviously in most parts of the world conspicuously manage to grow wild. It does not require any religion to encourage it, and by this religion it was definitely discouraged. I doubt whether it could ever have seemed self-evident to discourage it, in the absence of such an influence; and that was exactly what these controversialists did. The habit of taking for granted the duty of forgiveness was a Christian growth; and these people actually took it for granted as a reproach against Christianity.[119] There is something more peculiar and provocative in the Christian idea, and it is expressed in the words repentance and humility. It means that when we face the facts of the age, the first facts we face should be the faults of ourselves; and that we should at least consider, concerning any fact, the possibility that it is our fault.

I remember that very many years ago, when I was extremely young, I had an argument with an atheist in the porch of a post-office. We were total strangers, and were only standing there to be out of the rain. The aim of argument is differing in order to agree; the failure of argument is when you agree to differ. This mental collapse came upon us after an hour or so, and we fell back into ordinary speech, the atheist remarking, "It is still raining." To which I answered, with some irritation, "What is raining? Is it the same as what is reigning?" Then I suddenly remembered that the pun would not be apparent, except on paper, and walked hurriedly away.[120]

I also remember once arguing with an honest young atheist, who was very much shocked at my disputing some of the assumptions which

---

[119] *Illustrated London News*, Nov. 4, 1922.
[120] *Illustrated London News*, Apr. 1, 1911.

were absolute sanctities to him (such as the quite unproved proposition of the independence of matter and the quite improbable proposition of its power to originate mind), and he at length fell back upon this question, which he delivered with an honourable heat of defiance and indignation: "Well, can you tell me any man of intellect, great in science or philosophy, who accepted the miraculous?" I said, "With pleasure. Descartes, Dr. Johnson, Newton, Faraday, Newman, Gladstone, Pasteur, Browning, Brunetière[121]—as many more as you please." To which that quite admirable and idealistic young man made this astonishing reply— "Oh, but of course they *had* to say that; they were Christians." First he challenged me to find a black swan, and then he ruled out all my swans because they were black. The fact that all these great intellects had come to the Christian view was somehow or other a proof either that they were not great intellects or that they had not really come to that view. The argument thus stood in a charmingly convenient form: "All men that count have come to my conclusion; for if they come to your conclusion they do not count."[122]

You may or may not be able to reveal the divine secret; but at least you cannot let it leak out. If ever it comes, it will be unmistakable, it will kill or cure. Judaism, with its dark sublimity, said that if a man saw God he would die. Christianity conjectures that (by an even more catastrophic fatality) if he sees God he will live for ever. But whatever happens will be something decisive and indubitable. A man after seeing God may die; but at least he will not be slightly unwell, and then have to take a little medicine and then have to call in a doctor. If any of us ever do read the riddle, we shall read it in brutal black and blazing white, exactly as we do read the riddle of some sixpenny mystery of murder. If we ever do find the solution, we shall know that it is the right solution.[123]

I, personally, like sensational novels, sensational papers, sensational articles, and all the rest of it, as long as they give the right sensation, and in modern journalism, which I do sincerely believe to be in a dangerous state of ignorance and hypocrisy—in modern journalism I

---

[121] Yeah, I was wondering who that last one was, too. Ferdinand Brunetière (1849–1906) was a French academic and literary critic. Known as a rationalist and a freethinker, he surprised the intellectual community when he converted to Roman Catholicism in 1895.

[122] *Illustrated London News*, Apr. 20, 1907.

[123] *Daily News*, Apr. 20, 1907.

am not at all sure that the most honest part as a rule is not the police news. There you really read about human life and death and human beings tested against some reality. I think upon the whole the leading article is more immoral than the police news. At this moment I think modern English journalism tends simply to be dull. Political compromise, financial entanglements, cowardice have all made English journalism so cautious that at last there falls upon it that curse of God which falls upon all caution—that of becoming simply unintelligent. Half the journalists are concerned to write a sentence so that the first half of the sentence may say one thing and the second half say the opposite. That, putting it at the lowest and simplest, is not exciting, not sensational. There is no fun in that.[124]

I think the way for a man to get on is to bombard the editors indiscriminately with his best work, in the hope that something may take effect, much as a besieging army hurls its shells into the city it desires to capture. Some years ago, when quite inexperienced in Press work, I was asked to write some articles for a certain paper. Now when the old journalistic hand is required to do anything of the kind he immediately procures a copy of the paper in question, reads it and carefully notes the kind of matter that its editor seems to require. Then he proceeds to write in the same style, and the consequence is that it appears to the reader so like all the other contents of the journal that it passes quite unnoticed. But I took no such precautions; I simply sat down and wrote an article on some subject that happened to please me, putting, however, my very best work into it, and the result was quite a new sort of thing for that particular paper. It came with rather a shock to its readers, who were surprised and apparently pleased with the innovation.[125]

I lived in Fleet Street early in the Time of Transition. It is of some historical interest, as showing how the modern world marches onwards, and progress and improvement prove their claims as they advance. We came at the tail end of a journalism that was written in taverns, in dirty little eating-houses, in all sorts of holes and corners haunted by shabby and impecunious men. In these dens scholars and sometimes great scholars, men of culture and tradition, wrote

---

[124] *Evening Standard and St. James's Gazette*, Oct. 14, 1912.
[125] *Idler*, June 1903.

serious articles about serious things, law or liberty or economics or empire, stiffened with the strength of the Roman phrase, and full of the thoughts of thousands of years. We have lived to see the great improvement; the general clean-up. Journalists no longer write in low public houses or on the corners of coffee stalls. All have their appointed place and office in a colossal building resembling the palace of Tiberius Cæsar, though in worse taste; and in each of these cells sits a journalist who has never heard of Tiberius, but who laboriously prints in large letters, like a child, his message to the modern world, which is "Film Girl All Out For Kisses"; or "Flying Girl Fights Fourth Divorce." Such are the great changes that pass over a great society; and by this we know that Progress never wavers or looks back.

We were in the *Daily News* office, which had already been built as a big and impressive office, but not so big and impressive as those that have been built since. Meanwhile we had not deserted the taverns and eating-houses, which we much preferred the neighbourhood of the Cock or the Cheshire Cheese. For me the air that it awakens blows from the oldest and the newest of all countries; and recalls the days when large-hearted and unforgotten friends, in however crooked a street of however narrow a city, drank ale in the country of the young.[126]

I would not be going too far, in all probability, to assert that journalists as a whole are not reverenced. The iniquities of journalism, and the cheap and degraded character of those who follow that calling, occupy a very large part of the matter of the daily papers. Journalism is regarded with great contempt by those who have been journalists; it is regarded with an even more Olympian contempt by those who are trying to be journalists; but perhaps, after all, an even greater scorn is directed towards it by those who *are* journalists.

I am, like I imagine the greater part of the population of these islands, one who has experienced the sensations of writing for the papers. The only point in which I can claim a peculiar and, indeed, almost lurid isolation, is the fact that I am exceedingly proud of it. I am certainly quite as gratified at the thought that I have borne a part in the most romantic of all the developments of this most romantic age, as if I were a doctor, or a soldier, or a barrister, or a priest. And

---

[126] *Time and Tide*, Aug. 12, 1933.

I must admit that I have yet to learn that soldiers ever became better as a class for being regarded as cut-throats, or lawyers better as a class for being classed together as swindlers, or priests better for being denounced as hypocrites, or doctors better for being burnt as wizards.[127]

When I was a boy, which was just before the motorcar burst upon the world, I never dreamed of doubting that the railway-train dominated the whole future of the world. It was the latest great locomotive that man had invented. And that conservative spirit of childhood always makes the child think of the latest as the last.[128]

Hansom cabs were the gondolas of London.[129] I do not need to dwell on the essential romance of the hansom cab—that one really noble modern thing which our age, when it is judged, will gravely put beside the Parthenon. It is really modern in that it is both secret and swift. Once my hansom cab ran into the side of a motor omnibus, and I hope hurt it. My particular hansom cab was modern in the fact that it came to grief. But it was also English; not to be found abroad; belonging to a beautiful, romantic country where nearly everybody is pretending to be richer than they are, and acting as if they were. It was comfortable, and yet it was reckless, and that combination is the very soul of England. But although I had always realised all these good qualities in a hansom cab I had not experienced all the possibilities, or, as the moderns put it, all the aspects of that vehicle. My enunciation of the merits of a hansom cab had been always made when it was the right way up. Let me, therefore, explain how I felt when I fell out of a hansom cab for the first and, I am happy to believe, the last time.

I was riding one afternoon in a hansom cab down one of the sloping streets into the Strand, reading one of my own admirable articles with continual pleasure, and still more continual surprise when the horse fell forward, scrambled a moment on the scraping stones, staggered to his

---

[127] *Pall Mall Magazine*, February 1902.

[128] *Illustrated London News*, Oct. 27, 1928.

[129] *Daily News*, June 8, 1907. Chesterton had a romantic attachment to these horse-drawn taxis and regretted it when they were replaced by motorcars. He enjoyed a good relationship with the drivers during his early days as a journalist. They would give him rides for free when he had no money (which was often), but he in turn helped drivers out when they were in trouble, including giving money to a driver who had been released from prison and could not get work.

feet again, and went forward. The horses in my cabs often do this, and I have learnt to enjoy my own articles at any angle of the vehicle. So I did not see anything at all odd about the way the horse went on again. But I saw it suddenly in the faces of all the people on the pavement. They were all turned towards me, and they were all struck with fear suddenly, as with a white flame out of the sky. And one man half ran out into the road with a movement of the elbow as if warding off a blow, and tried to stop the horse. Then I knew that the reins were lost, and the next moment the horse was like a living thunderbolt. I try to describe things exactly as they seemed to me; many details I may have missed or mis-stated; many details may have, so to speak, gone mad in the race down the road.

I believe in preaching to the converted; for I have generally found that the converted do not understand their own religion. Thus I have always urged in this paper that democracy has a deeper meaning than democrats understand; that is, that common and popular things, proverbs, and ordinary sayings, always have something in them unrealised by most who repeat them. Here is one. We have all heard about the man who is in momentary danger, and who sees the whole of his life pass before him in a moment. In the cold, literal, and common sense of words, this is obviously a thundering lie. Nobody can pretend that in an accident or a mortal crisis he elaborately remembered all the tickets he had ever taken to Wimbledon, or all the times that he had ever passed the brown bread and butter.

But in those few moments, while my cab was tearing towards the traffic of the Strand, I discovered that there is a truth behind this phrase, as there is behind all popular phrases. I did really have, in that short and shrieking period, a rapid succession of a number of fundamental points of view. I had, so to speak, about five religions in almost as many seconds. My first religion was pure Paganism, which among sinful men is more shortly described as extreme fear. Then there succeeded a state of mind which is quite real, but for which no proper name has ever been found. The ancients called it Stoicism, and I think it must be what some German lunatics mean (if they mean anything) when they talk about Pessimism. It was an empty and open acceptance of the thing that happens—as if one had got beyond the value of it. And then, curiously enough, came a very strong contrary feeling—that things mattered very much indeed, and yet that they were something more than tragic. It was a feeling, not that life was unimportant, but that life was much too important ever to be anything but life. I hope that this was Christianity. At any rate, it occurred at the moment when we went crash into the omnibus. It seemed the hansom cab man simply turned over on top of me, like an enormous boot or hat. I then found myself crawling out from underneath it in [an] attitude so undignified that they must have added enormously to that great cause to which the Anti-Puritan League and I have recently dedicated ourselves. I mean the cause of the pleasures of the people. As to my demeanour when I emerged, I have two confessions to make, and they are both made merely in the interests of mental science. The first is that whereas I had been [in] a quite pious frame of mind the moment before the collision, when I got to my feet and found I had got off with a cut or two I began (like St. Peter) to curse and to swear. A man offered me a newspaper or something that I had dropped. I can distinctly remember consigning the paper to a state of irremediable spiritual ruin. I am very sorry for this now, and I apologise both to the man and to the paper. I have not the least idea what was the meaning of this unnatural anger; I mention it as a psychological confession. It was immediately followed by extreme hilarity, and I made so many silly jokes to the policeman that he disgraced himself by continual laughter before all the little boys in the street, who had hitherto taken him seriously.

There is one other odd thing about the matter which I also mention as a curiosity of intervals of about every three minutes I kept on reminding the policeman that I had not paid the cabman, and that I hoped he would not lose his money. He said it would be all right, and the man would appear. But it was not until about half-an-hour afterwards that it suddenly struck me with a shock intolerable that the man might conceivably have lost more than half-a-crown; that he had been in danger as well as I. I had instinctively regarded the cabman as something uplifted above accidents, a god. I immediately made inquiries, and I am happy to say that they seem to have been unnecessary.

But henceforward I shall always understand with a darker and more delicate charity those who rake tithe of mint, and anise, and cumin, and neglect the weightier matters of the law; I shall remember how I was once really tortured with owing half-a-crown to a man who might have been dead. Some admirable men in white coats at the Charing

Cross Hospital tied up my small injury, and I went out again into the Strand.[130]

I once wrote, unfortunately, a book called *Twelve Types*. The last I heard about the bundle of historical sketches was that one copy of it was bought by mistake for a library of technical works on printing; under the impression that it explained the differences of Small Pica and Long Primer. Perhaps this was the only copy of the book that ever was sold. Outside this somewhat mistaken generalisation, I fear that the book had nothing that could be called a general idea.[131]

I wrote a book about Robert Browning in my youth, or rather, a book that should have been about him; for, as far as I remember it (I have never dared to read it) it was mostly about other things. Still allusions to Browning were brightly introduced from time to time.[132]

I should never dream of defending my books, well knowing them to be utterly indefensible. But I shall always take every opportunity of defending my opinions, well knowing them to be entirely correct; which is the only possible meaning of having any opinions. I have had to say a word for some of my historical views, which by accident were expressed in a rambling pamphlet of my own, which I was reluctantly persuaded to call a history.[133]

I do find it amusing to watch the continual rise of new fashions, which is invariably the return of old fashions. The things I like arguing about are absolute things; whether a proof is logical or whether a practice is just. I do not want to quarrel with anybody about whether being greenery-yallery in the nineteenth century was worse than being orangey-magenta in the twentieth. Anybody can dress in what clothes he likes, or put up what decoration he likes, or look at what pictures he likes; and I have never understood why in this department, of all others, there should be so strong an element of pugnacity and even of persecution. I am therefore a pretty impartial critic, as critics go; and neither about the old revolution nor the new revolution have I ever been a very excited revolutionary—or reactionary.[134]

---

[130] *Daily News*, Nov. 3, 1906.
[131] *G.K.'s Weekly*, Apr. 23, 1932.
[132] *Daily News*, Nov. 2, 1907.
[133] *Illustrated London News*, July 26, 1919. The book was *A Short History of England*.
[134] *Illustrated London News*, Dec. 17, 1927.

That study of mine on Dickens—in which I talk sometimes about the French Revolution, sometimes about the immortality of the soul, and sometimes about a hundred other things—that book has a certain historic interest. At the end of the nineteenth century the English had got into a habit of despising Dickens and finding a thousand faults in him. It was a fashion to which all the intellectuals, the decadents, and snobs of every stripe rallied; but since my study appeared, the fashion has changed. To my mind he, with Shakespeare, is the greatest genius England has produced. Let the rest of them bow before that fact, and afterwards I do not mind all their fault-finding. But you do not get rid of a mountain by digging ditches into it.[135]

The aim of literature is to give something pointed in the mere form which shall correspond to something pointed, something inexpressibly pointed in the emotions. Verbal wit like Victor Hugo's has the same effect on the emotions as rhyme. Rhyme gives a ringing finality to a sentiment; the ear hears that something has been decided even before the brain can take it in. I believe some critics of Shakespeare blame him for ending a blank-verse scene with a rhymed couplet so often. It seems to me not only natural, but splendid, that the speech at the last should rise into a kind of recurrent song. That air of finishing the matter at a blow which verbal rhyme gives in the plays of Shakespeare, verbal wit gives in the plays of Victor Hugo and in the plays of Rostand. It is not in the least what we mean by wit, something frigid and fugitive; it is not only emotional, but violent with emotion.[136]

I myself have known and even suffered some odd misunderstandings. The other day somebody wrote to protest indignantly against my having made a mockery of St. Paul's Cathedral. Needless to say, I never made a mockery of St. Paul's Cathedral; and, even if I had, it seems just possible that St. Paul's Cathedral would have survived the incident, and that my words would not have been among the great natural forces that are said to be weighing it down. But the point is that my correspondent thought I was deriding St. Paul's, when I was deriding something quite different—and indeed, opposite. He thought I was criticising the cathedral when I was doing the contrary. I was criticising the Modernists or upholders of relativity in religion, the people who say that our

---

[135] *Living Age*, June 6, 1925.
[136] *Daily News*, Mar. 12, 1906.

faith about fundamental things must be always expanding and evolving and changing. And I said that, if we adopted that principle, there was really no reason why we should build permanent religious buildings at all. Why should we erect a temple to stand even two hundred years if all our conceptions of science and philosophy will be quite different in twenty years? I was careful to point out that our fathers who built the existing St. Paul's two hundred years ago did believe that the truth would last longer than the temple. I said not a word of disrespect about them or about the building that they made. What I said was that, if certain new notions were really adopted, such buildings never would or could be made. I said that, *if* those new notions were adopted, the only logical case would be to have no cathedral at all. It would be to put up a sort of stage scenery, which could be taken down again whenever we changed our minds in matters of religion.[137]

I think everybody, right in the middle of them, would sooner write poetry than anything else, but I am not sure that I don't enjoy controversy best of anything. I have no feeling for immortality. I don't care for anything except to be in the present stress of life as it is. I would rather live now and die, from an artistic point of view, than keep aloof and write things that will remain in the world hundreds of years after my death. What I say is subject to some modification. It so happens that I couldn't be immortal; but if I could, I shouldn't want to be. What I value in my own work is what I may succeed in striking out of others. *Heretics* isn't certainly a particularly good sort of book, but I enjoyed it because it was so very rude to all my contemporaries. I don't enjoy being rude in the ordinary way, but I think that good taste is the curse of the modern world. It's this at bottom. It's the adoption of ideals of other people. Take the English nation. Its vital fault is snobbish contempt for the poorer classes. One is thought more finely bred if one preserves a sort of reticence, both politically and other wise. Manners have become much more important than morals—a sign of decadence.[138]

A man expressing his opinions is by hypothesis trying to make them mine. But a man expressing his emotions is only asserting that they are his; and I cannot see how I can possibly contradict him.

---

[137] *Illustrated London News*, Apr. 18, 1925.
[138] *Public Opinion*, Sept. 29, 1905.

And that is why I cannot really review books of verse, though I once wrote a strong slating review of my own book of verse. I never published the review; but it was so convincing that I ought never to have published the book either.[139]

I was a great reader of novels until I began to review them, when I naturally left off reading them. I do not mean to admit that I did them any injustice; I studied and sampled them with the purpose of being strictly fair; but I do not call that "novel reading" in the old enchanting sense. If I read them thoroughly I still read them rapidly; which is quite against my instincts for the mere luxury of reading. When I was a boy and really had a new adventure story, when I was a young man and read my first few detective stories, I did not enjoy precipitation, but actually enjoyed delay. The pleasure was so intense that I was always putting it off. I loved to look at the mere solid bulk of a sensational novel as one looks at the solid bulk of a cheese; to open the first page, dally with the first paragraph, and then shut it again, feeling how little pleasure I had lost as yet. And my favourite novelists are still those great nineteenth century novelists who give an impression of bewildering bulk and variety, Scott or Dickens or Thackeray. I have artistic pleasure as keen or keener, I have moral sympathy as intense or more intense with many later writers; with the hard-hitting *mot juste* of Stevenson's stories or the insurgent irony of Mr. Belloc's. But Stevenson has one fault as a novelist, that he must be read quickly. Novels like Mr. Belloc's *Emmanuel Burden* must not only be read quickly but fiercely; they describe a short, sharp struggle; the mood both of writer and reader is heroic and abnormal, like that of two men fighting a duel. But Scott, Thackeray, and Dickens had the mysterious trick or talent of the inexhaustible novel. Even when we come to the end of the story we somehow feel that it is endless. People say they have read *Pickwick* five times or fifty times or five hundred times. For my part, I have only read *Pickwick* once. Since then I have lived in *Pickwick*; walked into it when and where I chose, as a man walks into his club. But whenever I have walked in, it seemed to me that I found something new. I am not sure that stringent modern artists like Stevenson or Mr. Belloc do not actually suffer from the strictness and swiftness of their art. If a book

---

[139] *To-day*, July 1919.

is a book to be lived in, it should be (like a house to be lived in) a little untidy.

Apart from such chaotic classics as these, my own taste in novel reading is one which I am prepared in a rather especial manner, not only to declare, but to defend. My taste is for the sensational novel, the detective story, the story about death, robbery, and secret societies; a taste which I share in common with the bulk at least of the male population of this world. There was a time in my own melodramatic boyhood when I became quite fastidious in this respect. I would look at the first chapter of any new novel as a final test of its merits. If there was a murdered man under the sofa in the first chapter, I read the story. If there was no murdered man under the sofa in the first chapter, I dismissed the story as a tea-table twaddle, which it often really was. But we all lose a little of that fine edge of austerity and idealism which sharpened our spiritual standard in our youth. I have come to compromise with the tea-table and to be less insistent about the sofa. As long as a corpse or two turn up in the second, the third, nay even the fourth or fifth chapter, I make allowance for human weakness and I ask no more. But a novel without any death in it is still to me a novel without any life in it.

Now I have read in my journalistic capacity multitudes of novels in which all the incidents were mild but in which the whole atmosphere was profoundly immoral. I have read light and frivolous novels which were quite serious upon their ultimate assumption that there is no God. I have read quiet and conversational novels which were quite fierce and dogmatic upon the idea that there ought to be no marriage. I have read every kind of terrible profanity and atrocity talked over the tea-cups. But I have never yet read a sensational story that was not on the side of Christian morals. I have never yet read or heard of a detective story that did not take common Christian decency for granted. I believe I have read nearly all the mystery stories there are, except those that I have written myself, which, unfortunately, are not mystery stories as far as I am concerned. If anybody knows any mystery stories that I have not read I implore him to send them along. But I believe that sensational novels are the most moral part of modern fiction, and I believe it upon two converging lines, such as make all real conviction. It is, I think, the fact that melodramatic fiction is moral and not immoral. And it is, I think, the abstract truth that any literature that represents our life as dangerous and startling is truer than any literature that represents it as dubious and languid. For life is a fight and not a conversation.[140]

There are a dozen reasons for despising a charge of plagiarism: One is the fact that all the most original art of the world was produced by schools in which plagiarism was a principle rather than a peccadillo. Another is that the absence of coincidence would be the greatest of all coincidences. But the reason on which I personally should most rely is the curious fact that I have never written anything out of what I call my head without its being plagiarised, not generally copied in literature (literature has better taste), but copied in real life. I wrote in my youth a foolish romance [*The Napoleon of Notting Hill*] about the occupants of a small street north of Kensington barricading themselves against some big Capitalist "improvements." I wrote it in a small square in Kensington hardly half a mile away; and when I had left this square to live in more barbaric places, the inhabitants of that very square did in very fact barricade themselves in it against similar Capitalistic improvements—and, I am happy to say, won. At another time I wrote a sort of farce [*The Man Who Was Thursday*], of which the point (God help it) was that a band of conspirators consisted entirely of disguised policemen, innocently spying on each other. Almost immediately afterwards I read the insane Azeff revelations; that nightmare of double selves, in which men seemed really to have forgotten whether they were police spying on the Anarchists or Anarchists spying on the police, so much had their heads been turned dizzy with treason.[141]

I wrote *The Man Who Was Thursday* with reference to notions that lay behind nationalism, and concerned not a country but a cosmos. And it is a very good example of how difficult I find it to describe my writing without boring everybody else about my thinking, or attempts at thinking. The peculiarity of that period was that while we were expected to be optimistic about Empire, we were also expected to be pessimistic about existence. The people who were painting the map red were also painting the universe black; and I was early moved

---

[140] *T.P.'s Weekly*, Apr. 7, 1911.

[141] *Daily News*, July 13, 1912. Yevno Asef was a double agent, spying and arranging assassinations for both the Russian secret police and the Socialist Revolutionary Party until he was exposed in 1909, after which he escaped to Germany.

to the heresy that the universe was not so black as it was painted. Even that brilliant pessimist, the Shropshire Lad,[142] was sardonically confident that "God would save the Queen" while thinking it rather unusual for God to save anybody. Now among these pessimists I was an optimist; and in *The Man Who Was Thursday* I tried to justify that phase of my optimism. I suggested that perhaps much of the apparent evil of the world was meant as a trial to our courage, and many foes if they were faced might turn out to be friends. I expressed this in a grotesque fantasia of masked Anarchists who turned out to be all of them policemen. But even at that stage I admitted the existence of a real enemy, and the whole was concerned to suggest that even optimism can hardly hold that everything is for the best, since one of the best things is a good fight.[143]

The Man Who Was Thursday was a very melodramatic sort of moonshine, but it had a kind of notion in it; and the point is that it described, first a band of the last champions of order fighting against what appeared to be a world of anarchy; and then the discovery that the mysterious master both of the anarchy and the order was the same sort of elemental elf; who had appeared to be rather too like a pantomime ogre. This line of logic, or lunacy, led many to infer that this equivocal being was meant for a serious description of the Deity; and my work even enjoyed a temporary respect among those who like the Deity to be so described. But this error was entirely due to the same cause; that they had read the book but had not read the title-page. In my case, it is true, it was a question of a sub-title rather than a title. The book was called *The Man Who Was Thursday: a Nightmare*. It was not intended to describe the real world as it was, or as I thought it was, even when my thoughts were considerably less settled than they are now. It was intended to describe the world of wild doubt and despair which the pessimists were generally describing at

---

[142] *A Shropshire Lad* was a collection of poems by A. E. Housman, which praises the bravery and sacrifice of young men who were soldiers but also speaks almost admirably about the decision of one of the very same characters to commit suicide—thus the mixed message of the poems. GKC was once asked about the difference between Housman's pessimism and Thomas Hardy's. "Housman's has the tang of fresh air about it, whereas Hardy's seems somewhat unpleasant." Then GKC, with great gusto, quoted the opening lines of verse from *A Shropshire Lad*: "O many a peer of England brews / Livelier liquor than the Muse."

[143] *T.P.'s and Cassell's Weekly*, Jan. 23, 1926.

that date; with just a gleam of hope in some double meaning of the doubt, which even the pessimists felt in some fitful fashion.[144]

What did I mean when I wrote *The Man Who Was Thursday*? I know that I meant it to be a detective tale. The reading of detective tales is my secret sin, and I had always wanted to write one myself. So in the end, partly to please myself and partly to please Mr. E. C. Bentley, I wrote it. He paid me the magnificent compliment of writing for me, in return, what I think is one of the best detective tales of the period, *Trent's Last Case*.

But I wanted to write a particular kind of detective tale. The usual thing is for your detective to track down some respectable citizen who wears top-hat, spats, and an umbrella, and subscribes to the fund for distressed dachshunds, and finally reveal him as the heartless murderer of a harmless laundress, film actress, or tax collector. Well, I thought it would be rather jolly to reverse the process, and have a number of characters who are apparently able-bodied villains who, when unmasked, prove to be decent citizens. That was the foundation of the story.

But a literary image always has an idea behind it. That is inevitable. And the idea behind this image of mine—the standing of the ordinary detective tale on its head—was that we who think we are fighting for justice are often aiming tremendous blows at villainous masks which hide people who have the same aim as we have, and think of us as we do of them. Most people, in fact, are on the right side, only they keep it dark.

All the same, I was convinced then, and I am convinced still, that there are people who have definitely taken sides with the devil, and in my book, there is one character, the real Anarchist, Lucien Gregory, who does stand for the forces of evil and despair. My villain—the real Anarchist of the story—is a decadent artist. He was very much with us at the time I wrote the book. It was a poisonous period, when all the ordinary normal ways of living were regarded as silly, and young men who spent most of their time in drinking strange liquors and imagining stranger sins—impeached God for not having made a universe to suit them.[145]

---

[144] *Illustrated London News*, June 13, 1936.
[145] *Illustrated Sunday Herald*, Jan. 24, 1926.

Very many years ago I wrote a book about orthodoxy. Until I read Mr. Bax's article on *Orthodoxy*, I had no idea how utterly and finally dead is the whole nineteenth century attack on Christianity.[146] I do not propose to discuss here the controversies with which it was concerned. But the word, as a word, as a convenient term out of the English dictionary to be used as a tool in the English workshop of words, is not without a certain interest of its own. I used it, to begin with, because it was the only word I could think of for something which is sometimes confused with tradition, and is sometimes confused with conservatism. It is the word for something which may be old and may be official, but is not right because it is old, and certainly not because it is official, but only right because it is right.[147]

I once wrote a sort of nonsense essay, urging that the saint or the true Christian ought to find nothing but childlike enthusiasm in running after his hat.[148]

I once wrote a string of small detective stories [*The Club of Queer Trades*]; mostly of the nature of horrible jokes: for it is my morality that horror is permissible if it is a joke. I do not know if anybody in particular read them; but certainly there could be no reason for anybody in particular objecting to them. Nobody in particular did; or at least nobody with one singular exception. One only, among all my acquaintances, confessed that he was shocked and disappointed at my prostituting what he was pleased to call my powers by writing vulgar tales about crime. He was a refined, sensitised sort of man; and it was plain that he was really wounded in his sympathies. Now it is the simple fact that this man, the only man I ever knew who thought it low in me to write about crimes, was also the only man

---

[146] *New Age*, Nov. 26, 1908. *The New Age* was the forum for a multiple-issue debate from 1908 to 1909 featuring multiple participants. It started with George Bernard Shaw and Cecil Chesterton defending socialism against Chesterton and Belloc. It was here where Shaw first dubbed the two as the "ChesterBelloc." Wells and others also joined the debate along with the now quite forgotten Belfort Bax. It was Bax who put GKC in what he called the "undignified" position of having to defend one of his own books. The book was *Orthodoxy*.

[147] *Illustrated London News*, July 6, 1935.

[148] *G.K.'s Weekly*, Apr. 25, 1931. (The essay "On Running After One's Hat" appeared in the *Illustrated London News*, July 21, 1906, and was later collected in *All Things Considered*. It contains the famous line "An inconvenience is only an adventure wrongly considered. An adventure is only an inconvenience rightly considered.") The three books just referred to—*The Man Who Was Thursday*, *Orthodoxy*, and *All Things Considered*—were three of GKC's most popular books, and they all came out the same year: 1908.

I ever knew who really went to gaol for committing a big, black, thumping felony.[149]

The London suburb of Kensington is the land of my birth, and Beaconsfield is the land of my adoption.[150] In the interim, we lived at Overstrand Mansions, Prince of Wales's-road, Battersea. That is a long, rolling, and interesting phrase; and it is literally true that the most striking thing about it is the fact that not one word of it means anything at all. "Overstrand" means nothing; it is not over any strand; it is named after some place in Norfolk, I believe. "Mansions" means nothing; the places are not mansions in any conceivable sense. "Prince of Wales's-road" means nothing. The Prince of Wales has, I am glad to say, nothing whatever to do with that road; almost as little as he has to do with Wales.[151] A very little way off from Battersea is the place where, by tradition, the brilliant Bolingbroke lived, and where (as some say) Pope wrote the *Essay on Man*. Across the river I can see the square tower of a church in which (it is said) the great Sir Thomas More lies dead. Right opposite me is the house of Catherine of Braganza.[152]

Some time ago my wife and I discovered that we were tired of London, and determined to set out for the land of no-where-in-particular. We simply bought two satchels, a brandy flask in case of accidents, some chocolate, a bit of candle, and some cigarettes. Thus equipped, and armed with a sword-stick and an Alpine-stock respectively, we set out, without having the slightest idea where we were going. We found an omnibus at Notting Hill which happened to pass Hanwell Railway Station. Thinking the name encouraging,[153] we waylaid an official and asked: "Where does the next train go to?"

---

[149] *New Witness*, Oct. 7, 1915. Although GKC uses some discretion in not naming the felon, he is referring to Charles Granville, who served as an editor of the *Eye Witness* and *New Witness*, and secretly disliked both Hilaire Belloc and Cecil Chesterton, and even testified against them and their newspapers during the Marconi hearings in 1913. But by that time, he was already in prison, having been convicted a few weeks earlier for both fraud and bigamy. Granville was not even his real name. It was Hosken.

[150] *New Witness*, Mar. 9, 1923.

[151] *Daily News*, May 21, 1904.

[152] Introduction to *Literary London*, by Elsie M. Lang (T. Werner, 1906), pp. ix–x. Henry St. John, Lord Bolingbroke (1678–1751), was a leading English political figure and a political philosopher whose ideas influenced Thomas Jefferson and James Madison. Catherine of Braganza was married to Charles II and was the last Catholic queen of England.

[153] Hanwell refers not just to the town of that name, but to the large insane asylum that was located there. Chesterton famously refers to both uses of the name in his chapter "The Maniac," in *Orthodoxy*.

"All depends where you want to go," replied the railway man.

"What has that got to do with you, my good friend?" I said, "where does the next train go to?"

"Away from London, or towards London?"

"Away from London."

"The next train is for Slough and Windsor."

"That will do nicely," I said, and to Slough we went, and setting out from there, tramped about all the morning going in any direction that pleased us for the moment, and at lunch time we found ourselves miles from anywhere and in the midst of a wild and desolate heath, without the faintest notion as to our whereabouts. An ancient man (who was, I am sure, a fairy), directed us to a hotel a little farther on, and we found an admirable country inn where we fared sumptuously, and then started on our travels again. I am quite certain myself that the hotel was a fairy thing, and disappeared as soon as we left its doors.

Finding ourselves once more in the open space, our gaze was arrested by a singularly ugly erection in the middle of a field. So ugly was it, that a responsive sympathy was awakened in my heart and I went to examine it, and to my surprise it turned out to be a memorial to Gray. We went a little further (as they say in the other, but kindred fairy-tales) and I walked into a church idly enough, and the first thing that met my eye was a pompous eighteenth century monument, on which was inscribed something to this effect: "Under this stone lies all that is perishable of Edmund Burke." And so, walking from my own door *via* Hanwell, I had gone straight to the grave of the greatest British figure of the eighteenth century. But do you suppose that if I had been carted in six hot wagonettes to see the tomb of Burke I should have felt as I felt then? [154]

I abominate and abjure the man who lives in London and wants to go [to] the country; I do it with all the more heartiness because I am that sort of man myself. I never liked a Battersea flat, except in so far as I liked living in Battersea. Of course, I can eat, sleep, and praise God in a flat. I can eat, sleep, and praise God in a railway carriage.

---

[154] *Idler*, June 1903. The town that GKC and Frances visited by chance that day in 1903 turned out to be Beaconsfield, where they would move five years later and make it their permanent home. The inn they stayed at was the White Hart. This account is from an interview GKC gave long before he would find his way home via Hanwell.

But a railway carriage is not a house because it is a house on wheels. A flat is not a house because it is a house on stilts.[155]

There has been an exodus into the country of those who could afford it, and some I could name who can't.[156]

Every man, though he were born in the very belfry of Bow and spent his infancy climbing among chimneys, has waiting for him somewhere a country house which he has never seen; but which was built for him in the very shape of his soul. It stands patiently waiting to be found, knee-deep in some Kentish garden or mirrored in some slow Norfolk stream; and when the man sees it he remembers it, though he has never seen it before. Even I have been forced to confess this at last, who am a Cockney, if ever there was one, a Cockney not only on principle, but with savage pride. I have always maintained quite seriously that the Lord is not in the wind or thunder of the waste, but in the still small voice of Fleet Street. I sincerely maintain that Nature-worship is more morally dangerous than the most vulgar man-worship of the cities; since it can easily be perverted into the worship of an impersonal mystery, carelessness, or cruelty. Thoreau would have been a jollier fellow if he had devoted himself to a greengrocer instead of to greens. Swinburne would have been a better moralist if he had worshipped a fishmonger instead of worshipping the sea. I prefer the philosophy of bricks and mortar to the mere philosophy of turnips. To call a man a turnip may be playful, but is never respectful. But when we wish to pay emphatic honour to a man, to praise the firmness of his nature, the squareness of his conduct, the strong humility with which he is interlocked with his equals in silent mutual support, then we invoke the nobler cockney metaphor, and call him a brick.

But, despite all these theories, I have surrendered; I have struck my colours at sight; at a mere glimpse through the opening of a hedge. I shall come down to living in the country, like any common Socialist or Simple Lifer. I shall end my days in a village, in the character of the Village Idiot, and be a spectacle and a judgment to mankind. I have already learnt the rustic manner of leaning upon a gate; and I was

---

[155] *New Age*, Apr. 15, 1909.
[156] *Daily News*, May 21, 1910. He's obviously referring to himself as one of those who cannot afford to live in the country.

thus gymnastically occupied at the moment when my eye caught the house that was made for me. It stood well back from the road, and was built of a good yellow brick; it was narrow for its height, like the tower of some Border robber; and over the front door was carved in large letters, "1908." That last burst of sincerity, that superb scorn of antiquarian sentiment, overwhelmed me finally. I closed my eyes in a kind of ecstasy. My friend (who was helping me to lean on the gate) asked me with some curiosity what I was doing.

"My dear fellow," I said, with emotion, "I am bidding farewell to forty-three hansom cabmen."[157]

After living two months in the country, I gathered the last rich autumnal fruit of a rural life, which is a strong desire to see London. Arriving in London for the first time as an outsider, I visited the Marble Arch, which had recently had all of the traffic around it rerouted so that no traffic could actually pass under it. I got into a conversation with an Anarchist and realised that the Marble Arch is a massive symbol of the modern mind; a door with no house to it; the gigantic gate of Nowhere.[158]

I am happy to say that I live in Beaconsfield; I mean, of course, that I live in Bekonsfield. I believe that there are some people who live in Beekonsfield, but I do not know where it is, and I cannot imagine why anybody should live there. Now about the origin of the name of this town there is some dispute; but about the pronunciation of the name, there is no dispute whatever. There is only knowledge as possessed by those who know; and the often invincible and therefore innocent ignorance of the world outside. I need hardly say that those who know are those who are now commonly called ignorant and uneducated people. When you have heard the name of your own town for twenty years on the tongues of hedgers, ditchers, rat-catchers, gamekeepers, poachers and village idiots, then you know absolutely for certain that it is the correct pronunciation. When the intellectual aristocracy of clerks, counter-jumpers, commission-agents, bucket-shop keepers, and the rest of the ruling class of our day, comes down to such a place and pronounces it as it is spelt, you know for a simple fact that they are wrong. If you have any real education, you know

---

[157] *Daily News*, Aug. 28, 1909.
[158] *Daily News*, Dec. 11, 1909. (This passage was heavily edited in order to condense it.)

that spelling was never in the past a great part of education; that it is now treated by these people as the whole of education; simply because it is the whole of their education, or the only education they have. It never occurs to them that, while Shakespeare would write his own name in two or three totally different but equally illegible scrawls, he trusted the whole great load of his glory to the sound of words, to be spoken by living men. In dealing therefore with a word like "Beaconsfield," they do not know how to choose between the men who can speak and the men who can only spell. It was always pronounced right. Only it is still spelt wrong. It is true that some at least maintain that the name is derived from an old word for a beech-tree. Certainly there could be no more appropriate name and no more symbolic and inspiring thing. For the beech-tree has a special representative quality in all this rolling wooded landscape, which makes up the central and southern parts of Buckinghamshire; and through the county a real relation to the country. A Sussex man [perhaps Belloc], himself boiling over with enthusiasm for Sussex, once said to me of the beech-woods about my Beaconsfield home; "This is really the most English part of England; I confess that, compared with this, Sussex is a thing quite separate and apart."

If I were choosing an entirely English emblem, I should choose the beech-tree. It is strong and expressive of strength; but its smoothness is also expressive of a certain slowness that is akin to mercy and mildness. Its curves are of the gradual sort found in everything in these parts; in the slow speech of the rustics; in the gradual curves in the hills, even far away to the downs of Hampshire and Sussex, that are the only mountains of the South. They have a power like that of lazy waves that are lifted slowly; and allow villages to grow up in their hollows, only because they are too lazy to fall. Here especially, in this section of Bucks, the beeches surround and overshadow us and cover our home; so that it is no accident that has called this particular stretch of England the Home Counties. The return to a real England would be a return to the beech-woods: which still make this town like a home. At least, they did until recently. I shall probably be told to-morrow that several beech-forests have been removed to enable a motorist, temporarily deaf and blind, to go from Birmingham to Brighton.[159]

---

[159] *G.K.'s Weekly*, Dec. 17, 1932.

When I lived at Overroads, I bought a plot of land across the road and built a studio on it. The point is that it was mine. The house I lived in belonged to a very decent little man. We were on the best of terms, he and I. But the place was his: nothing could change that, and across there was something quite my own.[160] While returning from the studio to Overroads one night, I fell over a flower-box which stood in the middle of the path in the dark; but I am far from claiming that if it had stood three yards from the path in broad daylight I might not have managed to fall over it some day or other. And as a weekly paper admirably said, people inquired after me, but no one had the common compassion to inquire after the flower-box. I am glad I broke my arm; chiefly because it is the safest thing to break; and broken heads and broken hearts are the later penalty for refusing all wisdom or wonder.[161]

One of the things that has made a difference to me is owning my own place in the country. I was born and bred a Cockney. I was altogether urban. And then I moved into the country and I bought a field. My own field! My very own! And then I built a studio on it. My very own studio. I could enact my own (or my wife's) plays in that studio, and whoever said to me nay could go to blazes. And then the house grew on to the studio. And now I am proud to say that I can grow in my garden enough to keep my family alive if our toppling system of credit went to pieces and our great cities were famine-stricken. Yes, I have learnt the meaning of ownership. I know what liberty really means.[162] What I know now is that the garden of private property is not a refuge, but rather a new world—as much of a new world as learning to read or to play the piano.[163]

There hangs on my wall one of those painted ikons which are carried by the soldiers of Russia and which has the private value that it was given to me by a friend whom I love, and who is a great lover of that land.[164]

In the Spring of 1914, a relative of my wife, who had married a German professor, came to England bearing a present from him,

---

[160] *New York Tribune*, Sept. 15, 1912 (edited to the past tense).
[161] *Daily News*, July 13, 1912.
[162] *Daily Sketch*, May 14, 1931.
[163] *Illustrated London News*, Feb. 25, 1922.
[164] *New Witness*, Nov. 16, 1916. The friend, no doubt, is Maurice Baring.

which took the form of one of those enormous picture pipes, with a painted head like a wooden doll. I beheld the pipe with some inward terror, but with outward bravado, and said I would smoke it solemnly the next day before the whole family circle, who would sit around worshipping this sacred rite. For it was, as I pointed out, a symbol. The diplomatic ice was already thin and slippery, even for conversation, and my own sympathies were rather French than German; but both the professor and I could join in prayers that Christendom might be spared the curse of war. So I pointed to the pipe, where I hung it on a nail in the wall for that one night, and said solemnly, "It is the Pipe of Peace."

That night, in the midst of a windless stillness, without visible agency, the pipe fell from the wall and was shattered into a score of fragments.

I am not a pagan, like so many of the bright young people of our rationalistic and sceptical age. I am not a pagan; and therefore I am not superstitious. I think these coincidences can sometimes be reminders; but that is all. But one of the real pagans, the old pagans who could write great poetry and carve great sculpture, would most certainly have said that I had received an omen and almost the answer of an oracle.[165]

Shortly after moving away from London and taking up my new residence, I was put up as Parish Constable of Beaconsfield, though I did not know it at the time; and though I managed to evade the honour afterwards. I based my *nolo Constabulari* on two grounds: first, that though I may possess some of the qualities of a pantomime policeman, I do not possess those of a real one; and second, that if a riot broke out in a modern English town my sympathies would almost certainly be on the side of the rioters. I did not know about it, because it is one of those old posts which inherit from the Middle Ages the tradition of summoning public officers without their assent, and even against their will. Anyhow, the result was that everybody had heard of my name being put up except myself. People rang me up on the telephone to congratulate me on being a Constable; and I denied it, saying, "Do I look like a man whom anybody would make Constable?" which was perhaps an illogical question to ask on the telephone. People from the illustrated papers came down with cameras

---

[165] *New York American*, Sept. 22, 1934.

to photograph me in my constabular uniform. My post-bag was full of letters about it, which I do not remember in detail, though I could reconstruct many of the more amusing kind in some approximate rendering. The best of them, of course, were of the hearty and candid sort, beginning, "No doubt you think yourself jolly fine swaggering about as a constable and not knowing what a fool you look. I saw the posters of your play, *You Never Can Tell*,[166] and they made me sick—Disgusted Ratepayer." Or another would run, in a more persuasive diction, "Now that you are Constable of Beaconsfield I am sure your will use your influence at Pekin [Bejing] on behalf of my nephew, who is very short-sighted and attached to the Observatory in that city, founded by the Jesuits in the sixteenth century, so that you will be doing a good Protestant work in that heathen land." Or another message would run, "We can print fifteen million words from you on *Life Garnerings of a Constable in the Old Country*,—Cable to Arkansas Elevator and Uplift." Or I might read something like: "Last Sabbath afternoon, while reading the Word with some earnest friends, I came upon the following text: 'Making him to skip like a small goat upon the mountains of Lebanon.' On the very next morning I read of your appointment as Constable of Beaconsfield." And the next, perhaps, might run: "Your appointment to the position of Beaconsfield Parish Constable recalls to me the fact that I once met the late Lord Beaconsfield at an hotel in Oban. It was soon after his great exploit in securing Peace with Honour, and I distinctly remember hearing him say to one of his friends, 'Don't touch Patagonian oyster beds. There's nothing in it.' Long may the Conservative party be guided by such far-sighted and patriotic considerations. I make no apology for drawing your attention to this observation, as I feel sure it will be of great service to you in the strenuous duties you have undertaken." Of such tenuous texture, alas! are all the memories I can collect of my own somewhat phantasmal tenure of office.[167]

My friend Mr. Bernard Shaw wanted me to stand as his colleague for the County Council. I often please myself with the thought of

---

[166] The play is by Shaw. GKC mentions this to show that in spite of their vast philosophical differences, in the public's eye, they were the same paradoxical person.

[167] Introduction to *Songs of the Specials*, by E. W. Fordham (C. Palmer & Hayward, 1916), pp. 4–5. Ironically, Fordham, GKC's friend from the JDC (Junior Debating Club), actually *was* a constable.

how the audience would have roared with laughter whenever we appeared on the platform side by side, like the Two Macs at the music-hall. I think I would really have accepted the candidature if I could have been quite certain of being defeated. But life is full of unforeseen disasters: I might even have got in, and a nice mess I should have been in then.[168] Anyone who has worked in a modern Parliamentary election knows that the most lamentable part of it is the person who is elected.[169]

Having taken part in a pageant of Nursery Rhymes; in the character of Old King Cole,[170] I was told that I was just like Dr. Johnson. Seeing that Dr. Johnson was heavily seamed with small-pox, had a waistcoat all covered with gravy, snorted and rolled as he walked, and was probably the ugliest man in London, I mention this identification as a fact and not as a vaunt.

The procession took place at night in a large garden and by torch-light. The garden was crowded with Puritans, monks, and men-at-arms, and especially with early Celtic saints smoking pipes, and with elegant Renaissance gentlemen talking Cockney. Suffice it to say, or rather it is needless to say, that I got lost. I wandered away into some dim corner of that dim shrubbery, where there was nothing to do except tumbling over tent ropes, and I began almost to feel like my prototype, and to share his horror of solitude and hatred of a country life.

I mixed with the men of the 18th century; and we fooled as one does at a fancy-dress ball. There was Burke as large as life and a great deal better looking. There was Cowper much larger than life; he ought to have been a little man in a night-cap, with a cat under one arm and a spaniel under the other. As it was, he was a magnificent person, and looked more like the Master of Ballantrae than Cowper. I persuaded him at last to the night-cap, but never, alas, to the cat and dog. When I came the next night Burke was still the same beautiful improvement upon himself; Cowper was still weeping for his dog and cat and would not be comforted; Bishop Berkeley was still waiting to be kicked in the interests of philosophy. In short, I met all my old friends.[171]

---

[168] *Illustrated London News*, Nov. 20, 1909.
[169] *Illustrated London News*, Oct. 11, 1919.
[170] *New Witness*, Dec. 10, 1920.
[171] *Daily News*, June 19, 1909.

I once wrote some journalistic sketches or stories which turned upon queer trades.[172] I have forgotten what they were, I am happy to say; but I am pretty sure I should not find in those lost tales any trade so extraordinary as one which I have just noted in an ordinary newspaper.[173]

I once wrote a very rambling romance called *The Flying Inn*, in which there was an aged Turk who was a sort of crank and preached the theory that everything in Christendom had really been founded upon Islam. Wishing to make it perfectly manifest that the man was mad, I made him say that the prevalence of Crescents among the streets of London was a mark of Moslem influence. He particularly mentioned Denmark Crescent, and pointed to it proudly as a proof of his contention. You would say that this is too farcical even for a farce. You would argue that there could not be even a crank so cranky as that. You would be wrong. Years afterwards I actually did hear Denmark Crescent specially mentioned in proof of a theory. Seated on a secluded seat in the beautiful hill-town of Rye, of all places in the world, I heard with my own ears, in the hush of the twilight, an elderly gentleman saying to a young friend the words "Denmark Crescent." For the instant I was too thrilled to disengage my attention; and the next sentence and a half were enough to fix the fact. The old gentleman was saying that Denmark Crescent was quite obviously named after the tribe of Dan, and was a clinching and conclusive proof that the English were the Lost Ten Tribes. I heard no more; I fled; I felt it was no place for me or perhaps for any mortal man. I went back to gargoyles and grotesque monstrosities to soothe my mind with a sense of sane and ordinary things. Insanity of that towering and tropical description is too much for a mere weaver of words into frail and tenuous fairy-tales.[174]

---

[172] As you surmised, *The Club of Queer Trades*.

[173] *Illustrated London News*, June 21, 1919.

[174] *Illustrated London News*, May 2, 1925. In the *Daily News*, Jan. 13, 1912, GKC describes, how ten years earlier, he found himself in the midst of a mob that was trying to crash a meeting of pro-Boers. He was outside with the mob, but he was actually a pro-Boer, part of the most unpopular group of people in England. "I wish I could ever be as unpopular as that again. It would prove that there is still a populace." He and a friend shouted out some pro-Jingo names, and the crowd roared its approval until the names became more ironic, like Eckstein, Beit, and Albu, the money powers behind the Boer War. He says he had a hard time extricating himself from the crowd. He got a black eye and had his watch stolen. He was proud of the black eye and relieved to be rid of his watch. But what he liked about the mob

I love waiting for trains. Such philosophies as I have, I have often evolved while waiting at Clapham Junction. I am one of those shameless beings who enjoy having nothing to do.[175] The only way of catching a train I have ever discovered is to be late for the one before. Do this and you will find in a railway station much of the quietude and consolation of a cathedral. It has many of the characteristics of a great ecclesiastical building; it has vast arches, void spaces, coloured lights, and above all, it has recurrence or ritual. It is dedicated to the celebration of water and fire, the two prime elements of all human ceremonial. Lastly, a station resembles the old religions rather than the new religions in this point, that people go there. In connection with this it should also be remembered that all popular places, all sites, actually used by the people, tend to retain the best routine of antiquity. When I get in a third-class carriage from the nearest circle station to Battersea to the nearest circle station to the *Daily News* the names of the stations are one long litany of solemn and saintly memories. Leaving Victoria I come to a park belonging especially to St. James the Apostle; thence I go to Westminster Bridge, whose very name alludes to the awful Abbey; Charing Cross holds up the symbol of Christendom; the next station is called a Temple; and Blackfriars remembers the mediaeval dream of a Brotherhood.

If you wish to find the past preserved follow the million feet of the crowd. At the worst the uneducated only wear down old things by sheer walking. But the educated kick them down out of sheer culture.

I feel all this profoundly as I wander about the empty railway station, where I have no business of any kind. I have extracted a vast number of chocolates from automatic machines; I have obtained cigarettes, toffee, scent, and other things that I dislike by the same machinery. I have weighed myself, with sublime results; and this sense not only of the healthiness of popular things, but of their essential antiquity and permanence is still in possession of my mind. I wander up to the bookstall, and my faith survives even the wild spectacle of modern literature and journalism. Even in the crudest and most clamorous aspects of the newspaper world I still prefer the popular

---

is that he could speak more freely than he could in the newspaper. His days on the *Daily News* were numbered at this point. He points out the irony that Albu was knighted. It is an event that perhaps inspires the plot of *The Flying Inn*.

[175] *Philosopher*, July–September 1927.

to the proud and fastidious. If I had to choose between taking in the *Daily Mail* and taking in *The Times* (the dilemma reminds one of a nightmare) I should certainly cry out with the whole of my being for the *Daily Mail*. Even mere bigness preached in a frivolous way is not so irritating as mere meanness preached in a big and solemn way. People buy the *Daily Mail*, but they do not believe in it. They do believe in *The Times*, and (apparently) they do not buy it. But the more the output of paper upon the modern world is actually studied the more it will be found to be in all its essentials ancient and human, like the name of Charing-cross. Linger for two or three hours at a station bookstall (as I do) and you will find that it gradually takes on the grandeur and historic allusiveness of the Vatican or Bodleian Library. The novelty is all superficial; the tradition is all interior and profound. The *Daily Mail* has new editions, but never a new idea. Everything in a newspaper that is not the old human love of altar or fatherland is the old human love of gossip. Modern writers have often made game of the old chronicles because they chiefly record accidents and prodigies; a church struck by lightning or a calf with six legs. They do not seem to realise that this old barbaric history is the same as new democratic journalism. It is not the savage chronicle that has disappeared. It is merely that the savage chronicle now appears every morning.

As I moved thus mildly and vaguely in front of the bookstall my eye caught a sudden and scarlet title that for the moment staggered me. On the outside of a book I saw written in large letters, "Get On or Get Out." The title of the book recalled to me with a sudden revolt and reaction all that does seem unquestionably new and nasty; it reminded me that there was in the world of to-day that utterly idiotic thing, a worship of success; a thing that only means surpassing anybody in anything; a thing that may mean being the most successful person in running away from a battle; a thing that may mean being the most successfully sleepy of a whole row of sleeping men. When I saw those words the silence and sanctity of the railway station were for a moment shadowed. Here, I thought, there is at any rate something anarchic and violent and vile. This title at any rate means the most disgusting individualism of this individualistic world. In the fury of my bitterness and passion I actually bought the book, thereby ensuring that my enemy would get some of my money. I opened it prepared to find some brutality, some blasphemy, which would really be an exception to the general silence and sanctity of the railway station. I was prepared to find something in the book that was as infamous as its title. I was disappointed. There was nothing at all corresponding to the furious decisiveness of the remarks on the cover.[176]

The other day, to my great astonishment, I *caught* a train; it was a train going into the Eastern Counties, and I only just caught it. And while I was running along the train (amid general admiration) I noticed that there were a quite peculiar and unusual number of carriages marked "Engaged." On five, six, seven, eight, nine carriages was pasted the little notice: at five, six, seven, eight, nine windows were big bland men staring out in the conscious pride of possession. Their bodies seemed more than usually impenetrable, their faces more than usually placid. It could not be the Derby, if only for the minor reasons that it was the opposite direction and the wrong day. It could hardly be the King. It could hardly be the French President. For though these distinguished persons naturally like to be private for three hours, they are at least public for three minutes. A crowd can gather to see them step into the train and there was no crowd here or any police ceremonial.

Who were these awful persons, who occupied more of the train than a bricklayers' beanfeast, and yet were more fastidious and delicate than the King's own suits? Who were these, that were larger than a mob, yet more mysterious than a monarch? Was it possible that instead of our Royal House visiting the Tsar he was really visiting us? Or does the House of Lords have a beanfeast? I waited and wondered until the train slowed down at some station in the direction of Cambridge. Then the large, impenetrable men got out, and after them got out the distinguished holders of the engaged seats. They were all dressed decorously in one colour; they had neatly cropped hair; and they were chained together.

I looked across the carriage at its only other occupant, and our eyes met. He was a small, tired-looking man, and, as I afterwards learnt, a native of Cambridge; by the look of him, some working tradesman there, such as a journeyman tailor or a small clock-mender. In order to make conversation I said I wondered where the convicts were going. His mouth twitched with the instinctive irony of the poor,

---

[176] *Daily News*, Jan. 12, 1907.

and he said: "I don't s'pose they're goin' on an 'oliday at the sea-side with little spades and pails." I was naturally delighted, and pursuing the same vein of literary invention, I suggested that perhaps dons were taken down to Cambridge chained together like this. And as he lived in Cambridge, and had seen several dons, he was pleased with such a scheme. Then when we had ceased to laugh we suddenly became quite silent; and the bleak, grey eyes of the little man grew sadder and emptier than an open sea. I knew what he was thinking, because I was thinking the same, because all modern sophists are only sophists, and there is such a thing as mankind. Then at last (and it fell in as exactly as the last note of a tune one is trying to remember) he said: "Well, I s'pose we 'ave to do it." And in those three things, his first speech and his silence and his second speech, there were all the three great fundamental facts of the English democracy, its profound sense of humour, its profound sense of pathos, and its profound sense of helplessness.

It cannot be too often repeated that all real democracy is an attempt (like that of a jolly hostess) to bring the shy people out. For every practical purpose of a political state, for every practical purpose of a tea-party, he that abaseth himself must be exalted. At a tea-party it is equally obvious that he that exalteth himself must be abased, if possible without bodily violence. Now people talk of democracy as being coarse and turbulent: it is a self-evident error in mere history. Aristocracy is the thing that is always coarse and turbulent: for it means appealing to the self-confident people. Democracy means appealing to the diffident people. Democracy means getting those people to vote who would never have the cheek to govern: and (according to Christian ethics) the precise people who ought to govern are the people who have not the cheek to do it. There is a strong example of this truth in my friend in the train. The only two types we hear of in this argument about crime and punishment are two very rare and abnormal types.

We hear of the stark sentimentalist, who talks as if there were no problem at all: as if physical kindness would cure everything: as if one need only pat Nero and stroke Ivan the terrible. This mere belief in bodily humanitarianism is not sentimental; it is simply snobbish. For if comfort gives men virtue the comfortable classes ought to be virtuous—which is absurd. Then, again, we do hear of the yet weaker and more watery type of sentimentalist: I mean the sentimentalist who says with a sort of splutter, "Flog the brutes!" or who tells you with innocent obscenity "what he would do" with a certain man—always supposing the man's hands were tied.

This is the more effeminate type of the two; but both are weak and unbalanced. And it is only these two types, the sentimental humanitarian and the sentimental brutalitarian, whom one hears in the modern babel. Yet you very rarely meet either of them in a train. You never meet anyone else in a controversy. The man you meet in a train is like this man that I met: he is emotionally decent, only he is intellectually doubtful. So far from luxuriating in the loathsome things that could be "done" to criminals, he feels bitterly how much better it would be if nothing need be done. But something must be done. "I s'pose we 'ave to do it." In short he is simply a sane man, and of a sane man there is only one safe definition. He is a man who can have tragedy in his heart and comedy in his head.

The train moved swiftly through the sunny English Fields. They took the prisoners away, and I do not know what they did with them.[177]

I know no better exercise in that art of wonder, which is the life of man and the beginning of the praise of God, than to travel in a train through a long dark almost uninterrupted tunnel: until the traveller has grown almost accustomed to dusk and a dead blank background of brick. At last, after long stretches and at long intervals, the wall will suddenly break in two; and give a glowing glimpse of the land of the living. It may be a chasm of daylight showing a bright and busy street. It may be a similar flash of light on a long lonely road of poplars, with a solitary human figure plodding across the vast countryside. I know not which of the two gives a more startling stab of human vitality. Sometimes the grey facade is broken by the lighted windows of a house, almost overhanging the railway-line; and for an instant we look deep into a domestic interior; chamber within chamber of a glowing and coloured human home. That is the way in which objects ought to be seen; separate; illuminated; and above all, contrasted against blank night or bare walls; as indeed these living creations do stand eternally contrasted with the colourless chaos out of which they came.

---

[177] *Daily News*, June 6, 1908.

Travelling in this fashion, the other day, I was continually haunted, and almost tormented, with an impression that I could not disentangle; nor am I at all confident that I can disentangle it here. It seemed to me that I saw very strange sights; which ought to have been significant sights. I looked suddenly through an open window into a little room that was filled with blue light; something much bluer than we see in moonlight, even once in a blue moon. It came apparently from the blue shade that completely hooded a lamp standing on the table; there was nothing else on the table but an open book, which gleamed almost pale blue in that bleak luminosity. There was nobody there; there was nothing else. And I had an indescribable subconscious sense that it ought to mean something; and there massed vaguely at the back of my mind like blue clouds, the colours that cling about the Blessed Virgin in the old pictures and the visions seen in narrow rooms and cells.

Then again I saw a square patch of burning red, which was but the red curtain covering a lighted room. But there was a shadow that moved sharply across it, lifting long arms, arms of an unnatural exaggerated length, and making the black pattern of a cross upon the burning scarlet. It was impossible not to feel that somebody had made a signal to the train. And yet somebody had only stretched his arms, probably with a yawn, before going indifferently to bed. All along that night journey there were these signals signifying nothing. And I grew conscious, in a way quite beyond expression, that there is indeed a poetry of modern life, and of the modern cities; but it is in some strange way a poetry of misfits; a tangle of misunderstood messages; an alphabet all higgledy-piggledy in a heap. Beautiful things ought to mean beautiful things. And the case for simpler conditions is that, on the whole, they do. That indestructibility of religion, and even of ritualism, which puzzles the poor old rationalist so much, is not a little due to the fact that in ritual, for the first time, modern men see forms and colours placed where they mean something. Anybody can see why the priest's vestment on common days is green like the common fields, and on martyrs' days red as blood. But that blood-red curtain I saw from the train either commemorated no martyrdom; or the man crucified within did not know that his martyrdom was commemorated.[178]

---

[178] *G.K.'s Weekly*, Nov. 29, 1930.

All this talk of a railway mystery has sent my mind back to a lost memory. The perplexity of life arises from there being too many interesting things in it for us to be interested properly in any of them: what we call its triviality is really the tag ends of numberless tales; ordinary and unmeaning existence is like ten thousand thrilling detective stories mixed up with a spoon. My experience was a fragment of this nature. I remember the details vividly.

About noon of an ashen autumn day some years ago I was standing outside the station at Oxford intending to take the train to London. And for some reason, out of idleness or the emptiness of my mind or the emptiness of the pale grey sky, or the cold, a kind of caprice fell upon me that I would not go by that train at all, but would step out on the road and walk at least some part of the way to London. I do not know if other people are made like me in this matter; but to me it is always dreary weather, what may be called useless weather, that stings into a sense of action and romance. On bright, blue days I do not want anything to happen; the sky is complete and beautiful, a thing for contemplation. I no more ask for adventures under that turquoise dome than I ask for adventures in church. But when the background of man's life is a grey background, then, in the name of man's sacred supremacy, I desire to paint on it in fire and gore. When the heavens fail man refuses to fail; when the sky seems to have written on it, in letters of lead and pale silver the decree that nothing shall happen, then the immortal soul, the prince of the creatures, rises up and decrees that something shall happen, if it be only the slaughter of a policeman. But that bleak sky awoke in me a hunger for some change of plans and I set out into the country lanes, out of the town of Oxford.

As I crossed the country everything was ghostly and colourless. The fields that should have been green were as grey as the skies: the tree-tops that should have been green were as grey as the clouds and as cloudy. And when I had walked for some hours the evening was closing in. A sickly sunset clung weakly to the horizon, as if pale with reluctance to leave the world in the dark. And as it faded more and more the skies seemed to come closer and to threaten. The clouds which had been merely sullen became swollen; and then they loosened and let down the dark curtains of the rain. The rain was blinding and seemed to beat like blows from an enemy at close quarters; the skies seemed bending over me and bawling in my ears. I walked on many more miles before I met a man, and in that distance my mind had been made up; and when I met him I asked him if anywhere in the neighbourhood I could pick up the train for Paddington. He directed me to a small silent station (I cannot even remember the name of it) which stood well away from the road and looked as lonely as a hut on the Andes. I do not think I have seen such a type of time and sadness and scepticism and everything devilish as that station was; it looked as if it were not water at all, but some loathsome liquid corruption of the wood itself; as if the solid station were eternally falling to pieces and pouring away in filth. It took me nearly ten minutes to find a man in the station. When I did he was a dull one, and when I asked him if there was a train for Paddington his affirmative was sleepy and vague. As far as I understood him, he said there would be a train in half-an-hour. I sat down and lit a cigar and waited, watching the last tail of the tattered sunset and listening to the everlasting rain. It may have been in half-an-hour or less, but a train came rather slowly into the station. It was an unnaturally dark train; I could not see a light anywhere in the long, black body of it; and I could not see any guard running beside it. I was reduced to walking up to the engine and calling out to the stoker to ask if the train was going to London. "Well-yes, sir," he said, with an unaccountable kind of reluctance. "It is going to London; but——." It was just starting, and I jumped into the first carriage: it was pitch-dark. I sat there smoking and wondering, as we steamed through the continually darkening landscape, lined with desolate poplars, until we slowed down and stopped, irrationally, in the middle of a field. I heard a heavy noise as of some one clambering off the train, and a dark, ragged head suddenly put itself into my window. "Excuse me, sir," said the stoker, "but I think, perhaps—well, perhaps you ought to know—there's a dead man in this train."

Had I been a true artist, a person of exquisite susceptibilities and nothing else, I should have been bound, no doubt, to be finally overwhelmed with this sensational touch, and to have insisted on getting out and walking. As it was, I regret to say, I expressed myself politely, but firmly, to the effect that I didn't care particularly if the train took me to Paddington. But when the train had started with its unknown burden I did do one thing and did it quite instinctively, without stopping to think, or to think more than a flash. I threw away my cigar. Something that is as old as man and has to do with all mourning and ceremonial told me to do it. There was something unnecessarily horrible, it seemed to me, in the idea of there being only two men in that train, one of them dead and the other smoking a cigar. And as the red and gold of the butt end of it faded like a funeral torch trampled out at some symbolic moment of a procession I realised how immortal ritual is. I realised (what is the origin and essence of all ritual) that in the presence of those sacred riddles about which we can say nothing it is often more decent merely to do something. And I realised that ritual will always mean throwing away something; destroying our corn or wine upon the altars of our gods.[179]

Here is a simple story, a little episode in the life of a journalist, which may be amusing and instructive. There are really two stories; the story as seen from the outside, by a man reading the paper; and the story seen from the inside, by the journalists shouting and telephoning and taking notes in shorthand through the night.

This is the outside story; and it reads like a dreadful quarrel.

> The notorious G.K. Chesterton, a reactionary Torquemada whose one gloomy pleasure is in the defence of orthodoxy and the pursuit of heretics, long calculates and at last launches a denunciation of a brilliant leader of the New Theology which he hates with all the furnace of his fanatic soul. In this document Chesterton, darkly, deliberately, and not having the fear of God before his eyes, asserts that Shakespeare wrote the line "that wreathes its old fantastic roots so high." This he says because he has been kept in ignorance by priests; or, perhaps, because he thinks craftily that none of his dupes can discover a curious and forgotten rhyme called "Elegy in a Country Churchyard." Anyhow, that orthodox gentleman makes a howling error; and receives some twenty-five letters and postcards from kind correspondents who point out the mistake.

But the odd thing is that scarcely any of them could conceive that it was a mistake. The first wrote in the tone of one wearied of epigrams, and cried, "What is the joke now?" Another professed (and practised, for all I know, God help him) that he had read through all Shakespeare and failed to find the line. A third wrote in a sort of moral distress, asking, as in confidence, if Gray was really a plagiarist.

[179] *Daily News*, Oct. 7, 1905.

They were a noble collection; but they all subtly assumed an element of leisure and exactitude in the recipient's profession and character which is far from the truth. Let us pass on to the next act of the external tragedy.

In Monday's issue of the same paper appeared a letter from the same culprit. He ingenuously confessed that the line did not belong to Shakespeare, but to a poet whom he called Grey. Which was another cropper—or whopper. This strange and illiterate outbreak was printed by the editor with the justly scornful title, "Mr. Chesterton 'Explains'"? Any many reading the paper at breakfast saw at once the meaning of the sarcastic quotation marks. They meant, of course, "Here is a man who doesn't know Gray from Shakespeare; he tried to patch it up and he can't even spell Gray. And that is what he calls an Explanation." That is the perfectly natural inference of the reader from the letter, the mistake and the headline—as seen from the outside. The falsehood was serious; the editorial rebuke was serious. The stern editor and the sombre, baffled contributor confront each other as the curtain falls.

And now I will tell you exactly what really happened. It is honestly rather amusing; it is a story of what journals and journalists really are. A monstrously lazy man lives in South Bucks partly by writing a column in the Saturday *Daily News*. At the time he usually writes it (which is always at the last moment) his house is unexpectedly invaded by infants of all shapes and sizes. His secretary is called away; and he has to cope with the invading pigmies. Playing with children is a glorious thing; but the journalist in question has never understood why it was considered a soothing or idyllic one. It reminds him, not of watering little budding flowers, but of wrestling for hours with gigantic angels and devils. Moral problems of the most monstrous complexity besiege him incessantly. He has to decide before the awful eyes of innocence, whether, when a sister has knocked down a brother's bricks, in revenge for the brother having taken two sweets out of his turn, it is endurable that the brother should retaliate by scribbling on the sister's picture-book, and whether such conduct does not justify the sister in blowing out the brother's unlawfully lighted match.

Just as he is solving this problem upon principles of the highest morality, it occurs to him suddenly that he has not written his Saturday article; and that there is only about an hour to do it in. He wildly calls to somebody (probably the gardener) to telephone to somewhere for a messenger; he barricades himself in another room and tears his hair, wondering what on earth he shall write about. A drumming of fists on the door outside and a cheerful bellowing encourage and clarify his thoughts; and he is able to observe some newspapers and circulars in wrappers lying on the table. One is a dingy book catalogue; the second is a shiny pamphlet about petrol; the third is a paper called *The Christian Commonwealth*. He opens it anyhow, and sees in the middle of a page a sentence with which he honestly disagrees. It says that the sense of beauty in Nature is a new thing, hardly felt before Wordsworth. A stream of images and pictures pour through his head, like skies chasing each other or forests running by. "Not felt before Wordsworth!" he thinks. "Oh, but this won't do ... bare ruined choirs where late the sweet birds sang ... night's candles are burnt out ... glowed with living sapphires ... leaving their moon-loves maze ... antique roots fantastic ... antique roots wreathed high ... what is it in *As You Like It*?"

He sits down desperately; the messenger rings at the bell; the children drum on the door; the servants run up from time to time to say the messenger is getting bored; and the pencil staggers along, making the world a present of fifteen hundred unimportant words, and making Shakespeare a present of a portion of Gray's Elegy; putting "fantastic roots wreathed high" instead of "antique roots peep out." Then the journalist sends off his copy and turns his attention to the enigma of whether a brother should commandeer a sister's necklace because the sister pinched him at Little Hampton. That is the first scene; that is how an article is really written.

The scene now changes to the newspaper office. The writer of the article has discovered his mistake and wants to correct it by the next day: but the next day is Sunday. He cannot post a letter, so he rings up the paper and dictates a letter by telephone. He leaves the title to his friends at the other end; he knows that they can spell "Gray," as no doubt they can: but the letter is put down by journalistic custom in a pencil scribble and the vowel may well be doubtful. The friend writes at the top of the Letter " 'GKC' Explains," putting the initials in quotation marks. The next man passing it for press is bored with these initials (I am with him there) and crosses them out, substituting with austere civility, "Mr. Chesterton Explains." But—and now we hear the iron laughter of the Fates, for the blind bolt is about to fall—but he neglects to cross out the second "quote" (as we call it) and he goes up to press with a "quote" between the last words. Another question mark at the end of "explains" was the work of one merry moment for the printers upstairs. So the inverted commas were lifted entirely off one word on to the other and a totally innocent title suddenly turned into a blasting sneer. But that would have mattered nothing so far, for there was nothing to sneer at. In the same dark hour, however, there was a printer who was (I suppose) so devoted to this government that he could think of no Gray but Sir Edward Grey. He spelt it "Grey" by a mere misprint, and the whole tale was complete: first blunder, second blunder, and final condemnation.

That is a little tale of journalism as it is; if you call it egotistic and ask what is the use of it I think I could tell you. You might remember it when next some ordinary young workman is going to be hanged by the neck on circumstantial evidence.[180]

I can recall, in the decadent days of my youth, the wonder with which I read that Ibsen, or somebody of that sort, had suggested a doubt about whether "two and two may not make five in the fixed stars." It was my immediate impression that Ibsen, if it was Ibsen, might unquestionably know how to write, but most certainly did not know how to think. And that is the chief feature of current fashions, the number of people who do really know how to write, but who certainly do not know how to think. To say that two and two may make five in the fixed stars, is a confusion as well as a contradiction. The fixed stars are not fixed, if our fundamental perceptions are not fixed. If you say you have seen two groups of two stars each, it is simply senseless to say you are sure they are fixed, but are not sure they are four. If you are not sure they are four, you are not sure of anything; and certainly not of the immobility of distant worlds through eternal time. And to say that the same number may be five in those stars which is four in this star, is to impute a mere magic to locality which you do not allow to logic. Why the fixed stars? Why not the Five Towns? Why not say yes may be no in Maida Vale or Cricklewood, if we do not happen to have been there? Reason is real or unreal; but why should another unreality called space affect it; and why should it change in a million miles and not in one mile? This seemed to me elementary sanity when I was twenty years old; and it seems so still. I have indeed come to see that

[180] *Daily News*, Dec. 17, 1910.

there are mysteries on the border line both of mathematics and moral philosophy, which can only be conveyed by paradox.[181]

There it is: a sort of spell or magic word; it is a Greek tri-syllable which I should be sorry to be driven to describe as a Greek invocation to call fools into circle. What it means in English, in the minds of those who use it, I have not the faintest idea. The word is Paradox; and my rather dim memories of Greek would lead me to translate it as meaning something against dogma or traditional teaching; which is the very last thing that I am. When and where I have really written any paradoxes I do not know, and have searched my works for them in vain. As I told my American friends, I think of writing a sombre spiritual epic about it, called "Paradox Lost."[182] But an element of paradox runs through the whole of existence itself. It begins in the two facts that we cannot imagine a space that is infinite, and that we cannot imagine a space that is finite. It runs through the inmost complications of divinity, in that we cannot conceive that Christ in the wilderness was truly pure, unless we also conceive that he desired to sin. It runs, in the same manner, through all the minor matters of morals, so that we cannot imagine courage existing except in conjunction with fear, or magnanimity existing except in conjunction with some temptation to meanness.[183] Paradox is often only an answer to a fallacy that has become a habit.[184] "Jack the Giant-Killer" is the embodiment of the paradox of Courage; the paradox which says, "You must defy the thing that is terrifying; unless you are frightened, you are not brave." "Cinderella" is the embodiment the paradox of Humility which says "Look for the best in the thing, ignorant of its merit; he that abases himself shall be exalted." And "Beauty and the Beast" is the embodiment of the paradox of Faith—the absolutely necessary and wildly unreasonable maxim which says to every mother with a child or to every patriot with a country, "You must love the thing first and make it lovable afterwards."[185]

I don't deny that, man being a combative animal, there is a certain wild joy in saying things which one knows are calculated to startle and

[181] *Illustrated London News*, Dec. 13, 1919.
[182] *New Witness*, Feb. 9, 1923.
[183] *Daily News*, Feb. 14, 1902.
[184] *Spectator*, Nov. 20, 1926.
[185] *World*, Sept. 7, 1904.

antagonize those to whom they are addressed, simply because one is aware that those to whom they are addressed will insist upon perversely regarding them as paradoxes. The exhilaration which one derives in this way is, I maintain, perfectly legitimate, though I am bound to say that I think a much deeper spiritual ecstasy is to be attained by the utterance of platitudes. For your good, sound, stodgy, barefaced, baldheaded platitude is a thing that brings you instantly into touch and sympathy with the great mass of your fellow-men; and what ecstasy, after all, is equal to that which comes of such assurance of one's own part and lot in the unity of the great human family? But, granting that the enunciator of what his neighbours regard as paradoxes is a sincere man, he himself does not regard them as paradoxes at all. To him they are truisms, which it is his bounden duty, as a good citizen, to get others to recognise as truisms also. When I myself, for instance, am charged with indulging in feats of what some people seem to me—misguided enough to describe as feats of "verbal topsy-turveydom" and so forth, my answer is that I say the things to which such epithets are applied because, in the first place, I profoundly believe them to be true; and, in the second place, I want to make other people see that they are true as well. My aim, in fact, is to do what I can to get these so-called paradoxes not merely recognised for the truths they are, but accepted by common consent as platitudes no less unquestionable than "Temperance is a virtue" or "Pineapples don't grow in the Twopenny Tube."[186] Of one thing I am certain, that the age needs, first and foremost, to be startled; to be taught the nature of wonder.[187]

I wrote for a magazine story a sentence descriptive of the hero, which ran, "He talked a great deal about himself because he was not an egoist."[188] I found it rendered on the printed page in the amended and blameless form, "He talked a great deal about himself because he was an egoist."

---

[186] *World*, May 31, 1904.

[187] *Black and White*, Feb. 14, 1903. GKC wrote a series of essays for *Black and White*, kicking off with one that throws down the gauntlet at the title of the very publication he is writing for. His first proposition was "That Black Is—in a General Sense—White." This was followed with such titles as "That Respectable People Are More Interesting Than Bohemians," "That Bigoted People Have No Beliefs," "That the Simple Life Is an Artificial Nuisance," and so on.

[188] *Maclean's Magazine*, Nov. 1, 1924. The reference is to Gabriel Gale, and the story, "The Asylum of Adventure," was collected in *The Poet and the Lunatics* with typo corrected.

To the obscure scribbler in the background, who merely writes the story, there is a difference. But I do not suppose it made much difference to the reader of the story, if there ever was a reader of the story. Anyhow, at some stage of the long, mechanical modern process of copying and printing and proofreading, and so on, there must have been, I presume, a grave and careful character who thought it was obviously a mistake to say that a man talking of himself was not an egoist. He therefore made the reasonable and natural correction and said he was an egoist. As this is, by the whole depth of hell, the most hideous and infernal thing that a human being can be, it makes some little difference to the story considered as a story. But it was evidently supposed to improve the sense considered as the sense. Now, extraordinary as it may seem, I myself am under the impression that my original sentence was quite sensible. It is my experience that the egoist, or, at least, the really evil and poisonous sort of egoist, is not remarkable for talking a great deal about himself; or, indeed, for talking a great deal at all. The worst examples of the egoistic type are silent and watchful, and wait until they can say something which (as they think, and as others may possibly think) nobody could have said but themselves. But even when they do talk at large, it is not in the ordinary sense about themselves. They are much more likely to talk about a large number of different things, to show how wise and widely cultivated they are. Above all, the true egoist can generally be detected by this diabolic mark: that he is not only willing to talk on any subject, but on any side of any subject. He has no creed, no cause, no conception of truth which he thinks more important than himself.[189]

I have always heard of the brutality of publishers and how they crush and obscure the author; but my complaint has always been that they push him forward far too much. I will not say that, so far from making too little of the author, they make too much of him; that this phrase is capable of a dark financial interpretation which I do not intend. But I do say that the prominent personalities of the literary

---

[189] *Illustrated London News*, Nov. 3, 1928. Indeed, we have been able to create this book because GKC talks a great deal about himself and is not an egoist. His experiences are obviously interesting and are the fodder for many of his columns; he is as a writer inviting us to see the world through his eyes. But he is looking outward, not inward. He is not self-centered. He is God-centered. He sees more than anything his own inadequacy. It is why he can talk about himself and still be humble.

world are very largely the creations of their publishers, in so far as they are not solely the creations of their wives. Here is a small incident out of my own existence. I designed to write a sort of essay, divided into sections, on one particular point of political error. This fallacy, though small and scholastic at first sight, seemed to me to be the real mistake in most modern sociological works. It was, briefly, the idea that things that have been tried have been found wanting. It was my purpose to point out that in the entanglements of practice this is untrue; that an old expedient may easily be the best thing for a new situation; that its principle may be useful though its practice failed; that its practice may have failed because its principle was abandoned; and so on. Therefore, I claimed, we should look for the best method, the ideal, whether it is in the future or the past. I imagined this book as a drab-coloured, decorous little philosophical treatise, with no chapters, but the page occasionally broken by section-headings at the side. I proposed to call my analysis of a radical error "What is wrong," meaning where the mistake is in our logical calculation. But I had highly capable and sympathetic publishers, whose only weakness was that they thought my unhappy monologue much more important than I did. By some confusion of ecstasy (which entirely through my own fault I failed to check) the title was changed into the apocalyptic trumpet-blast *What's Wrong With the World*. It was divided up into three short, fierce chapters, like proclamations in a French riot. Outside there was an enormous portrait of myself looking like a depressed hairdresser, and the whole publication had somehow got the violence and instancy of a bombshell. Let it be understood that I do not blame the publishers in the least for this. I could have stopped it if I had minded my own affairs.[190]

I was asked to write a little book on Victorian literature, for a series edited by good academic authorities. They were very complimentary and courteous, but they thought it their duty to preface the book with a note explaining that they were not responsible for my opinions, with the implication that the opinions were rather wild. As a matter of fact, in so far as the opinions implied were more or less mystical, they belonged to what is by far the commonest, the most cosmopolitan, and the most popular sort of mysticism. Anyhow, they

---

[190] *T.P.'s Weekly*, Christmas Number, 1910.

thought it necessary to protect their own impartiality. Many of them were men whom I greatly admire; nor was their action one which I in any way resent. But I confess I was amused some time after in opening a book in the same series called *A History of Free Thought*, or some such name, by an ordinary academic agnostic. This book was devoted entirely, down to the last detail, to demonstrating the proposition that religion has been a nonsensical nightmare from first to last, that Christianity is dead, and that the world is well rid of it. There was no preliminary note of apology to that. There was no warning against that bias; there was no disavowal of that partisanship. Nor can it be explained by supposing that it referred to the facts and not the theories of the agnostic and myself. I could easily imagine that my information was sometimes incorrect; but it is quite sufficient to save me from supposing that his was always correct. There were no dates in my book, so they could not be put right; but it was afterwards shown that the dates in his book were wildly wrong. No; the simple explanation is that the editors did not think his bias was a bias. They thought that sort of secularism was simply sanity; what has been called the religion of all sensible men.[191]

What I deplore about publishers is not their way of beating me down, but their way of cracking me up. What they do is to write on the cover or poster is that Mr. Chesterton is witty and wise and wonderful; or that my new work is marked as usual by brilliant paradox. It is on these occasions that the rough outline of the murder of a publisher begins to sketch itself darkly in my mind.[192]

When I was quite young the whole intellectual fashion of the world was pessimism. It was the attitude expressed by the two young men in *Punch*, and a good many young men in real life, when one said, "After all, Smith, what would life be without coffee?" And the other answered, "True, Jones, true; and after all, what is life with coffee?" Now, the only answer to this is to inform the young men, in a low and hoarse voice, that you have discovered poison in the coffee they have just drunk. You will soon discover, from the greater animation of their movements, whether they attach any importance to life or not. I once wrote a romance on this theme, about a man who went

---

[191] *Illustrated London News*, Mar. 22, 1924. GKC's book was *The Victorian Age in Literature*.
[192] *G.K.'s Weekly*, Dec. 11, 1926.

about with a loaded pistol, presenting at the heads of people who said casually at tea-parties, "Is life worth living?" I indicated that the result would be that he would find there were a good many secret adherents of the sect of the Methuselahites. I implied that there were rather fewer real pessimists that might be implied in calling it an age of pessimism. But it was to a great extent an age of pessimism; and anybody saying, as I said then and should say now, that the sky is sometimes blue and not black, that the grass is often green and not grey, that life itself is a glorious experience and that by the wind of God in his nostrils man became a living soul, was then regarded as having let off in the universal darkness a sort of foolish firework called a paradox.[193]

I hope I may always be allowed to defend my opinions, so long as it is clearly understood that I do not defend my writings. My opinions, as opinions, are all quite correct. Any thinking person will see that to say this is only saying that they are my opinions. A man has not got a conviction if he is not convinced of it. But my books, as books, are very far from being all correct; and I wonder they are not more often corrected. I do not mean especially about details of fact, though, of course, I have from time to time mentioned details that were inaccurate, but I mean a much more serious sort of inaccuracy or insufficiency. I am conscious of having frequently written badly a book that another man would have written well if he could have been induced to write it at all. But, as these gentlemen have plenty of ideas of their own, I have often been driven to attempt the artistic adventures myself, with results which are far from satisfactory to myself. I am not sure whether it is a boast or an apology. But I do believe I have spoilt some very good ideas in my time.[194]

I am proud to say that I have by this time read more vulgar and sensational detective stories, both American and English, than would fill the shelves of that complete gentleman's library which should only be stocked with the classics. A taste for trash is of great value to the serious sociologist. By reading intellectual fiction we only find out what the intellectuals are saying, and saying somewhat self-consciously. By reading shockers and police novels we find out what the mass of the

---

[193] "On Optimism," in *Rosemary*, collected and compiled by F. de Burgh and Walter Stoneman (Sampson Low, Marston, 1924), p. 5. GKC's "romance" was his novel *Manalive*.

[194] *Illustrated London News*, Mar. 25, 1922.

people are saying—or, what is much more important, what they are not saying. We find out what they assume unconsciously, and therefore do not think it worth while to say.[195]

Murder is a private affair; indeed, in most cases a purely domestic matter.[196] I have walked along in front of those respectable railings or trim and tidy hedges, and looked in at one front garden after another, probably arousing suburban suspicions that I had an eye at least on the milk-can outside the door. Yet I was innocent of any intention of stealing so much as a stray cat. Though the owners would not have believed it if I had told them, I was really admiring their front-gardens. I was considering the suitability of each to be the scene of some lurid crime or ludicrous fiasco.[197]

I am very fond of detective stories, and some historical mysteries have every charm and virtue of a detective story, with the additional beauty of containing no detectives. While giving my deepest and worthiest powers to the reading of detective stories, I have not disdained altogether those lighter relaxations like history and biography.[198]

I very rapidly realised that as a murderer I should never make good. I then devoted myself to hymning and celebrating the murders of others, in the form of composing crime stories. In no less than fifty-three separate crime stories I have clearly proved myself incompetent in this department also.[199]

I remember I had the honour of solving, or pretending to solve, a riddle of crime propounded by Mr. Max Pemberton ["Father Brown and the Donnington Affair"]. He undertook by a certain date to deliver a fresh, attractive corpse; and I undertook by a certain date to tell him where he had got it from. But I have seen any number of detective stories in which the same writer first failed to mystify and then failed to elucidate. I was never puzzled by the problem as a problem; but it is only fair to say I was sometimes a little puzzled by the explanation as an explanation. This evil obviously arises from the

---

[195] *Illustrated London News*, Feb. 11, 1928.
[196] *Illustrated London News*, Apr. 5, 1925.
[197] *Illustrated London News*, Nov. 22, 1924.
[198] *Illustrated London News*, Jan. 16, 1926.
[199] *New York American*, May 30, 1935. These are only the *Father Brown* mysteries. The total, including *The Club of Queer Trades, The Poet and the Lunatics, The Man Who Knew Too Much, The Paradoxes of Mr. Pond,* and several one-offs, is ninety.

same literary man becoming first a criminal and then a policeman. I have often done it myself, but I do not think that is anything in its favour. Obviously his temptation is first to set himself an easy problem, and then to allow himself a far-fetched explanation. He is acting as a magistrate and capturing himself as a criminal.[200]

I happen to be one of the few and rather unpopular persons who like the cool and troubled temper of the English climate.[201] On the bright blue day my spirits go slightly down; there seems something pitiless about perfect weather. On the clear cool day, my spirits are normal. In the fog, my spirits go up; it feels like the end of the world, or better still, a detective story.[202] Unlike Father Brown, I could never reconcile myself to carrying an umbrella: it is a pompous Eastern business, carried over the heads of despots in the dry, hot lands. Shut up, an umbrella is an unmanageable walking-stick; open, it is an inadequate tent. For my part, I have no taste for pretending to be a walking pavilion; I think nothing of my hat, and precious little of my head.[203]

An editor once asked a number of writers to review their own books over their own names. I was one of the writers, and the book was, unfortunately, a play [*Magic*], and therefore even more amateurish than if it had been a book. I wrote what is called a slashing or slating review of it, cutting it up in a ferocious and derisive manner, which may have appeared to be something of a pose, but I really did not know what else to do.[204]

I have been myself attempting for some time past to complete a play in a small toy theatre, the sort of toy theatre that used to be called Penny Plain and Twopence Coloured; only that I drew and coloured the figures and scenes myself. Hence I was free from the degrading obligation of having to pay either a penny or twopence; I only had to pay a shilling a sheet for good cardboard and a shilling a box for bad water colours. The kind of miniature stage I mean is probably familiar to everyone; it is never more than a development of the stage which Skelt made and Stevenson celebrated.

But though I have worked much harder at the toy theatre than I ever worked at any tale or article, I cannot finish it; the work seems too

---

[200] *Illustrated London News*, Jan. 23, 1926.
[201] *Illustrated London News*, July 11, 1931.
[202] *Illustrated London News*, Sept. 26, 1908.
[203] *Daily News*, Nov. 5, 1910.
[204] *Illustrated London News*, Nov. 22, 1924.

heavy for me. I have to break off and betake myself to lighter employments; such as the biographies of great men. The play of "St. George and the Dragon," over which I have burnt the midnight oil (you must colour the thing by lamplight because that is how it will be seen), still lacks most conspicuously, alas! two wings of the Sultan's Palace, and also some comprehensible and workable way of getting up the curtain.

All this gives me a feeling touching the real meaning of immortality. In this world we cannot have pure pleasure. This is partly because pure pleasure would be dangerous to us and to our neighbours. But it is partly because pure pleasure is a great deal too much trouble. If I am ever in any other and better world, I hope that I shall have enough time to play with nothing but toy theatres; and I hope that I shall have enough divine and superhuman energy to act at least one play in them without a hitch.[205]

Toys are not childish, they are merely human. It is just as natural to want to make a beautiful scene in that theatre as to want to make a beautiful scene in your own house. The people who put up Morris papers and decorative panels, and copper and peacock hangings, are playing with toys just as much as I am. I am creating an imaginary world of beauty just as much as they are. The only practical advantage is altogether on my side, for I can have explosions of red fire in the theatre, and it is, I assure you, an awful nuisance to have them on a proportional scale in one's house.[206]

The best game I know is playing with a toy theatre. A toy theatre is a little world, and may involve the creation of little models of nearly everything in the world. I once constructed a whole city, which was to tumble down when the earth began to shake with the approach of a distant dragon; and it was great fun fixing the towers and spires with moveable clips, collar studs or anything else that would serve as pivots, and then pulling them over with threads of cotton. But as they were the buildings of a whole city, they could include any number of different kinds of building. They were designed in all the styles of architecture there are, and in many that there aren't.[207]

I had a primary tragedy at the age of two or three. It was that I could not get inside a theatre or on to the stage where things happen

---

[205] *Daily News*, Feb. 2, 1907.
[206] *Idler*, June 1903.
[207] *Merry-Go-Round*, May 1924.

immeasurably more interesting than in the real world. If I could not get on the stage then, it is even less feasible now. To try to work up a whole performance such as proposed at this exhibition calls for very serious virtues of patience, endurance, resolution, and so on. I come before you as a fraud, as one who has wasted life in writing articles and things of that kind, whereas if I had lived up to the ideals of my childhood I might have produced the finest toy theatre in the world. There is instead the depressing thought that he who goes in for literature, for journalism, politics, and so on, is not only losing his own great spiritual opportunities but involves others in his ruin because by writing books I occupy the time of a great many people, the publisher for instance. The things we do which are less worthy do not permit us to do the things which are really worth doing. Otherwise this kind of art would have risen to colossal proportions.[208]

The memory of childish joys does not make me melancholy (it is perhaps a fine shade of theology), and I am quite sure that I am remembering a reality that was real then as well as now. You could as soon persuade me that the taste of toffee was an illusion that only came to me in later years, or that I think I liked roast chestnuts then only because I like them now, as convince me that I did not have, even as a child, an overwhelming impression that the farcical world of the puppet show was fantastic, not merely in the sense of being comic, but also in the sense of being mystic. Though the scene might superficially seem completely constructed out of objects made as much as possible prosaic, I had an instant inward certainty that they were all poetic. The sky above those staggering chimneys was not the sky above the chimneys in the street outside; its stars would have been strange stars; for I had looked round another corner of the cosmos. To wander in the streets of that strange town would have been as unearthly an experience as to wander in the Blue Forest round Bluebeard's Sapphire Palace. Not verbally, but quite vividly, I knew then, exactly as I know now, that there is something mysterious and perhaps more than mortal about the power and call of Imagination. I do not think this early experience has been quite rightly understood,

---

[208] *Glasgow Herald*, Aug. 25, 1925. Remarks made at the opening of an exhibition of toy theatres, puppets, model designs for scenery, costumes, and properties for theatres, and other paraphernalia for use in presenting stage plays in miniature presented by the British Modern Theatre Guild.

even by those modern writers who have written the most charming and fanciful studies of childhood; and I am not so presumptuous as to think that I can scientifically succeed where I think they have somehow vaguely failed. But I have often fancied that it might be worth while to set down a few notes or queries about this difficult and distant impression. For one thing, the ordinary phrases used about childish fancies often strike me as missing the mark; and being, in some subtle way, quite misleading. For instance, there is the very popular phrase, "Make-believe." This seems to imply that the mind makes itself believe something; or else that it first makes something and then forces itself to believe in it, or to believe something about it. I do not think there is even this slight crack of falsity in the crystal clearness and directness of the child's vision of a fairy palace—or a fairy policeman. In one sense the child believes much less, and in another much more than that. I do not think the child is deceived; or that he attempts for a moment to deceive himself. I think he instantly asserts, his direct and divine right to enjoy, beauty; that he steps straight into his own lawful kingdom of imagination, without any quibbles or questions, such as arise afterwards out of false moralities and philosophies, touching the nature of falsehood and truth. In other words, I believe that the child has inside his head a pretty correct and complete definition of the whole nature and function of Art; with the one addition that he is quite incapable of saying, even to himself, a single word on the subject. Would that many other professors of aesthetics were under a similar restraint. Anyhow, he does not say to himself, "This is a real street, in which mother could go shopping." He does not say to himself, "This is an exact realistic copy of a real street, to be admired for its technical correctness." Neither does he say, "This is an unreal street, and I am drugging and deceiving my powerful mind with something that is a mere illusion." Neither does he say, "This is only a story, and nurse says it is very naughty to tell stories." If he says anything, he only says what was said by those men who saw the white blaze of the Transfiguration: "It is well for us to be here" [Mt 17:4].

The problem is very close to the real problem about images. A child knows that a doll is not a baby; just as clearly as a real believer knows that a statue of an angel is not an angel. But both know that in both cases the image has the power of both opening and concentrating the imagination. The child is perfectly clear about the difference, not only between truth and falsehood, but between fiction and falsehood. He understands the two essential types of truth: the truth of the mystic, which turns a fact into a truth, where it should be turned into a truth, because the alternative is a triviality; and the truth of the martyr, which treats a truth as a fact, where it should be treated as a fact, because the alternative is a lie. It is we who have grown confused about these categories; and cannot realise the swiftness and clarity with which the child accepts what we call the convention of art.

I know I knew that the scenery and costume of the puppet show were "artificial," because I deeply rejoiced that they were artificial. I liked the notion that things were made of painted wood or plastered by hand. These were the vestments and ornaments of the ritual; but they were not the rite, still less the revelation. I liked the magic-box called a stage, because there, for some reason, the light that never was on sea or land was on paint and pasteboard. But I knew perfectly well that it was paint and pasteboard. It would be impossible for anybody not to know that, who had a toy theatre of his own. There were tricks of mere stage carpentry which I enjoyed. There was one way of representing tossing waves, by rank behind rank of escalloped blue walls as ground-pieces, moved in opposite directions so that the crests seemed to cross and dance. I knew how it was done; because my father did it himself before my very eyes, in my own toy-theatre at home. But it gave me such ecstasy that even now, when I think of it for an instant, my heart leaps up like the wave. I knew it was not Water; but I knew it was Sea; and in that flash of knowledge I had passed far beyond those who suffer the fixed and freezing illusion, uttered by the pessimistic poet, that "the sea's a lot of water that happens to be there." In imagination there is no illusion; no, not even an instant of illusion. What I felt was that it was right; that it was a good and enlarging and inspiring thing to see; that it was an excellent experience to look down on the strange street where such things could be seen.[209]

Another game which filled me with joy when I was a child was playing with toy soldiers. I have heard that some poor children are not allowed to have any; but I am not going to argue here about pacificism or humanitarianism, for so far as one can ever explain why a

---

[209] *Life and Letters*, December 1934.

game is a good game, the fun of it is a fusion of three things: the real romance of the soldier, that he is brave and going into danger with steadfastness (and nothing could be more steadfast than the expression of most toy soldiers); that he wears bright colours and glittering weapons; and, last but not least, that he and his fellows are made to be arranged in lines and masses that suggest movement on a large scale; the excitement that there is in any sort of procession.[210]

When I was a little boy I used to keep a pack of snails.

I have of late introduced into my domestic life a four-legged innovation in the shape of an Aberdeen terrier. I have always imagined myself to be a lover of all animals, because I have never met any animal that I definitely disliked. Most people draw the line somewhere. Lord Roberts dislikes cats; the best woman I know objects to spiders; a Theosophist I know protects, but detests, mice; and many leading humanitarians have an objection to human beings.

But I cannot recall ever having shrunk from an animal; I do not mind a slug, however slimy he is, nor a rhinoceros, however much his horn is exalted. When I was a little boy I used to keep a pack of snails as representing what I thought the proper pace of hunting. Thus I fell into the mistake common to many modern universalists and humanitarians. I thought that I loved all God's creatures, whereas the only point was that I did not hate them. I did not dislike the camel for having a hump or the whale for containing blubber. But I could not seriously have supposed that the time would ever come when a whale's blubber would move my heart with a quiver of affection; or that I should know one camel's hump among others as one knows the profile of a beautiful woman. This is the first of the extraordinary effects of having a dog, upon one who has never had one before. One loves an animal like a man instead of merely accepting an animal like an optimist.

But then, again, if the dog is loved he is loved as a dog; not as a fellow-citizen, or an idol, or a pet, or a product of evolution. The moment you are responsible for one respectable animal, that moment an abyss opens as wide as the world between cruelty and the necessary coercion of animals.[211]

---

[210] *Merry-Go-Round*, May 1924.
[211] *Daily News*, Mar. 27, 1909.

There are things in this world of which I can say seriously that I love them but I do not like them. The point is not merely verbal, but psychologically quite valid. Cats are the first things that occur to me as examples of the principle. Cats are so beautiful that a creature from another star might fall in love with them, and so incalculable that he might kill them. Some of my friends take quite a high moral line about cats. Some, like Mr. Titterton, I think, admire a cat for its moral independence and readiness to scratch anybody "if he does not behave himself." Others, like Mr. Belloc, regard the cat as cruel and secret, a fit friend for witches; one who will devour everything, except, indeed, poisoned food, "So utterly lacking is it in Christian simplicity and humility." For my part, I have neither of these feelings. I admire cats as I admire catkins; those little fluffy things that hang on trees. They are both pretty and both furry, and both declare the glory of God. And this abstract exultation in all living things is truly to be called Love; for it is a higher feeling than mere affectional convenience; it is a vision. It is heroic, and even saintly, in this: that it asks for nothing in return. I love all the cats in the street as St. Francis of Assisi loved all the birds in the wood or all the fishes in the sea; not so much, of course, but then I am not a saint. But he did not wish to bridle a bird and ride on its back, as one bridles and rides on a horse. He did not wish to put a collar round a fish's neck, marked with the name "Francis," and the address "Assisi"—as one does with a dog. He did not wish them to belong to him or himself to belong to them; in fact, it would be a very awkward experience to belong to a lot of fishes. But a man does belong to his dog, in another but an equally real sense with that in which the dog belongs to him. The two bonds of obedience and responsibility vary very much with the dogs and the men; but they are both bonds. In other words, a man does not merely love a dog; as he might (in a mystical moment) love any sparrow that perched on his window-sill or any rabbit that ran across his path. A man likes a dog and that is a serious matter.[212]

I have a senile interest in the beginnings of things—in quaint questionings about why things exist, and whence they came, and what they were really supposed to be. I admit that a bungalow may be made out of a railway carriage, but I am not content that all mankind should live

---

[212] *Daily News*, Aug. 12, 1911.

in railway carriages without ever having heard of railways. I admit that the hat that was made for a man may end on a scarecrow, but I never can concentrate properly on the fashions for scarecrows, without some sort of backward glance at the philosophy of clothes for men. And when I look at Liberalism, or preferably at liberty, I never can avoid the same sort of backward glance at the philosophy of the first Libertarians. I ask myself what the men who brought this ideal into the world really imagined they were bringing, and what it was for which so many of them strove and starved and died on the scaffold or the barricade or the battlefield? And I think their real ideal is very much misunderstood to-day, especially by those who believe in it. Some say that every Liberal is continually engaged in adding something to Liberalism. It seems to me that most modern Liberals have been largely occupied in taking something away.... I shall probably be misunderstood, and even derided, if I say that most modern Liberals need to go back and study the old orators and poets of liberty. They will find that those great men had other ideals besides liberty, and especially ideals that balanced and corrected the ideal of liberty. And I would very specially and seriously draw their attention to one, which might well be described, to their grave astonishment, as the ideal of Poverty.[213]

In an advanced, scientific, enlightened industrial community like our own, the difficulty about the poor is that there are so many of them.[214] In various poor parts of London there are excellent institutions called "Guilds of Play," in which poor children (somewhat pathetically) sing the songs or dance the dances which were natural to their fathers when England was comparatively free. Here luckless but lively gutter-snipes, who have never seen anything but chimney-pots, sing old English songs which take for granted the greenwood and the meadow. Nay, the child sings songs in praise of the legendary London, which was paved with gold, in the very entrails of the real London, that is paved with mire. I once took a Stockbroker, who is a friend of mine, to enjoy this excruciating and poetic irony. We sat on a platform all by ourselves, and in front of us danced a large number of little girls in pointed caps of pink or white cotton, little girls from the London slums, many of them pretty and nearly all of

---

[213] *Illustrated London News*, Mar. 3, 1928.
[214] *New Witness*, Feb. 17, 1922.

them graceful. My friend the Stockbroker was much impressed. He had never met the English poor (that is, the English people) before in his life. He did not know that the English poor are polite to excess, and contain many middle-class and aristocratic traditions, being descended from all sorts of people who have been too honourable to get on in the world. We meet refinement among the poor about five times as often as we meet vulgarity among the rich.[215]

I haven't any children of my own, so I always have those of other people staying with me.[216] I believe that one of the most vital, one of the most honourable and let me add, one of the most difficult callings on earth is that of playing with children. I believe that it would be well if the whole bench of bishops played with children, if Professor Huxley played with children and Mr. Ruskin helped him. And I believe that if a man had climbed beyond the stars and found the secret that the angels do not know, he would have nothing more useful to do than to come back and play with children.[217]

I was brought up in the atmosphere of what we call in England the "Broad Church"—the Church that Kingsley and Morris represented. At a very early date I began to take an interest in Liberal politics, the influence of which I still feel. Even now I call myself a Liberal, though most people deny me the name. Even before I became a Catholic, I was always an advocate of Irish freedom.

The first and most important event in my life was the struggle in Ireland, which made a deep impression on me. This was during the years between 1898 and 1901. Professor Eccles, who had replaced M. Rudler in the chair of French at the University of London, was one of my great friends and contributed not a little to developing my sympathy for Ireland, but the determining influence in my life was the founding by Hilaire Belloc and my brother Cecil of a periodical which they called the *New Witness*. What was there interesting about the *New Witness*? It was the only journal which deliberately set out to attack political corruption. We had a good many libel suits, of which the Marconi affair was the most famous. It would be hard to make

---

[215] *Illustrated London News*, Oct. 16, 1909.

[216] *New York Tribune*, Sept. 15, 1912.

[217] This is from the subchapter "The Nurse" in a longish short story by GKC called "The Human Club" that was never published in his lifetime. It appears in the *Collected Works of G. K. Chesterton*, vol. 14, from Ignatius Press (1993).

a Frenchman understand the atmosphere of England before the *New Witness* was founded. It was good form to pretend to believe that politicians were not interested in the question of money. If that is no longer true to-day, the fact is largely due to the *New Witness*. If you had said, in those days, that a politician preferred one position to another because it was better paid, you would have stirred up a regular scandal. I wrote a good many satirical poems for the *New Witness*. I intend some day to write a history of the Marconi scandal.[218]

When Mr. Belloc became the first editor of *The Eye-Witness*, that paper announced, amid a universal optimistic silence of the Press, that secret gambling and jobbery were rampant in English politics. It was stated as a general truth, and as a generalisation it sounded insane. Then by a sort of blazing coincidence, the Marconi Case burst upon the world, and was so sensationally public that it could hardly be concealed, even in the public Press. The Marconi Ministers were forced to make their explanations, we might say their confessions, in the witness-box of the *Matin* Case;[219] and since that day everybody has known the truth.[220] The word "Marconi" does indeed stand to-day for a wireless system; a system of silent communications intercepting and embarrassing the men who pull the wires.[221]

The Press can no longer maintain that bad things do not matter. The Liberal creed must grow looser and looser, the Liberal code must sink lower and lower, after every answer of every witness in the affair. A man supposed to be defending Liberalism has to stand up and say: "We concealed an essential public fact from Parliament; but in this we did not violate Liberalism. We treated ourselves as privileged, and did things for which poorer officials are punished; but we are as Liberal as ever. We gambled, gained, and lost the State secret; but, Lord bless you, lots of Liberals do that. We concealed from our own faithful followers our own real line of defence; and what could be

---

[218] *Living Age*, June 6, 1925.
[219] *Matin* was the French newspaper that first broke the story of the Marconi Scandal. They were immediately sued and withdrew the story, but Cecil Chesterton and the *New Witness* picked it up and pursued it till it was revealed that David Lloyd George, Rufus Isaacs, and other cabinet members had engaged in insider trading before the government publicly announced that it had awarded exclusive wireless rights to the Marconi company.
[220] *G.K.'s Weekly*, July 12, 1930.
[221] *New Witness*, May 8, 1913.

more Liberal? We conspired to the advantage of a few rich men and to the disadvantage of the common investing public: and it was as fine a bit of Liberalism as I could see in a summer's day. We talked of imprisoning men for mentioning what we ourselves afterwards admitted to be true: I suppose no one will say *that* is inconsistent with Liberalism," and so on. And I have to listen to all this, knowing that troops and troops of silent Tories are listening to it also, and only thinking "I am glad I never was a Liberal."

I decline to listen in silence; for the honour of my own youth. I beg to state that the political philosophy which I inherited and held was not a string of excuses for privilege and intrigue. The men with whom I worked did not watch the labours and pauses of the national policy with an eye to a financial flutter. The men with whom I shall always connect the name of Liberalism, the men who demanded the independence of the Irish, who defended the independence of the Dutch, did not leave such lessons in my mind. Liberalism had its faults, but Liberalism was not such slime as the Liberal Press maintains.[222]

Having argued most of my life, with intervals for refreshment, I decided, when private accident put me among those who cannot fight directly for the flag, that there was work to be done for it in the way of intellectual fighting.[223] I am sorry to say that I was unable to be a soldier.[224]

I have come to have a sort of mystical feeling about the abstract justice of our case in the Great War. I mean that I am not less, but rather more, convinced that it was just. But I also mean that the feeling has grown more mystical and the justice more abstract; being abstracted from almost all the actors in it, even the actors on the right side. The mediaeval chronicler commemorating a Crusade (as it happens,

---

[222] *Daily Herald*, Apr. 19, 1913. This was written shortly after he left the *Daily News*, the Liberal paper with which he had gained his fame, but which he chided for not condemning the "Marconi Ministers" who were members of the Liberal Party. For the next year, he wrote for the *Daily Herald*, and his columns were colored by great anger. It may have led to his physical collapse. He finally popped a gasket, as it were. Over at the *Illustrated London News*, which was his bread and butter, he wrote on September 12, 1914, "This page, even in tragic times, is supposed to represent G. K. Chesterton's rambles through life, and not Dante's journey through hell." However, he was about to embark on a journey through hell, as he lay semi-comatose for almost six months. He woke up on a battlefield, as it were, in the middle of the Great War.

[223] *Illustrated London News*, Oct. 16, 1915.

[224] *Illustrated London News*, July 17, 1920.

a Crusade conducted by rather unscrupulous Crusaders) gave his whole book the magnificent title of *Gesta Dei Per Francos*; that is, Acts of God done through the French. I should call the Great War an Act of God done through the French, through the English, through the Russians, Serbs, Romanians, Italians and Americans. But I doubt whether any of them quite understood the Act of God; I even doubt whether any of them were even worthy to understand it. I have never discovered the rag of a reason for reversing my original view of the facts. Unlike so many of my stolid, steady-going and conservative countrymen, I agree with every word I said a few years ago; and I do not think that what was brutal barbarism as an experience has become beautiful brotherhood as a memory.

But the point is not that the cause of the Allies was much better than the Germans'. The point is that the cause of the Allies was much better than the Allies. I do not doubt for a moment that we were right; I know of no cause in history that was so right. But I have sometimes come to doubt whether we had any right to be so right.[225]

When I was writing through the crisis of 1914 and the great quarrel with Germany, I propounded certain principles which I held throughout all that terrible business and which I hold still. They were not merely concerned, though they were very much concerned, with maintaining that the cause of the Allies was just and that their insistence upon victory was justified. They also involved a certain view of the European quarrel, which was not exactly the same as that of a great many other patriotic people who were equally steady in pressing the same international claim. I always insisted, rightly or wrongly, that the war was not to be regarded as a vulgar commercial and colonial rivalry between the German Empire and the British Empire. I even insisted that it was possible to exaggerate the extent to which it turned on the British Empire at all. I said we were in it not only as Englishmen, but as Europeans; because a great European question was being settled; which was whether the predominance which Prussia and the northern tribes had gained by the surprise of 1870 could remain normal to our civilisation and that civilisation remain civilised. I, for one, was quite certain that Europe would be slowly barbarised if Prussia remained the predominant power in it. But it concerned the culture of the old Latin States even more than our own; though it concerned our

---

[225] *G.K.'s Weekly*, June 25, 1927.

own, because we also were heirs of the old Empire. To put it shortly, we said that the war was really Rome against the barbarians. But we admitted that this was symbolically true, because the provinces of Gaul and Britain were the symbols of Rome.[226]

There had been a controversy about what was called German atrocity in Belgium. If men I know had not told me they had themselves seen the bayoneting of a baby; if the most respectable refugees did not bring with them stories of burning cottages—yes, and of burning cottagers as well; if doctors did not report of the condition of girls in the hospitals; if there were no facts; if there were no photographs, I would not have believed that the Prussians are tyrants; tyrants in a peculiar and almost insane sense which makes them pre-eminent among the evil princes of the earth.[227] When I approved the war with Prussia, it was really as a war with Prussianism. And the difference between Prussia and Prussianism was this; I believed (and still believe) that there was in one corner of Europe a cold and cruel philosophy, sneering at chivalry and pity, believing only in science as an instrument of fear. It was that state of mind we were fighting, not the state of Saxony or the state of Württemberg.[228]

---

[226] *Illustrated London News*, July 17, 1926.

[227] *Daily Herald*, Oct. 31, 1914.

[228] *G.K.'s Weekly*, Apr. 5, 1930. GKC's hatred of Prussia is explained in part by his love of Belgium. He had firsthand accounts of the atrocities committed by German soldiers when they seized Belgium. The treatment of the Belgians was an outrage. It was "the stunning directness of a blow from hell." (*Manchester Guardian*, Aug. 7, 1915.) But what also outraged GK was the very idea of one country invading another and simply taking it over, claiming it for itself. It was especially poignant because only a few years earlier he had visited Belgium, enjoying the simple pleasures of its small towns. It was, he says, "a scene of peace and prosperity." (*Daily News*, May 2, 1908.)

He also takes pacifists to task because he considered their position to be aiding the enemy. The Cambridge pacifists particularly objected to being labeled pro-German. He harkens back to when he was called pro-Boer simply because he thought England did not have a just cause for going to war in South Africa. But he understands that this was taken to mean that he favored the Boers over the English. He does not object to the epithet. And he even understands the pacifists objecting to being called pro-German, because it associates them with something far more evil than the Boers. However, he says, what makes them angry should really make them ashamed. (*New Witness*, Mar. 31, 1917.)

While the armistice meant the end of the fighting, it did not mean the end of the war. He never thought of the Great War, as H. G. Wells and so many Americans did, as "the War that will end all war." GKC said that is like saying "the work that will end all work." He maintained that Germany was still a threat to Europe. Change the word "Prussianism" to "Nazism." For GKC, they are descriptions of the same thing.

There really is a very direct connection between my early fairy-tales about the thistledown and the pillar-box and our controversial case in the late war. Of course, a man cannot fill his life with fairy-tales; it is his business to take serious things seriously, to defend justice and do his best for his country. In such a war a romancer ought to be proud to become a controversialist, as a hair-dresser is proud to become a soldier. But in this case there is no inconsistency, but a very close connection. When I was called an optimist for saying we should wonder at the thistledown or thank God for the pillar-box, I was saying something that I should still say, and especially as to the real moral of the Great War. It is a moral that seems to be entirely missed; and I think it is hugely important.

The disappointment after the war seems to me to have been due to the very fact that the world went into it with a false notion of *progress*. We thought a man could fight to *improve* things; and especially to improve his own position. We forgot that a man may fight not to improve things, but to rescue them. He may fight, not to improve his position, but to save his life. It is not fantastically quixotic to say that he may sometimes even fight to save somebody else's life. To save things implies that they are worth saving; and the point is that their very peril makes us feel that they are worth saving.

Now, the war did point to that moral of the intrinsic preciousness of threatened things. This theory of the defence of human culture implies that there are enemies of human culture, people who are liable to attack human culture; and I think there are. And it is not in the least irrelevant to discuss whether they did it, if only because they are quite likely to do it again.[229]

In the sense of having an influence and making a difference, the *New Witness* certainly succeeded. The journalists outside have been influenced almost against their will, and often probably against their orders. I do not think that anyone who knows me will think me subject to pessimistic egomania or the dark delusion of being persecuted. I have always been on genial and even convivial terms with my fellows in Fleet Street, and knowing them to be a humorous race,

---

[229] *Illustrated London News*, May 5, 1923. Germany did do it again. Frank Sheed collected a book of Chesterton's essays under the title *The End of the Armistice* (Sheed & Ward, 1940), showing how well Chesterton predicted World War II.

I have little doubt they would admit the truth themselves that they have been influenced almost against their will, and often probably against their orders. We shall only have passed from a condition of ignoring corruption to a condition of approving it. When Mr. Belloc founded the paper under the name of the *Eye Witness*, the public honestly regarded the suggestion that our statesmen might be bribed by financial influence, against the national interests, as something like a suggestion that the Archbishop of Canterbury burgled a house every night, or that the Poet Laureate was a professional pickpocket. Nobody feels that about politicians now: the way in which any paper speaks of any politician is enough to prove it. But we have only destroyed the innocence without disturbing the guilt. It is a very terrible moral transition from denying it to defending it.[230]

The book *The Equipment of the Workers* (1919) is a compilation by social workers in Sheffield, containing the results of the cross-examination of some hundreds of poor people about their artistic tastes and moral and religious feelings. As a result, the poor people were classified, of course, like other creatures whose habits are watched by the naturalist; and are divided into the "mal-equipped," the "well-equipped" and the "inadequately equipped." I gather from this book, with no great surprise, that I must myself be one of the mal-equipped. I say it without any irritation, or indeed any ground for it; for I have myself the honour, along with Wells and Shaw, as well as Maeterlinck and Carpenter, to be mentioned as one of the modern writers whose names are a test of general reading. But I confess I commonly feel much more camaraderie with the mal-equipped, who have never heard of me, than with the well-equipped who have seen my name in a newspaper. For I really care a great deal, not merely for success as a writer, but for the success of the truths about which I try to write. And it is out of the mouths of the mal-equipped, as of babes and sucklings, that these truths seem chiefly to proceed. It is this curious coincidence that makes me realise, with a sigh of resignation, that I must really be one of them.[231] A paper fighting for the poor is pretty certain to be comparatively poor

---

[230] *New Witness*, Aug. 13, 1920.

[231] *New Witness*, Nov. 7, 1919. He proceeds to list the opinions of the poor which reflect his own: they think there is too much talk about education and not enough about life, they are not really free to do what they want, the government interferes with their lives, and the rich have too much influence in government.

itself.[232] So long as people had to write for the *New Witness* for nothing, or next to nothing, they naturally would write for the *New Witness* only the things that they could not write anywhere else.[233]

"At the Sign of the World's End" was the title of my personal column in *The New Witness*. I wrote the first of these articles in what seemed very like the end of the world. It seemed like the end of the world because it was only the beginning of the war. About a year after the first shot was fired, my brother asked me to contribute a regular item to his paper; and I have since glanced at the introductory essay I then wrote about all that my title might suggest; glimpses of the ends of the earth unvisited except in vision, and especially of some mystical inn bearing for its sign a dark picture of the Day of Judgment. I noted, as a mystery or secret in my life, that I had never been to Cricklewood. I said that several people had asked me to go to America and that many had told me to go to Jericho. Re-reading these things is not without some of the idle ironies of memory. Since that day I have really and truly gone to Jericho; I have even gone so far in the same desperate career as to go to America. But Cricklewood still stands mysterious and virgin and inviolate. Omnibus after omnibus passes me with that strange and elvish inscription. But I have never gone there. I hope that nobody will ever go there. I conceive it vaguely, in a dream, as a grey, twisted, thorny forest such as Albert Dürer might have drawn; and in the grey there are touches of silver, either of starlight or the white corners of the daybreak. But in truth I think I was attracted to the title of this series because there is really a history of triple meaning in the word end as applied to the world. It may mean a limit in space, as in those legendary landscapes of the last wood or the ultimate isles. It may mean a point of time, even if it be

---

[232] *New Witness*, Jan. 8, 1914.

[233] *New Witness*, Jan. 12, 1923. While this may have been true of the other writers on his staff, particularly Belloc, who had to make a living as a writer, GKC himself was in fact writing about the same themes in the *New Witness* that he was writing about everywhere else, which included every major paper he wrote for during his entire career. Maybe he felt he was pulling his punches in those other papers, but he was speaking out against corruption in politics from the beginning, starting with his position as a pro-Boer. He was defending democracy from the beginning, which means he was attacking aristocracy and a rule by the elite, who do their deals in private rather than in public. He was speaking out against the sale of peerages and the unaudited secret party funds as early as 1907. "The only thing we know about our public life is that it is conducted in private." (*Albany Review*, November 1907.)

the end of time. And it may mean something yet higher and deeper, to which I referred then in saying: "For the world really has an end, since it has an aim."

As a point of personal and even poetical sentiment I am very fond of ends. As this is a study in almost remote retrospect, I will recall a story I must have heard at my great grandmother's knee; a thing of such unthinkable antiquity that it must have grown on the chestnut-tree that grew in the Garden of Eden, from which Adam helped himself so freely before he troubled the Tree of Knowledge. You will all remember the sea-captain who was serving a long sausage-shaped pudding to his first officer and a distinguished guest, and who asked the latter which end he would like. But the distinguished guest was probably a great publicist and Parliamentary statesman; anyhow he was one of those who warned us against the violence of Extremists; one of those who call themselves Moderate in municipal affairs; one of those who wish to be broad-minded in Church affairs without going all the lengths of the lawless party in the Church; one of those who most sincerely wish well to Labour and hope it will see that all its true interests are entirely bound up with those of Capital; one of those who believe in true liberty and true religion and true Christianity and have a horror of extremes. In short, he was that kind of man; and he said that he would like a little of the middle.

Whereon that noble mariner, full of the dash and decision of the Nelson touch, merely said: "Me and the Mate like ends," and cut the pudding in two, allotting one half to himself and the other to his professional subordinate.

So I may say of myself and my supporters in this sort of enterprise; that in that sense we like ends. We like to know what end a man proposes to himself, or at which end he begins. We do not like the man who begins in the middle, because he will not take the trouble to begin at the beginning. But also in another sense, more individual and imaginative, I happened to be so constituted as to like ends. I like ends in the sense of edges; in the sense that the morning and evening are the first day. I think the first thing that made me dislike Imperialism was the statement that the sun never sets on the British Empire. Long ago, almost as soon as I heard it, I was moved to exclaim: "What is the good of a country with no sunset?" I can imagine nothing more ghastly than that glaring endless illumination, like the stare of lidless eyes. It would seem that Imperialism is insomnia. I like things to have their appointed limits and changes, and I no more desire to have a country that curls all round the terrestrial globe than to have a house that runs all round the city in the shape of a city wall. And just as I felt about the attempt of the colonial expansionists to overawe the mother-country by appealing to the ends of the earth, so I felt about the attempt of the cosmic sceptics to overawe our mother-earth by visions of the endlessness of the sky. I am a Little Earther as well as a Little Englander. I always thought it very vulgar of Herbert Spencer and the agnostics to suggest that man must be overawed by space. If Einstein succeeds in persuading people that space is limited as well as curved, I shall never be sorry; and shall not undertake one of my sanguinary raids of Anti-Semitic persecution on that account.

I remember in the crisis of the Marconi mystery, when every decent person from Mr. Massingham to the man in the street was startled by the confessions in the *Matin* case, that the *Daily News*, as the official government organ, had a queer little leading article about it. The article was called "The End of a Rumour." I wrote to the paper to say that it might be the end, but the interesting question was which end. As a matter of fact, of course, it was only the beginning. It was but the first rift of rending revelations, that had not ended until they had destroyed the whole self-respect or self-deception of modern politics; which had not ended until the late editor of the *New Witness* had dared imprisonment and been let off with a light fine, because it was then too late. Perhaps it did not really end until he died in the Great War; certainly his life was all of a piece and moved to its own end simply, like the fulfillment of a promise.

But that same question of "Which end?" which I asked in those days, is not altogether inapplicable. For me individually it happens to be particularly and almost alarmingly true that what is an end is also a beginning. As I undertook in that autumn of 1915 to start a new series of articles signed with my name, I have now undertaken a whole new paper, defaced with my own name in a still more disgusting fashion. I have in some sense to make a new world of my own and begin it at the other end; that logical and terrible end which is called the beginning. I only slid by stages into a semi-official position on the *New Witness*. Its real editor, as the phases of the war went on, began by asking me to write a weekly article, went on to ask me to write a leading article, ended by asking me to put my name on the front page of the paper, not so much as a substitute but rather as a symbol of his own. So much of the work was left for me to do and I continued to do it; but the foundation and framework of the whole thing was not mine, and I never regarded it as mine.[234]

It was financed without a financier; and edited without an editor. It told the truth that no one else would print. There was not a single paper which attacked Socialism in defence of small property, as distinct from large property. We supported nationalism against cosmopolitanism; we supported Poland against Bolshevism; we applied the same principle to certain views of France and of Ireland. We may sum up many of them in contrast to a considerable undercurrent in the whole Press to-day, by saying that we at least do not feel the faintest regret for the cause of the Great War. Conductors of the paper had right to speak so of the war, considering what they lost in it.[235]

---

[234] *New Witness*, May 4, 1923. GKC's final column in the final issue of the paper.

[235] *New Witness*, Sept. 15, 1922. What Chesterton lost was his brother. While Mrs. Cecil Chesterton merited an extensive footnote above, we have not really said much about her husband, Mr. Cecil Chesterton, GKC's younger brother. The siblings were famous for their arguments, which commenced as soon as Cecil achieved the facility of speech and continued until his untimely death in France just after the end of the Great War, where he had been serving in the infantry.

Cecil made his public debut debating at the National Liberal Club in May 1902. The topic was French Nationalism compared to British Imperialism. Cecil's argument, whatever it was, got muddled and he had to correct himself. It prompted a letter to the editor of *Daily News* (May 8, 1902) from one F. Victor Fisher: "With more valour than discretion, Mr. Cecil Chesterton has rushed into print." As Cecil began, so he continued, and so he ended, with more valour than discretion. Cecil took sides with Shaw in *The New Age*, defending socialism in a written debate with GKC and Belloc, who were defending democracy and ownership (what would become known as Distributism). GKC was saying that socialism is against property, but also against democracy, true popular rule. "My noble relative comforts himself by thinking that we shall not get State ownership until the people fight. I think we shall get something very like State ownership before the people ever dream of fighting." (*New Age*, Apr. 15, 1909.)

Cecil penned an anonymous book, *G. K. Chesterton: A Criticism*, which came out in 1908, at the same time as *Orthodoxy*, thereby upstaging one of GKC's greatest books at the worst possible moment. The timing was typical of Cecil's history of miscues, but his thesis was nonetheless provocative. He argued that although GKC claimed to be a liberal, most of his positions were conservative.

GKC told the *New York Tribune* (Sept. 15, 1912): "My brother is a man of the highest moral character and the most abominable opinions."

While GKC lay near death in 1914, Cecil was on a lecture tour in the U.S. It led the way to his book on the history of the United States, which was published after Cecil's death, with

When I became the first, and presumably last, editor of the little paper which (to my profound disgust) bears my initials, I had a different primary object from *The Eye-Witness* and *New Witness*, suited to the different political conditions. I was concerned to warn the public, not of political corruption (of which it was already well aware) but of the new and enormous peril of monopoly, and the growth of great combines destined to destroy all independent trade and individual property. This monopoly was especially threatening and repulsive in the case of the Press; and we said again and again that when a few men owned many newspapers, or most newspapers, they would only have to agree about something in order to impose it on millions without check or appeal.[236]

I certainly never contemplated the title when I conceived *G.K.'s Weekly*. I had always thought that there ought to be a paper expressing a certain serious body of opinion that has no other organ. But it

---

an introduction by GKC. After Cecil's untimely and tragic death, GKC recalled that Cecil was never bitter about the libel case that had gone against him, nor did it slow him down in any way. "More pugnacious even than I, a more daring chap, finer altogether. He never minded the result to himself so long as he succeeded in exposing corruption in high places.... He just went on telling the truth about those people. Oh, he was a splendid fellow." (*New York Times*, June 8, 1924.)

It could be argued that his loyalty to Cecil, more than anything else, is what got him into endless trouble with the critics who claimed he was anti-Semitic because of Cecil's intemperate and ceaseless comments about Jewish bankers and businessmen. Ironically, filial allegiance is what GKC maintained was one of the great strengths of the Jews.

What is often forgotten is that his brother converted before him. Cecil was received into the Church in 1912, right in the midst of his legal troubles with Godfrey Isaacs, manager of the Marconi Wireless Telegraph Company. Cecil enjoyed his greatest popularity over the next few years. The public saw him as a hero and martyr for calling out the Marconi scandal. He was the celebrity Catholic convert a decade before his brother, invited to speak at many Catholic events, and naturally was the more visible Chesterton when GKC lay ill for half a year. As editor of the *New Witness*, he had a regular platform from which to preach. Then he marched off to war and died, and like so many fallen soldiers, was forgotten. It was about the time of Cecil's conversion when GKC told Fr. O'Connor that he also intended to become Catholic, but that he had to wait for Frances to join him. He waited ten years, and in the end, had to make the step alone.

While his loyalty to Cecil never wavers, by 1922 that loyalty in the form of maintaining Cecil's paper is no longer sustainable. It is interesting that this change comes just after what Chesterton calls "the chief event" of his life: his own entering the Roman Catholic Church. Is there a connection? By making a spiritual communion with his brother, could GKC at last sever the journalistic, that is to say, the temporal one?

The important subject of GKC's conversion will be covered in chapter 11.

[236] *G.K.'s Weekly*, July 12, 1930.

would be expressing it mildly to state I am not a business man; and I had and still have to consult friends who are much more businesslike. When they answered my question by saying earnestly that the only way it could be worked would be as a personal organ with my initials on the front page, I naturally thought it was a joke. It took me two years to realise and be reconciled to the cold and blood-curdling fact that they really were practical men; and it was a practical joke. That practical joke went into operation. The reader has seen the booby-trap at work; though I have disquieting doubts about who is the booby. I was too much exhausted with my hopeless struggle against business efficiency to resist the further outrage of my portrait being put on the outer cover of the first number. I am told that this also is a part of efficiency; though I have not the least idea of what it is supposed to effect. Perhaps it has something to do with the principle by which a dubious character is expected to put his photograph on his passport. In that case, perhaps it would lie even better to have a large finger-print or an even larger foot-print. And with these brighter thoughts my mood changed; and I began to see my duty in a clearer and more cheerful fashion. If I must sell the paper in order to spread the opinions, and perform these mysterious antics in order to sell the paper, I will cut my capers heartily and in a more varied and vigorous fashion. It is evidently no time to be hampered by my middle-class traditions. I must abandon all this affectation of the fine and fastidious self-respect of a Bohemian journalist of Fleet Street. I must be rolled in the mud just as if I were a great nobleman, a great Minister of State, the ruler of a historic nation or the bearer of a historic name.[237]

To my personal and informal contributions to *G.K.'s Weekly*, I gave the general title of "Found Wandering,"[238] because I believe that is the official description often given of persons of weak intellect when found by the police, into whose arms I shall probably eventually wander.

It was said that the Chicago pork-machine used every part of a pig except the squeal. It might be said that the Fleet Street press-machine

---

[237] *G.K.'s Weekly*, Mar. 21, 1925.
[238] "Found Wandering" was the original title of GKC's column in his newspaper, but he later changed it to "Straws in the Wind," a phrase that in English journalism refers to an incident that may be a sign of what will happen next. It turned out to be a fitting title for GKC's often prophetic writing.

uses only the squeal. When I compare the journalist to a pig I mean it, of course, as a compliment and I include myself in the compliment. Pork is a truly traditional symbol of Christian morals and peasant civilisation; and it is true to say that by the present process of elimination all such inherited and substantial things have vanished. We have lost a pig and have nothing left but a pig's whisper. We have lost the substance, the experience, the real humour and knowledge of the world of the jolly old journalist; and have nothing left but some small separate thing squeezed out of his necessity or his fear. That is what many solemn scientific asses have called the "Division of Labour." It means that a man must always be divided from the labour he could really do. It means producing nothing except a by-product.

In short, nobody reading the newspapers could form the faintest notion of how intelligent we newspaper people are. The whole machine is made to chop up each mind into meaningless fragments and waste the vast mass even of those. Such a thing as one complete human being appearing in the Press is almost unknown; and when an attempt is made at it, it necessarily has a certain air of eccentric egotism. That is a risk which I am obliged to run. But it is inevitable that I should seem to indulge egotism in many forms. Even to meet practical problems of space I have to write far more of the paper myself than I had expected. But over and above that. I have resolved to put the whole of myself into this paper; and if there is too much of me, it is a joke to which I am accustomed.[239]

I write three paragraphs for the *Daily Mail* out of sheer necessity and two paragraphs for *G.K.'s Weekly* out of sheer fanaticism.[240]

It would be truer nowadays to say that a newspaper is printed on the back of an advertisement than that an advertisement is printed on the back of a newspaper. It is more and more obvious which is really the front of the page. And in time, no doubt, nothing will be seriously and systematically printed except commercial advertisements; but poets and prophets and such poor devils will pay for permission to write their remarks on the backs or blank spaces of advertisements of pills and hair-wash. Anyhow, the point is that this little advertisement is not advertising anything except itself. It has never had any

---

[239] *G.K.'s Weekly*, Mar. 28, 1925.
[240] *G.K.'s Weekly*, July 7, 1928.

indirect motive or any indirect support. *G.K.'s Weekly* may have been all the more deplorable or damnable for being *G.K.'s Weekly*; but it was *G.K.'s Weekly*. I may be a dummy but I am not a puppet. I may exasperate a constituency; but I do not merely satisfy a patron. There are no other ambitions or interests or individual purposes, honest or dishonest, behind my name. It means exactly what it says. Now I do not mean to be in the least superior when I state, simply as a historical fact, that this condition is now astonishingly uncommon. Almost every editor, every paper, every party leader, has something or somebody behind him, whose name is not displayed in front of him. He has something not himself, which does not always make for righteousness.[241] I should be only too proud if anyone regarded my paper as in any sense a sequel or successor to the *Eye Witness* and the *New Witness*. But I doubt whether the problem before it can entirely correspond to the problem before its predecessors. Their business was to tell the public of the existence of corruption in politics; and point to that corruption wherever it was. To-day it would be far more startling and dramatic to point to somewhere where it wasn't. But while the corruption is widespread, the knowledge of it is also widespread. Little more can be done by mere revelations; for the main fact is already revealed. Men have actually begun to talk everywhere as if rottenness were the rule rather than the exception. The question is whether they will cease to talk and begin to act.[242]

The truth is that tremendous changes are passing over the world; the sort of changes that appear in history because men struggled with them; but which do not appear in journalism. Our fathers sometimes exaggerated their own wars and revolutions; we are perhaps the first generation of men who underrate them, or are even unconscious of them. Some may doubt this generalisation, and may murmur that our great scientific discoveries are fully demonstrated and displayed. This is true; but these are not the really remarkable changes; and it is not the remarkable part of them that is displayed. In so far as they are a continuation of the comparatively commonplace notion of increasing speed and decreasing space, we do indeed boast of them; but it is already a very old boast. For centuries it has been a recognised matter of gossip

---

[241] *G.K.'s Weekly*, Aug. 7, 1926.
[242] *G.K.'s Weekly*, Jan. 7, 1928.

that the new coach is quicker than the old coach, that the new steam-engine is quicker than the new coach, and so on and so on. It is only because we have got thoroughly used to this sort of self-flattery that we can accept it from the newspapers in any quantities. But any real news about events that are really new is still for all practical purposes forbidden. Our ancestors would have been astounded at the open story of monopoly and tyranny that we all take for granted. There was a moment when the new power of the Word, given by the Wireless, might have broken the whole servile silence which the printed word preserves. For one wild instant a man might have told the truth to ten thousand people; and a roar from the whole Press and Parliament could never have covered or recalled the secret that had broken loose. The next moment the government, grumbling at and haggling and delaying all sorts of other nationalizations, lost not an hour or a minute in nationalizing the new telegraphy. On that sort of thing, at least, we are all Socialists now. It is wicked to nationalize mines or railroads; but we lose no time in nationalizing tongues and talk. The public of to-day had that huge opportunity without knowing it. They had that huge disappointment without knowing it. We might once have used, and we shall now never use, the twentieth century science against the nineteenth century hypocrisy. It was prevented by a swift, sweeping, and intolerant state monopoly; a monster suddenly swallowing all rivals, alternatives, discussions, or delays, with one snap of its gigantic jaws. That is what I mean by saying we cannot see the monsters that overcome us. But I suppose that even Jonah, when once he was swallowed, could not see the Whale.[243]

I have always supported frank and free dispute among Distributists. The truth we touch is much too deep and intelligent to be forced through with gag and guillotine and the strangling of all discussion.[244] It is impossible for me to know, even so much as a person in my position would normally know, about the details of dispute; and the difficulty is bound up with the economic facts of the position. The reason is very simple. It is that I also have a particular part to play in the historical drama. I suppose it might be called, by the fastidious, the part of the villain; for it is my own highly inadequate rendering of the

---

[243] *G.K.'s Weekly*, Jan. 28, 1928.
[244] *G.K.'s Weekly*, July 16, 1927.

part of the Financier. I am the thin and shadowy approximation to a Capitalist; the best imitation that our rather ragged stage can produce. I am a Capitalist without any Capital; I have no rent or interest; I have nothing but one trivial advantage, which I only mention in order to make the situation clear; the fact that I can write in other papers, for the sake of keeping this paper [G.K.'s Weekly] to write in. I could only manage, at least until very lately, to keep this paper in existence at all, by earning the money in the open market; and more especially in that busy and happy market where corpses are sold in batches; I mean the mart of Murder and Mystery: the booth of the Detective Story. Many a squire has died in a dank garden arbour, transfixed by a mysterious dagger, many a millionaire has perished silently though surrounded by a ring of private secretaries, in order that Mr. Belloc may have a paper in which he is allowed to point out that a great Empire does not default because it is growing richer. Many a shot has rung out in the silent night, many a constable has hurled himself through a crashing door, from under which there crawled a crimson stain, in order that there might be a page somewhere for Mr. Kenrick's virile and logical expositions of the principles of Distributism. Many an Imperial jewel has vanished from its golden setting, many a detective crawled about in the carpet for clues, before some of those little printers' bills could be settled, which enabled the most distinguished and intelligent of Distributists to denounce each other as Capitalists and Communists, in the columns of the Cockpit and elsewhere. This being my humble and even highly irrelevant contribution to the common team-work, it is obvious that it could not be done at the same time as a close following of the varying shades of thought in the Distributist debates. And this ignorance of mine, though naturally very irritating to people better informed, has at least the advantage of giving some genuineness to my impartiality. I have really never belonged distinctively to any of the different Distributist groups; I have never had time.[245]

I recently had occasion to write to the leading Labour newspaper to protest against a most astonishing statement, to the effect that I had not only joined the official Liberal Party, but had abandoned his antagonism to the Secret Party Fund, as well as to Lloyd George and Isaacs and the present group at the new Liberal headquarters.

---

[245] G.K.'s Weekly, Sept. 3, 1932.

Considering that we abuse these people nearly every week, it is a mystery to us how any such notion can have occurred to anybody anywhere. We are perhaps the only people who do go on persistently talking against the Secret Party Fund. We are certainly the only people who still go on talking about the Marconi scandal. What possible indication we are supposed to have given of any intention to leave off we cannot imagine. But, anyhow, we have not left off.[246]

There are other places where I may properly press the definite claims of my own very definite private convictions about politics, economics, ethics, and religion. In the *Illustrated London News* I deal chiefly with what is common to all views of these things. I deal with the use and abuse of logic; the use and abuse of language; the duty of talking sense even on the wrong side; the duty of not talking nonsense even on the right side. There may be things I think so absolutely abnormal as to deserve to be treated as monstrosities. I thought so of the servile ideal of Prussianism; I think so of the servile ideal of Prohibition. But by far the greater part of what I have written there has been directed, not against things, but against theories supposed to support those things; not against the government, but against this or that howling headline glorifying the government; not against the opposition, but against this or that noisy sophistry employed by the opposition.[247]

Infinite years ago, at an age almost infantile, I began to call myself a Radical; and I have called myself so ever since. It is a name not without its real vices and limitations. It has been associated with a shallow and cocksure attack upon the divine part of man which alone gives him leave to be human. It has been mixed up with a stingy and flat-footed philosophy of supply and demand, indifferent to art and honour. There has been a small Radicalism, founded not so much on every man having two eyes or two ears, as on every man having two quite symmetrical mutton-chop whiskers. But when we have got back past all this crawling conventionality, the real meaning of the word remains. A Radical was a man who was convinced that the wrong was in the root of the system, and must be uprooted; in other

---

[246] *G.K.'s Weekly*, Aug. 20, 1927. GKC speculated that the *Daily Herald* had reported him rejoining the Liberal Party because he had given a talk at a social event attended by "young Liberals" (who may have had some of their ideals still intact). It shows that GKC would be invited everywhere and was always happy to accept the invitation.

[247] *Illustrated London News*, Feb. 20, 1934.

words, he was a man who thought things so bad that they required something as bad as a revolution to cure them. In that sense I am a Radical at this moment; and was never more of one in my life.[248]

When I say that I am neither a Reactionary nor a Red, when I say that I have the same dislike of the Imperialist and Capitalist as I have of the Internationalist and Communist, I fear that many may come to the shocking conclusion, and may do me the ghastly wrong, of supposing that I am a Moderate.[249] I am the most orthodox Liberal in the world.[250] I do not think at present I have a party; I do not think there is a party that owns me, so to speak.[251] I am a Radical Nationalist Anti-Imperialist Anti-Collectivist Distributivist Christian Social Democrat. I am all that; and there are about three more of me.[252]

It may or may not do good to go to a hall packed with one's own sort of people and hit a table and say that the will of the people must prevail. It will certainly do unmixed harm if by the "people" we mean the people in the hall and not the people in the street. We tend insensibly to judge ourselves by what we do best, not solely out of silly vanity, but also because it is naturally the thing we take pleasure in, and our closest friends are likely to take pleasure in, too. We thus tend to commit a blasphemy even worse than that of magnifying ourselves; the blasphemy of diminishing the universe.[253]

I was once concerned in controversy, along with Mr. Belloc and my friends, and did what I could to help a campaign against the old Party System, which reduced all the possibilities of politics to the rotation of the Two Front Benches. We dared to dispute the sacred oracle which declared that every little boy and girl was either a little Liberal or else a little Conservative.[254]

One of the old sayings repeated eternally by everybody, and rather especially by those who pride themselves on novelty and originality, is the statement that old people tend to be Conservative, and that it is

---

[248] *Daily News*, Mar. 11, 1911.
[249] *G.K.'s Weekly*, June 21, 1930.
[250] *New Witness*, July 10, 1913.
[251] Speech at the National Catholic Congress, Sept. 25, 1926.
[252] *Illustrated London News*, July 16, 1921. When once asked who the "other three" were, GKC paused, and then answered: "Hilaire Belloc, Cunningham Grahame and Quiller Couch." (*New York Tribune*, Sept. 15, 1912.)
[253] *Daily News*, Jan. 11, 1913.
[254] *Illustrated London News*, Jan. 27, 1934.

only the young who can really believe in change. And yet this saying seems to me to be rather less than a half-truth—so much less as to be very nearly two-thirds of a lie. To the very young the world they see really seems to be eternal; and that, however much they may talk a current cant about novelty and mutability, they do not really expect the externals of their world to be profoundly altered by time.[255]

Looking back on my life, I find that its final divergence occurred when Liberalism deserted liberty.[256] I sometimes have a whimsical fancy that I shall end as I began, trying to make some sense out of what is called Liberalism in politics. There is a Fleet Street story about me, which may be a fact though I have entirely forgotten it, that when I was asked if I was a Liberal, I answered, "I am the only Liberal." The Liberal Party now consists entirely of leaders—or rather misleaders. And all they want, all they have left to pray for, is one single simple solitary human being who is willing to be misled.[257]

Having called myself a Liberal all my life, having written regularly for the great Liberal paper, the *Daily News*, for a great part of my life, and being still a Liberal in the stiff rejection of the philosophies of Imperialism and Socialism, I found myself in a queer and eccentric position. I found, as I said at the time, that I was not only a Liberal, but the only Liberal. I was the only person left who seemed in any way moved by the conception of liberty; with the exception of two or three of my friends, some of whom had never had anything to do with Liberalism, and some of whom actively detested it.[258] And it is to me a melancholy fact, but one to be confessed, that at this moment the word "Liberalism" is as Newman used it—the name of the enemy.[259] It is queer to note in what a number of cases modern Liberalism is the *opposite* of what it should be by its theory and its history.[260]

Again, I have always believed in liberty. But I noticed that all those who said that they believed in liberty and nothing else proceeded at

---

[255] *Illustrated London News*, Oct. 27, 1928. That is, he could not in his youth ever have imagined that the coal mines would run out of coal, or that automobiles would replace the trains. In this way, he sees young people in every generation conservative in the same way, not really believing in change.
[256] *G.K.'s Weekly*, Oct. 11, 1934.
[257] *G.K.'s Weekly*, July 27, 1933.
[258] *G.K.'s Weekly*, Oct. 11, 1934.
[259] *New Witness*, May 1, 1913.
[260] *New Witness*, July 30, 1914.

once to shackle themselves. What they did was adopt an economic creed (which the Russians hold to-day) that everything that happens *must* happen—that, in fact, nobody can be free. It seemed a poor way to use your freedom. And I have noticed that the modern idea of freedom seems to be that you are not to be allowed to bring up your family as you choose, that you are not to be allowed to marry as you choose, that you are not to be allowed to drink as you choose.

I soon came to realise that liberty was a more complicated thing than I imagined and that it seemed to need somebody (perhaps God) standing outside human life as an arbiter.[261]

That a man should have one God, one wife, one country, so far as possible one house, and certainly not more than one vote—in these truisms I do indeed grow more conservative, or to use a better word, contented.[262] We grow conservative as we grow old, it is true. But we do not grow conservative because we find so many new things spurious. We grow conservative because we find so many old things genuine.[263]

I am one of the few who do still believe in the many. I am one of the intelligent but rapidly disappearing minority which actually trust the majority. We who believe in the mob are forlorn and forsaken figures now; and the mob mocks at us in the street. But, I repeat, I am still of the intelligent minority which does not believe in the intelligent minority. I believe that, given saner and simpler conditions, there is no better government than self-government, and that the citizens should normally rule the city. I apologise for the antiquated nature of this creed; but I hold it. But I always held it along with a recognition of certain real difficulties, which were almost entirely neglected, when it was the fashion to deafen us all with shouts for democracy, and which are now likely to be neglected again in the neglect of democracy itself. And, to begin with, it always seemed to me that there was a vital distinction between the citizens managing their own affairs and the citizens managing all conceivable affairs, not only all the affairs of the city, but all the affairs of the world.[264]

In discussing Distribution I do not insist on Catholicism; but I do insist on candour about Catholicism. I do not propose to conceal my

[261] *Daily Sketch*, May 14, 1931.
[262] *Illustrated London News*, Aug. 26, 1911.
[263] *Daily News*, Oct. 14, 1904.
[264] *G.K.'s Weekly*, Nov. 17, 1928.

religion; and I do not expect any sincere Protestant to conceal his. I do not assume that every Distributist is a Catholic; nor, I will add, that every Catholic is a Distributist. But I do think I have a perfect right to try to convert a Distributist to Catholicism, as I have to try to convert a Catholic to Distributism. There is no sort of comparison between the importance of the two things; but the point is that it was the big thing and not the little thing that we were always told to conceal. Even in the eye of the world, it has grown much too big to be concealed.

My country has reached a great religious crisis; in which I happen to believe that mine is the true religion. Anything I write must necessarily be marked with so momentous a belief; and anything that other people write ought equally to be marked with their beliefs. The more simply that situation is realised, the more frankly it is faced, the better for everybody. I do not propose to conceal my views about these things; and I do not ask any Protestant to conceal his.

The truth is that the modern world would like to force upon us that very secrecy of which it falsely accuses us. So a man in my position is allowed to play about as a universal critic, so long as he will not embarrass anybody by mentioning his relations to a universal creed.[265]

The views I maintain here are connected with the views I have maintained elsewhere, in private as well as public; and I should like to explain something of that inner consistency. I began with what I should then have called Democracy; I end with what I should now call Distributism; and I have not changed. It is a blunder to imagine, as many do, that those who agree with me wish to make every man a Robinson Crusoe, making all his own clothes and living only for himself. As a fact, the peasant, though he has much of the handy universality of Robinson Crusoe, can never be content with the solitude of Robinson Crusoe. A peasant lives in a peasantry and not on a desert island. He is by nature as ready for co-operation as he is resolute against Communism. Still, there is something symbolic in the figure of Robinson Crusoe, and especially in its fascination for the innocent imagination in the most creative period of childhood. Why is it that a child is delighted with the idea of Robinson Crusoe, complete with his gun and umbrella, his goat and parrot, his axe and antiquated sword? It is precisely because he is complete and also compact; that

---

[265] *G.K.'s Weekly*, Feb. 18, 1928.

he has a limited number of things, but these things immediately at hand and directly under his control. It is equally, or perhaps even more, because these things have been barely snatched from the bottomless peril of shipwreck and the dark infinity of the sea. That is the right view of the good things of life; we would possess them directly; but we should possess them thriftily; and above all, we should possess them thankfully. They and we have been saved by God out of the sea of nothing and the night that was before the world. Now, in the course of my life, I have seen this compact conception, symbolised by Robinson Crusoe in the children's books, attacked by two opposite enemies but with equal enmity. The old enemy called itself Pessimism; the new enemy calls itself Progress and Optimism; but both invade the desert island with the destructive frenzy of the cannibals. The sin of the optimist is that he does not recognise the wreck; as the sin of the pessimist is that he does not recognise the rescue.[266]

I fancy that a man grows less controversial as he grows more convinced. Perhaps the moment when he is most controversial is when he is convincing himself. I know that since my own views have grown much more settled and satisfied, I am less inclined than I was to go about incessantly contradicting everybody who contradicts them. There are several critics who have written amusingly about me, and whom it would amuse me very much to answer; but somehow there seems to be less and less time for such amusements. There are several learned and excellent persons with whom I have begun debates and afterwards allowed them to drop; but it does not disturb me as it might once have done. And this is not because I am any more drawn towards thinking they are right, but because I am far more securely and serenely certain that they are wrong. But I think it is most of all because, with fuller convictions, one comes to have larger views, and to see the wrongness not as an individual wrongness, but as a vast field of rich and abundant wrongness—an entrancing landscape and radiant vista of error.[267]

I am not one of those who wake up in the night with a wild shriek that a Bolshevist or an atheist must be shot like a burglar. When people hold false theories of life, I prefer to prove them to be false, rather

---

[266] *G.K.'s Weekly*, Oct. 11, 1930.
[267] *Illustrated London News*, July 24, 1926.

than cut short the lives or even the language of their honest victims before they can live to be enlightened. If a grown-up man, writing for grown-up men, chooses to write a Bolshevist article, I will try to answer him with another article and not with a howl of horror. Nor am I myself at one with the conventional views underlying most of the official history I learnt at school, or most of the official newspapers that I read now. I also am in a minority in many things; as a Distributist, as a Catholic, as a man opposing Capitalism from the opposite extreme to that of Communism. But I should not think it fair to put these controversial views of mine into something professing to be a mere primer of ordinary objective scientific instruction.

As I say, if somebody writes a Communist pamphlet, I will write an Anti-Communist pamphlet; and in the same way I have often written a Distributist pamphlet, not to mention a Papist pamphlet. But if I were to write a sort of technical encyclopedia of the nature of the Boys' Own Handy Handbook of Boat-Building, or A Hundred Ways of Making Paper Boats, I should not think myself justified in insinuating into it my own case against Capitalism and monopoly in the Paper Trade, nor in introducing parenthetical theological propaganda about the bark of St. Peter. This seems to me a simple matter of principle; of not doing one thing when everybody supposes you are doing another. If I hold different views from those of my countrymen, it is my business to convert my countrymen, if possible, by direct and straightforward arguments addressed to them and addressed to the question. The tradition of my country, the religion of my fathers, the existing system of property and law in a great nation deserve at least to be directly and avowedly challenged, and not merely undermined in a series of lectures on Fretwork or Electricity for the Little Ones. Frankly, therefore, I do not like this method of educational propaganda very much. I should not like it as a way of popularizing the unpopular opinions I hold, and I naturally like it even less as a way of popularizing the unpopular opinions I hate. The people who produced this particular work probably meant no harm. Their opinions are doubtless sincere, and their methods may well be such as they themselves can approve sincerely. Possibly they think their moral or metaphysical views are now self-evident to every sensible person.

Indeed, this is probable as well as possible. For people with those views are commonly simple-minded. They do not know how much of the modern intellectual world continues to regard their simple notions as impudent assumptions. But I repeat that I do not like the method myself. It partakes too much of a sort of spiritual kidnapping.[268]

Religious liberty is tied to freedom of speech. England is under the strange impression that such freedom exists. Anybody who has ever tried, as I have tried, to take a part in the exposure of real political corruption, or help those trying to tell the truth in the public Press in the interests [of] the public, will be heartily entertained by this idea.[269]

Ever since I began, almost ever since I was a baby, I have been familiar with the statement that the creeds are crumbling. And, having watched the world from my first to my second childhood, I have come to the conclusion that the statement is quite untrue. The creeds, when they really are creeds, seem to me much the hardest and most indestructible material made by man, if they were made by man. Huge crowds of people are still reciting word for word the creeds that were composed before a single existing kingdom had a king, before a single existing nation had a name, when chariot-races still swept round the Roman amphitheatre, when legionaries still watched the eagles on the Roman Wall. That may have nothing to do with the truth of the creeds, but it surely has something to do with their tenacity.[270]

The object of travel is to visit varied and attractive places. Popular and even vulgar speech testifies to that truth; as in speaking about somebody "going away for a change." But it would be infinitely more worth while to walk into the nearest village, so long as that village retained its own natural diversity, than to travel a hundred miles through a hundred villages which the very act of travelling was flattening out into uniformity.[271]

---

[268] *Illustrated London News*, Oct. 29, 1932.

[269] *America*, July 27, 1929.

[270] *Illustrated London News*, Nov. 26, 1927.

[271] *G.K.'s Weekly*, Mar. 19, 1927. Whenever he visited other countries, and for that matter, when he visited his own, GKC would seek out small villages and countrysides, where he would walk and draw and write and think and drink the local wine and eat the local cheese. He would amuse children by drawing pictures for them, usually pictures of two men swordfighting, which would amuse them very much. He often got lost, which he greatly enjoyed doing. He visited seaside towns, where he would enjoy walking along the stone walls or piers, watching the crashing waves. Though he wrote travel books on America, Italy, Ireland, and the Holy Land, he did not write books on three countries he especially loved: Poland, France, and Spain. Poland he only visited once, but the latter two several times. In two trips to America, he saw Niagara Falls, the Grand Canyon, the Rocky Mountains, and the Pacific Ocean, but he never mentions the experiences in his writings. When he saw the lights of Broadway,

In America the fact of my landing and lecturing was evidently regarded in the same light as a murder or a great fire, or any other terrible but incurable catastrophe, a matter of interest to all pressmen concerned with practical events. One of the first questions I was asked was how I should be disposed to explain the wave of crime in New York. Naturally I replied that it might possibly be due to the number of English lecturers who had recently landed.[272]

America has never been quite normal.[273] The country began with the Declaration of Independence and ends with Prohibition! As I passed the Statue of Liberty I had an inclination to want to see all the liquor on board ship poured out in an act of pagan oblation.[274] It might be suggested that American citizens do at least so far love freedom as to like to have their hands free. It might be suggested, on the other hand, that they keep their hands for the handles of many

---

all he cared about was the lights, and not Broadway. His comment that it would be beautiful if only one could not read was reprinted in papers around the world.

Although he always lectured to packed houses, and his arrival was front-page news in that city, he played to mixed reviews. Some were in awe of his genius. Some were merely baffled by him. Some of the editors of the Midwestern papers resented that the lecture tour seemed to be a source of easy money for him. But none of them hesitated to fill a blank space in their paper with a good Chesterton quip.

He was taken to task by one reporter who criticized "The Ignorance of the Educated" talk, pointing out that GKC had wrongly attributed the quote " 'It ain't so much men's ignorance that does the harm as their knowing so many things that ain't so" to Artemus Ward, when it apparently came from Josh Billings. However, while the reporter got the quoter right, he got the quote wrong. What Josh Billings actually said was, "I honestly beleave it iz better tew know nothing than two know what ain't so." Chesterton would continue to quote the line incorrectly in his writings but would correctly attribute it to Josh Billings. Ironically, the East Coast liked GKC better. In Boston, one editor said that Chesterton is one of the few Englishmen who is persona grata in America, and that his writings are in sympathy with the whole world. (*Boston Sunday Post*, Jan. 9, 1921.)

There was a notable change of attitude ten years later. Chesterton had gone from being merely famous to being distinguished. His attitude toward America won him over especially to the staid Midwesterners, as Chesterton criticized the criticisms of Sinclair Lewis and actually defended Main Street. It is the difference between an alienated insider and a sympathetic outsider. Chesterton had stayed for six weeks in a typical middle-class home, "an ordinary, jolly little frame house," in South Bend, Indiana, and found it utterly charming, wholesome, and egalitarian. One editor admitted, "Maybe the real Main Street that most of us live on isn't so bad, after all." (*Bradford Era* [PA], Dec. 20, 1930.) More somberly, another editor admitted that "the clear-eyed Chesterton" had come along as a counterpoint to the American confidence in the machine age. He approvingly quotes Chesterton's assessment: "We have given ourselves over to an insatiable monster who serves us at the price of our slavery." (*Olean Times*, Nov. 28, 1930.)

[272] *New Witness*, Mar. 11, 1921.
[273] *G.K.'s Weekly*, May 16, 1931.
[274] *Philadelphia Inquirer*, Feb. 13, 1921.

machines. And that the hand on a handle is less free than the hand on a stick or even a tool.[275] I regret the curious evolution of the human form in America, where wheels have completely taken the place of legs.[276] Americans are the most idealistic people in the whole world. Their only danger is that the idealist can easily become the idolator. And the American has become so idealistic that he even idealises money.[277] However, I fancy that the American, quite apart from any love of money, has a great love of measurement. He will mention the exact size or weight of things, in a way which appears to us as irrelevant.[278] The very largeness of America isolates and therefore imprisons them. For it is large things that really limit us, because they prevent us even from seeing anything beyond.[279]

America is the last of the monarchies, much more of a monarchy than Great Britain. The president has almost complete authority and complete responsibility. He gets blamed for everything.[280] But one of the very real American virtues is a most fiery readiness to fight.[281]

I travelled about America with two sticks, like a Japanese nobleman with his two swords. I fear the simile is too stately. I bore more resemblance to a cripple with two crutches or a highly ineffectual version of the devil on two sticks. I carried them both because I valued them both, and did not wish to risk losing either of them in my erratic travels. One is a very plain grey stick from the woods of Buckinghamshire, but as I took it with me to Palestine it partakes of the character of a pilgrim's staff. When I can say that I have taken the same stick to Jerusalem and to Chicago, I think the stick and I may both have a rest. The other, which I value even more, was given me by the Knights of Columbus at Yale, and I wish I could think that their chivalric title allowed me to regard it as a sword.[282]

---

[275] *New Witness*, Apr. 8, 1921.
[276] *Illustrated London News*, Apr. 6, 1935.
[277] *Daily News*, July 6, 1907.
[278] *New Witness*, Apr. 29, 1921.
[279] *Illustrated London News*, Feb. 5, 1927.
[280] *Baltimore Sun*, Feb. 24, 1921.
[281] *G.K.'s Weekly*, Aug. 13, 1927.
[282] *New Witness*, Apr. 8, 1921. He chose the Knights of Columbus "snakewood" stick to accompany him the day he was received into the Catholic Church on July 30, 1922. He got some hand-carved Polish walking sticks in 1927 when visiting Zakopane, and he generally carried one of these the rest of his life.

In America a walking stick is commonly called a cane. There is about it a faint flavour of luxury and lounging, and most of the energetic citizens of this energetic society avoid it by instinct. Now, in an Englishman like myself, carrying a stick may imply lounging, but it does not imply luxury, and I can say with some firmness that it does not imply dandyism. In a great many Englishmen it means the very opposite even of lounging. By one of those fantastic paradoxes which are the mystery of nationality, a walking stick often actually means walking.[283]

Americans have enthusiastically embraced boot-legging, with all their modern taste for profiteering and their national taste for lawlessness. I wrote a book which was called on the cover, *What I Saw in America*. All my impressions are subject to correction by other things that I did not see. I did see rich people drinking cocktails and costly wines in a great proportion of the houses I visited. I did not see poor people manufacturing drink from wood-pulp or swallowing poisonous beer; I only heard the rumour of it on every side. I was not, I deeply regret to say, taken down into dark cellars in the criminal quarter, where hell-broths were brewed underground.[284] But I really did feel as if I were on another planet when I was in the United States.[285]

America had a great political idea, but it had a small religious idea.[286] What is really peculiar to America, by this time, is that Puritanism and faddism, originally the poisons of the towns, have here even poisoned the villages. Everywhere else in the world the villages are either pagan or Christian; that is, they are healthy. Here alone they are Puritan; that is, they derive not from general human folk-lore or from a universal Church, but solely from the dirty bye-product of seventeenth-century sectarianism, developing into nineteenth-century faddism.

This accounts for almost all that is defective or destructive in America; this is the darker spirit that has striven with the brighter spirit of democracy and simplicity and adventure. This was the curse that was mingled from the first with the blessing of life, liberty and the pursuit of happiness; and it is now working itself out all over America in the form of hygienic panics and insane taboos; monkey chatter about

---

[283] *New Witness*, Apr. 8, 1921. GKC never used his walking stick as a cane. It wound not have supported him!
[284] *Illustrated London News*, Dec. 2, 1922. This was obviously during Prohibition.
[285] *Illustrated London News*, Feb. 2, 1924.
[286] *G.K.'s Weekly*, May 16, 1931.

utterly meaningless psychology; and a universal wallowing in that most unhealthy of all topics, the topic of health.[287]

When I was in America, for instance, some lunatics were actually trying to teach children to take care of their health. In other words, they were teaching babies to be valetudinarians and hypochondriacs in order that they might be healthy. They were even proud of their half-witted and wicked amusement; and one of them actually boasted that his schoolchildren were "health-mad." That it is not exactly the aim of all mental hygiene to be mad did not occur to him.[288] Sections of what was once the American democracy have already begun to play the fool with Eugenics; so that a fantastic perversion of science by the State has already begun.[289]

There does exist a group of new religions which have grown up in America, which may be not unfairly classified as being essentially the religions of pride. Being inspired by pride they are naturally allied to prosperity. There are individuals in all these creeds who have nothing the matter with them except their creeds. Now it is very important to know the enemy's religion; and still more important to know the enemy's religious atmosphere. For every man has a religious atmosphere even if he has not a religion. And these plutocrats probably will have a religion. Whatever its external forms, it will be full of what the Americans call optimism. Optimism means that the master of slaves likes the slaves to look cheerful, because a sad slave is a reproach to slavery.[290] America does still manage to believe that Capitalism is normal. It is natural, because Capitalism does always begin with what is normal; with private property and political liberty. Owing to greed of property in some and neglect of liberty for all, it becomes mere plutocracy.[291]

Individualism bordering on anarchism was let loose, especially in America. It has ended in standardization bordering on slavery, especially in America.[292] I do not say that the wealth of America was a vice; it was merely a calamity.[293]

---

[287] *G.K.'s Weekly*, Apr. 18, 1931.
[288] *New Witness*, Oct. 28, 1921.
[289] *New Witness*, Apr. 7, 1922.
[290] *New Witness*, Mar. 2, 1923.
[291] *G.K.'s Weekly*, Dec. 17, 1927.
[292] *G.K.'s Weekly*, July 21, 1928.
[293] *G.K.'s Weekly*, May 16, 1931.

We have sometimes been driven by the logic of social theories to treat America as a sort of enemy. In so far as she is, at the moment, the habitat of the huge Trusts (or Corporations) and howling advertisements and base standardisation of our day, it was almost inevitable that such a mistake should be made. I am more glad to record here a deep, a real, a rending difference between the two societies, in which I strongly suspect that America is on the side of the angels. I do not advance this point as a satire on New York and Chicago. I have my national affections, as is natural; but I have a sense of justice too. And I suspect that in this respect, the utter blank incomprehension by all Americans of what we mean by Rank, they are really and truly better than we; and New York and Chicago, if not God's Own Country, are a good many miles nearer to the Garden of Eden.[294]

The best American people are in the back-blocks and the bye-streets; where even the rich Americans do not look for them, let alone the European travellers. It is in them that there endures an indescribable decency and security of soul; not poisoned by servility; not poisoned by pessimism. The good that is in them is naturally not known to globe-trotters, for it is not known to themselves. A Catholic priest said to me of some people in the Middle West, "They know nothing of their virtues, and that must be pleasing to God." Main Street has been held up to the world as the worst thing in America. I think it is almost the best.[295]

In America the skyscrapers have something in them recalling primeval Babylon or Assyria; but it is a mistake to suppose that America as a whole is merely dominated by skyscrapers. I lived for some weeks in a little town in the Middle West; and when I first entered its quieter streets, I certainly was not reminded of anything in England. As a matter of fact, I was reminded of Poland. There were the same rather shabby looking houses of grey thin wood; and even churches built of such shaving of pine and fir, as I have seen them in the wild country beyond the Carpathians. Most English people would regard Poland as the last word in mouldering mediaeval poverty and the Middle West as the latest word in bustling business and prosperity. But the town was much more like a Polish town than an English town. It was also (I might add) like a Polish town in containing several thousands of Poles.

---

[294] *G.K.'s Weekly*, Jan. 18, 1930.
[295] *G.K.'s Weekly*, May 16, 1931.

The jolliest thing about American framehouses, and one of the jolliest things about America, is the institution of the Porch; worthy to be that great Porch which gave its name to a whole school of Greek philosophers. It is a splendid place in which to philosophise, without being a Greek; and even American business men have been caught philosophising in it. It is a sort of open gallery or covered platform outside each of the houses; primarily valued for coolness, I suppose, in the heavy American summers. But, when I first saw it, I was instantly reminded of that outer court or covered entrance which introduces the stranger to so many houses in Spain. To sit in it is much more of a Spanish than an English sensation; and might make a man fancy he was in South rather than North America.[296]

When I was wandering about in the market of an old town in Spain, I came upon a sort of ramshackle bookstall and paperstall full of odds and ends of novelettes and penny-dreadfuls, in languages and local dialects all strange and baffling to me; and among them I saw with a start of surprise (followed, I need not say, by a burst of tears) an odd number of *Illustrated London News*, which is found wherever the traveller may wander, probably at the North Pole, and almost certainly in the Cannibal Islands. Naturally, I proceeded, drying my tears, to purchase the document; as it was almost the only English document I had seen for some time.[297]

I did not go to see any bullfights, for a reason which I explained to my Spanish friends on the spot. I said I should be very much annoyed if one of my Spanish friends came to England, and instantly put on pink that he might rush to the meet and be in at the death of a poor little fox, and then turn round and say, "How hideous! How repulsive! What brutes in human form are the English, whose whole lives are passed in this degrading sport!" We can indulge in all sorts of controversy and casuistry about bull-fighting or fox-hunting, and there is a great deal to be said against both. But, whatever be the right way of treating a bull or a fox, there is a very wrong way of treating a man or a nation of men. And that is to make your first dash to see something that you know you will dislike, in order to tell him that you dislike it. That is not the way to begin to understand anybody

---

[296] *G.K.'s Weekly*, Dec. 6, 1930.
[297] *Illustrated London News*, May 29, 1926.

or anything; it is simply taking a pride in prolonging your own prejudices and in learning nothing that might balance or correct them. All countries have anomalies that strike us as abnormalities, or even abominations; but it is not seeing a country to look for the things that you abominate.[298]

There are two kinds of travellers who enjoy their travels, even over roads that they have travelled before. The first is the man who remembers everything; and the second is the man who forgets everything. I myself belong to the second class; and when my companion exclaims that this is exactly the cross-roads where we went wrong in 1913, I have no feeling except that this is a place that no human foot has ever trod, and that my own feet are quite certain to go right. The first type of traveller has the rich enjoyments of experience and memory; the second enjoys all the advantages of arrested development. The world is an everlasting fairyland to the man who can forget. The companion[299] with whom I commonly set forth from Beaconsfield upon foreign travel is my exact contrary in all this, which is just as it should be; and remembers Jerusalem when I have completely forgotten Gerrards Cross. In any case, when escaping for a holiday. I always forget everything. I do not actually forget my name, like Mr. Petre;[300] but I have a profound hope that everybody else has forgotten it; and I go by preference to the innumerable innocent and happy places where nobody can possibly have heard of it. When I am on a holiday, I find it difficult even to remember holidays. Certain dark superstitions, on which we need not dwell, lead me to inquire occasionally of my fellow-creatures whether it is Sunday or Friday; but, except for such inquiries, I should not have the wildest idea of what was the day of the week. The consequence is that I can really crowd into a week or two a whole cosmos of distances and remote separations; which is the whole purpose of what popular language very rightly calls "a change."[301]

I have heartily enjoyed motoring, in many different motors and manners. I have staggered in a ricketty Ford over the wilderness of Palestine, when the roads were more impassable than the rocks; with

---

[298] *Illustrated London News*, June 19, 1926.
[299] That would be his wife, Frances.
[300] The main character from Belloc's novel of that name, which was illustrated by GKC.
[301] *G.K.'s Weekly*, June 13, 1935.

a little Jewish professor who talked all day about Zionism, except once when he paused to tell me (more cheerfully) that he believed that our driver across that desert was a murderer. I have driven round the West Country in a Rolls Royce; I need not say in somebody else's Rolls Royce; and been received everywhere with a respect and reverence that nobody has ever paid me before or since. But the fact which I strongly and vividly associate with my early motor trips is the fact that motoring can really give to man a new sensation; an experience that man has never had before. In that sense it was more immediately and arrestingly novel than flying.[302] I have been driven in a motor-car over mountain-passes that carried every suggestion of being as separate as the mountains of the moon. I had crossed abysses which seemed as bottomless as the abysses between the stars; I had followed the trail of a white mountain road that seemed to vanish into an eternal void like the white tail of a comet. I really did feel as if I had passed beyond all the world that I knew; as if it were a matter of vision and of the valley of the shadow of death. There are points in such toppling and perilous landscapes, when the most comfortable traveller does almost wonder whether he died at the last corner of the cliff; and it is only his ghost that goes on.[303]

I was in Warsaw on the Third of May, the national festival which commemorates the one really astounding historical incident of our time: the day when Poland rose from the dead.[304] I had left Warsaw for about a week, and was sketching out in Belgium a series of articles on somewhat more serene and permanent aspects of Poland, when the news reached me of the political crime in the city I had just left.[305] I have more than once had this ironic experience of leaving a place of interest just before it became really interesting. In the first days of the Zionist quarrel in Jerusalem, I saw the mobs gathering and heard the cries against the Jews; but the first real riot in which Jews were killed broke out a few days after my departure. There were also

---

[302] *G.K.'s Weekly*, Jan. 9, 1932.

[303] *G.K.'s Weekly*, June 13, 1935.

[304] *Illustrated London News*, June 25, 1927. Poland had defeated the Soviet Union in 1920 and had regained its status as an independent nation.

[305] The Soviet ambassador to Poland, Pyotr Voykov, had been assassinated at a Warsaw railway station by a nineteen-year-old Russian exile who was acting in retaliation for Voykov having signed the death warrants for Tsar Nicholas II and his family.

interesting developments in the Spanish capital soon after I left it; but just then there were even more interesting developments in the English capital to which I tried in vain to return. This may sometimes be a relief to a humanitarian; but it is something of a tragedy to a journalist. If I were a real vigorous, unconquerable American Journalist, if I were a Man Who Means To Get On, a self-confident superman of the sort recently described in "Jesus Christ as a Publicity Agent," I should doubtless regard this as a proof of virtue or (what seems to mean the same thing) something to my own advantage. I should say that the moment my moral influence is withdrawn from any city, it breaks out into crime. When my purifying presence is removed, Anti-Semitism instantly appears; when the Poles can no longer look to me for guidance they console themselves with the blood of Bolshevists; when I leave England for a week or two there is a General Strike. How glorious it must be to have the real Publicity Sense; and say these things of oneself and perhaps believe them! What fun to have no sense of humour! It would be no sillier than the boasts made by newspapers about their influence or politicians about their policy. If on the other hand I were an ascetic of extravagant humility (which is also not the case) I should say that a curse and a nemesis of sin followed me everywhere; and that wherever I went murder, rapine, and ruin blazed in my track. But as I cannot offer the excitement of either of these extremes, I can only say that as a citizen I regret hearing of murder, and as a journalist I regret missing it.[306]

Upon returning to England, I read a newspaper article that was a furious attack on Poland, full of the wildest historical falsehoods and a gross ignorance of the realities of Europe. It represented a curious modern mentality which is a hatred of the heroic, a highly sentimental hatred. It always appeals to humanitarianism against heroism. It detests anything savouring of miracle and especially of resurrection. What it hates about Poland is that Poland has been murdered and is still alive. The smooth and successful achievement of such murders as

---

[306] *G.K.'s Weekly*, July 2, 1927. GKC wrote a few articles about his 1927 trip to Poland and intended to write more (which may have become a book), but he had to attend to making peace among the Distributists. He found among other things Eric Gill trying to correct Fr. McNabb. So even though GKC wanted to emphasize the importance of Poland, he could not—and once again Poland was neglected, just the rest of Europe neglected it throughout the twentieth century—until Poland (and a pope from Poland) brought down the Soviet Empire.

maybe convenient to its conception of history is rudely broken and reversed, when one out of the customary batch of corpses happens to come to life. For this sort of pacifist never objects to violence so long as it takes the form of tyranny.[307]

When I first learnt lessons they were out of a history book full of the very things that always fascinated me most—fighting and coloured pageantry. I learnt the tales of Bruce and the Black Prince, and liked them so much that I acted them all the rest of the day and (when alone) for the rest of my life. But for all that I hated the hour of work as it arrived every morning with a hatred which I retain heartily to this day. The basic nuisance of work is not that the thing is intrinsically dull; it is that you want to do something else. My own present trade is more amusing than most, but I am often cursing an article as fast as I write it, because I have an important appointment with myself on the top of a neighbouring hill that overlooks the flats towards the sea.[308] And there are other things. For instance, when writing an article on John Milton, one of the most difficult subjects in the world, what could be more appropriate for my purpose, when I am dictating desperately to a typewriter in order to catch a train?"[309]

Alas, I am myself a rude and unlettered creature; I have lived a vain and thoughtless life without reading Perry on Cause or Beckitt on the Laws of Nature; I never pretended that I had been slap through Kelvin, Maxwell and Poincaré lately. Deprived of all these supports of authority, I have too often been driven back on the expedient of using my own judgment on many matters, talking with many kinds of people, trying to learn something from their faces and the apparent facts of their lives, noticing the number and duration of their fashions, trying to pick up something from the more obvious features of the street and even the school, and generally tending only too much, perhaps, to treat men of science as if they were men.[310]

Most of us have that difficulty of remembering people's faces or names sufficiently for the purposes of politeness. Personally I am in a curious position; it is neither their names, addresses, nor details of physique that I can remember. I always remember people by their

---

[307] *G.K.'s Weekly*, Nov. 26, 1927.
[308] *Daily News*, July 18, 1908.
[309] *Daily News*, Dec. 19, 1908.
[310] *New Witness*, Aug. 23, 1917.

opinions. I remember what the man said to me in some far-off argument which I must have had with him in the middle of Ludgate Circus. Therefore, if he says to me, with a sort of beaming cunning (as he almost always does), "Now you don't know who I am, you know," then I can truthfully assure him that I do know his most sacred thoughts, his central pillar of conviction, the very backbone of his soul. The trifling fact that I have not the faintest notion of his name, or what he is, or where I met him, the mere fact that in this popular phrase I do not know him from Adam (except by the costume), is in no sense an invalidation of my claim that I know him spiritually, as he would be known in heaven.

But I find that in practice this is not well received. It does not soothe such a man to say to him: "I don't know your name; but you are the man who believes that Mahomet was the real founder of Christianity." For the social purpose of breaking the ice such an opening is not to be compared to that of the weather. It is true, after all, in the most solemn and universal sense, that nothing but the weather can break the ice. Somehow my method does not work. A person is not pleased when I say to him: "I do not remember who you are; but I can tell you exactly what view of the Monroe Doctrine you had in the affair with Venesuela." Nor does it do when introducing the gentleman to somebody else to say: "This is the gentleman who believes that the Duke of Wellington was in the pay of Napoleon Bonaparte. I have not the pleasure of knowing his name." It ought to work out all right, like Parliamentary government, but somehow it doesn't. Hence it happens that my social tragedies in this respect increase rather than diminish; and men will not admit that I may reverence their intellects without remembering their surname.[311]

When a man figures for moment in the attitude of the *laudator temporis acti*,[312] he is almost always misunderstood. He is always supposed to be prepared to put everything back exactly as it was in the period which he praises. He is supposed to be holding an ancient society up as the exact model for a modern society. The truth is, of course, that his praise of the past is merely meant as a correction of the present, not as a complete substitute for it. He does not want to tie people to

---

[311] *Daily News*, Nov. 21, 1908.
[312] Latin for "one who praises the past times."

some particular dead century. But he does want to free people from this present existing century; to make them see it with independent eyes and judge it by larger comparisons. I want the modern middle class to see that its present compromise is nowhere the one possible scheme, and in many cases is becoming the one impossible.[313]

Intelligence is tested by the apprehension of truth, and raises the question of what is true; or by the relative importance of truths, and raises the question of what is important. I fancy the fundamental difference between Mr. H. G. Wells and myself is something like this. I believe in men beginning with a common basis of belief and going on to considerable development and variety. He seems to believe that men who have begun anyhow, and come from anywhere, and believe or disbelieve in anything, will by some process of pooling impressions arrive at an agreement at the end, though not at the beginning. I cannot see how this is really consistent with any rational process of thought at all; I certainly cannot imagine what the ultimate condition of thought is like. The only thing that appears quite tangible, in the general conception of control, is what is grimly and very priggishly called Birth-Control. And that, which is the one solid rock, is also the rock we split on. It is alone enough to illustrate the fact that people who differ at the beginning still differ at the end. Not merely by authority, but by every aboriginal instinct of my being, I feel this social solution to be bad. Anything healthy in me, that dislikes treason and assassination, tells me that if it could be proved that the full pleasure of producing life was forbidden to us, we should rise to the height of our tragedy and refuse the pleasure as well as the production. I wish I had as much intellectual as moral sympathy with his unquestionable humanity and earnestness and hope.[314]

Mr. George Bernard Shaw always criticises man from the position of one not of mankind. He never takes his stand with his fellow-creatures. He talks, acts and feels as one apart. He has no more conscience than Henry VIII had. Brilliant men like Shaw ought to be honoured with deferential calmness, but don't think of them as democratic. Personally, I'd rather be tried by a jury of ordinary men than by Shaw if I wanted justice and understanding.[315]

---

[313] *Daily News*, June 3, 1911.
[314] *G.K.'s Weekly*, June 2, 1928.
[315] *New York Tribune*, Sept. 15, 1912.

Bernard Shaw and I were both accused of something called Paradox. This merely meant that, being quite capable of reasoning, and even perhaps supposing (in our youth and innocence) that everybody else was capable of reasoning, we amused ourselves with short cuts and elliptical exaggerations, stating something really reasonable under a figure of unreason; on the model, say, of that fine paradox: "Give us the luxuries of life and we will dispense with the necessities." But the man who said that was quite lucid enough to know that "dispense" and "necessities" involve a formal-contradiction. So when Shaw said, "She was a born wife and mother; that is why her children left home," he expressed something super-rationally which he could have expressed rationally, and really thought rational. When I said, "Whatever is worth doing is worth doing badly," I meant merely to defy, but I could defend; and defend with reason.[316]

I hate to be influenced. I like to be commanded or to be free. In both of these my own soul can take a clear and conscious part: for when I am free it must be for something that I really like, and not something that I am persuaded to pretend to like: and when I am commanded it must be by something I know, like the Ten Commandments. But the thing called Pressure, of which the polite name is Persuasion, I always feel to be a hidden enemy. It is all a part of that worship of formlessness, and flowing tendencies, which is really the drift of cosmos back into chaos. I remember how I suddenly recoiled in youth from the influence of Matthew Arnold (who said many things very well worth saying) when he told me that God was "a stream of tendency." Since then I have hated tendencies: and liked to know where I was going and go there or refuse.[317]

---

[316] *G.K.'s Weekly*, May 7, 1932. GKC often misquotes other writers, but here he manages to misquote himself, and even misquote one of most famous quotations. The original is "If a thing is worth doing, it is worth doing badly." He first used the line in the *Daily News*, Oct. 18, 1901. When he used it again in the chapter "Folly and Female Education," in *What's Wrong with the World* (1910), it was already well known. In an interview in 1907, P. W. Wilson of the *Daily News* says to Frances: "The best thing your husband ever wrote [so he began] was that 'if a thing is worth doing at all—'" "It is worth doing badly," replied Mrs. Chesterton. "I know it well, because I have opened debates on the point and got everyone to agree. Look at children playing with paints," she continued, "and you will realise the truth of the paradox. Music and dancing and singing have all been banished from our lives because we are all afraid to do things badly." (But the interviewer also gets the quote wrong.)

[317] *G.K.'s Weekly*, Aug. 18, 1928.

We have read of some celebrated philosopher who was so absent-minded that he paid a call at his own house. My own absent-mindedness is extreme, and my philosophy, as is plain enough, is ecstatic in its sublimity. But I never quite managed to be as absent-minded as that. Of course I have quite constantly walked into another man's house, thinking it was my own house; my visits became almost monotonous. But walking into my own house and thinking it was another man's house is a flight of poetic detachment still beyond me.[318]

Sir Arthur Conan Doyle, by spreading the notion that practical logic must be unpoetical, may have encouraged the notion, too common already, that imagination must be absent-minded. It is a false and dangerous doctrine that the poet must be absent-minded.

I know all about it, because I am absent-minded myself. In fact, I once planned out a series of short stories, exactly on the same model as the short stories about Sherlock Holmes, and having titles similar to *The Adventure of the Speckled Band,* or *The Adventure of the Engineer's Thumb.* Only my stories were all intended to narrate not instances of marvelous observation, but instances of marvelous lack of observation. I was the Sherlock Homes of this series, and I had a Watson who continually broke out into respectful astonishment at the things that I failed to notice and the small details that I did not observe. He asked me in dazed admiration how I had managed not to post the letter that was given me that morning, or not to see the man into whom I had run in the street. Of course, I only waved my hand at him airily, and said, "You know my methods."

Once I remember changing into evening dress at the house of a friend of mine who is a priest of the Church of England.[319] On this occasion I largely arrayed myself in clerical costume, which I mistook

---

[318] *Daily News,* Jan. 28, 1911. GKC was famously absent-minded. Although he explains, "To be absent-minded is to be present-minded about something else," he does not excuse himself, because he does not consider being absent-minded to be a virtue. A true mystic, he says, should notice everything. He should be "socially alert" and "correctly dressed," because to be otherwise is to draw attention to oneself, which is not what he wanted. And yet he cannot help but draw attention to himself. ("Everyone seems to know you, Mr. Chesterton." "If they don't," with a sigh, "they ask.") But this does not prevent him from being able to laugh along with everyone else at the stories about his having to send a telegram to his wife asking where he is supposed to be, attempting to unlock his door with a corkscrew, and hailing a cab to take him to an address that was across the street.

[319] Rev. Conrad Noel, who married GKC and Frances, and was a longtime friend.

for my own dress clothes, because of the blackness of both suits. This incident (noted in my series under the title of *The Adventure of the Curate's Trousers*) would have made a very subtle study in the psychology of absentmindedness. I have also once asked for a cup of tea at the ticket office; this was narrated as *The Adventure of the Unreasonable Request*. There was another very good story which was called *The Adventure of the Pro-Boer's Corkscrew*. But I think I will not tell this, as, except among my friends, it might lay me open to misunderstanding. I can claim, therefore, to speak with a certain amount of authority on the subject of "Absence of Mind," and even to be under all the temptations that are possible in the case to represent absence of mind as allied to inspiration or nobility of character. But I do not believe it. I refuse to admire this characteristic in myself, merely confining myself with a grand and manly self-restraint to continue indulging it to its full extent. I should certainly be more poetical if I had more of the observation of Mr. Sherlock Holmes, just as he would be a better observer if he were a more poetical observer.[320]

It is but seldom that I read what I have written; and when I do, I generally find that I did not write it right. A panic seizes me in the presence of my own disproportionate pronouncements; and I think this fear must be fairly common among those who have to express themselves with haste. He who runs may read; but he who writes may have every reason to run. I have never repented of the principle maintained in anything I wrote; it is of my practice that I repent.[321]

Every man who writes (frequently and with any success) does drop into a trick of style; upon which he probably learns to rely too much, especially if he lives by writing and therefore writes in a hurry. That I have such a trick, a trick of sharp inversions and short sentences, is quite obvious; and is often a nuisance I can very well believe.[322] A really good epigram should be as carefully placed and as telling as a great gun in action. The most trivial woman cannot appear, so to speak, without being like the breaking of dawn. But a careful study of the ways of Nature has led us to be content with one dawn for one

---

[320] *Daily News*, Mar. 23, 1907.
[321] *G.K.'s Weekly*, Dec. 5, 1935. "He who runs may read" is a reference to Habakkuk 2:2. But you knew that.
[322] *New Age*, Nov. 26, 1908.

day.³²³ The art of rhetoric is one which I specially enjoy.³²⁴ Having certain arguments to offer, I make them as amusing as I can; that is, I am a buffoon to avoid being a bore. But I do not say these silly superficial things against an opponent.³²⁵ Most of us, I suppose, discover the badness of a cause chiefly by hearing the argument in favour of it. That, at least, is the quickest and most convenient way.³²⁶ I believe that the moralists arguing with the immoralists will have the best of the argument, because men cannot argue without doctrine any more than they can fight without discipline.³²⁷ I am in these matters a somewhat detached and almost academic person, and chiefly concerned to find out if people's ideas make sense, quite apart from whether they make peace or war. I am chiefly interested in knowing what thoughts are behind their actions, and whether those thoughts are clear and consistent along their own line.³²⁸

Personally, I am all for propaganda; and a great deal of what I write is deliberately propagandist. But even when it is not in the least propagandist, it will probably be full of the implications of my own religion; because that is what is meant by having religion. So the jokes of a Buddhist, if there were any, would be Buddhist jokes. So the love-songs of a Calvinistic Methodist, should they burst from him, would be Calvinistic-Methodist love-songs.

Catholics have produced more jokes and love-songs than Calvinists or Buddhists. That is because, saving their holy presence, Calvinists and Buddhists have not got so large or human a religion. But anything they did express would be steeped in any convictions that they do hold; and that is a piece of common sense which would seem to be quite self-evident; yet I foresee a vast amount of difficulty about it in the one isolated case of the Catholic Church.

To begin with, what I have said would be true of any other real religion; but so much of the modern world is full of a religiosity that is rather a sort of unconscious prejudice. Buddhism is a real religion

---

³²³ *Daily News*, Apr. 25, 1901. GKC knows the value of a good epigram, but part of that value is its rarity. To his critic's annoyance, he cannot follow his own advice, and his writing is bursting with epigrams. But I doubt it that makes it less effective. I appreciate a mountain of jewels. My goal is to distribute the riches.
³²⁴ *Illustrated London News*, Apr. 4, 1914.
³²⁵ *New Witness*, May 19, 1922.
³²⁶ *Daily News*, Apr. 28, 1906.
³²⁷ *Illustrated London News*, Apr. 2, 1927.
³²⁸ *Illustrated London News*, Sept. 16, 1933.

or at any rate a real philosophy. Calvinism was a real religion, with a real theology. But the mind of the modern man is a curious mixture of decayed Calvinism and diluted Buddhism; and he expresses his philosophy without knowing that he holds it.

We say what it is natural to us to say; but we know what we are saying; therefore it is assumed that we are saying it for effect. He says what it is natural to him to say; but he does not know what he is saying, still less why he is saying it. So he is not accused of uttering his dogma with the purpose of revealing it to the world; for he has not really revealed it to himself. He is just as partisan, he is just as particularist, he is just as much depending on one doctrinal system as distinct from another. But he has taken it for granted so often that he has forgotten what it is. So his literature does not seem to him partisan, even when it is. But our literature does seem to him propagandist, even when it isn't.

Suppose I write a story, let us hope a short story, say about a wood that is haunted by evil spirits. Let us give ourselves the pleasure of supposing that at night all the branches have the appearance of being hung with hundreds of corpses, like the orchard of Louis the Eleventh, the spirits of travellers who have hanged themselves when they came to that spot; or anything bright and cheery like that.

Suppose I make my hero, Gorlias Fitzgorgon (that noble character), make the sign of the cross as he passes this spot. Making the sign of the cross seems to me not only religiously right but artistically appropriate and psychologically probable. It is what I should do; it is what I conceive that my friend Fitzgorgon would do. I rather fancy it might be effective if the traveller saw with the mystical eye, as he saw the forest of dead men, a sort of shining pattern or silver tangle of crosses hovering in the dark, where so many human fingers had made that sign upon the empty air. But though I am writing what seems to me to be natural and appropriate and artistic, I know that the moment I have written it a great roar and bellow will go up with the word "Propaganda" coming from a thousand throats; and that every other critic, even if he is kind enough to comment on the story, will certainly add, "But why does Mr. Chesterton drag in his Roman Catholicism?"

My book on Chaucer, I fear is a rather rambling performance; great parts of it originally written from memory and afterwards insufficiently pulled together. However, I have a perfectly clear, logical, and consistent reason for regarding real democracy as the best government and our present sham democracy as worse than the feudal

Middle Ages. It certainly would not take me long to explain how there is more liberty in the Catholic Church than in the Modern State. But I do not explain all this in the book. My poor old book on Chaucer—already so parenthetical and diffuse. After all, it was supposed to be a book on Chaucer! It would have given me the wildest joy to interpose four or five chapters on the very hopeful prospect of a modern Catholic. Only—surely the critic would then have a real right to complain. But has he a right to complain because I happened to be writing about a mediaeval Catholic? There is no more question of "grabbing" Chaucer for Catholicism than of "grabbing" Confucius for China or Abraham Lincoln for America. The man came straight out of the very middle of the systems. Can it be wrong to discuss the systems in dealing with the man? We all have our limitations. I know nothing about music or mathematics; but I should not think a writer odd for dragging music into a book on Browning or mathematics into a book on Lewis Carroll. But the practical question of what is to be done with theology, when it does quite definitely come into history or biography, is particularly pressing in any case, because of the whole plan and point of my book.

At the very beginning I propound a problem of Chaucer, which is this: That the poet of ruder, harsher and (some say) more superstitious days was certainly more sane, more serene, more sensible than the poets in later days. Can anybody dispute it? From Shakespeare to Shelley, from Milton to Byron, the poet has grown more wild or bitter or extremist or exaggerative; till the very word poet almost came to mean madman. To this problem I propound, more or less tentatively, two or three solutions, or at least suggestions. (1) That Boethius and the philosophy of antiquity mixed more with mediaeval thought in practice than we commonly suppose. (2) That we now overrate the soothing effect of a simple religion; which is really a single religion and often a single doctrine. A man reposing in a rich and complex religion, with many balancing dogmas, may himself be more happy; nay, may himself be more simple. (3) One difference between mediaeval and post-mediaeval religion is this. The later system swept away all sins together. The man who was "saved" was saved simultaneously from his sense of having poisoned his mother and having got drunk at the fair. The older system tabulated sins; distinguished between the mortal and the venial and so on. Now I suggested that, just as this later certainly led to abuses of relativity and laxity, as in the Indulgences of "the gentle Pardoner," so it may have led to the Chaucerian knack of looking at all sides of a fault, and of taking some lightly, too, being a gentle Pardoner in a better sense.

Now these suggestions may be right or wrong; the critic probably thinks them wrong; nor did I at all aggressively offer them as right. But they are not irrelevant; they are not idiotic; they are not absurdities without reference to the argument. Above all, they are about Chaucer. They are my answers to the problem of Chaucer; and the question is not whether I have dragged them in when they are "only" religious; but whether I must cut them out because they are religious. What, in the name of common sense, is to be the attitude towards these great human influences of writers who happen to believe in them? Are they to be suppressed out of respect for the delicacy of those who do not believe in them? Is it irrelevant to connect Chaucer with Chaucer's religion, because it happens also to be my religion? Am I not to tell what I think is the truth about the poet because I also think it is the truth about the world?[329]

I may remark that all the quotations I give are probably wrong. I quote from memory both by temper and on principle. That is what literature is for; it ought to be a part of man.[330] There is a difference between misquotation from memory and misquotation from quoting a quotation. Misquotation is a proof that you love an author, that you do not need to read him. Verifying a quotation is done in offices by sub-editors, who look up books which they have not read before.[331] It is the most sincere compliment to an author to misquote him. It means that his work has become a part of our mind and not merely of our library. I have a strong suspicion that I forgot altogether to verify one or two quotations from Robert Louis Stevenson in a book I recently wrote on that subject; but I know it does not affect the argument and I cannot say that it very much affects me. The question is whether a critic misquotes an author because he has not read him, or because he has read him. In practice, as I have said elsewhere, it resolves itself into a division between two quite opposite types of error; those who quote

---

[329] *Observer*, Apr. 17, 1932.
[330] *Daily News*, Sept. 28, 1912.
[331] *Leeds Mercury*, Nov. 26, 1927.

from memory and those who only quote from quotations. But I prefer even the latter type, who is at least a sort of twisted traditionalist, to the correct person who looks up everything as if it were entirely new; and consults an author as he might consult a directory. He is the sort of man who never misquotes and always misunderstands.[332]

Most people would agree that even good writers can write too much, and that bad writers cannot write too little. Nevertheless, a particular problem has arisen in our own epoch, apart from the obvious practical complications that may arise in any epoch. Those who earn their living by writing, as I do, always write too much; on the other hand, there are writers at once more leisured and more laborious who write the same poem a hundred times, or even bring out three or four entirely different editions of the same book.

This modern habit of taking a detached image, with or without the elucidation of its indwelling idea, is to supersede the old reasoned arrangement of themes and thoughts. There is nothing to be said against it, except that there seems to be no end to it.

I was looking the other day through a large anthology, or collection, of the most modern and advanced American poems. Most of them consisted of short impressions, with one or two arbitrary details in irregular verse; and that was all. I do not mean that they were worthless; a thousand things of the sort are worth seeing and may be worth saying. A brown trickle from a gutter makes a pool in the street, reflecting half a scrap of sky; a black cluster of lamp-posts and top-hats is relieved against a strip of cold green sunset; the passing lights of a tram paint one side of a grey horse in a field a golden colour; a splash of green slime on a wall looks like sprawling fingers; and so on. Now, whether it sound egotistical or no, it is a fact that if I began to write little paragraphs in free verse on such things, I should never stop writing them. I should write thousands and thousands of them. I do not deny the truth of such sights; I am always seeing them. I do not deny the suggestiveness of such sights; I am often moved by them. I only say that if the mere recording of them constitutes poetry, there ought to be a vast amount more poetry and a great many more poets. But whether that prospect be a glorious or an alarming one, I will not venture on my own isolated example, to decide.[333]

---

[332] *G.K.'s Weekly*, Dec. 31, 1927.
[333] *Illustrated London News*, May 21, 1932.

Anyone who wishes to be an artistic journalist must enjoy the disadvantages of his trade; he must like the journalistic quality in journalism, its impressionism, its rapidity, its instinct for sensation, its eye upon the ordinary man. To consider "the man in the street" is not cynicism; it is democracy; I might almost say it is Christianity. Write for all the people, but do not write down to the people. Write up to the people, for the people is a king. These cynical editors would get far better work out of their subordinates if instead of telling them to take their work cynically, they told them to take it seriously; to get some sympathy with the awful humanity in the streets outside. A cynical journalist will give the people what they want when they ask for it. A serious journalist would give it [to] them before they asked for it. He would be at one with the thing for which he spoke; he would be himself the man in the street. A man may find out a great deal about public opinion if he is an extraordinary observer, but he will find out far more by being an ordinary one.[334]

I have occasionally in my life made jokes, and I have also occasionally been serious. And this, I had always understood, was the not unusual practice of my fellow-creatures. But I have discovered that this explanation is not considered sufficient in my case; I am always supposed to be engaged with some tortuous or topsy-turvy intention. When I state the dull truth about anything, it is said to be a showy paradox; when I lighten or brighten it with any common jest, it is supposed to be my solid and absurd opinion. If I ask a rational question of an opponent, it is considered a wild frivolity. But if I make an ordinary idle pun, it is gravely explained to me that my analogy is rather a verbal parallelism than a philosophic example of the operations of a common law. Thus I was in controversy lately with some writers on a certain journal who maintain that such a doctrine as that of miracles (let us say) is not a truth, but the symbol of a truth. I merely asked them, "What is the truth of which it is a symbol?" You would think that was a courteous, relevant, and reasonable question. The answer of the journal was to cast up its eyes and clasp its hands, and ask distractedly how it could be expected to argue with such a wild, elusive, ever-changing, fantastical, and irresponsible jester as myself. On the other hand, I casually summed up the distinction between the supernatural and the unreasonable by the phrase that one

[334] *Cassell's Magazine*, December 1906.

might believe that a Beanstalk grew up to the sky without having any doubts about how many beans make five. For this a writer, intelligible and presumably human, actually rebuked me, gravely asking me whether I believed in the Beanstalk! When I make common jokes they are regarded as highly uncommon opinions. When I state solid opinions, they are regarded as giddy jokes.[335]

My business here is to warn people against being caught by catchwords.[336] I do not pose as a pioneer of new things; but really the things I say still seem quite new to quite a number of people. I have no particular pretence or pride in being a revolutionist; it is my opponents who represent me as a revolutionist. I come with nothing but the mildest platitudes; the obvious idea of one man one hat and one man one house. It is the enemy who flatters my aged vanity, by telling me that these things are the paradoxes of an earthly paradise. I come uttering homely and somewhat banal sentiments about the charm of children or the old fireside. It is the critics who assure me that by encouraging children I am calling up demons of destruction; or that poking at the old fireside will certainly set fire to the house.[337] One of the chief problems of our time is the prevalence of popular ideas which are really only the reversal of normal ideas.[338] Every revolution is only a reversion to the normal; every rebel is only trying to be human; every extraordinary man is making a wild effort to be ordinary.[339]

For decades we have been tolerating things that all ages have denounced. We have not been progressing towards a morality that nobody understood; we have been violating a morality that everybody understood. And our real progress will begin when we know we are on the wrong road.[340] When I say "we" I do not mean "I." When I say "we" I mean corporate human society, male and female: the public, in short, to which all journalists are supposed to address themselves.[341]

I was once invited to participate in a debate, but the sponsor expressed the earnest wish that nothing should be introduced that was at all controversial. I naturally went away in a thoughtful mood, considering

---

[335] *Illustrated London News*, May 21, 1910.
[336] *Illustrated London News*, Feb. 20, 1932.
[337] *G.K.'s Weekly*, Oct. 1, 1927.
[338] *Illustrated London News*, Apr. 27, 1935.
[339] *Daily News*, Nov. 13, 1901.
[340] *New Witness*, Aug. 15, 1919.
[341] *New Witness*, June 5, 1913.

how I could most carefully ensure that there should be nothing controversial in a controversy. What is a controversial statement? Is it something that somebody might controvert, or something that we ourselves should controvert, or something that the majority would controvert? It seems obvious that anybody can make a non-controversial statement controversial simply by contradicting it. In practice the rule is practical enough, no doubt. It is simply that anything criticising the rich is controversial and anything justifying the rich is non-controversial.[342]

I have spoken on a hundred platforms, not only lecturing to Americans, who are nearly always kind, but to Jingo patriots and political opponents who are not always kind. I know the only way to speak then is to hold your head up and shout and be violent and very emphatic; and it is very great fun. But the whole point of broadcasting is that it is just the opposite. It is best when quiet and conversational.[343]

At the central wireless station in London I have sometimes been allowed to indulge in what is called broadcasting; an art much less difficult than the art of broadcast sowing, its agricultural counterpart, which can only be done by really clever peasants and farmers' labourers. However, I generally got through my job without catastrophe, for it is a social relation in which the audience cannot possibly hit you back. And the other day, to my profound astonishment, I was informed that those who had already suffered the experience of hearing me were supposed to crave the additional experience of seeing me. Whether or no the crowd really craved to see the monsters from whom these strange sounds had come forth, all the more notorious broadcasters were to be paraded in a sort of film, to show to cinema frequenters all the darkest secrets of the inner life of Broadcasting House.

I was first photographed making horrible faces into the microphone, and then they very politely asked if I would be photographed again walking into the room. I said I could perhaps do it with a lighter and more buoyant step if I were supposed to be walking out of the room.

And just then all my unworthy criticisms were struck dumb on my lips by the sight of the very small boy who was to escort me. He was like the boy who wanders through American hotels with the cry of "Calling Mr. Pickleson." But this boy at least had found his

---

[342] *G.K.'s Weekly*, Nov. 19, 1927.
[343] *New York American*, July 26, 1935.

Mr. Pickleson. Never have I seen such radiant complacency on a human countenance.

And then I suddenly thought: Of course, *he* will be in the film. He will actually like being in the film. His mother will come to see it. His grandmother will come to see it. I felt ashamed of my reluctance in the face of that direct democratic enjoyment.

I followed him reverently, for he was the star performer. I was not much of a Dante, however appropriate the Inferno. But for Virgil, my guide through the abyss, it was really a poem.[344]

It is not always wrong even to go, like Dante, to the brink of the lowest promontory and look down at hell. It is when you look up at hell that a serious miscalculation has probably been made.[345] Dante defended the Roman Empire as the best human government, on the definite ground that the best human government would probably crucify God. Caesar had to be lawful; because Christ had to be killed by law.[346]

There is a great passage in the *Paradiso* of Dante, which I wish I knew enough Italian to appreciate or enough English to translate. But I would commend it to those who may fancy that my emphasis on this exceptional quality of man in the universe is a mere modern whitewashing of a mediaeval superstition; and especially to those who have been taught in laborious detail, by learned and very stupid historians, to regard mediaevalism as narrow and enchained. For it runs roughly like this:

> The mightiest gift that God of his largesse
> Made in creation, perfect even as He,
> Most of His substance, and to Him most dear,
> He gave to the Will and it was Liberty.[347]

---

[344] *New York American*, June 27, 1935. The clips of GKC walking through a hallway with his young escort at BBC and speaking in the microphone are in the 1935 documentary *BBC: The Voice of the Nation.*

[345] *Daily News*, Oct. 16, 1909.

[346] *Hearth and Home*, Oct. 17, 1912.

[347] *America*, Mar. 23, 1929. This indicates that GKC read Dante in the original, as he has made his own translation of this passage rather than quoting from some other published translation, and he is remembering the original Italian as he performs his translation. He does this with other foreign writers such as Victor Hugo, and even manages to keep their rhyme scheme while doing an extemporaneous translation.

We live now among poets who cannot conceive of the universal power containing any larger feelings than their own; they cannot imagine, in the tremendous words of Dante, "the love that drives the sun and all the stars," for the loves of which they write would not drive thistledown.[348]

I do rather doubt whether young journalists are joyously capping each other's quotations from Toplady's sermons on Calvinism. But eager young men do still quote Aquinas, just as they still quote Aristotle. I have heard them at it. And certain ideas are flying about, even in the original prose of St. Thomas, as well as in the poetry of Dante.[349] Dante, being a deeper thinker than Milton, said that the worst punishment of the demons was that they were unable to philosophise.[350]

There is plenty of philosophy in A. A. Milne's books, when they are not books of philosophy. I myself have adopted as a sort of sacred motto or maxim one of the rhymed meditations of the Pooh, when he was considering whether he should call on his friend Roo or not. Many a time I have murmured to myself, when a day of leisure gave me the chance of walking about the garden or taking the train to town:

> I could spend a happy morning
> Seeing Roo.
> I could spend a happy morning Being Pooh.
> So it doesn't really matter
> If I don't get any fatter (And I don't get any fatter)
> What I do.

It is not only the personal appropriateness of the last stipulation that has wedded me to these words. It is also the grasp of a reality not often expressed in poetry; save perhaps by Burns when he wrote boldly: "I have been happy thinking." One of the truly good and glorious things, for which to thank God, is the possession of that power to spend a happy morning being Pooh. Robert Hugh Benson expressed it, a little too tartly, I think, when he said, "There are only two kinds of people, those who like solitude and those who hate it;

---

[348] *Daily News*, June 11, 1901.
[349] *G.K.'s Weekly*, Nov. 3, 1928.
[350] *G.K.'s Weekly*, Apr. 6, 1933.

because there are only two kinds of people, the full and the empty." But I prefer Monsignor Benson to Mr. Milne when it comes to a logical and intelligible explanation of the relation of these things to theology. Meanwhile, those of us who really happen to have a theology and a philosophy will find ourselves in an ironical position. All the irreligious people will be drawing attention to religion; and it will soon be left to us to draw attention to the importance of other things.

Believing in fidelity to an ancient tradition of truth, about the fundamentals of faith and morals, I am trying to bring a little light and liberty into the discussion of daily politics. I am trying to get people to think for themselves about the things on which they can think fruitfully; their own homes and habits and local rights and relation to the township and the land. But the plutocratic Press, which brags of being emancipated about theology and philosophy, is tame and timid enough about politics and economics. It will swagger about sweeping away doctrine and dogma and boast of ranging over all religions and soaring above all creeds. But when it comes to the plain facts about the shops in the street or the shares in the market, it walks in a very narrow rut and it walks delicately.[351]

There are moods when I can sympathise with a quivering nerve of nobility running through the unnatural state of Nietzsche; especially when it quivered in protest against something really ignoble in the smug utilitariansim of the nineteenth century. If I were locked up alone for ten years with Herbert Spencer, I might come out feeling a little like Nietzsche. But that is only another way of saying that if I were locked up for ten years with Herbert Spencer, I might come out raving mad. So long as I consider myself sane I shall consider myself superior, merely in point of spiritual freedom and flexibility, to these prophets in constrained and fantastic postures. For the madman might almost be defined as the man in whom the mood has become the mind.

The one most exalted and enthusiastic mood, merely considered as a mood, is that of the man who can affirm and witness to a truth above all his moods. To enjoy this a man must have a philosophy. But the narrow philosophy is that which only allows of one mood, such as rebellion, or disdain, or even despair. The large philosophy is that

[351] *G.K.'s Weekly*, May 12, 1928.

which allows of many moods; such as charity, or zeal, or patience. And it is so with what I count the largest of philosophies; which can be in revolt against the Prince of the World while it is loyal to the Creator of the World; which can love the world like St. Francis, or renounce the world like St. Jerome. The point is that the Christian not only has mirth and indignation and compassion and comradeship and individual isolation; but he has them consistently; and each of them has a clear place in his theory of things.

It was a common saying among the old Victorian agnostics that men were better than their creeds. It is a fortunate feature of modern confusion that men are better than their doubts. But above all, it is certainly true that men are broader than their doubts. For Man is a much larger thing than myriads of modern philosophies; and the philosophy that can contain him must be something larger than the world.[352]

The hardest kind of work is really to work with one's head, not with one's pen or spectacles or paste-pot or scissors or British Museum reading ticket. To write down no word that does not mean something; to write no sentence without a point to it; to echo no mere fashionable phrases; to pick living adjectives; to select real analogies; not to pad by so much as an inch; this is really to work hard. Being accurate can be delegated. It is not dishonourable to put some private error into a book, but it is dishonourable not to put any private truth into it. We writers are paid to cut off bits of ourselves, and we must deliver the goods, if they are pounds of flesh.[353]

Most of those who know me have been able to distinguish me at a glance from a haggard and emaciated genius, starving in a garret and spitting out curses against the critics and the human race. Many could testify that I am not haggard; most would add that I am not a genius; some would conceive that I am not naturally a hater of my kind. But there is always a danger of calling up this image before the mind if ever a man who has written a book makes any remark about the reviews upon the book. Generally speaking, it is a very good rule not to do it. It is true that the genius who never replies to critics is an even more offensive person than the genius who is always replying to critics. But an ordinary human being who happens to write books may

---

[352] *New Witness*, Oct. 15, 1920.
[353] *Nation* (UK), Oct. 3, 1908.

happen also to read newspapers. He may happen to notice something in a newspaper that interests him, and he should not, I think, be compelled to renounce his interest because the note concerns a book he had written. Anyhow, I noticed a remark in a newspaper the other day in connection with something I had perpetrated called *The Everlasting Man*, and, while I should not dream of attempting to defend my book, I consider myself entitled to defend my opinion.

It concerned the mysterious but also amusing subject of animals. My thesis was roughly summed up in the statement: "The more we look at a man as an animal the less he will look like one." But it also suggested that when we look at him for the very first time, in the full and frank use of our common-sense before it is complicated with sophistry, we never *do* look at him as an animal. It is proved by the very fact that we say "animals" when we mean the other animals. If somebody said, "There is another animal in the garden," and you found it was the Vicar, you would be surprised; and no subsequent explanation about the Vicar's evolutionary origin and biological structure could completely efface the memory of a departure from common speech. If somebody said, "Come and see the animals," and you found that his animals were his aunts, you would think it was a joke; you might possibly think it was a disrespectful joke; but you would not think it was simply a serious thesis about the unity of nature. I say we are in danger of forgetting this first fact, the enormous distinction and disproportion of man in relation to other creatures. In other words, the animality of man is an afterthought. Say, if you like, that the achievements of this animal have been so amazing and miraculous that they have stunned and stupefied us, so that we forget that he is an animal. We do not in a racial sense remember our relation to the animals, or our rise out of the animals, if there was one. It is just barely possible, of course (as I also delicately suggested) that we do not remember it because it never happened. But I am not specially concerned with that doubt here; and even in my unfortunate book I was not mainly concerned with it. I was concerned with pointing out that, if man is a beast, he is something like a monster—an exceptional and extravagant apparition preternatural, and quite out of the scale of things.

Now, I should have thought that point was simple, for it professedly only points out what is self-evident. And yet it is exactly that simple and self-evident thing that I do not seem to have been able to convey.

For an excellent evolutionary critic in the *Morning Post* gave a reply that somehow startles me, as it startles one to find one is talking to a stone-deaf person. His review was very well written and far more friendly than I had any particular right to expect. He wrote like a scholar and a man who understood ideas. What puzzled me was that the critic told me, with great gravity, that it was not quite true that the lower animals were entirely without traces of our spiritual or artistic tendencies, because if I would read about the researches of M. Fabre,[354] or some distinguished biologist, I should find that such signs had already been noted and tabulated.

Now that is exactly what I mean by not seeing the self-evident. That is what I mean by missing the point. For the point I mean is a point like the peak of the Matterhorn. It is a gigantic spike standing up sharp and solid in the sky; and that is apparently why people cannot see it. All that my critic can tell me is that if I were to follow out certain experiments recorded by a particular naturalist in a particular book, I might begin to find for the first time what some suppose to be traces of a resemblance between the human and the sub-human mind. But I do not need to follow anything, or read anything, or specially go out of my way even to notice anything, in order to notice the superiority of the human to the sub-human mind. He tells me that if I had watched a monkey, say, for as many years on end as did an inexhaustible French naturalist, I should see he was in some ways like a man. But that is the whole point. How long should I have to watch a man before I saw he was not a monkey?

The man would have managed in the first fifteen minutes to do a whole wonderland of things that exist nowhere in the world except in him. It is this striking and outstanding disproportion that I think is in danger of being forgotten. Whether he put on his hat, or looked at his watch, or lit a cigarette, or sat down in a chair, or did any other ordinary action, he would be working miracles as compared with the world before he came. There is no question of *studying* that prodigy in order to see that it is a prodigy. These are not facts we find out, but facts from which we could not flee; these are not disputable traces, but indisputable truths. Nobody could be so stupid as not to see them, though people sometimes become so clever as to forget them.

---

[354] Jean-Henri Fabre (1823–1915) was a French entomologist.

Now I do not need to be told that many of the higher animals have been discovered by some distinguished French naturalist to have many of the moods and fine shades of human nature. I am not a distinguished French naturalist, but I have a dog. Nobody could be a week in the house with my dog without knowing that he performs some mental operations in much the same fashion as his master, only a little quicker. He loves his friends, though I am inclined to doubt whether he prays for his enemies. He certainly feels, and in his way he certainly thinks. Whether he reasons rather depends on the definition of the term. In one sense he reasons as well as anybody else—that is, he infers one thing from another thing, as that there may be a cat in a tree to-day because there was one yesterday, or that picking up a hat points probably to going for a walk. I should be inclined to say that he does not concern himself with reason in the sense of abstraction. He knows that a ball rolls in different directions, and so do those who have to throw it for him. He knows that the wheels of motorcars go round, and he has discovered by a slight and salutary accident that it is well to allow them to do so unimpeded. That is certainly the scientific method of discovery, and he has made that discovery in practical mechanics. But I do not think he ever says, "A ball is round all ways, and that is why it rolls all ways; a wheel is only a section of a globe, and that is why it goes one way."

But whatever causes the difference, there is the difference; and I say that the difference is a division—a real distinction of kind and not a degree. A vague sense of degree may produce only an impression of similarity. A sense of proportion shows us a prodigy. It is a question of fact about one of the outstanding features of the universe. And it is not an answer to a man staring in admiration at the Matterhorn to say that he might see crystals of the same shape through a microscope.[355]

Miss Maud Royden reviewed *The Everlasting Man*, and was in a state of pardonable indignation about that literary outrage. She said, in the first place, that reading my book was like moving through a fog, with occasional detonations and flares. I am far from suggesting that the only fog through which I am moving is the fog of Miss Royden's mind; but I think it might be said, in a more general sense, of that thing (already rather old-fashioned) which calls itself the modern

[355] *Illustrated London News*, Oct. 31, 1925.

mind. Whatever else the world is in at present, it is in a fog; and the future of this society, this controversy, and, I will add, this organ of controversy, is increasingly difficult to predict from hour to hour. But it is not our fault that there is a fog. The train knows where it wants to go to well enough. Only it cannot get there quickly, because there are very serious surrounding dangers in a society full of a sort of silent explosion, where refuse hangs in the very air; which is the definition of a fog. But Miss Royden does not know where we want to go to, and she pulls the communication cord with something resembling frenzy. But most of her shocks are merely due to our not running exactly in the old grooves. That is why she naturally prefers Wells's World-Wide Excursion Tour. She is wrong, by the way, in saying I dismissed Mr. Wells's history as having no outline. In my final criticism of *The Outline of History* I did not say it had no outline; I said it had the wrong outline.

But her other image is still more important and profound; so much so that I will quote her own words. "To many of us history reads an ambiguous lesson. It shows progress and reaction so balanced as to make the future uncertain indeed. But to such, the longer view of science gave a different hope. We might, with hope renewed, look at the whole of the pit whence we were digged, and looking, take courage to believe that at last Mankind might grow to the measure of the stature of the fullness of Christ." There seems to be an idea that my book denied Evolution; though I explained two or three times in the course of it that it did not. But if this is Miss Royden's assertion of Evolution, as against someone denying it, it is a most extraordinary one. Because a certain creature cannot improve when he is really trying to improve (or at least when he knows what he is doing and has the science and social direction to do it)—therefore we must believe that a creature improved through unknown ages, when he did not know what he was doing, when he had neither will nor wits nor principle of improvement in himself; when he was something like a blind monster of the slime or the sea. Well, such a creature may have so evolved, for all I know, and for all I ever said to the contrary. But I'm hanged if I can see why we must believe that he has evolved merely because he has not progressed. And apparently we must also believe that in some strange future (after we have failed to progress or left off trying) the same prehuman trend will inevitably go on, until merely by the biological process (whatever it was) which eventually gave a giraffe a long neck or a rhinoceros a horn on his nose, we shall all have reached the same divine nature as Jesus Christ. And when I venture to doubt this extraordinary dogma, and decline to admit that I must believe anything of the sort, Miss Royden pathetically reproaches me with "jeering" at her only "hope." She wants there to be evolution, as others want there to be inspiration or immortality or infallibility or all sorts of things; but most of us have some sort of reason beyond our own wish. We used to be told that Darwinism was proved and we must accept it, even if it seemed hopeless. Now it is being disproved,[356] Miss Royden clings to it as her only hope. But I shudder to think what Huxley would have said to her, if she had told him that evolution followed the line of ethics and that biology would some day turn every man into Jesus Christ.

But there is another interesting point in her remarks; which is the real reason why I mentioned them here. She says that man, though apparently discouraged by contemplating that part of his history which he happens to know anything about, can yet revive his spirits and feel cheerful again by "looking into the pit" from whence he came; that is, comparing himself with slugs and slimy seabeasts; and feeling that he is better than that anyhow. Now, in saying that, I do believe she has put her finger on the nerve; she has exposed, I had almost said betrayed, the truth about the whole subconscious excitement round the evolutionary legend. It is a way of comforting ourselves, amid the wickedness and the unclean cruelty of all the modern industrial world, by deliberately dwelling on things lower

---

[356] It is important to note that GKC makes a distinction between Darwinism in particular and evolution in general. "There is an element of evolutionism in the universe; and I know of no religion or philosophy that ever entirely ignored it." (*Daily Herald*, Jan. 19, 1914.) "Darwinism was only biological conjecture for overcoming some difficulties in the very ancient doctrine of evolution." (*Daily News*, June 26, 1909.) "It is obvious that there is an element of evolution in nature.... But the actual effect of Darwinism, on the generation following Darwin, was only a vague fashionable feeling that everything was evolution and that evolution was everything." (*Illustrated London News*, May 29, 1920.) "A vague Darwinism has communicated its doubt without fully communicating its doctrine, has succeeded in its attempt to question, while failing in its attempt to explain. Of the narrow, materialistic Darwinism, one may say that nothing remains of it except the damage it has done." (*Illustrated London News*, Aug. 24, 1912.) He says evolution may be a description, but it is not an explanation. But he does not dispute evolution; he disputes Darwinism. And as a matter of fact, while there are various schools of evolutionary thought, there are almost no scientists who fully embrace classic Darwinism.

than ourselves, whether they are legendary or real. It is more pleasant to think about slugs than about slums; and to be able to say that even a man in a slum is able to do many things, such as talk and bet and read the *Daily Mail*, which are rare in the daily life of a slug. The man who puts up the slum rents is supposed to murmur to himself, "But I am already more idealistic than a jelly-fish." The man who has to pay the slum rent is expected to whisper, "But at least I have more money than was possessed by a mammoth." That is why the plutocratic powers, the newspaper-proprietors and the self-educated millionaires, the big publishers and especially the American sort of philanthropists, are all so keen on such "culture." That is why they insist that people should have what they call Education especially about what they call Evolution. That is why the world knows more about Mr. H. G. Wells as a second-rate historian than as a first-rate artist and visionary. That is why his Utopias are less widely circulated than his Outline of History. That is why the modern patrons of letters will always eagerly publish, advertise, illustrate, translate, re-duplicate and syndicate an evolutionary history of that sort, and announce and adorn it with fictitious portraits of primitive apes and pre-historic men. It is obviously the interest of the rich and the rulers to blacken the past; and they have to blacken it very much to make it worse than the present.

All this evolutionary education on the cheap is simply the propaganda of Capitalism. Simple-minded Capitalists are sometimes heard to say that we should teach the discontented workers political economy. It is far more effective to teach them biology or history; and teach it wrong. The plutocrat will always bring wealth in bulk to back up this sort of cheap science against literature and philosophy. That is why the libraries of Carnegie were always conditioned by exclusions, aimed against the language of Plato or the theology of St. John. That is why big newspapers do not ask for theology from theologians who possess it, but from popular novelists who have none. Of course, this is not the motive of Mr. Wells when he ties himself to the theory of Natural Selection or of Miss Royden when she ties herself to the philosophy of Mr. Wells. But it is the reason why one of his worst books is one of his best-sellers. It is the reason why the sort of backing he could never have got for the noble nightmare of *The Time Machine* is given to a larger and later work, which is in a very different sense a machine, and in a very different sense a figment of time. That is why so much less fuss was made about his supremely true fictions than about his very fictitious history. And if we were only concerned with telling slaves to be cheerful because they were once chimpanzees, and not concerned with telling them to be ashamed because they were once free men, if we could tell them that the disappearance of the yeoman was a happy prelude to the arrival of the superman, and that by shedding the tests and standards of the Guilds we are only going on towards evolving into Jesus Christ, we also could utter a more comfortable prophecy and achieve a more practical reward. But we shall remain in what seems to us a more responsible function; not looking down into the pit from which we were digged; but into that other and deeper pit into which we may yet descend.[357]

While I was writing *The Everlasting Man*, I came across a very learned, and I doubt not a very reliable, article on "Religion and Primitive Culture." What does the word "primitive" mean? Does it mean that the modern savages have only just begun to exist? Does it mean that the Sandwich Islanders have only just left the Garden of Eden, or that their tails have only just dropped off in accordance with Darwinian evolution? Or does it mean that we take it for granted that prehistoric men were just like Sandwich Islanders, and then start out to prove from Sandwich Islanders exactly what prehistoric men were like? There might be a sense in the word "primitive" if it meant "near the beginning." But what are the Sandwich Islanders near the beginning of, as they are obviously not near the beginning of the universe or the Sandwich Islands? There must be a meaning in the word prehistoric, if it means before the beginning of our history. But it obviously cannot apply to the Sandwich Islanders, who were only discovered at the end of our history. If it be a benefit to be written about in books, the Sandwich Islanders are in full enjoyment of that felicity.

I think it will be found that these terms, so far from being scientific terms, are literary and colloquial terms of the very loosest sort. The truth is that the whole misuse of the term "primitive" rests on an assumption; the assumption that the men we call savages have remained exactly in the condition of the first men on the earth. I have often seen

---

[357] *G.K.'s Weekly*, Jan. 2, 1926.

this assumed, but I have never seen it proved. It does not seem to me particularly probable on the face of it. If we have changed so much, surely they may have changed at least a little. But anyhow, the philosopher cannot argue in a circle, and first assume that the two things can be called by the same name in order to prove they are the same.[358]

I grieve to say that I must again exhibit the exceedingly bad taste of mentioning *The Everlasting Man* and answering another journalistic comment upon it. My real motive is simply that I think the subject much more interesting than the book.

A critic in the *Times* said, with many graceful concessions, that it was all very well for me to glorify Christendom because it had resisted Islam, but it would be equally easy to retort that Islam had resisted Christendom. He almost playfully suggested that I should write as a companion volume a History of Islam. It was doubtless a very legitimate piece of chaff at the expense of my journalistic readiness to write on all sorts of subjects of which I know nothing. That, I imagine, is almost the definition of a journalist. But, though I may not know very much about Islam, I do know something about what I said about Islam. And I venture to say that on this point the *Times* reviewer is not very accurate. If he can bring himself to the exceedingly tiresome effort of opening my book again after he has reviewed it (a thing inevitably revolting to any reviewer of proper tastes and traditions) he will see he is mistaken about what I actually said. I never based my sense of the *superiority* of Christendom to Islam on the fact that it had resisted Islam. And, curiously enough, the only thing I was really trying to prove, in the passage about Christendom resisting Islam, was one which could be proved quite as well from Islam resisting Christendom.

What I maintain about resistance to Islam is this. I said that people have tried to explain Christianity in various ways by saying it was not merely Christian. Some say it was Roman; as they put it, the Church is but the ghost of the Empire sitting on the ruins of Rome. Others say it is merely Buddhist or Manichean, an infusion out of Asia in the general melting down of the old civilisation. And others, again, say it is merely what Matthew Arnold called the influence of Hebraism. He would have said that Hebraism prevailed over Hellenism, when

---

[358] *Illustrated London News*, May 9, 1925.

Christianity prevailed over Paganism. Or, as Disraeli put it, the Semitic spirit prevailed and imposed its one God in place of all the gods of Greece. To this I answer that the Christian Church proved itself independent of all these things because it was at war with all these things. Christianity was Christianity; it was not Hebraism, because it struggled to the death with Hebraism; it was not Manicheanism, because it fought like fury against the Manichees. The Church was the Church; it was not the Empire, because it defied the Empire—not only at the beginning, when the Emperors were pagan, but also afterwards, when the Emperors became Arian. It is not the ghost of the Roman Empire sitting on its own grave, for a very simple reason. Amid all the wild and weird ghost-stories that have been told, nobody ever told a story about a man fighting for his life and being killed by his own ghost. And the world did see enacted the actual story of the heretic Emperors fighting for their life against the religion risen from the dead. So, in the same way, I argued about Islam. I said the Church was certainly not merely an attack of Hebraism upon Hellenism, because when there really was such an attack the Christians may be said to have fought fiercely on the side of Hellenism. The Christian creed was not merely the Semitic spirit rushing West, because, when the Semitic spirit did undoubtedly and unmistakably rush West, all the Christians lived and longed and strove only to drive it back into the East. In other words, if the Church was only a vanguard of Eastern fanaticism, it was a vanguard that unaccountably waged war on its own rearguard without stopping for a thousand years. It seems only sane to suppose that these were not two forms of the Semitic spirit, but two very different spirits. I will not say that one of them was an Anti-Semitic spirit, for the word has another and much sillier significance, and is a signal for all the fools on both sides.

Now that argument may be right or wrong, but it is merely a matter of fact that the *Times* criticism does not touch it.

My reasons for thinking Christendom *superior* to Islam are stated in a totally different part of the book, and are a totally different sort of reasons. They have nothing to do with the fact that Christendom resisted Islam, either successfully or unsuccessfully. I am not such a fool as to suppose that mere fighting could prove a creed to be true, especially in a fight where both the false creed and the true produced such splendid fighters. I think Christianity truer than Islam on a general view of truth. And this also was what I said in my very rambling and unsatisfactory book, as anybody can find out by the painful and laborious experience of reading it. But since a barefoot pilgrimage to the Holy Land, or the sufferings of the Crusaders in the burning desert, may well seem a less toilsome way of arriving at the truth, I will quote one or two of the things that I really did say when I really was trying to show that our religion is more philosophical than the creed of the great Arabian. I said that Christianity contains more; that things exist in it side by side which are separated and solitary in other systems. "Islam may be equally military; it does not even pretend to be equally metaphysical and subtle." Or, again, I said, "Where is Our Lady of the Moslems, a woman made for no man and set above all angels?" It is therefore, I would submit, an injustice to represent me as basing the Christian case upon a mere boasting about the battlefields of Syria or brandishing of the battleaxe of King Richard. I base the Christian case not upon a war, but upon a peace; and especially on that most paradoxical of all forms of peace, the harmony between peace and war. I prefer the Crusader to the Sheik and the Cross to the Crescent, because (if I may repeat the outrage of quoting myself) "in the soul of St. Louis the lion lay down with the lamb." But this shall be my last outrage; save under intolerable provocation, I will not offend again by a defence. I merely think it worth while to note that on a not unimportant historical question the real case for Christendom still stands, and that it may be defensible to defend what I actually said, where even the most scholarly and responsible critics may attack what I did not say.[359]

If the egoism is excusable, I am myself an Englishman (which some identify with an egoist) and I have done my best to praise and glorify a number of English things; English inns, English roads, English jokes and jokers; even to the point of praising the roads for being crooked or the humour for being Cockney; but I have invariably written, ever since I have written at all, against the cult of British Imperialism; especially at the acute crises when it was being practically applied to the Irish or the Boers.[360]

---

[359] *Illustrated London News*, Nov. 7, 1925.
[360] *G.K.'s Weekly*, May 16, 1931.

If I may again be permitted a piece of egoism, I generally am consistent.[361] I am not a number of other things on which I have been complimented by friends, and, strangely enough, especially by foes. I hate paradoxes; it was a slander to say that I was dazzling and elusive; none but a few sneering enemies have called me brilliant; but I am consistent. I have, as had my happier fathers, some notion of a general plan of human life, the parts of which are rationally related to each other; and what I say in one place about one point will generally be found to have a connection with anything I said in another place on another point. I mention the matter, merely because this seems to be the one normal and even prosaic quality of the mind, which has disappeared entirely from a multitude of much more brilliant minds. It is really a paradox (I say it with reluctance) that the modern world has completely failed in its mental communications, at the very moment when it has perfected its material communications. It can carry a cable across the Atlantic or conduct an expedition to the North Pole. But it cannot carry an argument across the tea-table without getting it entangled like a cat's-cradle; or conduct a search for truth without going to pieces at the start instead of the finish. And then it can only pick up the pieces, and say that one or two of them do not fit, without attempting to find the pattern.[362]

I know not whether the egotistical reflection ought to cause rejoicing or remorse. But I cannot help reflection on a real fact: that many things I once regarded as unpopular truths have since achieved triumphs, and yet I do not feel altogether triumphant. I have been in some fairly hard-hitting controversies in my time; nor were the heads to be hit altogether inconspicuous. But since then the things or

---

[361] Indeed, GKC knew he was consistent, which is why he was surprised one day when he opened a paper and saw the headline "G.K.C.'s Retreat" by a writer who went by "H.S." He responded: "On some popular papers, I believe, the article is written by one person and the headline by somebody else. But whoever wrote it, nobody made the smallest attempt to support what it states or justify anything that it implies. To talk of my retreating from somewhere obviously implies that I have retracted something. 'H.S.' cannot produce, and does not attempt to produce, any example of anything that I have retracted. He does not quote a single word, or suggest the existence of a single thing, which I have stated formerly and do not state now. He does not attempt to show that what I recently said was anything but what I have always said. This does not surprise me, of course; because I know it is what I have always said. But surely it is for him to make some faint attempt to suggest what my previous position was, before he accuses me of retreating from it." (*G.K.'s Weekly*, Nov. 19, 1927.)

[362] *G.K.'s Weekly*, May 30, 1931.

persons which I set out with a Christian hope of hitting lightly in the nose have often been hit much harder than I ever wanted them hit. Or they have been hit in the wrong place or in the wrong way, or in such a manner that the repercussion hit somebody else much better than themselves. I have hated the spirit of Prussianised Germany all my life, and in times when my countrymen largely professed to like it. And I am happy to say that I have lived to see it overthrown and partially punished in a great war. But I have never understood why civilised Austria and Hungary were treated worse than the northern barbarians who are now once more besieging Vienna. I have been accused in my youth of a desire to bait or beat the Jews: but they have since been actually baited and beaten by the same northern barbarians, and things have been done to them that I should never have dreamed of defending. I have hated the multi-millionaire type of Capitalism, with its Trusts and rings, as it flourished most prosperously in America; but I hated much more the flattery which favoured these things, and was known to all that period as the Spirit of Optimism.

Since then I have seen America itself reduced to a condition in which it is difficult to be an optimist, and not so cosy as it was even to be a multi-millionaire. But this has not been reached without ruining thousands of much more respectable and representative Americans who were too honest ever to be multi-millionaires. I am glad that the whole tone of science has changed from materialism to something more like mysticism. But I am not entirely glad that this has been in practice effected much more by a sort of fashionable legend about Einstein than by any sober facing of the facts and the processes of logic about Haeckel. I have got into trouble in my time, along with friends far more useful than I, for denouncing representative government as unrepresentative; and Parliament as a place where nobody is allowed to speak, or, at any rate, to speak the truth. I have lived to see this controversial statement become a commonplace in the mouths of countless young men, eager and energetic, to the point of putting on black shirts. But even this funeral parade does not convince me that all political liberty is quite so black as they have painted it. On the whole, it would seem that I have no cause for regrets, though I might suggest some readjustments. The things I once accepted as lost causes are certainly not lost. But they have been gained in such a way that there is still some doubtful reckoning about loss and gain.

But of all the cases in which I have seen an enemy completely knocked out, but not knocked in the right direction (as when we speak of his being knocked into the middle of next week), the most catastrophic case is that of my old friend and enemy the Puritan. I remember a time when I think I was perfectly justified in giving to the Puritan the title of the Pharisee. I can remember when he really possessed the brute political power to prevent millions of perfectly moral and moderate Englishmen from enjoying the most ordinary joys of life. Ludicrous laws were passed through Parliament, professing to prevent anybody anywhere from amusing himself with a toss-up or a turn of chance. I need hardly say, since the Puritan government was almost entirely a plutocracy, that it was really an arrangement of the rich at the expense of the poor. Still less need I say that nobody who shrieked about the necessity for stopping gambling dreamed of trying to stop the gambling on the Stock Exchange. But all that is a side issue; the point is that there was really a time when not only was a raffle or a trivial bet forbidden, but that the whole tone of society was really kept not only sober but sombre, out of fear of a few fanatics. Discussion about whether the County Council should tolerate this or that entertainment did not mean what it means now. It meant, on one occasion, denouncing the immorality of wooden puppets about a foot high, which had to be looked at very closely by a Councillor to see whether there was any sort of suggestiveness that he could suggest.

But if we compare that sort of thing with the social manners of today, we shall see at a glance that the boot is now on the other leg. It is obvious that the old Puritan has been conquered, if not converted; but has been conquered or converted in such a muddle-headed way that the triumph has passed to people who do not know the difference between Puritanism and Purity. The only apparent alternative to worrying about whether little dolls on a distant stage had quite long enough dresses is the modern proposal that grown-up people should walk about the streets without any dresses at all. So completely lost is that principle of proportion, which keeps civilisations erect, that our civilisation can only fall and flounder in one direction when it has done falling and floundering in the other. The objection to an excessive fuss about indecency is that it is not decent. That is, it is not dignified or decorous or fitting. The atmosphere of the nosing Puritans of the nineties was thoroughly undignified and indecorous and indecent. But surely no normal person wants such a problem solved by the mere negative oblivion of decency. That is merely to abandon the arts of life and the constructive side of civilisation.

In most of these cases the trouble was that both sides were sentimental and neither side philosophical. It is still the unmistakable mark of the whole thing; that it is equally easy to gush on the Puritan and the Anti-Puritan side. The same stream of facile denunciation, in more than a verbal sense to be described as vulgar abuse, the same piling up of adjectives to the disappearance of their own weak nouns and verbs, the same garrulity of disgust, flow from the man who denounces the wrong and the man who denounces the suggestion of the wrong. Both of them will say anything about the wrong except that it is wrong. In other words, both of them will do anything to avoid drawing up anything like a definite and coherent creed or code about right and wrong; nor is the human intellect allowed even to enter the sphere of human ethics. Men who only follow their feelings can be trusted to realise that they suffer from a disease: but it needs more than feelings to find a cure.[363]

It is very difficult for a man not to talk about himself when he is challenged to defend himself. I do not apologise for explaining here what has been the fundamental principle of my action in recent European troubles although it may seem so fundamental as to be merely personal. Now the real tragedy of the twentieth century is that it threatens to relapse into the nineteenth century. The huge horrible and real danger is that it will leave the English as insular as ever; the European as suspicious of England as ever; and the hope that all the nations might feel their unity and fight out their various difficulties by a common conscience, further away than it was at the worst moment of the disaster of the division of Christendom. That is the test that I have applied to all the terrible crises that have tried us in the last few years. My hopes were increased because, until a very short time ago, it did really appear that our ancient civilisation was growing together once more. This was effected by thousands of people who thought about what they saw or felt in their travels or their reading; and very little affected by the few who talked about what they had never seen and could not feel; and called themselves Internationalists

---

[363] *Illustrated London News*, July 14, 1934.

because they were intensely disliked by every nation, but especially their own. Bands of prigs vowed themselves never to resist being killed; and though normal men would dislike the idea of killing anybody who did not resist, it is probable that in their case the reluctance would be overcome. An elaborate machinery, entirely devoid of any morality, was set up to keep the peace between nations; without even attempting to decide whether there is any relation between peace and justice. But these were not the forces that we felt were really re-establishing a fellowship of Christian men.[364]

It seems to me that changes happen slowly. We need time to think. And it has struck me as curious that although the modern world insists that we should have leisure to play tennis or to work out crossword puzzles, the modern world does not insist that we should have time to think. And, probably owing to congenital laziness, I have always given myself time to think.[365]

At this fairly late stage of my experience, I feel an enormous exhilaration. This is really a psychological fact; and perhaps requires some explanation. It arises out of the crisis of the world, which I have lived to see, as I see it.

When I began to write, I was called an optimist; and may have deserved, or possibly accepted, the epithet. This was not, as will be said by the cynic, the sceptic, the materialist, the modern psychologist, and the whole herd of wild asses, merely because I was young. As a fact, it was precisely because nearly all the other young men were pessimists, that I consented to call myself an optimist. It was precisely because they boasted so arrogantly of being completely in the dark, that I pointed out that there is something to be said for the daylight.

But perhaps it is true that my vision was then much too much limited to a mere acceptance of the daylight. Yet it is, on its own legitimate level, the light that lighteth every man that cometh into the world, and at least I prefer it to the black candles which led so many enlightened, or benighted, suicides out of the world. Those who remember the Age of Schopenhauer will always attach a vivid sense to that great phrase; about a yesterday that lighted fools the way to dusty death.

---

[364] *G.K.'s Weekly*, June 4, 1936. He says he plans to address specific attacks on his position in a subsequent article. But he will not live to write it. He ends the article by saying he is trying to get people to wake up.

[365] *Daily Sketch*, May 14, 1931.

But then, after naturally enjoying the daylight, I came to be troubled with the twilight. It was no longer a war between light and darkness, as between hope and hopelessness; but only a conflict of hopes, many of which I thought pretty hopeless. I found myself apparently among divided counsels; as for instance, I liked patriotism; I hated pacifism; but I hated Imperialism more. And now, at this much later stage, I am beginning to find that most of the things I really like are on one side; and most of the things I dislike on the other.

I regretted that Religion should be against Liberalism; when I really imagined that Liberalism was in favour of Liberty. So far as I can see now, there is not the remotest chance of the restoration of Liberty except through the return of Religion. All that there is, in substance, on the other side, is a row of official optimists, boasting of the liberties they have not got, and defending the religion they do not believe.[366]

Now if I were to ask myself where and when I have been happiest, I could of course give the obvious answers, as true of me as of everybody else; at some dance or feast of the romantic time of life; at some juvenile triumph of debate; at some sight of beautiful things in strange lands. But it is much more important to remember that I have been intensely and imaginatively happy in the queerest because the quietest places. I have been filled with life from within a cold waiting-room in a deserted railway-junction. I have been completely alive sitting on an iron seat under an ugly lamp-post at a third-rate watering-place. In short, I have experienced the mere excitement of existence in places that would commonly be called as dull as ditch-water. And by the way, is ditch-water dull? Naturalists with microscopes have told me that it teems with quiet fun. Even that proverbial phrase will prove that we cannot always trust what is proverbial when it professes to describe what is prosaic. I doubt whether the fifteen gushing fountains to be found in your ornamental garden contain creatures so amusing as those the microscope reveals; like the profiles of politicians in caricatures. Anyhow, I am even prepared to fight for ditch-water as well as beer; if any scientific scheme of hydraulics would sweep it away, I shall resist. I shall die in the last ditch. And that is only one example out of a thousand, of the thing in daily life we call dull that are not really so dull after all.

[366] *Sign*, April 1936.

Until a man can enjoy himself he will grow more and more tired of enjoying everything else. What we have to teach him is to amuse himself. At this moment he only asks what will amuse him. And to judge by the expression of his face, it does not amuse him very much. When we consider what he receives, it is indeed a most magnificent concentration of amusement. He can travel in a racing-car almost as quick as a cannon-ball, and still have his car fitted up with wireless from all the ends of the earth. But all this does not help him when the car stops; and he has to stand stamping about in a lane, with nothing to think about. All this does not help him even when the wireless stops, and he has to sit in a silent car with nothing to talk about. But if you consider what comes out of him, as a result of all this absorption, the result we have to record is rather curious. In the vast majority of cases, nothing. Not even conversation, as it used to be. Certainly not correspondence, as it used to be. He does not conduct long arguments, as young men did when I was young. The first and startling effect of all this noise is silence.

When he speaks it is with irritation; and there is irritation and irritation. For instance, a man of genius of the same generation, for whom I have a very special admiration, is Mr. T. S. Eliot. But nobody will deny that there was a sense in which, originally, even his inspiration was irritation. He began with pure pessimism; he has since found much finer and more subtle things; but I hardly think he has found repose. And it is just here that I will have the effrontery to distinguish between his generation and mine. You know, it used to be thought impudent for a boy to criticise an old gentleman. It now requires far more sublime impudence for an older man to criticise a younger. I know very well that Mr. Eliot described the desolation he found more than the desolation he felt. But I think that "The Waste Land" was at least a world in which he had wandered. And as I am describing the recent world, I may as well describe it as he has described it, in "The Hollow Men"—though nobody would describe him as a hollow man. This is his impression of many impressions.

> This is the way the world ends
> This is the way the world ends
> This is the way the world ends
> Not with a bang but a whimper.

Now forgive me if I say, in my old-world fashion, that I'm damned if I ever felt like that. I recognise the great realities Mr. Eliot has revealed; but I do not admit that this is the deepest reality. I am ready to admit that our generation made too much of romance and comfort, but even when I was uncomfortable I was more comfortable than that. I was more comfortable on the iron seat. I was more happy in the cold waiting-room. I knew the world was perishable and would end, but I did not think it would end with a whimper, but, if anything, with a trump of doom. It is doubtless a grotesque spectacle that the great-grandfathers should be still dancing with indecent gaiety, when the young are so grave and sad; but in this matter of the spice of life I will defend the spiritual appetite of my own age. I will even be so indecently frivolous as to burst into song, and say to the young pessimists:

> Some sneer; some snigger; some simper;
> In the youth where we laughed and sang,
> And *they* may end with a whimper
> But *we* will end with a bang.[367]

---

[367] *Listener*, Mar. 18, 1936. This was originally a BBC broadcast, and although he had one more broadcast after this one, it seems that this one was a more fitting farewell to the world.

Chapter 2

With Monstrous Head

All I Survey

> *I enjoy stars and the sun or trees and the sea, because they exist in spite of me; and I believe the sentiment to be at the root of all that real kind of romance which makes life not a delusion of the night, but an adventure of the morning.*
>
> —*Illustrated London News*, November 22, 1913

Philosophy is either eternal or it is not philosophy. The modern habit of saying "This is my opinion, but I may be wrong" is entirely irrational. If I say that it may be wrong, I say that is not my opinion. The modern habit of saying "Every man has a different philosophy; this is my philosophy and it suits me"—the habit of saying this is mere weak-mindedness. A cosmic philosophy is not constructed to fit a man; a cosmic philosophy is constructed to fit a cosmos. A man can no more possess a private religion than he can possess a private sun and moon.[1]

I do not take down huge volumes from my shelves to decide whether Imperialism is possible or whether Christianity is true. I do not do so for the very simple yet modest reason that I believe my opinion on these matters to be of more value than all the books in the world.[2]

---

[1] Introduction to *The Book of Job*.
[2] *Black and White*, Jan. 2, 1904.

Credo[3]

As things go in modern thought, it is a very bold and solid thing even to be able to say "This is true; I believe it."[4] I perceive life to be logical and workable with these beliefs, and illogical and unworkable without them.[5]

I believe in the supernatural as a matter of intellect and reason, not as a matter of personal experience.[6] I believe myself that the universe is monotonous like a child's game because there is behind it an unexhausted Will.[7]

I believe many things which I have not seen.[8] I believe (merely upon authority) that the world is round.[9] I believe that the earth goes round the sun.[10] I believe in that philosophy which claimed to come that we might have life, and that we might have it more abundantly. And I think it is because of our defects and disaffections that we weary of life, and not because life itself would not always be glorious to men truly alive.[11]

I believe that Christianity was a great vision of reality by people passing through a tragedy and confronted with death. When a man decides a thing on his death-bed, it is taken for granted that he is serious. It is customary to be serious on one's death-bed. Now while there are those who claim that the ancient world was dying and hardly itself when it decided in favour of Christianity, I am convinced by the nature of the men who were converted to Christianity, that the ancient world was seriously convinced of the truth of Christianity. I am the more fortified in this view by knowing the claims of Christianity upon the mind to be very convincing.[12]

---

[3] "A man who professes a creed confesses a partiality for the creed; when he loves it he is necessarily partial. But when he hates it he generally professes to be impartial. He pretends that the thing he hates is obstructing his way to other things; such as education or hygiene or science or social reform." (*New Witness*, June 30, 1922.)

[4] *Daily News*, Oct. 24, 1908.
[5] *Daily News*, Dec. 19, 1903.
[6] *Daily News*, Aug. 11, 1906.
[7] *Daily News*, Jan. 24, 1906.
[8] *Daily News*, Dec. 14, 1907.
[9] *Daily News*, May 7, 1910.
[10] *Illustrated London News*, Apr. 8, 1911.
[11] *Illustrated London News*, July 7, 1928.
[12] *Our Sunday Visitor*, Aug. 2, 1931.

I believe in the brotherhood of men; I also believe in the communion of saints. It so happens that in the street to-day one of these is called a truism and the other called a dogma. But to me they are both dogmatic and both true.[13] I do believe in natural rights; perhaps it would be truer to say in supernatural rights. I do not say they came from nature, for I am by no means clear what people mean by nature; apart from a fabulous female dragon red in tooth and claw. I believe they came from God.[14] I believe that the moralists arguing with the immoralists will have the best of the argument, because men cannot argue without doctrine.[15]

I believe in reflecting a little not on what we have done with the great heritage, but on what we have neglected to do with it; not upon how closely we have copied a master, but on the things in which we have not copied him; not on how faithfully we have followed, but upon how far we have betrayed the dead.[16]

I believe that freedom, as such, is good; I believe it is the part of man that in all myths and mysteries has put man highest above nature and nearest to the divine.[17] I believed in Apollo when I was quite little; and I believe in Christmas now that I am very, very big.[18] I believe in Santa Claus.[19] I believe that St. Nicholas is in heaven, accessible to our prayers for anybody; if he was supposed to be specially accessible to prayers of children, as being their patron, I see no reason why he should not be concerned with human gifts to children.[20] I believe that the gods who feast on ambrosia would have some special ambrosia on Christmas Day, probably in the form of a pie. And I am sure that an angel, on entering the private apartment of another angel, would take off his halo.[21]

---

[13] *Daily News*, June 3, 1905.
[14] *New Witness*, May 27, 1921.
[15] *Illustrated London News*, Apr. 2, 1927.
[16] *Daily News*, Feb. 10, 1912.
[17] *Daily News*, Sept. 7, 1912.
[18] *Illustrated London News*, Jan. 1, 1910.
[19] *Daily News*, Dec. 21, 1907.
[20] *Commonweal*, Dec. 20, 1935.
[21] *Daily News*, Dec. 26, 1903.

On Politics

I have the misfortune to be interested in politics, and not merely in politicians; politics are eternal and politicians luckily are not.[22] If I were a magistrate—well, I suppose I should resign.[23]

Like all sane men and most mad ones I am concerned about social reform.[24] I believe most of the great social reforms of our time will remain in history as Follies.[25]

If there is one thing I believe in with a solid certainty, it is in discussing the abstract question before what is called the practical question. In other words, it is clearing up the matter while it is moral and before it becomes merely political.[26]

To me the only perfect pleasure in life is the pleasure of fighting for something in which one passionately believes.[27] I am on the side of the vulgar majority.[28] I believe that the people can rule, and that when it does rule, it does so better than any of its rulers. Even where it is unjustly forbidden to rule, and appears only to dissolve and destroy, I am disposed to defend it; I believe that no human institution in history has really so little to be ashamed of as the mob.[29] My own sympathies are sometimes with the revolutionary and sometimes with the reactionary.[30] I have always believed very much in local government; but I believe even more in local revolution.[31] If ever we did touch and stir that dark heart of the people and that human underworld rose in arms, I think we should see some strange judgments upon our modernity. I think the priest would be left alone; I fear the tyrants might escape; but I believe that the gutters would be simply running with the blood of philanthropists.[32]

---

[22] *Daily News*, Jan. 1, 1910.
[23] *Illustrated London News*, Apr. 4, 1914.
[24] *Daily News*, Jan. 18, 1908.
[25] *Illustrated London News*, May 3, 1919.
[26] *Illustrated London News*, Jan. 7, 1928.
[27] *Daily News*, Oct. 10, 1903.
[28] *Illustrated London News*, Nov. 11, 1916.
[29] *North American Review*, April 1918.
[30] *Illustrated London News*, Oct. 17, 1931.
[31] *New Witness*, Nov. 25, 1915.
[32] *Daily News*, June 3, 1905.

I believe that, given saner and simpler conditions, there is no better government than self-government, and that the citizens should normally rule the city.³³ I believe that pure democracy is the manliest government for men.³⁴ I wish to acquit myself of the charge of contemptuousness. All my life I have endeavoured to explain that my sympathies are entirely with the mass of people in their ordinary instincts. I am not a highbrow. I realise that it is this mass of normal people which keeps the world straight and that, without them, the world would soon qualify for a lunatic asylum.³⁵ Give me the common human jolly healthy fool and let him govern me. I would rather be governed by nine million people mostly fools than by nine people mostly mono-maniacs.³⁶

I believe in the universal extension of rights, but not in the universal extension of privileges.³⁷ I possess a certain proportion of popular sympathies. I think democracy is commonly direct, even in error; that the popular instinct generally goes to the point. In short, I have not only a sneaking tenderness for the common people, but a weakness for confiding in their common sense.³⁸

I believe in liberty.³⁹ I believe the system to be the darkest and dreariest hole in which oppressors hide themselves from human anger.⁴⁰ I believe, as the mediaevals did, that the only authority of government is moral, that the chief object of government is to get the most wicked man, the oppressor of the poor, into the pillory.⁴¹

I believe that the whole education trouble has come from people trying to be loose and universal, not from people trying to be dogmatic and particular. We could all respect each other's faith; but it is too much to ask us to respect each other's doubt and hesitation.⁴²

I believe in the right of national self-defence.⁴³ It is true (as my enemies may malignantly urge) that I have never been in an army.⁴⁴

---

³³ *G.K.'s Weekly*, Nov. 17, 1928.
³⁴ *Illustrated London News*, June 12, 1915.
³⁵ *Philosopher*, July–September 1927.
³⁶ *Manchester Guardian*, Jan. 21, 1907.
³⁷ *Daily News*, Mar. 12, 1910.
³⁸ *New Witness*, May 31, 1917.
³⁹ *America*, Jan. 30, 1937.
⁴⁰ *Daily News*, Jan. 18, 1908.
⁴¹ *Daily News*, May 8, 1909.
⁴² *Daily News*, Nov. 28, 1908.
⁴³ *G.K.'s Weekly*, Nov. 14, 1925.
⁴⁴ *Illustrated London News*, Jan. 10, 1914.

I believe we must see the intrinsic value of the nation before we see its international value to other nations.⁴⁵ I myself believe that a nation can be criminal, and can be punished for crime. I believe it because I am a nationalist, and still more because I am a democrat—or, if the phrase be more exact, a republican. That is, I believe a commonwealth has a common will, a corporate spirit which can be loved, and which therefore can be blamed.⁴⁶

I believe that it was always common ground to people of common sense that the enslavement and importation of negroes had been the crime and catastrophe of American history.⁴⁷ I believe that all men have equal rights, including the right to a thing called justice, which is attested by a thing called conscience; and I agree with the American Declaration of Independence, that this recognition in every man of a certain dignity refers ultimately to a certain divinity.⁴⁸ I fear my own tastes are for the tradition of Jefferson rather than of Franklin.⁴⁹ I myself am one of those poor, lost lingering sentimentalists who do still believe in liberty. I believe in liberty very much as Jefferson did, allowing for the fact that a hundred years of history and experience have taught me to believe a little more than he did in original sin.⁵⁰

I believe that the external differences between Americans and Englishmen are not enough to keep them apart, and their similarities are not enough to bring them together.⁵¹ I am a Little Earther as well as a Little Englander.⁵² I believe that men in large and victorious societies like the Roman Empire or the British Empire see less of the miscellaneous excitement of humanity than anybody else. And I believe that the people who see most of this miscellaneous excitement are the people who live in some tiny community, the people who live in some small walled city, the people who live in some sleepy village in the hills.⁵³ I believe that the whole modern industrial and commercial system, of which America is the wealthiest, most powerful and most energetic leader, is at least relatively barbarous. I say relatively barbarous,

---

⁴⁵ *Illustrated London News*, June 4, 1921.
⁴⁶ *Illustrated London News*, May 31, 1919.
⁴⁷ *New Witness*, Sept. 16, 1921.
⁴⁸ *New Witness*, Dec. 3, 1920.
⁴⁹ *New York American*, Apr. 17, 1935.
⁵⁰ *New York American*, Oct. 10, 1931.
⁵¹ *America*, Jan. 8, 1927.
⁵² *New Witness*, May 4, 1923.
⁵³ *Daily News*, Feb. 11, 1905.

meaning that it is the beginning of a decline which would lead us, if left to itself, to all that is absolutely barbarous.[54]

It may seem absurd, but I believe I am a fair controversialist.[55] I never claim for my opinions the vice of impartiality, and in the question of divorce I most certainly do not profess to be impartial. In my modest manner, however, I do claim most emphatically to be right. I also claim to be representative; that is democratic.[56] I am against anything or everything, which may contain many worthy people, but which is founded on a falsehood, and whose existence insults reality.[57] I believe that the common sense of the common people is, after all, the best test of rule that human imperfection permits, and that the nearer the normal man gets to the organ of government the better.[58]

I will be a patriot even in my dreams.[59]

On Religion

I am so perverse that I think the religious squabbles are much less silly than the political squabbles.[60] I have a senile interest in the beginnings of things—in quaint questionings about why things exist, and whence they came, and what they were really supposed to be.[61] I am not an idolater. I do not worship a clock, or anything that is the work of man's hands. I believe it is perfectly possible for the man who made the clock to put back the clock, or stop the clock, or smash the clock to smithereens, if he chooses to do so; and therefore I have never cared a brass farthing about these measurements of moral ideas in terms of time. Some of the modern ideas are moral ideas that seem to me quite right because they are moral, not because they are modern.[62] Without morals there would be no justice in the world.[63]

---

[54] *G.K.'S Weekly*, June 13, 1931.
[55] *Illustrated London News*, Feb. 14, 1914.
[56] *Sun* (NY), June 25, 1916.
[57] *Daily News*, Mar. 26, 1910.
[58] *New Witness*, Apr. 22, 1921.
[59] *New Witness*, Aug. 4, 1922.
[60] *New York American*, Jan. 9, 1932.
[61] *Illustrated London News*, Mar. 3, 1928.
[62] *Illustrated London News*, Sept. 30, 1933.
[63] *Brooklyn Daily Eagle*, Nov. 26, 1930.

The things I like arguing about are absolute things; whether a proof is logical or whether a practice is just.[64] I will not engage in a verbal controversy with the sceptic, because long experience has taught me that the sceptic's ultimate scepticism is about the use of his own words and the reliability of his own intelligence.[65] I believe that this age wants philosophical argument, argument about fundamentals, more than anything else in the world, however urgent, more than steamboats on the Thames, more than dancing in religious services, more than a scheme of moral education for the rich, more than an English patriotism, more than it wants a poem I am just going to write on the subject of hard-boiled eggs.[66]

I have never been a Jew or a Buddhist or a Moslem, so I cannot say what it feels like.[67] I happen to be able to see in all sorts of odds and ends the universal truth of a universal religion.[68] Saving the grace of God, a mystery not within our measure, I believe the practical problem of whether people will become Catholics is simply the problem of whether they will think hard enough to become Catholics.[69] I believe in preaching to the converted; for I have generally found that the converted do not understand their own religion.[70]

I believe that even rationalist historians will be forced, under whatever phraseology, to use some theory of tremendous interruptions; of something behind life working not with an equal pressure but by cataclysms, things which even when they become universal remain unique. Those who classify Rome with other empires, or Christianity with other religions, or the Jews with other sects, strike me as missing proportion as in the classification of men with beasts.[71]

I cannot work miracles, but I think it probable that there are some people who can ... and I seem to remember somebody who (as I believe) could work miracles, but who was taunted in the hour of death with not working them, and taunted in vain.[72]

---

[64] *Illustrated London News*, Dec. 17, 1927.
[65] *Illustrated London News*, Oct. 30, 1909.
[66] *Daily News*, July 4, 1903.
[67] *Daily News*, July 17, 1909.
[68] *Daily News*, Dec. 19, 1903.
[69] *America*, June 9, 1928.
[70] *Daily News*, Nov. 3, 1906.
[71] *New Witness*, Apr. 6, 1916.
[72] *Illustrated London News*, Mar. 21, 1914.

For my part, I like morality; it is so exciting.[73] I do not myself think it is wrong to laugh even at a morality in which I do believe. I most certainly think it right to laugh at a morality in which I don't believe. And I shall certainly laugh my longest and loudest about a morality that nobody has yet discovered.[74] I have been happy in a minority in times when some New Theology leaders were very placidly in the majority. I do indeed believe that all rule rests on the divine hunger in all the hearts of men; and that the common conscience is that whereby we erect institutions or accept creeds. But I know quite well that whole tracts of humanity can be sunk in special ignorance or swept away with special delusions.[75] I do not believe that the critical activity of the West—and the changes induced by this activity—have been mainly due to the modern doctrine of progress. On the contrary, I believe they have been mainly due to the Christian doctrine of the Fall. That is, it comes not from a confidence that everything is continually rising, but from a suspicion that everything, left to itself, is continually falling.[76]

I annoy the sceptical philosopher by smiling; which is a sign, not of doubt, but of certitude.[77] I keep my faith for the things of another world. About this world I am a complete agnostic.[78]

On Being Human

I believe that this is how people really began to be savages. They progressed clean out of their clothes. They did so because they had already progressed clean out of their wits. Over-civilisation and barbarism are within an inch of each other. And a mark of both is the power of medicine-men.[79]

I believe that the Fall of Man was due to the introduction of the simple life. In a state of innocence our first ancestors (I suppose) ate

---

[73] *Nation*, Oct. 3, 1908.
[74] *Illustrated London News*, Jan. 27, 1912.
[75] *Daily News*, Jan. 21, 1911.
[76] *Forum*, June 1929.
[77] *Illustrated London News*, Jan. 31, 1931.
[78] *Illustrated London News*, Sept. 16, 1911.
[79] *Illustrated London News*, Sept. 11, 1909.

beef and drank beer like Christians. Then came the Tempter, the spirit of intellectual pride and intellectual perversity; he took the form of a Serpent because that form is full of an evil simplicity. And he said, with the elaborate lucidity of modern hygiene, "All these meals are unnecessary to health. Take one raw apple, Madam, in the early morning; another at noon. The apple best suited for our purpose is of particular chemical properties, at once nutritious and light; it grows on a tree which I will show you in a moment..."[80]

I believe that at this historic crisis property has become not only a just thing, but a sacred thing. Real Property will be all the more sacred because it will be rather rare. It will be an island of Christian culture in seas of senseless drifting and mutable social moods. In short, I believe we have reached the time when the family will be called upon to play the part once played by the Monastery. That is to say, there will retire into it not merely the peculiar virtues that are its own, but the crafts and creative habits which once belonged to all sorts of other people.[81] I believe there are a very large number of young men working in offices who are not far from raving in asylums, merely because they are not in the country when they ought to be.[82]

I believe that apology must play a great part in the world to-day. I might almost say that at present the most practical of all actions is an apology. So far from being a sign of weakness, it is the one thing that nobody seems strong enough to do. So far from being a useless regret for the past, it is the only definite departure for which there is anything like a future. Modern civilisation has a great many things to do which it will have great difficulty in doing; and every sympathy is due to it if it really tries to do them. But the very first thing that all modern civilisation has to do is to apologise. It has to apologise to God and man for the horrible muddle into which it has brought itself by its materialism, its mad sophistries, its cocksure theories and its cannibal economics.[83] I believe that the great source of the hideousness of modern life is the lack of enthusiasm for modern life. If we really loved modern life we

---

[80] *Illustrated London News*, July 7, 1906.
[81] *G.K.'s Weekly*, May 21, 1927.
[82] *G.K.'s Weekly*, Aug. 29, 1925.
[83] *G.K.'s Weekly*, Dec. 12, 1925.

should make it beautiful. For all men seek to make beautiful the thing which they already think beautiful.[84]

I believe in making thousands of things; making jokes, making pictures, making (as distinct from faking) goods, making books, and even articles (of which, as the reader will sadly perceive, there is no end), making toys, making tools, making farms, making homes, making churches, making sacred images; and, incidentally also, making war on people who would prevent me from doing these things.[85] I believe we have the right to wage war until we can do justice upon princes and captains as we do it upon thieves and assassins.[86]

I believe it is possible to reverse the evil of the excessive concentration of wealth, and that any reform that does not reverse that evil will only exaggerate it, just as the collectivist would remedy the concentration of wealth by concentrating it still further.[87] I believe that all our hopes hang just now on realising that there is not a black-and-white alternative between a dead Capitalism and an advanced Communism; that there is in history much more humanity, much more variety, and much more liberty; and that we can find a third alternative course, that is at once more traditional and more free.[88] I believe it is possible to restore and perpetuate a reasonable just distribution of private property.[89] I believe in giving money to beggars in the street as they stand.[90]

I believe that our civilisation is not only founded on Christianity, but is in its very material and texture Christian. In other words, I believe that, if there had been no Christianity at all, there would now be no such civilisation at all.[91] I believe not only in being politically democratic and theologically orthodox, but in being strongly democratic and strongly orthodox; not only in being against Bolshevism and against Big Business, but in being indignant against Bolshevism and indignant against Big Business. I believe in it, first because it is more honourable, and second because it is better fun; but I also believe it

---

[84] *Daily News*, Jan. 2, 1902.
[85] *G.K.'s Weekly*, Mar. 21, 1935.
[86] *Illustrated London News*, Sept. 16, 1916.
[87] *Illustrated London News*, May 12, 1923.
[88] *Illustrated London News*, July 21, 1923.
[89] "Apologia," *GKC as MC*.
[90] *Daily News*, Oct. 10, 1908.
[91] *Illustrated London News*, June 10, 1922.

is much better policy than many people imagine.⁹² I believe more and more that there are no trivialities but only truths neglected.⁹³ I believe material causes count for much less in history than is now supposed. I believe that moral causes count for much more than is now supposed. I believe that the supreme factor is not even the bodily framework, or the framework of environment, but the frame of mind.⁹⁴ I believe that of all the things that have ever frozen human charity and prevented healthy reform, one of the worst has been the complete reliance on what are called scientific facts.⁹⁵

I believe profoundly in tradition.⁹⁶ I believe in monogamy as the one complete adventure of man.⁹⁷ I believe that the child has inside his head a pretty correct and complete definition of the whole nature and function of Art; with the one addition that he is quite incapable of saying, even to himself, a single word on the subject.⁹⁸ I believe in fairy-tales; in the sense that I marvel so much at what does exist that I am the readier to admit what might.⁹⁹

I believe the body is good, but the soul bad enough to abuse all sorts of accidental aspects of the body.¹⁰⁰ I believe that sleep is a sacrament; or, what is the same thing, a food.¹⁰¹ I believe that when men are happy, they sing.¹⁰²

I believe in getting into hot water. I think it keeps you clean.¹⁰³

On Being a Writer

Those who read my books never ask me to lunch.¹⁰⁴ It happens that most of my literary admirers live in asylums.¹⁰⁵

---

⁹² *New Witness*, Jan. 19, 1923.
⁹³ *New Witness*, Mar. 8, 1918.
⁹⁴ *Illustrated London News*, Apr. 16, 1932.
⁹⁵ *Daily News*, Dec. 12, 1902.
⁹⁶ *Illustrated London News*, Nov. 23, 1929.
⁹⁷ *Daily News*, Oct. 28, 1905.
⁹⁸ *Life and Letters*, December 1934.
⁹⁹ *New Witness*, June 15, 1916.
¹⁰⁰ *Illustrated London News*, June 30, 1934.
¹⁰¹ *Daily News*, Mar. 27, 1909.
¹⁰² *Everyweek*, Aug. 29, 1918.
¹⁰³ *Illustrated London News*, Mar. 10, 1906.
¹⁰⁴ Quoted in *Hampshire Advertiser*, July 8, 1922.
¹⁰⁵ *Illustrated London News*, Dec. 4, 1909.

I like detective stories, you know, and when I can't find any to read I write them myself. That is somewhat pathetic, too, because one can hardly enjoy reading what one writes, because there are no surprises in it.[106] I vastly prefer the police novel to the pseudo-philosophical exposition. The amateur detective has to give some sort of answer to his own question. The amateur theologian never gives any at all.[107]

Anyone playing at anything has to be serious. Whereas, I have only too good reason to know, if you are writing an article you can say anything that comes into your head.[108] I take the liberty of using the wits which God (I apologise for the term) has given me.[109] Through sheer laziness I always say what I think.[110] If I make a mistake in writing an article, I can cross it out, though I very seldom do, as you know.[111] I hate to read what I have written.[112] I have never felt certain of my writing, but only quite certain of my opinions.[113] I have never been burned alive for my opinions; I have never been tortured for my opinions; only from time to time have I even been sacked for my opinions.[114]

I think the artist is the man who ought to be able to say what everybody else means.[115] I could never understand why it should be considered as anything against the truth of an idea that it was funny: to me it appears that its funniness should be rather in its favour.[116] I have a sincere enthusiasm for the obvious.[117]

I have reviewed a great many books, nay, I have read them.[118] Heaven forbid that I should feel superior to reviewers; for I know I am the worst reviewer of all. I do not claim to be a reviewer but only

---

[106] *St. Louis Post-Dispatch*, Mar. 19, 1921.
[107] *G.K.'s Weekly*, Dec. 3, 1927.
[108] *Daily News*, Feb. 2, 1907.
[109] *G.K.'s Weekly*, Apr. 5, 1930.
[110] *Daily News*, Apr. 13, 1907.
[111] *Illustrated London News*, June 15, 1907.
[112] *Living Age*, June 6, 1925.
[113] Preface to *A Miscellany of Men*.
[114] *Illustrated London News*, Nov. 14, 1908.
[115] *Observer*, Feb. 26, 1911.
[116] *Speaker*, June 1, 1901.
[117] *Daily News*, Nov. 2, 1912.
[118] *Pall Mall Magazine*, February 1902.

to be a reader; and one who can see the perfectly obvious point of what he reads.[119]

I am of the antiquated creed which holds that saying something is often connected with having something to say. And, right or wrong, serious conviction is a great help to humorous expression. It is because it is controversial that it is convivial.[120] When a man has an original point of view of his own, it will appear in everything he writes.[121]

We authors are a miserable, emaciated race, hunted, living a dog's life. The other half of the world, the readers, are a silent, subtle, philosophic people.[122] I admit that we writers, wretched beings, have only to blame ourselves: though we generally prefer to blame each other.[123] I am always writing letters to apologise for not having written letters.[124]

The only poetry which is real fun to compose is the poetry addressed to intimate friends. So far as poetic form is concerned I am very old-fashioned—very much behind the times. I employ all the old rhythms and I use rhyme.[125] I speak as a child, that is, as an impartial witness.[126]

On Being a Journalist

I am a journalist and never believe the newspapers.[127] I am a journalist and so am vastly ignorant of many things, but because I am a journalist I write and talk about them all.[128] I fear I gravitate naturally towards all the easiest jobs which require no particular education, just as it is much easier to be a journalist than to be a journeyman tailor or a journeyman carpenter.[129] I am a sedentary, casual, self-indulgent

---

[119] *G.K.'s Weekly*, Apr. 26, 1930.
[120] *New York American*, Dec. 8, 1934.
[121] *Week-end Review*, June 24, 1933.
[122] *Leeds Mercury*, Nov. 26, 1927.
[123] *New York American*, Oct. 27, 1934.
[124] *New York American*, Mar. 6, 1935.
[125] *Living Age*, June 6, 1925.
[126] *Daily News*, Sept. 14, 1912.
[127] *Century Magazine*, May 1913.
[128] *New York Times*, Jan. 11, 1921.
[129] *New York American*, June 27, 1935.

person, as are most journalists.[130] If I criticise journalism it is rather to check or dilute my own insupportable arrogance in being a journalist than to join in any of the commonplace charges against it.[131]

The trouble with the journalist is that he has to work as hard as a millionaire; while he hates work as heartily as a mystic. It is a dangerous trade to be at once lazy and busy. The effect is that things are finished at the last moment—sometimes (if you can bear the thought) begun at the last moment, and have to end anyhow, cut short, by themselves or someone else.[132]

I believe in the judgment of all uncultured people; but it is my misfortune that I am the only quite uncultured person in England who writes articles.[133] I will not pass any matter on which I have pronounced opinions without saying what they are, for not saying one's own opinions is the temptation, and therefore the treason, of my trade.[134]

I am fairly brazen being a journalist, but I really am for ever conscious of how badly and clumsily I am using the English language in writing and speaking except when I am at the white heat of controversy, and at the hammer and tongs stage I get the illusion that I am doing things rather well. It's the best fun in life this argument business, and what makes being a journalist really worth while.[135] I can say abnormal things in modern magazines. It is the normal things that I am not allowed to say.[136]

It is one of the journalist's tragedies that whenever he introduces a thing purely as an impossibility, somebody writes to say that it really occurred. If I use a foolish metaphor at random I generally receive two letters—one complaining that the thing is too violent and absurd, the other saying that it happened to the writer's aunt.[137]

I think a great deal could be done by giving away money in the street. I would give a public exhibition of how it should be done myself; only, as I said before, I am a journalist. I have no money.[138]

---

[130] *New Witness*, July 10, 1913.
[131] *Illustrated London News*, Oct. 12, 1906.
[132] *New Witness*, May 15, 1913.
[133] *Daily News*, May 18, 1907.
[134] *Illustrated London News*, Jan. 3, 1914.
[135] *Montreal Gazette*, Feb. 14, 1921.
[136] *Daily News*, Aug. 21, 1909.
[137] *Illustrated London News*, Sept. 22, 1906.
[138] *Illustrated London News*, Dec. 22, 1906.

I am the worst editor in the world. I no more expected to be an editor than to be the policeman who stops the traffic in the Strand.[139] I do not believe in the moral significance of modern success; I do not believe, in the sense of taking it seriously, in my own journalistic importance; I do not believe in my editorial powers. But I do believe in my beliefs. I do believe that somebody ought to make a stand or strike a blow for certain civilised certitudes in times of terror and doubt. I do believe that certain human and historic necessities are perishing before our eyes in vast whirlpools of monopoly and slavery.[140]

A journalist at his worst (as at present) is often, if only through hurry, an honester man.[141] I have had a very jolly time as a journalist, and never ask to be anything better.[142]

On Being Large

The disadvantage of "the sunny side" is that when you walk on it you generally cover it with your shadow. At least, I do.[143] The chair I sit on is really romantic—nay, it is heroic, for it is eternally in danger.[144]

I need not say I do not mind being called fat; for deprived of that jest, I should be almost a serious writer. I do not even mind being supposed to mind being called fat. But being supposed to be contented, and contented with the present institutions of modern society, is a mortal slander I will not take from any man.[145] There was once a happy fable in Fleet Street to the effect that I illustrated my defence of the chivalric prejudice by standing up in an omnibus and offering my seat to three ladies. Gallantry upon so gargantuan a scale seems almost to have an alarming flavour of polygamy.[146]

The chief gift of hot weather to me is the somewhat unpopular benefit called a conviction of sin. All the rest of the year I am

---

[139] *New Witness*, Dec. 7, 1916.
[140] *New Witness*, Feb. 9, 1923.
[141] *Illustrated London News*, July 20, 1912.
[142] *New Witness*, Oct. 21, 1915.
[143] *Illustrated London News*, Aug. 15, 1914.
[144] *Illustrated London News*, July 24, 1909.
[145] *Everyweek*, Aug. 29, 1918.
[146] *New Witness*, Feb. 8, 1917.

untidy, lazy, awkward, and futile. But in hot weather I feel untidy, lazy, awkward, and futile. Sitting in a garden-chair in a fresh breeze under a brisk grey and silver sky, I feel a frightfully strenuous fellow: sitting on the same garden-chair in strong sunshine, it begins slowly to dawn on me that I am doing nothing. In neither case, of course, do I get out of the chair. But I resent that noontide glare of photographic detail by the ruthless light of which I can quite clearly see myself sitting in the chair. I prefer a more grey and gracious haze, something more in the Celtic twilight style, through which I can only faintly trace my own contours, vast but vague in the dusk and distance.[147]

Going out for the first time into the wintery sunlight, I met a much esteemed neighbour, who remarked on the large open spaces which I had lately left in the streets, by remaining inside the house.[148] The Christmas pudding is still quite as big as it was when I was a baby; it is only that I in my turn have taken on the contours of a yet larger Christmas pudding.[149]

I am not short myself, though the popular image is one of latitude rather than longitude.[150] Leaping is scarcely my most characteristic gesture.[151] Nature has designed me on the lines of a boxing glove or a punch ball.[152] I have been accused of standing on my head; which is not a tribute to the solidity of my skull but an exaggeration of the lithe and serpentine agility of my figure.[153] I am not a Mahatma; and the occasions on which my bodily presence has been mistaken for that of Mr. Gandhi in a loin-cloth have been few and far between.[154] I propose to model myself on the Skeleton Dude.[155]

I don't mind being ugly, but I have a strong objection to being sad.[156]

---

[147] *Illustrated London News*, June 11, 1910.
[148] *G.K.'s Weekly*, Mar. 24, 1928.
[149] *Illustrated London News*, Jan. 8, 1910.
[150] *Pax*, no. 89, 1927.
[151] *New Witness*, Nov. 1, 1917.
[152] *New Witness*, Mar. 8, 1917.
[153] *London Magazine*, August 1923.
[154] *G.K.'s Weekly*, Nov. 28, 1931.
[155] *New Witness*, Apr. 20, 1923.
[156] *Daily News*, Feb. 11, 1911.

On Eating, Drinking, and Smoking[157]

I am not a person especially prone by nature to be a nuisance in hotels; I am not a vegetarian; I am not an epicure; I can eat and drink and smoke the ordinary things provided in ordinary places.[158] I am a vegetarian between meals.[159]

I am very fond of spiced beef and all the spices; I always dread that the Puritan reformers will suddenly forbid mustard and pepper as they did malt and hops.[160] I am a great enthusiast for the English breakfast. Bacon and eggs seem to me to have been wedded by a god in the morning of the world.[161] I cannot imagine that Shakespeare began the day with rolls and coffee, like a Frenchman or a German. Surely he began with bacon or bloaters. In fact, a light bursts upon me; for the first time I see ... bacon did write Shakespeare.[162]

Continue to eat pork (sooner or later the doctors will say that pork is the only food that is perfectly digestible). Continue to drink port (sooner or later a man will arise in medical circles who will prove that port is the only certain safeguard against gout).[163] The young student should not attempt eating soup with the fingers.[164] When giving treats to friends or children, give them what they like, emphatically not what is good for them.[165] Salt is not a pièce de résistance. It is a corrective. It is the priest, not the man. The meaning of salt is that there exists something which we cannot live on, but cannot live without.[166]

---

[157] In spite of Chesterton's great weight, the record shows he was not a glutton. His wife, his secretary, and his lifelong friend Bentley all testify to how surprisingly little he ate and drank. And a visitor observed: "No one can stay at Top Meadow without the realization of how abstemious in food and drink is 'G.K.' He declares himself 'fonder of beer' and more anti-Prohibitionist than ever, but that seems largely a matter of word than of deed! He says he can eat 'almost anything,' and he never fusses about food, but he eats lightly and almost unnoticingly. His whole manner of life is, in fact, one of amazing simplicity, at home and abroad." (May Bateman, "Top Meadow—Where the Chestertons Live," *Extension Magazine*, January 1927.)

[158] *New Witness*, Mar. 31, 1922.
[159] *Illustrated London News*, Dec. 4, 1909.
[160] *Listener*, Mar. 18, 1936.
[161] *G.K.'s Weekly*, Apr. 12, 1934.
[162] *Daily News*, July 6, 1907.
[163] *Illustrated London News*, Jan. 19, 1907.
[164] *New Witness*, June 18, 1914.
[165] *Forum*, February 1909.
[166] *Illustrated London News*, Oct. 23, 1913.

Let a man walk ten miles steadily on a hot summer's day along a dusty English road, and he will soon discover why beer was invented.[167] If I die worth millions (which again is only a hypothesis) and leave a huge legacy of pots of beer to all the people in workhouses—for that is the form of charity I should choose—then my motives might be considered to be my own affair. Granted that I had done good to other people's bodies, it might be left to a higher tribunal whether I had done good to my own soul.[168]

Causing all the fountains to run with wine is probably expensive, but sounds to me pleasing.[169] I have no objection to wine, and no objection to vodka except the fact that I once tasted it.[170] I do not drink whisky.[171] Most of my own work is, I will not venture to say, literary, but at least sedentary. I never do anything except walk about and throw clubs and javelins in the garden. But I never require anything to give me an appetite for a meal. I never yet needed a tot of rum to help me to go over the top and face the mortal perils of luncheon.[172]

I know two or three of those great solemn words which hold our European civilisation together—one of which is "cigar."[173] If I generally smoke cigars I can smoke all sorts of cigars, in the American or German manner; and the habit does not connote the degree of luxury or fashion it commonly connotes in England. I do not, so to speak, dress up to my cigar.[174] I myself smoke like a chimney, though I trust not quite like a factory-chimney, but the notion that this idle pleasure in itself involves progress, truth and intellectual courage seems to me quite as mad as the notion that it involves in itself vice and vulgarity and mortal sin. Smoking is a relaxation.[175] I have never inhaled my smoke.[176]

I have passed a great part of my life with the immediate intention of learning to smoke a pipe. Unfortunately, I am one of those people

---

[167] *Illustrated London News*, Apr. 20, 1907.
[168] *Illustrated London News*, May 29, 1909.
[169] *Daily News*, July 23, 1904.
[170] *Illustrated London News*, Nov. 21, 1914.
[171] *New Witness*, Mar. 19, 1914.
[172] *Nash's Pall Mall Magazine*, June 1930.
[173] *Daily News*, June 16, 1906.
[174] *New York American*, Sept. 22, 1934.
[175] *New York American*, Feb. 27, 1935.
[176] *Illustrated London News*, Aug. 15, 1914.

who put off almost everything; and put off the things I want to do, as well as the things I have to do.[177]

On Travel

Some day I will write a thrilling book of travels about all the places I have never visited.[178] I am grossly ignorant of geography.[179] I believe it is of enormous spiritual advantage to know no geography. If you do not know where the lane at the end of your own garden leads, you are on the edge of eternity. And I think myself that it would be far better if there were fewer guide-books, and time-tables, and maps, and more travel. I always start off from my own door, like the third brother in the fairy-tale, and go anywhere.[180] Through some perversity of temper of which I am by no means proud, I am able to enjoy everything in a trip of sight-seeing except the sight that is to be seen.[181]

It is much easier to go to America than it was, but it is not any easier to understand it when you have got there.[182] The only glimpse I ever got in my life of the hell of unbearable monotony, of something I felt I would rather die than endure, was in some of those films describing the fast and fashionable life of New York.[183] When I first saw the skyscrapers of New York, I said to myself, "This is a city built by giraffes for giraffes."[184]

I was in Chicago for a time, but I couldn't see a murder, because you cannot get into real murder society there without an introduction.[185] Chicago was a pleasing disappointment. In England, they think of Chicago as a monster of manufacturing industry. I found it quite beautiful, especially the Lake Drive.[186]

---

[177] *New York American*, Sept. 22, 1934.
[178] *New Witness*, Sept. 9, 1915.
[179] *New Witness*, Dec. 8, 1922.
[180] *Idler*, June 1903.
[181] *Daily News*, Oct. 7, 1911.
[182] *Illustrated London News*, May 9, 1908.
[183] *Vanity Fair*, February 1929.
[184] *Berkeley Daily Gazette*, Mar. 6, 1931.
[185] *Oregonian*, Mar. 8, 1931.
[186] *New York Tribune*, Mar. 27, 1921.

I felt much more at home in Palestine than I did in America.[187] Palestine is really a strange and symbolic country; and in nothing more than its series of levels and climates. It is not so much a land as a ladder. Degrees of altitude take the place of degrees of latitude. The Jordan Valley really has the atmosphere of those tropics which seem like the suburbs of hell. But the holy mountain of Jerusalem has really an air of something lifted nearer to heaven. It has the clearness and coldness, not of being nearer to the poles, but of being nearer to the stars.[188]

Except for some fine works of art, which seem to be there by accident, the City of Brussels is like a bad Paris, a Paris with everything noble cut out, and everything nasty left in. When I had got into Brussels I began to make all necessary arrangements for getting out of it again.[189]

The filthiest sink of wickedness in the world is Berlin; where not only normal but abnormal vice is flaunted in the same fashion.[190] If I were a German lunatic, I should say it was "beyond good and evil."[191]

Nobody can walk through any part of a peasant state like Bavaria without receiving and seeing a thousand kindnesses.[192] An ordinary casual Bavarian would be content left alone with his beer and his music and his mediaevalism (which is the polite name for his religion).[193]

The French, in bulk, are the most respectable people in Europe; and sometimes the dullest. The Latin Quarter is probably the least Latin of all the quarters of Paris. That is why the English and Americans write books about it.[194]

The Spaniards discovered America; but the English have not yet discovered Spain.[195] The reputation of Spain is almost the reverse of the reality of Spain.[196] The Spanish are very jolly, happy people, but they eat rather on the principle of a boa-constrictor—an enormous

---

[187] *Illustrated London News*, Feb. 2, 1924.
[188] *Illustrated London News*, Dec. 25, 1920.
[189] *Daily News*, May 9, 1908.
[190] *Outline*, June 29, 1929.
[191] *Illustrated London News*, Nov. 11, 1916.
[192] *G.K.'s Weekly*, July 17, 1926.
[193] *Illustrated London News*, Dec. 5, 1931.
[194] *New Witness*, July 9, 1914.
[195] *G.K.'s Weekly*, Dec. 28, 1933.
[196] *G.K.'s Weekly*, Jan. 4, 1934.

meal, followed by a sleep. The Catalonians are far more fussy than the rest of their countrymen. They are distinguished for what I can only describe as fanatical cleanliness. I found their rabid hygiene distressing. There seemed to be an uncontrollable impulse to scrub everything. As a matter of fact, I have an idea that they practised this extreme cleanliness merely to annoy the rest of Spain. In Spain there is a survival of the elaborate old Spanish courtesy—the sort of courtesy which, we are told, impels a host to offer his entire household goods as a gift to the most casual visitor.[197] In Spain, everybody drinks wine, and it is almost impossible to discover a drunken man.[198]

Most Englishmen know nothing about Poland.[199] Poland is the central pillar of Europe.[200] A Pole will never admit, until the crack of doom, that a State which a few intellectuals have made for him is necessarily higher than a household that he has made for himself.[201]

I knew nothing about Holland except from pictures, and when I recently visited it was natural that the first impression should be that it had stolen its landscapes from the National Gallery. In Amsterdam, the traveller walks rather amid the ruins of a great State than the restrictions of a small one. Everywhere is the sort of magnificence that always marks an aristocracy founded on colonies and commerce, which marked Venice in the sixteenth and England in the eighteenth century; the private houses like palaces, and the personal genius for portrait-painting. But as Dutch dignity is connected with Dutch decay, an Englishman looks at it with an unquiet mind. It is as though he looked not at things of the past, but of the future.[202]

I do not understand Welshmen. I mean, quite simply and ingenuously, that I know nothing about Wales—not even (for certain) that there is such a place. I went, indeed, a few weeks ago to a curious place full of rocks; and the people there *said* it was Wales. But then, other people said that these people were very sly, and that you could not believe anything they said.[203]

---

[197] *Observer*, June 6, 1926.
[198] *Illustrated London News*, May 22, 1926.
[199] *G.K.'s Weekly*, July 9, 1927.
[200] *Illustrated London News*, Aug. 12, 1916.
[201] *New Witness*, Sept. 3, 1920.
[202] *Illustrated London News*, Apr. 29, 1922.
[203] *Illustrated London News*, Sept. 16, 1911.

Of all the great nations of Christendom, the Scotch are by far the most romantic. You do need to be very romantic to accept the industrial civilisation. The industrial dream suited the Scots. Here was a really romantic vista, suited to a romantic people; a vision of higher and higher chimneys taking hold upon the heavens, of fiercer and fiercer fires in which adamant could evaporate like dew. The Scotch were tempted by the enormous but unequal opportunities of industrialism, because the Scotch are romantic.[204] Scotch Presbyterians might claim the X as St. Andrew's Cross; true sons of the Kirk being well assured that St. Andrew was a Scotsman and Presbyterian.[205]

There is nothing that I enjoy so much, in the ordinary way, as taking a ticket and a train and a boat and going to Dublin.[206] If Ireland is conscious of the borderland of the reason which leads to the unreasonable and the divine, if Ireland is vain of a prehistoric glory, if Ireland listens to old wives' fables and calls upon the genius of the hill or stream, Ireland is not therefore a dreamer among nations. She is simply a nation, a common healthy nation like the other nations of the world. If England neglects these things, then England is not in the least the type of normal common sense. England is in this the morbid exception among peoples; England is the eccentric; England is the dreamer. That Ireland believes in the fairies is one of the proofs that she has to offer that she is a sane and vigorous community. Too many Celtophiles talk as if the man who believed in the fairies must be a fragile and over-sensitised artist. The general truth about the world as it is may be best expressed by saying that the man who believes in the fairies in any country might be trusted physically and morally to knock down two of the men who do not.[207] Very few people know how badly the Irish have been treated. That is the English way. They turn aside, they don't inquire, and they don't know. The fact is they don't want to know.[208]

Rome is a Holy City; unique and universal and towering over the tribes of men.[209] Italians are not in the least hysterical; they are only angry.[210] I do not know Italian, though I sometimes manage, by a

---

[204] *Daily News*, Mar. 23, 1912.
[205] *New York American*, Dec. 12, 1931.
[206] *America*, Aug. 6, 1932.
[207] *Speaker*, Oct. 31, 1903.
[208] *New York Times*, June 8, 1924.
[209] *Universe*, Feb. 24, 1928.
[210] *Illustrated London News*, Nov. 11, 1933.

mixture of French and Latin, with more than Italian gesticulation, violently to impose my meaning.[211] Italy is still a place more full of roughly balanced and reasonably proportioned things; of locality and liberty. Italy is still what England once was; what England may be again.[212]

I am not fond of the word British.[213] I have passed a great part of my life in pointing out that England happens to be a part of Europe.[214]

Whatever is it that we are all looking for? I fancy that it is really quite close.[215]

On G. K. Chesterton

It is not I that am paradoxical, but the facts that are paradoxical.[216] I never use paradox. The statements I make are wearisome and obvious common sense. I have even been driven to the tedium of reading through my own books, and have been unable to find any paradox. In fact, the thing is quite tragic, and some day I hope to write an epic called "Paradox Lost."[217] I should like to write an enormous Miltonic epic about the universe and call it "Paradox Regained."[218]

I have often been congratulated on talking nonsense when I believe I am talking sense.[219] I am accused of being "mediaeval"; I do not know what it means, but perhaps the one respect in which I do truly and heartily admire mediaevalism may be found in the fact that it invented the phrase "common sense," and never, so far as I know, used the word "paradox."[220]

My mind being incurably frivolous, I find my fancies straying towards lighter things like history, philology, philosophy, metaphysics and moral theology, when my countrymen are concerned with really serious subjects, such as money.[221] I have not, as the Society says,

---

[211] *New York American*, June 30, 1934.
[212] *G.K.'s Weekly*, Aug. 22, 1925.
[213] *Illustrated London News*, Nov. 7, 1931.
[214] *New York American*, Feb. 28, 1934.
[215] *Daily News*, Mar. 9, 1907.
[216] *Daily News*, Aug. 24, 1907.
[217] *New York Times*, Feb. 7, 1921.
[218] *Illustrated London News*, May 22, 1915.
[219] Introduction to *The New World of the Theatre*.
[220] *Illustrated London News*, Feb. 12, 1927.
[221] *New York American*, Dec. 5, 1931.

much special knowledge; but there are some things that it requires precious little knowledge to know.[222] I have not read St. Thomas any more than I have read the Encyclopedia Britannica.[223]

I am one of those absent-minded people who never notice anything unless it is concealed.[224] I do not think it can be fairly said that I have neglected the most recent realities of the real world. It seems rather the real world that neglects them.[225] I confess I guard rather jealously everything that the world does not value.[226]

I do from time to time see my name in the papers; indeed, in these days of political liberty, I am always expecting to see it in the police news.[227] I jolly well know that I would not turn out at night to hear myself lecture even if it was a free entertainment.[228] I like theatres theatrical, as I like poems poetical.[229] I have no objection to earnest modern dramas being acted early in the morning, for I am a late riser myself.[230]

I generally make my New Year resolutions somewhere towards the end of May, for I belong to that higher order of beings who not only forget to keep promises, but forget even to make them.[231] I am a typical Englishman and therefore lazy and illogical.[232] I love croquet, but you do not love croquet until you love being beaten at croquet.[233] I never beat anyone at billiards. A very distinguished novelist and social philosopher took me the other day to a club in Piccadilly solely in order that we might finally decide which was the worst billiard player in Europe. I won.[234] I have played ordinary games like skittles, always badly. I have even played golf in Scotland before it became a fashion and then a religion.[235] I know chess well enough to

---

[222] *Daily News*, Sept. 7, 1912.
[223] *New Witness*, Aug. 18, 1922.
[224] *Daily Herald*, May 10, 1913.
[225] *Illustrated London News*, Mar. 8, 1930.
[226] *G.K.'s Weekly*, Nov. 1, 1934.
[227] *Daily News*, Jan. 11, 1913.
[228] *Burlington Gazette*, Feb. 16, 1921 (during his first American lecture tour).
[229] *Illustrated London News*, Jan. 27, 1912.
[230] *Illustrated London News*, Sept. 18, 1909.
[231] *Daily News*, Jan. 11, 1913.
[232] *New York American*, Mar. 6, 1935.
[233] *Daily News*, Aug. 11, 1906.
[234] *Illustrated London News*, Sept. 1, 1906. It probably was H. G. Wells.
[235] *Listener*, Mar. 18, 1936.

do it badly.²³⁶ I can play chess and even enjoy it enormously; though it is generally the generous enjoyment of being beaten. But poker is too intellectual for me.²³⁷

I have long ago discovered, in the actual or earthly sense, that I can never be a gardener, because of my delight in a garden—when it is covered with weeds. I cannot see why the wildness of the dandelion, any more than the wildness of the other kind of lion, should make men miss the splendour of its golden name: but when I have employed some such expressions to the professional gardener, they have been coldly received.²³⁸

I like to read the sane and solid fairy-tales, where men are celebrated for an honest animal valour or for a cunning allied to the animals. That is why I read the football news, of which I do not understand a single word.²³⁹ I will not promise not to laugh at a rhinoceros.²⁴⁰ I for one will willingly confess that the only thing on earth I am frightfully afraid of is a little girl.²⁴¹

The mirror of a very moderate sense and sanity is all I have claimed to possess.²⁴² I judge by my own human nature, which is human and ordinary enough.²⁴³ The boots I wear are, I will not say beautiful upon the mountains, but, at least, highly symbolic in the street, being the boots of one that bringeth good news.²⁴⁴

On Life and Death

I can truly say that I have hardly ever been bored in my life.²⁴⁵ Nearly the chief trouble of life is that there is nothing dull in it: it is not a waste of monotony but a jungle of distractions.²⁴⁶

---

²³⁶ *New Witness*, Nov. 4, 1915.
²³⁷ *New York American*, Jan. 27, 1934.
²³⁸ *New Witness*, Dec. 7, 1916.
²³⁹ *Daily News*, July 28, 1906.
²⁴⁰ *Illustrated London News*, Jan. 17, 1914.
²⁴¹ *Nation*, Dec. 7, 1907.
²⁴² Introduction to *Fancies vs. Fads*.
²⁴³ *New Witness*, Jan. 19, 1923.
²⁴⁴ *Illustrated London News*, July 24, 1909.
²⁴⁵ *Vanity Fair*, February 1929.
²⁴⁶ *New Witness*, Dec. 7, 1916.

I am not so frightened of life that I dare not obstruct it, like the Nature-worshipper. Nor am I so frightened of life that I have to tie it down with hundreds of little cords, like the hygienist. My test is whether the life is what can decently be called human life, life neither choked with anarchy nor enslaved by fear.[247] As becomes any healthy man, I fear death.[248] I had a relative who came late for the Battle of Waterloo; and I sometimes almost hope that I myself may come late for the Day of Judgment.[249]

I have had, to my shame, a happier life than most men; and should therefore be the sorrier to lose it.[250]

---

[247] *Daily News*, Sept. 11, 1909.
[248] *Illustrated London News*, Jan. 11, 1913.
[249] *Illustrated London News*, Mar. 16, 1912.
[250] *Daily News*, Dec. 21, 1912.

Chapter 3

The Devil's Walking Parody
An Alternative Biography

He was, among other things, emphatically what we call a character, almost as we speak of a character in a good novel or play. He was not only a humanist but a humourist, a humourist especially in the old English sense of a man always in his humour, going his own way and doing what nobody else would have done.

—*"The Little Poor Man," St. Francis of Assisi*

Editor's Note: This chapter is based on a talk I gave on my first trip to England when I addressed the Annual General Meeting of the Chesterton Society in London on April 19, 2002. It has been modified with quite a bit of additional material.

I have never been satisfied with any of my own descriptions of G. K. Chesterton. But I have been collecting from other sources a sentence here or a short passage there that captures him, or at least some aspect of him, with unmistakable precision. I finally assembled these, the best descriptions of Chesterton that I have ever read, and the result is a condensed and concise mini-biography. Perhaps it is less a biography than a character study, but perhaps biography in that it is a collection of writings—or even better, drawings, word pictures—not of the events of his life but of his life, the life that he lived from the inside.

These passages are quite short and succinct, which is probably their greatest strength, but if they seem a bit disjointed, it is because they are from several different sources. I will explain where they came from at the conclusion of the chapter. (Try to resist the temptation to look at the sources at the end of the chapter until you finish reading—they will *only be a distraction ahead of time.) I have edited them only slightly in stitching them together. It is not a seamless work; the seams show, as they show on Frankenstein's monster. But the creature here is nothing like that. He is not so frightening. But he is much more unbelievable and unlikely, and certainly more full of life. He is G. K. Chesterton.*

Chesterton was a huge heavy man, fat and slow and quiet, very mild and magnanimous, shy, even apart from the humility of holiness; and abstracted. He was so stolid that the teachers in the schools which he attended regularly, thought he was a dunce. His stature was more remarked than his stoutness. His head gave the impression of caverns of thought.[a] He unconsciously inhabited a large heart and a large head, and exercised there an equally generous if rather absent-minded hospitality.[b]

Chesterton was a hospitable giant; a good ogre whose very man-eating was a form of hospitality. He was a huge human being whom men could inhabit like a house, whose eyes were like windows from which they could behold the whole world.[c] He had a power of seeing the world as the highly poetical thing that it quite obviously is.[d] He had a genial and musical style that heightens the most prosaic fragments and achieves that awful and beautiful thing which is the dream of all democracy, the seeing of all things as wonderful.[e]

Being by birth an Englishman, he took pleasure in being an Englishman; being by rank a member of the middle class, he took a pride in its ancient scruples and its everlasting boundaries. He was everything that he was with a definite and conscious pleasure.[f]

It is a curious tribute to the quite curious greatness of Chesterton that in the period of his youthful strain we do not feel the strain but feel only the youth. His own amazing wish to write equaled or outstripped even his readers' amazing wish to read.[g] One of the worst of the disadvantages of the rich and random fertility of Chesterton is the fact that it is very difficult to trace or recover all the things that he has written.[h] It is very ungracious to complain of the amazing multiplicity of the output which a man like Chesterton manages to achieve. It is like complaining that a really good ale-house provides too much ale; which would seem not only a blasphemy but almost a contradiction in terms. It is like complaining that a really good popular singer can sing too many different songs; a complaint that is entirely a compliment.[i] He suffered from his versatility, not, as is loosely said, by not doing every department well enough, but by doing every department too well.[j]

It is quite true that our modern world does not adequately understand the benevolence of Chesterton. It is quite true that most modern critics instinctively dislike his perpetual friendliness.[k] He is accused of superficiality by those who cannot grasp that there is foam upon deep seas.[l] His enormous capacity for joy flowed directly out of his profoundly religious temperament. He conceived himself as an unimportant guest at one eternal and uproarious banquet, and, instead of grumbling at the soup, he accepted it with that careless gratitude which marks the baby and the real man of the world. He rode on the great galloping gift-horse of existence with the joy of a horseman at once dexterous and reckless, and did not, like so many more ambitious philosophers, nearly fall off in his desperate efforts to look the gift-horse in the mouth. His gaiety was neither the gaiety of the pagan nor the gaiety of the bon vivant. It was the greater gaiety of the mystic. He could enjoy trifles, because to him there was no such thing as a trifle. He was a child who respected his dolls because they were the images of the image of God, portraits at only two removes. He was a boy who thought his fireworks were as splendid as the stars, but it was only because he thought the stars were as youthful and as festive as the fireworks.[m]

He was perhaps the one writer, certainly the one poet, who gave the impression of writing slap-dash and always finding the right word. He was a man of the people. He was an earthquake.[n] He combines being epigrammatic with being dogmatic.[o] Built into his very bones is that old English last-century thing which the flimsy moderns cannot endure or understand—the didactic spirit, the spirit which tells the great man to tell other men simply and fully the whole of his mind.[p] He was a man who could write what nobody else could have written, and often at a time when nobody else would have dared to write it. He could tell the truth about a time in which perhaps more lies were told, and about which perhaps more lies have since been taught, than any other episode in English history. He could say the right thing, and say it exactly rightly.[q]

Every great man must go through a period of unpopularity, not while he is alive, but shortly after he is dead. If he is a great man he returns, and he returns for the right reasons.^r The real reason of the temporary eclipse of Chesterton is not that he was a faulty artist but that he expresses almost faultlessly a certain class of thoughts and emotions which happen at this moment to be almost absent from the cultivated class. It was not that he had a deficiency in his art, it is we that have a deficiency in our experience.^s He will not fit into any of the obvious categories we employ; because he will not fit into anything, hardly into the world itself.^t When corruption and chaos are disturbing ordinary minds, and many good men are only worried and serious, it has often happened that a great man could apparently be frivolous; and appear in history almost as a great buffoon.^u That is the mark of the truly great man: that he sees the common man afar off, and worships him. The great man tries to be ordinary, and becomes extraordinary in the process. But the small man tries to be mysterious, and becomes lucid in an awful sense—for we can all see through him.^v

Chesterton has the freshness to enjoy a fresh fact, the freshness to enjoy an old one. He can feel that the common thing prose is an accomplishment like verse; it is the miracle of language. He can feel the subtle taste of water, and roll it on his tongue like wine. His innocent love of living, his ignorant love of learning, are things far fuller of romance than the weariness and foppishness of the sniggering cavaliers.^w He devoted his genius in a somewhat special sense to the description of happiness.^x With the clear eyes of humility he perceives the whole world as it is. He prefers goodness to strength, as do all masculine men.^y He utters the secret anger of the humble.^z

It is in broken outbreaks that his greatness appears. If a man has flung away bad ideas he has shown his sense, but if he has flung away good ideas he has shown his genius. Critics have called Keats and others who died young "the great Might-have-beens of literary history." Chesterton certainly was not merely a great Might-have-been. Chesterton, to say the least of him, was a great Was. Yet this fails fully to express the richness of his talent; for the truth is that he was a great Was and also a great Might-have-been. He said what he had to say, and yet not all he had to say.^aa We must consider the books that he wrote but we also have to consider the books that he might have written, but that he did not since he took on the duties of an editor and he was not by any means naturally fitted for that position. It was not that he was careless; rather it was that he was too conscientious.^bb

He was not content with being original, he had a wild wish to be true.^(cc) But it was as a journalist that he attacked the world, as a journalist that he conquered it.^(dd)

Whether Chesterton was a great poet I shall not discuss. I understand that one has to wait about eight hundred years before discussing that. But that he was an astonishingly good poet is solid and certain. And by all common chances Chesterton ought to be preserved as a pleasure.^(ee) He had the one great requirement of a poet—he was not difficult to please. To the man who sees the marvellousness of all things, the surface of life is fully as strange and magical as its interior.^(ff)

But while Chesterton is always large and humorous, his critics are often small and serious. They not only get hold of the wrong end of the stick, but of the diminishing end of the telescope; and take in a detail when they should be taking in a design.^(gg) Authors both great and small are, like everything else in existence, upon the whole greatly underrated. They are blamed for not doing, not only what they have failed to do to reach their own ideal, but what they have never tried to do to reach every other writer's ideal.^(hh) In one sense Chesterton is taken too seriously and in the other sense not seriously enough.^(ii)

He was much more sane and cheerful and normal than most other English writers.^(jj) There is a sort of penumbra of playfulness round everything he ever said or penned: a halo of humour. Much of his work is marked by what can only be called a quiet exaggeration, even a quiet extravagance. The greatest poets of the world have a certain serenity, because they have not bothered to invent a small philosophy, but have rather inherited a large philosophy. It is, nine times out of ten, a philosophy which very great men share with very ordinary men. The poet makes men realize how great are the great emotions which they, in a smaller way have already experienced.^(kk) His own touch was as light as a feather; but the feather came truly from an angel's wing.^(ll)

He is as large as the land. It is impossible not to feel something mystical about his magnitude. He took things as they came, and the world as he found it, and men as God made them or even as they made themselves.^(mm) He was always a happy man, since he had a God^(nn) Chesterton inherited the tradition of a Church which had condemned heresies on the right hand and the left; and always claimed to stand for the truth as a whole and not for concentration on a part^(oo) And he had the one thing needful; he had the frame of mind that is the ultimate result of right reason and a universal philosophy; the temper that is the flower and fruit of all the tillage and the toil of moralists and theologians. He had Charity; that is the heart and not merely the mind of our ancient Christendom.^{pp}

Chesterton had a memory like the British Museum Library.^{qq} It was only when he wrote about himself that he dealt with a subject of which he, like all good and brave men, was profoundly ignorant^{rr} He contrived by sheer poetry to picture himself as prosaic. He was so imaginative that he imagined himself to be merely a plain man.^{ss}

He thought the world good because he had found so many things that were good in it—religion, the nation, the family.^{tt} The faces in the street were to him all the masks of a Deity.^{uu} He believed in the traditions of the past and the instincts of the people.^{vv} He represented a revolt of the normal against the abnormal.^{ww} He was pickled in common sense.^{xx}

With him the great concrete experiences which God made always come first; his own deductions and speculations about them come second.^{yy} He held that it is necessary to listen to all sides of a question in order to discover the truth of it. But he held that there was a truth to discover. He held that justice was a mystery, but not, like the decadents, that justice was a delusion.^{zz} Like every true romantic, he loved the irrevocable. He was a fanatic on the subject of the firm line. The thing he loved most in art was that lucidity and decision of outline which can be seen best in the cartoons of Raphael, in the Elgin Marbles, and in the designs of Michelangelo. The thing he hated most was the thing which we now call Impressionism—the substitution of atmosphere for shape, the sacrifice of form to tint, the cloudland of the mere colourist. He was literally packed with ideas—with ideas which required unpacking. And as a thief might steal a diamond and turn it into twenty farms, so the plagiarist of Chesterton might steal a sentence and turn it into twenty volumes. The brilliant man seems more lumbering and elaborate than anyone else, because he has something to say about everything. The very quickness of his mind makes the slowness of his narrative. For he finds sermons in stones, in all the paving stones of the street he plods along. Every fact or phrase that occurs in the immediate question carries back his mind to ages and initial power. Because he is original he is always going back to the origins.^{aaa} A mind like Chesterton's was full of light like a house made of windows; but the windows looked out on all sides and in all directions. We might say that, as the jewel has many facets, so the man had many faces; only none of them were masks.[bbb]

He saw what we see, but he saw it when it was not there. And some cannot see it—even when it is there. It is the paradox of his life that he loved the past, and he alone really lived in the future. As a dead man fighting with dead men, he can still very easily be covered with derision; but if we imagine him still alive and talking to living men, his remarks are rather uncomfortably like life.[ccc] The world, in the sense of the ordinary political and literary world, could not understand him or what he said. People could not understand it because it was not obscure enough. He did not soothe them with those formless but familiar obscurities which they expected.[ddd]

Being himself resolved to argue, to argue honestly, to answer everybody, to deal with everything, he produced books enough to sink a ship or stock a library, though he died comparatively early.[eee] This uneducated man was too well educated for all his contemporaries. He stood in a world which believed it was broadening; and the whole mind of that world was narrower than his own. It believed itself to be growing modern and many-sided; and he alone saw that it was growing monomaniac and mean. His mind is a place where extremes meet. It was because he was original; but also because he was universal.[fff] He was a poet whose whole life was a poem. The whole point of his point of view was that it looked out freshly upon a fresh world that might have been made that morning. He understood down to its very depths the theory of thanks.[ggg]

He had a stupendous certitude, in the presence of which all his writings on philosophy, and even theology, were but a litter of pamphlets. It is certain that this thing was in him from the first, in the form of a conviction, long before it could possibly have even begun to take the form of controversy. He had from the first that full and final test of truly orthodox Catholicity; the impetuous, impatient, intolerant passion for the poor; and even that readiness to be rather a nuisance to the rich, out of a hunger to feed the hungry.[hhh]

He lifts Faith above Reason; but does not lower Reason. He puts the supernatural higher than the natural; but does not lower the natural. He says that the lower thing is in every sense worthy; except that compared with the higher it is worthless.[iii] He is both a mystic and a rationalist. The Mystic is right in saying that the relation of God and Man is essentially a love-story. The rationalist is equally right in saying that the intellect is at home in the topmost heavens; and that the appetite for truth may outlast and even devour all the duller appetites of man. I do seriously believe that what protected him was very largely the prodigious power of his simplicity and his obvious goodness and love of truth.[jjj]

The habit of talking too much about his life has already led to thinking far too little of his literature. His ideas are being underrated, precisely because they are not being studied separately and seriously as ideas. The new criticism of Chesterton is still a criticism of Chesterton rather than of Chesterton's work; it is always a personal criticism, and often, I think, rather a spiteful criticism.[kkk] It is impossible to speak of Chesterton without becoming a little combative.[lll] Those happy few of us who happen to have read him have generally come to the conclusion that those who refer to him have not read him.[mmm]

Chesterton is a peculiarly difficult man for any biographer to estimate fairly. The reason lies in the fact that his personality was, as it were, singularly light and slippery, and that this slipperiness and levity arose not from eccentricity, but from a swift and unconquerable common sense. We are so rooted in open and systematic morbidities, in inhuman prejudices, in respectable monomanias, that a sane man terrifies us all like a lunatic. Chesterton was peculiarly an embodiment of this elvish sanity. He is continually startling us, not because his remarks are peculiar, but because they are a little more sensible than anything we had ever thought of. He was a sincere moralist and a sincere artist, but neither the old morality of light and darkness nor the new morality of light and shade could capture or contain him. He danced beyond them all with that divine frivolity which is the best definition of faith. It is said in some quarters that Chesterton has been overpraised, that a reaction has set in against him, that he will not fascinate the next generation. It matters not one rap whether he does or not to anyone who has perceived his absolute solidity and his eternal use to mankind. If we in this age had a little more faith in certainties and a little less dread of caprice and reaction and changes of public opinion, we should gain more credit for sense in the long run. Chesterton will win, not because he has friends or admirers or the approval of the public or the assent of the aesthetes. He will win because he is *right*—a word of great practical import which needs to be rediscovered. He may or may not be eclipsed for a time; it would be a truer way of putting it to say that the public may or may not be eclipsed for a time.ⁿⁿⁿ The world will return to him and will always return to him, almost as it returns to Aristotle; because he also judged all things with a gigantic and detached good sense.^{ooo}

* * *

Editor's Note: Now, I said these passages came from different sources, and they did. But they were all written by the same author. You probably figured out that they could only have been written by one writer. That writer is G. K. Chesterton. I said I edited them slightly, and I did. Instead of the name Chesterton, the name in the original source was Dickens, or Chaucer, or Browning, or Cobbett, or Blake, or Stevenson, or Newman, or Whitman, or Austen, or St. Francis of Assisi, or St. Thomas Aquinas. Or someone else.

We can look at these passages two ways. Either Chesterton admired these qualities in the subjects he was writing about, and he imitated them. Or else, because he already had these qualities, he connected with these writers in part because of what he had in common with them.

In either case, he is never so autobiographical as when he is biographical. Chesterton has revealed something of himself in his admirable and admiring descriptions of others. And it is a wonderful paradox that we can use the humble man's own words in order to praise him, in order to explain his own importance, his own greatness.

What is particularly striking is that he not only describes himself in the authors; he describes the world's reaction to himself in describing its reaction to them. So many of these authors were treated the same way as Chesterton is treated by his critics: underrated and underappreciated, misunderstood in spite of a crystal clarity of thought and expression.

Many of the authors he writes about died too soon, with some of their work still in them. This is also true of Chesterton himself. If he had lived longer, he would no doubt have finished the books he had been commissioned to write on Shakespeare and Napoleon and Savonarola (and try to imagine any other writer in history who would have been asked to write books on three figures so diverse as that trio). He would have completed an agreed-upon exchange on faith and doubt with the agnostic G. G. Coulton. And he would have continued his weekly contributions to the *Illustrated London News* and *G.K.'s Weekly*, as well as his irregular contributions to other periodicals and his introductions to other people's books, and his fortnightly reviews on BBC radio. And he would have continued to toss off poems and Father Brown stories and probably introduce other amateur sleuths, such as Mr. Pond, to the world of detective fiction. He would have commented on the encroaching darkness of Nazi Germany and the widening pit of Soviet Communism, and his analysis would have been as profound and provocative and prophetic as ever.

But though we do not have the privilege of this added material from Chesterton, who died too young at the age of sixty-two, it is probably a good thing. We have too much material as it is, much more than we know what to do with. We have already ill-served his legacy. It is an act of mercy that his legacy is not even larger and greater than it already is, because then our sin against his legacy would be even greater.

I would like to conclude this exercise with three more references from Chesterton, where his words about others could apply to himself.

In his book on Chaucer, Chesterton quotes William Caxton, the printer who published Chaucer. Caxton's apt description of Chaucer could well be applied to Chesterton: "For he writeth no void words; but all his matter is full of high and quick sentence."

And though I've already taken the liberty to compare Chesterton with two saints, Francis of Assisi and Thomas of Aquino, I think we can use Chesterton's own words about another saint that certainly describe Chesterton himself. I'm thinking of his description of Saint Peter, when he was crucified upside down: "I've often fancied his humility was rewarded by seeing in death the beautiful vision of . . . the landscape as it really is: with the stars like flowers, and the clouds like hills, and all men hanging on the mercy of God"[PPP]—the advantage of seeing the world upside down from the master of paradox.

Finally, there is one other person about whom Chesterton writes and says things that to me also evoke Chesterton himself. He says of this person that he sometimes seems wrong to us and would seem wrong to anyone in any time, and sometimes seems so amazingly right that he seems to be more fitted for our time than his own. For some of his utterances he could almost be called a maniac, but for others, we might justly call him a prophet. He seems extreme because he sees a further development in virtue that to us is untried. He seems to speak in contradictions, but that is because he sees the whole picture; he looks at life like a map and he sees a connection between things which to us are disconnected. He gives us the sensation that he is turning all our standards upside down, and also a sensation that he has undeniably put them the right way up.[qqq]

That bit was slightly edited, too. And it is probably a stretch to use it as a description of Chesterton, especially when you consider that it is Chesterton's description ... of Jesus. But draw your own conclusions.

NOTES

[a] "The Real Life of St. Thomas," *St. Thomas Aquinas*. This is Chesterton's description of St. Thomas Aquinas. For the remainder of the notes to this chapter, the actual person being described will appear in brackets, followed by the citation of the Chesterton work. I have also broken one of the rules I made for myself in preparing this book. In this chapter I do not confine myself only to GKC's journalism, but I also use references from Chesterton's books. However, since the use of those books is ironic, I will allow myself the exception.

[b] [St. Thomas Aquinas] "On Two Friars," *St. Thomas Aquinas*.
[c] [Walt Whitman] *T.P.'s and Cassell's Weekly*, Jan. 23, 1926.
[d] [Alexandre Dumas] *Daily News*, Jan. 2, 1907.
[e] [St. John Henry Newman] *Speaker*, Sept. 24, 1904.
[f] [Robert Browning] "Browning in Italy," *Robert Browning*.
[g] [Charles Dickens] Introduction to *Barnaby Rudge*.
[h] [Bret Harte] *Critic*, August 1902.
[i] [Edgar Wallace] *Illustrated London News*, Aug. 17, 1929.
[j] [Robert Louis Stevenson] *Daily News*, Mar. 14, 1901.
[k] [Dickens] *Morning Post*, Mar. 7, 1907.
[l] [Dickens] Introduction to *Reprinted Pieces*.
[m] [Stevenson] *Daily News*, Oct. 18, 1901.
[n] [Robert Burns] *Glasgow Herald*, Jan. 26, 1923.
[o] [George Bernard Shaw] *Illustrated London News*, Aug. 29, 1931.
[p] [William Watson] *Speaker*, Jan. 14, 1905.
[q] [Jonathan Swift] *Illustrated London News*, Oct. 15, 1932.
[r] [Thomas Babington Macaulay] *Daily News*, June 12, 1909.
[s] [Dickens] "Disputes on Dickens," *The Spice of Life*.
[t] [Not a specific author, but a general reference to great writers] "The Great Victorian Poets," *Victorian Age in Literature*.
[u] [Geoffrey Chaucer] "The Moral of the Story," *Chaucer*.
[v] [George Meredith] *Illustrated London News*, June 5, 1909.
[w] [Dickens] "Pickwick Papers," *Charles Dickens*.
[x] [Dickens] Introduction to *Christmas Books*.
[y] [Dickens] Introduction to *Dombey and Son*.
[z] [Dickens] "Dickens and Christmas," *Charles Dickens*.
[aa] [Dickens] Introduction to *Christmas Stories*.
[bb] [Dickens] "The Time of Transition," *Charles Dickens*.
[cc] [Dickens] Ibid.

^{dd} [Dickens] Introduction to *Sketches by Boz*.
^{ee} [Alfred Lord Tennyson] *Tennyson*.
^{ff} [Browning] "Browning in Later Life," *Robert Browning*.
^{gg} [Chaucer] "The Greatness of Chaucer," *Chaucer*.
^{hh} [Browning] "Browning as a Literary Artist," *Robert Browning*.
ⁱⁱ [Chaucer] "The Greatness of Chaucer," *Chaucer*.
^{jj} [Chaucer] Introduction to *Chaucer*.
^{kk} [Chaucer] "The Greatness of Chaucer," *Chaucer*.
^{ll} [Chaucer] "The Age of Chaucer," *Chaucer*.
^{mm} [Chaucer] "Chaucer as an Englishman," *Chaucer*.
ⁿⁿ [William Blake] *William Blake*.
^{oo} [Chaucer] "Chaucer and the Renaissance," *Chaucer*.
^{pp} [Chaucer] "The Religion of Chaucer," *Chaucer*.
^{qq} [Browning] "Browning in Early Life," *Robert Browning*.
^{rr} [Browning] "Early Works," *Robert Browning*.
^{ss} [William Cobbett] "The Rural Rider," *William Cobbett*.
^{tt} [Browning] "Browning in Later Life," *Robert Browning*.
^{uu} [Browning] "The Philosophy of Browning," *Robert Browning*.
^{vv} [Cobbett] "The Rural Rider," *William Cobbett*.
^{ww} [Browning] "Early Works," *Robert Browning*.
^{xx} [Chaucer] "Chaucer and the Renaissance," *Chaucer*.
^{yy} [Browning] "The Philosophy of Browning," *Robert Browning*.
^{zz} [Browning] "The Ring and the Book," *Robert Browning*.
^{aaa} [Blake] *William Blake*.
^{bbb} [St. Thomas More] *America*, May 11, 1935.
^{ccc} [Cobbett] "The Revival of Cobbett," *William Cobbett*.
^{ddd} [Cobbett] "The Amateur Historian," *William Cobbett*.
^{eee} [Aquinas] "The Real Life of St. Thomas," *St. Thomas Aquinas*.
^{fff} [Cobbett] "Last Days and Death," *William Cobbett*.
^{ggg} [St. Francis of Assisi] "The Little Poor Man," *St. Francis of Assisi*.
^{hhh} [Aquinas] "The Real Life of St. Thomas," *St. Thomas Aquinas*.
ⁱⁱⁱ [Chaucer] "The Religion of Chaucer," *Chaucer*.
^{jjj} [Aquinas] "The Aristotelian Revolution," *St. Thomas Aquinas*.
^{kkk} [Stevenson] "The Myth of Stevenson," *Robert Louis Stevenson*.
^{lll} [Dickens] *Dickensian*, November 1912.
^{mmm} [Jane Austen] *Illustrated London News*, June 1, 1929.
ⁿⁿⁿ [Stevenson] "Robert Louis Stevenson," *A Handful of Authors*.
^{ooo} [Dr. Samuel Johnson] "Dr. Johnson," *GKC as MC*.
^{ppp} "The Fantastic Friends," *The Poet and the Lunatics*.
^{qqq} *Hibbert Journal*, July 1909.

Chapter 4

All Four-Footed Things

The ChesterBelloc

> *"I reckon," he continued gaily, "that there are only five men who can talk me down, and one of the men is a woman. Certainly Belloc can't"*—*he added significantly.*
>
> *"I am not so sure," said Mrs. Chesterton, after a pause. "You only talk level with Mr. Belloc when you get in first. If he has the start you never catch up."*
>
> —Interview in *Daily News*, December 13, 1907

While it is easy to make fun of a friend in his presence, it is much easier to praise him seriously behind his back.[1] Mr. Belloc is a classicist, or rather, a classic.[2]

---

[1] *G.K.'s Weekly*, Nov. 26, 1927.

[2] *G.K.'s Weekly*, Nov. 8, 1924. Educated at Oxford, hoping to be a don but forced to make a living writing what he called "hackwork," Hilaire Belloc was as mixed a bag as you could find. Born to a French father and an English mother, he served in the French army but considered the hills of Sussex his home. But he hiked across America to woo an American bride from the wine country of northern California.

During Belloc's rise to fame, an anonymous journalist described him as having "a lust for battle," doing the thankless work of opposing the National Insurance Act and the "financial considerations in the distribution of honours" (i.e., the selling of peerages). "There is certainly no more vivid and vivacious talker in London.... Even Mr. G. K. Chesterton is silent in the presence of Mr. Belloc—they are the closest of friends, possibly because they disagree so well." (*West Sussex County Times*, July 27, 1912.)

GKC was indeed a devoted friend and perhaps even a more devoted admirer and defender of Belloc. What some saw as Belloc's tactlessness, GKC regarded as courage and a dedication to truth.

There was certainly a time in their early Fleet Street days when they were almost always together. But while Chesterton left London, it should be noted that Belloc also left London

Colonel Repington, in his memoirs, told an anecdote about me and Mr. Belloc to the effect that we were talking so much at dinner that an air raid occurred without our noticing it. I confess an English weakness, when I say that this flattered me.[3]

Mr. Bernard Shaw invented the Chesterbelloc, that pantomime elephant.[4] But I do not always agree with all Mr. Belloc says; and

---

and lived even farther away in Sussex. As the Timeline demonstrates, as they grew older, they saw each other on fewer and fewer occasions. They were connected by the written word, not by writing *to* each other, but by writing *about* each other, and otherwise writing about the same things—and ultimately, the same thing.

There is an oft-told tale that at Chesterton's funeral, Belloc sold exclusive rights to a personal article on Chesterton to four different papers. It's not true. He was at the White Hart crying inconsolably in front of a glass of beer. But if it were true, it would be understandable. Belloc was one of the most abused writers in journalism and had to rely on any writing job at all to pay his bills. However, the idea that a publisher would actually seek him out for an article would have been rare. It would have been an astonishment.

In some ways, it's a pity that Chesterton died before Belloc. It was left to Belloc to write a tribute to GKC, and it was not in any way adequate. Chesterton may have been better suited to have written a tribute to his friend and partner in all that they fought for side by side. But let us leave that aside and hear briefly from Belloc's certainly heartfelt eulogy of GKC: "I knew him, I think as well as any man ever knew another, not only from the depth of my affection, nor only for the intimacy and very long acquaintance of that intimacy—close on forty years—you may say the lifetime of a man, but most of all because so thoroughly did my mind jump with his, so fully did his answer meet the question my own soul was always asking, that his conclusions, the things he found and communicated, his solutions of the great riddles, his stamp of certitude, were soon part of myself." (*Saturday Review*, July 4, 1936.)

[3] *New York American*, Apr. 30, 1935.

[4] *G.K.'s Weekly*, Nov. 8, 1924. In contrast to Shaw's characterization of GKC and Belloc, Robert Lynd called them "the Heavenly Twins," comparing them with Castor and Pollux: "Great Twin Brethren, / Who fought so well for Rome." (Robert Lynd, *Old and New Masters* [T. F. Unwin, 1919], p. 25.)

He says the titles of their books and essays could be interchangeable. They are clearly defending the same thing; "however, Mr. Chesterton and Mr. Belloc are as unlike as possible in the spirit in which they proclaim it. If Mr. Chesterton gets up on his box to prophesy against the times, he seems to do so out of a passionate and unreasoning affection for his fellows. If Mr. Belloc denounces the age, he seems also to be denouncing the human race. Mr. Chesterton is jovial and democratic; Mr. Belloc is (to some extent) saturnine and autocratic. Mr. Chesterton belongs to the exuberantly lovable tradition of Dickens; indeed, he is, in the opinion of many people, the most exuberantly lovable personality which has expressed itself in English literature since Dickens. Mr. Belloc, on the other hand, has something of the gleaming and solitary fierceness of Swift and Hazlitt. Mr. Chesterton's vision, coloured though it is with the colours of the past, projects itself generously into the future. He is foretelling the eve of the Utopia of the poor and the oppressed when he speaks of the riot that all good men, even the most conservative, really dream of, when the sneer shall be struck from the face of the well-fed; when the wine of honour shall be poured down the throat of despair; when we shall, so far as to the sons of flesh is possible, take tyranny, and usury, and public treason, and bind them into bundles, and burn them.

when I do I do not always say it as he says it. Friends, thank God, are not so much alike as that; and fellow-Catholics can include the widest contrasts in the world.[5] But thank God there has never been any contradiction between our public and private relations. We are not rivals calling ourselves colleagues or conspirators calling ourselves opponents; foes disguised as friends or friends disguised as foes. We are not great imperial and international statesmen. The world has known something of our friendship, as naturally as it knew of the friendships of a simpler time.[6]

Mr. Belloc is disliked, not for any defence of ancient superstitions, but for a denunciation of modern superstitions.[7] He is a pugnacious, but also pertinacious and industrious animal.[8] He likes his history to be Roman Catholic, not only because he likes it to be Catholic, but partly because he likes it to be Roman.[9] I think the *Nation* rebuked Mr. Belloc for suggesting that drinking was best practised and understood in Catholic countries; and told him he could have found plenty of it in Scotland. He would answer, I imagine, that he could find it practised, but not understood. Mr. Belloc would not say that Catholics generally drank; but that they generally know how to drink.[10]

Mr. Belloc was perhaps the first to point out, in this country, that the State Education, so much praised as emancipating and enlightening, is in fact a far more crushing and flattening instrument of a centralised tyranny than the mere negative, scrappy and exceptional

---

"There is anger, as well as affection, in this eloquence—anger as of a new sort of knight thirsting to spill the blood of a new sort of barbarian in the name of Christ. Mr. Belloc's attack on the barbarians lacks the charity of these fiery sentences. He concludes his essay on the scientific spirit, as embodied in Lombroso, for instance, with the words, 'The Ass!' And he seems to sneer the insult where Mr. Chesterton would have roared it. Mr. Chesterton and he may be at one in the way in which they regard the scientific criminologists, eugenists, collectivists, pragmatists, post-impressionists, and most of the other 'ists' of recent times, as an army of barbarians invading the territories of mediaeval Christendom. But while Mr. Chesterton is in the gap of danger, waving against his enemies the sword of the spirit, Mr. Belloc stands on a little height apart, aiming at them the more cruel shafts of the intellect. It is not that he is less courageous than Mr. Chesterton, but that he is more contemptuous." (Ibid., pp. 27–28.)

[5] *G.K.'s Weekly*, Jan. 22, 1927.
[6] *New Witness*, Apr. 27, 1923.
[7] *New Witness*, Oct. 22, 1920.
[8] *New Witness*, Apr. 26, 1917.
[9] *New Witness*, June 11, 1920.
[10] *New Witness*, July 9, 1914.

action of a trifle like the Spanish Inquisition. The old persecutors could only arrest heresy in somebody; the new officials can impose orthodoxy on everybody.[11]

I have never, or hardly ever, seen in any paper a review of a book by Mr. Belloc. I have seen long or short notices in newspapers and elsewhere; I presume they are called notices because they never notice anything. Nearly all of them look as if they had been written before reading the book and not afterwards. To the rest, there are three generally accepted principles for reviewing Mr. Belloc's books. The first is to say nothing whatever about the point of the book; though it is generally quite clear and solid; a point that sticks out like a spike. The second is to assume beforehand that the book is full of furious and flamboyant praise of Popery; though it often, in fact, errs very much on the side of dry recital and carefully limited statements. And the third is to discover, if possible, some sentence in which the author has said that Louis the Fourteenth's shaving-brush was held by the second footman, when some don has decided that it was held by the third footman. The consequence is that nobody has any notion of the nature of Mr. Belloc's books, except by reading them; which is perhaps a good thing.[12]

Hilaire Belloc has written a good deal in very different styles. I think the best of his books is *The Path to Rome*. It is the story of a trip on foot across France. Then, too, there is his *Emmanuel Burden*, a satire on political corruption. But it is hard to prophesy what third of his works will survive. Belloc is too much engaged in the battle. He is fighting against certain vices, and once—thanks to his onslaughts—they have disappeared it will be harder to realise how valuable his pamphlets have been. His glory will vanish with the shame of the vices he attacks. His poetry, especially his sonnets, will certainly live.

Belloc has a very great importance in the militant life of the Catholic Church in England. Many a convert would never have crossed the threshold but for him. His personal influence is enormous, and is primarily due to his astounding vitality and his extraordinary learning. How did he influence me and the others? By simply showing us the truth. He pointed out that the Catholic Church is there, like the

---

[11] *G.K.'s Weekly*, Sept. 20, 1934.
[12] *G.K.'s Weekly*, Apr. 26, 1930.

gas lamp in the street. You pass by on one side, but if someone calls it to your attention you never afterwards think of denying its existence.

Belloc has an extraordinary gift of exposition. He is a born master of the art of teaching his equals. For example, at the beginning of the war he began a series of articles in *Land and Water* on the art of war. He showed what an army is, how it is formed and organised, all of which he knew better than anyone else because he had been in military service in France. He never left a single important aspect of the question in shadow. That is an unusual phenomenon.[13]

The Path to Rome is, to judge from Mr. Belloc's way of describing it to us, a very rambling, a very mazy, a very up-and-down and a particularly pleasant and exciting path. The travels of Mr. Belloc's body from Toul on the Moselle to Rome were sufficiently varied and picturesque, but the travels of his mind are something which altogether baffle description, sprawling, incalculable, splendidly vagrant and runaway. Mentally considered, the road from Toul to Rome runs through Oxford, Jerusalem, Croydon, Cincinnati, Hell, Heaven, and Purgatory. It has been stated (and it would seem to sum up Mr. Belloc's view of European civilisation) that all roads lead to Rome, and this entertaining volume gives rather the impression of a man trying to travel by all of them at once. He is, as a matter of mere bodily fact, walking along country roads in France and Italy, smoking and singing and drinking weak wine at small taverns. But in order to describe what really happened in that walk he has to speak of the termination of the Iliad, of proverbs, of the German army, of the Phoceans, of Cobbett's English, of mediaeval heretics, of the landscapes in Sussex, of the affectations of London culture, of Moliere's "Misanthrope," of the place of property in economics, of differences between the French and English army, of the goodness of worship and the badness of University dons. And these things are not touched upon apologetically in passing, but hunted separately through pages of disquisition as if the author were quite happy in an everlasting parenthesis. I will not call this uproarious and admirable mode of writing irrelevant, for it belongs, in truth, to that god-like mood in which everything is relevant to everything else. We all know that golden temper when we lean back and smoke a cigar and look at the heavens, and all things come

[13] *Living Age*, June 6, 1925.

together naturally, so that we would as soon pass to one thought as to another. Suppose that we are looking at sunset clouds and a man says abruptly, "Gorgonzola," we do not feel it a discord, we can see gorgonzola and the clouds united in one law of man's natural repletion, the cheese as nobly coloured as the clouds, the clouds as sensible and solid as the cheese. If we were, as we so often are, reading Buckle's *History of Civilisation* and somebody suggested "Ping-Pong," the connection would seem relevant; both occupations would be redolent of the futile activities of man. The mood is dominated with a certain universal relevance which is, when one comes to think of it, the essence of theism. It is impossible to keep to the subject, for it is impossible to get outside of it. It is idle to stick to the point, for all points on the circumference are equidistant from the centre.

The Path to Rome is quite the most sumptuous embodiment of this universal gaiety and erratic wisdom that has been written for many years past, but its peculiar originality and difference from the rut of such light literature in our day requires somewhat more careful definition. We have, of course, a school of nonsense—literary men of a high order are interested in the aesthetics of unreason, and the most fastidious of our decadents condescend to write nursery rhymes with a flavour of the symbolistic school. Nonsense—the true expression of gaiety—attracts the literary men of the day because it is a borderland, and therefore a mystic thing. Just as Mr. W. B. Yeats is interested in the frontier between earth and Paradise, so Mr. Max Beerbohm is interested in the frontier between earth and topsy-turvydom, the frontier where the trees begin to straggle strangely and the dark houses to lean away. So far as Mr. Belloc's book partakes of the character of nonsense, so far as it is the use of disorder and irrelevance as artistic weapons, the employment of designlessness itself as a design, so far as it is this, it would seem at first sight that his work was in a current modern spirit. But all the sensations of the reader tell him that this is not so, that the madness of Mr. Belloc is a peculiar madness, and the distinction when once realised is abysmal indeed. *The Path to Rome* is written recklessly. The typical modern book of nonsense is written so as to appear reckless. *The Path to Rome* is the product of the actual and genuine buoyancy and thoughtlessness of a rich intellect; whereas the young decadent takes more trouble over his nursery rhymes than even over his sonnets. And this is the paltriest and vilest of all the many vile works of the ultra-aesthetic school, with its care for technicality and finish. We have learnt to put up with clever men who handle English as if it were something that would come to pieces in their hands. We can manage to put up with a careful fiction and a careful poetry, and a careful comedy and tragedy; but the insulted human spirit does finally and absolutely rebel against being called upon to accept a careful hilarity. The objection to a book like *The Green Carnation* is that it is the very embodiment of something which is meaningless and even horrible; nonsense without joy—a cold nonsense, a priggish, foppish, heartless, inhuman nonsense. The dandies in *The Green Carnation* stand on their heads for the same reason that the dandies in Bond Street stand on their feet—because it is a thing that is done; but they do it with the same expression of fixed despair on their faces, the expression of fixed despair which you will find everywhere and always on the faces of frivolous people and men of pleasure.

He will be a lucky man who can escape out of that world of freezing folly into the flaming and reverberating folly of *The Path to Rome*. Here is a man who is using humour, not as a stimulant to get rid of this depression, but rather as a dance to get rid of his superfluous joy. After the traveller has told us all his wild tales and propounded all his fantastic opinions, and even overwhelmed us in torrents of mere gibberish, we still feel that he has not told us the best of his journey. Like Rabelais, his master, he has much love of the mere brute force of language. He breaks out into long screeds of verse that have and profess to have no other merit than that they serve as a kind of tune for the beat of his foot upon the road.

A compliment to his intellect Mr. Belloc might not relish, as his views on the purely intellectual classes are emphatic. "Would you like," he says "to know why Universities suffer from this curse of nervous disease? Why the greatest personages stammer, or have St. Vitus's dance, or jabber at the lips, or hop in their walk, or have their heads screwed round, or tremble in the fingers, or go through life with great goggles like a motor-car. Eh? I will tell you. It is the punishment of their intellectual pride, than which no sin is more offensive to the angels." And again: "They never can keep sane in a discussion; they will go wild on matters they are wholly unable to judge, such as the Armenian religion, or the politics of Paris, or what not. Never do they use one of those three phrases which keep a man steady and balance his mind. I mean the words: (1) After all, it is not my business; (2) Tut! tut! You don't say so; and (3) Credo in unum Deum, Patrem ominpotentem, Factorem omnium visibilium atque invisibilium." ["I believe in one God, the Father Almighty, Maker of all things visible and invisible."] That trio of talismans the reader will consider the maddest thing he has ever read; and also, if he comes to think of it, the sanest.[14]

When Mr. Belloc wrote a book about The Servile State, many people disagreed with it without reading it; some people agreed with it without reading it. If they had really read it, they would have found something entirely distinct, different and unexpected with which to agree or disagree. Strangest of all, they would have found that the book on The Servile State was a book about the Servile State and not about the Socialist State or even the Bureaucratic State.[15]

Only a few bold economic inquirers even knew what Mr. Belloc meant by the Servile State.[16] If it be a triumph to have popularised a name, Mr. Belloc might truly claim that nearly everybody by this time has heard of him and his Servile State. But Mr. Belloc, as it happens, had something to say. And I fear that few of these people have anything but the very vaguest notion of what it was that he said. Some credit him with something like the very contrary of what he said. The supporters of Socialism generally assume that he continues the criticism of Herbert Spencer, and says that our social future will be Servile because it will be Socialist. On the contrary, he says it will not be Socialist because it will be Servile. Nor is the Servile State, as some suppose, a mere condemnation of a too rigid or coercive State; a protest against what is official because it is officious. On the contrary, one of its essential points is that the tremendous transition to a servile society is entirely unofficial. It arises out of the private relations of employers and employed; as distinct and different from the public relations in which they are all supposed to be fellow-citizens. The thesis is that the servant might become in practice a slave, even before he had ceased to be in theory a citizen.

[14] *World*, Apr. 30, 1902.
[15] *New Witness*, Apr. 14, 1922.
[16] *Listener*, Dec. 4, 1935.

But if the supporters of Socialism miss the point, the supporters of conventional Capitalism miss it quite as wildly. Their favourite phrase is that Mr. Belloc is haunted by some horrible disaster that is going to fall on us in the future, and the name of this nightmare is the Servile State. This is rather like saying that Darwin warned us all that we should soon be eaten by the Missing Link. Just as the whole point of Darwin was that evolution was gradual and began a long time ago, so the whole point of Belloc is that the Servile tendency is gradual, and has already begun. So far from suggesting that some unnatural catastrophe threatens us, Mr. Belloc is chiefly concerned to show that the whole servile tendency is now SO natural to us that we have already begun to act on it without knowing it.

And all the time the thesis of the book is quite simple and straightforward, and could easily be explained to any reasonable person. Those who talk about the Servile State, who repeat its title, refer to it, rebuke it, revolve round it in various attitudes of speculation, mystification, remonstrance, or despair—for them it would seem that one possible expedient would be to read it. If this be too daring a solution of the difficulty, another way would be to look at the facts in front of our eyes at this very moment, and make an effort to think it out for ourselves. At this moment there is an enormous and terrible problem of the unemployed, and much discussion about the anomaly of their being paid and the tragedy of their being unpaid. Now it is not unnatural to suggest that an ordinary Capitalist, conventional but not without common sense, may be saying something like this: "I am honestly very sorry for the unemployed, and wish we could give them employment. But suppose we do give them employment, and then they go on strike or hold us up with some quarrel about wages? In short, I would give them work or even wages till they got work, if I were quite sure they would accept the work." Now in saying that he is, quite innocently, coming very close to the ancient logic of slavery, such as supported the pagan civilisation. It is almost the definition of a slave that he does receive unemployment pay. That is, he receives board and lodging, whether his master wants him to work at that moment or no. The whole point of the servile relation is that the master does undertake the whole support of the slave, idle or busy, but receives in return the right to decide when he shall be busy and when idle. Expressed in modern terms, the slave-owner agreed to give unemployment pay, on condition of getting rid of strikes. To a very large proportion of perfectly humane and intelligent business men to-day, it would seem a very workable compromise. It would be a very workable compromise. It would also be slavery—or the Servile State.[17]

The Servile State is characterized by the fact that its statesmen are in their very mentality and morality servile. It consists in leaving to the employers all the power of plutocracy, while granting to the employed all the security of slavery. Since it extinguished independent institutions and individual re-action, it has all the disadvantages of honest Socialism, with the extra disadvantage of being dishonest. It has the same fallacy of assuming that all government will be good; with the additional certainty that it will be bad.[18]

Infanticide, that ancient heathen custom, has already been hinted at in the spiritual slums of Eugenics. The return of heathenry to the human race would not be complete without the re-establishment of that great social institution on which the great heathen civilisation reposed, and which the industry and persuasion of numerable priests in the Dark Ages gradually weeded from the world. It has been found generally convenient to describe this new but old rival to the Christian distribution of liberty and property by the name which Mr. Belloc used in his discovery and demonstration of this modern trend; and to call it the Servile State. Its essence is this: that the rich shall constitute the State; and the poor, their servants, be thus only the indirect servants of the State. So, in pagan times, the free men were the State and the slaves only its indirect servants. Its advantage would be that it would make impossible all that accidental agony which we call destitution. Its policy, or the direction of it, is well represented by the principle of Compulsory Insurance, begun in Germany and unfortunately imitated in England; by which the employee, solely as such, is compelled to a particular form of economic precaution, while his employer is under no such compulsion, but has to assist the compulsory operation with money. In short, the rich man is forced to buy medicine, but the poor man is forced to take it. This is literally slavery; and begins the claim for entire support on one side and entire obedience on the other. Slavery is scientific, it is workable,

---

[17] *Illustrated London News*, Sept. 10, 1921.
[18] *New Witness*, Oct. 29, 1920.

it is comfortable; and there is a temper which we call the Christian temper, to which it is intolerable.[19]

It would hardly be a practical policy that all Socialists should be shot; but it would be the most practical of all policies if many Socialists could be converted. Now by our method, and by no other, many Socialists have been converted. It is my experience that the sort of man who does really become a Distributist is exactly the sort of man who has really been a Socialist. As a mere fact of modern history, I believe it was by this sort of conversion that the whole huge movement of State Socialism, which looked so alarmingly strong in England at the end of the nineteenth century, was actually defeated and dissolved. I remember when it was roughly but really true to say in this country, "We are all Socialists now"; save for some outlying suburban herds that the Fabians were quite confident could be made Socialists without knowing it. Mr. Belloc was first in the field, and alone in the field, in the fight that has challenged and checked and broken up the main power of this vast advance. But Mr. Belloc himself had been a Socialist; my brother had been a Socialist; I had been a Socialist. In various ways, and varying degrees, it applied to numberless men of that sort. Indeed, I remember the days when a vast Fabian population was growing up under the name of the Fabian Nursery; in which little toddling Socialists were trained to toddle in the straight, but narrow, way of Socialism. As a fact, many of them toddled away in totally different directions; and not a few turned up in the Distributist Nursery, demanding to have their dolls back and the control of their own domestic dolls' houses. I do not wish to appear to boast, which is a most unmilitary thing to do; but I think we have really done something in a small way; we have only prevented the whole intellectual world of England in the twentieth century from going Socialist; and we have done it in a little way of our own. We have done it by leaving no doubt whatever that we also hated Dives like the Devil. "Unless your justice exceed the justice of the Scribes and Pharisees ..." [Mt 5:20].[20] Unless our indignation with injustice exceeds the indignation of the Bolshevists and Bohemians,

[19] *New Days*, Sept. 18, 1915.
[20] When GKC quotes Scripture, he generally uses the King James Version. However, he always uses the Catholic translation of *dikaiosuné* as "justice" rather than the Protestant "righteousness."

we shall carry no conviction to men whose conviction of the curse of Capitalism is not only genuine as far as it goes, but right as far as it goes. We cured them of the heresy that property is theft; but only by facing the truth that a great deal of plutocracy is theft; because it is.[21]

When Mr. Belloc became the first editor of *The Eye-Witness*, that paper announced, amid a universal optimistic silence of the Press, that secret gambling and jobbery were rampant in English politics. It was stated as a general truth, and as a generalisation it sounded insane. Then by a sort of blazing coincidence, the Marconi Case burst upon the world, and was so sensationally public that it could hardly be concealed, even in the public Press. The Marconi Ministers were forced to make their explanations, we might say their confessions, in the witness-box of the Matin Case; and since that day everybody has known the truth.[22]

In the case of Mr. Belloc, I have always found that my attempts at a criticism of his books tended to turn into a criticism of his critics. He is, in a sense far too real for what we call practical politics, a practical man. For this reason I despair of doing justice to his book *The Jews* as a book, to its literature, its learning, its imaginative justice, its generous casuistry. Only one thing I will say of it as a symbolic summary. Any man who says that Mr. Belloc has merely written a book against Jews is mad. Any man who says Mr. Belloc has a prejudice against Jews is mad; mad with prejudice. A prejudice plainly means a dislike for a thing before we know anything about it, and it is madness to say Mr. Belloc knows nothing about Jews. Historically, he knows more about Jews than they do. He knows more *in favour* of Jews than they do. They complain of massacres; but few are likely to dwell on those in Cyrenaica in the second century. They urge toleration and peace; but they are not likely to look for them, as he does, in a particular period of mediæval Poland. Finally and most emphatically, any man who says Mr. Belloc believes in a conspiracy of Jews is not even mad; he is simply lying. That there is *not* a conscious conspiracy, but only the sort of co-operation natural in a scattered nation, is here stated by the author in the plainest possible words; not for the first time, nor I fear for the last. His main

[21] *G.K.'s Weekly*, Nov. 28, 1935.
[22] *G.K.'s Weekly*, July 12, 1930.

thesis about that nation is that which has long been maintained in this paper; that the solution is in some separation of the Jews as a national unit or corporation. But the reception of the book resolves itself into one very simple question. Is it possible to get people to listen to reason? They will listen to rhetoric; they have long listened to rhetoric in favour of Jews; they are now more and more listening to rhetoric against Jews. If we go that wild way, there will be worse than rhetoric against them.

I am glad to say that Mr. Belloc's book has raised some reasonable discussion among intelligent Jews. There are some letters in the *Sunday Times* which are sincere and sensible enough as far as they go. They plead that particular Jews are really deeply embedded in English life. Some of them do indeed remind Mr. Belloc that he had external relations with the French tradition or the Roman obedience. Now even if this were true in their sense, it is really itself an answer to their question. I happen to know Mr. Belloc very well; and I know that he is an Englishman interested in France, and not a Frenchman interested in England. I know that his soul will really sing on Duncton Hill and not on the highest peak of the Pyrenees. But nobody will deny that, whichever way we put it, he is in a rather exceptional position among Englishmen; and that is exactly the point. The Jew, in living among Christian nationals, is *not* in an exceptional position among Jews; and *that* is exactly the point. If Belloc were really an exile or an alien or a hybrid, he would still only be Belloc; while the Jews would be a race of Bellocs. But there is no such community in his case. Suppose, for the sake of argument, that he is a French exile in England. Still, there is not another Belloc in Sweden, writing weekly articles for a *New Witness* in Stockholm as he does for the *New Witness* in London. There is not another Belloc in Russia, writing poems about the Caucasus as he writes poems about the Downs. There is not a fourth Belloc in Turkey having written military criticisms in a Turkish paper throughout the war; and a fifth Belloc in America having denounced a piece of political graft in New York in the manner of the Marconi Case; and a sixth Belloc in India having just written a book on Buddhism called "Asia and the Faith." In short, he would only be an individual instance even as a hard case. If he is really an exile, he is really an exception. Now nobody but a fool would deny that those individual exceptions do exist, in any international relation. A division of England from Ireland, for instance, will undoubtedly uproot some families rooted in both islands; but that alone does not prove that the Irish are not and ought not to be a separate union. Now I for one agree with the individual Jews about the individual cases which they describe. There are individual Jewish friends of mine, whom I know as well as I know Mr. Belloc, of whom I should be inclined to say that they *have* assimilated so much of the English soil and habit as to make it at least very difficult, and possibly very harsh, to detach them. These cases really are (in that sense) like the case of Mr. Belloc, or at least like his case as they honestly conceive it to be. To them at least he is an exception; and to me at least they are exceptions. They are the hard cases that can be found under any rule. But for that very reason they do not themselves constitute a rule. They do not destroy the general truth about the nomadic and cosmopolitan condition of the Jew.

For the moment my last word, as I expected, has to be given not to Mr. Belloc but to the Jews whom he is trying to save. But if it were truly my last word to them, that is what it would be; that Mr. Belloc is simply trying to save them. What is boiling up in England now on every side is sheer instinctive anarchical Anti-Semitism. The Jews have to choose between *that* and the other thing; which is listening to reason, and in this case means listening to Belloc.[23] Mr. Belloc raises his voice in public to warn us against Anti-Semitism; and he is called an Anti-Semite.[24]

There is still a literary legend that Mr. Belloc and I are ruthless Anti-Semites; though half the world is now full of a raging and reckless Anti-Semitism, which we never promoted, and against which we protest to this day.[25]

In the *Daily News'* review of Mr. Belloc's book *The Free Press*, I find this in the first few lines, stated as if it were common knowledge; "Mr. Belloc seems to live under an obsession of conspiracies. He regards the Jews as a conspiracy." Mr. Belloc has explained lucidly, I might say laboriously, in many places, that he does not regard them as anything of the sort. He says, in perfectly simple words, repeated

---

[23] *New Witness*, Apr. 28, 1922.
[24] *New Witness*, May 19, 1922.
[25] *G.K.'s Weekly*, June 22, 1933.

several times, that the Jews are *not* a conspiracy, but a nationality. That is to say, they work together, in the sense in which the Catholic Irish all over the world work together. The latter will be found everywhere saying about England the same sort of thing (much of it true, unfortunately, but not all): but this is not because they send each other cipher telegrams, but because they are all a certain sort of people. This distinction does not seem difficult to understand; but most critics seem unable even to read it in plain print. I need not go through all the other points about the other Mr. Belloc; for indeed, he is not a man but a myth. The man I know has, I should say, too classical a taste in art and excessively scientific taste in science. He has a great gift of hilarity; but less optimism, or faith in optimism, than any man I ever knew. Beyond the high spirits that should be the heritage of a healthier England, I think the most divergent thing is the touch of the French respectability, which is the most rigid in the world. He happens to be a man of genius, and has incidentally written fine humorous verse and prose; in which he has occasionally made fun of Jews, much as *Punch* made fun of Irishmen, but much better and rather less bitterly. He thinks the Jews are a serious problem: but every man in his five wits is coming to think that. If I were abusing instead of admiring, his sociological studies, I should profess to find them dull; for they are often as dry and compact as Aristotle. But though we hear much of Russian peasants who cannot read, it would seem almost equally true that English readers cannot read. Their primary idea in reading is to read into a book what they have been told to find there. They have been told that any man who for any reason admires the Middle Ages must himself be a sort of walking gargoyle. And therefore the critic in the *Daily News*, in the very act of quoting a sentence in which Mr. Belloc deprecates exaggeration, declares that he always exaggerates.

The effort of the writers is not so much to write against Mr. Belloc as to write about everything except the two or three very simple and solid things of which Mr. Belloc has written. The plutocratic Press deceives more dangerously by suppression than by positive untruth; and there are cases in which the critics seem specially anxious to avoid the use of some one particular word. This is common enough; there is such a thing as a word that gives a whole case away. I remember, in connection with some recent dramatic impersonation of Shylock, a long, interesting and many-sided controversy carried on in one of the great dailies; in which many able and eminent men discussed Shakespeare's moral intention about the character. Some, including Mr. Zangwill, I think, held that Shylock was made not only spirited but sympathetic; that Shakespeare was not only not himself Anti-Semite but might almost be called Pro-Semite. Others shook their heads sadly, saying that after all even Shakespeare could not wholly rise above the sixteenth century or share the blameless bliss of belonging to the twentieth. They illuminated in turn a hundred fascinating aspects both of Shakespeare and Shylock. And throughout the whole of that hundred-fold criticism, so far as I remember, nobody so much as mentioned the single word "usury." It is precisely as if men conducted a prolonged discussion on the character of Macbeth; in the course of which they were all forbidden to mention even the word "murder." The play called *The Merchant of Venice* happens to be about usury. It is founded on a mediaeval legend which was a healthy satire on usury; and the dramatist, while preserving that sound Christian condemnation of usury, also attempts, if with a more than mediaeval imagination and liberality, to suggest what even the usurer might reasonably have to say for himself; what sense of grievance and subtle self-respect might turn that type of sinner also from a monster to a man. But even if we were so absurd as to suppose that what Shylock has to say is all that Shakespeare has to say (in the teeth of some the most Shakespearian speeches in Shakespeare) it would still be the fact that it was about a usurer, and a problem of usury, that they were said. And it is these plain words, standing for primary facts, that are circuitously avoided in the present debate on the Press.

Just as the old newspaper discussion never so much as introduced the word usury, so this newspaper criticism of Mr. Belloc's book does not, from beginning to end, so much as mention the word "advertisement."

Advertisement is only one of the fundamental facts Mr. Belloc mentions as falsifying the claim of the current Press. But is great and growing and glaringly obvious; and therefore the critic does not grapple with it. Now it is the fact that criticism of crucial institutions, especially commercial institutions, is constrained and hampered in varying degrees by the weight of wealthy advertising interests, by which alone the big papers can pay. Every journalist knows it is a fact, and none more than the journalists who ignore it, or the journalists who attempt to deny it.

And if we wish to see a plain truth plainly, we must everywhere thus translate the affair into franker but less familiar terms. We have grown used to print as to a mere pattern. But when Mr. Belloc employs this very practical method of comparison, his critics are strangely puzzled. They seem to be moved to wonder or weak mirth, for instance, by his very reasonable remark that we must compare the newspaper with a more natural distribution of news. The *Daily News* critic turns up his nose with inimitable intellectual snobbishness over the "ignorant and illiterate man" in the village tavern, as compared with that classic monument of culture, the man who is "sufficiently educated to read the daily Press." It does not seem to occur to him, or to wiser critics than he, that the objection to news all coming in one form from one office is that if it is wrong it is rigidly and unalterably wrong. One of the advantages of the greater flexibility of gossip is that, if it can be shaped by exaggeration, it can also be reshaped by the incredulity of the common sense. In other words, the man in the tavern may not be so ignorant that he cannot throw a pot of beer at somebody who talks too transparent nonsense; and that by many such criticisms much nonsense is intercepted.[26]

English people are not getting the good out of Mr. Belloc's books as books, because there is a stupid journalistic legend that he is a partisan. It is totally untrue. There are things on which Mr. Belloc disagrees with his countrymen; but he is most emphatically not a man repeating the views of his party and insisting on your agreeing with them; he is a man advancing very original views entirely his own and you are perfectly free to disagree with them. Many of his party do disagree with them; but you might as well read them and realise that they are new.

We hear a good deal nowadays about resistance to new ideas. It seems to mean entirely certain negative and sceptical ideas that are not new at all. A man who disbelieves in God, a man who disbelieves in marriage, or disbelieves in the duty of fighting for his country, may be right or wrong, but he is not new. All the arguments against Providence are in the Book of Job, all the arguments against immortality

[26] *New Witness*, Feb. 14, 1918.

are in St. Thomas Aquinas, satires against marriage, and denunciations of war can be found in the most ancient pagan literature. What we commonly call modern ideas are all very ancient ideas; but if you want one or two new ideas you will find them in certain books, incidentally Mr. Belloc's book, and you can accept them or not as you choose. But they are not the stock-in-trade of a party. Mr. Belloc is opposed to Socialism, but his *Servile State* is not an attack on Socialism or any sort of State tyranny; it is an entirely original economic theory by which our social reforms tend, not to Socialism, but actually to the ancient status of masters and slaves. Mr. Belloc is a Catholic, but most Catholic writers, for instance, have described Queen Elizabeth as a tyrant. Mr. Belloc's whole point is that Queen Elizabeth was not a tyrant, but a victim of tyranny. Or again, Mr. Belloc does dislike Prussia, and, naturally, prefers France; but the friends and foes of Prussia would alike say that Bismarck's triumph was that he achieved the union of the German people. Mr. Belloc insists that Bismarck's triumph was that he prevented the union of the German people. If all the Germans had united, it would have been under Austria; Bismarck made sure that his Empire should be not large enough, but small enough, to leave the leadership to Prussia.

Now, all those are ideas to be judged in themselves, in books that you should read for yourselves. And it is not reading a book for yourself to open it with a newspaper prejudice that the writer writes nothing but Popish pamphlets when, in fact, he does nothing of the sort.[27]

The paradox of Belloc is this: That he is very well-known and most people are interested in him, but most people do not seem to know what is most interesting about him—or at least, about his books. Most recognise in him the picturesque figure of a fighter, yet few understand what he really fights; most quote him as a wit abounding in epigram, yet few see the point.

We have already mentioned the foolish notion that he fought against nothing but Jews; but nobody even noticed the joke of his last novel, one of his best, *The Post-Master-General*, in which the only good and noble characters are all Jews, and most of the swindlers and usurers (I grieve to say) are Scotchmen.

But it is so with more serious things. He has advanced important theses, and even his complimentary critics seldom criticise them. For

---

[27] *Listener*, Nov. 15, 1933.

instance, they know that he has been a French gunner and wrote a fine spirited poem to his old regiment which had fought for the French Revolution. *"You that put the mighty from their seat ... and trailed your scabbards in the halls of kings."* This naturally goes with some traditional hostility, not so much to Germans as to Prussians, whom he thinks the provocative force in Europe.

Right or wrong, that question seems more challenging than whether he has written a song or two about guns.

It is so with the Servile State. In England everybody uses his phrase, waiters and errand-boys talk about the Servile State. But they do not talk about what he wrote about. He wrote about a most interesting theory that Capitalism will not lead to Communism, but will harden into a system of employers, as such responsible for employees as such, empowered to prevent them starving, but also prevent them striking.

In short, Mr. Belloc is original and is admired, but he is not admired for what is most original. That seems to be too original for even admiring critics to understand.[28]

This is what is called "the Chester-Belloc view." We think that the modern evil is monopoly. Our objection to Socialism is that it is really only the culmination of Capitalism, and our objection to Capitalism is that it is likely to turn into Socialism, because what they have in common is that they both make wealth impersonal and centralised. Now it does not seem to me to matter much whether in practice all the land or all trade is owned by a ring of millionaires who are called private industry, though they are really a monopoly, or by a ring of officials who are called government or Socialism, though they are really oligarchy. The point is that both forms in the modern world, and particularly the industrial world, tend to keep power in the centre, because either in the form of Socialist officials, as in Bolshevik Russia, or in the form of trust magnates, as in industrial America, for instance, a few men do in practice not only rule, but own the lives of all other people; they own the things they eat and drink, as well as the machinery they use, and they pay them a wage. Our cure for this evil of monopoly is a reversal of the whole procedure, and an attempt to create as many small owners as possible. There is no organ in the Press that stands for that view at all. There are Socialist papers that stand, as we should say, for bureaucracy, and

[28] *New York American*, Apr. 3, 1935.

the ordinary Capitalist papers that stand for big business, or, in other words, for monopoly. But there is no one saying, "I am on the side of the independent shopkeeper against the stores," or "I am on the side of the small farmer against the landlord or the County Council, or anyone else who wants to unify the whole system." This is a view with which you may agree or disagree. You may think it desirable or undesirable; or, as is more likely to be the case with most people, you may think it possible or impossible. But considering that that form of well-distributed property exists already over an enormous part of the world—over all peasant countries, for instance—and has existed for all periods of the world's history, it seems extraordinary that there is no organ of opinion to express it at all, and all the more because it is the most sane and simple and ordinary of all human ideals.[29]

We have started people thinking; we have started people talking. We do not know how many there are of them; there are certainly many more than we know. That process of intellectual branching or breeding may go on until they have multiplied behind anything we could imagine. The world may wake up some day to find a new democracy of Distributists.[30] Hilaire Belloc was the only original hero and prophet of this process; and it was he who started the whole seminal and slowly branching growth that has stopped and strangled the Socialist movement, in the intellectual world which I remember in my youth. But it is true to say of that intellectual impulse that it converted thousands of thinking people from Socialism to Distributism. It converted me, for one.[31]

The courage of the intellect is a matter in which most of us are moral cowards. To testify thus and keep the faith in the most unsuitable surroundings, at the most unseasonable moment.

A very brilliant public man spoke to me recently in a most generous and admiring tone about Belloc; but added, "He offends people. One pays a lot for satirizing Jews." I answered, "One does; I have paid a little myself, but not so much." He also said, "Belloc has had no reward for all his talents." Somehow I suppressed the answer, "His reward is not here."[32]

[29] *Observer*, Feb. 11, 1923.
[30] *New Witness*, Apr. 27, 1923.
[31] *G.K.'s Weekly*, Dec. 5, 1935.
[32] *G.K.'s Weekly*, Nov. 26, 1927.

Chapter 5

Ancient Crooked Will

The Devil

God is a workman and can make things. The devil is a gentleman and can only destroy them.

—"The Face of Brass," Collected Works, vol. 14

Going mad is the slowest and dullest business in the world. I have very nearly done it more than once in my boyhood, and so have nearly all my friends, born under the general doom of mortals, but especially of moderns; I mean the doom that makes a man come almost to the end of thinking before he comes to the first chance of living.

But the process of going mad is dull, for the simple reason that a man does not know that it is going on. Routine and literalism and a certain dry-throated earnestness and mental thirst, these are the very atmosphere of morbidity. If once the man could become conscious of his madness, he would cease to be mad.[1] But I know distinctly less about my own sub-consciousness than I know about the devil.[2]

Even a bad play ought not to be blamed for a point it does not make; nor, I will add, praised for a point it does not make. I remember once sitting through an exceedingly bad play called *Magic*, during which my gloom was deepened by guilt; but while I could easily understand its author being received with rotten eggs, I still cannot understand some of the tributes he did receive. A highly intelligent, if too ingenious

---

[1] *Daily News*, Feb. 18, 1911.
[2] *Illustrated London News*, Nov. 27, 1909.

critic, falsely and brazenly pretending that this bad play was an interesting play, explained that the interest lay in an idea that faith could create a world better than the real one; which view however he corrected, with the sigh of a sceptic, sadly asking why, if God could descend to alter a coloured light, God did not alter all the evils of the earth. Now I should really have thought that anyone who managed to find such a play interesting might have noticed what happened in the wretched thing; and observed a few facts, as (1) that the light is not altered by God, but by his enemies the demons; (2) that they do a silly thing for a bad reason, because they are demons; (3) that, so far from it implying that things are as we wish, not a soul in the story believes in demons, except one who believes reluctantly because he knows.[3]

I have no sympathy whatever with the common boisterous sceptic. The sceptics only denounce Spiritualism because they do not believe in it. I only denounce Spiritualism because I do believe in it. I fear, the Spiritualist often open their doors to very disreputable deities. They entertain angels unawares—fallen angels. I do not deny the facts of Spiritualism. I wish I could.[4]

Believing that there are spirits, I am bound in mere reason to suppose that there are probably evil spirits; believing that there are evil spirits, I am bound in mere reason to suppose that some men grow evil by dealing with them.[5] I am not particularly proud in believing that there is positive evil in the world. I have no pride in it for the same reason that have no doubt of it. My shame and my certainty both come from the same thing; that I have found the evil in myself.[6]

The brute fact is that certain communications do come to entirely honest people through planchette, through table-rapping, through automatic writing, through professional mediums. The communications may be dishonest, but the people are not. In truth, the communications may be dishonest because they are genuine. They may be genuine messages from hell, the home of dishonesty. But a man is not dishonest because he receives them, because he believes them, or because he believes them to have come from heaven.

---

[3] *New Witness*, Dec. 6, 1917. His gloom was deepened by guilt because he was the author of the play.

[4] *Illustrated London News*, Oct. 30, 1909. He wrote this shortly after Frances had visited a medium in order to contact her dead brother.

[5] "The Unanswered Challenge," *Eugenics and Other Evils*.

[6] *New Witness*, Aug. 18, 1922.

When I was a boy I used to play with a planchette as carelessly as I played with a cricket-bat; I have never operated through a medium, but I suppose that the doubts and the certainties are much the same. If it had ever occurred to me to believe the things that the planchette wrote down I should be a raving maniac by this time. Gladstone pronouncing on the Budget would have been a very mild interlude in our old orgies of supernatural interviewing. Moses was perfectly ready to provide us with ten new commandments; Cromwell would be converted to Catholicism as soon as look at you. There was one story in particular about a secret marriage of one of my aunts to Cardinal Manning, which I am very glad did not find its way to Mr. Stead and the serious newspapers. One day, I remember, "Planchette," without the faintest justification, advised an acquaintance of mine to get a divorce. When we remonstrated, the oracle inscribed on the paper a long, illegible word beginning with O R R. Now, there is no word in English beginning O R R. We insisted on greater lucidity; and eventually the long word turned out like this— "Orrible revelations in 'igh life." ... I abandoned planchette as a toy, because even as a toy I found it left behind a strange and stale flavour of ignominy, as of a man who had been drunk the night before; and this smelt a little of evil. But I never dreamed at any time of believing in any of the Virgils, Newtons, and Isaiahs who used to come and give us information. I trust them no more than the monologues in a mad-house.[7]

Whether or not there are devils, there most certainly are devil-worshippers.[8]

What I have now to relate really happened; yet there was no element in it of practical politics or of personal danger. It was simply a quiet conversation which I had with another man. But that quiet conversation was by far the most terrible thing that has ever happened to me in my life. It happened so long ago that I cannot be certain of the exact words of the dialogue, only of its main questions and answers; but there is one sentence in it for which I can answer absolutely and word for word. It was a sentence so awful that I could not forget it if I would. It was the last sentence spoken; and it was not spoken to me.

---

[7] *Illustrated London News*, Nov. 27, 1909.
[8] *Illustrated London News*, Sept. 22, 1917.

The thing befell me in the days when I was at an art school. An art school is different from almost all other schools or colleges in this respect: that, being of new and crude creation and of lax discipline, it presents a specially strong contrast between the industrious and the idle. People at an art school either do an atrocious amount of work or do no work at all. I belonged, along with other charming people, to the latter class; and this threw me often into the society of men who were very different from myself, and who were idle for reasons very different from mine. I was idle because I was very much occupied; I was engaged about that time in discovering, to my own extreme and lasting astonishment, that I was not an atheist. But there were others also at loose ends who were engaged in discovering what Carlyle called (I think with needless delicacy) the fact that ginger is hot in the mouth.

I value that time, in short, because it made me acquainted with a good representative number of blackguards. In this connection there are two very curious things which the critic of human life may observe. The first is the fact that there is one real difference between men and women; that women prefer to talk in twos, while men prefer to talk in threes. The second is that when you find (as you often do) three young cads and idiots going about together and getting drunk together every day you generally find that one of the three cads and idiots is (for some extraordinary reason) not a cad and not an idiot. In those small groups devoted to a drivelling dissipation there is almost always one man who seems to have condescended to his company; one man who, while he can talk a foul triviality with his fellows, can also talk politics with a Socialist, or philosophy with a Catholic.

It was just such a man whom I came to know well. It was strange, perhaps, that he liked his dirty, drunken society; it was stranger still, perhaps, that he liked my society. For hours of the day he would talk with me about Milton or Gothic architecture; for hours of the night he would go where I have no wish to follow him, even in speculation. He was a man with a long, ironical face, and close and red hair; he was by class a gentleman, and could walk like one, but preferred, for some reason, to walk like a groom carrying two pails. He looked like a sort of Super-jockey; as if some archangel had gone on the Turf. And I shall never forget the half-hour in which he and I argued about real things for the first and the last time.

Along the front of the big building of which our school was a part ran a huge slope of stone steps, higher, I think, than those that lead up to St. Paul's Cathedral. On a black wintry evening he and I were wandering on these cold heights, which seemed as dreary as a pyramid under the stars. The one thing visible below us in the blackness was a burning and blowing fire; for some gardener (I suppose) was burning something in the grounds, and from time to time the red sparks went whirling past us like a swarm of scarlet insects in the dark. Above us also was gloom; but if one stared long enough at that upper darkness, one saw vertical stripes of grey in the black and then became conscious of the colossal façade of the Doric building, phantasmal, yet filling the sky, as if heaven were still filled with the gigantic ghost of Paganism.

The man asked me abruptly why I was becoming orthodox. Until he said it, I really had not known that I was; but the moment he had said it I knew it to be literally true. And the process had been so long and full that I answered him at once, out of existing stores of explanation.

"I am becoming orthodox," I said, "because I have come, rightly or wrongly, after stretching my brain till it bursts, to the old belief that heresy is worse even than sin. An error is more menacing than a crime, for an error begets crimes. An Imperialist is worse than a pirate. For an Imperialist keeps a school for pirates; he teaches piracy disinterestedly and without an adequate salary. A Free Lover is worse than a profligate. For a profligate is serious and reckless even in his shortest love; while a Free Lover is cautious and irresponsible even in his longest devotion. I hate modern doubt because it is dangerous."

"You mean dangerous to morality," he said in a voice of wonderful gentleness. "I expect you are right. But why do you care about morality?"

I glanced at his face quickly. He had thrust out his neck as he had a trick of doing; and so brought his face abruptly into the light of the bonfire from below, like a face in the footlights. His long chin and high cheekbones were lit up infernally from underneath; so that he looked like a fiend staring down into the flaming pit. I had an unmeaning sense of being tempted in a wilderness; and even as I paused a burst of red sparks broke past.

"Aren't those sparks splendid?" I said.

"Yes," he replied.

"That is all that I ask you to admit," said I. "Give me those few red specks and I will deduce Christian morality. Once I thought like you, that one's pleasure in a flying spark was a thing that could come and go with that spark. Once I thought that the delight was as free as the fire. Once I thought that red star we see was alone in space. But now I know that the red star is only on the apex of an invisible pyramid of virtues. That red fire is only the flower on a stalk of living habits, which you cannot see. Only because your mother made you say 'Thank you' for a bun are you now able to thank Nature or chaos for those red stars of an instant or for the white stars of all time. Only because you were humble before fireworks on the fifth of November do you now enjoy any fireworks that you chance to see. You only like them being red because you were told about the blood of the martyrs; you only like them being bright because brightness is a glory. That flame flowered out of virtues, and it will fade with virtues. Seduce a woman, and that spark will be less bright. Shed blood, and that spark will be less red. Be really bad, and they will be to you like the spots on a wallpaper."

He had a horrible fairness of the intellect that made me despair of his soul. A common, harmless atheist would have denied that religion produced humility or humility a simple joy: but he admitted both. He only said, "But shall I not find in evil a life of its own? Granted that for every woman I ruin one of those red sparks will go out: will not the expanding pleasure of ruin ..."

"Do you see that fire?" I asked. "If we had a real fighting democracy, some one would burn you in it; like the devil-worshipper that you are."

"Perhaps," he said, in his tired, fair way. "Only what you call evil I call good."

He went down the great steps alone, and I felt as if I wanted the steps swept and cleaned. I followed later, and as I went to find my hat in the low, dark passage where it hung, I suddenly heard his voice again, but the words were inaudible. I stopped, startled: then I heard the voice of one of the vilest of his associates saying "Nobody can possibly know." And then I heard those two or three words which I remember in every syllable and cannot forget. I heard the Diabolist say, "I tell you I have done everything else. If I do that I shan't know the difference between right and wrong." I rushed out without daring to pause; and as I passed the fire I did not know whether it was hell or the furious love of God.

I have since heard that he died: it may be said I think, that he committed suicide; though he did it with tools of pleasure, not with tools of pain. God help him, I know the road he went; but I have never known or even dared to think what was that place at which he stopped and refrained.[9]

I could fancy that men drew the Tempter with the curves of a serpent because they can be twisted into the shape of a question mark.[10] I have my doubts about all this real value in mountaineering, in getting to the top of everywhere and overlooking everything. Satan was the most celebrated of Alpine guides, when he took Jesus to the top of an exceeding high mountain and showed him all the kingdoms of the earth. But the joy of Satan in standing on a peak is not a joy in largeness, but a joy in beholding smallness, in the fact that all men look like insects at his feet.[11] What is the matter with the cult of Service is that, like so many modern notions, it is an idolatry of the intermediate, to the oblivion of the ultimate. It is like the jargon of the idiots who talk about Efficiency without any criticism of Effect. The sin of Service is the sin of Satan: that of trying to be first where it can only be second.[12]

The assertion that a man is possessed of a devil is the only way of avoiding the assertion that he is a devil.[13] The war in us is still going on between Falstaff, who did evil stupidly, and Satan, who desired evil intelligently. Falstaff is a mocker because he is incomplete; Satan is serious because he is complete.[14] Idolatry is committed, not merely by setting up false gods, but also by setting up false devils; by making men afraid of war or alcohol, or economic law, when they should be afraid of spiritual corruption and cowardice. The Moslems say, "There is no God but God." But we have to learn and remember also that there is no Satan but Satan.[15]

Where there is nothing there is Satan.[16]

---

[9] *Daily News*, Nov. 9, 1907.
[10] *Illustrated London News*, Jan. 27, 1917.
[11] "Tremendous Trifles," *Tremendous Trifles*.
[12] *The Forum*, February 1929.
[13] *Illustrated London News*, Apr. 28, 1917.
[14] *Illustrated London News*, May 18, 1907.
[15] *Illustrated London News*, Sept. 11, 1909.
[16] *Daily Herald*, Nov. 22, 1913.

Chapter 6

Starve, Scourge, Deride Me

The Accusation*

The world owes God to the Jews.... They preserved the primary religion of all mankind.

—"God and Comparative Religion," *The Everlasting Man*

I will take the opportunity here of correcting a curious mistake that clings to the minds of numbers of my correspondents. There is in particular a gloomy gentleman in America who keeps on asking me how my Anti-Semite prejudice is getting on, and generally displaying a curiosity about how many Hebrew teeth I have pulled out this week, and how often a Pogrom is held in front of my house. He appears to base it all on some statement of mine that Jews were tyrants and traitors. Upon this basis his indignation is eloquent, lengthy, and (in my opinion) just. The only weakness affecting this superstructure is the curious detail that I never did say that Jews were tyrants and traitors. I said that a particular kind of Jew tended to be a tyrant and another particular kind of Jew tended to be a traitor. I say it again. Patent facts of this kind are permitted in the criticism of every other nation on the

---

*Chesterton says that the nineteenth century would be easier to understand if Thomas Carlyle were not in it. Well, Chesterton himself apparently would be easier to understand if he had never mentioned the Jews. But he did. And now he has to be explained, not so much because of what Chesterton said, but because of what others have said he said. This chapter could be skipped, just as Carlyle could justifiably be skipped when studying the nineteenth century. But if you've ever heard the accusation against Chesterton—or if you've ever made it—then you should spend some time listening to Chesterton's own rebuttal to the accusation that he was anti-Semitic.

planet: it is not counted illiberal to say that a certain kind of Frenchman tends to be sensual or a certain kind of Prussian tends to be supercilious. It is as plain as a pikestaff that the Parisian tradition of life and letters has a marked element of sensuality; it is as plain as a pikestaff that the Prussian theory of the aristocracy and the army has an element of rather crude conceit. It is also as plain as a pikestaff that those who are creditors will always have a temptation to be tyrants, and that those who are cosmopolitans will always have a temptation to be spies. This has nothing to do with alleging that the majority of any people falls into its typical temptations. In this respect I should imagine that Jews varied in their moral proportions as much as the rest of mankind. Rehoboam was a tyrant; Jehosaphat was not. In what is perhaps the most celebrated collection of Jews in human history, the proportion of traitors was one in twelve. But I cannot see why the tyrants should not be called tyrants and the traitors traitors; why Rehoboam should not cause a rebellion or Judas become an object of dislike, merely because they happen to be members of a race persecuted for other reasons and on other occasions. Those are my views on Jews. They are more reasonable than those of the people that wreck their shops; and much more reasonable than those of the people who justify them on all occasions.[1]

The crank is never really interested in his subject, because he takes too stiff and biased a view of it. He knows nothing of the romantic hesitations, the rich reactions that there are in a really interesting subject. He cannot love and hate a thing at the same time; which is the root of half the poetry of the world. For instance, I should firmly claim that I am interested in Jews. I have not, indeed, the faintest serious dislike of them; nor can I be said to be on their side. But they attract me, they puzzle me; I find myself for ever fitting theories to them; I think they are a human triumph, a national danger, an intellectual inspiration, and a frightful nuisance. But the people who publish little pamphlets about the persecution of Jews in Russia are not interested in Jews at all. They are interested in certain imaginary good old men with patriarchal beards and ragged gaberdines who are made to wander about in the snow because they never did anyone any harm. All the interesting part of the Jewish problem, good as well as bad, is simply left out.[2]

---

[1] *Illustrated London News*, Sept. 16, 1911.
[2] *Illustrated London News*, July 19, 1913.

My friends and I originally shocked the Victorian conventions by saying that the Jews should be recognised as a separate nation, with their own national virtues and vices. Our critics howled with horror at the very suggestion that Benjamin Disraeli was not as English as the English primrose.³ A long controversy ensued, in the course of which they were gradually induced to listen to reason. But our critics invariably ended up by saying, with undiminished self-satisfaction, "The truth is, Jews may be different from us; but, after all, they have their good points and their bad points, just like Frenchmen and all sorts of foreigners. We must be broad-minded; they aren't all horrible heartless devils, *as you say they are.*"

Needless to say, I never said anything of the sort. I never said anything except the very thing he is himself saying. But when I first said it, he maintained that what I said was nonsense; and, now that he has found out for himself that it is sense, he chooses to say that I must have said something else. He makes a caricature of my caricature of the Jew, without even looking at it to see whether it was fair portrait; and later, when he sees the same portrait, he points it out to me as a model without even remembering that it is mine.⁴

There appeared in the *News-Chronicle* an only too merciful review of an only too vulnerable volume of sensational stories which I cast upon the world [*Four Faultless Felons*]. I hope I cannot be accused of taking such books of mine very seriously, and I hope I am not unduly puffed up when they happen to be criticised indulgently. But there is one thing which I do take seriously, and that is the one thing which was criticised critically. I do take my real opinions seriously, though not the stories that sometimes embody them. And I take especially seriously one particular opinion which has been universally misunderstood. I refer to my real views on the Jewish Problem and the Jews, and the critic in the *News-Chronicle* said the only thing to which I have any right to take exception when he deduced from one passage that I am "a professed Anti-Semite."

This is not true, and certainly the passage he quotes does not prove it to be true. He quotes a passage in which a financier declares that

---

³ The primrose was supposedly Disraeli's favorite flower and became the symbol for English conservatism.
⁴ *Illustrated London News*, May 26, 1923.

the Jewish vice is greed, or love of luxury or vanity; and concludes by saying that he knows this because he is a Jew himself. The critic declares that no Jew could ever talk like that. This is rather surprising, for I have, in fact, heard several Jews talk exactly like that. It seems to me that it is my critic who is the Anti-Semite, since he is apparently unaware of one of the very real virtues of the Jew—his capacity for detachment and objective criticism. Jews sometimes pursue (unwisely, as I think) an external policy of silence and suppression in the Press and the political world. They defend it in private on the ground of real peril from real persecution. But it is very rare to find a Jew who shows in private that shamefaced, muddle-headed half-hypocrisy and blustering evasion only too common in British and other Western patriots. The Jew may sometimes try to conceal the facts from the world, but he does not try to conceal them from himself, or even from his friends. I have any number of Jewish friends quite capable of saying that the Jewish temptation is greed and luxury. But, in any case, the critic misses the whole point by omitting the preceding sentence. The point was that the financier began by saying, "Avarice is not a Jewish vice."

In short, my Jew was not attacking Jews, though many Jews really do. He was defending Jews from the much more common but completely mistaken charge of being stingy and mean. In my story, somebody had suggested that a certain Jewish pawnbroker was a miser. The financier answers that a Jew is never a miser. His temptation is not to hoard money, but to grab it and spend it, if only in vulgarity or vice. To point out that Jews are not mean and miserly, even if they are showy and purse-proud, is to say something that might quite naturally be said by a Jew, and certainly not something that could only be said by an Anti-Semite.

For the rest, I maintain that it is perfectly sound psychology to make a man repel a charge against his race as untrue by admitting that another and almost contrary charge is true. It is what almost all patriots do who combine patriotism with any kind of balance and liberality of mind. I do not know who wrote the review in the *News-Chronicle*, but my thoughts naturally strayed to the literary editor of that paper, the distinguished essayist Mr. Robert Lynd, and from thence to the problems of his own native land. Suppose that I, as an Englishman, were trying to explain things to Mr. Lynd as an Irishman. I might very well say, for instance, that the English are not really cruel, though they have given the Irish a very justifiable impression of their cruelty. But they have been, in effect, cruel through credulity, through laziness and ignorance. I might almost say they have been cruel through good nature. It was not so much that they had too low an opinion of the Irish as that they had too high an opinion of the Anglo-Irish, of the officials and the landlords and the Parliamentary secretaries and the police; of the Anglo-Irish garrison that was to them like the Anglo-Indian garrison. But to suppose that a silly spinster reading truculent articles actually and directly desires to massacre Hindus, like a fanatical Moslem, is to do her an injustice—or perhaps pay her too high a compliment. It is almost equally untrue that most of us were ever in a mood to enjoy the massacre of Catholics and Celts. But it was none the less true that we tolerated the massacre of Catholics and Celts. And we did so through sins and weaknesses that were really our own, and about these I should express myself as vehemently, and even violently, as any Irishman. I should make a particular point of being emphatic and even exaggerative in describing the snobbishness, the impotence, the intellectual inertia of my countrymen who consented to the enslavement of a Christian nation; to show that I was defending them from a particular false criticism, and not denying that any criticism could be true. I might even talk rather bitterly about slavery and political poltroonery, as the Jew in my little story talks bitterly about vice and greed. But the Jew in my story does not talk more bitterly about them than several Jews in history have talked about them.

I prefer to make a note of this mild protest against a very satisfactory critique of a not very satisfactory book. For it concerns a really serious problem, and misrepresents me in a matter in which I do not wish to be misrepresented, though I generally am misrepresented. If I were an enemy of the Jews, I should call myself an enemy of the Jews.[5] Personally, I deny the charge of racial rancour.[6] The brotherhood of men is a fact: which in the long run wears down all other facts.[7]

There is one thing that nobody seems to notice about Anti-Semitism; and that is that the very name is a surrender to Semites.

[5] *Illustrated London News*, Sept. 20, 1930.
[6] *New Witness*, Sept. 16, 1915.
[7] *New Witness*, June 18, 1914.

Anti-Semitism, so far from being a cry of fanaticism, is a feeble and frightened euphemism. One of the ninety-nine reasons for not calling oneself an Anti-Semite is that it is so wretchedly polite and apologetic a thing to be. A man implies that he dislikes the Semitic race, he dares not admit that dislikes the Jewish people. That there are such things as Jews is a fact of immediate integration and experience, of which we are all certain. That there are such things as Semites is a theory of indirect and partial scientific syntheses, of which we are not certain at all. There are people who dislike Jews; though I am not one of them. But I doubt if there are any people who dislike Semites. I doubt whether any human being looks first at an Arab to see whether he is a Semite; whether he has certain craniological or other marks, supposed to connect him with the same large human division as the Jews. No Anti-Semite expects the vices of a Semite. No Zionist glories in the triumphs of a Moslem Arab who is supposed to be a Semite. Nobody goes poking about in Egypt or the Levant to find any qualities that are Jewish among any people that are not Jews. All men know in their hearts that Jews are Jews, and there is nothing like them in the world. Israel, like the Lord her God, is one; and there is no other tribe to share with her either the admiration or the power or the persecution that attend her on her wandering way.

The truth is that the very name of Anti-Semitism dates from the same artificial age as the contention of Anti-Anti-Semitism. The very title records the time when people were afraid to touch the Jewish problem. While the majority talked as if there were no problem even the minority tried to talk as if it were not a Jewish problem. They tried, unconsciously perhaps, to imply that it was merely an anthropological problem, to be discussed by professors: like the problem of why the Patagonian is tall, or why the Hairy Ainu is hairy. In other words, the very term Anti-Semite bears all the marks of the "liberal" age which denounces it. It is, in the bad sense, a very Victorian expression; a phrase that strikes the note of the middle of the nineteenth century. And is so chiefly in this: that it takes refuge in science to escape from truth.

It is needless here to recapitulate all the shifts to which that sham science lent itself. Just as it confused the Jewish problem by generalisations about Semites, so it confused the Irish problem by generalisations about Celts. But muddled as it was, it had in it a certain magnetic power strangely akin to magic. And the worst of it is that the learned are more liable to this extraordinary delusion than the ignorant. If anyone were to ask me why I trust a peasant or any such plain man more than most intellectual aristocracies, I should be content to answer with this case alone. The man I mean, and the man I trust, is the man who knows quite well that a Jew is a Jew; whether or no he was ever a Semite; and that Irishman is an Irishman, whether or no he was ever a Celt.

All this obsession with the origins resolves itself into the habit of leaving out the story. If you ask the common conscience of men, "What has made Smith a rascal?" nine times out of ten it will answer "Smith has made Smith a rascal." After that, it will in due proportion make all decent alliance for heredity and environment, for race or for climate. But no sane man, who does not know Smith, will dream of deducing where he is or is not a rascal from the facts of race or climate; from the skull of his great-grandfather or the weather-chart of his parish. That is, the same man will recognise that the most important thing about Smith is what he has done with himself; that the next most important thing is what other people have done to him. He will want to know what has happened; and not merely what conditions existed before anything happened. In short, he will want history; and all this talk of primitive conditions of climate or anthropology is a dodge for leaving out history. And this is the first fact to note if anyone asks, "What has made the Jew secretive or tenacious or restless or inspiring, or whatever we may think him to be?" The first answer is that the Jew has made the Jew secretive or tenacious or whatever he may be. The next most important fact is what the Gentiles have done to the Jews. This had nothing to do whether where we do in fact blame the Jew or the enemies of the Jew. It only means that what he is mainly the result of what he does and what other people do; not merely the result of the physical type of the remote tribe from which he sprang. It may be creditable to him, for instance that through the Christian ages he remained in isolation. But his problem is due to the fact that he did remain in isolation; not to the fact that people with Semitic skulls are bound to remain in isolation. He cannot be explained by the theory of race; and he is himself sufficient to expose and explode the theory of climate. For he has continued to be himself, for centuries, in all the climates of the world.

Even those who accuse me of being Anti-Semitic will hardly accuse me of being particularly Anti-Celtic. And the same point about the importance of the historic will, as compared with the prehistoric and conjectural conditions, applies to the other very different case which I have coupled for convenience with this one. The Irish may have come from the Celts; but it was not in the least necessary for the Celts to turn into the Irish. That was done partly by their own conduct and partly by other people's conduct; but at any rate by conduct and not merely by conditions. Ireland made Ireland; with some unintentional assistance from England. It was the Irish and not the Celts who chose to remain Catholic; and being Catholic is a choice, while being Celtic is not. I have taken these two working examples merely as being both familiar and dissimilar. But this is one more odd thing to note about the comparison; a thing I have never understood. If you tell an Irishman that he is an Irishman and not an Englishman, he will say he has insisted he is not an Englishman; possibly he thanked God [he] is not an Englishman. But if you tell a Jew he is not an Englishman, he says you're an Anti-Semite.[8]

I am not going to persecute any Jews. But I am going to go on talking about them. I shall talk about them as freely as I should about Germany or Japan; saying what, in my opinion, are their dangers, defects, or neglected merits. I shall say that a group of financial Jews urged on the African war, because they did: I heard them doing it. But I shall also say that I heard many of the equally unmistakable artistic and Bohemian Jews denounce the war fiercely. One is not supposed to insult America by discussing Trusts or France by discussing

---

[8] *New Witness*, Sept. 23, 1921. Chesterton's argument that the Irish are a distinct people from the English and entitled to their own nation won him praise from the Irish. But the same argument when applied to the Jews got him labeled as anti-Semitic. Chesterton even argues that the English treatment of the Irish is worse than its treatment of the Jews. He says that England (under Edward I) once expelled the Jews in order to stop usury, but it never tried to exterminate the Jews, as did Hitler. But England did try to exterminate a people once: the Irish. This policy "was stated in cold print as late as the nineteenth century and in a great newspaper like *The Times*, which actually expressed the hope that 'a Catholic Celt would be as rare on the banks of the Liffey as a Red Indian on the banks of the Manhattan.' In simpler times it had not been a question of misgovernment, but of massacre.... Ireland is not a dominion or a dependency or a colony. Ireland is a nation that we tried to kill and did not kill." (*G.K.'s Weekly*, May 21, 1932.) He never hesitates to remind England of its injustice to Ireland. And his defense of the Irish and respect for them has never been questioned. He has never been called anti-Irish (or anti-Celtic). And yet he is not afraid to criticize the Irish, saying things such as: "The Irish have great faults and are too slow to forgive." (Ibid.) But in spite of his expressed admiration and appreciation of the Jews whom he calls "a noble and historic race," any criticism he makes of them earns him the brand of anti-Semite.

dueling; why should the Jews be the only people who refuse to be talked about intelligently?[9]

Hastily as I write, I do not write so hastily as some people read. I fancy it often happens that a critic, sincerely convinced of the danger of my doctrines, does not pause to note in detail the safeguards in my statements.[10] Any generalisation I make—about America or other historical things—is subject to all sorts of cross divisions and exceptions, to be considered in their place. The negroes are a special problem, because of what white men in the past did to them. The Japanese are a special problem, because of what men fear that they in the future may do to white men. The Jews are a special problem, because of what they and the Gentiles, in the past, present and future, seem to have the habit of doing to each other.[11] The business of a critic is to discover the importance of men and not their crimes.[12]

The mediaeval civilisation had its crudities and cruelties, but it had simplicity and the power to create. The first thing it felt about the Jews, whether they were nice or nasty, whether they were impotent or omnipotent, was that they were different; and it expressed this by a physical artistic act, giving them a definite dwelling place and a definite dress. The incapacity for clear courage in expressing oneself by a bodily symbol will for the present prevent our society dividing itself, as mediaeval society did, under such crests, colours, guilds, costumes, patron saints as may seem to it to express its real differences. In the modern mood the deliberate *incarnation* of any fact would seem comic.

I am a Liberal, and I dislike the idea of Jews being excluded from any civic rights when they obey the civic order. By all means let a Jew be Prime Minister. But what a good taste Disraeli might have had in Oriental dress! And what a damnable taste he had in English dress! By all means let a Jew be Lord Chief Justice. I cannot quite grasp why the most discredited Jew should be specially selected for that post; but in this precisely what puzzles me is the existence of so many more worthy Jewish lawyers. By all means let him be Lord Chief Justice; but let him not sit in wig and gown, but in turban and flowing robes.[13]

---

[9] *Daily News*, June 14, 1911.
[10] *New Witness*, Oct. 31, 1919.
[11] "What Is America?," *What I Saw in America*.
[12] *Daily News*, Aug. 5, 1901.
[13] Ironically, Rufus Isaacs, the Jewish cabinet member who was a key figure in the Marconi scandal, was appointed Lord Chief Justice just three months after this article was written.

Now, if anyone be so far from simplicity as not to understand ritualism, let him consider this concrete case. Among the many Jews with whom I am on terms of old affection, there have been some who observed the exact rite of the Jewish grace before a meal, for which it is necessary to put on a top-hat, or some such thing, when sitting at the table. Many Gentiles to whom I have told this have laughed. But I pointed out to them that the laugh is really against the Gentile and not the Jew. Israel did not invent top-hats; it is we who have reared that bestial Tower of Babel. It is our fault if the hat we wear is not fit to be worn in the presence of God. But if we imagine the man in some loose Oriental draperies, the act of covering the head could be as natural and graceful as the act of lifting a light Western cap to a lady. I will not enter here into the question of whether there be some symbolism (as I sometimes think there may be) in the difference between the acts of covering the head from Jehovah and uncovering it to Christ. I will only say that both could be as dignified as the Iliad if they were done in the proper dress. If the Jew were dressed differently we should know what he meant; and when we were all quite separate we should begin to understand each other.[14]

---

[14] *New Witness*, July 24, 1913. This is six years before Chesterton wrote *The New Jerusalem*, in which he was (and still is) taken to task for the suggestion that contemporary English Jews should wear their historical dress (which has caused him to be compared with Hitler forcing Jews to wear yellow symbols identifying themselves as Jews). He says he made the suggestion as a joke (and he says elsewhere that his serious observations are taken as jokes, whereas his jokes are taken seriously). In this passage he explains the reason he has to offer it as a joke: because no one understands the Middle Ages, where traditional dress was a form of dignity.

While the suggestion immediately strikes many readers as offensive, the idea of a particular group wearing their own colors or distinctive clothes has been and still is common, whether it be ethnic groups, special interest groups, gangs, sports fans, Catholic religious orders, Amish farmers, Muslims, Mormon missionaries—or Orthodox Jews. All wear their garb as a declaration and without shame. Mark Twain, in *The Innocents Abroad*, describing his 1867 travels to Europe and the Holy Land, remarks with warm fascination about the Jews he sees in their natural dress and how it goes back three thousand years.

But does that mean there is something wrong with a people *not* calling attention to themselves, choosing *not* to wear the colors or distinctive dress associated with themselves, and just wanting to fit in to the surrounding culture? For Chesterton, it depends on the motive, and it depends on what "fitting in" means. One of the reasons Chesterton is accused of anti-Semitism is that he regards Jews as foreigners, as a nation without a country, that they are as distinct from the English as the Irish are distinct from the English. It is his opinion, mostly based on his own experience, whether it is justified or not, that he sees certain Jews not as trying to assimilate or "fit in" to English culture but as trying to hide within the culture where, by their own admission and choices, they are still outsiders.

Anti-Semitism is a sour fruit—but it is the fruit of Crypto-Semitism. If anyone doubts this, let him compare the picture of a Jew as painted a few centuries ago, when Jewry was as isolated as the Chinese Embassy, with the picture of a Jew as painted a few years ago, when Jewry was as "British" as Buckingham Palace. Compare a Jew as sketched by Rembrandt with a Jew as sketched by Sargent! In the old picture there is nothing of Anti-Semitism; the old Rabbi sits august in grey or black with the light lingering on him like silver; secure in that royal reverence the great artist gave to every gypsy and beggar. In the modern picture, apart from brilliant technique, there is nothing but Anti-Semitism, Anti-Semitism in black and white, in red and yellow, in purple and gold; perhaps unconscious, assuredly deep-seated; a crypto-Anti-Semitism to match the Crypto-Semitism it assails.[15]

A friend of mine, a warm and lifelong champion of Labour and a large-minded and charitable person, told me seriously that some of the Communists really are wicked; as wicked as the old lady in Cheltenham thinks they are. He held that their complete intellectual isolation from normal religion and morals had really left them free to play any political trick, and I know there is a type of homeless Jew intellectual of whom this is true.[16] Some day people may admit psychology into fact as well as fiction. Some day there may be a little realism in the newspapers dealing with public life, as well as in the novels dealing with private life. Then we may hear something of the type that really is Marxist and generally is Jewish. Now there is a type, generally sound at heart though not very clear in the head, that does become an atheist from a vague idea that it is part of being a revolutionist. Of him we can really ask why he needlessly adds this inhuman negation to his very human hopes. But there is another type, less common but more clear-headed, who has really become a revolutionist only as part of being an atheist. It is not good to ask him why he tacks on atheism to his idealism; because he would never have had any idealism except as something tacked on to atheism. His materialism is the main thing; he would not even be a Marxist except as a way of being a materialist. It is vain to ask this particular type of

---

[15] *New Witness*, Apr. 10, 1913.

[16] *G.K.'s Weekly*, Aug. 2, 1930. By "homeless Jew," he means a Jew who is not attached to his own country, his own religion, his own culture, as he explains in the next passage.

man why he should especially exhort the poor to attack the priest, who is often poorer than they are. It was only in order to attack the priest that he ever troubled about the poor. This special sort of young Jew is rare even among revolutionists. But though he is rare he is real; and he still awaits a realistic study. Nobody has put the truth about him even into a novel, let alone a newspaper. Yet he is a strangely interesting though a strangely depressing type. The first two facts that strike, and even shock us about him, are that he is really young, and that there is about him something which is nowhere else found in combination with youth. His soul is homeless. He talks of economics; but he does not mean what the word means, the laws of a home. He talks of psychology; but he does not mean what the word means, the study of a soul. He knows his own religion is dead; and he hates ours for being alive. His eyes are bright with something other than we mean when we speak of eyes like stars; and if we look, we shall see that they are like falling stars, meteoric stones drifting and disconnected, wandering and falling through the void in vain.[17]

Without making any very bombastic pretences of chivalry, I think most people who know me would expect me to remedy any real grievance I had caused.[18] The editor of the *Jewish Chronicle* and the *Jewish World* wrote to me touching some remarks in the *New Witness* on the Jewish crowds in the Tube Station during the air-raids, asking if the experience was my own, or on what testimony I relied. I answered his questions, as it seemed to me, quite as simply as he asked them. He asked me for the name of any station; and I gave him the name of three stations. He asked me whence this information came, and I told him; explaining that I was not one of the witnesses; but that (while I fully trusted them and took responsibility for their report) they were as ready, if he liked, to write their own experience over their own names. What more evidence of such events could be expected I cannot conceive; but the editor of the *Jewish World* says

---

[17] *New Witness*, June 30, 1922.

[18] *Daily Herald*, Oct. 25, 1913, "The Ethics of an Apology." An official from the Labour Party, apparently stung by GKC's criticism, had written a letter making rather limp excuses about some particular action and expected an apology from GKC. Chesterton wanted to know to whom he should apologize and for what, since none of that is made clear. GKC shows that he is a man who will make an apology if he has wronged someone. But he simply needs to know what it is he's done wrong and what he is apologizing for.

with extraordinary bitterness that it would not convince a court of law. About this I will not speculate; it is a sad truth, perhaps, that I have not a perfect faith in the realism of the ritual of our courts of justice, for measuring the plainest popular facts. But I have no such fine pride in being ignorant of what everybody knows.

Of the rest of the editor's remarks on the personal matter, I really cannot make head or tail through the twisted and almost tortured sarcasm which he seems to suffer.

But I should hardly touch on this but for another matter, more important because more impersonal. In concluding my reply, I remarked that though I saw no reason to withdraw any *New Witness* criticism as an item, a reasonable Jew might get a better impression by considering those criticisms as a whole. In effect, I suggested that while a certain psychological effect of a Gotha on a Ghetto cannot be denied, it can be defended, or a least excused and explained. I have myself defended the Jew so situated; comparing him, for instance, to a Red Indian who might possibly be afraid of fireworks, to which he was not accustomed, and yet not afraid of slow fires, to which he was accustomed. "After all," I wrote some time ago, "it is not their funeral; and may well seem to them to partake of the character of a premature burial." But this attempt to allow for the Jewish position evokes no answering attempt to allow for our position. The Jewish editor replies with one simple and sweeping statement; which is vastly interesting, because it is the root of all the trouble. He says that what I have called "these unhappy racial collisions" are due solely to malice against Jews; in other words that Christians hate Jews without cause; and have only to leave off hating. This, I believe, is the sincere, not to say innocent, opinion of many influential Jews; and it is utter balderdash.

A race simply rushes on to ruin when it thus ignores all that other people say about it. It does not follow that what the other people say is wholly true; yet when we sharply remind such a race of the current criticism, we necessarily produce the impression of suggesting that it is wholly true.

There is a strange failure of the Semites to think of what the Anti-Semites think; and they have a blind assumption that the Anti-Semites do not think at all. The implication in *The Jewish World*, is that there is nothing whatever against the Jews, except some odd superstitious spite.

For anybody facing realities, the Jews are a race in a unique and unnatural difficulty, cutting them off from the creative functions of a soil and the fighting responsibilities of a flag and therefore breeding certain evils. The chief, though by no means the only, evils are a nomadic money-lending in time of peace and a disaffection and indiscipline in time of war. I do not assert that it is entirely the fault of the Jews; I do assert that it is mere nonsense to talk as if it were not at least as much the misfortune of the Christians. Our own aim has always been to disentangle the two traditions from each other; and in this effort many thoughtful Jews have joined and probably would still join. But if the Jews insist on talking as if they had always been entirely right, they will most certainly end by being treated as if they had been entirely wrong.[19]

Another Jewish critic has compared me to Torquemada and the Spanish Inquisitors, saying that I want the wholesale conversion of the Jews to Roman Catholicism. He dared me to deny it. Well, I have not the smallest intention of denying that I wish for the wholesale conversion of the Jews and everybody else to Roman Catholicism.

The Jewish critic does not, however, think this probability one that presses so closely upon us as to be a substitute for any other policy about Jews. I have explained my own view of that policy very often to any Jews who may have the patience to read it; and none of it ever bore any resemblance to any part of the critic's account of my position. We never dreamed of saying that the Jews produced all the murders of the world, or anything of the sort. What we said was that they produced a friction in the world by being alien to the moral tradition around them. The critic chooses to assume that when we say that Jewish Capitalism is a special danger and that Jewish Socialism is also a special danger, we mean merely that we hate a Jew whether he is rich or poor; that we attack him equally for being on the one side and for being on the other. Now we say that this is a very natural error in a Jew; and that the very naturalness of it illustrates the difference we mean. To him, being a Communist and being a Capitalist are contrary things. To us they are very nearly the same thing. For him it is natural that the Jew sympathising with the poor should be a Socialist and the other Jew a Capitalist. We say he feels instinctively like this because

[19] *New Witness*, June 21, 1918.

his people (whether by their own fault or ours) have not been in the position to insist on certain traditions of the soil and small ownership, which we think the real antithesis to Collectivism and Capitalism together. To think this is not to think a Jew wrong whatever he does; it is simply to think him wrong in his traditional view of what there is to be done. Nor do we say that no Jew can understand our ideal; we only say that most Jews do not. Now it is quite possible, at any rate it is very arguable, that if the Jews had a country of their own, they might think a little more in terms of what lawyers, with unconscious truth, call real property. For that reason we have always been in favour of their having a country if possible; and [the] critic is quite mistaken in supposing that we ever suggested anything else. We have explained at some length that we have always been in favour of Zionism.[20]

On the same subject, another critic, as we understand it, complains that we think the world was made for non-Jewish races, because we said that the Jewish State ought to be established on a larger scale. She thinks we are denying life to the Jews, because we say that such a State ought to be more solidly and consistently Jewish. She thinks we are merely prejudiced against that race or religion, because we say that it ought if possible to have a real nation, and not be put off with some half-way house called a national home.

Suppose, in an almost exact parallel, we had said that the Irish could not be put off with the compromise called Home Rule, but must have a complete nation and even an independent republic. Would our critics have condemned us chiefly for our cruel prejudice against the Irish? In short, our present critic condemns us because we wish there could be a real Zionist policy instead of a sham Zionist policy. She is entirely mistaken in supposing we are without sympathy with the Zionist vision. We have often expressed our sympathy with Jewish nationalism; quite apart from friendship with many Jews. We wish that the Jews had half as much sympathy with the Christian feeling about the Holy Sepulchre or the Moslem feeling about the Holy Places as we have with the Zionist feeling about the Holy Hill of Zion. If they had, they would see what we see, the extraordinary difficulty of doing what ought to be done in the place where in many ways we should most like to do it. What is the matter with the

---

[20] *G.K.'s Weekly*, July 18, 1925. This is an edited version of GKC's response to a letter to the editor.

attitude with many Jews is the extraordinary delusion that there is no problem except the problem of the meaningless malice of Gentiles. Even if this were true, the lady would still have her problem. It would be the problem of why people all over the world should go mad on the subject of the Jews any more than of the Javanese. As long as a certain sort of quite intelligent Jew goes on maintaining that he and his people have never contributed at all to the misunderstanding, he will be more misunderstood than ever. That denial of all provocation is itself a provocation; that denial of the problem is itself a problem.[21]

Mr. Belloc and I did actually dare to criticise a particular Jew of privilege. What we objected to was not the fact that he was a Jew; but the fact that he was allowed to be a rascal because he was a Jew. Attacking other rascals was reform; but attacking that rascal was "Anti-Semitism." We objected to a curious contemporary mixture of shallow lying and shifty sentimentalism. In short, we were not so much preaching Anti-Semitism as protesting against Pro-Semitism, which was a prejudice and a privilege and a piece of pompous and pointless secrecy.[22]

The consequence was that we were denounced as demented fanatics, who wished to torture Jews in the cells of the Spanish Inquisition. Then Mr. Hitler comes; and has better luck. He only proposes to steal all the horses, asses, mules, camels and dromedaries of this unfortunate nomadic nation, all the chariots of Israel and horses thereof, all the normal national possessions to which even nomads have a natural right. Or rather, to use a more exact figure, he proposes to beat and belabour Jews like mules, to treat all Jews as such, at best as beasts of burden and more often as beasts of prey. We never hinted, or dreamed of hinting, at any mere herd-hatred of this kind. We never proposed to batter men merely because they were Jews; to hound out or exterminate hundreds and thousands of harmless little fiddlers and schoolmasters and actors and poor students, because they were Jews who were honest enough to keep their Jewish names. We never

---

[21] *G.K.'s Weekly*, Apr. 11, 1925. Another edited version of a response to a letter to the editor.
[22] *G.K.'s Weekly*, Mar. 30, 1933. The "particular Jew" is either Sir Rufus Isaacs (later Lord Reading), a member of the British cabinet, or his brother Godfrey, who was a businessman (and perhaps more of a "rascal"). GKC's argument is that the rich and influential Jews are protected by their fellow aristocrats, while poor, working Jews are the real ones who suffer from anti-Semitism. "We are accused, very unjustly, of a mere hatred of the Jewish race; but we certainly never exhibited so rabid and irrational hatred of the Jewish race as to say that either Rufus or Godfrey Isaacs were typical Jews." (*New Witness*, Mar. 7, 1919.)

had any quarrel with the non-financial Jews; we had both of us many friends among them. We thought the intermediate commercial position of the Jewish nation created a very real thing called the Jewish Problem. But we were never such fools as to think it could be solved by massacre. But when Mr. Hitler jumps over all the hedges, and steals all the horses, good or bad, well-treated or ill-treated, nearly everybody in England casts about to find excuses for him. They never tried to find such excuses for us; when we set forth with perfect sobriety and responsibility social solutions based on the reality of the Jewish Problem. Why is Mr. Hitler allowed to cross Jews, when Mr. Belloc was not allowed to criticise them? The answer is that, according to the vague traditions of this country, there is somebody who is even more sacred than the Jew. And that is what is called the German; who is, in actual practice, the Prussian.[23]

Prussia is a patch of eighteenth century heathenry and heresy, which never did believe, nor (to do it justice) generally pretend to believe, in any sort of international ideal or common code of Christendom. From the first command of Hohenzollern to the last appeal of Hitler, it is the most simple, one-sided, savage tribal patriotism;

---

[23] *G.K.'s Weekly*, Mar. 30, 1933. Chesterton's criticism of the Jews amounts to a drop in the bucket in comparison to what he says about the Prussians. His constant and consistent criticism of Prussianism takes up a large percentage of his political writings, including virtually all his *Illustrated London News* columns from 1914 to 1918, and then picking up again in the late 1920s and early '30s with the rise of Hitler. And as the reader can surmise, he argues that Nazism is just a different name for the same political and cultural philosophy. Whereas GKC regards Jews as "aliens" or outsiders in Europe, he regards Prussians as enemies to Europe. He repeatedly admonishes English academics for embracing "the German professors" with not only their skepticism, pessimism, and atheism, but their racial pride. "Up to the very edge of the Great War, our schools and colleges all taught various forms of the Teutonic Theory; and told the Englishman to pride himself primarily on being an Anglo-Saxon. A schoolmaster had no more hesitation about teaching Germanism than about teaching German. The professors of Oxford and Cambridge were perpetually flattering the professors beyond the Rhine; and the standard they set up in education was of the sort which has been called the sincerest form of flattery." (*Illustrated London News*, Apr. 7, 1917.) "That which cannot be restored to its own shape perishes, and if European civilisation cannot be restored to its own shape it will perish. The evolutionary idea of an animal unendingly changing into other animals is a German fable from the forests. It is because the German professor did think that man was such an animal that he became the enemy of the creative outline, of the sacred boundary, of the pledged word, of pity, of memory, of all that is magnificent in man. All this positive and creative concept of our civilisation as something with a special shape and value ... was concentrated in one central [idea] of the historic post and function of old Europe. But exactly the question the German professor was asking was whether there need be anything resembling the old Europe, or, indeed, anything resembling Europe at all." (*New Witness*, Sept. 14, 1916.)

and nothing else. The consequence is that Prussia is the one European State that may at any moment wage an aggressive war.[24] The Prussian has followed the advice of Nietzsche.[25] Prussians cannot laugh at anybody, because they cannot laugh at themselves.[26] Prussians always stand in rows to commit their crimes.[27] The Prussian in his uniform belongs to a different world; a world of gaudy and barbarous vanity where violence is worshipped without doubt or shame. It is a world where the Faith has never really been accepted—or abandoned. And for anyone who understands what I mean, the best proof of it is not in any catalogue of crimes, but simply in the way in which the man wears his uniform and walks down the street.[28] Prussia was supposed to be weak: and she again threatens the world.[29]

I am appalled by the Hitlerite atrocities. They have absolutely no reason or logic behind them. It is quite obviously the expedient of a man who has been driven to seeking a scapegoat, and has found with relief the most famous scapegoat in European history, the Jewish people.[30]

I doubt whether Israel can be killed—even by Israelites.[31] Even a man who did not believe in Jehovah would be obliged to believe in Jews. And the secular undisputed history of the Jews is, if possible, more extraordinary than their scriptural and miraculous history. They are quite unlike anything else in the world; and fire or manna falling visibly on them from heaven could hardly make them more unique than they are. For instance, the British Empire has rightly or wrongly made the experiment of Zionism; that is of re-establishing for the Jews their national position in Zion. But empires seem to have been making Zionist experiments, in one form or another, from the first ages of the world. In the doubtful liberation by Pharaoh for the march

---

[24] *G.K.'s Weekly*, Mar. 2, 1933.

[25] *New Witness*, Sept. 17, 1914. "The German soldiers agree with the German professors; or rather the German professors agree with the German soldiers." (*G.K.'s Weekly*, May 18, 1933.) GKC is amazed that the Germans could take Nietzsche's ideas seriously, but he is absolutely stupefied that Jewish intellectuals also promoted Nietzsche's philosophy, particularly Dr. Oscar Levy, a German-born Jew who translated Nietzsche into English and along with Shaw helped popularize Nietzsche in England.

[26] *Illustrated London News*, Nov. 7, 1914.

[27] *G.K.'s Weekly*, Jan. 30, 1932.

[28] *New Witness*, Mar. 16, 1923.

[29] *G.K.'s Weekly*, Aug. 13, 1932.

[30] Interview with the *Jewish Chronicle*, Sept. 22, 1933.

[31] *Illustrated London News*, Feb. 28, 1914.

of the Promised Land, there is very much the same combination of the desire to do justice to Jews with the desire to get rid of them. Then Babylon made the old Egyptian mistake and Persia tried the old Egyptian remedy. Babylon carried the Jews into exile that they might melt into other slave populations, and produce nothing except that noble psalm about the waters of Babylon; which is the song of all exiles and therefore of all patriots. Dispersion then, as now, only made the real Jew more Jewish. So when the Persians conquered Babylon, the great Darius adopted the Balfour Declaration. He sent the Jews back to rebuild their own city; and the story began all over again, as it is beginning all over again to-day. Every historical ruler has been a Zionist, and never more than when he has begun by being an Anti-Semite. I am not going to argue here about whether the Zionist solution is the right one; for this is only the sketch of simple and self-evident things, and not of disputable and disputed ones. I only point out that whether it is Rameses letting the people go or Darius bringing them back, Edward the First driving them from England or Napoleon the Great planning their return to Palestine, Lord Balfour promising them a national home or Mr. Ford denouncing them as an international danger, there is always the same sort of preoccupation with the same problem, in all the princes of the world. I only say that Jews, like Jerusalem, have been attacked and admired and oppressed and persuaded, but they could never be ignored. They are like their own city that is set upon a hill and cannot be hid.

Within the circle of the walled city, which is as contained as a cup and hardly larger than a hamlet, are Islam and the Roman Empire and the international nation of the Jews and the Catholic Church throughout the world. I have said nothing of sacred things in their sacred aspect, or of anything which a man of our religion feels when he stands upon that soil. But taking the bare facts, in the driest and most detached fashion, about what Palestine has actually done for men and what men have actually done for Palestine, I find it impossible to imagine any other explanation of the part it has played, and is still playing, except that it was set apart in some way for a divine adventure, and was the gate by which God entered the world.[32]

[32] "Palestine," in *The Guiding Book*, ed. Ann Kindersley (Hodder and Stoughton, 1923), p. 146.

Chapter 7

I Keep My Secret Still

The Echoes of Words

So little, I realise with a groan, after an obscure and laborious life of writing, does anybody know about anything that I think or feel.

—"The Holy Island," *The Resurrection of Rome*

Editor's Note: The subtitle is taken from GKC's own definition of poetry as "the echoes of words rather than the words themselves" (Illustrated London News, Jan. 8, 1927). GKC read poetry and wrote poetry and wrote about poetry. He wrote poems to his wife, to his friends, and to his enemies. He wrote poems as book inscriptions, as political commentary, as amusements for children. He wrote epic poetry, nonsense verse, love poems, hymns, and Christmas carols. He wrote ballades and sonnets and limericks and clerihews. And triolets. He wrote parodies of poetry. But does he write about himself in his poems? Yes. Things can be hidden in a poem but also revealed. In some cases, the only place they can be revealed is in a poem. GKC says, "If we were only real enough, we'd talk in rhyme" (Daily News, Jan. 30, 1909).

THOU SHALT NOT KILL[1]

I had grown weary of him, of his breath
And hands and features I was sick to death.
Each day I heard the same dull voice and tread;

---

[1] While struggling with depression in 1893–1894, GKC actually considered suicide. This serious poem is quite in contrast with the flippant "Ballade of Suicide," which contains the refrain "I think I will not hang myself today."

I did not hate him: but I wished him dead.
And he must with his blank face fill my life—
Then my brain blackened, and I snatched a knife.

But 'ere I struck, my soul's grey deserts through
A voice cried, "Know at least what thing you do."
"This is a common man: knowest thou, O soul,
What this thing is? somewhere where seasons roll
There is some living thing for whom this man
Is as seven heavens girt into a span,

For some one soul you take the world away—
Now know you well your deed and purpose. Slay!"
Then I cast down the knife upon the ground
And saw that mean man for one moment crowned.
I turned and laughed: for there was no one by—
The man that I had sought to slay was I.

I AM

There is a Knowledge wilder than the creeds
Of this, though all hope scatter like the seeds
Am I more proud than any tongue can tell
On this, though all hope scatter like the chaff
Would I abide as on a mighty staff—
Yea for this thing lift up my head and laugh
In everlasting hell.

"I am": men lightly utter it: but I
Saying "I am" to any sod or sky
Raise a new self, vaster yet the same
Stars crown my head: imperial and alone
In my own ears my voice is not my own
And he that sitteth on the last great throne
Sayeth his own name.

THE CONVERT[2]

After one moment when I bowed my head
And the whole world turned over and came upright,

---

[2] Written on July 30, 1922, the day GKC was received into the Catholic Church.

And I came out where the old road shone white,
I walked the ways and heard what all men said,
Forests of tongues, like autumn leaves unshed,
Being not unlovable but strange and light;
Old riddles and new creeds, not in despite
But softly, as men smile about the dead.

The sages have a hundred maps to give
That trace their crawling cosmos like a tree,
They rattle reason out through many a sieve
That stores the dust and lets the gold go free:
And all these things are less than dust to me
Because my name is Lazarus and I live.

THE HERITAGE OF WONDER

I have loved my land yet hailed it as a stranger
When birth-wracks wrecked me on a faerie shore:
I have kept the Faith yet hardly grasped it more
Than groping shepherds when they found the Manger.
I have loved my friends yet feared them more than foes
Lest they should ask the name God only knows;
And in long years of mating have been blest
Restlessly wondering why I was at rest.

CROOKED[3]

The little picture of the Mother of God
Hangs crooked upon the wall,
Blue and bright gold like a butterfly pinned askew
Only it does not fall,
As, stooping ever and falling never, an eagle
Hangs winged over all.
And it suddenly seemed that the whole long room was tilted
Like a cabin in stormy seas;

---

[3] GKC writes surprisingly little prose about the Blessed Virgin Mary, to whom he had great devotion even before his conversion. But he wrote quite a bit of poetry about her, including a major episode in *The Ballad of the White Horse*, and an entire book of poems, *The Queen of Seven Swords*. This little poem appeared only in *G.K's Weekly* and was never collected in any of the volumes of poems published during his life. It not only describes how she affects his outlook, but also affords a glimpse of his study, where her picture hangs on the wall.

The solid table and strong upstanding lamp and the inkstand
Leaned like stiff shrubs in a breeze
And the windows looked out upon slanted plains and meadows
As on slanted seas.
And I knew in a flash that the whole wide world was sliding;
Ice and not land.
And men were swaying and sliding, and nations staggered
And could not stand:
Going down to the ends of the earth, going down to destruction,
On either hand.
And knowing the whole world stiff with the crack of doom,
I pick up my pen and correct and make notes, and write small:
And go on with the task of the day, seeing unseeing
What hangs over all:
The awful eyes of Our Lady, who hangs so straight
Upon the crooked wall.

TO F. C. IN MEMORIAM PALESTINE, '19[4]

Do you remember one immortal
Lost moment out of time and space,
What time we thought, who passed the portal
Of that divine disastrous place
Where Life was slain and Truth was slandered
On that one holier hill than Rome,
How far abroad our bodies wandered
That evening when our souls came home?

The mystic city many-gated,
With monstrous columns, was your own:
Herodian stones fell down and waited
Two thousand years to be your throne.
In the grey rocks the burning blossom
Glowed terrible as the sacred blood:
It was no stranger to your bosom
Than bluebells of an English wood.

---

[4] Just as Mary seems purposely kept out of GKC's prose while she appears in his poetry, so does the other woman at the center of his life: his wife, Frances. He wrote many poems to her from the beginning to the end. This is the dedicatory poem of his lesser-known epic, *The Ballad of St. Barbara*, and celebrates not only their life together but especially the couple's trip to the Holy Land in 1919.

Do you remember a road that follows
The way of unforgotten feet,
Where from the waste of rocks and hollows
Climb up the crawling crooked street
The stages of one towering drama
Always ahead and out of sight ...
Do you remember Aceldama
And the jackal barking in the night?

Life is not void or stuff for scorners:
We have laughed loud and kept our love,
We have heard singers in tavern corners
And not forgotten the birds above:
We have known smiters and sons of thunder
And not unworthily walked with them,
We have grown wiser and lost not wonder;
And we have seen Jerusalem.

THE TWO KINDS[5]
(To one who long hesitated in her conversion on this point)

To others and of old I would have said
That dogmas deep as questioning Christendom
Sleep in the sundering of the wine and bread,
And that Incarnate Christ in every crumb.
For you I find words fewer and more human:
Content to say of him that guards the Shrine
"To drink this Wine he has lost the Love of Woman
Yea, even such love as yours: to drink this Wine."

A SECOND CHILDHOOD

When all my days are ending
And I have no song to sing,
I think I shall not be too old
To stare at everything;
As I stared once at a nursery door
Or a tall tree and a swing.

---

[5] Written to Frances when she was received into the Catholic Church in 1926, after having doubted the doctrine of the Real Presence of Christ in the Eucharist.

Wherein God's ponderous mercy hangs
On all my sins and me,
Because He does not take away
The terror from the tree
And stones still shine along the road
That are and cannot be.

Men grow too old for love, my love,
Men grow too old for wine,
But I shall not grow too old to see
Unearthly daylight shine,
Changing my chamber's dust to snow
Till I doubt if it be mine.

Behold, the crowning mercies melt,
The first surprises stay;
And in my dross is dropped a gift
For which I dare not pray:
That a man grow used to grief and joy
But not to night and day.

Men grow too old for love, my love,
Men grow too old for lies;
But I shall not grow too old to see
Enormous night arise,
A cloud that is larger than the world
And a monster made of eyes.

Nor am I worthy to unloose
The latchet of my shoe;
Or shake the dust from off my feet
Or the staff that bears me through
On ground that is too good to last,
Too solid to be true.

Men grow too old to woo, my love,
Men grow too old to wed:
But I shall not grow too old to see
Hung crazily overhead
Incredible rafters when I wake
And find I am not dead.

A thrill of thunder in my hair:
Though blackening clouds be plain,

Still I am stung and startled
By the first drop of the rain:
Romance and pride and passion pass
And these are what remain.

Strange crawling carpets of the grass,
Wide windows of the sky:
So in this perilous grace of God
With all my sins go I:
And things grow new though I grow old,
Though I grow old and die.

AUTUMN[6]

The woods are bronzed with autumn
When all the leaves are gold
The year grows old around me
And I am passing old
The walls are gilt with mosses
Leaves are a golden sea
The world is fair and ancient
And all is sweet to me.

When I was young and yearning
I chased a drifting dream
I saw a world's ideal
Through mere and tangled gleam
But now the common millions
That trust and toil and grieve
Are flushed in one great sunset
The light I soon must leave.

The young heart, wild and windy
May chase the fresh-blown seed
May seek the lonely blossom
That burns upon the mead.
But stricken hearts grow gentle
And I am passing old
And now I sit in autumn
When all the leaves are gold.

[6] *G.K.'s Weekly*, Sept. 7, 1933.

Chapter 8

Fools

A Brief Word on Critics

It is unfair to judge an author, especially a good author, through his critics.

—*New Witness*, August 4, 1922

Editor's Note: In an unremembered 1915 book, Criticisms of Life, *one Horace J. Bridges dismisses Chesterton as "a weak logician, a poor reasoner, a dishonest controversialist and an unsound theologian." Bridges says that orthodoxy is "unverifiable either by history or by present-day experience," and considers Christianity a "materialistic fairy tale." An anonymous reviewer in* The Catholic World *responded: "The chief reason why Mr. Bridges fails to understand the reasoning of Mr. Chesterton lies in the former's bitter hatred of all supernaturalism and his lack of any sense of humor." (*The Catholic World, *November 1915.) We could fill many pages with such somber thrusts and light-hearted parries, but the long-forgotten Horace Bridges epitomizes Chesterton's critics who have not only lost their faith but their joy. They take themselves so entirely seriously that they are more important than God and too important to laugh. Chesterton's unnamed defender still answers them all. But here we will devote ourselves to letting Chesterton himself answer his critics.*

I have had, if I may say so, a very happy and lucky literary life; and have often felt rather the indulgence than the impatience of critics; and it is in a perfectly amiable spirit that I note that it has involved a certain transition or change. Up to a certain point, I was charitably chaffed for saying what I could not possibly mean; and I was then rather more sharply criticised, when it was discovered that I did really mean it.[1]

In the course of many controversies, something has often occurred to me which I cannot for the life of me understand. As I have littered the land with a vast amount of spoilt paper in my time, I can easily believe that I have often exasperated people, and still more easily that I have often bored them. But why should I exasperate people into paying me extravagant compliments? Why do they pretend, when I have bored them, that I have bewildered them? If I say "The camel is a quadruped," why should somebody else say: "Mr. Chesterton's imaginative fairyland of centaurs and hippogriffs doubtless delights him to the point of delirium, but, etc." If I say "Lord Devonport is a grocer," why should my critics say: "Few can be expected to cope with a fancy that can weave the wildest and most mediaeval romance round, etc." How does it make my remark more dull to pretend that I think it clever? Why does my critic try to convict me of stupidity by representing himself as stupid?[2]

I apologise if my frivolous figures of speech have served to disguise what they were only intended to display. For it is clear that statements of mine which I had imagined to be simple must in truth be singularly obscure, since the most eminent critics are unable to understand them.[3]

Objections have been raised against my verses in the battle poem *The Ballad of St. Barbara*, but strangely enough, not upon the simple and solid and self-evident ground that they are bad verses. So far as I follow the criticism, it is not so much a question of bad verse as of bad taste. And so far as I understand the test, it is regarded as bad taste for anybody to appear to be in any way enjoying himself, let alone his compositions. One excellent critic on an excellent paper reminded me gently that most people in the modern world are agnostics, and very sensitive in their feelings; and it seems that to use religious language in a loud voice in their presence is like disregarding the warning hush on the entrance to a sick-room. That the modern world is in many ways very like a sick-room I should be the last to deny; but I am not sure

---

[1] Introduction to *The Well and the Shallows*.
[2] *New Witness*, May 24, 1917.
[3] *New Witness*, May 7, 1920.

that all the invalids need nothing but the sedative treatment. Another critic retorted upon me a remark I had made about Swinburne and said that my statements were contradicted by the cheerfulness of the metre I employed. I do not altogether admit the parallel; for I think that my sentiments are almost as superior to Swinburne's sentiments as my verse is inferior to Swinburne's verse. But I do not think there is any contradiction between a cheerful metre and a combative meaning, even if there is between a cheerful metre and a pessimistic meaning; and none of my remarks are meant to have a pessimistic meaning.

Nothing would induce me to say a word in defence of my poetry, even in the sense of seriously calling it poetry. But a man should always be ready to say a word for his philosophy; for if it is really a philosophy, it is not merely his. And to the gentleman who wished me to lower my voice lest the sensitive sceptic should overhear me, I think it only fair to confess that I have every hope that he will. It seems to me a little unfair that liberty of opinion should take the form of somebody saying to me, "It is highly indecent that your religion should be still alive, when my religion has been dead for some time." I am quite ready to condole with him; but I cannot yet see that he has any right to complain of me. And to the critic who considered that verses of protest or denunciation should always be accompanied by a metre like a dirge, I must also express an apologetic incapacity to agree. I do not understand why any verse that suggests a battle must necessarily suggest a defeat. Even these few words would be an extravagant exaggeration of the importance of the subject, if the subject were merely the verses themselves. But it is at least connected in my mind with the most important subject in the world; and I merely wish to put it on record, as it were, that all that has been most reviled as dismal and decayed superstition can at least produce something that is rebuked for vainglorious levity and vulgar high spirits.[4]

If any one of my works were a work of art, it would be very inartistic to defend it from critics. A work of art ought to be finished in every sense, good and bad; it should be either done well or done for, or both. This is true of art but not of argument; for I am happy to say that argument is never finished.[5] When I think my critic is wrong,

---

[4] Preface to the American edition of *The Ballad of St. Barbara*.
[5] *New Witness*, May 7, 1920.

when I think heartily he is wrong, I care nothing for anything except which of us is right.[6]

However, one of my critics evidently regards himself as something of an authority on my secret intentions and emotions. When he says that I used an admittedly inoffensive term with an offensive though secret intention, he says something of which the truth or falsehood can never be cleared up till the Day of Judgment. But when he says that I treated his refutation as something that "could be disregarded," he makes a statement without even the shadow of truth. I did not treat his refutation as a thing to be disregarded. It was not disregarded. It was answered in detail, in a long article of nearly one thousand five hundred words, in which I answered all his arguments, point by point; offering counter-arguments which he does not now attempt to counter, and asking questions to which he does not now attempt to reply.[7]

When my critic can only say in a withering way that I am "dirty," I know he has not much else to say.[8]

It is the tendency of the critic to deal with what he expects rather than what he experiences.[9] Many of my critics answer what they imagine that I meant, rather than what I really said.[10] The critic fixes some person with a label and then proceeds to deduce everything from the label.[11] A writer on a High Church paper, being full of the lyric muse, recently described me as a "prolix Papist professor of paradox"; a line which it is my firm intention to extend into a poem of no less than nine verses depending upon the letter p; by which alliterative industry the unaccountable absence of any allusion to polygamous Popes, poisoning Pontiffs, piratical prelates and pestilent peasantries, will be supplied and made good at my own expense. And though the editor very gracefully apologised for having been accidentally prevented, doubtless by my prolixity, from discovering what I actually said in the passage he criticised, another critic has since then broken out on the same paper in the same literary style; and

---

[6] *America*, July 31, 1915.
[7] *Illustrated London News*, Sept. 19, 1931. GKC does not name the critic, but it is a writer for the *Homiletic Review*.
[8] *Illustrated London News*, June 8, 1918.
[9] *New Witness*, May 7, 1920.
[10] *New Witness*, June 24, 1921.
[11] *Illustrated London News*, Jan. 5, 1929.

described the same statement as going "beyond such terminological inexactitude as is permissible in the most putrid paradox"; and saying I devote myself to the propaganda of the gutter. I rather wish I knew what it is that makes the most distant prospect of me (of me, a mere dot on the crowded horizon) throw an honest gentleman into such astonishing convulsions.[12] I did not make the world, and I did not make it paradoxical.[13]

Missing the point is a very fine art; and has been carried to something like perfection by politicians and Pressmen to-day. For the point is generally a very sharp point; and they would probably impale themselves in an uncomfortable manner if they did not manage to avoid it altogether.[14] I think I shall try some day to write a huge philosophical and critical work called *The Point: Its Position, Importance, Interest and Place in our Life and Letters*. It would have separate sections On Seeing the Point; On Missing the Point; On Getting to the Point; On Wandering from the Point, and so on. The subject would be so vast and various that I think it would have to be arranged in the form of a sort of Encyclopaedia. Thus we should have: Point, the, obvious to born fool; see Fool. Point, is it rude to? Points, kindred, of heaven and home; see Ornithology. Point of pin, use of, when justified; and so on. Point evaded by Professor Robinson, and all the rest. But, anyhow, the subject of this great work is very real, much more real than the work itself. It concerns the whole of that great search for reality which is the main adventure of the mind. So many people, especially learned people and even clever people, seem to be quite unable to see the upshot of a thing; or what the French call its reason of being. They see everything in the story except the story.[15]

A man is not a fool because he has believed some pedantic but plausible derivation to be the fact. He is only a fool if he finds the fact and still prefers the derivation.[16] I am not pretending to be learned; nor is it a question of learning. It is a question of quite superficial information, but of information that is fairly well spread out over the whole surface. I have not been right slap-bang through *The Decline*

---

[12] *Universe*, Aug. 2, 1935.
[13] *Daily News*, July 6, 1907.
[14] *Daily Herald*, Feb. 7, 1914.
[15] *Illustrated London News*, Oct. 30, 1926.
[16] *Illustrated London News*, Apr. 21, 1917.

and Fall of the Roman Empire lately; I have not read every word of the *Acta Sanctorum* within the last week or so; I have not even read very closely the relatively modern romance of *The Seven Champions of Christendom*. I have nothing but general information; but it is fairly general. What surprises me in people younger, brighter, and more progressively educated than myself is that their general information is very patchy.[17]

"The wise few" must mean either the few whom the foolish think wise or the very foolish who think themselves wise.[18]

There is a certain solid use in fools. It is not so much that they rush in where angels fear to tread, but rather that they let out what devils intend to do. Some perversion or folly will float about nameless and pervade a whole society; then some fool gives it a name, and henceforth it is harmless. With all really evil things, when the danger has appeared the danger is over.[19] I think it foolish to be always guarding against the perils of life, because life itself is a peril. But I think it equally foolish to argue from what life would be if it were never interfered with, because it is perpetually interfering with itself. Life itself is a revolt against Nature. Nature and hygiene correspond to the two vague periods which scientists love; the prehistoric past of which we know very little, and the future of which we know nothing.[20]

It is not my fault that existence is a strange and dim affair, and not adapted to the intellectual delight of shallow people.[21] There is an apostolic injunction to suffer fools gladly. We always lay the stress on the word "suffer," and interpret the passage as one urging resignation. It might be better, perhaps, to lay the stress on upon the word "gladly," and make our familiarity with fools a delight, and almost a dissipation.[22] The world has made a fool of itself in all sorts of ways from the beginning of time, but its rich stores of foolery are by no means exhausted yet.[23] When it comes to folly we are all at home.[24]

---

[17] *Illustrated London News*, June 18, 1932.
[18] *Daily News*, Apr. 15, 1911.
[19] *Daily News*, Nov. 13, 1909.
[20] *Daily News*, Sept. 11, 1909.
[21] *Daily News*, Dec. 19, 1903.
[22] "The Great Dickens Characters," *Charles Dickens*.
[23] *Illustrated London News*, Apr. 13, 1929.
[24] *Speaker*, June 1, 1901.

Chapter 9

I Also Had My Hour

Manalive

Men acted quite differently according to whether they had met him or not.
— "The Little Poor Man," *St. Francis of Assisi*

Editor's Note: In GKC's original autobiography, it seems he wrote as little about himself as possible, but spent most of his attention on other people. In this, his alternative autobiography, we have tried to reverse the process and force him to write about himself as much as possible and everyone else as little as possible. However, there is no way to get Chesterton to speak well of his own character and accomplishments and unique charm. So, in this chapter, we take the pen out of his hand and give it to some of those who met him, who saw him, who heard him, who knew him. This is the testimony of the eyewitnesses.

Edmund Clerihew Bentley was an author, journalist, groundbreaking poet, and lifelong friend of GKC.

When Gilbert Chesterton and I became friends, during our early schooldays, he was already in the habit of writing essays. His parents' house in Kensington was a place which, happily for me, I came to know almost as well as he did; and in the sitting rooms of that house, in the hall, in the conservatory, on the table under the big tree in the garden, one was always likely to find at least a manuscript book with a few or many of its pages filled by his sprawling, energetic writing. If in those boyhood days the traces of literary activity were lying about everywhere, it was in his own big bedroom at the top of the house that they were concentrated. All along one wall of this room ran a breast-high shelf which was packed with "exercise books" of the kind used in schools, with ruled pages. The writing within, always done in pencil, consisted of essays mainly, though the output of verse was already beginning, there were some fragments of plays, and a much fatter book was devoted to a vast work of extravagant fiction in which we collaborated, writing alternative chapters. Whenever I asked what he had been writing about since our previous meeting he would tell me, but only very unwillingly would he let me read it: to the end of his days he hated to have his work read by any one else when he was present, and to have it read aloud was torture for him.[1]

Poet Alfred Noyes, who wrote "The Highwayman," recounts when he met GKC at the home of R. C. Lehman, editor of the Daily News *in 1902.*

I have a vivid recollection of Chesterton standing in the library, which had two large windows at opposite ends; the sun was shining in at one side and there was a slight April shower on the other, which induced Chesterton to quote the lines from William Morris ["Earthly Paradise"]:

> Folk say a wizard to a Northern King
> At Christmastide such wondrous thing did show
> That through one window men beheld the Spring
> And through another saw the summer glow,
> And through a third the fruited vine a-row,
> While still unheard, but in its wonted way
> Piped the drear wind of that December day.

At lunch that day Chesterton suddenly produced from his pocket and arranged on the table before him a number of little brass figures, Mr. Pickwick, Mr. Micawber, Sam Weller and other characters from Dickens, giving one an almost uncanny sense that Gulliver held them alive in his hands.[2]

---

[1] E. C. Bentley, introduction to *Selected Essays of G. K. Chesterton*, chosen by Dorothy Collins (Methuen, 1949), pp. v–vi.
[2] Alfred Noyes, *Two Worlds for Memory* (Lippincott, 1953), pp. 28–29.

A. G. Gardiner was the editor of the Daily News *following Lehman.*

He was like a child shouting with glee at the sight of the flowers and the sun and chalking on every vacant hoarding he passed with a jolly rapture of invention and no thought beyond. Nothing recalls him more vividly to mind than the remark of a waiter in one of the Fleet Street cafes which he frequented on Fridays when his Saturday article for the *Daily News* was on the anvil. That article was always belated, and one evening when Charles Masterman ran him to earth in one of his haunts the waiter who was hovering round the vast Balzacian figure at the table remarked to Masterman: "Your friend, he very clever man. He sit and laugh and laugh. And then he write. And then he sit and laugh at what he write." Who that knew the laugh will ever forget it? It came like a cascade of pure joy from the head notes to the middle voice and went out in a rumble and gurgle of affable thunder. It filled the atmosphere with the sense of sunshine and the singing of birds, so eloquent was it of the riches of a joyous and generous nature untouched by any thought of self or the calculations of meaner minds.[3]

When Chesterton first rose to journalistic fame at the dawn of the twentieth century, one of the earliest literary portraits of him came from Bertram Thomas, writing for The Idler.

He has a keen delight in all manner of swords. Never by any chance does he stir a yard from his stronghold without an absurd sword-stick; even if only taking a morning stroll in his ancestral park of Battersea, the steel is never left behind and serves to hail a cab, amuse a crowd of children, or mystify a policeman. Swords of all sorts are to be found everywhere about Mr. Chesterton's home. The umbrella stand in the hall bristles with foils; singlesticks litter the study, while in the dining-room are to be found a French sword-bayonet and a painted wooden sword, for of all swords, Mr. Chesterton loves best the wooden sabre of childhood; in truth, his love for children amounts almost to the fantastic.

In the study in Mr. Chesterton's flat at Battersea he is at work on the brown-paper covered walls with a chalk design which he calls "And a little child shall lead them," and which shows King

---

[3] *English: The Magazine of the English Association* 1, no. 3 (1936).

Arthur, Robin Hood, and other more or less mythical heroes following the lead of a small infant, who, mounted on a wooden horse, is pointing onwards and upwards with a toy sword. On another wall he has written in chalk, in large letters, "Lest We Forget," and underneath he marks up his appointments.

Mr. Chesterton always carries some crayons in his pocket, and when the mood is on him, will draw anywhere and on anything—in fact I am told that a diligent search on the blank walls in the squares on the south side of Kensington High Street, would reveal some examples of his work.[4]

Sir Phillip Gibbs, who achieved fame as a courageous war correspondent in World War I, was GKC's neighbor at the beginning of their writing careers.
G. K. Chesterton, who lived in the Overstrand Mansions, immediately over my head—I used to pray that he would not fall through—once remarked that if he ever had the good fortune to be shipwrecked on a desert island he would like it to be with the entire population of Prince of Wales road, whom he thought the most interesting collection of people in the world. I thought so, too.

Every time I saw him I admired more profoundly the range of his knowledge, his immense wit and fancy, his genial, jolly and passionately sincere idealism. From my ground floor flat every morning at 10 I used to observe a certain ritual in his life. There appeared an old hansom cab, with an old horse and an old driver. Then GKC would descend, a spacious and splendid figure in a big cloak and a slouch hat, like a brigand about to set forth on a great adventure, and though he was bound no further than Fleet Street it was adventure enough, leading to great flights of fancy and derring do. After him came Mrs. Chesterton, a little figure almost hidden by her husband's greatness. When Chesterton got into the cab the old horse used to stagger in its shafts and the old cab used to rock like a boat on a rough sea.

At luncheon time I often used to see GKC at an Italian restaurant in Fleet Street where, with a bottle of port wine at his elbow and a scribbling pad at his side, he used to write one of his articles for the *Daily News*, chuckling happily over some mighty paradox

---

[4] *The Idler*, June 1903.

which had just taken shape in his brain and totally unconscious of any public observation of his private mirth.[5]

Lucy Masterman, widow of Charles F. G. Masterman, who was also a fellow writer in the glory days of Chesterton's emergence on the literary scene, told a story about her husband and GKC.

Soon after the Boer War a Liberal magazine was started called the *Albany Review* for which Masterman promised a poem by GKC to appear on the first page of the first number. The poet promised readily but the days went by and no poem came. The printers became restive, the editor worried, and accordingly Masterman journeyed to the Chesterton flat in Battersea to see what could be done.

He found Gilbert in bed. It was not that he was ill; he had merely been thinking of other things and forgotten to get up. He was very apologetic, but stated that the poem was complete in his head; if someone would just take it down Charlie could have it at once. This Frances, his wife, prepared to do, somewhat hindered by a shortage in the supply of writing-paper. By dint of Masterman's tearing half-sheets of letters and splitting used envelopes down the sides there was no breakdown, and Gilbert, lying back on his pillow, poured out the first canto of *The Ballad of the White Horse*.[6]

Some seven years before Chesterton first visited the U.S., an anonymous reporter in The Sun *(NY), gave American readers a generous description of GKC.*

Gilbert Keith Chesterton, the most conspicuous figure in British Journalism today—unsystematic philosopher; maddening master of paradox, epigram and anti-climax; sensational, reactionist, always entertaining, brilliant, good tempered, and belligerent—is just 38 years old. For the last 14 years of it his mission in life has been to speak for two things: the romance of life, and the value of that which is old.

The predominant, personal characteristic of Mr. Chesterton is an enormous vitality, which appears in his powerful voice, his good humor, his pugnacity, his prodigal production of stories, essays, lectures, and poems, and in his dogma and practice of the joy of life. He is so incurably romantic that he is even said to have had

---

[5] *Sunday Star* (Washington, D.C.), July 22, 1923.
[6] *Manchester Guardian*, Apr. 11, 1955.

the habit of carrying a revolver and a sword stick in preparation for adventures which he might meet in the heart of London.

Mr. Chesterton is a democrat in sympathies, being convinced that vulgar notions are valid notions, and that common people possess common sense. In politics, he is a liberal, according to Holbrook Jackson, or if one prefers to believe Cecil Chesterton, a "Tory of the 17th or early 18th century, born out of his due time."

Chesterton is a man of positive opinions and tastes. Some of his favorite aversions are "the mad imp of modernity", teetotalism and vegetarianism, freak religions, British imperialism and the two power standard, anonymous journalism, contemporary Calvinism, French short stories, eugenics, Nietzsche, the zeitgeist, Darwinism, pedantry, the "dismal wine of Puritan determinism," seriousness and modern German philosophy. Among his admirations and affirmations are humility, the Catholic Church, the French revolution, the games of childhood, festivals and pageantry, democracy (a thing which he does not find in England), food and wine, fighting, the dignity of the physical senses and desires, truisms and romantic literature of all sorts from old ballads to penny dreadfuls.

GKC is recognized as a minor poet. *The Ballad of the White Horse* embodies the theme to which the author has returned time and again, King Alfred's great work for civilization and Christianity. The author has succeeded in catching the ballad spirit, yet he has colored his *Ballad of the White Horse* with quaint Chestertonian ideas, and has employed a type of verse which differs subtly, but essentially from that of the old ballade. The movement is neither easy nor rapid, and there is too strong a suggestion everywhere that the author is writing a consciously elaborate metaphysical poem. Being at once simple, like a ballad writer, and clever, like GKC, is a thing of no small difficulty.

The gospel according to G. K. Chesterton is embodied, especially in *Heretics* and *Orthodoxy* but it appears also in scraps of every book he has written. It is unsystematic, yet dogmatic and interesting. His enthusiasm for the Catholic Church is evident in every book he has written for some years.

It is not surprising that Mr. Chesterton is humorously averse to sociologists, pessimists, reformers, criminologists, eugenicists, official or institutional philanthropy of whatever sort. The weakness of most sociologists, he thinks, is an insufficient knowledge of man and society. Philanthropy, avers Mr. Chesterton, is religious persecution, and philanthropists (like bankers) are a curse. Their pity is "cold and repugnant", the vast mass of modern pity is pitiful, but not respectful.

Chesterton has written an "unobtrusive sociological essay" called *What is Wrong* (unfortunately renamed by the publishers, *What's Wrong with the World*), a work in which he has expressed opinions in regard to such matters as housing reforms, imperialism, "feminism, or the mistake about women," and "education, or the mistake about the child." He thinks there are too many clever things which need to be undone. He admits the possibility of "progress" only so far as people know where they are going. "Nobody has any business to use the word progress, unless he has a definite creed and a cast iron code of morals. Progress by its very name indicates a direction; and the moment we are the least doubtful about the direction we become in the same degree doubtful about the progress."[7]

Dixon Scott went to interview Chesterton at his Overstrand Mansions flat on the very day that GKC was being moved out of the building and to his new home in Beaconsfield.

G. K. Chesterton's capacity for brilliant work under even the most distracting circumstances was amazing. There was no midnight oil about his epigrams. Young Dixon Scott wrote beseeching an interview with him. Though GKC did not then know Scott from Adam, he good-humouredly made an appointment at his Battersea flat. Dixon Scott arrived to find men carting off furniture, and his literary idol scribbling away at a table in a study which contained only that and the chair on which Chesterton was seated. Even the chair and the table were spirited away next. But GKC, standing in Olympian ease at the fireplace, and using the mantelpiece to continue his scribbling, talked for half an hour to Dixon in the kindest and also most brilliant way. When Scott left, he handed him the scribble, and asked him to drop it in the office letterbox. It was a coruscating *Daily News* column![8]

---

[7] *The Sun* (NY), Apr. 4, 1914.

[8] *Plymouth and Exeter Gazette*, June 19, 1936. GKC's essay "On Being Moved" appeared in the *Daily News*, Oct. 2, 1909, and is collected in *Lunacy and Letters* and *In Defense of Sanity: The Best Essays of G. K. Chesterton*.

When Chesterton was writing for the Daily Herald *in 1914, critic Gerald Cumberland had the chance to observe him at work.*

On one occasion I saw him emerge from Shoe Lane, hurry into the middle of Fleet Street, and abruptly come to a standstill in the centre of the traffic. He stood there for some time, wrapped in thought, while buses, taxis and lorries eddied about him in a whirlpool and while drivers exercised to the full their gentle art of expostulation. Having come to the end of his meditations he held up his hand, turned round, cleared a passage through the horses and vehicles and returned up Shoe Lane. It was just as though he had deliberately chosen the middle of Fleet Street as the most fruitful place for thought. Nobody else in London could have done it with his air of absolute unconsciousness, of absent-mindedness. And not even the most stalwart policeman, vested with full authority, could have dammed up London's stream of traffic more effectively.

The more one sees of Chesterton the more difficult it is to discover when he is asleep and when he is awake. He may be talking to you most vivaciously one moment and the next he will have disappeared: his body will be there of course, but his mind, his soul, the living spirit within him, will have sunk out of sight.

One Friday afternoon I went to *The Daily Herald* office to call on a friend. As I entered the building a taxi stopped at the door, and I found GKC by my side.

"I have half-an-hour for my article," said he, rather breathlessly. "Wait here till I come back."

The first sentence was addressed to himself, the second to the taxi-driver, but as we were by now in the office the driver heard nothing. Chesterton called for a back file of *The Daily Herald*, sat down, lit a cigar and began to read some of his old articles. I watched him. Presently, he smiled. Then he laughed. Then he leaned back in his chair and roared. "Good—oh, damned good!" exclaimed he. He turned to another article and frowned a little, but a third pleased him better. After a while he pushed the papers from him and sat a while in thought. "And as in uffish thought he" sat, he wrote his article, rapidly, calmly, drowsily. Save that his hand moved, he might have been asleep. Nothing disturbed him—neither the noise of the office nor the faint throb of his taxi-cab rapidly ticking off twopences in the street below. He finished his article and rolled dreamily away.⁹

E. V. Lucas was editor of Punch.
The orchestra of [GKC's] brain is always in tune, ready instantaneously to begin. I know no one, except perhaps Bernard Shaw, whose reaction is so swift and whose arguments are in such good order. But the difference is that Shaw has had them ready for a long while, whereas Chesterton summons them from space....

On another lunching occasion, when Chesterton was beyond doubt my guest, we sat down at one o'clock and were still talking at three when the hall-porter came with a message from the taxi-driver, who would like to know if the gentleman—GKC—would pay him off now as he wanted to eat too.¹⁰

The following are glimpses of GKC from anonymous journalists.
When G. K. Chesterton ambles like a happy elephant along the pavements, it is no wonder that people emulate the Red Sea and clear a path before him. He was seen recently at London Victoria Station looking more than ever like a creation of his own fantasies. He examined the brightly coloured books on the stalls with the tender care of Father Brown searching for a clue. He took them up and put them down as if he was juggling with one of his own paradoxes.¹¹

One of the pleasantest sights imaginable is that of G. K. Chesterton, walking down Fleet Street, with his coat flying wide, his round-brimmed hat perched on his curly hair. There is about Mr. Chesterton an air of good fellowship, of being on good terms with the world at large, and the sight of him is like a tonic.¹²

Fleet Street crowds have been used to the ways of great men since Dr. Johnson and Dean Swift trod the paving stones. Chesterton is enveloped in an abstraction so mighty that it neutralises the attention

---

⁹ Gerald Cumberland, *Set Down in Malice: A Book of Reminiscences* (Brentano's, 1919), pp. 71–72.

¹⁰ E. V. Lucas, *Reading, Writing, and Remembering* (Methuen, 1932), pp. 26, 204.

¹¹ *Dundee Courier*, Jan. 13, 1928.

¹² *Gloucester Citizen*, May 4, 1925.

of the passer-by. His huge figure, enveloped in its cloak and shaded by a slouch hat, rolls through the streets unheeding his fellow beings. His eyes stare before him in a troubled dream; his lips move, muttering, composing, arguing. He is an imposing figure; of immense proportions, almost balloon-like with a fine impetuous head which rises over the surrounding crowds; his hair is properly shaggy, countenance open and frank, wearing indeed a curious childlike unconsciousness in spite of the thought intensity that clouds his brow.[13]

Probably every link boy in London knew Dr. Samuel Johnson and exchanged their views about him with some familiarity mixed with awe. Certainly every taxi driver knows G. K. Chesterton. He came into his old haunts in Fleet Street this Christmas and this is what happened.

The taxi-driver drove up to his destination, and got out to open the door with quite knightly courtesy. The great GKC alighted, squat hat, familiar black cloak, and all. Then he told the driver to wait, and disappeared.

Now the driver confided to a small van man the identity of his distinguished fare. The driver of a tea van which stood in front joined in to learn the secret. The news-vendor came forth and added his stock of reminiscences. And not one of these men drove their vans away until they had seen Mr. Chesterton once more. It was a spontaneous tribute to a great man of letters.[14]

The bulk of Mr. Chesterton, a physical feature regarding which he is himself ready to be jocular, is perhaps too often the occasion of his friend's chaff. To describe him as Falstaffian, however, is to do no injustice to his form; and one cannot but be amazed that so much vitality, activity, and unflagging industry abide in so great a body. Mr. Chesterton has been described by one who knows him as an overgrown boy without a scrap of artifice or pose. His chuckle alone disarms criticism; it seems to well from a naive, confiding, and affectionate nature.[15]

---

[13] Not quite anonymous: Constance Smedley, writing in *T.P's Weekly*, Nov. 12, 1909.
[14] *Market Harborough Advertiser*, Jan. 1, 1932. A link boy was a boy who carried a torch to light the way for pedestrians at night.
[15] *Musselburgh News*, July 29, 1910.

I saw G. K. Chesterton the other afternoon browsing at a bookshop near Leicester Square in London. He appeared to be going systematically over a number of weekly journals—comic, feminine, and otherwise—most of which he dismissed at one glance. Perhaps this explains how GKC in his writings always seems to be so familiar with the tendencies of popular taste, though so many people think of him as a confirmed medievalist.[16]

Nobody enters the company of GKC without a feeling of entering into good conversation as easily as a duck takes to water. Ideas pervade him; he shakes them off with a chuckle of enjoyment as if they were yours instead of his. Nor does he need to choose a subject for himself, as so many good talkers do. He is content to take up the "service" you send him, and return it with interest. You never come away from him without feeling as if you had climbed a hill-top and relished the fullness of life and thought at its best.[17]

Fellow Fleet Street journalist Bernard Falk shared his reminiscences.
My favorite place for lunch was the Wellington Tavern in Fleet Street, the proprietor, a kindly Italian with a most pleasant voice. Here I was used to having as a neighbor, G. K. Chesterton, an Ulster cloak falling gracefully around his agreeable and not inconsiderable proportions. Usually with a bottle of Burgundy or Chianti in front of him, he sat confiding his merry inventions to a large-size notebook, and, as he wrote, he rocked with laughter so infectious that I might have been pardoned for joining in. Sometimes, watching his rounded form expanded with these lusty twists of enjoyment, I feared for the contents of the table. The writing done, and the bill paid, the tremendous fellow retired into the capacious folds of his ulster, and, thus protected against the weather, emerged into Fleet Street, where his further progress was marked by a swinging cane whose pendulous movement conducted some unseen orchestra.[18]

---

[16] *Belfast Telegraph*, May 11, 1928.
[17] *Book Window*, June 1928.
[18] Bernard Falk, *He Laughed in Fleet Street* (Hutchinson, 1933), p. 78.

Long before she became a celebrated detective novelist and colleague of GKC, Dorothy L. Sayers wrote a letter to her parents from Somerville College in May 1914.

I had to leave a tennis party early to hear GKC at the School. I was very agreeably surprised in him. I had been afraid he would be untidy in his person and aggressive in his manner. He was very huge and ugly, of course, but it is a nice ugliness, and he was well dressed, with plenty of nice white linen, and he looked well-brushed and put together. He had a terrible cold, poor dear, but all the same one liked his voice—it was the voice of a gentleman, and suggested not only culture but breeding. His delivery, perhaps on account of the cold, was not very good—rather hesitating and slow, but he spoke very clearly. We were some distance away, and heard every syllable. His lecture was very Chestertonian, but much sounder than I had expected and not so fire-worky. He said some really excellent things. I have noted for future use, that his books ought to be read as he speaks—rather slowly, and delivering the paradoxical statements tentatively. His speaking has none of that aggressive and dogmatic quality which his writings are apt to assume when read aloud. Altogether, a most pleasant lecture.[19]

Harandraneth Maitra, editor of The Voice of India, *visited Chesterton for an interview in 1916.*

There is certainly nothing ordinary about his appearance. His face is that of a thinker. His eyes are deeply penetrating, but his smile is full of sympathy and affection. The genuineness of his laughter is infectious. His continual struggle with his eyeglasses, which seemed to be constantly wanting to come off, humorously suggested to my mind the many difficulties encountered by a nature like his in adapting itself to the manifold petty conventions of "civilization."[20]

Herbert H. Asquith was Prime Minister of England from 1908 to 1916. His son, also named Herbert, was a poet and novelist, who recalled Chesterton

---

[19] *The Letters of Dorothy L. Sayers, Vol. 1, 1899–1936: The Making of a Detective Novelist,* ed. Barbara Reynolds (Hodder & Stoughton, 1995), pp. 87–88.

[20] *Gilbert* magazine, January–February 2011.

visiting the senior Asquith's home during a children's house party and spending hours devising a treasure hunt for the amusement of the boys and girls.

The treasure was a portrait of a public character for whom Chesterton had never shown any marked enthusiasm; it was dismembered for purposes of the hunt; legs, arms, and body were concealed in different parts of the house and garden, and it was only when the last clue—contained in verses which he had composed for the occasion—was guessed that its identity could be established by the shocking discovery of the head.

He gave his task the grave concentration of an artist, and the result was a success that I have never seen equalled in a game of this kind.[21]

Hilaire Belloc's daughter, Eleanor Jebb, recalled her childhood memories of GKC.

Uncle Gilbert we called him. We saw him as he was—a giant—genial, lofty and concerned about all the things desired but beyond our reach—more static than mobile. He would come over the river with Auntie Frances and give us absorbing displays of phantasy through puppets with plaster heads and appropriate gowns. They came to life in those gifted hands of Uncle Gilbert—by the use of his fingers—by the accompanying antics and whims which enlivened them. They appeared to need no stage or scenery. Uncle Gilbert sat perilously on the edge of a nursery chair and rumbled off into the story of action! Oh that delightful rumble! Oh that groaning joy that carried us with it into long since vanished and forgotten lands! We have still treasured a little sword of gilt and mosaic handle, with which he made the hero wield many a thrust in the cause of Right and gallantly cause the death of many a villain—much to our satisfaction. Gilbert could always murder without malice, savagery or hate!

Then once he stood upon the long, wet sands at Felpham looking out across the Channel on a sunless summer afternoon. He saw far, far beyond that narrow sea with those short-sighted eyes—we were behind him, looking up in wonder and comfort, and knew he was a poet, his massive form reared against the crinkled shining

---

[21] H. H. Asquith, *Moments of Memory: Recollections and Impressions* (Hutchinson, 1937), pp. 170–71.

puddles, and the wind blew through his hair. I was four years old. Some years after we had left London for Shipley we were taken up to Town to see the Circus, and while passing through Victoria to the cab I saw in the distant gloom of the Station the familiar, and always comforting, figure of Gilbert Chesterton, cloaked and behatted. It seemed to me so normally part of London—London which he so loved—that I merely murmured looking at the fleeting figure "There is Uncle Gilbert" without surprise or emphasis. But my father electrified immediately, and with clamant and ringing cries of "Hi Gilbert! Gilbert!" shot off in his direction, captured him and brought him back to us, whereupon we were all kissed with groaning affection and blinking of the eyes, and the exciting erudite talk went on above our heads.

He rumbled off as the cab trundled away. He remains vividly in my memory, whereas the arrival of the elephants has not. That is as it should be, because you and I shall see Uncle Gilbert again.[22]

Robert Lynd was an Irish writer and nationalist.
Mr. Chesterton belongs to the exuberantly lovable tradition of Dickens; indeed, he is, in the opinion of many people, the most exuberantly lovable personality which has expressed itself in English literature since Dickens.[23]

Illustrator Thomas Derrick drew some famous caricatures of Chesterton as a quill-bearing knight.
I remember a lecture Chesterton spoke on the medieval State. In the discussion that followed, a young barrister called Blanco White told us that the medieval State which we had heard described was a figment of Mr. Chesterton's imagination. That such a state had never, as a matter of historical fact, ever really existed—and so on. As he spoke, I remember G.K. rolling about on his inadequate chair, and chuckling, and making strange noises; and when Blanco White had finished, G.K. rose and told him that he had only to go to the British Museum to see miles and miles of contemporary documents substantiating all that he had said about the law and structure of the medieval State. Then he proceeded—and this was

---

[22] In Maisie Ward, *Return to Chesterton* (Sheed and Ward, 1953), pp. 101–3.
[23] Robert Lynd, *Old and New Masters* (T. Fisher Unwin, 1919), p. 27.

the interesting and impressive thing—to repeat verbatim, in its Old English, the terms of the Magna Carta. I remember the pitiful and entirely humourless look of dismay on the face of the completely punctured Blanco White.[24]

T. W. Mercer describes Chesterton at a meeting of the Distributist League in 1930.

No author in Great Britain is less well-groomed than he. When he mounted the little platform he was warmly cheered; and it was great fun to watch him as he listened to the four speakers who preceded him. He shook with laughter at their jokes, sniffed, with a knowing air, when their logic went awry, and made notes eagerly and with joyous haste as each new opportunity for him to shatter their assertions unwittingly appeared.... When GKC addressed the meeting, he made hay of all the editor of the *Daily Herald* had said. I cannot remember when I heard a speaker's arguments so completely shattered. For fifteen minutes we watched the battle—Chesterton against the world! While he, like Don Quixote, his favourite hero, charged against Collectivists and Statists of all schools. When he laughed we knew another roaring joke was coming. His smile was a sign that laughter was on the way. And when he stood erect and shook his wild hair as a charger shakes its mane, all saw that another opponent would soon be rolling in the dust.[25]

An unnamed reporter for the Boston Globe *described Chesterton at the first lecture of his 1921 American speaking tour.*

Mr. Chesterton peered facetiously at his audience of several hundred from behind an enormous pair of glasses which persisted in coming loose, while he rambled entertainingly through his subject matter which was entitled "The Ignorance of the Educated."

He began by telling the audience that they were wrong. He wasn't a lecturer. He never was. He never would be. "I must confess that I know so little about anything that I am obliged to talk about everything," explained Mr. Chesterton. He then explained

---

[24] Unpublished letter to Maisie Ward, 1944. (It might have been the medieval charter that GKC quoted, since that would have better supported his thesis.)
[25] *Gilbert* magazine, December 2005.

minutely and in detail that he didn't know what he was talking about, sending the audience into roars.

Referring to prohibition, he asserted that "some of us think that if Patrick Henry could return to the earth and look about him at some the social problems of our day, it is possible that he might modify his observation and confine himself to saying, 'give me death.' "[26]

Southern poet and critic John Crowe Ransom also heard GKC lecture on the American tour of 1921.

Either Mr. Chesterton is the most modest man alive, or somebody has been telling him false tales about his merits as a lecturer. He is one of the best lecturers I have ever heard. He has a real feeling for the reaction of his audience, and can adapt very difficult material. Yet he told his audience with the utmost conviction that he could not lecture.[27]

When G. K. Chesterton was in New York in 1921, he spent one evening with some writers, including Robert Cortes Holliday.

His utterance was rapid, melodious. The modulations of his softly flowing voice had curiously somewhat the effect of a very cheerful music-box. His easy and very natural command of a great multitude of words was striking. And yet there was something decidedly boyish about the effect of his talk. I think the cause of this was, for one thing, the rather gurgling enjoyment with which he spoke, and for another thing, in his impulsive concern for the point of his idea he frequently did not trouble to begin nor end sentences. He just let 'er go. But the fundamental source of this boyishness of spirit I think was this: I do not believe I have ever seen a man who had borne the brunt of life for some forty-five years and still retained such complete, abounding, unaffected and infectious good humor as Mr. Chesterton.[28]

In Boston, GKC met journalist Myles Connolly, upon whom he made a deep and lasting impression. Connolly would go on to write several "Chestertonian"

---

[26] *Boston Globe*, Jan. 13, 1921.
[27] *Nashville Tennessean*, Mar. 23, 1921.
[28] Robert Cortes Holliday, *Turns About Town* (George H. Doran, 1921; Project Gutenberg, 2011), chap. 11, https://www.gutenberg.org/files/36085/36085-h/36085-h.htm.

novels, including Mr. Blue. *Of that initial encounter, Connolly wrote the following.*

"Be humble to be happy," says Gilbert K. Chesterton.

He is huge, gigantic though not as gigantic as you have been led to believe. He towers over tall men, is broader than broad men. And yet—and this is strange thing—his voice is soft and gentle and obliging, and his eyes are a young boy's eyes.

He has been called the boisterous Mr. Chesterton, the medieval Mr. Chesterton, the militant Mr. Chesterton, and the Mr. Chesterton what-not. But I do not think he has ever been called the meek Mr. Chesterton. Yet, meek he is.

There's nothing terrible or noisy about him. Even his laughter—which is ever-ready and jovial—is quiet laughter. He is a humble and simple man.

And—this is strange, too—for some peculiar reason, he is delighted to see you. How he seems to feel that this is a rare opportunity! How jolly he is about it!

I wish there was some device by which I could reproduce the exact effect that this man has when he talks. Perhaps, it is that elusive evanescent thing called personality that does the trick. Anyway, he has such a habit of enjoying just what he himself says in such a jolly way, that you are inclined to forget just what he is saying, and chuckle and laugh with him as says it. At times it is like laughing at a joke. You know it is a good joke, a marvelously strange joke. But, for the life of you, you just can't understand what it is about.[29]

GKC gave three lectures at the Bellevue Hotel ballroom in Philadelphia at the end of January 1921.

At the end of one of them, a woman from the audience asked, "What do you consider the weakest point in our civilization?" She sat down and waited with the rest of the audience for a dissertation on religion or government, but Chesterton chuckled and answered, "Well, I have always felt that it is the duty of everyone of us to consider himself the weakest point."[30]

---

[29] *Boston Sunday Post,* Jan. 9, 1921.

[30] The account is given in *Philadelphia Evening Public Ledger,* Feb. 18, 1921. This is a variation on "What's wrong with the world?"
 "I am."

Writer Patrick Braybrooke was a son of one of Frances Chesterton's cousins. He often visited GKC's home.

Chesterton is so remarkable-looking that anyone seeing him cannot fail to be impressed by his splendid head, his shapely forehead, his eyes that seem to look back over the forgotten centuries or forward to those yet to come.

If there is one thing that is characteristic of Chesterton, it is that he always seems genuinely pleased to see you.... He has the happy advantage of making you feel that he really is glad that you have come to his house.... Great men do not always trouble to be polite to smaller ones.

What a wonderful laugh Chesterton has. It is like a clap of thunder that suddenly startles the echoes in the valley; it is the very soul of geniality. There is nothing that so lays bare a man's character as his laugh—it cannot pretend....

It is remarkable the amount of work that Chesterton gets through. He has masses of correspondence, he has articles to write, books to get ready for press, and yet he finds time to help in local theatricals, to give lectures in places as wide apart as Oxford and America (and what is wider in every way than those two places?), that means all that is best in the ancient world and all that is best in the modern. He can also find time to take a long tour to Palestine to find the New Jerusalem, that city that Christ wept over....

What are the general impressions that a stranger visiting Chesterton would get? He would, I think, be impressed by his genial kindliness; he would be amazed by his extraordinary powers of memory and the depths of his reading; he would be gratified by the interest that Chesterton displays in him; he would be charmed by the quaintness of his home. That Chesterton has humour is abundant by his conversation; that he has pathos is not so apparent. I am not perfectly sure that he can appreciate the things that make ordinary men sad. It has been said that he is not concerned with the facts of everyday life; if he is not, it is because he can see beyond them—he can see that this is a good world, which makes him a good host; he can look forward across the ages to the glorious stars that shine in the night sky for those who are optimists, as Chesterton is, and are great men in their own homes....

I have often sat at his table.... There is no subject upon which he has not something worth while to say. His memory is remarkable;

he can quote poet after poet, or compose a poem on anything that crops up at the table.... He is a good host in the niceties of the table; he knows if you want salt; he does not forget that wine is the symbol of hospitality.[31]

St. John Ervine was a writer and critic. (He adopted the abbreviation "St." when he began his literary career.)

Mr. Chesterton is a fat man. There is a rumour in England that many Americans felt they had been defrauded of their money when they went to hear him lecture lately because he was hardly so fat as they had been led to believe! He certainly is not so bulky now, because of a serious illness, as he was when I first knew him, but in those days he was undeniably an enormous man. And in himself he is a complete refutation of the legend that fat men are dull men.

Mr. Chesterton was sent into the world by an All-Just God for the exclusive purpose of saying the opposite to Mr. Shaw. With the most complimentary intention I say that Mr. Chesterton's job in the world is, when Mr. Shaw speaks, to reply, "On the contrary!..." He has to restore the balance which Mr. Shaw very vigorously disturbs.[32]

George Bernard Shaw was a playwright and philosophical opponent of GKC in most things.

I enjoyed him and admired him keenly; and nothing could have been more generous than his treatment of me. Our controversies were exhibition spars, in which nothing could have induced either of us to hurt the other.[33]

H. G. Wells was a novelist and another friend and philosophical opponent of GKC.

G. K. Chesterton is a joyous whirl of brushwork. When he is there, I remark, the whole ceiling is by a sort of radiation convivial. We drink limitless old October from handsome flagons, and we argue mightily about Pride and the nature of Deity.

---

[31] Patrick Braybrooke, *Gilbert Keith Chesterton* (Chelsea Publishing, 1922), pp. 100–101, 103–4.
[32] St. John Ervine, *Some Impressions of My Elders* (George Allen & Unwin, 1923), pp. 91–92.
[33] *Mark Twain Quarterly*, Spring 1937.

We all three [Chesterton, Belloc, Wells] want people to have property of a real and personal sort, to have the son, as Chesterton put it, bringing up the port his father laid down, and pride in the pears one has grown in one's own garden. And I agree with Chesterton that giving—giving oneself out of love and fellowship—is the salt of life.[34]

Canon Wilkinson, writing for the Glasgow Herald *in 1924, called Chesterton "A Man of Cheerful Yesterdays."*
I love him for his beauty, but not for that alone. The magnet that draws me to him is his heart's gladness, the joy that ripples in his voice and trips with gay abandon from his pen and flows flashingly and foamingly all round him, until, in the midst of a naughty and perverse generation, he remains gloriously stranded on an island of delight. If my metaphors seem extravagant, please ascribe them, not to the senseless sin of idolatry, but to the charitable urge that compels me to remind a weary and sophisticated old world that it is worth while being on nodding terms with a man who believes—as Chesterton, I am sure, believes—that God is really glad to be glad, and that joy cometh in the morning because it is meant to bide with us all day.

It might be to our advantage to treat Mr. Chesterton seriously. He is much more than a portly gentleman with an amusing passion for turning pyramids upside down. He is a great interpreter; more, he is a reconciler. He reveals the simplicities that we thought the world had no longer any use for.[35]

Andrue Berding attended a Chesterton lecture at Oxford in 1927.
No one could more truthfully and literally be said to be in constant touch with his audience than G. K. Chesterton. His enormous person, which he brought with him to Oxford to accompany his brain while he lectured one recent Saturday night, protruded out into the audience and made them feel that Mr. Chesterton was indeed very much among them. Mr. Chesterton might have stepped from an illustrated edition of Thackeray as he stood before his audience in

---

[34] H. G. Wells, *An Englishman Looks at the World* (Cassell, 1914), p. 175.
[35] *Glasgow Herald*, Dec. 27, 1924.

a fourth-floor hall in the ancient university city of Oxford. Genial, expansive to the point where his stiff shirt-front found it impossible to maintain its dignity and hopelessly gave up the struggle, witty beyond imitation, and withal deeply philosophic and observant, he made a steel engraving in my mind.

If I could sketch with lines as well as with words I could draw him now from memory ... his steel-gray hair, which flows down the back of his huge head; his twinkling eyes behind the spectacles whose ribbon dangled to his shirt-front; his high forehead which shone in the brilliance of the unshaded English electric lights; his nervous, though pudgy, hands, and the ring that seemed to give him inspiration while he talked, for he lifted it up and glanced at it whenever he paused for thought. Having drawn the cartoon of this big man whose big thoughts went out to a big audience, I might put words in his mouth, cartoon-fashion. But they would be in very small letters, for his voice seems out of proportion to his size and its sounding board. During the lecture Mr. Chesterton became somewhat hazy, for in English show-houses and lecture-rooms one is permitted to smoke; but his words came through the mist, clear if not strong, and powerful in thought if not in sound.[36]

Lawyer Reginald Hine said that he knew Chesterton (if you can "claim to know a man by virtue of shaking his hand").

One day at the Poetry Society, as president, he lectured us on Alexander Pope, a poet the very opposite to himself; but out of mere perverseness, or possibly because Pope was a Catholic, GKC was resolved to make us bow down and worship him. But the members were not willing to bow the knee. We could admire the diabolical cleverness, the satirical talent of Pope. Most of us had smiled over the *Rape of the Lock* and chuckled over his *Dunciad*. But where was there any magic, where was the "pleasance and half wonder"? We grew restive and rebellious, and of this our president was made aware.

Then came the best conclusion that ever I heard. "Gentlemen," he said, looking more like a giant than ever, "I can dispute with you no longer. My time is up. But if you will do me the honour to meet me outside this hall"—and here he brandished his fist—"I

---

[36] *America,* Jan. 8, 1927.

will prove upon your shameful bodies what I have failed to impress upon your stupid minds."

Well aware of Johnsonian proportions, Chesterton was pleased to play the *ursa major*. But this truculent attitude was more than mere bravado. The bigness in him went deep. Below the glittering surface of his style, too prone to paradox, you came upon a roundabout common sense, a largeness of vision, a broad, wholesome outlook upon men and things. Tall he was, so tall that his head hit against the stars; yet so massive was he that his feet sank down into common soil. He had a fat man's impatience at thin and skinny views. Even poetry, he held, should keep close to mother earth. Let the maker see that it had a body; the soul could look after itself. How entirely he agreed with the stout fellow William Morris: "Half a dozen stanzas of ballad poetry are worth a cartload of the whining introspective pieces of today." As for his own work, the best of it would stand. Possibly he had grown too epigrammatic. The habit of juggling with words had laid him open to the charge which the idle citizen in the *Spectator* brought against his pudding: "Mem. Too many Plumbs and no Sewett." But the critics have been misled by his style. Somehow the plums had all gone to the top. There was plenty of suet below.

I have made it appear as though I looked upon Chesterton but once, and at one of his most Gilbertian moments. But I was forgetting that I was present at the last meeting he attended—a religious conference held at Letchworth. Advertised to take the chair, he did so in a fashion all his own. Having wedged himself comfortably into an armchair of absurdly insufficient size, he then essayed to speak, but the chair rose with him, and stuck to him devotedly despite the efforts of two priests to disengage him. At last it was done, and the great man began:

"Now that I am free to speak to you, I am wondering whether I should not have done better to have stuck to my chair. To have been seen and heard! What an ideal chairman I could have made! All I can hope is that I shall adhere to the points at issue in this debate, and that we shall get to the bottom of our more pressing problems."[37]

[37] Reginald Hine, *Memoirs of an Uncommon Lawyer* (J. M. Dent, 1946), pp. 165–66.

A columnist who went by "C. P." attended more than one of GKC's speeches.
There are some men who can speak anywhere, at any time, and seemingly about anything. These are the masters of the art, and are the precious minority. The man who can make a lively, witty, and provocative speech extemporaneously is in possession of one of the rarest gifts of the gods.

I know no greater test of friendship than the misery we endure with stoical resignation when an otherwise lovable fellow gets up to make a speech so inane that his audience is dumbfounded.

Public banquets, in the main, can be placed in two categories: either the dinner is good and the speeches unbearable, or the dinner and speeches alike are bad. However, I would eat the worst dinner in London if it afforded me the opportunity of listening to a speech by G. K. Chesterton.[38]

Famed rare-book dealer David Magee said that no author impressed him as much as Chesterton. As a young boy, Magee spent the summer of 1913 in Beaconsfield, and he and his sister were invited one afternoon to Chesterton's home.
He resembled nothing so much as a vast unmade bed. I remember at that table he told us a tale of falling down stairs. I forget the point, if it ever had one, but I do recall the difficulty I had in hearing him. He talked into his chins which seemed to muffle all sound. Pointless or not, he enjoyed his own story, for when it was over his great body shook with silent laughter and tears of merriment ran down his cheeks.[39]

Almost twenty years later, Magee returned to Beaconsfield to ask Chesterton to write an introduction to a book he was publishing.
He was a charming host and I was immediately struck by his modesty which was absolutely genuine. He was at that time my favorite author and I had read practically everything he had written. When I told him this he threw up his hands in mock horror. "But, my

---

[38] *Lincolnshire Echo*, Oct. 28, 1932.
[39] David Magee, *Infinite Riches: The Adventures of a Rare Book Dealer* (Eriksson, 1973), p. 230.

dear sir, that is an ordeal *no one* deserves." He honestly didn't think much of his Father Brown stories. "Potboilers," he said. "But I must admit they were fun to write."[40]

In September of 1929, GKC visited his cousin, Rev. J. A. Chesterton, who was the Anglican Vicar in Tenbury Wells. Rev. Chesterton invited the local Catholic priest, Father H. E. G. Rope, to meet GKC. Father Rope recounted the meeting in his diary.

He was just as his portrait suggested, only taller than I expected. Chesterton's hair is silvery; he suffers acutely from rheumatism, I think, and rose with great difficulty from the narrow chair on which he preferred to sit. He said he always found it most difficult in the early morning. What especially charmed me was his old world courtesy, and his utter freedom from affectation or pose of any kind (contrary to what many have imagined of him).

I found his own feelings about machinery were the same as mine, his ideal would be no machinery at all. But in every movement there must be a right and a left of those inclined to a compromise. "At present it is a case of nothing but machines." When I suggested that the change we hope for could only come, like the conversion of England, by a miracle, I think he fully concurred, saying "But it is worthwhile keeping up a protest."

Chesterton's conversation was just like his writings, both utterly sincere and always informed by true charity.[41]

James Lansdale Hodson spent a summer holiday in the coastal village of Lyme Regis, where GKC often spent his holiday.

I once came upon that wise man G.K. Chesterton sitting like a full-blown Dickens character in the doorway of a hotel on a steep street in Lyme Regis. Day after day I saw him there, eyeglasses

---

[40] Ibid., p. 232. The book for which he had asked GKC to write the introduction was never published. Magee became a bookseller in San Francisco, where, in 1955, he sold a copy of Holbrook Jackson's *Platitudes in the Making* that contained GKC's comments in the margins, written in green pencil. The buyer was Charlotte Kessler, who purchased it for her husband Alfred, who was an avid GKC fan. A facsimile of the book was published by Ignatius Press as *Platitudes Undone* (1997). It is not known how Magee obtained the original.

[41] *Gilbert* magazine, January–February 2019.

on his nose, his frame overflowing his basket chair, about his feet books piled—fine books and paperbacks.

When at last I ventured to speak to him and ask him what he was doing, he said blandly: "Nothing. I can never get enough of nothing. Look at these motor cars rushing up the hill and rushing down, going only to return."

He sighed, as if at the inscrutability of human nature, and resumed his reading. I spent several days at that place, but every time I passed his hotel, there he was, magnificently immobile, taking his ease, resting and (no doubt) being thankful.[42]

Much to her surprise, the press wanted to interview Frances Chesterton several times when the Chestertons first visited America in 1921. When she asked a reporter why, he responded, "Because you are the wife of a celebrity." Following is her response.

And that's the very thing I have been trying to forget.

It astounds Mr. Chesterton, too, who is the simplest sort of person. Why, we are just ordinary people, and over in England, just a couple of members of a large group of people who are honestly trying to do good work.

We live in a little house, out in the country, five and twenty miles from London, which we call Overroads, because it looks out on a couple of roads. Mr. Chesterton has the peculiarity of some big men physically and of his temperament, that he can't be really happy in doing work except in a very small room. I have tried again and again to get him to fix up a decent study where he could receive people and in which he would have a decent desk and decent furniture. But, he simply won't do it. He has a room so small he that can practically sit at his desk and reach all around the room what he wants. And his desk is nothing but an old kitchen table. He likes that, because he can draw on it or hack it to his heart's content. It has been covered with oilcloth but that is all hacked up. In the study he has the things valuable to him that wouldn't be worth a tuppence [twopence] to any one else.[43]

---

[42] *Aberdeen Journal*, June 1, 1939.
[43] *Vancouver Daily World*, Mar. 15, 1921.

W. R. Titterton, who was assistant editor of G.K.'s Weekly, *describes the paper's weekly editorial meeting.*

I am sitting in the editorial chair, when the door opens, and discloses Chesterton, floppy hat in one hand, sprouting cigarillo and sword-stick in the other. Of course, his pince-nez hang sideways on his nose. A beaming smile, half of surprise, half of joy is on his face, as if, on a long and hazardous voyage of discovery, most unexpectedly he'd found *us!*

The next few moments are taken up with his depositing his impedimenta carefully anywhere and his apologies for disturbing us. And then he is seated in the editorial chair, happy and at ease.

Usually he feels in an inside pocket and takes out some manuscripts done in that marvelous Gothic handwriting. He hands the articles to me, and probably his work in town is finished. But now and then he'd say to the secretary, "Oh, Miss Dunham, would you mind taking down this for me?" and he'd stride up and down the small office, hands behind his back, while Bunny Dunham typed his conversation.

Every now and then would come a chuckle, ending in a roar and a squeak. When his talk had ended, and he'd quickly read it through, he'd chat for a while and then with infinite reluctance vanish. Afterwards I have (but not often) seen him in a dim corner of a Fleet Street tavern, or in El Vino's wineshop, blissfully contemplating the universe.[44]

In 1932, Maria Petrie was commissioned to sculpt a bust of Chesterton, which is now in London's National Gallery of Art.

Although I had brought along more than the usual supply of clay for a large bust, I found it quite inadequate and had to build up over a foundations of five flowerpots. My work proceeded to the dictation of a Father Brown story without any pause for reflection, for Gilbert wrote exactly as he talked, ideas pouring forth in well-finished sentences like liquid metal in a mould and no revision was needed.[45]

---

[44] W. R. Titterton, *The World Is So Full: Of a Number of Things, I Think We Should All Be as Happy as Kings* (W. R. Titterton, 1961), pp. 37–38.
[45] *Manchester Guardian*, June 11, 1955.

Sculptor and graphic artist Eric Gill would eventually sculpt the original headstone for Chesterton's grave. He also created a stained glass window of St. Francis of Assisi as a memorial to Gilbert and Frances in their home parish.

In my Fabian days I much disliked GKC. Arguing with him seemed like beating the air. I was quite out of tune with him. But as the years passed I got past that and came to revere and love him, as a writer and as a holy man, beyond all his contemporaries. Thanks be to God he also loved and befriended me.[46]

Belgian poet and translator Emile Cammaerts became a close friend of GKC.
Those who remember him as a boy tell me that he was rather thin and loose-limbed, but when I met him, in his thirties, he had already acquired the large bulk to which he liked to refer good-humouredly. My first impression was the contrast between his amazingly quick mind and slow-moving body. It took him half a minute to take a few steps, but it did not take him a second to hit upon the conclusion of the most involved argument, and as he liked to talk while walking about the room, the result was nothing short of staggering. I had met before men who thought as they moved, slowly or quickly. I had never met a man who allied such intellectual agility with such physical clumsiness.[47]

Grace Carey was a resident of Beaconsfield when GKC lived there.
G. K. Chesterton was a familiar figure in the town, beloved of both his fellow Catholics and those who did not share his religious views. He was never too busy to open a fete or attend a local show, or give his support and patronage to some society struggling to establish itself in the community. Small wonder that everyone loved this man, great in mind and in stature. His courtesy and kindness were for all, not just for the few. No-one was too humble for his attention. I have seen him chatting to someone's cook-general, who had asked him to autograph one of his books presented for

---

[46] Eric Gill, *Autobiography* (J. Cape, 1940), p. 197.
[47] Emile Cammaerts, *The Laughing Prophet: The Seven Virtues & G. K. Chesterton* (ACS Books, 1937), pp. 11–12, https://www.chesterton.org/wp-content/uploads/2020/04/The-Laughing-Prophet_ACS-Books.pdf.

sale at a bazaar, as though she were a grande dame and the only person in the world at that moment.[48]

Monsignor Charles Boldrick was a priest in the Archdiocese of Louisville, Kentucky. In preparation for the priesthood, he studied at the North American College in Rome and was there in 1929, when G. K. Chesterton was a guest for dinner and gave a speech to the American seminarians.

We were all anticipating Chesterton's visit tonight. When we came down to supper, he was at the post of honor, and among several Bishops. He is a towering man of colossal proportions, with a gray mane of hair and a black string on his eye-glasses. He eats with his left hand. At the lecture following, the library was nicely decorated, and crowded with ourselves and alumni. Mr. Chesterton apologized for presenting such a ridiculous sight, and for having carried up that torch of a cigar, which bore no resemblance to the torch of truth. One of the striking ways, he said, in which the Church differed from earthly powers was its ability to have strong support farthest from its center, such as glorious Ireland, Scandinavia, Scotch Highlands, and now America. America has always been regarded, he went on, as a Utopia in England. And he recited a doggerel he heard in his youth to prove it. He referred to H. G. Wells's writing frequent Utopias all different, some about distant fixed stars, but he was sure that, if Mr. Wells would pay a visit to some of these, his distant colonies, he'd find Catholics there, to his discomfort. He referred amusingly to the Pilgrim Fathers, to Glorious Maryland, and Virginia, and Sir Walter Raleigh, who was he said the only approximately respectable person who ever had anything to do with Queen Elizabeth. He said America is the only country which started with a clean slate, with a creed for its foundation, down in black and white. He referred to the text "Many shall come from the East and the West" [Mt 8:11], and he was glad to salute some who have arrived. Everyone enjoyed him immensely. I was so glad to see and hear him who, I think, is the outstanding Catholic writer of today, one of the world's great minds, perhaps the greatest convert since Newman. The Church is fortunate in calling him her son.[49]

[48] *Heritage Magazine*, January 1956.
[49] Charles Boldrick diary, Dec. 6, 1929.

Malcolm Muggeridge was a legendary British journalist.

When I was still a schoolboy my father took me to a dinner at a Soho restaurant at which G. K. Chesterton was being entertained. It was an occasion of inconceivable glory. I observed with fascination the enormous bulk of the guest of honour, his great stomach and plump hands; how his pince-nez on a black ribbon were almost lost in the vast expanse of his face, and how when he delivered himself of what he considered to be a good remark he had a way of blowing into his moustache with a sound like an expiring balloon. His speech, if he made one, was lost on me, but I vividly recall how I persuaded my father to wait outside the restaurant while we watched the great man make his way down the street in a billowing black cloak and old-style bohemian hat with a large brim.[50]

C. Northcote Parkinson was a British historian and essayist who was famous for formulating Parkinson's Law ("Work expands to fill the time available for its completion"). He considered G. K. Chesterton his mentor and hero and made the decision to follow his example as "a literate Englishman and practicing essayist."

I met Chesterton when I was a young man and he was old, and it was from him that I derived the whole idea of conveying serious thoughts in the form of a joke. The humor made the whole thing more digestible and gave it great publicity.[51]

Frank Sheed, along with his wife Maisie Ward (Chesterton's official biographer), ran a publishing house that published most of GKC's later books.

Chesterton was wholly without vanity. A friend of mine asked him which he thought his most important book. He answered, "I don't think any of my books important." And he was putting on no act. I never heard him refer to a review that praised him.[52]

---

[50] Malcolm Muggeridge, *Chronicles of Wasted Time: An Autobiography* (Gateway Books, 1989), p. 13.

[51] *New York Times*, June 11, 1971. Parkinson's Law is used to explain the inevitability of bureaucratic expansion. For instance, Parkinson correctly predicted that the Royal Navy would eventually have more admirals than ships, and while living in California, he was invited by Governor Ronald Reagan to explain "why the San Francisco-Oakland Bay Bridge's original repainting crew of 14 members grew to 72 once a labor-saving paint sprayer had been introduced."

[52] Frank Sheed, *The Church and I* (Doubleday, 1974), pp. 114–15.

Maurice Reckitt, who was the editor of Christendom: A Journal of Christian Sociology, *served on the board of G.K.'s* Weekly.

It is usually unwise to meet one's heroes face to face, yet this was a test which G. K. Chesterton triumphantly survived. As one sat in his company his books came alive; their wit was matched in a dozen casual pleasantries, the resources behind them were vindicated by a prodigious allusiveness, their magnanimity was confirmed by an unfailing generosity of every kind. While auditors and secretaries confronted board meetings of *G.K.'s Weekly* with bewildering and often unpromising statistics, an unruffled editor decorated the blotting paper with brilliant cartoons (which I more than once rescued from the floor at the end), and was too shy to hint that the deficits would be met out of his own pocket. Chesterton was in everything a little more than you had hoped he could be, and those who had hoped the most were perhaps the least disappointed.[53]

When he was a young man, Brocard Sewell worked as an apprentice for G.K.'s Weekly.

About once a month "The Old Man", as he was called in the office, would put in an appearance, to discuss the next few issues of the paper. These editorial visits were highly informal. GKC would wheeze ponderously up the steep and narrow stairs, sink into an an all too small chair, and pour out a stream of jokes and witticisms on every subject under the sun while he smoked a cigar or doodled on the office stationery or blotting paper.

G.K.'s Weekly never developed a wide appeal, and the number of readers remained well below what it deserved. Perhaps its standard was too high, and its policies too much against the current trend of things, for it ever to have become popular; and there was never enough money to advertise it properly. For a time one of the big firms of wholesale agents refused to handle it; its assaults on big business and capitalism in general made it unpopular in such quarters. In fact for a while Chesterton and Belloc were regarded as revolutionary firebrands, and the editors of two of the big London daily papers had orders from their noble proprietors never to allow these two names to be mentioned.

---

[53] Maurice Reckitt, *As It Happened: An Autobiography* (J. M. Dent & Sons, 1941), p. 185.

None of the directors was able to back the paper financially beyond a certain point, and usually each successive crisis in the paper's affairs was resolved by a subsidy from GKC's own pocket.[54]

Arthur Bryant succeeded GKC as the "Our Note-Book" columnist for the Illustrated London News *(between the two of them, they penned the column for seventy years, GKC for thirty-one, and Bryant for forty).*

I never met a more generous man, and I never saw a happier. I do not believe there is anyone who had the inestimable privilege of knowing Gilbert Keith Chesterton who would not say the same.[55]

Lawyer and writer E. S. P. Haynes knew GKC throughout his entire career.

G. K. Chesterton was not only of the most brilliant and humourous men I have known but also one of the noblest. He touched nothing that he did not illuminate and in some sense bless and glorify. He was a fine poet and his drawings (of which I am proud to possess one original) have a genius all their own. I read his weekly essays in the *Illustrated London News* for more than thirty years, and every article he wrote for *G.K.'s Weekly* without ever becoming bored, as one sometimes is by too much of a good thing.

I met him first at lunch with Belloc and Masterman in 1900, Belloc being host. I have seldom warmed to anyone so much at first sight. Every quality in him—his wit, his love of human beings, his irony—was so vitally spontaneous. His magnanimity was securely founded on real humility.

When I last saw him he told me that his secretary had asked the foreman of some workmen next door whether he was aware that they were making such a noise that Mr. Chesterton could not write. "Yes," said the foreman, "we are quite aware of that." G. K. chuckled with joy over the wonderful career that must await this master of repartee.

He embodied all the virtues; but charity in the best sense is what principally shone through all that he said, wrote and did.[56]

---

[54] Brocard Sewell, *My Dear Time's Waste* (St. Albert's Press, 1966), p. 35.

[55] Arthur Bryant, introduction to *The Glass Walking Stick*, by G. K. Chesterton (Methuen, 1955), p. ix.

[56] E. S. P. Haynes, *The Lawyer: A Conversation Piece* (Eyer and Spottiswoode, 1949), pp. 180–81.

J. P. De Fonseka, a scholar from Ceylon, lived in London for two years, befriending Chesterton and editing the collection GKC as MC.

At Westminster Cathedral he was frequently a worshipper at 12 o'clock Mass and towered above the congregation at the gospel. He was the soul of goodness in a thousand ways.[57]

Sir John C. Squire was editor of the London Mercury *from 1919 to 1934.*
A publisher who should endeavor to divide the Chestertonian sheep and goats would soon discover most of them to be hybrids. Comic poetry is as rare as comic verse is common; Mr. Chesterton has written more comic poetry than any Englishman on record. And, to complicate the achievement, he has contrived to make a great deal of it didactic, without falling into the perils that beset didacticism.

His greatest distinction lies in the hold he has upon the fundamentals of human life, considered both its social and its metaphysical aspects. In an age of new questions he has reiterated old answers; in an age of scepticism has laughed at the laughers with a hilarity less hollow than theirs; in an age which tends to excuse baseness, even when it does not explain it away, he has flown the banners of honour, fidelity, and generosity; in an age of mass-regimentation he has stood for the sanctities of the individual soul. And above all—a fact in whose presence all his levities, quibbles, occasional injustices, easy assumptions, and prejudices pale into insignificance—living in a period when the value of life itself has been widely questioned (and, by that very fact, impoverished) he has maintained that "it is something to have been," showing the world the spectacle of one man enjoying the thousand miracles of the day, though the sword of Damocles hangs over his head as it hangs over the heads of all.[58]

R. A. Scott-James was editor of the London Mercury *from 1934 to 1939.*
In most respects, as a man and as a friend, he seemed to be as near perfection as fallible human nature is capable of. For a few years, before he removed to Buckinghamshire, he filled an incomparable place in the literary and journalistic life of London—in the days when he was always in and out of newspaper offices, writing

---

[57] *The Month*, January 1938.
[58] *Observer*, July 3, 1927.

essays in restaurants, or exploring their ground in conversation with friends. He had the rare quality of being brilliant in talk without seeking to shine, of being always gay, without ever not being serious—Olympian in magnanimity and mirth, and endearingly less than Olympian in his chivalry, his quixotry, his constancy to ideas and to friends.[59]

Monsignor John O'Connor, the priest who received Chesterton into the Catholic Church and who was the inspiration for the Father Brown *character, recalled Chesterton's charm for children and theirs for him.*

Uncle Gilbert slid into their souls with the naturalness of music. He never talked down to them so far as I could observe or even suspect, and he never made them self-conscious. Only good playmates together, and the play was quiet and contained, making one want to join in if one could but guess how to set about it.

His voice took on a special timbre in his talks with children: I feared to impair the stillness which reigned about them when engrossed, for the child was stilled or hypnotised by the large Uncle.

His wife had much the same affinity for the little ones, and she could give delicious imitation of Cockney children, but Gilbert never seemed to see a funny side to them at all. This is revealing indeed and symptomatic of the childhood he always kept within his soul.[60]

Father Martin D'Arcy, S.J., was Master of the Jesuit College at Oxford in the 1930s and '40s.

I often say of Chesterton that God must have been looking the other way when he was conceived, because you'd think the man didn't have any original sin in him. Chesterton remained to his dying day a beloved genius still something of a child. There was always a certain innocence about him.

This great, enormous three-hundred pound man would roll about on the floor playing with little children. There was an unwritten law that if any child called at Beaconsfield, where he lived, he was to be immediately admitted. And all writing and everything

---

[59] *London Mercury*, July 1936.
[60] *The Nineteenth Century and After*, June 1946.

else was forgotten while the children would clamber about his neck and roll about the floor with him, and he simply roared with laughter, enjoying it thoroughly. He couldn't make an enemy. Everybody felt he was a likeable person. He could say sharp things occasionally, but not often, because he was full of charity.

Chesterton was much more affectionate (or should I say gentle?) than Belloc. But Chesterton would himself have said the he owed a great deal to Belloc. He would have maintained, "I'm only a journalist. I know nothing. My ideas are borrowed from Belloc, then I adorn them and write about them in my own way." He did transfigure them with this extraordinary gift that he had.

Chesterton, of course, had this amazing gift of picking the core out of book in no time. He ... was a pure genius though he is very much out of fashion now. I'm constantly coming across sneers at him in reviews and periodicals. But what I also notice is that very frequently, when someone wants to make a point in a very sharp saying, he will say, "As G.K. Chesterton said ..." You see, they can't keep away from him.[61]

Monsignor Ronald Knox was a notable Anglican clergyman and scholar whose conversion to Catholicism was nearly as famous as Chesterton's.

My most cherished memory of the late Gilbert Chesterton is that of a luncheon-party with friends in Hertfordshire, after which he was asked if would walk down to the end of the garden, so that a bed-ridden old lady upstairs might see, from her window, the great Mr. Chesterton. He acceded readily enough, though it was with more difficulty that we persuaded him to remove the wastepaper basket with which he had modestly obscured his features. To relieve his self-consciousness, I suggested walking with him. "Oh, do come," he said, "then you will look like *the ordinary person.*" He was (it is be remembered) not only a fat man and proud of it, but very tall and broad. And I honestly think it was this physical greatness which he had the intention of parading, set off by contrast with the ordinary person, myself. But as I walked down such

---

[61] Quoted in William S. Abell, ed., *Laughter and the Love of Friends: Reminiscences of the Distinguished English Priest and Philosopher Martin Cyril D'Arcy, S.J.* (Christian Classics, 1991), pp. 118–20.

a garden path as he would have loved to describe, flaming with poppies and delphiniums by the side of an old millstream, I was vividly conscious that his intellectual greatness might have been set off, not by such an ordinary person as myself, but by almost any figure in contemporary life. Almost anybody was an ordinary person compared with him.[62]

Long before his meteoric fall from grace, Father Leonard Feeney was the best-selling Catholic writer in America in the late 1930s and early 1940s and the literary editor of the Jesuit magazine America.

In point of kindliness, Chesterton had one of the biggest hearts that has ever lived. And yet I am told the doctors found it undersized physically when they examined him in one of this illnesses. Nothing daunted, he went right on using what share of heart he had to love the world largely and lavishly until the hour of his death.

When Chesterton stood up he was impressive. But it was even more marvelous to watch him sit down. He sat down with an air [of] supreme humility, as if totally collapsing in the arms of God. In the difficult assignment of being both huge and human he needed lots of support. Once seated he seemed constantly distracted by the incessant rush of his own thoughts.

One archbishop, even during Chesterton's lifetime, was for calling him a Doctor of the Church. However unofficial, this compliment may be taken as more than a mere pleasantry. For if the requirements of a Doctor of the Church are *eximia scientia et sanctitas* ["exceptional knowledge and sanctity"], surely something perilously near to both must be ascribed to a man who could roam without an *imprimatur* through all Catholic theology, hagiography and apologetics and never make a statement which the most meticulous Ultra-montane could suspect of heresy; and who could fill a hundred books with an almost beer-garden joviality and never write a line that would cause a child to blush. It would be nice to have a St. Gilbert taking rank with St. Augustine, St. Bernard and St. Thomas.[63]

---

[62] Ronald Knox, "G. K. Chesterton," *The Spoken Word: A Selection from Twenty-Five Years of "The Listener"*, ed. Richard Church (Collins, 1955).

[63] "The Metaphysics to Chesterton," *The Leonard Feeney Omnibus: A Collection of Prose and Verse Old and New* (Sheed & Ward, 1943), p. 208.

The Dominican friar Father Vincent McNabb was a great friend of Chesterton and a leader in the Distributist movement.

One high activity of this humble soul was his unruffled patience. One incident may suffice. At the Eucharistic Congress in Dublin he sat beside a priest whilst a Bishop gave an hour's address in Gaelic. At the end of the hour, during which he had been almost motionless, he heaved a smile and said, with a characteristic chuckle: "The finer points of that discourse escaped me." That smile and whimsicality were the fine, patient craftsmanship of humility.

It was hard to speak with Gilbert Chesterton and not to think—and think of God. Even the atheist who spoke with him, and who would have despised the God of Abraham, the God of Isaac, the God of Jacob, felt he would like to know about the God of Gilbert Chesterton—this God whom the very laughter of Gilbert Chesterton seemed to prove was such a lovably human, though transcendent being.[64]

He was a great Englishman and one of the greatest thinkers and writers of our time. His writings will be even better appreciated in years to come than they are now.[65]

Reverend C. C. Martindale, S.J., gave a tribute and remembrance following GKC's death.

I met G. K. Chesterton but seldom, but I hoped that I knew him, and knew that I loved him. I think first, that no man within our memory has been so universally loved, let alone one who was very pugilistic. He cannot have had an enemy who hated him.

And he must have been universally trusted. Not even a lunatic could have supposed that he ever once played for his own hand.

And even the general Press recognised his "gravitas": his profoundness of conviction, under all the "paradoxes"—a word that used to worry him. He could not see that he was being paradoxical!

Chesterton wrote *The Everlasting Man*, neglected for *Father Brown*. But, in any case, you have in his writings Man transfused

---

[64] Quoted in Francis Edward Nugent, ed., *A Vincent McNabb Anthology: Selections from the Writings of Vincent McNabb, O.P.* (Blackfriars, 1955).

[65] Quoted in E. A. Siderman, *A Saint in Hyde Park: Memories of Father Vincent McNabb, O.P.* (Geoffrey Bles, 1950), p. 136.

by God; and I hope I am not wrong in seeing in Chesterton something to be called Sanctity.[66]

Jesuit priest Daniel Lord was one of the most active and influential American Catholics of the twentieth century. As national director of the Sodality movement, he traveled the entire country, lecturing and leading spiritual retreats as well as writing and producing plays. He was an advisor to Cecil B. DeMille.

Chesterton is not likely to be canonized. But I personally should love to see him canonized and made Doctor of the Universal Church and Doctor of Universal Laughter.[67]

Edward Shanks was a war poet, literary critic, and science fiction writer. In his "Homage to Chesterton," he goes down the list, praising Chesterton's greatness as a writer on every genre he touched. But that is not what most impresses him.

He did want to be read. He wanted to give pleasure and he wanted to communicate ideas. He was the most genuinely humble great man I have ever known—it was sometimes embarrassing to those who could not meet him on that ground.

G. K. Chesterton himself is a subject I approach with diffidence and which I wish I could approach with a humility like his own. I have heard someone saying that Chesterton can hardly have had an enemy. But could he have had *one*—one honest one, I mean? There may have been people who never met him but were wounded in their guilty consciences by the generalizations he sometimes made. Probably it would have distressed him to think that there were any such persons.

He had an infinite pity for poor human beings like himself. It extended even to callers at inopportune times—the severest test of a philosopher, or of a saint. No one who knew him, I think, will dispute my assertion that there was something saint-like about him. And he was saint-like both in his private and in his public character.

He hated no man in person but only sometimes what a man stood for. To the individual, however small, he was magnanimity itself. While you spoke to Chesterton you were the only creature

---

[66] *Tablet*, June 20, 1936.
[67] *The Fleur de Lis* (St. Louis University), September 1936.

to whom his attention was given, and that was not a trick, it was the man himself. He sent out from his great body a warmth of interest which his death has irreplaceably removed from the world. The causes for which he fought have lost a notable champion. But he would not have troubled about that, because he was so serenely certain of their ultimate triumph. Still less would he have stopped to think that the good work will be carried on by what he has left behind him. But it will.[68]

---

[68] *John O'London's Weekly*, June 27, 1936.

Chapter 10

One Far Fierce Hour and Sweet

The Man Who Was Sunday

It is embarrassing, talking with God face to face, as a man speaketh to his friend.
—Letter to Edmund Clerihew Bentley, 1894

Who is Sunday?[1] Well, you may call him Nature, if you like. But you will note that I hold that when the mask of Nature is lifted you find God behind. All that wild exuberance of Nature, all its strange pranks, all its seeming indifference to the wants and feelings of men, all that is only a mask. It is a mask which your Lucien Gregorys paint, but can never raise. I think it is well that we should not know all about those around us, that we should fight in the dark, while having the faith that most men are on the right side, for to possess courage the soul of man must be lonely until at last it knows all.[2]

As an old-fashioned person, who still believes that Reason is a gift of God and a guide to truth, I must confine myself to saying that I do not want a God whom I have made, but a God who has made me.[3] I happen to believe, not by any merit of mine but rather the reverse, that the veritable objective truth of all things is also that which can satisfy all hearts. But I quite agree that truth is to be preferred to mere satisfaction. And I cannot see why a sceptic should pretend to be satisfied with mere negation, any more than a sentimentalist should pretend to

---

[1] The other main character in GKC's 1908 novel *The Man Who Was Thursday*.
[2] *Illustrated Sunday Herald*, Jan. 24, 1926.
[3] *Illustrated London News*, Dec. 31, 1932.

be convinced by mere sentiment.[4] It is the curse of our epoch that the educated are uneducated, especially in the study of history—which is only the study of humanity. Their ignorance is less logical than the ignorance of the Dark Ages, because those ages filled the place of history with legends, which at least professed to deal with the first things, while we only fill it with news, which can only deal with the latest.[5] Religion may be defined as that which puts the first things first.[6] It is the fundamental principle of true Modern Thought to put first things last.[7]

A modern agnostic thinks he is broadminded when he says that all religions or revelations, Catholic or Protestant, savage or civilised, are alike mere myths and guesses at what man can never know. But I think that is a narrow negation, sprung from special spiritual conditions in Upper Tooting.[8] Agnosticism, the ancient confession of ignorance, was a singularly sane and healthy thing so far as it went. Unfortunately it has not gone as far as the twentieth century. It has declared in all ages, as a heathen chief declared in the dark ages, that the life of a man is like the flight of a bird across a firelit room, because we know nothing of whence it comes or whither it goes. It would seem natural to apply it not only to man but to mankind. But the moderns do not apply the same principle but the very opposite principle. They specialize in the unknown origins and in the unknown future. They dwell on the prehistoric and on the post-historic or prophetic; and neglect only the historic.[9] Agnostics are not merely men who know that they know nothing. More often they are men who know that nobody else can ever know anything. That is a very different thing; and one of the most dogmatic of dogmas: a universal negative. Nevertheless, there is about such agnostics a real and often respectable ignorance. They really do not know how sectarian they are, or in other words, how small a section of human thought and experience they really present.[10] It is assumed that the agnostic is impartial; whereas the agnostic is merely ignorant.[11]

---

[4] *Illustrated London News*, Jan. 12, 1929.
[5] *Illustrated London News*, Mar. 22, 1919.
[6] *Illustrated London News*, Apr. 26, 1930.
[7] *Illustrated London News*, Feb. 15, 1936.
[8] *Fife Free Press*, Feb. 9, 1929.
[9] *New Witness*, July 14, 1922.
[10] *G.K.'s Weekly*, July 19, 1930.
[11] *Illustrated London News*, May 4, 1907.

To-day real Agnosticism has declined along with real theology.[12] To teach people to believe in God may be in its highest sense a hard task even among Christians. But to prevent people from thinking about God will be an impossible task even among agnostics; or perhaps especially among agnostics.[13] I am not at all disturbed about the future of the Faith; but I am disturbed about the future of the doubters.[14] No one has ever answered the question without surrendering the whole agnostic philosophy of experience. We all do wake up in our cradles with an attitude of confidence in the course of our experiences, which is, in its nature, anterior to those experiences. The assumption that what is in memory was in experience, is not an experience. It is an assumption. Faith in the past is not an experience; it is a faith.[15] Faith is something superior to reason but not contrary to it.[16]

Faith, of its own nature, wants to worship a real god.[17] In ages of faith all men who believe work together, and the result is common sense; in an age of doubt, the one man who believes has to work alone, and the result is an insane exaggeration.[18]

It is no disgrace to Christianity, it is no disgrace to any great religion, that its counsels of perfection have not made every single person perfect. If after centuries a disparity is still found between its ideal and its followers, it only means that the religion still maintains the ideal, and the followers still need it.[19] Every man carries with him the standard by which we judge him, even if he always falls short of it. That is one of the things in which all men are equal; and it is a sort of implicit image of man, which the mystics called the image of God.[20] Most Christians fail to fulfill the Christian ideal. This bitter and bracing fact cannot be too much insisted upon in this and every other moral question. But, perhaps, it might be suggested that this failure is not so much the failure of Christians in connection with the

---

[12] *Daily News*, Sept. 17, 1910.
[13] "Utopias," *GKC as MC*.
[14] "The Rout of Reason," in *Where Are the Dead?*, Arnold Bennett et al. (Cassell, 1928), p. 24.
[15] *Dublin Review*, January–March 1912.
[16] *Illustrated London News*, Jan. 15, 1910.
[17] *Daily News*, Nov. 9, 1912.
[18] *T.P.'s Weekly*, Christmas Number, 1907.
[19] *Illustrated London News*, Mar. 2, 1929.
[20] *Columbia*, May 1925.

Christian ideal as the failure of any men in connection with any ideal. That Christians are not always Christian is obvious; neither are Liberals always liberal, nor Socialists always social, nor Humanitarians always kind, nor Rationalists always rational, nor are gentlemen always gentle, nor do working men always work. If people are especially horrified at the failure of Christian practice it must be an indirect compliment to the Christian creed.[21]

I do believe in Christianity, and my impression is that a system must be divine which has survived so much insane mismanagement.[22] Faith is a thing to be respected, especially when it has no apparent supports but in the soul.[23] Every man feels the faith or the sin.[24] Faith is that which is able to survive a mood.[25] The only argument against losing faith is that you also lose hope—and generally charity.[26]

Happiness is a state of the soul; a state in which our natures are full of the wine of an ancient youth, in which banquets last for ever, and roads lead everywhere, where all things are under the exuberant leadership of faith, hope, and charity.[27] Christianity did *not* conceive Christian virtues as tame, timid, and respectable things. It *did* conceive of these virtues as vast, defiant, and even destructive things, scorning the yoke of this world, dwelling in the desert, and seeking their meat from God.[28]

The highest thing in the world is goodness.[29] Man is never genuinely at home except in goodness.[30] The whole object of poetry and mysticism, the whole object of all religions and of all philosophies not invented by the devil, is to make us value good things.[31] It is the point of all deprivation that it sharpens the idea of value.[32] Every

---

[21] *Daily News*, Feb. 13, 1906.
[22] *Illustrated London News*, Oct. 6, 1906.
[23] *Illustrated London News*, Mar. 1, 1930.
[24] *Bibliophile*, March 1908.
[25] *Daily News*, May 18, 1907.
[26] *Hearst's Magazine*, Jan. 13, 1918.
[27] G.K. Chesterton and F.G. Kitton, *The Bookman Booklets: Charles Dickens* (Hodder and Stoughton, 1903).
[28] *Daily News*, Nov. 4, 1911.
[29] *Daily News*, Feb. 27, 1904.
[30] *Daily News*, June 18, 1901.
[31] *Daily News*, Dec. 24, 1904.
[32] *Daily News*, Oct. 2, 1909.

hateful thing is a mimicry of something that is good.³³ To see good is to see God.³⁴

There are two blessings which belong to simplicity. The first blessing is that the simple man sees good suddenly. That grace we call gratitude. The other is that the simple man sees evil suddenly. That grace we call anger.³⁵ I am not one of those who wake up in the night with a wild shriek that a Bolshevist or an atheist must be shot like a burglar. When people hold false theories of life, I prefer to prove them to be false, rather than cut short the lives or even the language of their honest victims before they can live to be enlightened.³⁶ I am certainly not going to speculate [on what] are admittedly the most subtle problems of the trained theologian; all those questions about the will to believe and the operations of grace; and the fact that something more than reason is needed to bring any of us into the most reasonable of all philosophies.³⁷ I should say it was a first principle that men desire happiness. It is to be so described for fundamental reasons that might be expressed in several ways; but perhaps the simplest way is to say that anybody who denies it is cracked. Then, being granted the first principle that men desire happiness, we should go on to examine the curious manner in which they fail to get it; and so, through certain combinations of experience and authority, approach the conception of the Fall. Similarly we should pass to subsequent ideas of redemption and revelation after the Fall, and should consider the record of that revelation, and what it said, and in what sense it should be taken.³⁸ Men need a religion primarily to prevent them from worshipping idols.³⁹

What makes a real religion mystical is that it claims (truly or falsely) to be hiding a beauty that is more beautiful than any that we know, or perhaps an evil that is more evil. This gives another sort of intensity to common things, suggesting something that is redder than red, or more white than white.⁴⁰ The common and natural error is regarding mysticism as something mysterious. Mysticism, or a sense of the

---

³³ *Illustrated London News*, June 15, 1912.
³⁴ *Listener*, Jan. 4, 1933.
³⁵ *Daily News*, June 1, 1907.
³⁶ *Illustrated London News*, Oct. 29, 1932.
³⁷ *America*, Sept. 3, 1927.
³⁸ *America*, June 6, 1929.
³⁹ *Illustrated London News*, June 20, 1914.
⁴⁰ *Illustrated London News*, Feb. 17, 1923.

mystery of things, is simply the most gigantic form of common sense. We should not have to complain of any materialism if common sense were only common.[41]

Mysticism is the only enduring sanity of mankind. Mysticism is not to be commended merely as the only thing that gives a value to the soul; mysticism is the only that gives any certain value to the body.[42] The common man is a mystic. Mysticism is only a transcendent form of common sense. Mysticism and common sense alike consist in a sense of the dominance of certain truths and tendencies which cannot be formally demonstrated or even formally named. Mysticism and common sense are like appeals to realities that we all know to be real, but which have no place in argument except as postulates.[43]

Mysticism may be roughly defined as the belief that man lives upon a borderland: and mysticism, in this sense of an admission that anything may happen, is simply the legitimate deduction from Agnosticism. The old Agnosticism prided itself upon the fact that, like Socrates, at least it knew that it could know nothing. The new Agnosticism, is much more humble: it does not pretend to know even what things it cannot know. It holds itself ready to receive evidence of a ghost or a fairy, conscious that no ghost or fairy can be more intrinsically mysterious than a toadstool or a tuft of grass. Everybody knows, of course, and everybody feels (which is more convincing) that there are ultimately things beyond our ken, but there is no hard and fast line to be drawn in the matter. The error of current mysticism is that mysticism, religion and poetry have to do with the abstract. There is a tendency to believe that the concrete is the symbol of the abstract. The truth, the truth at the root of all true mysticism, is quite the other way. The abstract is the symbol of the concrete. This may possibly seem at first sight a paradox; but it is a purely transcendental truth. We see a green tree which we worship. Then because there are so many green trees, so many men, so many elephants, so many butterflies, so many daisies, so many animalculae, we coin a general term "Life." And then the mystic comes and says that a green tree symbolises Life. It is not so. Life symbolises a green tree. Just in so far as we get into the abstract, we get away from the reality, we get away from the mystery, we get away

---

[41] *Daily News*, Aug. 30, 1901.
[42] *Daily News*, June 22, 1905.
[43] *Daily News*, July 26, 1901.

from the tree. And this is the reason that so many transcendental discourses are merely blank and tedious to us, because they have to do with Truth and Beauty, and the Destiny of the Soul, and all the great, faint, faded symbols of the reality. And this is why all poetry is so interesting to us, because it has to do with skies, with woods, with battles, with temples, with women and with wine, with the ultimate miracles which no philosopher could create. The difference between the concrete and the abstract is the difference between the country and the town. God made the concrete, but man made the abstract. A truthful man is a miracle, but the truth is a commonplace.[44]

Mysticism is the art of seeing everything as supernatural, of seeing every material object encircled with a halo from a secret sun. It is not an exceptionally dark and secret thing, but an exceptionally luminous and open thing. It is in reality too clear for most of us to comprehend, and too obvious for most of us to see. Such an utterance as the utterance that "God is Love" does in reality overwhelm us like an immeasurable landscape on a clear day, like the light of an intolerable summer sun. We may call it a dark saying; but we have an inward knowledge all the time that it is we who are dark. True spirituality is as humble as a lover and as careless as a school-boy. Christian mysticism should at least stand for the principle that the moral life is not an egotistical scramble in which the devil catches the hindmost, but a great fellowship in which the devil generally catches the most confident person. When a man reaches, as St. Francis reached, the highest plane of spirituality the fact is signalised by his calling his own beast of burden "my brother the ass." Self-surrender is one of the essential points of true mysticism, but self-surrender, which is a plain and deliberate act, may easily in some cases be more insolently selfish than selfishness itself. The true key of Christian mysticism is not so much self-surrender, which is a painful and complex thing, as self-forgetfulness, which we all fall into in the presence of a splendid sunrise or a little child, and which is to our highest nature as natural as singing to a bird.[45]

The man who really thinks he has an idea will always try to explain that idea. The charlatan who has no idea will always confine himself

---

[44] *Speaker*, May 31, 1902.
[45] *Daily News*, Aug. 30, 1901.

to explaining that it is much too subtle to be explained. The first idea may really be very difficult to express to ordinary people. But because the man is trying to express it, it is most probable that there is something in it, after all. The honest man is he who is always trying to utter the unutterable, to describe the indescribable; but the quack lives not by plunging into mystery, but by refusing to come out of it.[46] A mediaeval mystic like Dante will say that in God's will is our peace. For everybody who believes that God is good must believe that our peace is in being reconciled with good. But that does not alter the fact that Dante describes the blessed as seeing and not as being God. It is still something sufficiently separate to be loved. And that idea of the element of separation in creation, and even in affection, seems to me a very vital distinction indeed; and especially a great distinction of the Christian creed. Christian mysticism, as it seems to me, has not said *merely* that we shall all melt into the divine life, but that we shall all ourselves remain sufficiently alive to measure the height and even the distance of its divinity.[47]

I cannot leave out God. For I have seen so many things go wrong when they left out God. Liberty became licence—desperate, sordid licence—or became sheer slavery. Property became monopoly. And the miracle of everyday life became of no account at all. And so I, who began as a Protestant, remain one, as a Catholic—a Protestant against the destruction of all the material, simple things. I have not changed. God made me; and here I am. Socialism failed me, and I have turned my back on that because it was not social. Protestantism failed me, and I have turned my back on that because it did not protest. These things endure: life and liberty and the boundless magic of night and day—and what comes after.[48] It is a very good thing for us to be compelled to wait, if it means that we are compelled to watch—I am even tempted to add, to watch and pray.[49] For it is only on those in the struggle for existence who hang on for ten minutes after all is hopeless, that hope begins to dawn.[50]

---

[46] *Illustrated London News*, Jan. 25, 1908.
[47] *Illustrated London News*, July 7, 1928.
[48] *Daily Sketch*, May 14, 1931.
[49] Introduction to *Purple Hours*.
[50] *Speaker*, Feb. 2, 1901.

Chapter 11

There Was a Shout About My Ears
The Convert

The chief event of my life.
—Preface to *The Everlasting Man*

I was brought up as an ordinary theist, that is in a practice a Unitarian; and the idea, for instance, that God could be cruel—Shelley's "Almighty Fiend"—is literally an idea that has never crossed my mind. I was a perfectly savage and truculent atheist at the age of fourteen, and a thoroughly matured and mellow agnostic at eighteen; and so far as these were a revolt against that sort of Calvinism which teaches that some people are damned before they are born, and that there is no efficiency in works, I sympathise with that rebellion, though I was brought up on a higher kind of theism. I can understand the revolt against Calvinism and the remains of a bitter and pungent sort of Puritanism, but not revolt against dogma.

I don't see any objection to the dogmatic temper, which is only another name, and not nearly such a good one, for the human intellect. The mind was made to dogmatize, to reach conclusions, just as a pair of pincers are made to pinch. One of the reasons why I believe in dogma is that literature is impossible without it. I cannot imagine myself putting pen to paper unless I had a creed to defend. Europe must now return to a Catholic unity, and it is a question whether the Anglican Church is right in claiming to be part of that unity.

However, whatever I have to say about Anglo-Catholics, it will not be an attack on them. My position is rather a delicate one in that connection. I have been an Anglo-Catholic, I am now a Catholic, therefore no longer "Anglo." But I have very great respect and sympathy for Anglo-Catholics,[1] entirely differing from some of my Roman friends who regard them as sham Catholics. Being now in the Roman Communion, I believe that to be the one True Church. But I do not share the view of those who regard most of the Anglo-Catholics of late years as merely silly people who like "playing with little boys in pink." I am sure they are civilised human beings groping their way back to the real secret of European civilisation and unity. They seem to be growing in all the Church of England that matters.

I believe the modern world is going to divide into two great armies of Catholicism and Paganism. In the Church of England, as in my own Church, there is a considerable drain away of people into sheer Paganism. Many people who call themselves Anglicans and go to church more or less regularly would just as willingly, if the circumstances were different, go to a temple of Apollo or Pan. Of course, that is what the more honest of them mean when they say they like to go into the fields to worship God under the blue dome of the sky, and so on; but of the people in the Church of England who are not performing a mere official ceremony but who have got a real religion and are on fire with it—I believe, from my own experience, that the overwhelming majority of that kind of people are Anglo-Catholic. If the True Church—if you will excuse my so putting it—were out of the way, the Anglo-Catholics sooner or later would win entirely. To me it is apparent that no other party in the Church of England has any principle of corporate life with which to grip and hold people. I should think that some leaders in the Church of England would be much happier and could get much nearer together if they confessed themselves agnostic.

There is a very personal side as to why I joined the Roman Catholic Church, which it is difficult to dismiss. One receives a kind of mystical assurance which is indescribable, but apart from that the general approach to my present position is that outside the Catholic authority at this moment there is a sheer welter of beliefs and practices. The Protestants, who were my ancestors thought they had found and

---

[1] Fr. John O'Connor says that Chesterton "never sat in judgment on his bygone Anglican tastes or feelings or friends, because he had made them all stepping-stones to the fullness of belief, and one does not despise the ladder by which one has climbed." *Father Brown on Chesterton* (Frederick Muller, 1937), p. 138.

sometimes actually did find secure ground for their religious convictions, but I am sure that ground has entirely gone. People are now trying to find all sorts of other grounds, such as humanitarianism and belief in progress—like poor old Bernard Shaw with his Life Force and evolution of things upwards, onwards and outwards. But all such ideas and theories seem to me to be intrinsically worthless, because they are relative and uncertain. There is no other short way of stating what seems to me to be common sense on a thousand subjects at the same moment than to say one is a Catholic. You can, of course, do it piecemeal. For instance, in answer to a man who says as some Germans said, that the nation is absolutely supreme, the State is the only thing you need to bother about, you can say: "No, that is not true; we owe something to all humanity, we owe something to God, to ourselves and the conscience within." And then you can turn round to somebody else who insists that everybody can do exactly what he likes, and that there is no State authority, no authority of any sort, who says: "Why should the State have any social authority? Why should I not go naked if I choose?'—you can say: "No, you are wrong, there is a State authority, we must have a social rule." In that sort of way you can work round hundreds of positions, answering one man after another, possibly from opposite sides; but the Catholic simply says: "You must not walk around naked because there is such a thing as original sin and man's passions are dangerous." As I say, the only short sharp way I know of answering such questions as I have mentioned and thousands of others is by saying: "I am Catholic."

One reason why I never could have been content to remain an Anglo-Catholic is that, though the Anglo-Catholics may be perfectly right upon all the questions on which they are fighting the Protestants, the Catholic Church is not only fighting Protestants or only right upon particular points. For instance, the Anglo-Catholic says there ought to be ritual, while the extreme Protestant says it is sheer hypocrisy and idolatry. In human psychology the Anglo-Catholic is absolutely right, but it might easily happen that one hundred years hence there might be a tendency to exaggerate ritualism and overload people with fantastic, impossible ceremonies. Then the Catholic Church would be found facing in the Puritan direction and drawing the line where it should be drawn. She goes back to older controversies and draws upon a much longer past. She fights on a hundred fronts, not only on one, and it is only an accident, as it were, that the Anglo-Catholic is right in a quarrel with particular heretics. There are other heretics and other quarrels, and on these I do not trust the Church of England to be right and I do trust the Church of Rome.

Everybody who has become a Catholic thinks that that has influenced him more than anything else. In its complete form it came to me fairly late in life, but I have an idea that I was always groping after it. Of the early things that influenced me, I should mention the sort of general atmosphere of fairy-tales. Some of the best of George MacDonald's fairy-tales had a determining influence upon me. Looking back now I am sure I was moved by a kind of instinct for the Catholic idea—and if there ever was a person who would have been a Catholic if he had the chance it was George MacDonald.[2]

In my early critical adventures I made a picturesque romance of my own about St. Francis of Assisi. I knew nothing about the most important part of him; I did not even know that it was there to be known. I no more thought of becoming a Catholic than of becoming a cannibal. It was an entirely personal but perfectly spontaneous attraction towards a certain sort of poetry. There was something in the first few lines of the Canticle of the Creatures that there was not, at least for me, in Shakespeare or in Shelley. It was the same gigantic firelight; here also it seemed that all sorts were welcome, and I could see haloes round hundreds of unconscious heads. Compared with these two, it seemed to me that most poets, and much greater poets, were frozen with pessimism and with pride.

St. Francis was as emotional and impulsive as anybody could be; but there was a reason for his emotion; there was a method in his madness. His mood of mysticism was connected with clear ideas that do endure; the idea that God had died for the common person. It was part of the nature of the world, that could be urged on all men in all moods.

And the history of my own mind, so far as it can be shortly stated, might be summed up as the discovery of that doctrine that will justify that enthusiasm. The saint can support the intuitions of the poet, but without that support they fade away like any other fancies, and are often replaced by quite the opposite fancies.

[2] *Churchman*, Oct. 23, 1926.

If I had in my youth flung myself entirely upon the future as unfolded by my favourite Whitman, I should have found that in fact my favourite Whitman had no future. There was a future for his fad, but none for his faith. It was in the past that I had to look for the future, in something more enduring, and I was glad in the end to again come upon St. Francis.[3]

Few of the conversations which lead up to conversions have been as public as mine.[4] Before reaching Catholicism, I passed through various stages and had a long struggle. That section of the Church of England that call themselves "Anglo-Catholics" believe that they have the true tradition of the Church of Christ. Thus, before becoming a Catholic—or, as we say, Roman Catholic—we have first to solve the problem of the legitimacy of this claim of the Anglo-Catholics, and that often takes a long time.

It is difficult to explain in detail the various stages through which I passed. After much study and thought I had reached the conclusion that all the evils from which England suffers—Capitalism, Imperialism wrongly understood, Industrialism, Plutocracy, Destruction of the Family, etc.—are due to the fact that England is not Catholic. But the whole Anglo-Catholic position was that England had remained Catholic in spite of, and even because of, the Reformation. Now, in my judgment, it is illogical to pretend that England is Catholic. I was bound, therefore, to turn to the real Catholicism, Roman Catholicism.

I had many Catholic ideas before my conversion, and my outlook in general has but little changed. Catholicism gives us doctrine. It gives a reasonable basis to life. It is not only a question of authority, but of first principles, on which our judgment can rest. For instance, people here are always talking about modern fashions and the indecency of female dress but all their criticism has no reasonable foundation, because these people no longer know what chastity is. Now, a Catholic knows and esteems chastity, and consequently he knows what is wrong with modern feminine fashions. That is merely an example of how Catholicism provides a solid basis for all our judgments, enabling us to test our ideas and our way of living. There is no aspect of life which cannot be harmonized with its principles.[5]

---

[3] *T.P.'s and Cassell's Weekly*, Jan. 23, 1926.
[4] *America*, Apr. 13, 1929.
[5] *Catholic Mind*, Aug. 8, 1925.

I have always believed, at least for twenty years, in the Catholic view of Christianity. Unless the Church of England was a branch of the Catholic Church I had no use for it. If it were a Protestant Church I did not believe in it in any case. The question always was whether the Church of England can claim to be in direct descent from the mediaeval Catholic Church. That is the question with every Anglo-Catholic or Higher Churchman.

Among the people who have most helped me to answer the question whether the Church of England is Catholic, and to whom I am most indebted, are the chief Protestant leaders in the Church of England, such as the Dean of St. Paul's[6] and Bishop Hensley Henson.[7] They have done me this good service, and I wish to express gratitude for it. They have done me the best service one man can do to another.

It appears to me quite clear that any church claiming to be authoritative, must be able to answer quite definitely when great questions of

---

[6] The Reverend Dr. William Inge (1860–1954), after being a professor of divinity at Cambridge, was appointed to the prestigious and public position of dean of St. Paul's Cathedral. Inge had gained the epithet "The Gloomy Dean" after using his pulpit to deliver an over-the-top pessimistic lecture in 1920 entitled "The Idea of Progress," in which he lashed out at everything ever accomplished by Western civilization and everything ever believed by those who went by the name of Christian. He was the prototypical "Broad Churchman" as opposed to "High Churchman." Tradition was bad, progress was good. Doctrine was bad because it divided people and was based on documents that were doubtful. He favored a more "spiritual" and "autonomous" form of Christianity, based on "experience and individual inspiration." He had no use for the common man whom Chesterton championed, and certainly not for the beliefs of the common man, which Chesterton affirmed. The dean dismissed "sacramentalism" because it was "obvious" that the lower classes were "natural idolaters" who believed in the Blessed Sacrament. In addition to throwing out the sacraments, he also threw out Scripture; that is, he embraced the "higher criticism," thereby emptying the Bible of any divinity. Thus, he rejected both "High Church" and "Low Church" Christians. Above all, he hated the Roman Catholic Church with "a raging hatred." He endorsed contraception and opposed organized labor, wringing his hands about "unwanted children" but once saying that strikers should be hanged. He was also an outspoken eugenicist. The Broad Churchmen like Dr. Inge, says Chesterton, "combine the widest cosmic doubts with the narrowest social sympathies. They will tell you blandly that they do not believe in the *vox populi vox dei*; but the truth is much more than that. The truth is; that they would hate the *vox populi* much more if they thought it was the *vox dei*: for they fear all ultimate realities. That is what is meant by being broad-minded." (*Daily News*, Feb. 24, 1912.)

[7] Herbert Hensley Henson (1863–1947), Anglican bishop of Hereford and then of Durham. He had very liberal views of what it meant to be a Christian and publicly encouraged doubt of the Virgin Birth and the Resurrection. After Chesterton's conversion, the Anglican paper *Church Times* intoned: "Hensonism has never, we believe, attracted one educated man to the church; it has, we believe, robbed that church of the genius of G. K. Chesterton and of lesser men who are not content with cold negations."

public morals are put. Can I go in for cannibalism, or murder babies to reduce the population, or any similar scientific and progressive reform? Any Church with authority to teach must be able to say whether it can be done. But Protestant churches are in utter bewilderment on these moral questions—for example on birth control, on divorce, and on Spiritualism.

You have people like Dean Inge coming out publicly and definitely to champion what I regard as a low and poisonous trick, not far removed from infanticide. It is perfectly true that there are in the Church of England and other Protestant bodies, men who would denounce these heathen vices as much as I can. Bishop Gore[8] would speak about them as strongly as the Pope.

But the point is that the Church of England does not speak strongly. It has no united action. I have no use for a Church which is not a Church militant, which cannot order battle and fall in line and march in the same direction.[9] Now that even High Churchmen have departed from their former attitude towards birth control, Catholics only remain to hold up the standards of married life.[10]

I did not myself become a Catholic without having found out something about what a Catholic was supposed to believe. This curious and cautious curiosity on my part covered a great many matters like that of the true doctrine of the Fall and of original sin; which is very much milder, more moderate and more optimistic (as the phrase goes) than the Puritan doctrine. Anyhow, I think I do know something about the orthodox doctrine and that I am quite orthodox about it. And the fact that Mr. Wells imagines I may be heretical is enough to show that he at least does not know anything about it. Without professing to speak with authority, I think the great authorities of the Church have substantially said this; that normally a story should be taken as it stands, that we should not look for allegories merely to suit our fancy; but that things in Scripture, notably the first Hebrew books, are in their nature capable of several interpretations, some

---

[8] Charles Gore (1853–1932), Anglican Bishop of Worcester, then Birmingham, then Oxford. He was considered orthodox in his defense of doctrine, but liberal in his views on Scripture and science.

[9] *Toronto Daily Star*, Oct. 4, 1922.

[10] *Western Morning News*, Aug. 20, 1930. The Anglican church approved contraception in 1930.

being symbolical; that they must be supposed to be symbolical if ever they really conflict with reason and fact when accepted as literal; and that in the case of Genesis, the story whether literal or symbolical must be taken as committing us to the real occurrence of the Fall of Man. And if Mr. Wells insists on imagining that this is some modernist hair-splitting of my own, I can only say it would not be much trouble to find the passages in Augustine or Aquinas which I am now quoting from memory. I think some of those passages would surprise Mr. Wells very much. St. Augustine, at the very beginning of Christian history, actually went so far, I think, as to use the word "puerile" of the material and matter-of-fact view of Eden afterwards taught to Protestants. St. Thomas Aquinas, the most approved and authoritative of mediaeval theologians, spoke of the limitation laid on Moses by the necessity of suiting his statement to a barbarous people. Some would say, I fear, that this again was why that sort of statement was suited to Protestants. But, as a matter of fact, Mr. Wells still misses the point even about the material story. It is not a question merely of my not believing, any more than of my believing, in that story. It is a question of where I place the importance of that story as compared with the moral of that story. This is a confusion in which modern impressionism will easily be entangled, though mediaeval logic would have disentangled it in an instant. To say that the Fall does not merely mean a garden and a snake, to say that it is something much more than any garden or any snake, is not even the same as saying there was no garden or no snake. It is simply saying what is of primary and what of secondary importance. I mean that it is unworthy of a philosopher to think more about the snake and less about the sin.[11]

Saving the grace of God, a mystery not within our measure, I believe the practical problem of whether people will become Catholics is simply the problem of whether they will think hard enough to become Catholics.[12]

I am a little tired of the profound thinkers who can only argue with me by calling me a fool. They do not tell me why it is more the mark of a fool to think the world designed than undesigned; to think

---

[11] *G.K.'s Weekly*, Oct. 23, 1926.

[12] *America*, July 9, 1928. "Saving the grace of God, my own conversion to Catholicism was entirely rational" (unpublished letter to Bertram Hyde).

the world the product of will rather than of fate; to think that the will could vary its operations as well as repeat its operations. I do not learn why what appears to me to be the working of a normal intelligence is in fact only that of abnormal unintelligence. The deep and delicate and almost mystical question, of whether I myself am a blithering ass, is one which it seems to me embarrassing to raise and difficult to settle. According to these simple controversialists, it is already settled. Intelligent people cannot believe in dogmas. That is a dogma that is only stated dogmatically. Nothing resembling a reason for the statement ever has been given, or ever will be. It rests on something that is very strange and mysterious and quite peculiar to our own time: anonymous authority.

I do not say that anybody exercising mental activity must come to the Catholic Faith. But I do say that many men will have to exercise great mental activity in order to come to the Catholic Faith. And I do say that most men are kept out of it for want of that mental activity. And I do think that this is the chief problem before us in the practical matter of conversion. So far from men entering the Church, as was alleged, because they are too weary to think, many remain outside because they are too weary to think their way in.

Put shortly and roughly, the problem of this great educated modern world is whether people are still bright enough to be converted. Fortunately there are other and better sorts of brightness and illumination. But saving the grace of God, as I said at the beginning, many might well fall into a mood of wondering whether science and rationalism and education and instruction, and all the rest, have not reduced a multitude of minds to such a pulp of impotence and incompetence that they cannot make the movement of reason needed to catch hold of unfamiliar truth. We do not deny to all our opponents, as they do to us, so mild a thing as ordinary intelligence. We only wonder whether all will have the supreme intelligence for the supreme act of the mind.[13]

If we want character, in the old unique sense of being "a character," we are much more likely to find it in Christians who accepted the Imitation of Christ than in all these millions of materialists who are taught to imitate each other.[14]

[13] *America*, July 9, 1928.
[14] *Illustrated London News*, Feb. 25, 1928.

When I became a Catholic, I was quite prepared to find that in many respects the Catholic Church really was behind the times. I was very tolerant of the idea of being behind the times, having had long opportunities of studying the perfectly ghastly people who were abreast of the times; or the still more pestilent people who were in advance of the times. I knew that being in the movement generally meant only being in the fashion. I knew that fashions had an extraordinary way of being first omnipresent and oppressive and then suddenly blank and forgotten. I know how publicity seems fixed like a spotlight and vanishes like a lightning flash.[15]

Stock phrases stop a man from thinking. They stuff up the hole in his head with rubbish so that he does not even know there is a hole. He is filled without being fed. There is something about this sort of catchword that prevents a man from ever developing it or from deducing anything from it or even asking any question about it. And the chief contrast between Catholics and such Non-Catholics now, it seems to me, is simply that we are still thinking and they have stopped thinking. And what has stopped them is the sort of barricade of the old bricks and stones and stale cabbages and rotten eggs that they heaved at us nearly a hundred years ago. We can still think because we have Dogmas; because we have Dogmas to think about; because we are still infested with these dreadful and dangerous animals, whose complete absence from their own homes is almost the only thing that they have to boast of.[16] I should very much like to ask a sincere and intelligent man what he thinks is to be the common philosophy of Europe if the Catholic tradition finally fades. Many modern words will be offered in place of that common philosophy; but they are either not common or not philosophic.[17] The man who picks out some part of Catholicism that happens to please him, or throws away some part that happens to puzzle him, does in fact produce, not only the queerest sort of result, but generally the very opposite result to what he intends.[18]

Though I have only been for a few years in the Catholic Church, I already know that the question "Why I am a Catholic" is by no means the same as the question "Why I became a Catholic." There is an

---

[15] *America*, May 4, 1929.
[16] *Glasgow Observer*, Oct. 10, 1925.
[17] *New Witness*, Nov. 12, 1920.
[18] *America*, Mar. 2, 1929.

ever-increasing number of reasons which only appear after the first reason has operated; they are so vast and varied that they sometimes might even make the original reason look relatively small and accidental.

In a real as well as a ritual sense, confirmation can come after conversion. There are endless converging and corroborative arguments, and the convert cannot always remember even the order in which they came. They are a multitude; but they have already become one thing. Artistic agnostics sometimes make a great fuss about which parts of a cathedral are old and which "restored"; where a Catholic is chiefly concerned about whether it has been restored to its use as a cathedral. In the same way, while the whole of my conviction is, like a cathedral, too large to be described, I should already have some difficulty in dating the different stones.

I think I should find that the very first things that attracted me to Catholicism were things meant to repel me from it. I remember two cases especially in which denunciations by more serious writers made the very thing they denounced seem to me a thing to be desired. One was a shuddering whisper, a hideous blasphemy which someone had found in some Catholic mystic, touching the Blessed Virgin: "All other creatures owe everything to God, but God Himself owes something to her." And I started up as at the sound of a trumpet and said almost aloud: "But what a splendid thing to say!" It seemed to me that the paradox of the Incarnation could hardly have been repeated on a more noble or ringing note.

And the other was when somebody on the *Daily News* (I was somebody on the *Daily News* myself in those days) gave as an example of the lifeless formality of Roman religion that some French bishop had told a number of soldiers and workmen, who could only go to early Mass under conditions of great exhaustion, that God would be glad of the presence of their bodies and would forgive the fatigue and distraction of their minds. And again I said to myself: "What a lot of common sense these people seem to have. If a man walked ten miles to please me I should naturally be pleased, even if he fell asleep when he got there." I could give many examples of this first phase, in which the first faint beginnings of my Catholic faith were practically entirely fed on anti-Catholic literature.

About the next among these early tendencies I have no doubt. It is a debt I have always admitted and always wished I could have done more to pay. Long before I had even met the two very remarkable men to whom I owe most in this matter, Fr. John O'Connor, of Bradford, and Mr. Hilaire Belloc, I had begun to move in that direction through an influence which I found in the midst of my ordinary political Liberalism; in the very citadel of the *Daily News*.

I owe those first stirrings, under God, to the story and spectacle of the Irish nation; I who have not a drop of Irish blood, who have only been twice in Ireland, and who have (in the graceful phrase of Buckingham) neither an Irish interest nor an Irish understanding. But I saw very early that the Irish question was the one thing keeping the Party System alive, because there was in the heart of it a religious reality; and I concentrated on that part of Liberal policy because it was real. And what I saw more and more clearly in history and experience was a Christian people long persecuted and still hated, for some inscrutable reason, till I began to think it must be simply for being the same original and irritating sort of Christians who were thrown to the lions of Nero.

In this personal way, as I have suggested, it might be possible to follow the reasons for being a Catholic as they actually accumulated. I might explain how I came to see that the great states which broke from Rome had exactly what people always have who break laws and natural bonds; a swift and immediate success followed by the feeling of waking up in a trap; of having got into a false position and not being able to get out again.

But this autobiographical method, while in a sense more easy, would be absurdly egotistical. And yet when I turn to the other method, of trying to summarise shortly the substance of the conviction in its complete form, I find myself at a loss; not for want of things to say, but about how to choose among them. However, I will try to note one or two points that chiefly affected me.

First, the world contains a thousand forms of mysticism which drive a man mad; and one which drives a man sane. It is not natural, it does not even feel natural, to be a materialist. It is not natural to be content with nature. A man is a mystic; he is born a mystic and certainly he always dies a mystic. But while all societies feel again, sooner or later, this appetite for these extraordinary things, I note that there is one in which it protects ordinary things. I note that the ordinary things always decay and are despised without it.

A famous novelist [Charles Reade] wrote a romance on the antithesis of The Cloister and the Hearth. For in his day, in the England of fifty years ago, it was actually possible to fancy that it was an antithesis. To-day the antithesis is quite obviously an alliance. Those who clamoured to break down the cloister have now openly gone on to trample out the hearth. That is only one of a thousand things that illustrate one truth; that in this religion alone the highest and (if you will) the wildest vows and vocations are nevertheless the friends and guardians of the good things of daily life.

Any number of mystical prodigies have staggered the world; but only one has steadied the world. The saint is on the side of the sane man; the pilgrim is on the side of home; the monk is on the side of marriage. With us the best is not the enemy of the good. With us the best is the best friend of the good.

All other visionary revelations tend ultimately to inhuman philosophies; to destructive simplifications; to pessimism; to optimism; to fatalism; to nothingness and nonsense. There are good things attached to all the religions; but *goodness*, the thing itself, the positive presence of humility and charity and a glowing gratitude to God—this is not in the heart of them. The more we understand them, the more we even respect them, the more we realise it. What is in the heart of them is something other than pure goodness; as a metaphysical doubt about matter, or a sense of the wild call of nature, or at the best a fear of the Law and the Lord.

These things when exaggerated are always distorted; and often distorted into diabolism. They are only tolerable when they are tame. They only remain respectable when they remain lukewarm, like Victorian Protestantism. But the most flaming zeal for Our Lady, or the most fantastic emulation of St. Francis of Assisi, is still in its vital essence a clean and wholesome thing; it can never drive a man to deny his humanity or despise his fellows; and goodness can never be too good.

That is one of the notes that seem to me at once unique and universal; here is another. Only the Catholic Church can save a man from the grinding and degrading slavery of being a child of his age. Mr. Bernard Shaw lately expressed the aspiration that in a happier time every man would live to be three hundred years old. It is rather amusing; for I am quite certain that if Mr. Bernard Shaw had lived for the last three hundred years, he would have been a Catholic long ago. He would have seen how the wheel of the world comes full circle and how little its pretentious progress can really be trusted. He would have seen the Church sacrificed to a superstition about the King, the King sacrificed to a superstition about the Bible, and the Bible sacrificed to a superstition of Darwinian anarchism against which he was one of the first to rebel.

But in any case, the point here is that he did wish every man to have the experience of three centuries. Every Catholic, as compared with every other man, has the experience of nineteen centuries. Every man, when he becomes a Catholic, becomes suddenly two thousand years old. Yet it would be still truer to say that, for the first time, he fills and rises to the full stature of man. He judges things as they affect mankind, in many lands and ages, and not merely by the latest squabbles in the newspapers.

The Catholic Church has long proved that it was not a creature of its age. It is a creature of its Creator and one that is as much alive in its last age as in its first; and even its enemies in their hearts have given up hoping to see it die.[19]

The Pope as a private person may believe all sorts of things that I do not believe at all. The point is not that I believe few or many things, but that I believe one thing: that there is on earth a man wielding the authority of another Man, who was also God.[20] I am strongly in favour of keeping the peace, not because I am a pacifist, but because I am a patriot. I am also, oddly enough, in favour of peace because I am a Christian, and should like to see a fuller reunion of Christendom.[21]

Men need an image, single, coloured and clear in outline, an image to be called up instantly in the imagination, when what is Catholic is to be distinguished from what claims to be Christian or even what in one sense is Christian. Now I can scarcely remember a time when the image of Our Lady did not stand up in my mind quite definitely, at the mention or the thought of all these things. I was quite distant from these things, and then doubtful about these things;

---

[19] *Catholic Times*, Aug. 6, 1926.
[20] *G.K.'s Weekly*, Apr. 11, 1935.
[21] *Illustrated London News*, Sept. 16, 1933.

and then disputing with the world for them, and with myself against them; for that is the condition before conversion. But whether the figure was distant, or was dark and mysterious, or was a scandal to my contemporaries, or was a challenge to myself—I never doubted that this figure was the figure of the Faith; that she embodied, as a complete human being still only human, all that this Thing had to say to humanity. The instant I remembered the Catholic Church, I remembered her; when I tried to forget the Catholic Church, I tried to forget her; when I finally saw what was nobler than my fate, the freest and the hardest of all my acts of freedom, it was in front of a gilded and very gaudy little image of her in the port of Brindisi, that I promised the thing that I would do, if I returned to my own land.[22]

Some four years after my conversion, I was privileged to be present at the ceremony of laying the foundation-stone of the first Catholic Church erected since the Reformation in the town of Beaconsfield. It was a ceremony profoundly moving as a thing of the present, and of a deep historical interest as a thing of the past, considered in its liturgical form alone; beginning, as it does, with the blessing of salt and water as creatures dedicated anew to their Creator, proceeding to the mystical marking of the Cross upon the corner-stone and the world-old ritual of burying under the building a record of its reason and origin and an offering of gold and silver.

It was affecting in the particular and even accidental circumstances of the case: the setting forth of that procession with the pomp of cross and candles, and crozier and mitre, through the quiet streets of that small country town, a procession that would once have seemed like a resurrection from the dead, like ancient Egyptian mummies walking out of a pyramid, but which is now every day a more and more familiar, and a more and more welcome, sight to the populace of a nation that was driven back on inventing pageants because it had been deprived of processions.

It was yet more moving because of the lucid and direct appeal of the Lord Bishop of Northampton, who recalled the days when such a ceremony would have been native to that town and intelligible to all the townsfolk. Even the weather added something to the high drama

---

[22] "Mary and the Convert," *The Well and the Shallows*. Chesterton visited the cathedral in Brindisi on Easter Sunday in 1919. It would be three years before he fulfilled the promise he made there while standing before the image of the Madonna and Child.

of the ritual, for it hung stormy and doubtful above the opening march and invocation, the sun breaking out with the abruptness of a burst of lightning when those unfinished walls had been named after St. Teresa of the Infant Jesus.

Finally, it was deeply interesting, and even curious, because of circumstances special and peculiar to the place itself. Beaconsfield, as it happens, is a particularly strong case of that paradox of the Church to-day, that, while the trail of its traditions is over all the older things, it has sprung up suddenly and with new power in the very midst of the new. The old town of Beaconsfield, and until recently the only town of Beaconsfield, has been Protestant for three centuries. Yet, the old town of Beaconsfield is plastered all over with names and memories of Catholicism. Two of the chief roads are still Candlemas and Christmas Lane. The old monastic foundation of Burnham gives its title to the chief country seat; in the old rectory, which is a haunt of antiquaries, the alleged ghost is a nun. The very names of the inns are an echo: "The Saracen's Head," that it comes from the Crusades; "The White Hart," that was the badge of Richard the Second.

And, in face of all this, Mass has only been said for the last twenty years in the middle of the New Town and in a shed at the back of the Railway Hotel.[23]

No Catholic thinks he is a good Catholic; or he would by that thought become a bad Catholic. I for one am not even tempted to any illusion in that matter; I fear that very often, when I have got up early to go to Mass, I have said with a groan, *Tantum religio potuit suadere malorum*, which, I may explain to the Moslem, is not a quotation from the Mass, but, in the grand Lucretian manner, "Religion alone can persuade men to such evils."[24]

But if we only believed that religion was useful, it would be of no use.[25] To a Catholic it is the necessary system of religion that is logical and marching and militant; but that the heart of all that system is a broken heart, the core of all that music a breaking voice; and that the last reality is that which is the most personal; which is not only love but pardon.[26]

[23] *Catholic Times*, July 30, 1926. It was in that shed where GKC made his first confession and was received into the Catholic Church on July 30, 1922.
[24] *G.K.'s Weekly*, Aug. 24, 1933.
[25] "Roman Catholicism," in *An Outline of Christianity*, vol. 3 (Universe Books, 1926), p. 124.
[26] *G.K.'s Weekly*, Mar. 24, 1928.

Chapter 12

And Palms Before My Feet

The Path to Holiness

To be a failure may be one step to being a saint.
—Introduction to *Little Dorrit*

If there be one principle for which I am willing to be persecuted in moderation, and to perish to a reasonable extent, it is the great dogma that a man sees more through a hole in the wall than he would see if there were no wall at all. Anything that makes him value his vision, by limiting and defining, does in fact add to it a new dimension of intensity and significance.[1] Man is a creature; all his happiness consists in being a creature; or, as the Great Voice commanded us, in becoming a child [Mt 18:3]. All his fun is in having a gift or present; which the child, with profound understanding, values because it is "a surprise." But surprise implies that a thing came from outside ourselves; and gratitude that it comes from someone other than ourselves. It is thrust through the letter-box; it is thrown in at the window; it is thrown over the wall. Those limits are the lines of the very plan of human pleasure.[2] Has not everyone noticed how sweet and startling any landscape looks when seen through an arch? This strong, square shape, this shutting off of everything else is not only an assistance to beauty; it is the essential of beauty. The most beautiful part of every

---

[1] *The Gate*, December 1931.
[2] "The Crime of Gabriel Gale," *The Poet and the Lunatics*.

picture is the frame.³ Every Christmas carol contains the suggestion that the Incarnation itself is a sort of colossal limitation.⁴

We are always hearing about the limits of realism in art; that is, of this or that respect in which a written thing can never be quite like an acted thing. It seems odd to me that nobody ever mentions the chief chasm or cleavage between the thing written and the thing done. It turns on the old pivot of what theologians call Free Will. The difference is that all events in genuine art are decided: all events in genuine life (in anything worth calling life) are undecided. What is written is written (to quote a Roman governor who showed his taste for epigram at a somewhat unlucky moment [Jn 19:22]); what is written is written; but what is doing need not be done. Every artistic drama is named on the first page a tragedy or a comedy. That is because in every artistic drama the last page is written before the first. But it is not so in that terrific drama which heaven has given us to play upon this earth, without any punctual cues, with a very invisible, and sometimes inaudible, prompter, and without the faintest notion about when the curtain will come down. If the drama of real life is more dreadful, it has at least one agreeable quality; it is more uncertain. Every human life begins in tragedy, for it begins in travail. But every human life may end in comedy—even in divine comedy. It may end in a joy beyond all our jokes; in that cry across the chasm, "Fear not, I have conquered the world" [Jn 16:33]. Real human life differs from all imitations of it in the fact that it can perpetually alter itself as it goes along. Art can hardly survive one such change. It could not possibly survive a series of such changes. Of a fictitious story we may say decisively that it should go as straight as possible to its end. Or, to put it another way, the sooner we have finished a novel the better. But of a real story, as distinct from a fictitious story, we may say that the more the stream straggles this way and that, the more likely it is to be a clean or even sacred stream. It proves its wish to go right by so often confessing that it has gone wrong.⁵

Most Christians fail to fulfill the Christian ideal. This bitter and bracing fact cannot be too much insisted upon in this and every other

---

³ *Daily News*, Feb. 2, 1907.
⁴ *New Witness*, Oct. 7, 1921.
⁵ *Illustrated London News*, Mar. 16, 1912.

moral question. But, perhaps, it might be suggested that this failure is not so much the failure of Christians in connection with the Christian ideal as the failure of any men in connection with any ideal. That Christians are not always Christian is obvious; neither are Liberals always liberal, nor Socialists always social, nor Humanitarians always kind, nor Rationalists always rational, nor are gentlemen always gentle, nor do working men always work. If people are especially horrified at the failure of Christian practice it must be an indirect compliment to the Christian creed.[6] Christianity, which has been ludicrously accused of being gloomy and the enemy of life, has distinguished itself among the creeds of the world by its quite peculiar insistence on the fact that life is sacred, even when it is sad; that a man is sacred, even when he is oneself.[7]

The power of being decisive first and being proved right afterward is exactly the quality a supernatural power would have.[8] The supernatural has been in a large number of cases the thing that rescued man from a gloom and terror that arose very easily out of the ordinary appearances of things. The natural instinct of a man is to take himself far too much as a part of his surroundings and of a piece with his past. It is only too easy to grow as grey as the fence or the streets, to fall with a falling city or decay with a decaying civilisation. The sense of personal immortality which Christianity brought so violently and vividly into the world, even when accompanied with all its coarsest terrors, was an exhilaration precisely because it cut a man free from the obvious destiny of the tribe, the animal tragedy, the thing that we call heredity. If a man was to be damned he would not at least be damned automatically along with all his dull relations.[9] If Christianity has failed (which I should not admit), it has failed by defiling itself with the world, but certainly not by feeling superior to it.[10]

Ten years ago Nietzsche might have been interesting to me as a philosopher. Now he is only interesting as a personality. I can find a saner and more vigorous philosophy in Joan of Arc. For I know that all that is true in Nietzsche is in Joan of Arc. Also I know that all that is

---

[6] *Daily News*, Feb. 13, 1906.
[7] *Daily News*, Sept. 17, 1904.
[8] Letter to Maurice Baring, Feb. 14, 1923.
[9] *Daily News*, Apr. 14, 1906.
[10] *Illustrated London News*, Feb. 21, 1914.

true in Tolstoy is in Joan of Arc. If in a certain sense Tolstoy does stand for a kind of simplicity and for the dignity of the peasants—so did Joan of Arc. And with the solid difference that Joan of Arc was a peasant whereas Tolstoy is an aristocrat studying peasants. If in a certain sense Nietzsche does stand for a European energy and the high-hearted in battle—so did Joan of Arc. And, again, with this sharp difference, that Joan of Arc did fight and win battles, whereas Nietzsche, for all we know, would have run away from a cow. Christianity is exactly the normal from which these two cranks both strayed. Christianity is much humbler than Tolstoy. Christianity is much prouder than Nietzsche.[11] Nietzsche abandons the human race and looks for the advent of the Overman, gigantic in stature and intellect. Tolstoy, too, in his way, destroys many of the cardinal virtues: he would not have us interfere to prevent a child being burnt alive, if violence were necessitated by such interference. It is said that Jesus Christ forbade retaliation, but He drove the money-changers out of the Temple by force.[12] The heathen wishes to worship strength, but the Christian to strengthen worship.[13]

In a sense we renew hope when we renounce expectation. Our happiness consists in seeing each thing as fresh and free; the effort of all poetry is to correct that mere calculation by custom, which by the process of foreseeing a thing, prevents us from seeing it. One objection to counting chickens before they are hatched is that it blinds the imagination to the wild beauty and abysmal mystery of a chicken; and makes us satisfied with the stupid and sullen tautology of being sure eggs are eggs. This generally decays in the conception that they were rotten eggs; but when the poet is at the breakfast table (so to speak) the eggs are always new laid. Even a very minor poet may help this work of re-awakening wonder; and I myself, though microscopically minor, will risk the vanity of saying that I have always tried to help it. I have always urged that the hundredth egg is as amazing as the first; and that merely to take it for granted is not even to see the round figures, let alone the round eggs. Merely to count on things is not even to count them; but rather to discount them. I have desired every separate thing in life to stand out like a picture and not to fall back

---

[11] *Daily News*, Dec. 15, 1906.
[12] *Middlesex Gazette*, Dec. 22, 1906.
[13] *Daily News*, June 26, 1909.

and fade like a pattern; and wished to look at life as a child looks at a picture-book.[14] This old attitude of mine, which used to be called optimism, should more properly be called thanks.[15]

It is only people who do not believe in Christianity who take it for granted.[16] People forget how to be grateful unless they learn how to be humble.[17]

I have not the faintest doubt that praise is the noblest thing in the world. Indeed, it is obviously the highest function in man, since it is the one function that he can properly employ towards God.[18] Wonder and humility and gratitude are good things, but they are not the only good things; justice and mercy and human dignity are good things too.[19]

I recognise that we shall have a hard struggle to establish Christianity, or anything else that is good.[20] The whole object of poetry and mysticism, the whole object of all religions and of all philosophies not invented by the devil, is to make us value good things.[21] The highest thing in the world is goodness.[22] Every hateful thing is a mimicry of something that is good.[23] Man is never genuinely at home except in goodness.[24] To see good is to see God.[25]

As a Christian, I think the dangers of equality, which are sloth or objectless anger, less poisonous to the soul than the moral dangers of subordination, which are a satanic pride and an inhuman fear.[26] Pride is a sin. Nearly everyone feels it as a fact when they consider sin objectively—that is, as they mostly do consider it, in other people.[27] Sin, whatever else it is, is not merely the dregs of a bestial existence.[28]

---

[14] *New Witness*, Mar. 15, 1918.
[15] Ibid.
[16] *Daily News*, Jan. 11, 1908.
[17] *Daily News*, Dec. 15, 1906.
[18] *Illustrated London News*, May 1, 1909.
[19] *Catholic World*, November 1922.
[20] *Lancashire Daily Post*, Mar. 22, 1906.
[21] *Daily News*, Dec. 24, 1904.
[22] *Daily News*, Feb. 27, 1904.
[23] *Illustrated London News*, June 15, 1912.
[24] *Daily News*, June 18, 1901.
[25] *Listener*, Jan. 4, 1933.
[26] *Daily News*, July 3, 1909.
[27] *Illustrated London News*, Feb. 26, 1916.
[28] *Illustrated London News*, Sept. 1, 1928.

Our own day has its unconscious dogmas and its universal prejudices; and it needs a special, a sacred and what seems to many an inhuman separation to stand above them or to see beyond.[29] There are two types of dogma in practice in the modern world. First, there is the dogma which we ignore because we do not believe it—like the Communion of Saints. Second, there is the dogma which we ignore because we do believe it—like the Brotherhood of Man.[30]

Truth does not merely stick pins into people to sting them to anger without stopping them from action; truth puts hooks into people, in the manner of that ancient and magnificent metaphor which sent man forth to be the fishers of men [Mt 4:19].[31] To a Catholic it is the necessary system of religion that is logical and marching and militant; but that the heart of all that system is a broken heart, the core of all that music a breaking voice; and that the last reality is that which is the most personal; which is not only love but pardon.[32] The Church created a machinery of pardon, where the State could only work by a machinery of punishment.[33]

We need a more fixed idea of truth to establish a reign of justice.[34] Peace will only begin to be possible when we try to do justice to the side with which we do not feel sympathy, and earnestly try to call up in our own imagination the sorrows we have not suffered and the angers we do not feel.[35]

In one sense I have never changed my mind. My mind is exactly the thing I have not changed. I think it was Newman who pointed out that people do not often change their first principles, but only the applications and consequences of them. For instance, I prefer a political authority that is popular rather than merely privileged or exclusive. When I believed, as a boy, that Oliver Cromwell was the leader of a popular protest against the arrogance of aristocrats in lace collars, I sympathised with Oliver Cromwell. Now I am certain that he was the leader of the grasping squires who stole the common land

---

[29] *Papal Annual*, January 1928.
[30] *Independent Review*, June 1906.
[31] *New Witness*, Apr. 27, 1923.
[32] *G.K.'s Weekly*, Mar. 24, 1928.
[33] *Illustrated London News*, Sept. 2, 1916.
[34] *Illustrated London News*, Feb. 1, 1930.
[35] *Illustrated London News*, June 25, 1932.

and the popular traditions, I am against Oliver Cromwell. But my mind is not changed; only my information about a certain individual. Or again, I think the present economic disproportion involves a gross oppression of the poor. When I thought it could only be remedied by Socialism, I was a Socialist; now I am sure it could be better remedied by a democratic distribution, I am a Distributist. But the mind, in the sense of the type of mind, has not changed; on the contrary, I have found something that is, strictly speaking, more to my mind.[36]

I feel rather ashamed of my good luck, in having succeeded through a Greek catchword and a few jokes about elephants. I do not believe in the moral significance of modern success; I do not believe, in the sense of taking it seriously, in my own journalistic importance; I do not believe in my editorial powers. But I do believe in my beliefs. I do believe that somebody ought to make a stand or strike a blow for certain civilised certitudes in times of terror and doubt. I do believe that certain human and historic necessities are perishing before our eyes in vast whirlpools of monopoly and slavery.[37]

I have been asked, Why am I still fighting? I do not know whether my ruthless and unrelenting habit of writing deserves to be compared to anything so Christian and holy as fighting. But in so far as I have been fighting, I have from the first, and especially at the first, been fighting on two fronts. That is, I have defended two sets of ideas, which seem to me to be closely connected; but seem to many people, perhaps most people, to be completely divided.

Now the amusing point about the position is this: If I answer that I still think the controversial campaign necessary, because some of my most sacred beliefs are likely to be lost or neglected by the march of modern progress, some things I hold dear derided and deserted by the change and novelty of the new world, most modern readers will imagine (quite correctly) that they know what I mean. They will say, "Oh, of course, you are attached to antiquated superstitions; you cling to the altars of an old supernatural creed, and naturally you are afraid those altars may be deserted and that creed crumble away. You are a Gothic ruin. Your figure has the ethereal attenuation of a stained-glass window. You are a gaunt ascetic, a fasting friar, a mere

---

[36] *John O'London's Weekly*, Sept. 29, 1923.
[37] *New Witness*, Feb. 9, 1923.

shadow of the past. No wonder you tremble like an autumn leaf, feeling that the wind of the world's future will soon blow you and your frail traditions away."

Not at all. By no means. Contrariwise. I am not in the least alarmed about the future of the sacred and supernatural part of my convictions. I am not at all anxious about the altars and the antiquated creeds; I know they are all right; and doing nicely, thank you.

I know that we shall not only have plenty of new stained-glass windows, but plenty of new saints to put in them.

And though I am not worthy to be a fasting friar, I have friends who are actually fasting friars,[38] and men who can shake any modern mob with questions it cannot answer.

But, as I say, I was fighting on two fronts; and I had another set of positions to defend. I had a political as well as a religious ideal; a human as well as a divine tradition; and on that side all my sympathies are what is called popular, but what I would much prefer to call revolutionary.

It is those popular political ideals which are now in danger of crumbling like ruins or disappearing like dreams. Fr. Ronald Knox in early youth, I think, wrote a rhymed account of Oxford groups, containing a couplet something like:

> The Chestertonians five things revere:
> Faith, Hope, the Church, Democracy and Beer.

It is not the Faith and the Church that are now in danger; it is the Hope and the Democracy. We will defer a discussion on the state of beer to some more suitable social occasion.

To-day, being a Democrat, I am naturally a Die-hard. Before the war I wrote, "Democracy is fighting in the last ditch." I well remember people who cried out against the paradox; I imagine most people would now accept the platitude.

When I say I still believe in liberty, in a commonwealth controlled by its citizens, and all the rest—then indeed I am a phantom from the past. I am really a Gothic ruin. I am indeed clinging to a cold and deserted altar. European civilisation has gone the other way with a

---

[38] A reference to the Dominican friar Fr. Vincent McNabb.

rush; the Communists quite as much as the Fascists. All the danger is now that the death of Liberalism will really be the death of liberty. It may be said that they will meet in death, after having been for a long time separated in life. It is true that popular institutions have suffered by the corruption of Parliamentary institutions. I think nobody whose memory goes back as far as the Marconi Case will accuse me of having failed to foresee that.

But I do still believe in Liberty, Equality and Fraternity; and I do still most emphatically disbelieve in the idolatry of the State; that is, the city crushing the citizens.

Thus, I have reached the conclusion that there is only one sort of real political liberty; and certainly only one sort of political equality. And that is the wide distribution, not of votes but of values, of things economically valuable; of the means of production. The only way by which Englishmen can be approximately equal in England is that each Englishman should own, if possible, some of England, and anyhow something in England. Private Property is the only practical Democracy; all the rest is political hypocrisy. I am still clinging to my mediaeval superstition of Freedom; I am still following the fantastic dream of the free man; and I am solidly certain that nothing could ever achieve it except small but solid property.

That is the thing for which I am fighting, for that is really in doubt; not the rather muddleheaded thing the nineteenth century called religious doubt; but the real doubt that attaches to all secular things, much more than to religious things.

To sum up: I found myself fighting against two things from the first. One was an atheism I thought would lead to fatalism and despair. The other was a concentrated Capitalism I thought would lead to slavery.[39] Both Capitalism and Communism rest on the same idea: a centralisation of wealth which destroys private property.[40] The basis of the whole Marxian business is the religion of monism and materialism. Every man gets his economics from his religion.[41]

Strange as it may sound, there is some real reason for rejoicing in the idea that what we see before us is a social decline. It is a most

---

[39] *Leader*, Mar. 12, 1935.
[40] *G.K.'s Weekly*, July 20, 1933.
[41] *New Witness*, Dec. 9, 1921.

happy and almost hilarious relief from the idea that what we see is social progress. It is better to believe that the Servile State is a morass into which we have strayed and sunk, than to believe that it is the goal and golden city to which all mankind is on the march. Modern plutocracy, materialistic culture, organised philanthropy, sexual science, we can recognise and resist these things as realities, but our mortal lot would be indeed a dark one if we had to recognise them as ideals. There may be spirited defence and defiance if the world is growing worse; but there is nothing but mourning and lamentation and woe if the world is improving.[42] This fallacy of false progress tends to obscure the old common sense of all mankind, which is still the common sense of every man in his own daily dealings: that everything has its place and proportion and proper use, and that it is rational to trust its use and distrust its abuse. Progress, in the good sense, does not consist in looking for a direction in which one can go on indefinitely. For there is no such direction, unless it be in quite transcendental things, like the love of God. It would be far truer to say that true progress consists in looking for the place where we can stop.[43] The Conservative has exactly the same error as the Progressive. It consists in the fact that each of them allows truth to be determined by time. That is to say, he judges a thing by whether it is of yesterday or to-day or to-morrow, and not by what it is in eternity.[44]

We are all of us supposed to be trying to be good men. None of us has actually succeeded. Many of us have not actually tried: most of us are not trying now. But we have all some more or less definite ideal before us in our better moments, and we have expended a good deal of time and a good deal of energy in discussing the means of perfection, and numerous arguments have arisen about the details of civilisation. But in our time there has sprung up a discussion of a different nature, which is not about the machinery of civilisation, or about what tools or instruments should be used in the process of perfecting humanity. Let us suppose ourselves young and healthy and walking down Kensington High-street, and we meet,—what shall I say, the Pope? or a policeman? or a Bishop with his mitre and crozier,

---

[42] *New Witness*, Aug. 5, 1921.
[43] *Illustrated London News*, Jan. 28, 1922.
[44] *Illustrated London News*, Oct. 30, 1920.

very pompous and very elaborately dressed. We wonder at these human arrangements, and up to a point everything is perfectly sensible and perfectly clear. But modern scepticism does not now ask whether bishops wear these things to promote holiness, but whether holiness ought to be promoted; not whether policemen do wholly support justice, but whether justice ought to be supported at all.[45]

A progressive critic has taken me to task for presuming to stand by my creed and my *tradition*—a word he treats with some disdain. The projector of the New Religion tries to evade the sanity of creed by all sorts of transcendental talk about the beauty of Becoming, and the inevitable blessings of Evolution, which is bound to bring something out of nothing. He suggests that Einstein "thought there was going to be a Fourth Dimension" either before there was or before there was any reason to suspect that there was.

I do not propose to discuss the Higher Mathematics, but all I can say is that, if Einstein's starting-point really was "dissatisfaction with the three-dimension conception of the universe," Einstein must be much more of a fool than I take him for. How could anybody outside a lunatic asylum be discontented with living under three dimensions?

What the critic means, which is quite different from what he says, is that Einstein (or any other scientific man) saw a number of new facts which he thought might fit better into some new theory than into the accepted one, and began to think of new theories into which they might fit.

If the progressive has any new facts to offer, I shall be delighted to discuss them. If he has any new theories to suggest, I shall hail them with delighted surprise. What I say is that there is nothing particularly new about going back fifty years to read Emerson; and certainly nothing new in talking about the Oversoul or *anima mundi*; which is part of a Pantheism as old as Paganism. What I complain of is not that he has given us hints of something new, but that he has only given us a cold hash of something already old; the old label of Christianity artificially tied on to all the old attacks on Christianity.

Nor was there ever anything new in the only novelty with which he credits Christianity. Apparently the only distinction that he leaves to Jesus of Nazareth is that He was the first person who ever suggested a kinship between Man and God.

---

[45] *Middlesex Gazette*, Dec. 22, 1906.

Now whatever may be said of his version of Christianity, he is grossly unjust to Paganism. I should say myself that the general sense of something divine in man, of some relationship between himself and the higher powers, was the one thing which even heathen humanity never entirely lost; or (as we Catholics would put it) was that part of the Primitive Revelation that survived even the Fall. Why, I fancy that St. Paul actually appeals to pagan literature as a witness to that divine kinship as a universal truth; "As certain of your own poets have said; for we also are His children" [Acts 17:28]. The very word Jupiter contains the word "Father."

It would be nearer the truth to say, as Browning did, that Christianity was the first to state clearly the disruption and not the union between God and Man. But I do not say this: I only say the Gospels are full of Catholic theology. My critic sneers, I know not why, at my calling the Gospel truths tremendous. Well, I call it tremendous, if true, to say, "Before Abraham was, I am" [Jn 8:58]. I call it tremendous, if true to say to any human being, "Whatever you bind on earth shall be bound in heaven" [Mt 18:18]; to say to poor fishermen, "Whose sins you remit, they are remitted; whose sins you retain they are retained" [Jn 20:23]. But I should not rely on these even to prove Jesus unique.

There is one thing in which He is unique, and that is that He made something unique. It is that He not only talked about a kingdom, but founded one; a kingdom that actually rules and orders and is responsible; a kingdom that remains as a reality for all its friends and foes; loved as nothing else is loved, hated as nothing else is hated; a permanent inspiration, a permanent irritant; and irritating men so much that, in order to escape from it, they will even join a New Religion before they know what it is.[46] Living in a world that worships swiftness and success no longer means living in a world of new things. Rather it means living in a world of old things; of things that very swiftly grow old. The actual sensation of novelty lasts for a much shorter time than it does in a world where there are fewer sensations.[47]

Religion is a battle; and to have your thinking unfinished is to be fighting unprepared. If there is an enemy in the field, he will not wait

---

[46] *Outline*, Apr. 13, 1929. The critic in question is Canon Charles Raven (1885–1964), a liberal theologian and Anglican priest who taught at Cambridge and wrote about modern science and modern theology.

[47] *Illustrated London News*, Aug. 3, 1935.

until we find truth, he will already be leading us into error.[48] It is not at all easy to analyse errors when they are so entirely erroneous. It is always their character that they do not err in the words or even err in the facts, but always err in the truth.[49] The falsification of the past and present all men must to some extent suffer; and even religious truth will not correct it entirely. But religious error exaggerates it extravagantly. It makes the mighty object in the distance not only small, but invisible; it makes the nearer object not only an interruption to the view, but the view itself.[50] I have never been able to understand why the Modernist, even if he can see nothing of the truths, does not begin to suspect something from seeing so many of his own errors.[51]

There is a threadbare joke which calls the gallery in a theatre "the gods." For my part I accept that joke quite seriously. The people in the gallery *are* the gods. They are the ultimate authority so far as anything human is the ultimate authority. I do not see anything unreasonable in the actor calling upon them with the same gesture with which he calls upon the mountain of Olympus. When the actor looks down, brooding in despair or calling up black Erebus or the evil spirits, then, in such moments, by all means let him bend his black brows and look down into the stalls, the front row seats. But if there be in any acted play anything to make him lift up his heart to heaven, then in God's name, when he looks up to heaven, let him see the poor.[52]

The great conception at the back of the oldest religions in the world is, of course, the conception that man is of divine origin, a sacred and splendid heir, the eldest son of the universe. But humanity could not in practice carry out this conception that everyone was divine. The practical imagination recoils from the idea of two gods swindling each other over a pound of cheese. The mind refuses to accept the idea of sixty bodies, each filled with a blazing divinity, elbowing each other to get into an omnibus. This mere external difficulty causes men in every age to fall back upon the conception that certain men preserved for other men the sanctity of man. Certain

---

[48] *Columbia*, October 1926.
[49] *Illustrated London News*, Feb. 7, 1914.
[50] *America*, Aug. 28, 1926.
[51] Preface to *Modernism and the Christian Church*, by Francis Woodlock, S.J. (Longmans, Green, 1925), p. vi.
[52] *Daily News*, May 18, 1907.

figures were more divine because they were more human. In primitive times of folklore, and in some feudal periods, this larger man was the conquering hero, the strong man who slew dragons and oppressors. To the old Hebrews this sacred being was the prophet: to the men of the Christian ages it was the saint.[53]

Whether we call it idealism or hypocrisy, Christian conquest has always found it necessary to profess some reason in general morality.[54] If no one should be left in the world except a million open malefactors and one hypocrite, that hypocrite will still remind them of holiness.[55]

There are saints indeed in my religion: but a saint only means a man who really knows he is a sinner.[56] What should we think of a saint who denounced sin without ever admitting that he was a sinner?[57] The great strength of Christian sanctity has always been simply this—that the worst enemies of the saints could not say of the saints anything worse than the saints said of themselves.[58]

I believe that the real history of the Catholic pioneer has been the same; to be first and to be forgotten.[59] Empires break; industrial conditions change; the suburbs will not last for ever. What will remain? I will tell you. The Catholic Saint will remain.[60] Speaking as a Catholic, I am very proud and happy to say that I know of no reason, in heaven or earth, why a barmaid should not some time or other be canonized as a saint by the Catholic Church. It is simply a question of in what way, with what motives, and in what spirit she minded the bar.[61] I wish there were an Ideal Postman, an Ideal Grocer, and an Ideal Plumber. It is undoubtedly true that we should laugh at the idea of an Ideal Postman; it is true, and it proves that we are not genuine democrats. There certainly should be an ideal image of health and happiness in any trade. But although no ideal obliterates the ugly drudgery and detail of any calling. It is a serious calamity that no such

---

[53] *Speaker*, Oct. 26, 1901.
[54] *Illustrated London News*, Oct. 21, 1911.
[55] *Daily News*, Nov. 10, 1906.
[56] *Daily News*, Sept. 24, 1910.
[57] *New York American*, Feb. 17, 1934.
[58] *Illustrated London News*, Oct. 26, 1907.
[59] *America*, May 4, 1929.
[60] "An Interlude of an Argument," *The Ball and the Cross*.
[61] *G.K.'s Weekly*, Oct. 6, 1928.

ideal exists in the case of the vast number of honourable trades and crafts on which the existence of a modern city depends. It is a pity that current thought and sentiment offer nothing corresponding to the old conception of patron saints. If they did there would be a Patron Saint of Plumbers, and this would alone be a revolution, for it would force the individual craftsman to believe that there was once a perfect being who did actually plumb.[62]

The heaven of the atheist makes the earth of the atheist, as much as the heaven of the saint makes the earth of the saint.[63] We do not believe that there are any lost causes; we do not admit that there are any hopeless loyalties; and we should come back to our religion at last, if its temples were as deserted as Stonehenge. It is this splendour of the hopeless hope; sometimes called the forlorn hope, which has made the peculiar chivalry of Christendom, which has given to us alone the true idea of romance; for the real romance was a combination of fidelity to the quest as a task, with perpetual and enormous inequality to the task.[64] One can tell the divine origin of common sense by this simple test; that it is always crucified.[65] The sign in which we conquer is the cross and not the weathercock.[66]

It takes a long time to get to heaven. Obstacles on the way to heaven are the romance of spiritual existence.[67] The secret we are all seeking is the secret of enjoying life. I am perfectly certain that all our world will end in despair unless there is some way of making the mind itself, the ordinary thoughts we have at ordinary times, more healthy and more happy than they seem to be just now, to judge by most modern novels and poems. You have got to be happy in those quiet moments when you remember that you are alive; not in those noisy moments when you forget. Unless we can learn again to enjoy life, we shall not long enjoy the spices of life. I once read a French fairy-tale that expressed exactly what I mean. Never believe that French wit is shallow; it is the shining surface of French irony, which is unfathomable. It was about a pessimist poet who decided to drown

---

[62] *Speaker*, Mar. 30, 1901.
[63] *New Witness*, Dec. 9, 1921.
[64] *G.K.'s Weekly*, Apr. 9, 1936.
[65] *Daily News*, Mar. 16, 1907.
[66] *Illustrated London News*, Dec. 16, 1916.
[67] *Bystander*, Apr. 6, 1904.

himself; and as he went down to the river he gave away his eyes to a blind man, his ears to a deaf man, his legs to a lame man, and so on, up to the moment when the reader was waiting for the splash of his suicide; but the author wrote that this senseless trunk settled itself on the shore and began to experience the joy of living. *La joie de vivre.* The joy of being alive. You have to go deep, and perhaps to grow old, to know how true that story is.[68] Great joy has in it the sense of immortality: the triumphant moments of our life may have been only moments, but they were moments of eternity.[69] A characteristic of the great saints is their power of levity. Angels can fly because they can take themselves lightly.[70]

---

[68] *Listener*, Mar. 18, 1936.
[69] *Daily News*, Mar. 7, 1901.
[70] "The Eternal Revolution," *Orthodoxy*.